The Book of Love

ALSO BY DIANE ACKERMAN

A Slender Thread
The Rarest of the Rare
A Natural History of Love
The Moon by Whale Light
Jaguar of Sweet Laughter: New and Selected Poems
A Natural History of the Senses
Reverse Thunder
On Extended Wings
Lady Faustus
Twilight of the Tenderfoot
Wife of Light
The Planets: A Cosmic Pastoral

FOR CHILDREN

Monk Seal Hideaway

ALSO BY JEANNE MACKIN

The Frenchwoman
The Queen's War
Dreams of Empire
The Cornell Book of Herbs

The Book of LOVE

EDITED BY

Diane Ackerman & Jeanne Mackin

W. W. NORTON & COMPANY

New York • *London*

Because this page cannot legibly accommodate all copyright notices, pages
793–804 constitute an extension of the copyright page.

The text of this book is composed in Centaur with the display set in
Charlemagne.
Composition and manufacturing by The Haddon Craftsmen, Inc.
Book design by Judith Stagnitto Abbate

Library of Congress Cataloging-in-Publication Data
The book of love / edited by Diane Ackerman, Jeanne Mackin.
    p.   cm.
  Includes index.
  ISBN 0-393-04589-7
  I. Love—Literary collections.   I. Ackerman, Diane.   II. Mackin, Jeanne.
PN6071.L7B65   1998
808.8'03543—dc21   97-23049
                                                                  CIP

W. W. Norton & Company, Inc., 500 Fifth Avenue, New York, N.Y. 10110
            http://www.wwnorton.com

W. W. Norton & Company Ltd., 10 Coptic Street, London WC1A 1PU

1 2 3 4 5 6 7 8 9 10

for Paul and Steve, with love

CONTENTS

Introduction
 Diane Ackerman The Words We Love xxv
 Jeanne Mackin The Book of Love xxx

In the Beginning
 Empedocles Love and Strife xxxv

FICTION

Anonymous, Ancient Egypt The King's Son 3
Anonymous Inscription in the tomb of Queen Ahmose,
 wife of Tuthmosis I 5
Anonymous from *Gilgamesh* 5
Longus from *The Loves of Daphnis and Chloe* 8
Apuleius of Madaura from *The Metamorphoses or
 Golden Ass* 12
Heliodorus from *The Aethiopica* 19
Anonymous from *Aucassins and Nicolette* 23
Marie de France The Lay of the Two Lovers 24
Sir Thomas Malory from *Le Morte D'Arthur* 28
Margaret, Queen of Navarre from *The Heptameron* 33
Miguel de Cervantes Saavedra from *Don Quijote de la
 Mancha* 37
P'u Sung-ling The Young Lady of the Tung-T'ing Lake 41

Aphra Behn   from *Love Letters Between a Noble-Man and His Sister*   45

Daniel Defoe   from *Moll Flanders*   52

Samuel Richardson   from *The History of Clarissa Harlowe*   58

Fanny Burney (Madame d'Arblay)   from *Evelina, or A Young Lady's Entrance into the World*   62

Mary Wollstonecraft Shelley   from *Frankenstein, or The Modern Prometheus*   69

Jane Austen   from *Pride and Prejudice*   75

Charlotte Brontë   from *Jane Eyre*   76

William Makepeace Thackeray   from *Vanity Fair*   85

Emily Brontë   from *Wuthering Heights*   86

Nathaniel Hawthorne   from *The Scarlet Letter*   86

Gustave Flaubert   from *Madame Bovary*   90

Thomas Carlyle   from *Sartor Resartus: The Life and Opinions of Herr Teufelsdröckh*   94

Benjamin Disraeli   from *Coningsby*   97

Charles Dickens   from *David Copperfield*   98

Anthony Trollope   from *An Old Man's Love*   98

George Eliot (Mary Ann Evans)   from *The Lifted Veil*   101

Mark Twain (Samuel Clemens)   from *The Diary of Adam and Eve*   104

Leo Tolstoy   from *Anna Karenina* and *Resurrection*   105

Ivan Turgenev   from First Love   112

Anton Chekhov   The Kiss   115

Anatole France   from *The Crime of Sylvestre Bonnard*   129

Richard Burton   from *The Book of the Thousand Nights and a Night*   132

Guy de Maupassant   Love: Three Pages from a Sportsman's Book   136

Thomas Hardy   from *Under the Greenwood Tree* and *Tess of the D'Urbervilles*   141

Sarah Orne Jewett   from *The Country of the Pointed Firs*   143

Henry James   from *Daisy Miller: A Study*   147

Kate Chopin   Caline   148

Willa Cather   A Resurrection   150

Oscar Wilde   from *The Importance of Being Earnest* and The Nightingale and the Rose   164

O. Henry   The Gift of the Magi   171

Edith Wharton   from *Summer*   175

Bruno Schulz   from *Sanatorium Under the Sign of the Hourglass*   177
Philippe Thoby-Marcelin and Pierre Marcelin
    from *The Beast of the Haitian Hills*   178
Thomas Wolfe   from *The Web and the Rock*   184
Alice Adams   Complicities   187
Kim Addonizio   Survivors   193
Anthony Caputi   from *To Know the Wind Is Mortal*   193
Nicholas Delbanco   from *Count Rumford: His Book*   197
E. L. Doctrow   Willi   199
Lamar Herrin   from *The Lies Boys Tell*   205
Edward Hower   Miriamu and the King   210
William Kennedy   from *Ironweed*   220
Milan Kundera   from *The Book of Laughter and Forgetting*   225
Alison Lurie   Something Borrowed, Something Blue   227
Jeanne Mackin   from *The Wise and Foolish Virgins*   230
Robert Morgan   from *The Truest Pleasure*   235
Bradford Morrow   from *The Almanac Branch*   238
Stephen F. Poleskie   Love and Janus Zyvka   243
Joanna Scott   from *The Manikin*   246
Amy Tan   from *The Hundred Secret Senses*   249
John Vernon   from *All for Love: Baby Doe and Silver Dollar*   252
Paul West   from *Life with Swan*   255
Hilma Wolitzer   Sundays   265

POETRY

Anonymous, Sanskrit
    Charm to Quell a Rival   275
Anonymous, Egyptian
    Stand Fast, O My Heart   275
    from *The Crossing*   276
The Bible
    from *The Song of Solomon*   277
Ono no Yoshiki
    My Love   278
Ts'ao Chih
    Sorrow, in Seven   278
    Drifting Duckweed   279
Tu Fu
    Restless Night   279

Liu Hsiao-wei
    For My Wife   280
Kamal ud-Din
    O Love, Thy Hair!   281
Sophocles
    from *Antigone*   281
Homer
    from *The Odyssey*   282
Lucretius
    The Posture   286
Virgil
    from *The Aeneid*   287
Petronius
    Doing, a Filthy Pleasure Is, and Short   290
Ovid
    To His Mistress   291
    Elegy 5   293
Catullus
    Let Us Live and Love   294
Sappho
    Sonnet XXVII   295
Petrarch
    Sonnet CCXXIV   295
Hafiz
    Ode 147   296
    Ode 173   297
Elizabeth I
    On Monsieur's Departure   298
William Shakespeare
    "My mistress' eyes are nothing like the sun"   298
    "When my love swears that she is made of truth"   299
    "Shall I compare thee to a summer's day?"   299
    "When in disgrace with fortune and men's eyes"   300
    "Let me not to the marriage of true minds"   300
    from *Antony and Cleopatra*   301
    from *The Merchant of Venice*   302
    from *Romeo and Juliet*   303
Ben Jonson
    Drink to Me Only with Thine Eyes   304

Clement Robinson
    Greensleeves 305
John Donne
    The Flea 306
    The Sun Rising 307
    Song 308
    The Ecstasy 309
Anonymous, Scottish
    Barbara Allen 311
John Gay
    To a Young Lady, with Some Lampreys 312
Andrew Marvell
    To His Coy Mistress 314
    The Definition of Love 315
William Cartwright
    No Platonic Love 316
Robert Herrick
    The Vine 317
    Kisses Loathsome 318
    To the Virgins, to Make Much of Time 318
    Upon Julia's Clothes 319
    Delight in Disorder 319
    Be My Mistress Short or Tall 319
John Clare
    First Love 320
John Milton
    from *Paradise Lost* 321
Abraham Cowley
    from *Anacreon* 321
Thomas Carew
    Mediocrity in Love Rejected 321
    Fear Not, Dear Love 322
Thomas Wyatt
    They Flee from Me 322
Sir Philip Sidney
    Heart Exchange 323
Christopher Marlowe
    The Passionate Shepherd to His Love 324
Sir Walter Ralegh
    The Nymph's Reply to the Shepherd 325

George Herbert
    Love   326
John Wilmot, Second Earl of Rochester
    Written in a Lady's Prayer Book   326
    The Imperfect Enjoyment   327
Anne Bradstreet
    To My Dear and Loving Husband   329
John Keats
    Modern Love   329
    "I cry your mercy"   330
Lord Byron
    She Walks in Beauty   331
    When We Two Parted   331
    We'll Go No More A-Roving   332
Percy Bysshe Shelley
    Love's Philosophy   333
William Blake
    Song   333
A. C. Swinburne
    Before Parting   334
Matthew Arnold
    Dover Beach   335
Samuel Taylor Coleridge
    Desire   337
    Love   337
Alfred, Lord Tennyson
    Summer Night   338
William Wordsworth
    Perfect Woman   339
    The Cottager to Her Infant   340
Robert Burns
    Ye Flowery Banks   340
    Sweet Afton   341
Edgar Allan Poe
    To Helen   342
    Annabel Lee   342
Emily Dickinson
    "My life closed twice"   344
    "I cannot live with You"   344
    "Wild Nights"   346

"It's such a little thing to weep—" 346
"The Rose did caper" 346
Ho Xuan Huong
  On Sharing a Husband 347
Elizabeth Barrett Browning
  How Do I Love Thee? 348
  Sonnets from the Portuguese, XIII 348
Robert Browning
  Meeting at Night 349
  The Lost Mistress 349
Oscar Wilde
  In the Gold Room 350
Gerard Manley Hopkins
  At the Wedding March 351
Ralph Waldo Emerson
  Give All to Love 351
Walt Whitman
  Press Close Bare-Bosom'd Night 353
  From Pent-up, Aching Rivers 353
  When I Heard at the Close of the Day 355
  We Two Boys Together Clinging 356
Thomas Hardy
  Neutral Tones 357
Leigh Hunt
  Jenny Kissed Me 357
E. E. Cummings
  i like my body when it is with your 358
  somewhere i have never travelled,gladly beyond 358
  love's function is to fabricate unknownness 359
  the mind is its own beautiful prisoner 359
Samuel Beckett
  Cascando 360
William Butler Yeats
  A Drinking Song 361
  When You Are Old 362
James Wright
  A Blessing 362
  To the Muse 363
John Berryman
  from *The Dream Songs* 364

Stephen Spender
    Daybreak   365
Edna St. Vincent Millay
    "What lips my lips have kissed"   366
    "Love is not all"   366
Kenneth Fearing
    Love 20¢ the First Quarter Mile   367
W. H. Auden
    "Lay your sleeping head, my love"   368
T. S. Eliot
    A Dedication to My Wife   369
Dylan Thomas
    If I Were Tickled by the Rub of Love   370
Robinson Jeffers
    Granddaughter   371
George Barker
    To My Mother   372
John Ciardi
    Men Marry What They Need   372
Theodore Roethke
    I Knew a Woman   373
Phyllis McGinley
    Launcelot with Bicycle   374
A. E. Housman
    When I Was One-and-Twenty   375
Anne Sexton
    The Ballad of the Lonely Masturbator   376
Sara Teasdale
    Barter   377
May Swenson
    In Love Made Visible   378
Richard Wilbur
    For C.   379
    The Writer   380
Mark Strand
    Our Masterpiece Is the Private Life   381
    The Coming of Light   382
Maxine Kumin
    We Are   383
    Relearning the Language of April   383

James Tate
   My Felisberto 384
   A Dangerous Adventure 385
Philip Appleman
   A Priest Forever 386
   Crystal Anniversary 390
Marjorie Appleman
   Love 390
   Another Beginning 391
John Updike
   Report of Health 392
Donald Justice
   Women in Love 393
   On an Anniversary 394
Philip Levine
   In the Dark 395
   February 14th 396
Anthony Hecht
   A Birthday Poem 396
   Peripeteia 399
Garrett Kaoru Hongo
   A Restless Night 401
Wendell Berry
   The Country of Marriage 402
   Air and Fire 405
Siv Cedering
   Country Music 405
   Ukiyo-E 407
   Crossing the Sound by Ferry One Night During the
      Gulf War 408
William Meredith
   The Ghosts of the House 409
   Poem 410
   Crossing Over 411
Richard Harteis
   Einsteinian Love 412
   Winter Lesson 412
   Star Trek III 414
Galway Kinnell
   Telephoning in Mexican Sunlight 415
   Rapture 416

Charles Simic
  Marked Playing Cards   417
  At the Cookout   418
Linda Hogan
  The Origins of Corn   419
  Nothing   420
Laurence Goldstein
  Aubade   421
  Eros in Long Beach   421
Jorie Graham
  Studies in Secrecy   423
Mona Van Duyn
  Late Loving   425
  Earth Tremors Felt in Missouri   426
W. S. Merwin
  Late Spring   426
  Before Us   427
Richard Howard
  L'Invitation au Voyage   429
  The Lover Showeth Wherefore He Is Abandoned of the
    Beloved He Sometime Enjoyed, Even in Sleep   431
Heather McHugh
  Dry Time   432
  Untitled   433
Robert Pinsky
  The Time of Year, the Time of Day   434
  The Want Bone   435
Linda Pastan
  Wildflowers   435
  Late Love Songs   436
David Wagoner
  At the Mouth of a Creek   437
  A Woman Photographing Holsteins   438
Lonnie Balaban
  The Poet's Wife Sends Him a Poem   439
John Balaban
  His Reply   440
Louis Simpson
  Birch   441
  Dvonya   441

John Hollander
Heat of Snow 442
White Above Green 443
Phyllis Janowitz
Fisherman's Wife 444
Reunion with Jake at Still Pond Creek 445
Nicholas Christopher
Rice Wine 445
Sleep 447
Diane Ackerman
Beija-Flor 448
Ode to the Alien 449
Zoë 451
Robert Bly
Listening to the Köln Concert 453
A Third Body 453
Erica Jong
Sentient 454
We Learned 455
William Matthews
Cooking for C. 457
The Cloister 457
Joyce Carol Oates
Public Love 458
You / Your 459
Carolyn Kizer
The Light 460
The Gift 460
Rod Jellema
Because I Never Learned the Names of Flowers 461
Note to Marina Marquez of El Paso, Who Sublet My
Apartment for the Summer 462
Albert Goldbarth
Seriema Song 462
The Two Parts of the Day Are, 464
Pattiann Rogers
Love Song 465
The Hummingbird: A Seduction 466
Marvin Bell
The Last Thing I Say 467
Sounds of the Resurrected Dead Man's Footsteps #9 467

Roald Hoffmann
How It Grows 468
Gerald Stern
Both of Them Were Sixty-five 469
June First 470
Donald Hall
Weeds and Peonies 471
Gold 472
Rita Dove
His Shirt 473
Jill Bialosky
Without 474
Gary Snyder
Cross-Legg'd 475
David Ignatow
The Men You've Loved 476
The Principle 476
John Gill
6/16/94 476
Louise Glück
The White Lilies 477
Happiness 478
Dara Wier
Dreamland 478
Nude Descending a Staircase 480
John Ashbery
Just Walking Around 481
A Blessing in Disguise 482
Agha Shahid Ali
Ghazal 483
Josephine Jacobsen
The Edge 484
The Wind in the Sunporch 485
It Is the Season 486

ESSAYS

Anonymous   A Father's Advice to His Daughter, from the
Aztec Codices 491
Plato   from *Phaedrus* 492

Aristotle   from *Ethica Nicomachea*   495
The Bible   from Proverbs and Corinthians   498
Seneca   On Grief for Lost Friends   499
Plutarch   from *The Lives of the Noble Grecians and Romans*   500
Vatsyayana   from *The Kama Sutra*   503
Boethius   from *The Consolation of Philosophy*   505
Hugh of Saint Victor   from Of the Nature of Love   506
Andreas Capellanus   from *The Art of Courtly Love*   508
Michel de Montaigne   That Our Desires Are Increased by
        Difficulty   511
Johannes Secundus   from *The Kisses*   517
Count Baldesar Castiglione   from *The Book of the Courtier*   523
Thomas Dekker   from *The Bachelor's Banquet*   525
Francis Bacon   The Myth of Cupid and Of Love   526
Sir Thomas Overbury   An Amorist   530
Robert Burton   from *The Anatomy of Melancholy*   531
John Donne   That Women Ought to Paint   532
Sir Richard Steele   Conversations on Marriage   533
Benjamin Franklin   Advising a Young Man as to the Selection
        of a Mistress   537
Joseph Addison   History of the Lover's Leap   538
George Colman and Bonnel Thornton   On Superstitions in
        Love   541
Voltaire (François-Marie Arouet)   from *A Philosophical
        Dictionary*   545
Samuel Taylor Coleridge   Passion and Order   548
Charles Lamb   A Bachelor's Complaint of the Behavior of
        Married People   550
Percy Bysshe Shelley   Love Is a Powerful Attraction   555
Washington Irving   The Broken Heart   557
Stendhal (Marie Henri Beyle)   from *Of Love*   561
William Hazlitt   from *Liber Amoris*   562
Ralph Waldo Emerson   Love   563
Robert Louis Stevenson   On Falling in Love   573
Thomas Bulfinch   from *Age of Fable*   580
William James   from *The Principles of Psychology*
        and *The Varieties of Religious Experience*   589
Henry Adams   from *Mont Saint-Michel*   592
G. K. Chesterton   Romantic Love   599
Havelock Ellis   from *Studies in the Psychology of Sex*   602

Sigmund Freud from *Delusion and Dream* 606
H. L. Mencken The Wedding: A Stage Direction 610
Denis de Rougemont from *Love in the Western World* 614
Frank Gonzalez-Crussi from *The Remedies of Love* 616
Albert Camus Losing a Loved One 617
Muriel Spark Love 619

MEMOIRS AND LETTERS

Anonymous Tomb inscription, Ancient Egypt 625
Sappho to Anactoria 625
Anonymous The Alexandrian Erotic Fragment 626
Propertius from *The Elegies* 626
Pliny to Calpurnia and Paulinus 630
Marcus Aurelius to Fronto 631
St. Augustine from *The Confessions* 632
Heloise to Abelard 633
Abelard to Bernard and Heloise 641
Dante Alighieri from *The New Life* 642
Margery Brews to John Paston 644
Pietro Bembo to Lucrezia Borgia 645
Lucrezia Borgia to Pietro Bembo 647
King Henry VIII to Anne Boleyn 648
John Donne In Kindness to an Absent Friend 649
Maximilien de Bethune, Duc de Sully from *Memoirs* 650
Ann Hamilton and Barbara Villiers to Lord Chesterfield 653
Margaret, Duchess of Newcastle from *The Life of Newcastle* 653
Samuel Pepys from *The Diary* 654
John Wilmot, Earl of Rochester, to Mrs. Barry 657
William Congreve to Arabella Hunt 659
George Farquhar to Anne Oldfield 660
Alexander Pope to Teresa Blount 663
Esther Vanhomrigh (Vanessa) to Jonathan Swift 663
Jonathan Swift To Love 665
Françoise Athenais, Marquise de Montespan
  from *Memoirs* 666
Émilie du Châtelet to Duc de Richelieu 671
The Earl of Chesterfield from *On the Fine Art of Becoming
  a Man of the World and a Gentleman* 672
Jacques Casanova from *The Memoirs* 675

Lawrence Sterne to Catherine de Fourmantel, Lady Percy,
  and Mrs. H.   683
Ninon de l'Enclos to the Marquis de Sévigné   686
Edward Gibbon   from *Memoirs of My Life*   687
Benjamin Franklin   from *The Autobiography* and a letter to
  Madame Helvetius   688
Wolfgang Amadeus Mozart to his wife   691
James Boswell   from *Life of Samuel Johnson*   693
Lord Nelson to Lady Hamilton   693
Sir William Hamilton to Lady Hamilton   694
Napoleon Bonaparte to Josephine Bonaparte   695
John Keats to Fanny Brawne   697
Stendhal (Henri Beyle) to Madame Dembowski   698
Jane Clairmont to Lord Byron   701
Lord Byron to the Countess Guiccioli   ·   702
Thomas Medwin   from *Conversations of Lord Byron*   703
George Sand to Alfred de Musset   706
Black Elk   High Horse's Courting   708
Nathaniel Hawthorne to Sophia Hawthorne   713
Sophia Hawthorne to Nathaniel Hawthorne   715
Queen Victoria   journal entries and letters to King
  Leopold   716
Robert Browning to Elizabeth Barrett   718
Elizabeth Barrett to Robert Browning   720
Sarah Margaret Fuller, Marchioness D'Ossoli
  from letters and memoirs   722
Harriet Beecher Stowe to Calvin Stowe   726
John Ruskin to Effie Gray and Lady Mount-Temple   728
Kwei-li to her husband   730
Charlotte Brontë to Constantine Heger   734
George Eliot (Mary Ann Evans) to Herbert Spencer and
  John Cross   736
Charles Baudelaire to Apollonie Sabatier   738
Walt Whitman to Anne Gilchrist   740
Emily Dickinson to "Master"   740
Sullivan Ballou to Sarah Ballou   742
George Sand to Gustave Flaubert   743
Lewis Carroll to Gertrude   744
Sarah Orne Jewett to Annie Fields   745
Samuel Butler   from *The Notebooks*   746

Oscar Wilde to Lord Alfred Douglas   748
Jack London to Charmian Kittredge   750
Rainer Marie Rilke   from *Letters to a Young Poet*   752
Colette   from *Earthly Paradise* and letters to Marguerite
    and Pierre Moreno   756
Agnes von Kurowsky to Ernest Hemingway   761 ·
Aline Bernstein to Thomas Wolfe   762
Katherine Anne Porter to Matthew Josephson   764
Henry Miller to Anaïs Nin   766
Anaïs Nin   from *The Diary of Anaïs Nin, Vol. Two,*
    1934–1939   767
Vladimir Nabokov   First Love   770
Brenda Petersen   Sex as Compassion—A New Eros in a
    Time of AIDS   778
James McConkey   Idyll   780
Jan Morris   God, Love and Abysinnian Cats   788

Permissions   793

Index   805

INTRODUCTION

The Words We Love

O V E   is the great intangible. In our nightmares, we create beasts out of pure emotion. Hate stalks the streets with dripping fangs, fear flies down narrow alleyways on leather wings, and jealousy spins sticky webs across the sky. In daydreams, we maneuver with equal poise, foiling an opponent, scoring high on fields of glory while crowds cheer, cutting fast to the heart of an adventure. But what dream state is love? Frantic and serene, vigilant and calm, wrung-out and fortified, explosive and sedate—love commands a vast army of moods. Hoping for victory, limping from the latest skirmish, lovers enter the arena once again. Sitting still, we are as daring as gladiators. "What is the most dangerous thing you have ever done?" someone recently asked a well-known actress, to which she replied: "Date."

When I set a glass prism on a windowsill and allow the sun to flood through it, a spectrum of colors dances on the floor. What we call "white" is the rainbow of colored rays packed into a small space. The prism sets them free. Love is the white light of emotion. It includes many feelings that, out of laziness and confusion, we crowd into one simple word. Art is the prism that sets them free, then follows the gyrations of one or a few. When art separates the thick tangle of feelings, love's bones are bared. But love cannot be measured or mapped. Everyone admits that love is wonderful and necessary, yet no one can agree what it is. I once heard a sportscaster say of a basketball player, "He does all the intangibles. Just watch him do his dance." As lofty as ideas of love can be, no image is too profane to help explain it. Years ago, I fell in love with someone who was both a sport and a pastime. At the end, he made fade-away jump shots in my life. But, for a while, love did all the intangibles. It lets us do our finest dance.

Love. What a small word we use for an idea so immense and pow-erful it has altered the flow of history, calmed monsters, kindled great works of art, cheered the forlorn, turned tough guys to mush, consoled the enslaved, driven strong women mad, glorified the humble, fueled na-tional scandals, bankrupted robber barons, and made mincemeat of kings. How can love's spaciousness be conveyed in the narrow confines of one syllable? If we search for the source of the word, we find a his-tory vague and confusing, stretching back to the Sanskrit *lubhyati* ("he de-sires"). I'm sure the etymology rambles back much farther than that, to a one-syllable word heavy as a heartbeat. Love is an ancient delirium, a desire older than civilization with taproots stretching deep into dark and mysterious days.

We use the word love in such a sloppy way that it can mean almost nothing, or absolutely everything. It is the first conjugation students of Latin learn. It is a universally understood motive for crime. "Ah, he was in love," we sigh, "well, that explains it." In fact, in some countries, even murder is forgivable if it was "a crime of passion." Love, like truth, is the unassailable defense. Whoever first said "love makes the world go round" (it was an anonymous Frenchman) probably was not thinking about ce-lestial mechanics, but the way love seeps into the machinery of life to keep generation after generation in motion. We think of love as a posi-tive force that somehow ennobles the one feeling it. When a friend con-fesses that he's in love, we congratulate him.

In folk stories, unsuspecting lads and lasses ingest a love potion and quickly lose their hearts. As with all intoxicants, love comes in many guises and strengths. It has a mixed bouquet and may include some pi-quant ingredients. One's taste in love will have a lot to do with one's cul-ture, upbringing, generation, religion, era, gender, and so on. Ironically, although we sometimes think of it as the ultimate Oneness, love isn't mo-notone or uniform. Like a batik created from many emotional colors, it is a fabric whose pattern and brightness may vary. What is one's daugh-ter to think when she hears her mother say "I love Ben & Jerry's Cherry Garcia ice cream"; "I really loved my high school boyfriend"; "Don't you just love this sweater?"; "I'd love to take the whole family to the lake for a week this summer"; "Mommy loves you." Since all we have is one word, we talk about love in increments or unwieldy ratios. "How much do you love me?" a child asks. Because the parent can't answer "I (verb that means unconditional parental love) you," she may fling her arms wide, as if welcoming the sun and sky, stretching her body to its limit, spreading her fingers to encompass all of Creation, and say, "This much!" Or, "Think of the biggest thing you can imagine. Now double it. I love you a hundred times that much!"

When Elizabeth Barrett Browning wrote her famous sonnet, "How Do I Love Thee?" she didn't "count the ways" because she had an arithmetical turn of mind, but because English poets have always had to search hard for personal signals of their love. As a society, we are embarrassed by love. We treat it as if it were an obscenity. We reluctantly admit to it. Even saying the word makes us stumble and blush. Why should we be ashamed of an emotion that is beautiful and natural? In teaching writing students, I've sometimes given them the assignment of writing a love poem. "Be precise, be individual, and be descriptive. But don't use any clichés," I caution them, "or any curse words." Part of the reason for this assignment is that it helps them understand how inhibited we are about love. Love is the most important thing in our lives, a passion for which we would fight or die, and yet we're reluctant to linger over its name. Without a supple vocabulary, we can't even talk or think about it directly. On the other hand, we have many sharp verbs for the ways in which human beings can hurt one another, dozens of verbs for the subtle gradations of hate. But there are pitifully few synonyms for love. Our vocabulary of love and lovemaking is so paltry that a poet has to choose among clichés, profanities, or euphemisms. Fortunately, this problem has led to some richly imagined works of art. It has inspired poets to create their own private vocabularies. Mrs. Browning sent her husband a poetic abacus of love that in a roundabout way expressed the sum of her feeling. Other lovers have tried to calibrate their love in equally ingenious ways. In "The Flea," John Donne watches a flea suck blood from his arm and then from his beloved's and rejoices that their blood marries in the flea's stomach.

Yes, lovers are most often reduced to comparatives and quantities. "Do you love me more than her?" we ask. "Will you love me less if I don't do what you say?" We are afraid to look love in the face. We think of it as a sort of traffic accident of the heart. It is an emotion that scares us more than cruelty, more than violence, more than hatred. We allow ourselves to be foiled by the vagueness of the word. After all, love requires the utmost vulnerability. We equip someone with freshly-sharpened knives; strip naked; then invite him to stand close. What could be scarier?

Egyptologists have found fifty-five anonymous love poems, on papyri and vases, dating back to around 1300 B.C. Certainly there were poems written earlier, but papyri and vases are extremely perishable. Although we don't know the authors of the poems, they were most likely written by both men and women. Some of them are alternating duets between lovers. Told first from one point of view, then the next, they show psyches torn by uncertainty, hearts on fire. Here is part of a typical hieroglyphic love poem, "Conversations in Courtship," in which a man describes his darling as

> More lovely than all other womanhood,
>   luminous, perfect,
> A star coming over the sky-line at new year,
>   a good year,
> Splendid in colours,
>   with allure in the eye's turn.
> Her lips are enchantment,
>   her neck the right length
>   and her breasts a marvel;
>
> Her hair lapislazuli in its glitter,
>   her arms more splendid than gold.
> Her fingers make me see petals,
>   the lotus' are like that.
> Her flanks are modeled as should be,
>   her legs beyond all other beauty.
> Noble her walking
>   (vera incessu)
> My heart would be a slave should she enfold me.

In another poem, "Pleasant Songs of the Sweetheart Who Meets You in the Fields," we find a woman hunting birds:

> My darling—my beloved—whose love empowers me,
> Listen to what I tell you:
> I went to the field where birds gather.

I held in one hand a trap, and in the other a net and spear.
I saw many birds flying from the land of Punt
Laden with sweet fragrance to alight on Egypt's soil.

The first snatched the bait from my hand.
He had a beautiful odor and his claws held incense.
But, for your sake, dear beloved, I will set him free,
Because I would like you, when far away,
To listen to the song of the bird
Scented with myrrh.
How wonderful to go to the fields when one's heart
is consumed by love!

The goose cries out, the goose that snatched the bait and was
　　trapped.
Your love distracted me and I could not keep it.
I will fold the nets, but what can I tell mother
When I return each day without birds?
I will say I failed to set my nets,
because the nets of your love have trapped me.

Although these poems were written over three thousand years ago, they weave together many of the same themes, worries, and rejoicings we find in love poems today. They tell us what mattered to Egyptian lovers (and still vexes us). We find in them such themes as love's alchemy and the power to transform, the idealizing of the beloved in images drawn from nature, love as enslavement, love as a disabling force, the need to keep love a secret (especially from one's parents), and sensuous descriptions of how love redoubles one's senses.

If you took a woman from ancient Egypt and put her in an automobile factory in Detroit, she would be understandably disoriented. Everything would be new, especially her ability to stroke the wall and make light flood the room, touch the wall elsewhere and fill the room with summer's warm breezes or winter's blast. She'd be astonished by telephones, computers, fashions, the language and customs. But if she saw a couple stealing a kiss in a quiet corner, she would smile. People everywhere understand the phenomenon of love, just as they understand the appeal of music and find music deeply meaningful, even if they can't explain exactly what the meaning is, or why they respond viscerally to one composer and not another. Our Egyptian woman who prefers the birdlike twittering of a lute, and a 20th-century man who prefers heavy metal's jaws of sound, share a passion for music that both would understand. So it is with love. The values, customs, and protocols may vary from ancient days to the present, but not the majesty of love. People are unique in the way they walk, dress, and gesture. Yet we're able to look at two people—one wearing a business suit, the other wearing a sarong— and recognize that both of them are clothed. Love also has many fashions, some bizarre and (to our taste) shocking, others more familiar, but all are part of a fantasmagoria we know. In the Serengeti of the heart, time and nation are irrelevant. On that plain, all fires are the same fire.

Remember the feeling of an elevator falling in your chest when you said goodbye to a loved one? Parting is more than sweet sorrow, it pulls you apart when you are glued together. It feels like hunger pains, and we use the same word, pang. Perhaps this is why Cupid is depicted with a quiver of arrows, because love feels at times like being pierced in the chest. It is a wholesome violence. Common as childbirth, it seems rare nonetheless, always catches one by surprise, and cannot be taught. Each child rediscovers it, each couple redefines it, each parent reinvents it. People search for love as if it were a city lost beneath the desert dunes, where pleasure is the law, the streets are lined with brocade cushions, and the sun never sets.

DIANE ACKERMAN

The Book of Love

Gathering together the diverse works that make up this anthology was a daunting labor of love. When all is said and done, what work of art or literature is *not* about love, or at least the absence of it? Diane and I agreed that this anthology could not be inclusive, if for no other reason than that it must be of a size and weight that would allow readers to pick it up. We also knew that we did not want to limit our selections to the twentieth century or the west; we wanted the freedom to wander through the ideas of different times and different places. Love is timeless and universal. We hope our selections reflect that premise.

When possible, we wrote directly to authors, asking them if they might like to contribute to an anthology about love; many of the contemporary works were selected by the writers themselves. We read and reread, frequenting libraries, bookstores, and our own memories and imagination, looking for selections like the one below that, like love itself, make our hearts beat a little faster with recognition and joy. We hope our choices do the same for you.

> The Taoists relate that at the great beginning of the No-Beginning, Spirit and Matter met in mortal combat. At last the Yellow Emperor, the Sun of Heaven, triumphed over Shuyung, the demon of darkness and earth. The Titan, in his death agony, struck his head against the solar vault and shivered the blue dome of jade into fragments. The stars lost their nests, the moon wandered aimlessly among the wild chasms of the night. In despair, the Yellow Emperor sought far and wide for the repairer of the Heavens. He had not to search in vain. Out of the Eastern sea rose a queen, the divine Niuka, horn-crowned and dragon-tailed, resplendent in her armour of fire. She welded the five coloured rainbow in her magic cauldron and rebuilt the Chinese sky. But it is also told that Niuka forgot to fill two tiny crevices in the blue firmament. Thus began the dualism of love—two souls rolling through space and never at rest until they join together to complete the universe. Everyone has to build anew his sky of hope and peace.
>
> Okakura Kazuko,
> from *The Book of Tea*

In the midpoint of my work on this anthology, when piles of paper covered most surface areas of my house and my husband began talking about building an addition, I sought a break from "love." I decided to amuse myself with a book from the kitchen shelves, something to do with cookery or gardening and other matters less ethereal than the divine passion.

The above passage greeted me as soon as I opened the book.

It seemed like both reprimand and reminder. Love is not to be run from, hidden from, or disdained. It is always there, waiting to take us by surprise, to delight us, enrage us, enchant us, dismay us, and finally, inevitably, define us. We are how we love. That, more than anything. I think, is the theme of our selections. Medieval philosophers thought that bears were born amorphous and pliable; their mothers licked them into the shapes of bears. Love is the mother's tongue that forms us. It rules our lives, whether we will or not, so that those who flee love, like the atheist who can think only of god, end up most obsessed by it. For the human race, love seems to be the topic and subject and raison d'être and cause and effect, all at once, that consumes us.

Love certainly has given us the most numerous, consistent and absorbing plots in literature, be it fiction, nonfiction, or poetry. Why flee such a delightful emotion? Why not surrender? Surely that is the sensible thing to do. Love, after all, is the winged god. He can always overtake us. One thread in this book is the presence of Cupid in many selections—Cupid with his wings for speed, his arrows for pain, and his beauty for joy. We moderns wholeheartedly appropriated this ancient pagan child and still send our beloveds cards with his picture on them, as may have Margery Brews, along with her selection in this anthology, which is believed to be the first known Valentine.

Love is winged and swift, and also troublesome, another thread that weaves our selections together. From the early creation myths of war and strife between the gods to the "Unstable equilibrium" of William James, love is the great destabilizer. It shakes us awake, makes us conscious of our incompleteness, and makes us yearn. Perhaps we need to be broken so that we can better appreciate the joy of being made whole again.

Love is enchanting; our selections include tales of spells and potions and illusions and of resurrection. Love is the miracle that brings us back to life after the emotional death of loss or indifference. There are tales of jealousy and deceit, fidelity and reunion, hope and despair.

How we love is one issue; who and what we love is the other, and in this, we also made wide-ranging selections. Love does not strike only the young and able, the beautiful, the acceptable. Romantic love is only one possibility among many on the menu of the heart. Lovers in this anthology include couples, of course, but also children and their toys, parents and their offspring, and animals. We treat love not as an act but as an emotion, an overwhelming impulse to be with and protect our beloved.

Since love is complicated enough, we decided the structure of this anthology should not be. We arranged our choices by genre and within those genres followed a loose chronology so that tales of love requited and love defeated, happy love and sad love, pure and carnal, mingle and add to each other's appeal.

When, after two years of work, we sat back to assess our labor, we found we had put together a look at how love has been celebrated, suf-

fered, begun, ended, and preserved—in prose and poetry selections rang-
ing from an ancient Egyptian love story to a contemporary essay on in-
terspecies love and companionship. There are selections to remind us of
the three great roots of the many philosophies of love: the transcendental
dispassion of Platonism, the intrigue-ridden anguish of romatic medieval courtly love, and the illuminating mysticism first and perhaps best
developed in early Islamic love poems. Most loves combine a bit of the
three; no single love story is ever all pain or all pleasure or, for that matter, all talk. Along the way we found some wondrous connections. Ovid's
instructions to his mistress on how to behave at a dinner party find their
jealous, obsessive counterpart in one of Lord Nelson's letters to Lady
Hamilton. Plutarch's anecdote about Cleopatra flattering Antony on his
skills as an angler sounds again centuries later as Capellanus explains that
the word *amour* is from a latin verb meaning "to hook." Montaigne begins his essay on desire by speaking of love and ends it with meditations
on war; twentieth-century philosopher de Rougemont points out the
similarities between love-talk and war vocabulary.

The selections traverse the mine fields of the ancient mistrust between men and women, the politic parliament of love, the cunning country of lust and adultery, and the utopia of love's philosophies. Love
truly is the uncharted land, the boundary beyond which dragons be, the
wilderness we all must map for ourselves. Love is sacred and profane,
erotic and sublime, comic and tragic, carnal and mystical. When we are
most fortunate, when we have found true soulmates, love is all those different states.

And now, as Kazuko proposed in *The Book of Tea*, "let us have a sip of
tea. The afternoon glow is brightening the bamboos, the fountains are bubbling with delight, the soughing of the pines is heard in our kettle. Let us
dream of evanescence, and linger in the beautiful foolishness of things. . . ."

. . . And in the most beautiful, the most serious, essential, and
needful foolishness of all, love.

JEANNE MACKIN

In the Beginning

EMPEDOCLES

Love and Strife

———————

I will tell you a twofold tale. At one time it grew to be one only out of many; at another, it divided up to be many instead of one. There is a double becoming of perishable things and a double passing away. The coming together of all things brings one generation into being and destroys it; the other grows up and is scattered as things become divided. And these things never cease continually changing places, at one time all uniting in one through love, at another each borne in different directions. . . .

FICTION

ANONYMOUS, ANCIENT EGYPT

The King's Son

This excerpt from a longer Egyptian romance of the 19th dynasty (c. 1300 B.C.) already reflects many elements of love literature that will remain constant through the centuries: the concealing of identities (perhaps so that a new identity, that of lover, can be created); the need to overcome an obstacle, often portrayed as a disapproving parent; the power of love over death (in this romance, the wife saves her husband from death on several occasions); and, ultimately, the impossibility of avoiding one's destiny. By the end of this tale, fate catches up to the prince, and not even his loving wife can save him.

There was once a king who had no son. He therefore prayed to the gods to give him a son, and they ordered that a son should be born to him. He slept at night with his wife and she became pregnant. When her months were accomplished, behold she bore a son. When now the Hathors came to decide upon his fortune, they said: "He shall die by a crocodile, a snake, or a dog." The people who were with the children heard these words. They related them to His Majesty. Then was His Majesty very very sad. Then His Majesty caused a castle to be built in the mountains; this castle was provided with servants and with all good things from the palace, and the child was never allowed to go out of the castle.

Now when the child had grown tall, he went up on the roof and saw a greyhound running after a man who was walking along the road. He said to the servant who was with him: "What is that following the man who is walking along the road?" He answered him: "That is a greyhound!" The child said to him: "Let them bring me one." Then the servant went and told the king. The king then said: "Let them take him a pup, that his heart may not grieve about it." Then they brought him the greyhound.

Now after many days were gone, the child waxed great in all his members, and sent to his father to say: "Why should I remain here? Behold I am predestined to the three fates, and whether I do according to my will or not, God will do as He wills." Then they gave him weapons of all kinds . . . they brought him to the eastern frontier and said to him: "Go then according to thy wish." His dog was with him, and he travelled according to his heart's desire in the mountains, and lived on the best mountain game. Then he came to the prince of Naharanna. The prince of Naharanna had an only child, a daughter. He had built a house for her with a window more than seventy cubits from the ground. He ordered all the children of all the princes of Charu to be brought before him, and said to them: "Whoever shall climb to the window of my daughter, shall have her for wife."

Now after many days had passed, and the princes were making their daily attempt, the youth came past. Then they brought the youth to their house, they washed him and gave his horse food. They did all manner of good to the youth, they anointed him, they bound up his feet, and gave him of their own bread. They then talked to him and said: "Whence comest thou, thou beautiful youth?" He answered them: "I am the son of an Egyptian officer, my mother died, and my father took to himself another wife. . . . Thereupon she hated me, and I ran away and fled before her!" Then they embraced him and kissed him.

The prince then learnt from his hosts what had brought them hither, and naturally he also became desirous to win the king's daughter. Then they went to climb, as was their daily endeavour, and the lad stood afar from them and watched, and the eyes of the daughter of the prince of Naharanna rested upon him.

Now after some time had passed, the youth went to climb with the children of the princes. He climbed and reached the window of the daughter of the prince of Naharanna. She kissed him and embraced him in all his limbs. Then the suitors went to rejoice the heart of her father, and said to him: "A man has reached the window of thy daughter." The prince then asked: "The son of which prince is it?" and they answered him: "It is the son of an officer who has fled from his stepmother in Egypt." Then the prince of Naharanna was exceeding angry. Then he said: "I give my daughter to no Egyptian fugitive; he may return to his house again," and they went and told him: "Go back again to the place whence thou hast come." But the daughter seized him and swore: "By Rê'-Harmachis, if they take him from me, I will neither eat nor drink until I die." Then the messenger went and told her father what she had said. The prince of Naharanna sent people to kill the youth whilst he was in his house. But the daughter said: "By Rê', (if they kill) him, then I (also) shall be dead by sunset—I will not live an hour without him." . . . Then the messenger told this to her father.

The father could not understand such love, and he gave his daughter to the youth. He embraced him and kissed him in all his limbs, and said to him: "Tell me then who thou art; behold, art thou not now my son?" He answered him: "I am the son of an Egyptian officer, my mother died, my father took to himself another wife, thereupon she hated me, and I fled before her." Then he gave him his daughter to wife, and gave him (servants) and fields together with cattle and all good things.

❦ ❦

ANONYMOUS

Inscription in the tomb of Queen Ahmose, wife of Tuthmosis I

He (Amun) found her as she slept in the beauty of her palace. She waked at the fragrance of the god, which she smelled in the presence of his majesty. He went to her immediately . . . he imposed his desire upon her, he caused that she should see him in his form of a god. When he came before her she rejoiced at the sight of his beauty; his love passed into her limbs, which the fragrance of the god flooded; all his odours were from Punt, the land of perfumes.

How great is thy fame! said Queen Ahmose. It is splendid to see thy front; thou hast united my majesty with thy favours, thy dew is in all my limbs.

After this, the majesty of this god did all that he desired of her.

❦ ❦

ANONYMOUS

from *Gilgamesh*

TABLET VI
narrates the celebration of the victory of Gilgamesh, and his repulse of Ishtar's love advances

He cleansed his weapons, he polished his arms.
He took off the armour that was upon him. He put away

his soiled garments and put on clean raiment;
clothed himself with his ornaments, put on his diadem
Gilgamesh placed upon his head the crown and put on his diadem
To win the favour and love of Gilgamesh, Ishtar, the lofty goddess
    desired (and said unto him):
"Come, Gilgamesh, be thou my spouse,
Give, O give unto me thy manly strength.
Be thou my husband, let me be thy wife,
and I will set thee in a chariot (embossed) with precious stones and
    gold,
with wheels made of gold, and shafts of sapphires
Large kudanu-lions thou shalt harness to it.
Under sweet-smelling cedars thou shalt enter into our house.
[And] when thou enterest into our house
[Thou shalt sit upon?] a lofty throne, and people shall kiss thy feet;
kings and lords and rulers shall bow down before thee.
Whatever mountain and country produces, they shall bring to thee as
    tribute.
    thy sheep shall bear twin-ewes.
    mules they shall bring as tribute.
Thy majesty shall sit upon a chariot that is splendid,
drawn by a span that has no equal."
But Gilgamesh opened his mouth and spoke unto her;
said unto the lofty goddess Ishtar:

[The beginning lines of his speech are almost lost, only a few fragments
being preserved. Gilgamesh refused the proffered love of Ishtar, reminding her that all her former lovers have come to grief through her,
and said that he was not willing to share their fate.]

"Where is thy husband Tammuz, who was to be forever?
What, indeed, has become of the allallu-bird?
Well, I will tell thee plainly the dire result of thy coquetries.
To Tammuz, the husband of thy youth,
thou didst cause weeping and didst bring grief upon him every year.
The allallu-bird, so bright of colours, thou didst love;
But its wing thou didst break and crush,
so that now it sits in the woods crying: 'O my wing!'
Thou didst also love a lion, powerful in his strength,
seven and seven times didst thou dig a snaring pit for him.

Thou didst also love a horse, pre-eminent in battle,
but with bridle (?), spur, and whip thou didst force it on,
didst force it to run seven double-leagues at a stretch.
And when it was tired and wanted to drink, thou still didst force it on,
thereby causing weeping and grief to its mother Si-li-li.
Thou didst also love a shepherd of the flock
who continually poured out incense before thee,
and, for thy pleasure, slaughtered lambs day by day.
Thou didst smite him, and turn him into a tiger,
so that his own sheep-boys drove him away,
and his own dogs tore him to pieces.
Thou didst also love a farmer, a gardener of thy father,
who continually brought unto thee dainties,
and daily adorned thy table for thee.
Thine eye thou didst cast on him and turn his mind, saying:
'Oh, my farmer boy, let us enjoy thy manly strength.
Let thy hand come forth and take away my virginity'
But the farmer spoke unto thee and said:
'Me!—what is this that thou askest of me?
Mother, thou hast not baked, and I will not eat;
The food that I shall eat is bad and bitter,
and it is covered with cold and numbness.'
And when thou didst hear such words,
thou didst smite him and change him into a cripple
And didst thus compel him to lie on a couch,
so that he could no more rise up from his bed.
And now thou wouldst also love me; but like unto them I would fare."
When Ishtar heard such words
she became enraged, and went up into heaven,
and came unto Anu [her father], and
To Antum (her mother) she went, and thus spoke (unto them):
"My father, Gilgamesh has insulted me;
Gilgamesh has upbraided me with my evil deeds,
my deeds of evil and of violence."
And Anu opened his mouth and spoke—
said unto her, the mighty goddess Ishtar:
"Thou shalt not remain so disconsolate,
even though Gilgamesh has upbraided thee with thy evil deeds,
thy deeds of evil and of violence."
And Ishtar opened her mouth and said,

she spoke unto Anu, her father:
"My father, create [for me] a heaven-bull."

Translated by William Muss-Arnolt

❦ ❦

LONGUS

from *The Loves of Daphnis and Chloe*

Daphnis (son of the god Hermes) and the nymph Chloe are adopted and raised by two shepherds, Lamon and Dryas. As they grow, they fall in love with each other, with a little help from Cupid.

The two children grew rapidly, and their personal appearance exceeded that of ordinary rustics. Daphnis was now fifteen and Chloe was his junior by two years, when on the same night Lamon and Dryas had the following dream. They thought that they beheld the Nymphs of the Grotto, in which the fountain was and where Dryas found the infant, presenting Daphnis and Chloe to a very saucy-looking and handsome boy who had wings upon his shoulders and a little bow and arrows in his hand. He lightly touched them both with one of his shafts, and commanded them henceforth to follow a pastoral life. The boy was to tend goats, the girl was to have the charge of sheep.

The Shepherd and Goat-herd, having had this dream, were grieved to think that these, their adopted children, were like themselves to have the care of flocks. Their dress had given promise of a better fortune, in consequence of which their fare had been more delicate, and their education and accomplishments superior to those of a country life.

It appeared to them, however, that in the case of children whom the gods had preserved, the will of the gods must be obeyed; so each having communicated to the other his dream, they offered a sacrifice to the "winged boy, the companion of the Nymphs" (for they were unacquainted with his name), and sent forth the young people to their pastoral employments, having first instructed them in their duties: how to pasture their herds before the noon-day heat, and when it was abated; at what time to lead them to the stream, and afterward to drive them home to the fold; which of their sheep and goats required the crook, and to which only the voice was necessary.

They, on their part, received the charge as if it had been some powerful sovereignty, and felt an affection for their sheep and goats beyond what is usual with shepherds: Chloe referring her preservation to a ewe, and Daphnis remembering that a she-goat had suckled him when he was exposed.

It was the beginning of spring, the flowers were in bloom throughout the woods, the meadows, and the mountains; there were the buzzings of the bee, the warblings of the songsters, the frolics of the lambs. The young of the flock were skipping on the mountains, the bees flew humming through the meadows, and the songs of the birds resounded through the bushes. Seeing all things pervaded with such universal joy, they, young and susceptible as they were, imitated whatever they saw or heard. Hearing the carol of the birds, they sang; seeing the sportive skipping of the lambs, they danced; and in imitation of the bees they gathered flowers. Some they placed in their bosoms, and others they wove into chaplets and carried them as offerings to the Nymphs.

They tended their flocks in company, and all their occupations were in common. Daphnis frequently collected the sheep, which had strayed, and Chloe drove back from a precipice the goats which were too venturesome. Sometimes one would take the entire management both of goats and sheep, while the other was intent upon some amusement

Their sports were of a pastoral and childish kind. Chloe sometimes neglected her flock and went in search of stalks of asphodel, with which she wove traps for locusts; while Daphnis devoted himself to playing till nightfall upon his pipe, which he had formed by cutting slender reeds, perforating the intervals between the joints, and compacting them together with soft wax. Sometimes they shared their milk and wine, and made a common meal upon the provision which they had brought from home; and sooner might you see one part of the flock divided from the other than Daphnis separate from Chloe.

While thus engaged in their amusements Love contrived an interruption of a serious nature. A she-wolf from the neighbourhood had often carried off lambs from other shepherds' flocks, as she required a plentiful supply of food for her whelps. Upon this the villagers assembled by night and dug pits in the earth, six feet wide and twenty-four feet deep. The greater part of the loose earth, dug out of these pits, they carried to a distance and scattered about, spreading the remainder over some long dry sticks laid over the mouth of the pits, so as to resemble the natural surface of the ground. The sticks were weaker than straws, so that if even a hare ran over them they would break and prove that instead of substance there was but a show of solid earth. The villagers dug many of these pits in the mountains and in the plains, but they could not succeed in capturing the wolf, which discovered the contrivance of the snare. They however caused the destruction of many of their own goats and sheep, and very nearly, as we shall see, that of Daphnis.

Two angry he-goats engaged in fight. The contest waxed more and more violent, until one of them, having his horn broken, ran away bellowing with pain. The victor followed in hot and close pursuit. Daphnis, vexed to see that his goat's horn was broken, and that the conqueror persevered in his vengeance, seized his club and crook and pursued the pursuer. In consequence of the former hurrying on in wrath, and the latter flying in trepidation, neither of them observed what lay in their path, and both fell into a pit, the goat first, Daphnis afterward. This was the means of preserving his life, the goat serving as a support in his descent. Poor Daphnis remained at the bottom lamenting his sad mishap with tears, and anxiously hoping that someone might pass by, and pull him out. Chloe, who had observed the accident, hastened to the spot, and finding that he was still alive, summoned a cowherd from an adjacent field to come to his assistance. He obeyed the call, but upon seeking for a rope long enough to draw Daphnis out, no rope was to be found: upon which Chloe, undoing her head-band, gave it to the cowherd to let down; they then placed themselves at the brink of the pit, and held one end, while Daphnis grasped the other with both hands, and so got out.

They then extricated the unhappy goat, who had both his horns broken by the fall, and thus suffered a just punishment for his revenge toward his defeated fellow-combatant. They gave him to the herdsman as a reward for his assistance, and if the family at home inquired after him, were prepared to say that he had been destroyed by a wolf. After this they returned to see whether their flocks were safe, and finding both goats and sheep feeding quietly and orderly, they sat down on the trunk of a tree and began to examine whether Daphnis had received any wound. No hurt or blood was to be seen, but his hair and all the rest of his person was covered with mud and dirt. Daphnis thought it would be best to wash himself, before Lamon and Myrtale should find out what had happened to him; proceeding with Chloe to the Grotto of the Nymphs, he gave her his tunic and scrip in charge.

He then approached the fountain and washed his hair and his whole person. His hair was long and black, and his body sun-burnt; one might have imagined that its hue was derived from the overshadowing of his locks. Chloe thought him beautiful, and because she had never done so before, attributed his beauty to the effects of the bath. As she was washing his back and shoulders his tender flesh yielded to her hand, so that, unobserved, she frequently touched her own skin, in order to ascertain which of the two was softer. The sun was now setting, so they drove home their flocks, the only wish in Chloe's mind being to see Daphnis bathe again. The following day, upon returning to the accustomed pasture, Daphnis sat as usual under an oak, playing upon his pipe and surveying his goats lying down and apparently listening to his strains. Chloe, on her part, sitting near him, looked at her sheep, but more frequently turned her eyes upon Daphnis; again he appeared to her beautiful as he was playing upon his pipe, and she attributed his beauty to the melody, so that taking the pipe she played upon it, in order, if possible, to appear beautiful herself. She persuaded him to bathe again, she looked at him when in the bath, and while looking at him, touched his skin: after which, as she returned home, she mentally admired him, and this admiration was the beginning of love. She knew not the meaning of her feelings, young as she was, and brought up in the country, and never having heard from anyone so much as the name of love. She felt an oppression at her heart, she could not restrain her eyes from gazing upon him, nor her mouth from often pronouncing his name. She took no food, she lay awake at night, she neglected her flock, she laughed and wept by turns; now she would doze, then suddenly start up; at one moment her face became pale, in another moment it burnt with blushes. Such irritation is not felt even by the breeze-stung heifer. Upon one occasion, when alone, she thus reasoned with herself: "I am no doubt ill, but what my malady is I know not; I am in pain, and yet I have no wound; I feel grief, and yet I have lost none of my flock; I burn, and yet am sitting in the shade. How often have brambles torn my skin, without my shedding a single tear! How often have the bees stung me, yet I could still enjoy my meals! Whatever it is which now wounds my heart must be sharper than either of these. Daphnis is beautiful, so are the flowers; his pipe breathes sweetly, so does the nightingale; yet I take no account either of birds or flowers. Would that I could become a pipe, that he might play upon me! Or a goat, that I might pasture under his care! O cruel fountain, thou madest Daphnis alone beautiful; my bathing has been all in vain! Dear Nymphs, ye see me perishing, yet neither do ye endeavour to save the maiden brought up among you! Who will crown you with flowers when I am gone? Who will take care of my poor lambs? Who will attend to my chirping locust, which I caught with so much trouble, that its song might lull me to rest in the grotto; but now I am sleepless, because of Daphnis, and my locust chirps in vain!"

Translated by Rowland Smith

✥ ✥

APULEIUS OF MADAURA

from *The Metamorphoses or Golden Ass*

As soon as the sun new-risen had banished night and restored the day, I woke from slumber and at once left my bed, for I was most anxious to make myself acquainted with the rarities and wonders of the place. I reflected that I was now in the heart of Thessaly, the native land of magical incantations, and celebrated as such by common consent through all the world. I thought also of the story told by my good comrade, Aristomenes, the scene of which was laid in this place; my hopes and my scientific interests alike combined to put me in a state of great excitement and I observed everything that I saw with curious eyes. Nothing met my gaze in that town which I believed to be what it really was. I thought that everything had been transformed by wizard murmurs to a shape other than its own, that the stones on which I stumbled were petrified men, that the birds which I heard were men encased in feathers, that the trees surrounding the walls were men who had sprouted into leaf, and that the waters of the fountains had once worn the semblance of men. I expected every minute to see statues and pictures walk, to hear walls talk, oxen and cattle prophesy, and sudden oracles to fall from heaven itself and from the orb of day.

In this state of excitement, in fact quite overwhelmed by the desire that tormented me, although I found not a trace or single vestige of what I longed to see, I still went the round of all the town and I strolled from door to door like some rich and leisured lounger staring at everything I saw. Suddenly unawares I found myself in the provision market, and there I came upon a woman closely attended by a number of slaves. She was walking briskly; the gold in which her jewels were set and with which her garments were embroidered proclaimed her to be a married woman of good birth. Close to her side walked an old man bowed down with years, who had no sooner set eyes upon me than he cried, "By Hercules, it's Lucius." He saluted me with a kiss and murmured something in the woman's ear that I could not catch. Then "Why," said he, "don't you come and salute your kinswoman?" "I hardly like to," I replied, "since I do not know the lady." A sudden blush suffused my cheeks and I stood where I was with head bowed. She turned to look at me and said, "See, he has all the noble modesty of that best of women, his mother Salvia; and in person too he's her very image; tall but nicely proportioned, slender without being thin, complexion rosy but not too red, yellow hair simply arranged, tawny eyes but watchful and with flashing glance just like an eagle's, face handsome in all its features, and a graceful and unaffected gait." She added, "Lucius, I brought you up with my own hands. For your mother and I are united by more than mere ties of blood; we were brought up under the same roof. Both of us spring from the family of Plutarch, the same nurse suckled us; and we grew up together like sisters. The only thing that separates us is rank, for while she made a most distinguished marriage, I married a private citizen. I am Byrrena, whose name, I dare say, you have heard pretty often as one of those who brought you up. Come then, don't be shy, but accept the hospitality of my house, or rather regard it as if it were your own."

Her words had given time for my blushes to disperse, and I answered, "Kinswoman, I cannot think of leaving my host Milo, against whom I have no ground of complaint; but I will promise you this, as I may without incivility. As often as I have to travel this way again, I will never miss an opportunity of staying with you."

In the course of this conversation and similar words that followed, we arrived at Byrrena's house, which was only a few steps off. The hall was marvellously beautiful. At each of its four corners stood a pillar bearing an image of the goddess of victory, with wings spread wide and dewy feet that held motionless the rolling sphere on whose unstable summit they rested. So lightly trod they thereon that it seemed they could not stand still; nay, thou hadst even thought they flew. And, lo! A block of Parian marble wrought into the likeness of Diana occupied the midst of the hall and lent balance and symmetry to the whole; a statue of perfect beauty, with raiment blown in the wind and feet that pressed nimbly forward, it fronted all who entered and the majesty of the deity made it worshipful. Dogs guarded the goddess on either side, and the dogs also were wrought in stone. Their eyes glared threats, their ears were pricked, their nostrils parted, their mouths grinned fiercely; and if ever some dog began to bark hard by, thou hadst thought the sound came from the throats of stone. But that excellent sculptor had shown the greatest proof of his craftsmanship by making the dogs rear up with breasts raised high in air, so that their forefeet seemed to run, while their hinder feet stood still. Behind the goddess rose a rock shaped like a cave, adorned with moss and grass and twigs and foliage, with shrubs there and vine-leaves here, all blossoming in stone. Within, the reflection of the goddess shone on the polished marble. From the outer edges of this rock there hung exquisitely sculptured apples and grapes, perfect copies displayed by art in rivalry with nature. Nay, some there were thou mightest have thought to pluck and eat, when autumn full of new wine should have breathed the hue of ripeness on them; and didst thou stoop and gaze on the stream that flowed from beneath the goddess's feet with gently rippling waters, thou wouldst deem those clusters were true clusters swinging in air, among all their attributes of truth lacking not that of motion. In the midst of the marble foliage Actaeon craned forward, his curious gaze fixed on the goddess; the shining marble and the stream alike reflected his image, as already half-transformed to the semblance of a stag he waited for Diana to bathe.

Again and again my eyes explored each detail with exquisite delight, till Byrrena said, "All that you see is yours." Then she bade every one leave us, as she would talk with me alone. When they were all gone, she said, "Dearest Lucius, I fear for you most anxiously, and would forewarn you while the peril yet is far from you, for I love you as my own son. By this goddess, I beseech you, be on your guard; I adjure you, be upon your guard with all your might against the evil arts and wicked spells of Pamphila, the wife of that Milo with whom you tell me you are lodging. She is believed to be a witch of the first order and to know all manner of incantations such as are sung over the tombs of the dead. By breathing on twigs and stones and trifling objects of that nature she can drown the light of the starry firmament in the depths of hell and plunge it in ancient chaos. As soon as she sets eyes on any handsome youth, she is taken with his charms and forthwith fixes her eyes and her whole soul upon him. She lays wait for him with her allurements, invades his soul and binds him with eternal fetters of passionate love. Those who do not fall in with her desires, but render themselves vile in her eyes by the rejection of her love, she transforms in the twinkling of an eye into stones and cattle and all manner of beasts, or in some cases makes them as though they had never been. It is this I fear for you, it is of this I bid you beware. For her passion burns continually, and your youth and beauty are such as might well excite it." Such were the words Byrrena uttered, showing herself not a little anxious for my sake.

Nevertheless, as soon as I heard mention of the name of magic, the name I had ever so longed to hear, I became all on fire with curiosity and was so far from being on my guard against Pamphila that I was even desirous of submitting myself to her instruction, whatever the cost, and would verily have hurled myself into the abyss with desperate leap. I freed myself from Byrrena's grasp as though it had been a chain that bound me, bade her a hurried farewell, and flew with all speed to Milo's house, my mind full of the wildest expectation. And while I walked with hurried steps like any madman, I said to myself, "Come, Lucius, keep your eyes open and sharpen your wits. The chance you desired is come. You may now fill yourself with tales of wonder to your heart's content, as you have long prayed to do. Away with childish fears, up and grapple with your fortune face to face. Avoid the embraces of your hostess, see that you do no wrong to the good Milo, but do all you can to win Fotis the maidservant. For she is quite pretty, has a sportive disposition and a charming wit. And when you were retiring to sleep last night, with what kindly courtesy she led you to your room! How nicely she put you to bed and how affectionately she tucked you up! How she kissed your face! and what reluctance to leave you was written on her countenance! And when she went, remember how she kept stopping and looking back at you. May the omen prove fair and fortunate; urge your suit with Fotis, perilous though it be!"

As I thus reasoned with myself I reached Milo's door and wasting no words, like the senators who vote without speaking, plied my feet to give effect to my resolution. I found neither Milo nor his wife at home, but only my sweet Fotis. She was cutting up some pigs' innards to make stuffing and preparing a hash together with some gravy, which, as my nose told me from a distance, was exceedingly savoury. She was clad in a neat linen tunic, her skirts girt rather high with a bright pink ribbon fastened prettily beneath her breast. She was spinning the basin of food round and round in her rosy hands, and as she shook it again and again with circular motion, she swayed her limbs gently to and for, and her supple back quivered softly and bent with comely undulation. I was struck dumb with admiration at the sight and stood marvelling. At length I addressed her. "How charmingly, how merrily you twirl that basin, my pretty Fotis. What delicious dainties you're making. Happy, nay, blest, if truth be true, is he who has your leave to dip his finger in them."

To this the saucy wench replied, for she had a very pretty wit, "My poor boy, get away from my fire, as far as you can. Quick! If the least spark of mine touch you, you'll be all on fire within and I shall be the only person who can put out the conflagration."

As she spoke she looked at me and laughed. I did not leave her till I had carefully surveyed all her beauties. But why do I speak of other beauties, when my sole thought has ever been first to look at the head and hair with eager staring gaze and to delight myself with dreaming of it when I am alone? I have a firm and settled conviction that I am right in my views on this point, since the hair is the fairest part of all the body, is placed in an open and conspicuous position and is the first thing to meet our eyes, while its natural sheen does for the head what the cheerful colours of bright raiment do for the other limbs. But—though it is a sin to speak of it, and I pray that so frightful a sight is nowhere to be seen—if you should despoil the head of an exquisitely beautiful woman of its hair and deprive her face of its natural adornment, though she had descended from heaven, or sprung from the sea and had the waves for nurses, nay, though she were Venus herself, attended by all the choir of graces and escorted by the whole tribe of Cupids and girt with her cestus, sweet as cinnamon and distilling balsam, and yet were bald, she would give no pleasure even to Vulcan, her amorous spouse. What shall one say, when the hair glistens with ravishing hues and resplendent sheen, flashes swift lightnings against the sunlight, or shines with calmer glow, or changes its hue from beauty to beauty, and now from glistening gold sinks to soft honey-coloured shade, now with its raven blackness rivals the dark purple shimmer on the necks of doves, or when, smeared with Arabian unguents, parted with the fine teeth of a sharp comb and gathered behind in a knot, it greets the lover's eyes and mirror-like sends back a reflection fairer than the truth? What shall one say when it is heaped thick in many a tress upon the crown or streams down the back with long far-floating locks? Such is the glory of the hair, that though a woman go forth in raiment adorned with gold and gems and all manner of ornament, yet, if she tire not her hair, she cannot be said to be adorned.

But it was no laboured ornament, but artless grace that lent an added charm to my sweet Fotis. Her locks streamed gently down in their profusion, and hung about her neck and were massed about her nape and sank softly down in intricate tresses, till at last they were gradually gathered to a coil and bound in a knot upon the crown of her head.

I could no longer endure the torment of such fierce delight, but bending over her I implanted the sweetest of all kisses just where the hair climbs to the summit of the head. She bent her neck back and looking at me out of the corners of her twinkling eyes, "Hallo! master student," said she, "you are getting a taste of the fruit that is bittersweet. Have a care lest the honey be so sweet that it will sour your bile for many a long day."

"What matters that, my heart's joy?" I replied; "I am ready for the smart; if only I may refresh myself now and again with one little kiss, love may put me on his gridiron and roast me." With the words I caught her in a closer embrace and began to kiss her. Then, as she warmed to passion like to mine, I cried, "I shall perish, nay, my fate is long since sealed, if thou console me not." At this she kissed me again, and said, "Be of good cheer! my heart is thine! Wait till dinner is over and I will come to thee."

After murmuring these words and their like to one another we parted. It was just noon and Byrrena sent me as tokens of her affection a fat pig, five young chickens, and a jar of rare old wine. The rest of the day was given up first to bathing and finally to dinner. For at the excellent Milo's invitation I sat down to dinner with him at his exquisite little table! Remembering Byrrena's warning I screened myself as far as possible from the sight of his wife. When I cast my eyes upon her face it was with a shudder as though I were looking on Avernus's lake. Instead, I cheered my soul by many a glance at Fotis, who was waiting upon us. Suddenly Pamphila, looking at the lamp—for it was now evening— said, "What heavy rain we shall have tomorrow." When her husband asked her how she had discovered that, she replied that the lamp had foretold it to her. At this remark Milo laughed and said, "We keep a fine Sibyl in the house in the person of that lamp, which from the observatory of its chandelier espies all the business of the skies and the sun itself."

At this I struck in, "This is my first experience of this kind of divination. But it is not to be wondered at if that tiny flame, small though it be and the work of men's hands, remembers none the less that greater flame that burns in heaven as being its parent, and is therefore divinely gifted to know and proclaim to us what he purposes to bring about in the far heights of air. Even at Corinth in my own country there is a certain Chaldean stranger whose marvellous responses have set all the world agog. For a fee he reveals the secrets of the fates to the people, telling them which days are propitious for a happy marriage, which for laying the foundations of walls that shall stand for ever, which shall bring profit to the merchant, success to the traveller, or fair voyage to ships. In fact, when I asked him what would be the outcome of this my journeying abroad, in reply he prophesied many most marvellous things of very varied import. Now he said that I should become a name of high renown, now that I should be the hero of a remarkable tale, an incredible romance, and that books should be written concerning me."

At this Milo smiled and said, "What is this Chaldean like to look upon and what is his name?" "He is tall, and rather dark," I replied, "and calls himself Diophanes." "That's the very man," said he. "He was here among us and uttered many similar prophecies to many persons. He pocketed very considerable fees, nay, I may say that he made a magnificent harvest. But, poor wretch, he met with a most unhappy mischance, I might even call it cruel disaster. One day when he was surrounded by a great throng of people and was foretelling the destinies to a ring of bystanders, a man of business called Cerdo approached him and asked him to name a lucky day on which he might start to travel abroad. He selected a day and told it him. Cerdo produced his purse, poured out the money and counted out a hundred denarii as a reward for his divination, when, lo and behold! A young man of good birth crept up behind the seer, plucked him by the cloak, and when he turned round embraced him and kissed him most affectionately. He returned his kiss and forthwith made him sit down beside him. So overcome was he with amazement at this sudden apparition that he forgot the business on which he was at the moment engaged and began to speak with him. 'I am indeed delighted to see you,' he said; 'when did you arrive?' 'Only last evening,' replied the other; 'but do you in turn tell me, dear comrade, what sort of journey did you have both by sea and land after you took ship so suddenly from the island of Euboea?' To this Diophanes the admirable Chaldean replied—for he had not yet recovered himself and his wits had deserted him—'I can only wish my enemies and all those that hate me so horrible a journey. It was worthy of Ulysses. For the ship in which I sailed was tossed this way and that by tempestuous whirlwinds, lost both its steering-oars and was with great difficulty run aground on the farther shore. There she sank at once and we had much ado to swim ashore with the loss of all our possessions. And then all we managed to scrape together by the charity of strangers or the kindness of friends was seized by robbers, and poor Arignotus my only brother had his throat cut before my eyes while he was attempting to resist their audacious onslaught.' As he told his melancholy story, Cerdo, the man of business of whom I spoke, snatched up the money that he had intended as a reward for his divination and decamped forthwith. Then at last Diophanes woke to the situation and, seeing all of us who stood round dissolved in loud laughter, perceived what a fool he had made of himself. But, Master Lucius, I hope that the Chaldean has told you the truth, though he has told it no one else. Good luck to you, and may you have a prosperous journey!"

While Milo discoursed thus tediously, I groaned inwardly and was furious with myself for having started him on these interminable stories at such an unsuitable moment. For they were robbing me of the best part of the evening and the delights which it had in store. At last, throwing shame to the winds, I said to him, "As far as I am concerned your friend Diophanes may just endure his evil fortune, and earth and sea are welcome yet a second time to swallow up the booty he wins from all the world. But I am still crippled by the fatigues of yesterday. So forgive me if I retire rather early." I suited the deed to the word and went to my room, where I found a most elegant repast had been prepared. My servants' beds had been laid on the ground outside my room and as far as possible from it, that we might have privacy for our conversation. Beside my bed was placed a small table on which was spread no mean display of viands, the remains of the various courses of our dinner, together with cups of ample size. These had already been half-filled with wine so that there was room only for a very moderate admixture of water, while hard by there stood a flagon with mouth cut wide and smooth and most apt for the drawing of wine.

I had scarcely sat me down upon my bed when lo! my darling Fotis entered the room, her mistress now being safe in bed. Her face shone with joy and roses hung garlanded or wandering at their sweet will about her shapely bosom. She caught me to her arms, kissed me, set wreaths about my brow and sprinkled me with flowers. Then she took up a goblet and pouring hot water on the wine gave me to drink. Before I had quite drunk it to the last drop she laid gentle hands upon it and slowly with her own fair lips drained what was left, and as she sipped it cast sweet glances at me. A second and a third cup followed, with many others, all of which we drank turn and turn about. Thus we made merry, and many were the evenings afterwards that we passed in like enjoyment.

୧୦ଟ ଟ୭ଟ

HELIODORUS

from *The Aethiopica*

Theagenes and Chariclea fall in love during a religious procession

V.   At first they remained dumbfounded and motionless; she, still holding out the torch, and he, extending his hand to take it. For a long time they continued thus, their eyes fixed upon each other, as if, instead of having now met for the first time, they had met before, and were trying to remember where. Then they smiled, gently and almost imperceptibly, which was only betrayed by the movement of their eyes; soon, as if ashamed, they both blushed; and, a moment later, when passion had reached their hearts, they grew pale. In a word, a thousand changes overspread their faces in a moment, a thousand changes of colour and features betrayed the agitation of their souls. All this, as may be imagined, escaped the notice of the multitude, whose thoughts and attention were devoted to other matters. Charicles himself, busy in reciting the customary prayer and invocation, saw nothing of it either; but as for me, my whole attention was devoted to watching the young people; for, after I had heard the oracle that had been given to Theagenes, at the time when he was offering sacrifice in the temple, their names awakened in me some suspicion of what was going to happen, although I could not clearly make out the meaning of that part of the prophecy that related to the future.

VI.   At last, Theagenes tore himself away from the maiden, as if under compulsion, placed the torch beneath the altar, and lighted the pile. The procession broke up; the Thessalians repaired to a banquet, and the rest dispersed to their own houses. Chariclea threw a white robe over her shoulders, and retired with some of her companions to her abode in the precincts of the temple; for she did not live with her supposed father, but apart, in order that she might devote herself entirely to the service of the temple. Filled with curiosity by what I had seen and heard, I purposely went to meet Charicles. "Well," said he, "have you seen Chariclea, my pride and the pride of Delphi?" "Yes, and not for the first time," I replied; "I had already frequently met her before in the temple; not merely in passing by, as the phrase goes; she has frequently offered sacrifice with me; she has often questioned me concerning things human and divine, when she came across anything that puzzled her, and I was pleased to assist her." "And what did you think of her today? Did she add any ornament to the procession?" "Hush, Charicles; you might as well ask me whether the moon outshines the stars." "But some praise was given to the Thessalian youth." "Yes, to him was given the second or third place, but all were agreed that your daughter was the pride and crown of the procession." Charicles was evidently pleased at my words, and, while I told the truth, I attained my object, which was to inspire him with perfect confidence in me. He smiled and said to me: "I am now going to her; if you would like it, do not hesitate to come with me and see whether

the crowd and the disturbance have fatigued her." I gladly consented, giving him to understand that I had nothing more at heart than the wish
to oblige him.

VII.   When we reached her room, we found her lying on her
couch in a state of languor and depression, her eyes moist with the
tears of love. Her father, having embraced her as usual, asked her what
ailed her. She complained of a violent headache, and said that she would
like to rest. Then Charicles left the room with me, ordered the servants
to keep quiet, and, going out into the front of the house, said: "What
does this mean, my dear Calasiris? What is this languor which has come
over my daughter?" "Do not be surprised," I replied, "if, while walking
in procession amidst so large a crowd, she has drawn upon her some evil
eye." At these words he smiled ironically: "And do you also, like the vulgar, believe in the influence of the evil eye?" "I believe in it implicitly,
and the following is my explanation of the matter. The air which surrounds us and penetrates into our bodies through the eyes, nose, respiration, and other passages, reaches us charged with external qualities,
and, according to the different nature of these qualities, we are variously
affected. After that, it is enough for anyone to look at a beautiful object with an envious eye to communicate pernicious qualities to the surrounding air; his breath spreads, full of bitterness, over his neighbour,
and, thanks to its subtilty, penetrates to the bones, even to the very
marrow. Thus it is that, frequently, this species of envy which has been
called by the name of "fascination," affects the health of those whom
it attacks. To convince you of this, Charicles, I would ask you to remember that we are frequently attacked by ophthalmia or some conta-
gious disease, without having touched persons afflicted by them, without
having been near their bed or sat at the same table with them, but simply because we have breathed the same air. Remember again—and there
is not a more evident proof—the manner of the birth of love; objects
perceived by the sight produce it; they spread around themselves a kind
of light mist, and cause the passion, which is to have its abode in the
soul, to penetrate through the channel of the eyes. And it is not difficult to see the reason of this: the sight, being the most fiery and mobile
of all our senses, is for that very reason most susceptible to the influences around it; and, by reason of its burning spirit, attracts the ema-
nations of love.

VIII.   "But, if you wish for an example out of natural history, I
will give you one out of the sacred books on animals: the Charadrius
possesses the property of curing the jaundice; when anyone afflicted

with this complaint looks at it, it turns aside, shuts its eyes, and runs away; not, as is sometimes said, because it is unwilling to bestow its assistance, but because, from the moment that an afflicted person looks upon it, it naturally attracts, as it were, a current of the disease; for this reason it avoids the person's eyes, like a dart. It is the same with the serpent called basilisk; you have no doubt heard that its breath and look alone dry up and infect everything that it touches. Nor must we be astonished if some persons fascinate even their dearest friends, those to whom they wish every happiness; for, being naturally envious, they do not do what they wish, but what their nature compels them to do."

IX.   After a moment's silence, Charicles rejoined: "You have solved the question in a reasonable and convincing manner; pray Heaven that the fascination which influences her may be that of love; far from considering that a malady, I should think that she was cured. You know that I have already begged your assistance in this. But, for the moment, there seems no reason to suspect this; she is the declared enemy of love and marriage. We must therefore believe that her malady is really due to the evil eye. I do not doubt that you will consent to cure her of it; for you are my friend, and your learning is vast." I promised that I would do all that lay in my power to help her, if I found that there was anything the matter with her.

X.   We were still discussing the matter when a messenger arrived in great haste: "My good friends," said he, "one would think you were invited to a fray instead of a feast, you are so slow in coming. Have you forgotten that it is the handsome Theagenes who has prepared it, and that the greatest of heroes, Neoptolemus, presides at it? Come, then; do not make us wait until evening; we are only waiting for you." Charicles whispered to me: "This man's invitation is somewhat rude; he shows no signs of the good manners of Bacchus, although he has imbibed pretty freely. But, let us go, for I am afraid that he may in the end proceed to violence." "You are joking," I said; "however, let us go." As soon as we had arrived, Theagenes placed Charicles next to himself, and also treated me with respect for his sake. But why need I weary you with lengthy details of the feast, the dances of maidens, the music, the Pyrrhic dance of the youths in armour, and other entertainments with which Theagenes graced his magnificent banquet, and the exquisite dishes which rendered the repast more agreeable and conduced to conviviality? I will, however, tell you things which it is necessary you should know, and which it will give me pleasure to relate. Theagenes assumed a look of cheerfulness, and forced himself to entertain the company, but I saw in what direction his thoughts were tending. He kept rolling his eyes; from time to time he heaved a deep sigh without any apparent reason; at one time dejected and deep in thought, he suddenly became more cheerful, as if he were conscious of his manner and wished to recover himself; in short, he passed rapidly from one extreme to the other. The mind of a lover, like that of a drunken man, is changeable and inconstant; both seem to be tossed upon the waves of passion; wherefore a lover is prone to intoxication, and a drunken man to love.

XI.   At last, when he appeared overcome by languor and ill at ease, all the guests were convinced that he was unwell. Then Charicles, who had observed nothing but his changes of humour, whispered to me: "Some evil eye has also looked upon him; he seems to me in the same state as Chariclea." "The very same, by Isis!" I replied; "and not without reason; for, next after her, he was the most observed in all the procession."

ANONYMOUS

from *Aucassins and Nicolette*

In Paradise, what have I to do? I do not care to go there unless I may have Nicolette, my very sweet friend, whom I love so much. For, to Paradise goes no one but such people as I will tell you of. There go old priests and old cripples and the maimed, who all day and all night crouch before altars and in old crypts, and are clothed with old worn-out capes and old tattered rags; who are naked and footbare and sore; who die of hunger and want and misery. These go to Paradise; with them I have nothing to do; but to Hell I am willing to go. For, to Hell go the fine scholars and the fair knights who die in tournies and in glorious wars; and the good men-at-arms and the well-born. With them I will gladly go; and there go the fair courteous ladies whether they have two or three friends besides their lords. And the gold and silver go there, and the ermines and sables; and there go the harpers and jongleurs, and the kings of the world. With these will I go, if only I may have Nicolette, my very sweet friend, with me.

MARIE DE FRANCE

The Lay of the Two Lovers

Once upon a time there lived in Normandy two lovers who were pass-ing fond and were brought by Love to Death. The story of their love was bruited so abroad, that the Bretons made a song in their own tongue, and named this song the Lay of the Two Lovers.

In Neustria—that men call Normandy—there is verily a high and marvellously great mountain, where lie the relics of the Two Children. Near this high place the King of those parts caused to be built a certain fair and cunning city, and since he was lord of the Pistrians, it was known as Pistres. The town yet endures, with its towers and houses, to bear witness to the truth; moreover the country thereabouts is known to us all as the Valley of Pistres.

This King had one fair daughter, a damsel sweet of face and gra-cious of manner, very near to her father's heart, since he had lost his Queen. The maiden increased in years and favour, but he took no heed to her trothing, so that men—yea, even his own people—blamed him greatly for this thing. When the King heard thereof he was passing heavy and dolent, and considered within himself how he might be de-livered from this grief. So then, that none should carry off his child, he caused it to be proclaimed, both far and near, by script and trumpet, that he alone should wed the maid who would bear her in his arms to the pinnacle of the great and perilous mountain, and that without rest or stay. When this news was noised about the country, many came upon the quest. But strive as they would they might not enforce them-selves more than they were able. However mighty they were of body, at the last they failed upon the mountain, and fell with their burthen to the ground. Thus, for a while, was none so bold as to seek the high Princess.

Now in this country lived a squire, son to a certain count of that realm, seemly of semblance and courteous, and right desirous to win that prize, which was so coveted of all. He was a welcome guest at the Court, and the King talked with him very willingly. This squire had set his heart upon the daughter of the King, and many a time spoke in her ear, pray-ing her to give him again the love he had bestowed upon her. So seeing him brave and courteous, she esteemed him for the gifts which gained him the favour of the King, and they loved together in their youth. But they hid this matter from all about the Court. This thing was very grievous to them, but the damoiseau thought within himself that it were good to bear the pains he knew, rather than to seek out others that might prove sharper still. Yet in the end, altogether distraught by love, this prudent varlet sought his friend, and showed her his case, saying that he urgently required of her that she would flee with him, for no longer could he endure the weariness of his days. Should he ask her of the King, well he knew that by reason of his love he would refuse the gift, save he bore her in his arms up the steep mount. Then the maiden made answer to her lover, and said,

"Fair friend, well I know you may not carry me to that high place. Moreover should we take to flight, my father would suffer wrath and sorrow beyond measure, and go heavily all his days. Certainly my love is too fond to plague him thus, and we must seek another counsel, for this is not to my heart. Hearken well. I have kindred in Salerno, of rich estate. For more than thirty years my aunt has studied there the art of medicine, and knows the secret gift of every root and herb. If you hasten to her, bearing letters from me, and show her your adventure, certainly she will find counsel and cure. Doubt not that she will discover some cunning simple, that will strengthen your body, as well as comfort your heart. Then return to this realm with your potion, and ask me at my father's hand. He will deem you but a stripling, and set forth the terms of his bargain, that to him alone shall I be given who knows how to climb the perilous mountain, without pause or rest, bearing his lady between his arms."

When the varlet heard this cunning counsel of the maiden, he rejoiced greatly, and thanking her sweetly for her rede, craved permission to depart. He returned to his own home, and gathering together a goodly store of silken cloths most precious, he bestowed his gear upon the pack horses, and made him ready for the road. So with a little company of men, mounted on swift palfreys, and most privy to his mind, he arrived at Salerno. Now the squire made no long stay at his lodging, but as soon as he might, went to the damsel's kindred to open out his mind. He delivered to the aunt the letters he carried from his friend, and bewailed their evil case. When the dame had read these letters with him, line by line, she charged him to lodge with her awhile, still she might do according to his wish. So by her sorceries, and for the love of her maid, she brewed such a potion that no man, however wearied and outworn, but by drinking this philtre, would not be refreshed in heart and blood and

bones. Such virtue had this medicine, directly it were drunken. This simple she poured within a little flacket, and gave it to the varlet, who received the gift with great joy and delight, and returned swiftly to his own
land.

The varlet made no long sojourn in his home. He repaired straightway to the Court, and, seeking out the King, required of him his fair
daughter in marriage, promising, for his part, that were she given him,
he would bear her in his arms to the summit of the mount. The King was
no wise wrath at his presumption. He smiled rather at his folly, for how
should one so young and slender succeed in a business wherein so many
mighty men had failed. Therefore he appointed a certain day for this
judgment. Moreover he caused letters to be written to his vassals and his
friends—passing none by—bidding them to see the end of this adventure. Yea, with public cry and sound of trumpet he bade all who would,
come to behold the stripling carry his fair daughter to the pinnacle of
the mountain. And from every region round about men came to learn the
issue of this thing. But for her part the fair maiden did all that she was
able to bring her love to a good end. Ever was it fast day and fleshless
day with her, so that by any means she might lighten the burthen that her
friend must carry in his arms.

Now on the appointed day this young dansellon came very early
to the appointed place, bringing the flacket with him. When the great
company were fully met together, the King led forth his daughter before
them; and all might see that she was arrayed in nothing but her smock.
The varlet took the maiden in his arms, but first he gave her the flask
with the precious brewage to carry, since for pride he might not endure
to drink therefrom, save at utmost peril. The squire set forth at a great
pace, and climbed briskly till he was halfway up the mount. Because of
the joy he had in clasping his burthen, he gave no thought to the potion.
But she—she knew the strength was failing in his heart.

"Fair friend," said she, "well I know that you tire: drink now, I pray
you, of the flacket, and so shall your manhood come again at need."

But the varlet answered,

"Fair love, my heart is full of courage; nor for any reason will I
pause, so long as I can hold upon my way. It is the noise of all this folk—
the tumult and the shouting—that makes my steps uncertain. Their
cries distress me, I do not dare to stand."

But when two thirds of the course was won, the grasshopper would
have tripped him off his feet. Urgently and often the maiden prayed him,
saying,

"Fair friend, drink now of thy cordial."

But he would neither hear, nor give credence to her words. A mighty anguish filled his bosom. He climbed upon the summit of the mountain, and pained himself grievously to bring his journey to an end. This he might not do. He reeled and fell, nor could he rise again, for the heart had burst within his breast.

When the maiden saw her lover's piteous plight, she deemed that he had swooned by reason of his pain. She kneeled hastily at his side, and put the enchanted brewage to his lips, but he could neither drink nor speak, for he was dead, as I have told you. She bewailed his evil lot, with many shrill cries, and flung the useless flacket far away. The precious potion bestrewed the ground, making a garden of that desolate place. For many saving herbs have been found there since that day by the simple folk of that country, which from the magic philtre derived all their virtue.

But when the maiden knew that her lover was dead, she made such wondrous sorrow, as no man had ever seen. She kissed his eyes and mouth, and falling upon his body, took him in her arms, and pressed him closely to her breast. There was no heart so hard as not to be touched by her sorrow; for in this fashion died a dame, who was fair and sweet and gracious, beyond the wont of the daughters of men.

Now the King and his company, since these two lovers came not again, presently climbed the mountain to learn their end. But when the King came upon them lifeless, and fast in that embrace, incontinent he fell to the ground, bereft of sense. After his speech had returned to him, he was passing heavy, and lamented their doleful case, and thus did all his people with him.

Three days they kept the bodies of these two fair children from earth, with uncovered face. On the third day they sealed them fast in a goodly coffin of marble, and by the counsel of all men, laid them softly to rest on that mountain where they died. Then they departed from them, and left them together, alone.

Since this adventure of the Two Children this hill is known as the Mountain of the Two Lovers, and their story being bruited abroad, the Breton folk have made a Lay thereof, even as I have rehearsed before you.

❧❧❧

SIR THOMAS MALORY
from *Le Morte D'Arthur*

THE WAR BETWEEN KING ARTHUR AND SIR LAUNCELOT

How Sir Launcelot was taken in the Queen's Chamber.

In May, when every lusty heart flourisheth and burgeneth; for as the season is lusty to behold and comfortable, so man and woman rejoice and
gladden of summer coming with his fresh flowers: for winter, with his
rough winds and blasts, causeth a lusty man and woman to cower and sit
fast by the fire. So in this season, as in the month of May, it befell a great
anger and unhap that stinted not till the flower of chivalry of all the
world was destroyed and slain: and all was long upon two unhappy
knights, the which were named Sir Agravaine and Sir Mordred that were
brethren unto Sir Gawaine. For this Sir Agravaine and Sir Mordred had
ever a privy hate unto the queen dame Guenever, and to Sir Launcelot,
and daily and nightly they ever watched upon Sir Launcelot.

So it mishapped Sir Gawaine and all his brethren were in King
Arthur's chamber, and then Sir Agravaine said thus openly, and not in no
counsel, that many knights might hear it, I marvel that we all be not
ashamed both to see and to know how Sir Launcelot goeth with the
queen, and all we know it so, and it is shamefully suffered of us all, that
we all should suffer so noble a king, as King Arthur is, so to be shamed.
Then spake Sir Gawaine, and said, Brother, Sir Agravaine, I pray you, and
charge you, move no such matters no more said King Arthur, for I warn
you ye shall find him wight. Let us deal, said Sir Agravaine and Sir Mordred.

So on the morn, King Arthur rode on hunting, and sent word to
the queen that he would be out all that night. Then Sir Agravaine and
Sir Mordred gat to them twelve knights, and did themselves in a chamber, in the castle of Carlisle. So when the night came, Sir Launcelot told
Sir Bors how he would go that night, and speak with the queen. Sir, said
Sir Bors, ye shall not go this night, by my counsel. Why? said Sir
Launcelot. Sir, said Sir Bors, I dread me ever of Sir Agravaine, that wait-
eth you daily, to do you shame, and us all, and never gave my heart
against no going that ever ye went to the queen, so much as now, for I

mistrust that the king is out this night from the queen, because, perad-
venture, he hath lain some watch for you and the queen, and therefore I
dread me sore of treason. Have ye no dread, said Sir Launcelot, for I shall
go, and come again, and make no tarrying. Sir, said Sir Bors, that me sore
repenteth, for I dread me sore that your going out this night shall wrath
us all. Fair nephew, said Sir Launcelot, I marvel me much why ye say thus,
sithen the queen hath sent for me, and wit ye well that I will not be so
much a coward, but she shall understand I will see her good grace. God
speed you well, said Sir Bors, and send you sound and safe again.

So Sir Launcelot departed, and took his sword under his arm, and
so in his mantle that noble knight put himself in great jeopardy, and so
he passed till he came to the queen's chamber. And then, as the French
book saith, there came Sir Agravaine, and Sir Mordred, with twelve
knights with them of the Round Table, and they said with crying voice,
Traitor knight, Sir Launcelot du Lake, now art thou taken. And thus they
cried with a loud voice that all the court might hear it: and they all fourteen were armed at all points as they should fight in a battle. Alas, said
Queen afore me; for wit ye well, said Sir Gawaine, I will not be of your
counsel. Truly, said Sir Gaheris, and Sir Gareth, we will not be knowing,
brother Agravaine, of your deeds. Then will I, said Sir Mordred. I believe well that, said Sir Gawaine, for ever unto all unhappiness, brother
Sir Mordred, thereto will ye grant, and I would that ye left all this, and
made you not so busy, for I know, said Sir Gawaine, what will fall of it.
Fall of it what fall may, said Sir Agravaine, I will disclose it to the king.
Not by my counsel, said Sir Gawaine, for and there rise war and wrake
betwixt Sir Launcelot and us, wit you well, brother, there will many
kings and great lords hold with Sir Launcelot. Also, brother Sir Agravaine, said Sir Gawaine, ye must remember how ofttimes Sir Launcelot
hath rescued the king and the queen, and the best of us all had been full
cold at the heartroot, had not Sir Launcelot been better than we; and that
hath he proved himself full oft. And as for my part, said Sir Gawaine, I
will never be against Sir Launcelot, for one day's deed, when he rescued
me from king Carados of the dolorous tower, and slew him, and saved
my life. Also, brother Sir Agravaine, and Sir Mordred, in likewise Sir
Launcelot rescued you both, and three-score and two, from Sir Turquin.
Me thinketh, brother, such kind deeds and kindness should be remembered. Do as ye list, said Sir Agravaine, for I will hide it no longer.

With these words came to them King Arthur. Now, brother, stint
your noise, said Sir Gawaine. We will not, said Sir Agravaine and Sir
Mordred. Will ye so? said Sir Gawaine, then God speed you, for I will

not hear your tales, nor be of your counsel. No more will I, said Sir Gareth and Sir Gaheris, for we will never say evil by that man: for because, said Sir Gareth, Sir Launcelot made me knight, by no manner ought I to say ill of him. And therewithal they three departed, making great dole. Alas, said Sir Gawaine and Sir Gareth, now is this realm wholly mischieved, and the noble fellowship of the Round Table shall be dispersed. So they departed.

And then Sir Arthur asked them what noise they made. My lord, said Agravaine, I shall tell you that I may keep no longer. Here is I and my brother, Sir Mordred, brake unto my brother Sir Gawaine, Sir Gaheris, and to Sir Gareth, how this we know all, that Sir Launcelot holdeth your queen, and hath done long, and we be your sister's sons, and we may suffer it no longer; and all we wot that ye should be above Sir Launcelot, and ye are the king that made him knight, and, therefore, we will prove it that he is a traitor to your person. If it be so, said Sir Arthur, wit you well he is none other, but I would be loth to begin such a thing, but I might have proofs upon it; for Sir Launcelot is an hardy knight, and all ye know he is the best knight among us all, and, but if he be taken with the deed, he will fight with him that bringeth up the noise, and I know no knight that is able to match him. Therefore, and it be sooth as ye say, I would he were taken with the deed. For, as the French book saith, the king was full loth thereto, that any noise should be upon Sir Launcelot and his queen; for the king had a deeming, but he would not hear of it, for Sir Launcelot had done so much for him and for the queen so many times, that, wit ye well, the king loved him passing well. My lord, said Sir Agravaine, ye shall ride tomorrow on hunting, and doubt ye not, Sir Launcelot will not go with you. Then when it draweth toward night, ye may send the queen word that ye will lie out all that night, and so may ye send for your cooks; and then, upon pain of death, we shall take him with the queen, and either we shall bring him to you dead or quick. I will well, said the king, then I counsel you, take with you sure fellowship. Sir, said Agravaine, my brother, Sir Mordred, and I will take with us twelve knights of the Round Table. Beware, Guenever, now are we mischieved both. Madam, said Sir Launcelot, is there here any armour within your chamber that I might cover my poor body withal, and if there be any, give it me, and I shall soon stint their malice. Truly, said the queen, I have none armour, shield, sword, nor spear, wherefore I dread me sore our long love is come to a mischievous end; for, I hear by their noise, there by many noble knights, and well I wot they be surely armed, against them ye may make no resistance; wherefore ye are likely to be slain, and then shall I be burnt. For, and ye might escape them, said the queen, I would not doubt but that ye would rescue me in what danger that ever I stood in. Alas said Sir Launcelot, in all my life was I never bested that I should be thus shamefully slain for lack of mine armour. But ever in one Sir Agravaine and Sir Mordred cried, Traitor knight, come out of the queen's chamber, for wit thou well thou art so beset that thou shalt not escape. Oh mercy, said Sir Launcelot, this shameful cry and noise I may not suffer, for better were death at once, than thus to endure this pain.

Then he took the queen in his arms, and kissed her, and said, Most noble Christian queen, I beseech you, as ye have ever been my special good lady, and I at all times your true poor knight unto my power, and as I never failed you in right nor in wrong, since the first day that King Arthur made me knight, that ye will pray for my soul if that I here be slain. For well I am well assured that Sir Bors my nephew and all the remnant of my kin, with Sir Lavaine and Sir Urre, that they will not fail you to rescue you from the fire, and therefore, mine own lady, recomfort yourself whatsoever come of me, that ye go with Sir Bors my nephew, and Sir Urre, and they all will do you all the pleasure that they can or may, that ye shall live like a queen upon my lands. Nay, Launcelot, said the queen, wit thou well I will never live after thy days, but, and thou be slain, I will take my death as meekly for Jesu Christ's sake, as ever did any Christian queen. Well, madam, said Launcelot, sith it is so that the day is come that our love must depart, with you well I shall sell my life as dear as I may, and a thousand fold, said Sir Launcelot, I am more heavier for you than for myself. And now I had lever than to be lord of all Christendom, that I had sure armour upon me, that men might speak of my deeds or ever I were slain. Truly, said the queen, I would and it might please God that they would take me and slay me, and suffer you to escape. That shall never be, said Sir Launcelot. God defend me from such a shame, but Jesu be thou my shield and mine armour.

And therewith Sir Launcelot wrapped his mantle about his arm well and surely; and by then they had gotten a great form out of the hall, and therewithal they rashed at the door. Fair lords, said Sir Launcelot, leave your noise and your rashing, and I shall set open this door, and then may ye do with me what it liketh you. Come off then, said they all, and do it, for it availeth thee not to strive against us all, and therefore let us into this chamber, and we shall save thy life until thou come to King Arthur. Then Launcelot unbarred the door, and with his left hand he held it open a little so that but one man might come in at once. And so anon, there came striding a good knight, a much man and large, and his name was Colgrevance of Gore, and he with a sword strake at Sir Launcelot mightily, and he put aside the stroke, and gave him such a buffet upon the helmet that he fell groveling dead within the chamber door, and then Sir Launcelot with great might drew that dead knight within the chamber door; and then Sir Launcelot with the help of the queen and her ladies was lightly armed in Sir Colgrevance's armour. And ever stood Sir Agravaine and Sir Mordred, crying, Traitor knight, come out of the queen's chamber. Leave your noise, said Sir Launcelot unto Sir Agravaine, for wit ye well, Sir Agravaine, ye shall not prison me this night, and therefore and ye do by my counsel, go ye all from this chamber door, and make not such crying and such manner of slander as ye do, for I promise you by my knighthood, and ye will depart and make no more noise, I shall as tomorn appear before you all, before the king, and then let it be seen which of you all, either else ye all, will accuse me of treason, and there I shall answer you as a knight should, that hither I came to the queen for no manner of mal-engine, and that will I prove and make it good upon you with mine hands. Fie on thee, traitor, said Sir Agravaine and Sir Mordred, we will have thee and slay thee if we list, for we let thee wit, we have the choice of King Arthur, to save thee or to slay thee. Ah sirs, said Sir Launcelot, is there none other grace with you? Then keep yourself.

So then Sir Launcelot set all open the chamber door, and mightily and knightly he strode in amongst them, and anon at the first buffet he slew Sir Agravaine, and twelve of his fellows within a little while after he laid them cold to the earth, for there was none of the twelve that might stand Sir Launcelot one buffet. Also Sir Launcelot wounded Sir Mordred, and he fled with all his might. And then Sir Launcelot returned again unto the queen, and said, Madam, now wit you well all our true love is brought to an end, for now will King Arthur ever be my foe, and therefore, madam, and it like you that I may have you with me, I shall save you from all manner adventures dangerous. That is not best, said the queen, me seemeth now ye have done so much harm, it will be best ye hold you still with this. And if ye see that as tomorn they will put me unto the death, then may ye rescue me as ye think best. I will well, said Sir Launcelot, for have ye no doubt while I am living I shall rescue you. And then he kissed her, and either gave other a ring, and so there he left the queen and went unto his lodging.

Margaret, Queen of Navarre
from *The Heptameron*

Geburon relates how a Milanese lady tested her lover's courage, and afterwards loved him heartily.

"At the time when the Grand-Master of Chaumont was governor of Milan, there was a lady there who passed for one of the most respectable in the city. She was the widow of an Italian count, and resided with her brothers-in-law, not choosing to hear a word about marrying again. Her conduct was so correct and guarded that she was highly esteemed by all the French and Italians in the duchy. One day, when her brothers and sisters-in-law entertained the Grand-Master of Chaumont, the widow could not help being present, contrary to her custom of never appearing at any festive meeting. The French could not see her without praising her beauty and her grace; one among them especially, whom I will not name. It is enough to inform you that there was not a Frenchman in Italy more worthy to be loved, for he was fully endowed with all the beauties and graces which a gentleman could have. Though he saw the widow dressed in black crape, apart from the young people, and withdrawn into a corner with several old ladies, yet, being one who had never known what it was to fear man or woman, he accosted her, took off his mask, and quitted the dance to converse with her. He passed the whole evening with her and the old ladies her companions, and enjoyed himself more than he could have done with the youngest and sprightliest ladies of the court. So charmed was he with this conversation, that when it was time to retire he hardly believed he had had time to sit down. Though he talked with the widow only upon common topics, suited to the company around her, she failed not to perceive that he was anxious to make her acquaintance, which she was so resolute to prevent, that he could never afterwards meet with her in any company, great or small.

"At last, having made inquiries as to her habits of life, and learned that she went often to the churches and religious houses, he set so many people on the watch that she could not go to any of those places so secretly but that he was there before her, and stayed as long as he could see her. He made such good use of his time, and gazed at her with such hearty good-will, that she could not be ignorant of his passion; and to prevent these encounters she resolved to feign illness for some time, and hear mass at home. This was a bitter mortification to the gentleman, for he was thus deprived of his only means of seeing her. At last, when she thought she had baffled his plans, she returned to the churches as before, and Love took care forthwith to make this known to the gentleman, who then resumed his habits of devotion. Fearing lest she should throw some other obstacle in his way, and that he should not have time to make known to her what he felt, one morning, when she was hearing mass in a little chapel, where she thought herself snugly concealed, he placed himself at the end of the altar, and turning to her at the moment when the priest was elevating the host, said, in a voice of deep feeling, 'I swear to you, madam, by Him whom the priest holds in his hands, that you are the sole cause of my death. Though you deprive me of all opportunity to address you, yet you cannot be ignorant of the passion I entertain for you. My haggard eyes and death-like countenance must have sufficiently made known to you my condition.' The lady pretended not to understand him, and replied, 'God's name ought not to be taken in vain; but the poets say that the gods laugh at the oaths and falsehoods of lovers, wherefore women who prize their honor ought neither to be credulous nor pitiful.' So saying, she rose and went home.

"Those who have been in the like predicament will readily believe that the gentleman was sorely cast down at receiving such a reply. However, as he did not lack courage, he thought it better to have met with a rebuff than to have missed an opportunity of declaring his love. He persevered for three years, and lost not a moment in which he could solicit her by letters and by other means; but during all that time she never made him any other reply, but shunned him as the wolf shuns the mastiff; and that not by reason of any aversion she felt for him, but because she was afraid of exposing her honor and reputation. The gentleman was so well aware that there lay the knot of the difficulty, that he pushed matters more briskly than ever; till, after a world of trouble, refusals, and sufferings, the lady was touched by his constancy, took pity on him, and granted him what he had so long desired and waited for.

"The assignation having been made, and the requisite measures concerted, the gentleman failed not to present himself at the rendezvous, at whatever risk of his life, for the fair widow resided with her relations. But as he was not less cunning than handsome, he managed so adroitly that he was in the lady's chamber at the moment appointed. He found her alone in a handsome bed; but as he was undressing in eager haste he heard whisperings outside the chamber door, and the noise of swords clashing against the walls. 'We are undone,' cried the widow, more dead than alive. 'Your life and my honor are in mortal peril. My brothers are coming to kill you. Hide yourself under the bed, I beseech you; for then they will not find you, and I shall have a right to complain of their alarming me without cause.'

"The gentleman, who was not easily frightened, coolly replied, 'What are your brothers that they should make a man of honor afraid? If their whole race was assembled at the door, I am confident they would not stand the fourth lunge of my sword. Remain quietly in bed therefore, and leave me to guard the door.'

"Then, wrapping his cloak round his left arm, and with his sword in his hand, he opened the door, and saw that the threatening weapons were brandished by two servant maids. 'Forgive us, monsieur,' they said. 'It is by our mistress's orders we do this; but you shall have no more annoyance from us.' The gentleman, seeing that his supposed antagonists were women, contented himself with bidding them go the devil, and slamming the door in their faces. He then jumped into bed to his mistress without delay. Fear had not cooled his ardor, and without wasting time in asking the meaning of the sham alarm, he thought only of satisfying his passion.

"Towards daylight he asked his bedfellow why she had so long delayed his happiness, and what was her reason for making her servants behave so oddly? 'I had resolved,' she said, laughing, 'never to love; and I have adhered to that resolution ever since I became a widow. But the first time you spoke to me, I saw so much to admire in you that I changed my mind, and began from that hour to love you as much as you loved me. It is true that honor, which has always been the ruling principle of my conduct, would not suffer love to make me do anything which might blemish my reputation. But as the stricken deer thinks to change its pain by change of place, so did I go from church to church, hoping to fly from him whom I carried in my heart, the proof of whose perfect love has reconciled honor with love. But to be thoroughly assured that I gave my heart to a man who was perfectly worthy of it, I ordered my women to do as they have done. I can assure you, if you had been frightened enough to hide under the bed, my intention was to have got up and gone into another room, and never have had anything more to do with you. But as I have found you not only comely and pleasing, but also full of valor and intrepidity to a degree even beyond what fame had reported you; as I have seen that fear could not appal you, nor in the least degree cool the ardor of your passion for me, I have resolved to attach myself to you for the rest of my days; being well assured that I cannot place my life and my honor in better hands than in those of him whom of all men in the world I believe to be the bravest and the best.'

"And if human will could be immutable, they mutually promised and vowed a thing which was not in their power—I mean, perpetual affection, which can neither grow up nor abide in the hearts of men, as those ladies know who have learned by experience what is the duration of such engagements. Therefore, ladies, if you are wise, you will be on your guard against us, as the stag would be against the hunter if the animal had reason; for our felicity, our glory, and delight, is to see you captured, and to despoil you of what ought to be dearer to you than life."

"Since when have you turned preacher, Geburon?" said Hircan. "You did not always talk in that fashion."

"It is true," replied Geburon, "that I have all my life long held a quite different language; but as my teeth are bad, and I can no longer chew venison, I warn the poor deer against the hunters, that I may make amends in my old age for the mischiefs I have desired in my youth."

"Thank you, Geburon, for your warning," retorted Nomerfide; "but after all, we doubt that we have much reason to be obliged to you; for you did not speak in that way to the lady you loved so much; therefore, it is a proof that you do not love us, or yet wish that we should love. Yet we believe ourselves to be as prudent and virtuous as those you so long chased in your young days. But it is a common vanity of the old to believe that they have always been more discreet than those who come after them."

"When the cajolery of one of your wooers," retorted Geburon, "shall have made you acquainted with the nature of men, you will then believe, Nomerfide, that I have told you the truth."

"To me it seems probable," observed Oisille, "that the gentleman whose intrepidity you extol so highly must rather have been possessed by the fury of love, a passion so violent, that it makes the greatest poltroons undertake things which the bravest would think twice before attempting."

"If he had not believed, madam," said Saffredent, "that the Italians are readier with their tongues than with their hands, me thinks he must have been frightened."

"Yes," said Oisille, "if he had not had a fire in his heart which burns up fear."

Translated by Walter K. Kelly

MIGUEL DE CERVANTES SAAVEDRA

from *Don Quijote de la Mancha*

Don Quijote sends his servant, Sancho, to Dulcinea to ask if she will accept the don as her knight

". . . observe her every action and movement; which if you faithfully report, I shall divine what's hid in the secret places of her heart, bearing on her attitude toward my passion. For you should know, Sancho, if you don't already, that 'twixt two lovers their actions and motions when the beloved is named are most faithful messengers of what is transpiring within. Go, friend, and many better fortune than mine attend you, bringing you more success than I fear and look for, while I abide in the cruel solitude wherein you leave me."

"I'll go and come quickly," promised Sancho; "let your worship cheer up this little heart of yours, which can be no bigger than a hazelnut. Consider the proverb, A stout heart breaks bad luck, and, No flitches are, where there are no hooks, and how also it is said, The hare leaps where least he is looked for. I mean by all this that though in the night we failed to find the castles or palaces of Dulcinea, now that 'tis day I think to find them when least I expect, and when found, leave the lady to me." "Verily, my son, you are ever so pat with your proverbs, so may God grant me better fortune in my desire." With this Sancho wheeled about and pricked his Dapple, leaving his master mounted, braced in stirrups and leaning on his lance, at bay with sad and troubled fancies. There too we shall leave him and accompany Sancho Panza.

No less troubled and sad was the squire setting out than the knight remaining: so anxious was he indeed that scarce had he left the wood when, turning to see that his master was out of view, he alighted from Dapple and seating himself at the foot of a tree began to commune with himself saying: "Be kind enough to tell us, brother Sancho, whither your worship is bound; look you perchance for some lost ass or other?" "Not at all." "Then for what?" "To say the least of her I am looking for a princess and she the sun of beauty and the whole sky combined." "And where think you to find this wonder of wonders?" "Where? why in the great city of el Toboso of course." "Good; and on whose behalf do you run this errand?" "On behalf of the famous knight Don Quijote de la

Mancha, he that redresses wrongs, gives the thirsty to eat and the hungry to drink." "That sounds very well but know you her house?" "My master says 'tis some royal palaces or other, or a haughty castle."

"Possibly you've seen the lady once upon a time?" "Neither I nor master have e'er set eyes on her grace." "Then wouldn't you think it well and wisely done if the Tobosans, finding that you had come to pester their ladies and allure away their princesses, pounded your ribs with bare sticks till they left no whole bone in your body?" "They certainly would be right unless they bethought them in time that I acted under orders and that:

> Friend, as a messenger you came
> And therefore shall not meet with blame."

"Don't trust to that, my son, for Manchegans are as choleric as cunning and take jokes from none. My God, if they scent you, I promise you hard times." "The devil, man, let the bolt fall yonder; not if I know it shall I look for three feet on a cat for another man's pleasure, the more that looking for Dulcinea in el Toboso is like hunting for Maria in Ravenna or the bachelor in Salamanca. 'Tis the devil I say that has got me into this scrape and nobody else."

This conference occurred between himself and Sancho and the upshot was that as it broke up he declared: "Come now, all things have remedy save death, beneath whose yoke, in spite of ourselves, all must pass when life is over and done. A thousand proofs have been submitted that this my master is as mad as they make them and that even I am not so far behind. Indeed I, since I follow and serve him, am more fool than he, if the proverb be true, Tell me the company you keep and I will tell you what you are; and that other, Not with whom thou art bred but with whom thou art fed. Mad, then, as he is, and with a madness that is wont to take some things for others, calling black white and white black, as appeared when he said the windmills were giants, the friars' mules dromederies and the flocks of sheep hostile armies and much more to the same tune, it won't be so difficult to make him believe that a peasant woman, the first I come across, is the lady Dulcinea. And if he don't, I can swear she is, and if he swear back, I'll take a second oath, and if he keep it up, so will I and mine eye will not leave the mark, come as it will. Perhaps by mine obstinacy I shall end this sending me on embassies, when he sees the bad news I bring. Or maybe he'll think, and this is more likely, that some naughty enchanter, of those he says wish him ill, has changed her looks to make him mischief and trouble."

With this last thought Sancho became more at ease, feeling the job good as done. He waited till afternoon that sufficient time should seem to have elapsed for his trip to and fro. And so well did things fall out that when he rose to mount Dapple, he saw approaching from the city three peasant-women riding three he-asses or she-asses—the author doesn't state which, though the latter is more probable, being the usual mount of countrywomen, but, as 'tis of small concern, there's no reason we should stop to enquire. To be brief, as soon as Sancho saw the peasants, he galloped back to his master, whom he found sighing and uttering a thousand love-laments. When the knight saw him he exclaimed: "What news, Sancho friend? Shall I mark this day with white stone or black?" "Better mark it with red chalk, sir, as they do the college lists, to be more plainly seen."

" 'Tis good news, then, you bring me?" "So good that your worship has only to spur Rocinante and ride into the open to behold the lady Dulcinea with two of her maidens coming to wait upon you." "Blessed be God what do you say? remember and don't deceive me nor with false cheer try to ease my veritable sorrow." "Why should I try to deceive, especially when you are so near to learning the truth? Spur on, sire; come, and you will see the princess our mistress on the way, all dressed up and adorned—in short just like the lady she is. Her damsels and she are a blaze of gold, they look like corn-cobs of pearls and besides are covered with diamonds, rubies and brocades more than ten-folds thick. Their hair hangs loose upon their shoulders like so many sunbeams that go playing with the wind, and above all they come mounted on three piebald whacknees, the finest sight conceivable." "Hackneys you should say, Sancho." "There's small difference 'twixt whacknees and hackneys. But let their mount be what it may, coming they are, the showiest ladies you could ask for, especially my lady the princess Dulcinea, who makes one faint." "Come then, Sancho son, and as reward for this unexpected as 'tis good news I grant you the best spoil won in the next adventure. If this be not enough, yours are the three fillies my three mares give me this year; they're in foal on our town-meadow as you know." "I choose the fillies, for the spoils of our next adventure aren't very certain."

By this time they found themselves out of the wood and near the three peasant-girls. Don Quijote's eyes followed the road to el Toboso and seeing only the three grew nervous, asking Sancho if 'twere outside the city he left them. "How outside?" cried the other; "have you your eyes in the back of your head perchance that you fail to recognise her among these at hand, resplendent as the sun at noon?" "Naught can I see, squire, save three peasant-women on three asses." "Now God deliver me from the devil!" quoth the other; "and is it possible that three hackneys or however you call them, as white as the snow, should look to you like asses? As the Lord liveth, may they pluck out my beard if such be the truth." "Friend Sancho, it's as true that they are he or she-asees as that I am Don Quijote and you Sancho Panza; at least so they appear to me."

"Peace, señor, speak it not; snuff those eyes of yours and come and make obeisance to the lady of your thoughts that already draws nigh;" and saying this he advanced to meet the three women. Dropping from his Dapple he seized one of the three asses by the halter and kneeling said. "O queen, princess and duchess of beauty, may your haughtiness and majesty be pleased to receive in your grace and good-will your captive cavalier that stands there like marble, utterly puzzled and pulseless at finding himself before your magnificent presence. I am his squire Sancho Panza and he the wayworn knight Don Quijote de La Mancha, otherwise known as the Knight of Sorry Aspect." Don Quijote was now on his knees beside Sancho, staring with bulging eyes and bewildered look at her his squire called queen and lady. As he could see only a peasant-girl and not a very good-looking one at that (a flat nose on a round face), in his confusion he dared not open his lips.

The peasants were equally dumfounded at seing two such unlike men kneeling before and holding back their companion. But she, annoyed to the point of anger, broke the silence by saying: "Bad luck to you, get out of the way and let us pass on for we're in a hurry." And Sancho replied: "O princess and universal lady of el Toboso, how does your magnaminous heart not soften at seeing the prop and pillar of errantry kneeling before your sublimated presence?" To which one of the others retorted: "Whoa there, my father-in-law's ass, till I currycomb you. Look how these dandiprats come to poke fun at us poor country-girls, as though we knew not how to crack jokes as well as they. Go your way and let us go ours; 'twill be better for you."

"Rise, Sancho," sighed Don Quijote, "for I see that fortune, not yet sated with my sorrows, has blocked all roads whereby comfort might come to this wretched soul I bear in my flesh. But O thou crown of all imaginable excellence, thou limit of all human grace, sole consolation of the afflicted heart that adores thee, now that an evil enchanter persecutes me, placing clouds and cataracts in mine eyes and perverting thy peerless beauty and features into those of a poor peasant, unless he have at the same time changed mine into those of a wild beast to appear hateful in thy sight, fail not to look softly and lovingly upon me, detecting in this knee-bending and submission which I make to thy hidden beauty the humility wherewith my soul adores thee."

"Tell that to my grandfather!" retorted the wench; "I'm no woman to listen to love-jabber. Clear the road and we'll thank you." Sancho stood aside to let her pass, overjoyed at being well out of his entanglement. She that had done duty for Dulcinea no sooner found herself free than she pricked her whacknee with her pointed stick, making her dash over the meadow, till the jenny, feeling the extraordinary sting, began to cavort, at length landing her ladyship on the ground. When this was seen of Don Quijote, he hastened to assist her and Sancho to adjust the girth and pannel, which had slipped beneath the beast's belly. When this was secured and the knight was about to lift his enchanted lady-love back onto her seat, she took a quick run and clapping both hands on the jenny's haunches, more lightly than a falcon landed astride.

"By Roque!" exclaimed Sancho; "if the lady our mistress isn't nimbler than a hawk! I swear she can teach the most dexterous Cordovan or Mexican to mount jennet-wise. With one leap she sailed over the crupper and without spurs now makes her hackney run like a zebra. Nor do her damsels stay behind: all are travelling like the wind." Such was the case, for seeing Dulcinea mounted again the others pricked after and all shot off like a flash, not turning their heads for more than half a league. Don Quijote followed them with his eyes, and when they had passed beyond sight, he turned to his squire and said: "How does it look to you, Sancho, that I am so little loved by enchanters?"

Translated by Robinson Smith

❧ ❧

P'U SUNG-LING

The Young Lady of the Tung-T'ing Lake

The spirits of the Tung-t'ing lake are very much in the habit of borrowing boats. Sometimes the cable of an empty junk will cast itself off, and away goes the vessel over the waves to the sound of music in the air above. The boatmen crouch down in one corner and hide their faces, not daring to look up until the trip is over and they are once more at their old anchorage.

Now a certain Mr. Lin, returning home after having failed at the examination for Master's degree, was lying down very tipsy on the deck of his boat, when suddenly strains of music and singing began to be heard. The boatmen shook Mr. Lin, but failing to rouse him, ran down and hid themselves in the hold below. Then someone came and lifted him up, letting him drop again on to the deck, where he was allowed to remain in the same drunken sleep as before. By-and-by the noise of the various instruments became almost deafening, and Lin, partially waking up, smelt a delicious odour of perfumes filling the air around him. Opening his eyes, he saw that the boat was crowded with a number of beautiful girls; and knowing that something strange was going on, he pretended to be fast asleep. There was then a call for Chih-ch'êng, upon which a young waiting-maid came forward and stood quite close to Mr. Lin's head. Her stockings were the colour of the kingfisher's wing, and her feet encased in tiny purple shoes, no bigger than one's finger. Much smitten with this young lady, he took hold of her stocking with his teeth, causing her, the next time she moved, to fall forward flat on her face. Someone, evidently in authority, asked what was the matter; and when he heard the explanation, was very angry, and gave orders to take off Mr. Lin's head. Soldiers now came and bound Lin, and on getting up he beheld a man sitting with his face to the south, and dressed in the garments of a king. "Sire," cried Lin, as he was being led away, "the king of the Tung-t'ing lake was a mortal named Lin; your servant's name is Lin also. His Majesty was a disappointed candidate; your servant is one too. His Majesty met the Dragon Lady, and was made immortal; your servant has played a trick upon this girl, and he is to die. Why this inequality of fortunes?" When the king heard this, he bade them bring him back, and asked him, saying, "Are you, then, a disappointed candidate?" Lin said he was; whereupon the king handed him writing materials, and ordered him to compose an ode upon a lady's headdress. Some time passed before Lin, who was a scholar of some repute in his own neighbourhood, had done more than sit thinking about what he should write; and at length the king upbraided him, saying, "Come, come, a man of your reputation should not take so long." "Sire," replied Lin, laying down his pen, "it took ten years to complete the Songs of the Three Kingdoms; whereby it may be known that the value of compositions depends more upon the labour given to them than the speed with which they are written." The king laughed, and waited patiently from early morning till noon, when a copy of the verses was put into his hand, with which he declared himself very pleased. He now commanded that Lin should be served with wine; and shortly after there followed a collation of all kinds of curious dishes, in the middle of which an officer came in and reported that the register of people to be drowned had been made up. "How many in all?" asked the king. "Two hundred and twenty-eight," was the reply;

and then the king inquired who had been deputed to carry it out; whereupon he was informed that the generals Mao and Nan had been appointed to do the work. Lin here rose to take leave, and the king presented him with ten ounces of pure gold and a crystal square, telling him that it would preserve him from any danger he might encounter on the lake. At this moment the king's retinue and horses ranged themselves in proper order upon the surface of the lake; and His Majesty, stepping from the boat into his sedan-chair, disappeared from view.

When everything had been quiet for a long time, the boatmen emerged from the hold and proceeded to shape their course northwards. The wind, however, was against them, and they were unable to make any headway; when all of a sudden an iron cat appeared floating on the top of the water. "General Mao has come," cried the boatmen, in great alarm; and they and all the passengers on board fell down on their faces. Immediately afterwards a great wooden beam stood up from the lake, nodding itself backwards and forwards, which the boatmen, more frightened than ever, said was General Nan. Before long a tremendous sea was raging, the sun was darkened in the heavens, and every vessel in sight was capsized. But Mr. Lin sat in the middle of the boat, with the crystal square in his hand, and the mighty waves broke around without doing them any harm. Thus were they saved, and Lin returned home; and whenever he told his wonderful story, he would assert that, although unable to speak positively as to the facial beauty of the young lady he had seen, he dared say that she had the most exquisite pair of feet in the world.

Subsequently, having occasion to visit the city of Wu-ch'ang, he heard of an old woman who wished to sell her daughter, but was unwilling to accept money, giving out that any one who had the fellow of a certain crystal square in her possession should be at liberty to take the girl. Lin thought this very strange; and taking his square with him sought out the old woman, who was delighted to see him, and told her daughter to come in. The young lady was about fifteen years of age, and possessed of surpassing beauty; and after saying a few words of greeting, she turned round and went within again. Lin's reason had almost fled at the sight of this peerless girl, and he straightway informed the old woman that he had such an article as she required, but could not say whether it would match hers or not. So they compared their squares together, and there was not a fraction of difference between them, either in length or breadth. The old woman was overjoyed, and inquiring where Lin lived, bade him go home and get a bridal chair, leaving his square behind him as a pledge of his good faith. This he refused to do; but the old woman laughed, and said, "You are too cautious, Sir; do you think I should run away for a square?" Lin was thus constrained to leave it behind him, and hurrying away for a chair, made the best of his way back. When, however, he got there, the old woman was gone. In great alarm he inquired of the people who lived near as to her whereabouts; no one, however, knew; and it being already late he returned disconsolately to his boat. On the way, he met a chair coming towards him, and immediately the screen was drawn aside, and a voice cried out, "Mr. Lin! why so late?" Looking closely, he saw that it was the old woman, who, after asking him if he hadn't suspected her of playing him false, told him that just after he left she had had the offer of a chair; and knowing that he, being only a stranger in the place, would have some trouble in obtaining one, she had sent her daughter on to his boat. Lin then begged she would return with him, to which she would not consent; and accordingly, not fully trusting what she said, he hurried on himself as fast as he could, and, jumping into the boat, found the young lady already there. She rose to meet him with a smile, and then he was astonished to see that her stockings were the colour of a kingfisher's wing, her shoes purple, and her appearance generally like that of the girl he had met on the Tung-t'ing lake. While he was still confused, the young lady remarked, "You stare, Sir, as if you had never seen me before!" but just then Lin noticed the tear in her stocking made by his own teeth, and cried out in amazement, "What! are you Chih-ch'êng?" The young lady laughed at this; whereupon Lin rose, and, making her a profound bow, said, "If you are that divine creature, I pray you tell me at once, and set my anxiety at rest." "Sir," replied she, "I will tell you all. That personage you met on the boat was actually the king of the Tung-t'ing lake. He was so pleased with your talent that he wished to bestow me upon you; but, because I was a great favourite with Her Majesty the Queen, he went back to consult with her. I have now come at the Queen's own command." Lin was highly pleased; and washing his hands, burnt incense, with his face towards the lake, as if it were the Imperial Court, and then they went home together.

Subsequently, when Lin had occasion to go to Wu-ch'ang, his wife asked to be allowed to avail herself of the opportunity to visit her parents; and when they reached the lake, she drew a hairpin from her hair, and threw it into the water. Immediately a boat rose from the lake, and Lin's wife, stepping into it, vanished from sight like a bird on the wing. Lin remained waiting for her on the prow of his vessel, at the spot where she had disappeared; and by-and-by, he beheld a houseboat approach, from the window of which there flew a beautiful bird, which was no other than Chih-ch'êng. Then some one handed out from the same window gold and silk, and precious things in great abundance, all presents to them from the Queen. After this, Chih-ch'êng went home regularly twice every year, and Lin soon became a very rich man, the things he had being such as no one had ever before seen or heard of.

❧ ☙

APHRA BEHN

from *Love Letters Between a Noble-Man and His Sister*

TO SYLVIA

Though I parted from you resolv'd to obey your impossible Commands, yet know oh charming *Sylvia!* that after a thousand Conflicts between Love and Honour, I found the God (too mighty for the Idol) reign absolute Monarch in my Soul, and soon banish'd that Tyrant thence. That cruel Counsellor that would suggest to you a thousand fond Arguments to hinder my noble Pursuit; *Sylvia* came in view! her unresistable *Idea!* with all the Charm of blooming Youth, with all the Attractions of Heav'nly Beauty! Loose, wanton, gay, all flowing her bright Hair, and languishing her lovely Eyes, her Dress all negligent as when I saw her last, discovering a thousand ravishing Graces, round white small Breasts, delicate Neck, and rising Bosom, heav'd with Sighs she would in vain conceal; and all besides, that nicest Fancy can imagine surprizing—Oh I dare not think on, lest my Desires grow mad and raving; let it suffice, oh adorable *Sylvia!* I think and know enough to justifie that Flame in me, which our weak Alliance of Brother and Sister has render'd so criminal; but he that adores *Sylvia*, should do it at an uncommon rate; 'tis not enough to sacrifice a single Heart, to give you a simple Passion, your Beauty should like it self produce wondrous Effects; it should force all Obligations, all Laws, all Ties even of Natures self: You, my lovely Maid, were not born to be obtain'd by the dull Methods of ordinary loving; and 'tis in vain to prescribe me Measures; and oh much more in vain to urge the Nearness of our Relation. What Kin, my charming *Sylvia*, are you to me? No Ties of Blood forbid my Passion? and what's a Ceremony impos'd on Man by Custom? what is it to my divine *Sylvia*, that the Priest took my Hand and gave it to your Sister? What Alliance can that create? Why should a Trick devised by the wary old, only to make Provision for Posterity, tie me to an Eternal Slavery? No, no, my charming Maid, 'tis Nonsense all; let us (born for mightier Joys) scorn the dull *beaten Road,* but let us love like the first Race of Men, nearest ally'd to God, promiscuously they lov'd, and possess'd, Father and Daughter, Brother and Sister met, and reap'd the Joys of Love without Controul, and counted it Religious Coupling, and 'twas encourag'd too by Heav'n it self: Therefore start not (too nice and lovely Maid) at Shadows of things that can but frighten Fools. Put me not off with these Delays; rather say you but dissembled Love all this while, than now 'tis born, to die again with a poor Fright of Nonsense. A Fit of Honour! a phantom imaginary, and no more; no, no, represent me to your Soul more favourably, think you see me languishing at your Feet, breathing out my last in Sighs and kind Reproaches, on the pitiless *Sylvia;* reflect when I am dead, which will be the more afflicting Object, the Ghost (as you are pleas'd to call it) of your murder'd Honour, or the pale and bleeding one of

The lost
PHILANDER

I have liv'd a whole Day, and yet no Letter from Sylvia.

TO PHILANDER

Oh why will you make me own (oh too importunate *Philander!*) with what Regret I made you promise to prefer my Honour before your Love?

I confess with Blushes, which you might then see kindling in my face, that I was not at all pleas'd with the Vows you made me, to endeavour to obey me, and I then even wish'd you would obstinately have deny'd Obedience to my just Commands; have pursu'd your criminal Flame, and have left me raving on my Undoing: For when you were gone, and I had Leisure to look into my Heart, alas! I found whether you oblig'd or not, whether Love or Honour were preferr'd, I, unhappy I, was either way inevitably lost. Oh! what pitiless God, fond of his wondrous Power, made us the Objects of his Almighty Vanity? Oh why were we two made the first Precedents of his new found Revenge? for sure no Brother ever lov'd a Sister with so criminal a Flame before. At least my unexperienc'd Innocence ne'er met with so fatal a Story. And 'tis in vain (my too charming Brother) to make me insensible of our Alliance; to persuade me I am a Stranger to all but your Eyes and Soul.

Alas, your fatally kind Industry is all in vain. You grew up a Brother with me; the Title was fix'd in my Heart, when I was too young to understand your subtle Distinctions, and there it thriv'd and spread; and 'tis now too late to transplant it, or alter its native Property. Who can graft a Flower on a contrary Stalk? The Rose will bear no Tulips, nor the Hyacinth the Poppy, no more will the Brother the Name of Lover. Oh! spoil not the natural Sweetness and Innocence we now retain, by an Endeavour fruitless and destructive; no, no, *Philander*, dress your self in what Charms you will, be powerful as Love can make you in your soft Argument—yet, oh yet, you are my Brother still,—But why, oh cruel and eternal Powers, was not *Philander* my Lover before you destin'd him a Brother? or why, being a Brother, did you, malicious and spightful powers, destine him a Lover! Oh, take either Title from him, or from me a Life which can render me no Satisfaction, since your cruel Laws permit it not for *Philander*, nor his to bless the now

Unfortunate
Sylvia

Wednesday Morning.

To Philander
After I had dismiss'd my Page this Morning with my Letter, I walk'd (fill'd with sad soft Thoughts of my Brother *Philander*) into the Grove, and commanding *Melinda* to retire, who only attended me, I threw my self down on that Bank of Grass where we last disputed the dear but fatal Business of our Souls: Where our Prints (that invited me) still remain on the press'd Greens. There with ten thousand Sighs, with Remembrance of the tender Minutes we pass'd then, I drew your last Letter from my Bosom, and often kiss'd and often read it over; but oh, who can conceive my Torment, when I came to that fatal Part of it, where you say you gave your Hand to my Sister? I found my Soul agitated with a thousand different Passions, but all insupportable, all mad and raving; sometimes I threw my self with Fury on the Ground, and press'd my panting Heart to the Earth; then rise in Rage and tear my Heart, and hardly spare that Face that taught you first to love; then fold my wretched Arms to keep down rising Sighs that almost rend my Breast, I traverse swiftly the conscious Grove; with my distracted show'ring Eyes directed in vain to pitiless Heav'n, the lovely silent Shade favouring my Complaints, I cry aloud, Oh God! *Philander*'s marry'd, the lovely charming thing for whom I languish is marry'd!—That fatal Word's enough, I need not add to whom. Marry'd's enough to make me curse my Birth, my Youth, my Beauty, and

my Eyes that first betray'd me to the undoing Object. Curse on the Charms you have flatter'd, for every fancy'd Grace has help'd my Ruin on; now like Flowers that wither unseen and unpossess'd in Shades, they must die and be no more, they were to no end created, since *Philander's* marry'd: Marry'd! oh Fate, oh Hell, oh Torture and Confusion! Tell me not 'tis to my Sister, that Addition is needless and vain. To make me eternally wretched, there needs no more than that *Philander's* marry'd! than that the Priest gave your Hand away from me; to another, and not to me; tir'd out with Life I need no other Pass-port than this Repetition, *Philander's* marry'd! 'Tis that alone is sufficient to lay in her cold Tomb,

The wretched and despairing
SYLVIA

Wednesday Night, *Bellfont.*

TO SYLVIA

Twice last Night, oh unfaithful and unloving *Sylvia!* I sent the Page to the old Place for Letters, but he returned the Object of my Rage, because without the least Remembrance from my fickle Maid. In this Torment, unable to hide my Disorder, I suffered my self to be laid in Bed; where the restless Torments of the Night exceeded those of the Day, and are not even by the Languisher himself to be express'd; but the returning Light brought a short Slumber on its Wings; which was interrupted by my atoning Boy, who brought two Letters from my adorable *Sylvia.* He wak'd me from Dreams more agreeable than all my watchful Hours could bring, for they are all tortur'd.—And even the softest mix'd with a thousand Despairs, Difficulties and Disappointments, but these were all Love, which gave a loose to Joys undeny'd by Honour! And this way my charming *Sylvia,* you shall be mine, in spite of all the Tyrannies of that cruel Hinderer; Honour appears not, my *Sylvia,* within the close drawn Curtains, in Shades and gloomy Light the phantom frights not, but when one beholds its Blushes, when it's attended and adorn'd, and the Sun sees its false Beauties; in silent Groves and Grottoes, dark Alcoves, and lonely Recesses, all its Formalities are laid aside; it was then, and there methought my *Sylvia* yielded, with a faint Struggle and a soft Resistance; I heard her broken Sighs, her tender whispering Voice, that trembling cry'd,—Oh! Can you be so cruel.—Have you the Heart—Will you undo a Maid, because she loves you? Oh! Will you ruin me because you may?—My faithless—My unkind—then sigh'd and yielded, and made me happier than a triumphing God! But this was still a Dream, I wak'd and sigh'd, and found it vanish'd all! But oh, my *Sylvia*, your Letters were substantial Pleasure, and pardon your Adorer if he tell you, even the Disorder you express is infinitely dear to him, since he knows it all the Effects of Love; Love, my Soul! which you in vain oppose; pursue it, Dear, and call it not Undoing or else explain your Fear, and tell me what your soft, your trembling Heart gives that cruel Title to? Is it undoing to love? And love the Man you say has Youth and Beauty to justifie that Love? A Man that adores you with so submissive and perfect a Resignation; a Man that did not only love first, but is resolv'd to die in that agreeable Flame; in my Creation I was form'd for Love, and destin'd for my *Sylvia*, and she for her *Philander*. And shall we, can we disappoint our Fate? No, my soft Charmer, our Souls were touch'd with the same Shafts of Love before they had a Being in our Bodies, and can we contradict Divine Decree?

Or is it undoing, Dear, to bless *Philander* with what you must some time or other sacrifice to some hated, loath'd Object (for *Sylvia* can never love again;) and are those Treasures for the dull conjugal Lover to rifle? Was the Beauty of Divine Shape created for the cold Matrimonial Embrace? And shall the Eternal Joys that *Sylvia* can dispense, be return'd by the clumsy Husband's careless, forc'd, insipid Duties? Oh, my *Sylvia*, shall a Husband (whose Insensibility will call those Raptures of Joy! Those heavenly blisses! The drudgery of Life) shall he I say receive 'em? While your *Philander*, with the very thought of the Excess of Pleasure the least Possession would afford, faints o'er the Paper that brings here his Eternal Vows.

Oh! where, my *Sylvia*, lies the undoing then? My Quality and Fortune are of the highest Rank amongst Men, my Youth gay and fond, my Soul all soft, all Love; and all *Sylvia's*! I adore her, I am sick of Love and sick of Life, 'till she yields she is all mine!

You say, my *Sylvia*, I am marry'd, and there my Happiness is shipwreck'd; but *Sylvia*, I deny it, and will not have you think it. No, my Soul was marry'd to yours in its first Creation, and only *Sylvia* is the Wife of my sacred, my everlasting Vows, of my solemn considerate Thoughts, of my ripen'd Judgment, my mature Considerations. The rest are all repented and forgot, like the hasty Follies of unsteady Youth, like Vows breath'd in Anger, and die perjur'd as soon as vented, and unregarded either of Heaven or Man. Oh! why should my Soul suffer forever, why Eternal Pain for the unheedy short-liv'd Sin of my unwilling Lips? Besides, this fatal thing call'd Wife, this unlucky Sister, this *Myrtilla*, this stop to all my Heav'n, that breeds such fatal Differences in our Affairs, this *Myrtilla*, I say, first broke her Marriage Vows to me. I blame her not, nor is it reasonable I should; she saw the young *Cesario*, and lov'd him. Ce-

sario, whom the envying World in spite of Prejudice must own, has irresistible Charms, that Godlike Form, that Sweetness in his Face, that
Softness in his Eyes and delicate Mouth, and every Beauty besides that
Women dote on and Men envy. That lovely Composition of Man and
Angel! with the Addition of his eternal Youth and illustrious Birth, was
form'd by Heaven and Nature for universal Conquest! And who can
love the charming Hero at a cheaper rate than being undone? And she
that would not venture Fame, Honour, and a Marriage Vow for the
Glory of the young *Cesario's* Heart, merits not the noble Victim. Oh!
would I could say so much for the young *Philander,* who would run a thousand times more hazards of Life and Fortune for the adorable *Sylvia,* than
that amorous Hero ever did for *Myrtilla,* though from that Prince I learn'd
some of my Disguises for my Thefts of Love, for he like *Jove* courted in
several Shapes. I saw 'em all, and suffer'd the Delusion to pass upon me,
for I had seen the lovely *Sylvia;* yes I had seen her, and lov'd her too. But
Honour kept me yet Master of my Vows; but when I knew her false,
when I was once confirm'd,—when by my own Soul I found the dissembled Passion of hers, when she could no longer hide the Blushes or
the Paleness that seiz'd at the Approaches of my disorder'd Rival, when
I saw Love dancing in her Eyes, and her false Heart beat with nimble
Motions, and soft trembling seiz'd every Limb, at the Approach or Touch
of the Royal Lover, then I thought my self no longer oblig'd to conceal
my Flame for *Sylvia.* Nay, e'er I broke Silence, e'er I discover'd the hidden Treasure of my Heart, I made her Falsehood plainer yet: Even the
Time and Place of the dear Assignations I discover'd. Certainty! happy
Certainty! broke the dull heavy Chain, and I with Joy submitted to my
shameful Freedom, and caress'd my generous Rival. Nay, and by Heav'n
I lov'd him for't, pleas'd at the resemblance of our Souls, for we were secret Lovers both, but more pleas'd that he lov'd *Myrtilla,* for that made way
to my Passion for the adorable *Sylvia!*

　　Let the dull, hot-brain'd, jealous Fool upbraid me with cold Patience: Let the fond Coxcomb, whose Honour depends on the frail Marriage Vow, reproach me, or tell me that my Reputation depends on the
feeble Constancy of a Wife, persuade me it is Honour to fight for an un-
retrievable and unvalu'd Prize, and that because my Rival has taken leave
to Cuckold me, I shall give him leave to kill me too; unreasonable Nonsense grown to Custom. No, by Heav'n! I had rather *Myrtilla* should be
false, (as she is) than with and languish for the happy Occasion; the Sin's
the same, only the Act's more generous. Believe me, my *Sylvia,* we have all
false Notions of Virtue and Honour, and surely this was taken up by
some despairing Husband in Love with a fair Jilting Wife, and then I

pardon him; I should have done as much. For only she that has my Soul can engage my Sword, she that I love and my self, only commands and keeps my Stock of Honour: For *Sylvia!* the Charming, the Distracting *Sylvia!* I could fight for a Glance or Smile, expose my Heart for her dearer Fame, and with no Recompence, but breathing out my last Gasp into her soft, white, delicate Bosom. But for a Wife! That Stranger to my Soul, and whom we wed for Interest and Necessity.—A Wife, a light, loose, unregarding Property, who for a momentary Appetite will expose her fame, without the noble End of loving on; she that will abuse my Bed, and yet return again to the loath'd conjugal Embrace, back to the Arms so hated, that even strong Fancy of the absent Youth belov'd, cannot so much as render supportable. Curse on her, and yet she kisses, fawns and dissembles on, hangs on his Neck, and makes the Sot believe.—Damn her, Brute; I'll whistle'r off, and let her down the Wind, as Othello says. No, I adore the Wife, that when the Heart is gone, boldly and nobly pursues the Conqueror, and generously owns the Whore.—Not poorly adds the nauseous Sin of Jilting to't: That I could have born, at least commended; but this can never pardon; at worst then the World had said her Passion had undone her, she lov'd, and Love at worst is worthy of Pity. No, no, *Myrtilla,* I forgive your Love, but never can your poor Dissimulation. One drives you but from the Heart you value not, but t'other to my eternal Contempt. One deprives me but of thee, *Myrtilla* but t'other entitles me to a Beauty more surprizing, renders thee no Part of me; and so leaves the Lover free to *Sylvia,* without the Brother.

Thus, my excellent Maid, I have sent you the Sense and Truth of my Soul, in an Affair you have often hinted to me, and I take no Pleasure to remember. I hope you will at least think my Aversion reasonable; and that being thus undisputably freed from all Obligations to *Myrtilla* as a Husband, I may be permitted to lay Claim to *Sylvia,* as a Lover, and marry my self more effectually by my everlasting Vows, than the Priest by his common Method could do to any other Woman less belov'd, there being no other way at present left by Heav'n, to render me *Sylvia's*

Eternal happy Lover, and
PHILANDER

I die to see you.

TO PHILANDER
Another Night, oh Heav'ns, and yet no Letter come! Where are you, my *Philander?* What happy Place contains you! If in Heaven, why does not

some posting Angel bid me haste after you? If on Earth, why does not some little God of Love bring the grateful Tidings on his painted Wings! If sick, why does not my own fond Heart by sympathy inform me? But that is all active, vigorous, wishing, impatient of delaying, silent, and busy in Imagination. If you are false, if you have forgotten your poor believing and distracted *Sylvia*, why does not that kind Tyrant Death, that meager welcome Vision of the despairing, old and wretched, approach in dead of Night, approach my restless Bed, and toll the dismal Tidings in my frighted listning Ears, and strike me for ever silent, lay me for ever quiet, lost to the World, lost to my faithless Charmer! But if a sense of Honour in you has made you resolve to prefer mine before your Love, made you take up a noble fatal Resolution never to tell me more of your Passion; this were a Trial, I fear my fond Heart wants Courage to bear; or is it a Trick, a cold Fit only assum'd to try how much I love you? I have no Arts, Heav'n knows, no Guile or double Meaning in my Soul, 'tis all plain native Simplicity, fearful and timorous as Children in the Night, trembling as Doves pursu'd; born soft by Nature, and made tender by Love; what, oh! what will become of me then? Yet would I were confirm'd in all my Fears: For as I am, my Condition is yet more deplorable; for I'm in doubt, and Doubt is the worst Torment of the Mind. Oh *Philander*, be merciful, and let me know the worst; do not be cruel while you kill, do it with Pity to the wretched *Sylvia*; oh let me quickly know whether you are at all, or are the most impatient and unfortunate.

SYLVIA'S

I rave, I die for some Relief.

🙞 🙜

DANIEL DEFOE

from *Moll Flanders*

Moll, after learning that Robert, her lover and the elder son of her employers, will not marry her, takes to her bed only to discover that the younger son, Robin, is in love with her.

The bare loss of him as a Gallant was not so much my Affliction, as the loss of his Person, whom indeed I Lov'd to Distraction; and the loss of all the Expectations I had, and which I always had built my Hopes upon, of having him one Day for my Husband: These things oppress'd my Mind so much, that in short, I fell very ill; the agonies of my Mind, in a word, threw me into a high Fever, and long it was that none in the Family expected my Life.

I was reduc'd very low indeed, and was often Delirious and light Headed; but nothing lay so near me, as the fear that when I was light Headed, I should say something or other to his Prejudice; I was distress'd in my Mind also to see him, and so he was to see me, for he really Lov'd me most passionately; but it could not be; there was not the least Room to desire it, on one side, or other, or so much as to make it Decent.

It was near five Weeks that I kept my Bed, and tho' the violence of my Fever abated in three Weeks, yet it several times Return'd; and the Physicians said two or three times, they could do no more for me, but that they must leave Nature and the Distemper to fight it Out, only strengthening the first with Cordials to maintain the Struggle: After the end of five Weeks I grew better, but was so Weak, so Alter'd, so Melancholly, and recover'd so Slowly, that the Physicians apprehended I should go into a Consumption; and which vex'd me most, they gave it as their Opinion, that my Mind was Oppress'd, that something Troubl'd me, and in short, that I was IN LOVE; upon this, the whole House was set upon me to Examine me, and to press me to tell whether I was in Love or not, and with who? but as I well might, I deny'd my being in Love at all.

They had on this Occasion a Squable one Day about me at Table, that had like to have put the whole Family in an Uproar, and for sometime did so; they happen'd to be all at Table, but the Father; as for me I was Ill, and in my Chamber. At the beginning of the Talk, which was just as they had finish'd their Dinner, the old Gentlewoman who had sent me somewhat to Eat, call'd her Maid to go up, and ask me if I would have any more; but the Maid brought down Word I had not Eaten half what she had sent me already.

Alas, *says the* old Lady, that poor Girl; I am afraid she will never be well.

Well! *says the* elder Brother, How should Mrs. *Betty* be well, *they say* she is in Love?

I believe nothing of it *says the* old Gentlewoman.

I don't know *says the* eldest Sister, what to say to it, they have made such a rout about her being so Handsome, and so Charming, and I know not what, and that in her hearing too, that has turn'd the Creatures

Head I believe, and who knows what possessions may follow such Doings? for my Part I don't know what to make of it.

Why Sister, you must acknowledge she is very Handsome, *says the* elder Brother.

Ay, and a great deal Handsomer than you Sister, *says* Robin, and that's your Mortification.

Well, well, that is not the Question, *says his* Sister, the Girl is well enough, and she knows it well enough; she need not be told of it to make her Vain.

We are not a talking of her being Vain, *says the* elder Brother, but of her being in Love; it may be she is in Love with herself, it seems my Sisters think so.

I would she was in Love with me, *says* Robin, I'd quickly put her out of her Pain.

What d' ye mean by that, Son, *says the* old Lady, How can you talk so?

Why Madam, *says* Robin again, very honestly, Do you think I'd let the poor Girl Die for Love, and of one that is near at hand to be had too?

Fye Brother, *says the* second Sister, how can you talk so? would you take a Creature that has not a Groat in the World?

Prithee Child *says* Robin, Beauty's a Portion, and good Humour with it, is a double Portion; I wish thou hadst half her Stock of both for thy Portion: So there was her Mouth stopp'd.

I find, *says the* eldest Sister, if *Betty* is not in Love, my Brother is; I wonder he has not broke his Mind to *Betty,* I warrant she won't say NO.

They that yield when they're ask'd *says* Robin, are one step before them that were never ask'd to yield, Sister, and two Steps before them that yield before they are ask'd: And that's an Answer to you Sister.

This fir'd the Sister, and she flew into a Passion, and said, things were come to that pass, that it was time the Wench, *meaning me,* was out of the Family; and but that she was not fit to be turn'd out, she hop'd her Father and Mother would consider of it as soon as she could be remov'd.

Robin reply'd, That was business for the Master and Mistress of the Family, who were not to be taught by One that had so little Judgment as his eldest Sister.

It run up a great deal farther; the Sister Scolded, *Robin* Rally'd and Banter'd, but poor *Betty* lost Ground by it extremely in the Family: I heard of it, and I cry'd heartily, and the old Lady came up to me, some body having told her that I was so much concern'd about it: I complain'd to her, that it was very hard the Doctors should pass such a Censure upon me, for which they had no Ground; and that it was still harder, considering the Circumstances I was under in the Family; that I hop'd I had done nothing to lessen her Esteem for me, or given any Occasion for the Bickering between her Sons and Daughters; and I had more need to think of a Coffin than of being in Love, and beg'd she would not let me suffer in her Opinion for any body's Mistakes, but my own.

She was sensible of the Justice of what I said, but *told me,* since there had been such a Clamour among them, and that her younger Son Talk'd after such a rattling way as he did, she desir'd I would be so Faithful to her as to Answer her but one Question sincerely; I told her I would with all my heart, and with the utmost plainess and Sincerity: Why then the Question was, Whether there was any thing between her Son *Robert* and me? I told her with all the Protestations of Sincerity that I was able to make, and as I might well do, that there was not, nor ever had been; I *told her* that Mr. *Robert* had rattled and jested, as she knew it was his way, and that I took it always as I suppos'd he meant it, to be a wild airy way of Discourse that had no Signification in it: And again assured her that there was not the least title of what she understood by it between us; and that those who had Suggested it had done me a great deal of Wrong, and Mr. *Robert* no Service at all.

The old Lady was fully satisfy'd, and kiss'd me, spoke chearfully to me, and bid me take care of my Health and want for nothing, and so took her leave: But when she came down, she found the Brother and all his Sisters together by the Ears; they were Angry even to Passion, at his upbraiding them with their being Homely, and having never had any Sweethearts, never having been ask'd the Question, and their being so forward as almost to ask first: He rallied them upon the subject of Mrs. *Betty;* how Pretty, how good Humour'd, how she Sung better than they did, and Danc'd better, and how much Handsomer she was; and in doing this, he omitted no Ill-natur'd Thing that could vex them, and indeed, push'd too hard upon them: The old Lady came down in the height of it, and to put a stop to it, told them all the Discourse she had had with me, and how I answer'd, that there was nothing between Mr. *Robert* and I.

She's wrong there, *says* Robin, for if there was not a great deal between us, we should be closer together than we are: I told her I Lov'd her hugely, *says he,* but I could never make the Jade believe I was in Earnest; I do not know how you should *says his* Mother, no body in their Senses could believe you were in Earnest, to Talk so to a poor Girl, whose Circumstances you know so well.

But prithee Son *adds she,* since you tell me that you could not make her believe you were in Earnest, what must we believe about it? for you ramble so in your Discourse, that no body knows whether you are in

Earnest or in Jest: But as I find the Girl by your own Confession has answer'd truely, I wish you would do so too, and tell me seriously, so that I may depend upon it; Is there any thing in it or no? Are you in Earnest or no? Are you Distracted indeed, or are you not? 'Tis a weighty Question, and I wish you would make us easie about it.

By my Faith Madam, *says* Robin, 'tis in vain to mince the Matter, or tell any more Lies about it; I am in Earnest, as much as a Man is that's going to be Hang'd. If Mrs. *Betty* would say she Lov'd me, and that she would Marry me, I'd have her to morrow Morning fasting, and say, *To have, and to hold,* instead of eating my Breakfast.

Well, *says the Mother,* then there's one Son lost; and she said it in a very mournful Tone, as one greatly concern'd at it.

I hope not Madam, *says* Robin, no Man is lost, when a good Wife has found him.

Why but Child, *says the* old Lady, she is a Beggar.

Why then Madam, she has the more need of Charity *says* Robin; I'll take her off of the hands of the Parish, and she and I'll Beg together.

It's bad Jesting with such things, *says the Mother.*

I don't Jest Madam, *says* Robin: We'll come and beg your Pardon Madam; and your Blessing Madam, and my Father's.

This is all out of the way Son, *says the Mother,* if you are in Earnest you are Undone.

I am afraid not *says he,* for I am really afraid she won't have me, after all my Sisters huffing and blustring; I believe I shall never be able to persuade her to it.

That's a fine Tale indeed, she is not so far out of her Senses neither; Mrs. *Betty* is no Fool, *says the youngest Sister,* Do you think she has learnt to say NO, any more than other People?

No Mrs. *Mirth-Wit* says Robin, Mrs. *Betty's* no Fool; but Mrs. *Betty* may be Engag'd some other way, And what then?

Nay, *says the eldest Sister,* we can say nothing to that, Who must it be to then? She is never out of the Doors, it must be between you.

I have nothing to say to that *says* Robin, I have been Examin'd enough; there's my Brother, if it must be *between us,* go to Work with him.

This stung *the elder Brother* to the Quick, and he concluded that *Robin* had discover'd something: However, he kept himself from appearing disturb'd; Prithee *says he,* don't go to sham your Stories off upon me, I tell you, I deal in no such Ware; I have nothing to say to Mrs. *Betty,* nor to any of the *Miss Betty's* in the Parish; and with that he rose up and brush'd off.

No, *says the eldest Sister,* I dare answer for my Brother, he knows the World better.

Thus the Discourse ended; but it left *the elder Brother* quite confounded: He concluded his Brother had made a full Discovery, and he began to doubt whether I had been concern'd in it or not; but with all his Management, he could not bring it about to get at me; at last, he was so perplex'd, that he was quite Desperate, and resolv'd he wou'd come into my Chamber and see me, whatever came of it: In order to this, he contriv'd it so, that one Day after Dinner, watching *his eldest Sister* till he could see her go up Stairs, he runs after her: *Hark ye Sister, says he,* Where is this sick Woman? may not a body see her? YES, *says the Sister,* I believe you may, but let me go first a little, and I'll tell you; so she run up to the Door and gave me notice; and presently call'd to him again: BROTHER, *says she,* you may come if you please; so in he came, just in the same kind of Rant: Well, *says he,* at the Door *as he came in,* Where is this sick Body that's in Love? How do ye do Mrs. *Betty?* I would have got up out of my Chair, but was so Weak I could not for a good while; and he saw it and his Sister too, and she said, *Come do not strive to stand up,* my Brother desires no Ceremony, especially, now you are so Weak. No, No, Mrs. *Betty,* pray sit still *says he,* and so sits himself down in a Chair over-against me, and appear'd as if he was mighty Merry.

He talk'd a deal of rambling Stuff to his sister and to me; sometimes of one thing, sometimes of another, on purpose to Amuse his Sister; and every now and then, would turn it upon the old Story, directing it to me: Poor Mrs. *Betty, says he,* it is a sad thing to be in Love, why it has reduced you sadly; at last I spoke a little; I am glad to see you so merry, Sir, *says I,* but I think the Doctor might have found some thing better to do than to make his Game at his Patients: If I had been Ill of no other Distemper, I know the Proverb too well to have let him come to me: What Proverb *says he?* O! I remember it now: What,

> *Where Love is the Case,*
> *The* Doctor's *an Ass.*

Is not that it Mrs. *Betty?* I smil'd, and said nothing: Nay, *says he,* I think the effect has prov'd it to be Love, for it seems the Doctor has been able to do you but little Service; you mend very slowly they say, I doubt there's somewhat in it Mrs. *Betty,* I doubt you are sick of the Incureables, and that is Love; I smil'd and said, No, *indeed Sir,* that's none of my Distemper.

SAMUEL RICHARDSON

from *The History of Clarissa Harlowe*

MR. LOVELACE TO JOHN BELFORD, ESQ.

M. Hall, Thursday, Sept. 14.

Ever since the fatal seventh of this month, I have been lost to myself and to all the joys of life. I might have gone further back than that fatal seventh; which, for the future, I will never see anniversarily revolve but in sables; only till that cursed day I had some gleams of hope now and then darting in upon me.

They tell me of an odd letter I wrote to you. I remember I did write. But very little of the contents of what I wrote, do I remember.

I have been in a cursed way. Methinks something has been working strangely retributive. I never was such a fool as to disbelieve a Providence: yet am I not for resolving into judgments everything that seems to wear an avenging face. Yet if we must be punished either here or hereafter for our misdeeds, better *here*, say I, than *hereafter.* Have I not then an interest to think my punishment already not only begun but completed, since what I have suffered, and do suffer, passes all description?

To give but one instance of the *retributive*—here I, who was the barbarous cause of the loss of senses for a week together to the most inimitable of women, have been punished with the loss of my own—preparative to—who knows to what?—When, O when, shall I know a joyful hour?

I am kept excessively low; and excessively low I *am.* This sweet creature's posthumous letter sticks close to me. All her excellencies rise up hourly to my remembrance.

Yet dare I not indulge in these melancholy reflections. I find my head strangely working again—pen, begone!

Friday, Sept. 15.

I resume, in a sprightly vein, I hope—Mowbray and Tourville have just now—

But what of Mowbray and Tourville!—What's the world?— What's anybody in it?—

Yet they are highly exasperated against thee, for the last letter thou wrotest to them—such an unfriendly, such a merciless—

But it won't do! I must again lay down my pen.—O Belford!—Belford!—I am still, I am still, most miserably absent from myself! Shall never, never more be what I was!

✵   ✵   ✵

Saturday, Sunday, nothing done. Incapable of anything.

Monday, Sept. 18.

Heavy, d—nably heavy and sick at soul, by Jupiter! I must come into their expedient. I must see what change of climate will do.

You tell these fellows, and you tell me, of repenting and re-forming: but I can do neither. He who *can*, must not have the *extinction* of a Clarissa Harlowe to answer for.—Harlowe!—Curse upon the name!—And curse upon myself for not changing it, as I might have done!—Yet have I no need of urging a curse upon myself—I have it ef-fectually.

"To say I once respected you with a preference"—In what stiff lan-guage does maidenly modesty on these nice occasions express itself!—*To say I once loved you*, is the English, and there is truth and ease in the expression.—"To say I once loved you," then let it be, "is what I ought to blush to own."

And dost thou own it!—Excellent creature! and dost thou then own it!—What music in these words from such an angel!—What would I give that my Clarissa were in being, *and could* and *would* own that she loved me?

"But indeed, sir, I have long been greatly above you."

Long, my blessed charmer!—Long indeed—for you have been *ever* greatly above me, and above your sex, and above all the world.

"That preference was not grounded on ignoble motives."

What a wretch was I, to be so distinguished by her, and yet to be so unworthy of her hope to reclaim me!

Then, how generous her motives! Not for her *own* sake merely, not altogether for *mine*, did she hope to reclaim me, but equally for the sake of innocents who might otherwise be ruined by me.

And now, why did she write this letter, and *why* direct it to be given me when an event the most deplorable had taken place, but for my good, and with a view to the safety of innocents she knew not?—And *when* was this letter written? Was it not at the time, at the very time, that I had been pursuing her, as I may say, from place to place; when her soul was bowed down by calamity and persecution; and herself was denied all forgiveness from relations the most implacable?

Exalted creature!—And couldst thou, at *such a time* and *so early*, and in *such circumstances*, have so far subdued thy own just resentments, as to wish happiness to the principal author of all thy distresses? Wish happiness to him who had robbed thee "of all thy favourite expectations in this life?" To him who had been the cause, "that thou wert cut off in the bloom of youth?"

Heavenly aspirer!—What a frame must thou be in, to be able to use the word ONLY, in mentioning these important deprivations!—And as this was before thou puttest off mortality, may I not presume that thou now,

> with pitying eye,
> Not derogating from thy perfect bliss,
> Survey'st all heaven around, and wishest for me?

"Consider my ways"—Dear life of my life! of what avail is consideration now, when I have lost the dear creature, for whose sake alone it was worth while to *have* consideration?—Lost her beyond retrieving—swallowed up by the greedy grave—for *ever* lost her—that, *that's* the sting—matchless woman!—How does this reflection wound me!

"Your golden dream cannot long last."—Divine prophetess! my golden dream is *already* over.—"Thought and reflection" *are* no longer to be kept off,—no *longer continues* that "hardened insensibility" thou chargest upon me.—"Remorse *has* broken in upon me.—Dreadful *is* my condition;—it *is* all reproach and horror with me!"—A thousand vultures in turn are preying upon my heart!

But no more of these fruitless reflections—since I am incapable of writing anything else; since my pen will slide into this gloomy subject, whether I will or not; I will once more quit it; nor will I again resume it, till I can be more *its master* and my own.

All I took pen to write for is however unwritten. It was, in few words, to wish you to proceed with your communications, as usual. And why should you not?—Since, in her ever-to-be-lamented death, I know everything shocking and grievous—acquaint me, then, with all thou knowest, which I do *not* know: how her relations, her cruel relations, take it; and whether now, the barbed dart of after-reflection sticks not in their hearts, as in mine, up to the very feathers.

✻   ✻   ✻

I will soon quit this kingdom. For now my Clarissa is no more, what is there in it (in the world indeed) worth living for?—But shall I not first, by some masterly mischief, avenge her and myself upon her cursed family?

The accursed woman, they tell me, has broken her leg. Why was it not her neck?—All, all, but what is owing to her relations, is the fault of that woman, and of her hell-born nymphs. *The greater the virtue, the nobler the triumph*, was a sentence forever in their mouths.—I have had it several times in my head to set fire to the execrable house, and to watch at the doors and windows, that not a devil in it escape the consuming flames. Had the house stood by itself, I had certainly done it.

But, it seems, the old wretch is in the way to be rewarded, without my help. A shocking letter is received of somebody's, in relation to her—your's, I suppose—too shocking for me, they say, to see at present.

They govern me as a child in strings: yet did I suffer so much in my fever, that I am willing to bear with them, till I can get tolerably well.

At present, I can neither eat, drink, nor sleep. Yet are my disorders nothing to what they were: for, Jack, my brain was on fire day and night, and had it not been of the *asbestos* kind, it had all been consumed.

I had no distinct ideas, but of dark and confused misery: *it was all remorse and horror* indeed! Thoughts of hanging, drowning, shooting; then rage, violence, mischief, and despair took their turns with me. My lucid intervals still worse, giving me to reflect upon what I *was* the hour before, and what I was likely to be the next, and perhaps for life—the sport of enemies! the laughter of fools! and the hanging-sleeved go-carted property of hired slaves; who were perhaps to find their account in manacling, and (abhorred thought!) in personally abusing me by blows and stripes!

Who can bear such reflections as these? To be made to *fear* only, to such a one as me, and to fear *such wretches* too?—What a thing was this, but *remotely* to apprehend! And yet for a man to be in such a state as to render it necessary for his dearest friends to suffer this to be done for his own sake, and in order to prevent further mischief?—There is no thinking of these things!

I will *not* think of them, therefore: but will either get a train of cheerful ideas, or hang myself by tomorrow morning.

To be a dog, and dead,
Were paradise to such a life as mine.

❦ ❦

FANNY BURNEY (MADAME D'ARBLAY)

from *Evelina, or A Young Lady's Entrance into the World*

LETTER LVIII

Evelina in continuation

BERRY HILL, 21 *July.*

You accuse me of mystery, and charge me with reserve. I cannot doubt but I must have merited the accusation;—yet, to clear myself,—you know not how painful will be the task. But I cannot resist your kind entreaties,—indeed, I do not wish to resist them, for your friendship and affection will soothe my chagrin. Had it arisen from any other cause, not a moment would I have deferred the communication you ask;—but as it is, I would, were it possible, not only conceal it from all the world, but endeavour to disbelieve it myself. Yet, since I *must* tell you, why trifle with your impatience?

I know not how to come to the point; twenty times have I attempted it in vain;—but I will *force* myself to proceed.

Oh, Miss Mirvan, could you ever have believed that one who seemed formed as a pattern for his fellow-creatures, as a model of perfection,—one whose elegance surpassed all description,—whose sweetness of manners disgraced all comparison,—Oh Miss Mirvan, could you ever have believed that *Lord Orville* would have treated me with indignity?

Never, never again will I trust to appearances,—never confide in my own weak judgment,—never believe that person to be good who seems to be amiable! What cruel maxims are we taught by a knowledge of the world!—But while my own reflections absorb me, I forget you are still in suspense.

I had just finished the last letter which I wrote to you from London, when the maid of the house brought me a note. It was given to her, she said, by a footman, who told her he would call the next day for an answer.

This note,—but let it speak for itself.

"To Miss Anville

"With transport, most charming of thy sex, did I read the letter with which you yesterday morning favoured me. I am sorry the affair of the carriage should have given you any concern, but I am highly flattered by the anxiety you express so kindly. Believe me, my lovely girl, I am truly sensible of the honour of your good opinion, and feel myself deeply penetrated with love and gratitude. The correspondence you have so sweetly commenced I shall be proud of continuing, and I hope the strong sense I have of the favour you do me, will prevent your withdrawing it. Assure yourself that I desire nothing more ardently, than to pour forth my thanks at your feet, and to offer those vows which are so justly the tribute of your charms and accomplishments. In your next, I entreat you to acquaint me how long you shall remain in town. The servant whom I shall commission to call for an answer, has orders to ride post with it to me. My impatience for his arrival will be very great, though inferior to that with which I burn, to tell you, in person, how much I am, my sweet girl,

"Your grateful admirer,

"ORVILLE."

What a letter! how was my proud heart swelled, every line I have copied! What I wrote to him you know; tell me then, my dear friend, do you think it merited such an answer?—and that I have deservedly incurred the liberty he has taken? I meant nothing but a simple apology, which I thought as much due to my own character, as to his; yet, by the construction he seems to have put upon it, should you not have imagined it contained the avowal of sentiments which might, indeed, have provoked his contempt.

The moment the letter was delivered to me, I retired to my own room to read it, and so eager was my first perusal, that,—I am ashamed to own it gave me no sensation but of delight. Unsuspicious of any impropriety from Lord Orville, I perceived not immediately the impertinence it implied,—I only marked the expressions of his own regard; and I was so much surprised, that I was unable, for some time, to compose myself, or read it again,—I could only walk up and down the room, repeating to myself, "Good God, is it possible?—am I, then, loved by Lord Orville?"

But this dream was soon over, and I awoke to far different feelings; upon a second reading I thought every word changed,—it did not seem the same letter,—I could not find one sentence that I could look at without blushing. My astonishment was extreme, and it was succeeded by the utmost indignation.

If, as I am very ready to acknowledge, I erred in writing to Lord Orville, was it for *him* to punish the error? If he was offended, could he not have been silent? If he thought my letter ill-judged, should he not have pitied my ignorance? have considered my youth, and allowed for my inexperience?

Oh Maria, how have I been deceived in this man! Words have no power to tell the high opinion I had of him; to that was owing the unfortunate solicitude which prompted my writing,—a solicitude I must forever repent!

Yet perhaps I have rather reason to rejoice than to grieve, since this affair has shown me his real disposition, and removed that partiality, which, covering his every imperfection, left only his virtues and good qualities exposed to view. Had the deception continued much longer, had my mind received any additional prejudice in his favour, who knows whither my mistaken ideas might have led me? Indeed I fear I was in greater danger than I apprehended, or can now think of without trembling,—for oh, if this weak heart of mine had been penetrated with too deep an impression of his merit,—my peace and happiness had been lost forever!

I would fain encourage more cheerful thoughts, fain drive from my mind the melancholy that has taken possession of it,—but I cannot succeed; for, added to the humiliating feelings which so powerfully oppress me, I have yet another cause of concern;—alas, my dear Maria, I have broken the tranquillity of the best of men!

I have never had the courage to show him this cruel letter. I could not bear so greatly to depreciate in his opinion, one whom I had, with infinite anxiety, raised in it myself. Indeed, my first determination was to confine my chagrin totally to my own bosom; but your friendly enquiries have drawn it from me, and now I wish I had made no concealment from the beginning, since I know not how to account for a gravity which not all my endeavours can entirely hide or repress.

LETTER LXXVII

Evelina in continuation

CLIFTON, 7 *October.*

You will see, my dear Sir, that I was mistaken in supposing I should write no more from this place, where my residence, now, seems more uncertain than ever.

This morning, during breakfast, Lord Orville took an opportunity to beg me, in a low voice, to allow him a moment's conversation before I left Clifton; "May I hope," added he, "that you will stroll into the garden after breakfast?"

I made no answer, but I believe my looks gave no denial; for, indeed, I much wished to be satisfied concerning the letter. The moment, therefore, that I could quit the parlour, I ran upstairs for my calash; but before I reached my room, Mrs. Selwyn called after me, "If you are going to walk, Miss Anville, be so good as to bid Jenny bring down my hat, and I'll accompany you."

Very much disconcerted, I turned into the drawing-room, without making any answer, and there I hoped to wait unseen, till she had otherwise disposed of herself. But, in a few minutes, the door opened, and Sir Clement Willoughby entered.

Starting at the sight of him, in rising hastily, I let drop the letter which I had brought for Lord Orville's inspection, and, before I could recover it, Sir Clement, springing forward, had it in his hand. He was just presenting it to me, and, at the same time, enquiring after my health, when the signature caught his eye, and he read aloud "Orville."

I endeavoured, eagerly, to snatch it from him, but he would not permit me, and, holding it fast, in a passionate manner exclaimed, "Good God, Miss Anville, is it possible you can value such a letter as this?"

The question surprised and confounded me, and I was too much ashamed to answer him; but, finding he made an attempt to secure it, I prevented him, and vehemently demanded him to return it.

"Tell me first," said he, holding it above my reach, "tell me if you have, since, received any more letters from the same person?"

"No, indeed," cried I, "never!"

"And will you also, sweetest of women, promise that you never *will* receive any more? Say that, and you will make me the happiest of men."

"Sir Clement," cried I, greatly confused, "pray give me the letter."

"And will you first satisfy my doubts?—will you not relieve me from the torture of the most distracting suspense?—tell me but that the detested Orville has written to you no more!"

"Sir Clement," cried I, angrily, "you have no right to make any conditions,—so pray give me the letter directly."

"Why such solicitude about this hateful letter? Can it possibly deserve your eagerness? Tell me, with truth, with sincerity tell me; Does it really merit the least anxiety?"

"No matter, Sir," cried I, in great perplexity, "the letter is mine, and therefore—"

"I must conclude, then," said he, "that the letter deserves your utmost contempt,—but that the name of Orville is sufficient to make you prize it."

"Sir Clement," cried I, colouring, "you are quite—you are very much—the letter is not—"

"Oh, Miss Anville," cried he, "you blush!—you stammer!—Great Heaven! it is then all as I feared!"

"I know not," cried I, half frightened, "what you mean; but I beseech you to give me the letter, and to compose yourself."

"The letter," cried he, gnashing his teeth, "you shall never see more! You ought to have burnt it the moment you had read it!" And in an instant, he tore it into a thousand pieces.

Alarmed at a fury so indecently outrageous, I would have run out of the room; but he caught hold of my gown, and cried, "Not yet, not yet must you go! I am but half-mad yet, and you must stay to finish your work. Tell me, therefore, does Orville know your fatal partiality?—Say *yes*," added he, trembling with passion, "and I will fly you forever!"

"For Heaven's sake, Sir Clement," cried I, "release me!—if you do not, you will force me to call for help."

"Call then," cried he, "inexorable and most unfeeling girl; call, if you please, and bid all the world witness your triumph!—but could ten worlds obey your call, I would not part with you till you had answered me. Tell me, then, does Orville know you love him?"

At any other time, an enquiry so gross would have given me inexpressible confusion; but now, the wildness of his manner terrified me, and I only said, "Whatever you wish to know, Sir Clement, I will tell you another time; but for the present, I entreat you to let me go!"

"Enough," cried he, "I understand you!—the art of Orville has prevailed;—cold, inanimate, phlegmatic as he is, you have rendered him the most envied of men!—One thing more, and I have done:—Will he marry you?"

What a question! My cheeks glowed with indignation, and I felt too proud to make any answer.

"I see, I see how it is," cried he, after a short pause, "and I find I am undone forever!" Then, letting loose my gown, he put his hand to his forehead, and walked up and down the room in a hasty and agitated manner.

Though now at liberty to go, I had not the courage to leave him: for his evident distress excited all my compassion. And this was our situation, when Lady Louisa, Mr. Coverley, and Mrs. Beaumont entered the room.

"Sir Clement Willoughby," said the latter, "I beg pardon for making you wait so long, but—"

She had not time for another word; Sir Clement, too much disordered to know or care what he did, snatched up his hat, and, brushing hastily past her, flew downstairs, and out of the house.

And with him went my sincerest pity, though I earnestly hope I shall see him no more. But what, my dear Sir, am I to conclude from his strange speeches concerning the letter? Does it not seem as if he was himself the author of it? How else should he be so well acquainted with the contempt it merits? Neither do I know another human being who could serve any interest by such a deception. I remember, too, that just as I had given my own letter to the maid, Sir Clement came into the shop; probably he prevailed upon her, by some bribery, to give it to him, and afterwards, by the same means, to deliver me an answer of his own writing. Indeed, I can in no other manner account for this affair. Oh, Sir Clement, were you not yourself unhappy, I know not how I could pardon an artifice that has caused me so much uneasiness!

I know not how long I might have continued in this situation, had I not been awakened from my melancholy reverie by the voice of Lord Orville. "May I come in," cried he, "or shall I interrupt you?"

I was silent, and he seated himself next me.

"I fear," he continued, "Miss Anville will think I persecute her; yet so much as I have to say, and so much as I wish to hear, with so few opportunities for either, she cannot wonder,—and I hope she will not be offended,—that I seize with such avidity every moment in my power to converse with her. You are grave," added he, taking my hand; "I hope you do not regret the delay of your journey?—I hope the pleasure it gives to *me*, will not be a subject of pain to *you*?—You are silent?—Something, I am sure, has afflicted you:—Would to Heaven I were able to console you!—Would to Heaven I were worthy to participate in your sorrows!"

My heart was too full to bear this kindness, and I could only answer by my tears. "Good Heaven," cried he, "how you alarm me!—My love, my sweet Miss Anville, deny me no longer to be the sharer of your griefs!—tell me, at least, that you have not withdrawn your esteem!—that you do not repent the goodness you have shown me!—that you still think me the same grateful Orville whose heart you have deigned to accept!"

"Oh, my Lord," cried I, "your generosity overpowers me!" And I wept like an infant. For now that all my hopes of being acknowledged seemed finally crushed, I felt the nobleness of his disinterested regard so forcibly, that I could scarce breathe under the weight of gratitude which oppressed me.

He seemed greatly shocked, and in terms the most flattering, the most respectfully tender, he at once soothed my distress, and urged me to tell him its cause.

"My Lord," said I, when I was able to speak, "you little know what an outcast you have honoured with your choice!—a child of bounty,—an orphan from infancy,—dependent, even for subsistence dependent, upon the kindness of compassion!—Rejected by my natural friends,—disowned forever by my nearest relation,—Oh, my Lord, so circum-stanced, can I deserve the distinction with which you honour me? No, no; I feel the inequality too painfully;—you must leave me, my Lord, you must suffer me to return to obscurity,—and there in the bosom of my first, best,—my only friend,—I will pour forth all the grief of my heart!—while you, my Lord, must seek elsewhere—"

I could not proceed; my whole soul recoiled against the charge I would have given, and my voice refused to utter it.

"Never!" cried he, warmly; "my heart is your's, and I swear to you an attachment eternal!—You prepare me, indeed, for a tale of horror, and I am almost breathless with expectation,—but so firm is my con-viction, that, whatever are your misfortunes, to have merited them is not of the number, that I feel myself more strongly, more invincibly devoted to you than ever!—Tell me but where I may find this noble friend, whose virtues you have already taught me to reverence,—and I will fly to ob-tain his consent and intercession, that henceforward our fates may be in-dissolubly united,—and then shall it be the sole study of my life to endeavour to soften your past,—and guard you from future misfor-tunes!"

I had just raised my eyes, to answer this most generous of men, when the first object they met was Mrs. Selwyn!

"So my dear," cried she, "what, still courting the rural shades!—I thought ere now you would have been satiated with this retired seat, and I have been seeking you all over the house. But I find the only way to meet with *you*,—is to enquire for *Lord Orville*. However, don't let me disturb your meditations; you are possibly planning some pastoral dialogue."

And, with this provoking speech, she walked on.

In the greatest confusion, I was quitting the arbour, when Lord Orville said, "Permit *me* to follow Mrs. Selwyn,—it is time to put an end to all impertinent conjectures; will you allow me to speak to her openly?"

I assented in silence, and he left me.

I then went to my own room, where I continued till I was summoned to dinner; after which, Mrs. Selwyn invited me to her's.

The moment she had shut the door, "Your Ladyship," said she, "will, I hope, be seated."

"Ma'am!" cried I, staring.

"O the sweet innocent! So you don't know what I mean?—but, my dear, my sole view is to accustom you a little to your dignity elect, lest, when you are addressed by your title, you should look another way, from an apprehension of listening to a discourse not meant for you to hear."

Having, in this manner, diverted herself with my confusion, till her raillery was almost exhausted, she congratulated me very seriously upon the partiality of Lord Orville, and painted to me, in the strongest terms, his disinterested desire of being married to me immediately. She had told him, she said, my whole story; and yet he was willing, nay, eager, that our union should take place of any further application to my family. "Now, my dear," continued she, "I advise you by all means to marry him directly; nothing can be more precarious than our success with Sir John; and the young men of this age are not to be trusted with too much time for deliberation, where [their] interests are concerned."

❧ ☙

MARY WOLLSTONECRAFT SHELLEY

from *Frankenstein, or The Modern Prometheus*

The monster confronts his creator, Frankenstein

"I generally rested during the day, and travelled only when I was secured by night from the view of man. One morning, however, finding that my path lay through a deep wood, I ventured to continue my journey after the sun had risen; the day, which was one of the first of spring, cheered even me by the loveliness of its sunshine and the balminess of the air. I felt emotions of gentleness and pleasure, that had long appeared dead, revive within me. Half surprised by the novelty of these sensations, I allowed myself to be borne away by them; and, forgetting my solitude and deformity, dared to be happy. Soft tears again bedewed my cheeks, and I even raised my humid eyes with thankfulness towards the blessed sun which bestowed such joy upon me.

"I continued to wind among the paths of the wood, until I came to its boundary, which was skirted by a deep and rapid river, into which many of the trees bent their branches, now budding with the fresh spring. Here I paused, not exactly knowing what path to pursue, when I heard the sound of voices that induced me to conceal myself under the shade of a cypress. I was scarcely hid, when a young girl came running towards the spot where I was concealed, laughing, as if she ran from some one in sport. She continued her course along the precipitous sides of the river, when suddenly her foot slipt, and she fell into the rapid stream. I rushed from my hiding-place; and, with extreme labour from the force of the current, saved her, and dragged her to shore. She was senseless; and I endeavoured by every means in my power to restore animation, when I was suddenly interrupted by the approach of a rustic, who was probably the person from whom she had playfully fled. On seeing me, he darted towards me, and tearing the girl from my arms, hastened towards the deeper parts of the wood. I followed speedily, I hardly knew why; but when the man saw me draw near, he aimed a gun, which he carried, at my body, and fired. I sunk to the ground, and my injurer, with increased swiftness, escaped into the wood.

"This was then the reward of my benevolence! I had saved a human being from destruction, and, as a recompense, I now writhed under the miserable pain of a wound, which shattered the flesh and bone. The feelings of kindness and gentleness which I had entertained but a few moments before gave place to hellish rage and gnashing of teeth. Inflamed by pain, I vowed eternal hatred and vengeance to all mankind. But the agony of my wound overcame me; my pulses paused, and I fainted.

"For some weeks I led a miserable life in the woods, endeavouring to cure the wound which I had received. The ball had entered my shoulder, and I knew not whether it had remained there or passed through; at any rate I had no means of extracting it. My sufferings were augmented also by the oppressive sense of the injustice and ingratitude of their infliction. My daily vows rose for revenge—a deep and deadly revenge, such as would alone compensate for the outrages and anguish I had endured.

"After some weeks my wound healed, and I continued my journey. The labours I endured were no longer to be alleviated by the bright sun or gentle breezes of spring; all joy was but a mockery, which insulted my desolate state, and made me feel more painfully that I was not made for the enjoyment of pleasure.

"But my toils now drew near a close; and in two months from this time I reached the environs of Geneva.

"It was evening when I arrived, and I retired to a hiding-place among the fields that surround it, to meditate in what manner I should apply to you. I was oppressed by fatigue and hunger, and far too unhappy to enjoy the gentle breezes of evening, or the prospect of the sun setting behind the stupendous mountains of Jura.

"At this time a slight sleep relieved me from the pain of reflection, which was disturbed by the approach of a beautiful child, who came running into the recess I had chosen, with all the sportiveness of infancy. Suddenly, as I gazed on him, an idea seized me, that this little creature was unprejudiced, and had lived too short a time to have imbibed a horror of deformity. If, therefore, I could seize him, and educate him as my companion and friend, I should not be so desolate in this peopled earth.

"Urged by this impulse, I seized on the boy as he passed and drew him towards me. As soon as he beheld my form, he placed his hands before his eyes and uttered a shrill scream: I drew his hand forcibly from his face, and said, 'Child, what is the meaning of this? I do not intend to hurt you; listen to me.'

"He struggled violently. 'Let me go,' he cried; 'monster! ugly wretch! you wish to eat me, and tear me to pieces—You are an ogre—Let me go, or I will tell my papa.'

" 'Boy, you will never see your father again; you must come with me.'

" 'Hideous monster! let me go. My papa is a Syndic—he is M. Frankenstein—he will punish you. You dare not keep me.'

" 'Frankenstein! you belong then to my enemy—to him towards whom I have sworn eternal revenge; you shall be my first victim.'

"The child still struggled, and loaded me with epithets which carried despair to my heart; I grasped his throat to silence him, and in a moment he lay dead at my feet.

"I gazed on my victim, and my heart swelled with exultation and hellish triumph: clapping my hands, I exclaimed, 'I, too, can create desolation; my enemy is not invulnerable; this death will carry despair to him, and a thousand other miseries shall torment and destroy him.'

"As I fixed my eyes on the child, I saw something glittering on his breast. I took it; it was a portrait of a most lovely woman. In spite of my malignity, it softened and attracted me. For a few moments I gazed with delight on her dark eyes, fringed by deep lashes, and her lovely lips; but presently my rage returned: I remembered that I was for ever deprived of the delights that such beautiful creatures could bestow; and that she whose resemblance I contemplated would, in regarding me, have changed that air of divine benignity to one expressive of disgust and affright.

"Can you wonder that such thoughts transported me with rage? I only wonder that at that moment, instead of venting my sensations in exclamations and agony, I did not rush among mankind and perish in the attempt to destroy them.

"While I was overcome by these feelings, I left the spot where I had committed the murder, and seeking a more secluded hiding-place, I entered a barn which had appeared to me to be empty. A woman was sleeping on some straw; she was young: not indeed so beautiful as her whose portrait I held; but of an agreeable aspect, and blooming in the loveliness of youth and health. Here, I thought, is one of those whose joy-imparting smiles are bestowed on all but me. And then I bent over her, and whispered, 'Awake, fairest, thy lover is near—he who would give his life but to obtain one look of affection from thine eyes: my beloved, awake!'

"The sleeper stirred; a thrill of terror ran through me. Should she indeed awake, and see me, and curse me, and denounce the murderer? Thus would she assuredly act, if her darkened eyes opened and she beheld me. The thought was madness; it stirred the fiend within me—not I, but she shall suffer: the murder I have committed because I am for ever robbed of all that she could give me, she shall atone. The crime had its source in her: be hers the punishment! Thanks to the lessons of Felix and the sanguinary laws of man, I had learned now to work mischief. I bent over her, and placed the portrait securely in one of the folds of her dress. She moved again, and I fled.

"For some days I haunted the spot where these scenes had taken place; sometimes wishing to see you, sometimes resolved to quit the world and its miseries forever. At length I wandered towards these mountains, and have ranged through their immense recesses, consumed by a burning passion which you alone can gratify. We may not part until you have promised to comply with my requisition. I am alone, and miserable; man will not associate with me; but one as deformed and horrible as myself would not deny herself to me. My companion must be of the same species, and have the same defects. This being you must create."

The being finished speaking, and fixed his looks upon me in expectation of a reply. But I was bewildered, perplexed, and unable to arrange my ideas sufficiently to understand the full extent of his proposition. He continued—

"You must create a female for me, with whom I can live in the interchange of those sympathies necessary for my being. This you alone can do; and I demand it of you as a right which you must not refuse to concede."

The latter part of his tale had kindled anew in me the anger that had died away while he narrated his peaceful life among the cottagers, and, as he said this, I could no longer suppress the rage that burned within me.

"I do refuse it," I replied; "and no torture shall ever extort a consent from me. You may render me the most miserable of men, but you shall never make me base in my own eyes. Shall I create another like yourself, whose joint wickedness might desolate the world! Begone! I have answered you; you may torture me, but I will never consent."

"You are in the wrong," replied the fiend; "and, instead of threatening, I am content to reason with you. I am malicious because I am miserable. Am I not shunned and hated by all mankind? You, my creator, would tear me to pieces, and triumph; remember that, and tell me why I should pity man more than he pities me? You would not call it murder if you could precipitate me into one of those ice-rifts, and destroy my frame, the work of your own hands. Shall I respect man when he condemns me? Let him live with me in the interchange of kindness; and, instead of injury, I would bestow every benefit upon him with tears of gratitude at his acceptance. But that cannot be; the human senses are insurmountable barriers to our union. Yet mine shall not be the submission of abject slavery. I will revenge my injuries: if I cannot inspire love, I will cause fear; and chiefly towards you my arch-enemy, because my creator, do I swear inextinguishable hatred. Have a care: I will work at your destruction, nor finish until I desolate your heart, so that you shall curse the hour of your birth."

A fiendish rage animated him as he said this; his face was wrinkled into contortions too horrible for human eyes to behold; but presently he calmed himself and proceeded—

"I intended to reason. This passion is detrimental to me; for you do not reflect that *you* are the cause of its excess. If any being felt emotions of benevolence towards me, I should return them an hundred and an hundred fold; for that one creature's sake, I would make peace with the whole kind! But I now indulge in dreams of bliss that cannot be realised. What I ask of you is reasonable and moderate; I demand a creature of another sex, but as hideous as myself; the gratification is small, but it is all that I can receive, and it shall content me. It is true we shall be monsters, cut off from all the world; but on that account we shall be more attached to one another. Our lives will not be happy, but they will be harmless, and free from the misery I now feel. Oh! my creator, make me happy; let me feel gratitude towards you for one benefit! Let me see that I excite the sympathy of some existing thing; do not deny me my request!"

I was moved. I shuddered when I thought of the possible consequences of my consent; but I felt that there was some justice in his argument. His tale, and the feelings he now expressed, proved him to be a creature of fine sensations; and did I not as his maker owe him all the portion of happiness that it was in my power to bestow? He saw my change of feeling and continued—

"If you consent, neither you nor any other human being shall ever see us again: I will go to the vast wilds of South America. My food is not that of man; I do not destroy the lamb and the kid to glut my appetite; acorns and berries afford me sufficient nourishment. My companion will be of the same nature as myself, and will be content with the same fare. We shall make our bed of dried leaves; the sun will shine on us as on man, and will ripen our food. The picture I present to you is peaceful and human, and you must feel that you could deny it only in the wantonness of power and cruelty. Pitiless as you have been towards me, I now see compassion in your eyes; let me seize the favourable moment, and persuade you to promise what I so ardently desire."

"You propose," replied I, "to fly from the habitations of man, to dwell in those wilds where the beasts of the field will be your only companions. How can you, who long for the love and sympathy of man, persevere in this exile? You will return, and again seek their kindness, and you will meet with their detestation; your evil passions will be renewed, and you will then have a companion to aid you in the task of destruction. This may not be: cease to argue the point, for I cannot consent."

"How inconstant are your feelings! but a moment ago you were moved by my representations, and why do you again harden yourself to my complaints? I swear to you, by the earth which I inhabit, and by you that made me, that, with the companion you bestow, I will quit the neighbourhood of man, and dwell as it may chance in the most savage of places. My evil passions will have fled, for I shall meet with sympathy!"

JANE AUSTEN

from *Pride and Prejudice*

After a week spent in professions of love and schemes of felicity, Mr. Collins was called from his amiable Charlotte by the arrival of Saturday. The pain of separation, however, might be alleviated on his side by preparations for the reception of his bride, as he had reason to hope that shortly after his next return into Hertfordshire, the day would be fixed that was to make him the happiest of men. He took leave of his relations at Longbourn with as much solemnity as before, wished his fair cousins health and happiness again, and promised their father another letter of thanks.

On the following Monday, Mrs. Bennet had the pleasure of receiving her brother and his wife, who came as usual to spend the Christmas at Longbourn. Mr. Gardiner was a sensible, gentlemanlike man, greatly superior to his sister as well by nature as education. The Netherfield ladies would have had difficulty in believing that a man who lived by trade, and within view of his own warehouses, could have been so well bred and agreeable. Mrs. Gardiner, who was several years younger than Mrs. Bennet and Mrs. Philips, was an amiable, intelligent, elegant woman, and a great favourite with all her Longbourn nieces. Between the two eldest and herself especially there subsisted a very particular regard. They had frequently been staying with her in town.

The first part of Mrs. Gardiner's business on her arrival was to distribute her presents and describe the newest fashions. When this was done, she had a less active part to play. It became her turn to listen. Mrs. Bennet had many grievances to relate, and much to complain of. They had all been very ill-used since she last saw her sister. Two of her girls had been on the point of marriage, and after all there was nothing in it.

"I do not blame Jane," she continued, "for Jane would have got Mr. Bingley, if she could. But, Lizzy! Oh, sister! it is very hard to think that she might have been Mr. Collins's wife by this time, had not it been for her own perverseness. He made her an offer in this very room, and she refused him. The consequence of it is that Lady Lucas will have a daughter married before I have, and that Longbourn estate is just as much entailed as ever. The Lucases are very artful people indeed, sister. They are all for what they can get. I am sorry to say it of them, but so it is. It makes me very nervous and poorly to be thwarted so in my own family, and to have neighbours who think of themselves before anybody else. However, your coming just at this time is the greatest of comforts, and I am very glad to hear what you tell us of long sleeves."

Mrs. Gardiner, to whom the chief of this news had been given before, in the course of Jane and Elizabeth's correspondence with her, made her sister a slight answer, and in compassion to her nieces turned the conversation.

When alone with Elizabeth afterwards, she spoke more on the subject. "It seems likely to have been a desirable match for Jane," said she. "I am sorry it went off. But these things happen so often! A young man, such as you describe Mr. Bingley so easily falls in love with a pretty girl for a few weeks, and when accident separates them, so easily forgets her that these sort of inconstancies are very frequent."

"An excellent consolation in its way," said Elizabeth, "but it will not do for *us*. We do not suffer by *accident*. It does not often happen that the interference of friends will persuade a young man of independent fortune to think no more of a girl, whom he was violently in love with only a few days before."

"But that expression of 'violently in love' is so hackneyed, so doubtful, so indefinite, that it gives me very little idea. It is as often applied to feelings which arise from an half-hour's acquaintance as to a real, strong attachment. Pray, how *violent was* Mr. Bingley's love?"

"I never saw a more promising inclination. He was growing quite inattentive to other people, and wholly engrossed by her. Every time they met, it was more decided and remarkable. At his own ball he offended two or three young ladies by not asking them to dance, and I spoke to him twice myself, without receiving an answer. Could there be finer symptoms? Is not general incivility the very essence of love?"

❧ ❧

CHARLOTTE BRONTË

from *Jane Eyre*

A splendid Midsummer shone over England: skies so pure, suns so radiant as were then seen in long succession, seldom favour, even singly, our wave-girt land. It was as if a band of Italian days had come from the

South, like a flock of glorious passenger birds, and lighted to rest them on the cliffs of Albion. The hay was all got in; the fields round Thornfield were green and shorn; the roads white and baked; the trees were in their dark prime; hedge and wood, full-leaved and deeply tinted, contrasted well with the sunny hue of the clear meadows between.

One Midsummer-eve, Adèle, weary with gathering wild strawberries in Hay Lane half the day, had gone to bed with the sun. I watched her drop asleep, and when I left her I sought the garden.

It was now the sweetest hour of the twenty-four:—"Day its fervid fires had wasted," and dew fell cool on panting plain and scorched summit. Where the sun had gone down in simple state—pure of the pomp of clouds—spread a solemn purple, burning with the light of red jewel and furnace flame at one point, on one hill-peak, and extending high and wide, soft and still softer, over half heaven. The east had its own charm of fine, deep blue, and its own modest gem, a rising and solitary star: soon it would boast the moon; but she was yet beneath the horizon.

I walked a while on the pavement; but a subtle, well-known scent—that of a cigar—stole from some window; I saw the library casement open a hand-breadth; I knew I might be watched thence; so I went apart into the orchard. No nook in the grounds more sheltered and more Eden-like; it was full of trees, it bloomed with flowers: a very high wall shut it out from the court, on one side; on the other, a beech avenue screened it from the lawn. At the bottom was a sunk fence, its sole separation from lonely fields: a winding walk, bordered with laurels and terminating in a giant horse-chestnut, circled at the base by a seat, led down to the fence. Here one could wander unseen. While such honey-dew fell, such silence reigned, such gloaming gathered, I felt as if I could haunt such shade forever: but in threading the flower and fruit-parterres at the upper part of the inclosure, enticed there by the light the now-rising moon casts on this more open quarter, my step is stayed—not by sound, not by sight, but once more by a warning fragrance.

Sweet briar and southern wood, jasmine, pink, and rose, have long been yielding their evening sacrifice of incense: this new scent is neither of shrub nor flower; it is—I know it well—it is Mr. Rochester's cigar. I look round and I listen. I see trees laden with ripening fruit. I hear a nightingale warbling in a wood half a mile off; no moving form is visible, no coming step audible; but that perfume increases: I must flee. I make for the wicket leading to the shrubbery, and I see Mr. Rochester entering. I step aside into the ivy recess, he will not stay long: he will soon return whence he came, and if I sit still he will never see me.

But no—eventide is as pleasant to him as to me, and this antique garden as attractive; and he strolls on, now lifting the gooseberry-tree branches to look at the fruit, large as plums, with which they are laden; now taking a ripe cherry from the wall; now stooping towards a knot of flowers, either to inhale their fragrance or to admire the dew-beads on their petals. A great moth goes humming by me; it alights on a plant at Mr. Rochester's foot: he sees it, and bends to examine it.

"Now, he has his back towards me," thought I, "and he is occupied too; perhaps, if I walk softly, I can slip away unnoticed."

I trod on an edging of turf that the crackle of the pebbly gravel might not betray me: he was standing among the beds at a yard or two distant from where I had to pass; the moth apparently engaged him. "I shall get by very well," I meditated. As I crossed his shadow, thrown long over the garden by the moon, not yet risen high, he said quietly without turning:—

"Jane, come and look at this fellow."

I had made no noise: he had not eyes behind—could his shadow feel? I started at first, and then I approached him.

"Look at his wings," said he, "he reminds me rather of a West Indian insect; one does not often see so large and gay a nightrover in England: there! he is flown."

The moth roamed away. I was sheepishly retreating also; but Mr. Rochester followed me, and when we reached the wicket, he said:—

"Turn back: on so lovely a night it is a shame to sit in the house; and surely no one can wish to go to bed while sunset is thus at meeting with moonrise."

It is one of my faults, that though my tongue is sometimes prompt enough at an answer, there are times when it sadly fails me in framing an excuse; and always the lapse occurs at some crisis, when a facile word or plausible pretext is specially wanted to get me out of painful embarrassment. I did not like to walk at this hour alone with Mr. Rochester in the shadowy orchard; but I could not find a reason to allege for leaving him. I followed with lagging step, and thoughts busily bent on discovering a means of extrication; but he himself looked so composed and so grave also, I became ashamed of feeling any confusion: the evil—if evil existent or prospective there was—seemed to lie with me only; his mind was unconscious and quiet.

"Jane," he recommenced, as we entered the laurel walk, and slowly strayed down in the direction of the sunk fence and the horse-chestnut, "Thornfield is a pleasant place in summer, is it not?"

"Yes. sir."

"You must have become in some degree attached to the house,——you, who have an eye for natural beauties, and a good deal of the organ of Adhesiveness?"

"I am attached to it, indeed."

"And though I don't comprehend how it is, I perceive you have acquired a degree of regard for that foolish little child Adèle, too; and even for simple dame Fairfax?"

"Yes, sir; in different ways, I have an affection for both."

"And would be sorry to part with them?"

"Yes."

"Pity!" he said, and sighed and paused. "It is always the way of events in this life," he continued presently: "no sooner have you got settled in a pleasant resting-place, than a voice calls out to you to rise and move on, for the hour of repose is expired."

"Must I move on, sir?" I asked. "Must I leave Thornfield?"

"I believe you must, Jane. I am sorry, Janet, but I believe indeed you must."

This was a blow: but I did not let it prostrate me.

"Well, sir, I shall be ready when the order to march comes."

"It is come now——I must give it tonight."

"Then you are going to be married, sir?"

"Ex-act-ly——pre-cise-ly: with your usual acuteness, you have hit the nail straight on the head."

"Soon, sir?"

"Very soon, my——that is, Miss Eyre: and you'll remember, Jane, the first time I, or Rumour, plainly intimated to you that it was my intention to put my old bachelor's neck into the sacred noose, to enter into the holy estate of matrimony——to take Miss Ingram to my bosom, in short (she's an extensive armful: but that's not to the point——one can't have too much of such a very excellent thing as my beautiful Blanche): well, as I was saying——listen to me, Jane! You're not turning your head to look after more moths, are you? That was only a lady-clock, child, 'flying away home.' I wish to remind you that it was you who first said to me, with that discretion I respect in you——with that foresight, prudence and humility which befit your responsible and dependent position——that in case I married Miss Ingram——both you and little Adèle had better trot forthwith. I pass over the sort of slur conveyed in this suggestion on the character of my beloved; indeed, when you are far away, Janet, I'll try to forget it: I shall notice only its wisdom; which is such that I have made it my law of action. Adèle must go to school; and you, Miss Eyre, must get a new situation."

"Yes, sir, I will advertise immediately: and meantime, I suppose"— I was going to say, "I suppose I may stay here, till I find another shelter to betake myself to," but I stopped, feeling it would not do to risk a long sentence, for my voice was not quite under command.

"In about a month I hope to be a bridegroom," continued Mr. Rochester; "and in the interim I shall myself look out for employment and an asylum for you."

"Thank you, sir; I am sorry to give"—

"Oh, no need to apologise! I consider that when a dependant does her duty as well as you have done yours, she has a sort of claim upon her employer for any little assistance he can conveniently render her; indeed I have already, through my future mother-in-law, heard of a place that I think will suit: it is to undertake the education of the five daughters of Mrs. Dionysius O'Gall of Bitternutt Lodge, Connaught, Ireland. You'll like Ireland, I think: they're such warm-hearted people there, they say."

"It is a long way off, sir."

"No matter—a girl of your sense will not object to the voyage or the distance."

"Not the voyage, but the distance: and then the sea is a barrier"—

"From what, Jane?"

"From England and from Thornfield: and"—

"Well?"

"From *you*, sir."

I said this almost involuntarily; and, with as little sanction of free will, my tears gushed out. I did not cry so as to be heard, however; I avoided sobbing. The thought of Mrs. O'Gall and Bitternutt Lodge struck cold to my heart; and colder the thought of all the brine and foam, destined, as it seemed, to rush between me and the master at whose side I now walked; and coldest the remembrance of the wider ocean—wealth, caste, custom intervened between me and what I naturally and inevitably loved.

"It is a long way," I again said.

"It is, to be sure; and when you get to Bitternutt Lodge, Connaught, Ireland, I shall never see you again, Jane: that's morally certain. I never go over to Ireland, not having myself much of a fancy for the country. We have been good friends, Jane; have we not?"

"Yes, sir."

"And when friends are on the eve of separation, they like to spend the little time that remains to them close to each other. Come—we'll talk over the voyage and the parting quietly, half an hour or so, while the stars enter into their shining life up in heaven yonder: here is the chestnut tree: here is the bench at its old roots. Come, we will sit there in peace tonight, though we should never more be destined to sit there together." He seated me and himself.

"It is a long way to Ireland, Janet, and I am sorry to send my little friend on such weary travels: but if I can't do better, how is it to be helped? Are you anything akin to me, do you think, Jane?"

I could risk no sort of answer of answer by this time: my heart was full.

"Because," he said, "I sometimes have a queer feeling with regard to you—especially when you are near me, as now: it is as if I had a string somewhere under my left ribs, tightly and inextricably knotted to a similar string situated in the corresponding quarter of your little frame. And if that boisterous channel, and two hundred miles or so of land come broad between us, I am afraid that cord of communion will be snapped; and then I've a nervous notion I should take to bleeding inwardly. As for you,—you'd forget me."

"That I *never* should, sir: you know"—impossible to proceed.

"Jane, do you hear that nightingale singing in the wood? Listen!"

In listening, I sobbed convulsively; for I could repress what I endured no longer; I was obliged to yield, and I was shaken from head to foot with acute distress. When I did speak, it was only to express an impetuous wish that I had never been born, or never come to Thornfield.

"Because you are sorry to leave it?"

The vehemence of emotion, stirred by grief and love within me, was claiming mastery, and struggling for full sway; and asserting a right to predominate: to overcome, to live, rise, and reign at last; yes,—and to speak.

"I grieve to leave Thornfield: I love Thornfield:—I love it, because I have lived in it a full and delightful life,—momentarily at least. I have not been trampled on. I have not been petrified. I have not been buried with inferior minds, and excluded from every glimpse of communion with what is bright and energetic, and high. I have talked, face to face, with what I reverence; with what I delight in,—with an original, a vigorous, an expanded mind, I have known you, Mr. Rochester; and it strikes me with terror and anguish to feel I absolutely must be torn from you forever. I see the necessity of departure; and it is like looking on the necessity of death."

"Where do you see the necessity?" he asked, suddenly.

"Where? You, sir, have placed it before me."

"In what shape?"

"In the shape of Miss Ingram; a noble and beautiful woman,—your bride."

"My bride! What bride? I have no bride!"

"But you will have."

"Yes:—I will!—I will!" He set his teeth.

"Then I must go:—you have said it yourself."

"No: you must stay! I swear it—and the oath shall be kept."

"I tell you I must go!" I retorted, roused to something like passion. "Do you think I can stay to become nothing to you? Do you think I am an automaton?—a machine without feelings? and can bear to have my morsel of bread snatched from my lips, and my drop of living water dashed from my cup? Do you think, because I am poor, obscure, plain, and little, I am soulless and heartless? You think wrong!—I have as much soul as you,—and full as much heart! And if God had gifted me with some beauty, and much wealth, I should have made it as hard for you to leave me, as it is now for me to leave you. I am not talking to you now through the medium of custom, conventionalities, or even of mortal flesh:—it is my spirit that addresses your spirit; just as if both had passed through the grave, and we stood at God's feet, equal,—as we are!"

"As we are!" repeated Mr. Rochester—"so," he added, enclosing me in his arms, gathering me to his breast, pressing his lips on my lips: "so, Jane!"

"Yes, so, sir," I rejoined: "and yet not so; for you are a married man—or as good as a married man, and wed to one inferior to you—to one with whom you have no sympathy—whom I do not believe you truly love; for I have seen and heard you sneer at her. I would scorn such a union: therefore I am better than you—let me go!"

"Where, Jane? To Ireland?"

"Yes—to Ireland. I have spoken my mind, and can go anywhere now."

"Jane, be still; don't struggle so, like a wild, frantic bird that is rending its own plumage in its desperation."

"I am no bird; and no net ensnares me; I am a free human being with an independent will; which I now exert to leave you."

Another effort set me at liberty, and I stood erect before him.

"And your will shall decide your destiny," he said: "I offer you my hand, my heart, and a share of all my possessions."

"You play a farce, which I merely laugh at."

"I ask you to pass through life at my side—to be my second self and best earthly companion."

"For that fate you have already made your choice, and must abide by it."

"Jane, be still a few moments: you are over-excited: I will be still too."

A waft of wind came sweeping down the laurel-walk, and trembled through the boughs of the chestnut: it wandered away—away to an indefinite distance—it died. The nightingale's song was then the only voice of the hour: in listening to it, I again wept. Mr. Rochester sat quiet, looking at me gently and seriously. Some time passed before he spoke: he at last said:—

"Come to my side, Jane, and let us explain and understand one another."

"I will never again come to your side: I am torn away now, and cannot return."

"But, Jane, I summon you as my wife: it is you only I intend to marry."

I was silent: I thought he mocked me.

"Come, Jane—come hither."

"Your bride stands between us."

He rose, and with a stride reached me.

"My bride is here," he said, again drawing me to him, "because my equal is here, and my likeness. Jane, will you marry me?"

Still I did not answer, and still I writhed myself from his grasp: for I was still incredulous.

"Do you doubt me, Jane?"

"Entirely."

"You have no faith in me?"

"Not a whit."

"Am I a liar in your eyes?" he asked passionately. "Little skeptic, you *shall* be convinced. What love have I for Miss Ingram? None: and that you know. What love has she for me? None: as I have taken pains to prove: I caused a rumour to reach her that my fortune was not a third of what was supposed, and after that I presented myself to see the result; it was coldness both from her and her mother. I would not—I could not—marry Miss Ingram. You—you strange—you almost unearthly thing!—I love as my own flesh. You—poor and obscure, and small and plain as you are—I entreat to accept me as a husband."

"What, me!" I ejaculated: beginning in his earnestness—and especially in his incivility—to credit his sincerity: "me who have not a friend in the world but you—if you are my friend: not a shilling but what you have given me?"

"You, Jane. I must have you for my own—entirely my own. Will you be mine? Say yes, quickly."

"Mr. Rochester, let me look at your face: turn to the moonlight."

"Why?"

"Because I want to read your countenance; turn!"

"There: you will find it scarcely more legible than a crumpled, scratched page. Read on: only make haste, for I suffer."

His face was very much agitated and very much flushed, and there were strong workings in the features, and strange gleams in the eyes.

"Oh, Jane, you torture me!" he exclaimed. "With that searching and yet faithful and generous look, you torture me!"

"How can I do that? If you are true and your offer real, my only feelings to you must be gratitude and devotion—they cannot torture."

"Gratitude!" he ejaculated; and added wildly—"Jane, accept me quickly. Say Edward—give me my name—Edward—I will marry you."

"Are you in earnest?—Do you truly love me?—Do you sincerely wish me to be your wife?"

"I do; and if an oath is necessary to satisfy you, I swear it."

"Then, sir, I will marry you."

"Edward—my little wife!"

"Dear Edward!"

"Come to me—come to me entirely now," said he: and added, in his deepest tone, speaking in my ear as his cheek was laid on mine, "Make my happiness—I will make yours."

"God pardon me!" he subjoined ere long, "and man meddle not with me: I have her, and will hold her."

"There is no one to meddle, sir. I have no kindred to interfere."

"No—that is the best of it," he said. And if I had loved him less I should have thought his accent and look of exultation savage: but sitting by him, roused from the nightmare of parting—called to the paradise of union—I thought only of the bliss given me to drink in so abundant a flow. Again and again he said, "Are you happy, Jane?" And again and again I answered, "Yes." After which he murmured, "It will atone—it will atone. Have I not found her friendless, and cold, and comfortless? Will I not guard, and cherish, and solace her? Is there not love in my heart, and constancy in my resolves? It will expiate at God's tribunal. I know my Maker sanctions what I do. For the world's judgment—I wash my hands thereof. For man's opinion—I defy it."

But what had befallen the night? The moon was not yet set, and we were all in shadow: I could scarcely see my master's face, near as I was. And what ailed the chestnut tree? it writhed and groaned; while wind roared in the laurel walk, and came sweeping over us.

"We must go in," said Mr. Rochester, "the weather changes. I could have sat with thee till morning, Jane."

"And so," thought I, "could I with you." I should have said so, perhaps, but a livid, vivid spark leapt out of a cloud at which I was looking, and there was a crack, a crash, and a close rattling peal; and I thought only of hiding my dazzled eyes against Mr. Rochester's shoulder.

The rain rushed down. He hurried me up the walk, through the grounds, and into the house; but we were quite wet before we could pass the threshold. He was taking off my shawl in the hall, and shaking the water out of my loosened hair, when Mrs. Fairfax emerged from her room. I did not observe her at first, nor did Mr. Rochester. The lamp was lit. The clock was on the stroke of twelve.

"Hasten to take off your wet things," said he: "and before you go, good-night—good-night, my darling!"

He kissed me repeatedly. When I looked up, on leaving his arms, there stood the widow, pale, grave, and amazed. I only smiled at her, and ran upstairs. "Explanation will do for another time," thought I. Still, when I reached my chamber, I felt a pang at the idea she should even temporarily misconstrue what she had seen. But joy soon effaced every other feeling; and loud as the wind blew, near and deep as the thunder crashed, fierce and frequent as the lightning gleamed, cataract-like as the rain fell during a storm of two hours' duration, I experienced no fear, and little awe. Mr. Rochester came thrice to my door in the course of it, to ask if I was safe and tranquil: and that was comfort, that was strength for anything.

Before I left my bed in the morning, little Adèle came running in to tell me that the great horse-chestnut at the bottom of the orchard had been struck by lightning in the night, and half of it split away.

ᘛᘚ

WILLIAM MAKEPEACE THACKERAY

from *Vanity Fair*

Be cautious then, young ladies; be wary how you engage. Be shy of loving frankly; never tell all you feel, or (a better way still) feel very little.

See the consequences of being prematurely honest and confiding, and mistrust yourselves and everybody. Get yourselves married as they do in France, where the lawyers are the bridesmaids and confidants. At any rate, never have any feelings which may make you uncomfortable, or make any promises which you cannot at any required moment command and withdraw. That is the way to get on, and be respected, and have a virtuous character in Vanity Fair.

✺ ✺

EMILY BRONTË

from *Wuthering Heights*

You teach me how cruel you've been—cruel and false. Why did you despise me? Why did you betray your own heart, Cathy? I have not one word of comfort. You deserve this. You have killed yourself. Yes, you may kiss me, and cry, and wring out my kisses and tears; they'll blight you— they'll damn you. You loved me; then what right had you to leave me? What right—answer me—for the poor fancy you felt for Linton? Because misery, and degradation, and death, and nothing that God or Satan could inflict would have parted us, you, of your own free will, did it. I have not broken your heart—you have broken it; and in breaking it you have broken mine. So much the worse for me that I am strong. Do I want to live? What kind of living will it be, when you—O God—would you like to live with your soul in the grave!

✺ ✺

NATHANIEL HAWTHORNE

from *The Scarlet Letter*

A FLOOD OF SUNSHINE

Arthur Dimmesdale gazed into Hester's face with a look in which hope and joy shone out, indeed, but with fear betwixt them, and a kind of horror at her boldness, who had spoken what he vaguely hinted at but dared not speak.

But Hester Prynne, with a mind of native courage and activity, and for so long a period not merely estranged, but outlawed, from society, had habituated herself to such latitude of speculation as was altogether foreign to the clergyman. She had wandered, without rule or guidance, in a moral wilderness; as vast, as intricate and shadowy, as the untamed forest, amid the gloom of which they were now holding a colloquy that was to decide their fate. Her intellect and heart had their home, as it were, in desert places, where she roamed as freely as the wild Indian in his woods. For years past she looked from this estranged point of view at human institutions, and whatever priests or legislators had established; criticising all with hardly more reverence than the Indian would feel for the clerical band, the judicial robe, the pillory, the gallows, the fireside, or the church. The tendency of her fate and fortunes had been to set her free. The scarlet letter was her passport into regions where other women dared not tread. Shame, Despair, Solitude! These had been her teachers,—stern and wild ones,—and they had made her strong, but taught her much amiss.

The minister, on the other hand, had never gone through an experience calculated to lead him beyond the scope of generally received laws; although, in a single instance, he had so fearfully transgressed one of the most sacred of them. But this had been a sin of passion, not of principle, nor even purpose. Since that wretched epoch, he had watched, with morbid zeal and minuteness, not his acts,—for those it was easy to arrange,—but each breath of emotion, and his every thought. At the head of the social system, as the clergymen of that day stood, he was only the more trammelled by its regulations, its principles, and even its prejudices. As a priest, the framework of his order inevitably hemmed him in. As a man who had once sinned, but who kept his conscience all alive and painfully sensitive by the fretting of an unhealed wound, he might have been supposed safer within the line of virtue than if he had never sinned at all.

Thus, we seem to see that, as regarded Hester Prynne, the whole seven years of outlaw and ignominy had been little other than a preparation for this very hour. But Arthur Dimmesdale! Were such a man once more to fall, what plea could be urged in extenuation of his crime? None; unless it avail him somewhat, that he was broken down by long and exquisite suffering; that his mind was darkened and confused by the very remorse which harrowed it; that between fleeing as an avowed criminal, and remaining as a hypocrite, conscience might find it hard to strike the balance; that it was human to avoid the peril of death and infamy, and the inscrutable machinations of an enemy; that, finally, to this poor pilgrim, on his dreary and desert path, faint, sick, miserable, there appeared a glimpse of human affection and sympathy, a new life, and a true one, in exchange for the heavy doom which he was now expiating. And be the stern and sad truth spoken, that the breach which guilt has once made into the human soul is never, in this mortal state, repaired. It may be watched and guarded; so that the enemy shall not force his way again into the citadel, and might even, in his subsequent assaults, select some other avenue, in preference to that where he had formerly succeeded. But there is still the ruined wall, and, near it, the stealthy tread of the foe that would win over again his unforgotten triumph.

The struggle, if it were one, need not be described. Let it suffice, that the clergyman resolved to flee, and not alone.

"If, in all these past seven years," thought he, "I could recall one instant of peace or hope, I would yet endure for the sake of that earnest of Heaven's mercy. But now,—since I am irrevocably doomed,—wherefore should I not snatch the solace allowed to the condemned culprit before his execution? Or, if this be the path to a better life, as Hester would persuade me, I surely give up no fairer prospect by pursuing it! Neither can I any longer live without her companionship; so powerful is she to sustain,—so tender to soothe! O Thou to whom I dare not lift mine eyes, wilt Thou yet pardon me!"

"Thou wilt go!" said Hester, calmly, as he met her glance.

The decision once made, a glow of strange enjoyment threw its flickering brightness over the trouble of his breast. It was the exhilarating effect—upon a prisoner just escaped from the dungeon of his own heart—of breathing the wild, free atmosphere of an unredeemed, unchristianized, lawless region. His spirit rose, as it were, with a bound, and attained a nearer prospect of the sky, than throughout all the misery which had kept him grovelling on the earth. Of a deeply religious temperament, there was inevitably a tinge of the devotional in his mood.

"Do I feel joy again?" cried he, wondering at himself. "Methought the germ of it was dead in me! O Hester, thou art my better angel! I seem to have flung myself—sick, sin-stained, and sorrow-blackened—down upon these forest-leaves, and to have risen up all made anew, and with new powers to glorify Him that hath been merciful! This is already the better life! Why did we not find it sooner?"

"Let us not look back," answered Hester Prynne. "The past is gone! Wherefore should we linger upon it now? See! With this symbol, I undo it all, and make it as it had never been!"

So speaking, she undid the clasp that fastened the scarlet letter, and, taking it from her bosom, threw it to a distance among the withered leaves. The mystic token alighted on the hither verge of the stream. With a hand's-breadth farther flight it would have fallen into the water, and have given the little brook another woe to carry onward, besides the unintelligible tale which it still kept murmuring about. But there lay the embroidered letter, glittering like a lost jewel, which some ill-fated wanderer might pick up, and thenceforth be haunted by strange phantoms of guilt, sinkings of the heart, and unaccountable misfortune.

The stigma gone, Hester heaved a long, deep sigh, in which the burden of shame and anguish departed from her spirit. Oh exquisite relief! She had not known the weight, until she felt the freedom! By another impulse, she took off the formal cap that confined her hair; and down it fell upon her shoulders, dark and rich, with at once a shadow and a light in its abundance, and imparting the charm of softness to her features. There played around her mouth, and beamed out of her eyes, a radiant and tender smile, that seemed gushing from the very heart of womanhood. A crimson flush was glowing on her cheek, that had been long so pale. Her sex, her youth, and the whole richness of her beauty, came back from what men call the irrevocable past, and clustered themselves, with her maiden hope, and a happiness before unknown, within the magic circle of this hour. And, as if the gloom of the earth and sky had been but the effluence of these two mortal hearts, it vanished with their sorrow. All at once, as with a sudden smile of heaven, forth burst the sunshine, pouring a very flood into the obscure forest, gladdening each green leaf, transmuting the yellow fallen ones to gold, and gleaming adown the gray trunks of the solemn trees. The objects that had made a shadow hitherto, embodied the brightness now. The course of the little brook might be traced by its merry gleam afar into the wood's heart of mystery, which had become a mystery of joy.

Such was the sympathy of Nature—that wild, heathen Nature of the forest, never subjugated by human law, nor illumined by higher truth—with the bliss of these two spirits! Love, whether newly born, or aroused from a death-like slumber, must always create a sunshine, filling the heart so full of radiance, that it overflows upon the outward world. Had the forest still kept its gloom, it would have been bright in Hester's eyes, and bright in Arthur Dimmesdale's!

GUSTAVE FLAUBERT

from *Madame Bovary*

It was the first week in October. A haze lay over the country. Where the outline of the hills left gaps, mists stretched themselves away to the horizon; and others, dissolving, rose, were lost. Sometimes through a break in the mists, made by a ray of sunshine, there could be seen the roofs of Yonville in the distance, with the gardens by the river-side, the yards, the walls, and the spire of the church. Emma half closed her eyes, the better to distinguish her own house, and never had that poor village where she dwelt seemed to her so small. From the height where they stood the whole valley looked one immense pale lake evaporating into the air. The clumps of trees here and there stood out like black rocks; and the lofty lines of the poplars, rising above the haze, suggested the sand of sea-shores driven by the wind.

Near them, over the sward, between the pines, a melancholy light wandered in the mild atmosphere. The earth, ruddy like snuff, deadened the sound of the horses' feet; and with the front of their shoes they scattered before them the fallen pine-cones as they walked.

Rodolphe and Emma followed thus the outskirts of the wood. From time to time, to avoid his glance, she turned away to see, however, nothing but the trunks of the pines which, with the endless succession of their regular rows, made her feel a little dizzy. The horses breathed lustily. The leather of the saddles creaked.

At the moment when they entered the forest the sun shone out.

"God is protecting us!" said Rodolphe.

"You think so?" she replied.

"Let us make haste! Forward!" he rejoined.

He clicked with his tongue. The two beasts responded.

Certain tall brackens, at the side of the path, kept becoming entangled in Emma's stirrup. Rodolphe, without pulling up, leaned over and released them as they caught. At other times, to put aside the branches, he passed close to her, and Emma felt the light touch of his knee on her leg. The sky was become blue. The leaves did not stir. There were great expanses covered by heather in full bloom, and beds of violets lay among the medley of the trees, which were gray, tawny, or golden, according to the variety of the foliage. Often under the lower bushes you could hear a little fluttering of wings as they slipped away, or perhaps, hoarse and soft, the cry of rooks as they flew off among the oaks.

They alighted. Rodolphe tethered the horses. She went before, walking on the moss between the ruts.

But, although she held up its train, she was embarrassed by the too great length of her habit, and Rodolphe, as he followed her, could gaze upon the daintiness of her white stocking.

She stopped.

"I am tired," said she.

"Come, one more effort!" was his response. "Courage!"

Then, a hundred paces farther on, she stopped afresh, and, through her veil, which, from her hat like a man's, descended slantingly to her hips, her features were discernible in a bluish transparency, as though she were swimming beneath azure waves.

"But where are we going?"

He answered nothing. She was breathing with irregular jerks. Rodolphe cast a glance around him and bit his moustache.

They reached a larger open space where staddling had been cut, and, as they sat there on the trunk of a fallen tree, Rodolphe began to speak to her of his love.

He took care not to frighten her at the beginning by compliments. He was calm, serious, melancholy.

Emma listened to him with bowed head, while with the tip of her shoe she idly pushed about the chips on the ground. But at this phrase:

"Are not our destinies henceforth one?"

"As for that, no!" she replied. "You know it well. It is impossible."

She rose to go. He seized her by the wrist. She stopped. Then, after gazing at him for some minutes with eyes that were loving and quite moist, she said quickly:

"Ah! there—let us speak of it no more. Where are the horses? Let us return."

He made a gesture of anger and weariness. She repeated:

"Where are the horses? Where are the horses?"

Then, smiling a strange smile, the pupils of his eyes fixed and with teeth set, he stepped forward, opening his arms. She recoiled, trembling. She murmured:

"Oh, you frighten me! you hurt me! Let us start."

"Since it must be so," replied he, his face changing. And immediately he was once more respectful, caressing in manner, timid. She gave him her arm. They turned back. He said:

"What was the matter? Why? I didn't understand. You must have received a false impression, I think. In my soul you are like a Madonna on a pedestal. Your place there is high, firm, stainless. But you are necessary to my very life. I need your eyes, your voice, your thoughts. Be my friend, my sister, my angel!"

And stretching out his arm he pressed it about her waist. The attempt she made to disengage herself was only feeble. He continued to support her thus as they walked.

But they heard the sounds made by the two horses as they browsed on the leaves.

"Oh! longer yet," said Rodolphe. "Don't let us go! Stay!"

He drew her farther away, round a little pool, where water lentils made the water's face green-leaved. Withered water-lilies hung motionless between the rushes.

At the sound of their steps on the grass, frogs sprang away to hide themselves.

"It is wrong of me, it is wicked," she said. "I am mad to listen to you."

"*Why?* . . . Emma! Emma!"

"Oh! Rodolphe! . . ." said the young woman slowly, as she leaned on his shoulder, while the cloth of her riding-habit caught upon the velvet of his coat.

Presently the shadows of the evening began to fall; the horizontal sun, passing between the branches, dazzled her eyes. Here and there, all around her, among the leaves or on the ground, there trembled luminous patches, as though humming-birds, as they flew, had been casting their plumes. Silence was everywhere; from the trees seemed to emanate something of harmony and peace; she became conscious again of the beating of her own heart, and felt the blood circulate through her flesh like a stream of milk. Then she heard in the far distance, beyond the woods, on the other hills, a vague and prolonged cry, a voice that hung in the air, and she listened to it silently as it mingled like music with the last vibrations of her agitated nerves. Rodolphe, meantime, cigar between his teeth, mended with his penknife one of the two bridles which was broken.

They returned to Yonville by the same road. They saw again, on the mud, the tracks of their horses, side by side, and the same bushes, the same stones among the grass. Nothing around them had changed; and yet, for her, something had happened of importance greater than though the mountains should have been moved from their places. Rodolphe from time to time leaned over and took her hand to kiss it.

She was charming on horseback! Erect there, with her slender figure, knee bent over her horse's mane, and her colour a shade heightened by the fresh air, in the ruddy evening light.

As they entered Yonville she caracoled over the paving-stones. People watched her from the windows.

Her husband, at dinner, remarked how well she looked; but she affected not to hear when he inquired about her ride; and she sat on, with elbow at the side of her plate, between the two candles that burned on the table.

"Emma!" said he.

"What?"

"Well, I called this afternoon at M. Alexandre's; he has an old mare, a still very handsome beast, though a trifle broken-kneed, which could be bought, I feel sure, for a hundred crowns. . . ."

He added:

"Indeed, thinking to please you, I bespoke it . . . I bought it . . . Did I do right? Tell me."

She nodded her head in token of assent; then, a quarter of an hour later:

"Are you going out this evening?" she asked.

"Yes. Why?"

"Oh, nothing, nothing, my dear."

And as soon as she was rid of Charles she went upstairs to shut herself in her bedroom.

At first what she experienced was a kind of dizziness; she saw the trees, the roads, the ditches, Rodolphe, and she felt once more the embrace of his arms while the leaves shuddered and the rushes whistled.

But, when she saw herself in the mirror, her face astonished her. Never had her eyes looked so large, so dark, or of such depth. Some subtle influence diffused over her person transfigured it.

"I have a lover! a lover!" she kept repeating to herself, delighting in this idea, as though 'twere in the thought of a second youth come to her. At last, then, she was about to possess those joys of love, that fever of bliss of which she had despaired. She stood on the threshold of some marvellous world where all was going to be passion, ecstasy, delirium; an immensity, blue-tinged, surrounded her; the heights of sentiment sparkled in the rays of her fancy, and ordinary existence appeared only far away, quite below, in the shade of the hollows between those peaks.

Next she summoned to mind the heroines of the books she had

read, and the lyric legion of those adulterous women began to sing in her memory with sisterly voices that fascinated her. Herself she became, as it were, a veritable part of these imaginings, and realized the long dream of her youth in joining herself to that type of amorous woman which had aroused in her so great an envy. Besides, Emma felt a certain satisfaction of revenge. How much had she not suffered! But now was her hour of triumph, and love, so long repressed, could burst forth at last unrestrained, with joyous overflowings. She sucked its sweet without remorse, without disquiet, without anxiety.

✥ ✥

THOMAS CARLYLE

from *Sartor Resartus: The Life and Opinions of Herr Teufelsdröckh*

"For long years," writes Teufelsdröckh, "had the poor Hebrew, in this Egypt of an Auscultatorship, painfully toiled, baking bricks without stubble, before ever the question once struck him with entire force: For what?—*Beym Himmel!* For Food and Warmth! And are Food and Warmth nowhere else, in the whole wide Universe, discoverable?—Come of it what might, I resolved to try."

Thus then are we to see him in a new independent capacity, though perhaps far from an improved one. Teufelsdröckh is now a man without Profession. Quitting the common Fleet of herring-busses and whalers, where indeed his leeward, laggard condition was painful enough, he desperately steers off, on a course of his own, by sextant and compass of his own. Unhappy Teufelsdröckh! Though neither Fleet, nor Traffic, nor Commodores pleased thee, still was it not a *Fleet*, sailing in prescribed track, for fixed objects; above all, in combination, wherein, by mutual guidance, by all manner of loans and borrowings, each could manifoldly aid the other? How wilt thou sail in unknown seas; and for thyself find that shorter Northwest Passage to thy fair Spice-country of a Nowhere?—A solitary rover, on such a voyage, with such nautical tactics, will meet with adventures. Nay, as we forthwith discover, a certain Calypso-Island detains him at the very outset; and as it were falsifies and oversets his whole reckoning.

"If in youth," writes he once, "the Universe is majestically unveiling, and everywhere Heaven revealing itself on Earth, nowhere to the

Young Man does this Heaven on Earth so immediately reveal itself as in the Young Maiden. Strangely enough, in this strange life of ours, it has been so appointed. On the whole, as I have often said, a Person *(Persön-lichkeit)* is ever holy to us; a certain orthodox Anthropomorphism connects my *Me* with all *Thees* in bonds of Love: but it is in this approximation of the Like and Unlike, that such heavenly attraction, as between Negative and Positive, first burns-out into a flame. Is the pitifullest mortal Person, think you, indifferent to us? Is it not rather our heartfelt wish to be made one with him; to unite him to us, by gratitude, by admiration, even by fear; or failing all these, unite ourselves to him? But how much more, in this case of the Like-Unlike! Here is conceded us the higher mystic possibility of such a union, the highest in our Earth; thus, in the conducting medium of Fantasy, flames-forth that *fire*-development of the universal Spiritual Electricity, which, as unfolded between man and woman, we first emphatically denominate LOVE.

"In every well-conditioned stripling, as I conjecture, there already blooms a certain prospective Paradise, cheered by some fairest Eve; nor, in the stately vistas, and flowerage and foliage of that Garden, is a Tree of Knowledge, beautiful and awful in the midst thereof, wanting. Perhaps too the whole is but the lovelier, if Cherubim and a Flaming Sword divide it from all footsteps of men; and grant him, the imaginative stripling, only the view, not the entrance. Happy season of virtuous youth, when shame is still an impassable celestial barrier; and the sacred air-cities of Hope have not shrunk into the mean clay-hamlets of Reality; and man, by his nature, is yet infinite and free!

"As for our young Forlorn," continues Teufelsdröckh, evidently meaning himself, "in his secluded way of life, and with his glowing Fantasy, the more fiery that it burnt under cover, as in a reverberating furnace, his feeling towards the Queens of this Earth was, and indeed is, altogether unspeakable. A visible Divinity dwelt in them; to our young Friend all women were holy, were heavenly. As yet he but saw them flitting past, in their many-coloured angel-plumage; or hovering mute and inaccessible on the outskirts of *Æsthetic Tea:* all of air they were, all Soul and Form; so lovely, like mysterious priestesses, in whose hand was the invisible Jacob's-ladder, whereby man might mount into very Heaven. That he, our poor Friend, should ever win for himself one of these Gracefuls *(Holden)*—*Ach Gott!* how could he hope it; should he not have died under it? There was a certain delirious vertigo in the thought.

"Thus was the young man, if all-sceptical of Demons and Angels such as the vulgar had once believed in, nevertheless not unvisited by hosts of true Sky-born, who visibly and audibly hovered round him wheresoever he went; and they had that religious worship in his thought, though as yet it was by their mere earthly and trivial name that he named them. But now, if on a soul so circumstanced, some actual Air-maiden, incorporated into tangibility and reality, should cast any electric glance of kind eyes, saying thereby, "Thou too mayest love and be loved;" and so kindle him,—good Heaven, what a volcanic, earthquake-bringing, all-consuming fire were probably kindled!'

Such a fire, it afterwards appears, did actually burst forth, with explosions more or less Vesuvian, in the inner man of Herr Diogenes; as indeed how could it fail?

❊   ❊   ❊

Let the Philosopher answer this one question: What figure, at that period, was a Mrs. Teufelsdröckh likely to make in polished society? Could she have driven so much as a brass-bound Gig, or even a simple iron-spring one? Thou foolish "absolved Auscultator," before whom lies no prospect of capital, will any yet known "religion of young hearts" keep the human kitchen warm? Pshaw! thy divine Blumine, when she "resigned herself to wed some richer," shows more philosophy, though but "a woman of genius," than thou, a pretended man.

Our readers have witnessed the origin of this Love-mania, and with what royal splendour it waxes, and rises. Let no one ask us to unfold the glories of its dominant state; much less the horrors of its almost instantaneous dissolution. How from such inorganic masses, henceforth madder than ever, as lie in these Bags, can even fragments of a living delineation be organised? Besides, of what profit were it? We view, with a lively pleasure, the gay silk Montgolfier start from the ground, and shoot upwards, cleaving the liquid deeps, till it dwindle to a luminous star: but what is there to look longer on, when once, by natural elasticity, or accident of fire, it has exploded? A hapless air-navigator, plunging, amid torn parachutes, sand-bags, and confused wreck, fast enough into the jaws of the Devil! Suffice it to know that Teufelsdröckh rose into the highest regions of the Empyrean, by a natural parabolic track, and returned thence in a quick perpendicular one. For the rest, let any feeling reader, who has been unhappy enough to do the like, paint it out for himself: considering only that if he, for his perhaps comparatively insignificant mistress, underwent such agonies and frenzies, what must

Teufelsdröckh's have been, with a fire-heart, and for a nonpareil Blumine! We glance merely at the final scene:

"One morning, he found his Morning-star all dimmed and dusky-red; the fair creature was silent, absent, she seemed to have been weep-ing. Alas, no longer a Morning-star, but a troublous skyey Portent, announcing that the Doomsday had dawned! She said, in a tremulous voice, They were to meet no more." The thunderstruck Air-sailor is not wanting to himself in this dread hour: but what avails it? We omit the passionate expostulations, entreaties, indignations, since all was vain, and not even an explanation was conceded him; and hasten to the cata-strophe. " 'Farewell, then, Madam!' said he, not without sternness, for his stung pride helped him. She put her hand in his, she looked in his face, tears started to her eyes; in wild audacity he clasped her to his bosom; their lips were joined, their two souls, like two dew-drops, rushed into one,—for the first time, and for the last!" Thus was Teufelsdröckh made immortal by a kiss. And then? Why, then—"thick curtains of Night rushed over his soul, as rose the immeasurable Crash of Doom; and through the ruins as of a shivered Universe was he falling, falling, towards the Abyss."

❧ ☙

BENJAMIN DISRAELI

from *Coningsby*

At school, friendship is a passion. It entrances the being; it tears the soul. All loves of afterlife can never bring its rapture, or its wretchedness; no bliss so absorbing, no pangs of jealousy or despair so crushing and so keen! What tenderness and what devotion; what illimitable confidence, infinite revelations of inmost thoughts; what ecstatic present and ro-mantic future; what bitter estrangements and what melting reconcilia-tions; what scenes of wild recrimination, agitating explanations, passionate correspondence; what insane sensitiveness, and what frantic sensibility; what earthquakes of the heart and whirlwinds of the soul are confined in that simple phrase, a schoolboy's friendship!

CHARLES DICKENS

from *David Copperfield*

All this time, I had gone on loving Dora, harder than ever. Her idea was my refuge in disappointment and distress, and made some amends to me, even for the loss of my friend. The more I pitied myself, or pitied others, the more I sought for consolation in the image of Dora. The greater the accumulation of deceit and trouble in the world, the brighter and the purer shone the star of Dora high above the world. I don't think I had any definite idea where Dora came from, or in what degree she was related to a higher order of being but I am quite sure I should have scouted the notion of her being simply human, like any other young lady, with indignation and contempt.

If I may so express it, I was steeped in Dora. I was not merely over head and ears in love with her, but I was saturated through and through. Enough love might have been wrung out of me, metaphorically speaking, to drown anybody in; and yet there would have remained enough within me, and all over me, to pervade my entire existence.

ANTHONY TROLLOPE

from *An Old Man's Love*

"To me you are everything. I have been thinking as I walked up and down the path there, of all that I could do to make you happy. And I was so happy myself in feeling that I had your happiness to look after. How should I not let the wind blow too coldly on you? How should I be watchful to see that nothing should ruffle your spirits? What duties, what pleasures, what society should I provide for you? How should I change my habits, so as to make my advanced years fit for your younger life? And I was teaching myself to hope that I was not yet too old to make this altogether impossible. Then you come to me, and tell me that you must destroy all my dreams, dash all my hopes to the ground,—because an old woman has shown her temper and her jealousy!"

This was true,—according to the light in which he saw her position. Had there been nothing between them two but a mutual desire to be married, the reason given by her for changing it all would be absurd. As he had continued to speak, slowly adding on one argument to another, with a certain amount of true eloquence, she felt that unless she could go back to John Gordon she must yield. But it was very hard for her to go back to John Gordon. In the first place, she must acknowledge, in doing so, that she had only put forward Mrs. Baggett as a false plea. And then she must insist on her love for a man who had never spoken to her of love! It was so hard that she could not do it openly. "I had thought so little of the value I could be to you."

"Your value to me is infinite. I think, Mary, that there has come upon you a certain melancholy which is depressing you. Your regard to me is worth now more than any other possession or gift that the world can bestow. And I had taken pride to myself in saying that it had been given." Yes;—her regard! She could not contradict him as to that. "And have you thought of your own position? After all that has passed between us, you can hardly go on loving him as you have done."

"I know that."

"Then, what would become of you if you were to break away from me?"

"I thought you would get a place for me as a governess,—or a companion to some lady."

"Would that satisfy your ambition? I have got a place for you;—but it is here." As he spoke, he laid his hand upon his heart. "Not as a companion to a lady are you required to fulfill your duties here on earth. It is a fuller task of work that you must do. I trust,—I trust that it may not be more tedious." She looked at him again, and he did not now appear so old. There was a power of speech about the man, and a dignity which made her feel that she could in truth have loved him,—had it not been for John Gordon. "Unfortunately, I am older than you,—very much older. But to you there may be this advantage, that you can listen to what I may say with something of confidence in my knowledge of the world. As my wife, you will fill a position more honourable, and more suitable to your gifts, than could belong to you as a governess or a companion. You will have much more to do, and will be able to go nightly to your rest with a consciousness that you have done more as the mistress of our house than you could have done in that tamer capacity. You will have cares,—and even those will ennoble the world to you, and you to the world. That other life is a poor shrunken death,—rather than life.

It is a way of passing her days, which must fall to the lot of many a female who does not achieve the other; and it is well that they to whom it falls should be able to accommodate themselves to it with contentment and self-respect. I think that I may say of myself that, even as my wife, you will stand higher than you would do as a companion."

"I am sure of it."

"Not on that account should you accept any man that you cannot love." Had she not told him that she did not love him;—even that she loved another? And yet he spoke to her in this way! "You had better tell Mrs. Baggett to come to me."

"There is the memory of that other man," she murmured very gently.

Then the scowl came back upon his face;—or not a scowl, but a look rather of cold displeasure. "If I understand you rightly, the gentleman never addressed you as a lover."

"Never!"

"I see it all, Mary. Mrs. Baggett has been violent and selfish, and has made you think thoughts which should not have been put in your head to disturb you. You have dreamed a dream in your early life,—as girls do dream, I suppose,—and it has now to be forgotten. Is it not so?"

"I suppose it was a dream."

"He has passed away, and he has left you to become the happiness of my life. Send Mrs. Baggett to me, and I will speak to her." Then he came up to her,—for they had been standing about a yard apart,—and pressed his lips to hers. How was it possible that she should prevent him?

She turned round, and slowly left the room, feeling, as she did so, that she was again engaged to him for ever and ever. She hated herself because she had been so fickle. But how could she have done otherwise? She asked herself, as she went back to her room, at what period during the interview, which was now over, she could have declared to him the real state of her mind. He had, as it were, taken complete possession of her, by right of the deed of gift which she had made of herself that morning. She had endeavoured to resume the gift, but had altogether failed. She declared to herself that she was weak, impotent, purposeless; but she admitted, on the other hand, that he had displayed more of power than she had ever guessed at his possessing. A woman always loves this display of power in a man, and she felt that she could have loved him had it not been for John Gordon.

GEORGE ELIOT (MARY ANN EVANS)
from *The Lifted Veil*

I was perpetually exasperated with the petty promptings of his conceit, with his love of patronage, with his self-complacent belief in Bertha Grant's passion for him, with his half-pitying contempt for me—seen not in the ordinary indications of intonation and phrase and slight action, which an acute and suspicious mind is on the watch for, but in all their naked skinless complication.

For we were rivals, and our desires clashed, though he was not aware of it. I have said nothing yet of the effect Bertha Grant produced in me on a nearer acquaintance. That effect was chiefly determined by the fact that she made the only exemption, among all the human beings about me, to my unhappy gift of insight. About Bertha I was always in a state of uncertainty: I could watch the expression of her face, and speculate on its meaning; I could ask for her opinion with the real interest of ignorance; I could listen for her words and watch for her smile with hope and fear: she had for me the fascination of an unravelled destiny. I say it was this fact that chiefly determined the strong effect she produced on me: for, in the abstract, no womanly character could seem to have less affinity for that of a shrinking, romantic, passionate youth than Bertha's. She was keen, sarcastic, unimaginative, prematurely cynical, remaining critical and unmoved in the most impressive scenes, inclined to dissect all my favourite poems, and especially contemptuous towards the German lyrics which were my pet literature at that time. To this moment I am unable to define my feeling towards her: it was not ordinary boyish admiration, for she was the very opposite, even to the colour of her hair, of the ideal woman who still remained to me the type of loveliness; and she was without that enthusiasm for the great and good, which, even at the moment of her strongest dominion over me, I should have declared to be the highest element of character. But there is no tyranny more complete than that which a self-centered negative nature exercises over a morbidly sensitive nature perpetually craving sympathy and support. The most independent people feel the effect of a man's silence in heightening their value for his opinion—feel an additional triumph in conquering the reverence of a critic habitually captious and satirical: no wonder, then, that an enthusiastic self-distrusting youth should watch and wait before the closed secret of a sarcastic woman's face, as if it were the shrine of the doubtfully benignant deity who ruled his destiny. For a young enthusiast is unable to imagine the total negation in another mind of the emotions which are stirring his own; they may be feeble, latent, inactive, he thinks, but they are there—they may be called forth; sometimes, in moments of happy hallucination, he believes that they may be there in all the greater strength because he sees no outward sign of them. And this effect, as I have intimated, was heightened to its utmost intensity in me, because Bertha was the only being who remained for me in the mysterious seclusion of soul that renders such youthful delusion possible. Doubtless there was another sort of fascination at work—that subtle physical attraction which delights in cheating our psychological predictions, and in compelling the men who paint sylphs, to fall in love with some *bonne et brave femme,* heavy-heeled and freckled.

Bertha's behaviour towards me was such as to encourage all my illusions, to heighten my boyish passion, and make me more and more dependent on her smiles. Looking back with my present wretched knowledge, I conclude that her vanity and love of power were intensely gratified by the belief that I had fainted on first seeing her purely from the strong impression her person had produced on me. The most prosaic woman likes to believe herself the object of a violent, a poetic passion; and without a grain of romance in her Bertha had that spirit of intrigue which gave piquancy to the idea that the brother of the man she meant to marry was dying with love and jealousy for her sake. That she meant to marry my brother, was what at that time I did not believe; for though he was assiduous in his attentions to her, and I knew well enough that both he and my father had made up their minds to this result, there was not yet an understood engagement—there had been no explicit declaration; and Bertha habitually, while she flirted with my brother, and accepted his homage in a way that implied to him a thorough recognition of its intention, made me believe, by the subtlest looks and phrases—feminine nothings which could never be quoted against her— that he was really the object of her secret ridicule; that she thought him, as I did, a coxcomb, whom she would have pleasure in disappointing. Me she openly petted in my brother's presence, as if I were too young and sickly ever to be thought of as a lover; and that was the view he took of me. But I believe she must inwardly have delighted in the tremors into which she threw me by the coaxing way in which she patted my curls, while she laughed at my quotations. Such caresses were always given in the presence of our friends; for when we were alone together, she affected a much greater distance towards me, and now and then took the opportunity, by words or slight actions, to stimulate my foolish timid hope that she really preferred me. And why should she not follow her inclination? I was not a year younger than she was, and she was an heiress, who would soon be of age to decide for herself.

The fluctuations of hope and fear, confined to this one channel, made each day in her presence a delicious torment. There was one deliberate act of hers which especially helped to intoxicate me. When we were at Vienna her twentieth birthday occurred, and as she was very fond of ornaments, we all took the opportunity of the splendid jeweller's shops in that Teutonic Paris to purchase her a birthday present of jewellery. Mine, naturally, was the least expensive, it was an opal ring—the opal was my favourite stone, because it seems to blush and turn pale as if it had a soul. I told Bertha so when I gave it her, and said that it was an emblem of the poetic nature, changing with the changing light of heaven and of woman's eyes. In the evening she appeared elegantly dressed and wearing conspicuously all the birthday presents except mine. I looked eagerly at her fingers, but saw no opal. I had no opportunity of noticing this to her during the evening; but the next day, when I found her seated near the window alone, after breakfast, I said, "You scorn to wear my poor opal. I should have remembered that you despised poetic natures, and should have given your coral, or turquoise, or some other opaque unresponsive stone." "Do I despise it?" she answered, taking hold of a delicate gold chain which she always wore round her neck and drawing out the end from her bosom with my ring hanging to it; "it hurts me a little, I can tell you," she said, with her usual dubious smile, "to wear it in that secret place; and since your poetical nature is so stupid as to prefer a more public position, I shall not endure the pain any longer."

She took off the ring from the chain and put it on her finger, smiling still, while the blood rushed to my cheeks, and I could not trust myself to say a word of entreaty that she would keep the ring where it was before.

I was completely fooled by this, and for two days shut myself up in my room whenever Bertha was absent, that I might intoxicate myself afresh with the thought of this scene and all it implied.

MARK TWAIN (SAMUEL CLEMENS)

from *The Diary of Adam and Eve*

FROM ADAM'S DIARY

Monday   This new creature with the long hair is a good deal in the way. It is always hanging around and following me about, I don't like this; I am not used to company. I wish it would stay with the other animals. . . . Cloudy today, wind in the east; think we shall have rain. . . . *We?* Where did I get that word?—I remember now—the new creature uses it.

Wednesday   Built me a shelter against the rain, but could not have it to myself in peace. The new creature intruded. When I tried to put it out it shed water out of the holes it looks with, and wiped it away with the back of its paws, and made a noise such as some of the other animals make when they are in distress. I wish it would not talk; it is always talking. That sounds like a cheap fling at the poor creature, a slur; but I do not mean it so. I have never heard the human voice before, and any new and strange sound intruding itself here upon the solemn hush of these dreaming solitudes offends my ear and seems a false note. And this new sound is so close to me; it is right at my shoulder, right at my ear, first on one side and then on the other, and I am used only to sounds that are more or less distant from me.

FROM EVE'S DIARY

Thursday   My first sorrow. Yesterday he avoided me and seemed to wish I would not talk to him. I could not believe it, and thought there was some mistake, for I loved to be with him, and loved to hear him talk, and so how could it be that he could feel unkind toward me when I had not done anything? But at last it seemed true, so I went away and sat lonely in the place where I first saw him the morning that we were made and I did not know what he was and was indifferent about him; but now it was a mournful place, and every little thing spoke of him, and my heart was very sore. I did not know why very clearly, for it was a new feeling; I had not experienced it before, and it was all a mystery, and I could not make it out.

AFTER THE FALL

The Garden is lost, but I have found *him*, and am content. He loves me as well as he can; I love him with all the strength of my passionate nature, and this, I think, is proper to my youth and sex. If I ask myself why I love him, I find I do not know, and do not really much care to know; so I suppose that this kind of love is not a product of reasoning and statistics, like one's love for other reptiles and animals. I think that this must be so. I love certain birds because of their song; but I do not love Adam on account of his singing—no, it is not that; the more he sings the more I do not get reconciled to it. Yet I ask him to sing, because I wish to learn to like everything he is interested in. I am sure I can learn, because at first I could not stand it, but now I can. It sours the milk, but it doesn't matter; I can get used to that kind of milk.

AT EVE'S GRAVE

ADAM: Wheresoever she was, *there* was Eden.

❧ ☙

LEO TOLSTOY

from *Anna Karenina*

Steps were heard at the entrance, and the Princess Betsy, knowing that it was Anna, glanced at Vronsky. He was looking at the door with a strange new expression on his face. He gazed joyfully, intently, and yet timidly at the lady who was entering, and slowly rose from his seat. Anna entered the room holding herself, as usual, very erect, and without changing the direction of her eyes, approached her hostess, walking with that quick, firm yet light step which distinguished her from other Society women. She shook hands, smilingly, and with the same smile looked round at Vronsky. He bowed low and moved a chair toward her.

Anna responded only by an inclination of the head, though she blushed and frowned. But immediately, nodding rapidly to her acquaintances and pressing the hands extended to her, she turned again to her hostess:

"I have just been at the Countess Lydia's. I meant to come sooner, but could not get away. Sir John was there—he is very interesting."

"Oh, that missionary?"

"Yes, he was telling us about Indian life. It was very interesting."

The conversation, interrupted by her entrance, again burnt up like the flame of a lamp that has been blown about.

"Sir John! Oh yes, Sir John! I have seen him. He speaks very well. The elder Vlasyeva is quite in love with him."

"And is it true that the younger Vlasyeva is going to be married to Topov."

"Yes; they say it's quite settled."

"I am surprised at her parents. They say it's a love match."

"Love match! What antediluvian ideas you have! Who talks of love nowadays?" said the ambassador's wife.

"What's to be done? That silly old fashion hasn't died out yet!" said Vronsky.

"So much the worse for those who follow the fashion! I know of happy marriages, but only such as are founded on reason."

"Yes, but how often the happiness of marriages founded on reason crumbles to dust because the very passion that was disregarded makes itself felt later," said Vronsky.

"But by 'marriages founded on reason,' we mean marriages between those who have both passed through that madness. It's like scarlet fever: one has to get it over."

"Then someone should invent a way of inoculating love, like vaccination."

"When I was young I was in love with a chorister," said Princess Myagkaya. "I don't know whether it did me any good."

"No, joking apart, I believe that to understand love one must first make a mistake and then correct it," said the Princess Betsy.

"Even after marriage?" said the ambassador's wife archly.

"It is never too late to mend!" said the attaché, quoting the English proverb.

"Exactly!" chimed in Betsy. "One has to make mistakes and correct them. What do you think?" she asked, addressing Anna, who with a scarcely discernible resolute smile was listening to this conversation.

"I think," replied Anna, toying with the glove she had pulled off, "I think . . . if it is true that there are as many minds as there are heads, then there are as many kinds of love as there are hearts."

Vronsky had gazed at Anna and with sinking heart waited to hear what she would say. He sighed, as after a danger averted, when she had uttered these words.

Suddenly Anna addressed him:

"I have received a letter from Moscow. They write that Kitty Shcherbatskaya is very ill."

"Really?" said Vronsky, frowning.

Anna glanced sternly at him. "It does not interest you?"

"On the contrary, it interests me very much! What exactly do they write, if I may ask?" he inquired.

Anna rose and went up to Betsy. "Give me a cup of tea," she said, stopping behind Betsy's chair.

While Betsy was pouring out the tea, Vronsky went up to Anna. "What do they write?" he asked again.

"I often think men don't understand honour, though they are always talking about it," said Anna, without answering his question. "I have long wanted to tell you," she added, and, moving a few steps to a side table on which lay some albums, she sat down.

"I don't quite understand your meaning," he said, handing her the cup.

"I wanted to tell you," she began again, without looking at him, "that you have behaved badly, very badly."

"Don't I know that I behaved badly? But who was the cause?"

"Why say that to me?" she asked, looking severely at him.

"You know why," he answered boldly and joyously, meeting her look and continuing to gaze at her.

It was not he, but she, who became abashed.

"That only proves you have no heart," she said. But her look said that she knew he had a heart and that she therefore feared him.

"What you have just referred to was a mistake, and not love."

Anna shuddered, and said: "Don't you remember that I forbade you to mention that word, that horrid word?" But then she felt that the one word *forbade* showed that she claimed certain rights over him, thereby encouraging him to speak of love. "I have long wanted to say that to you," she went on, looking resolutely into his eyes, her face all aglow and suffused with a burning blush, "and today I came on purpose, knowing I should meet you here. I have come to tell you that this must stop! I have never till now had to blush before anyone, but you make me feel as if I were guilty of something."

He looked at her, and was struck by the new, spiritual beauty of her face.

"What do you want of me?" he asked, simply and seriously.

"I want you to go to Moscow and beg Kitty's pardon," said she.

"You don't want that," he replied.

He saw that she was saying what she forced herself to utter and not what she wished to say.

"If you love me as you say you do," she whispered, "behave so that I may be at peace."

His face brightened.

"Don't you know that you are all my life to me? . . . But peace I do not know, and can't give to you. My whole being, my love . . . yes! I cannot think about you and about myself separately. You and I are one to me. And I do not see before us the possibility of peace either for me or for you. I see the possibility of despair, misfortune . . . or of happiness—what happiness! . . . Is it impossible?" he added with his lips only, but she heard.

She exerted all the powers of her mind to say what she ought; but instead she fixed on him her eyes filled with love and did not answer at all.

"This is it!" he thought with rapture. "Just as I was beginning to despair, and when it seemed as though the end would never come . . . here it is! She loves me! She acknowledges it!"

"Do this for me: never say such words to me, and let us be good friends." These were her words, but her eyes said something very different.

"Friends we shall not be, you know that yourself; but whether we shall be the happiest or the most miserable of human beings . . . rests with you."

She wished to say something, but he interrupted her.

"I ask only one thing: I ask the right to hope and suffer as I do now; but if even that is impossible, command me to disappear, and I will do it. You shall not see me if my presence is painful to you."

"I don't want to drive you away."

"Only don't change anything. Leave everything as it is!" he said with trembling voice. "Here is your husband."

Indeed, just at that moment Karenin, with his deliberate, ungraceful gait, entered the drawing-room.

He glanced at his wife and Vronsky, went up to the hostess, and having sat down with a cup of tea began talking in his deliberate and always clear tones, in his usual ironical way ridiculing somebody.

"Your Hotel Rambouillet is in full muster," said he, glancing round the whole company, "the Graces and the Muses."

But the Princess Betsy could not bear that tone of his: "sneering," she called it in English: so, like a clever hostess, she at once led him into a serious conversation on universal military service. Karenin was immediately absorbed in the conversation, and began defending the new law very earnestly against the Princess Betsy, who attacked it.

Vronsky and Anna remained sitting at the little table.

"This is becoming indecent!" whispered a lady, indicating by a glance Vronsky, Anna, and Anna's husband.

"What did I tell you?" replied Anna's friend.

Not these two ladies alone, but nearly all those present in the drawing-room, even the Princess Myagkaya and Betsy herself, several times glanced across at the pair who had gone away from the general circle, as if their having done so disturbed the others. Only Karenin did not once glance that way and was not distracted from the interesting conversation in which he was engaged.

Noticing the unpleasant impression produced on every one, the Princess Betsy manoeuvred for someone else to take her place and to listen to Karenin, and she herself went up to Anna.

"I am always amazed at your husband's clearness and exactitude of expression," she said. "The most transcendental ideas become accessible to me when he speaks."

"Oh yes!" said Anna, radiant with a smile of happiness and not understanding a single word of what Betsy was saying; and going across to the big table she joined in the general conversation.

After half an hour's stay Karenin went up to his wife and suggested that they should go home together; but, without looking at him, she answered that she would stay to supper. Karenin bowed to the company and went away.

❊   ❊   ❊

The Karenins' fat old Tartar coachman, in his shiny leather coat, was finding it hard to control the near grey horse that had grown restive with cold, waiting before the portico. The footman stood holding open the carriage door. The hall-porter stood with his hand on the outer front door, Anna with her deft little hand was disengaging the lace of her sleeve which had caught on a hook of her fur coat, and with bent head was listening with delight to what Vronsky, who accompanied her, was saying.

"Granted that you have not said anything! I don't demand anything," he was saying, "but you know that it is not friendship I want! Only one happiness is possible for me in life, the word you so dislike— yes, love . . . ."

"Love," she slowly repeated to herself, and suddenly, while releasing the lace, she added aloud: "The reason I dislike that word is that it means too much for me, far more than you can understand," and she looked him in the face. *"Au revoir!"*

She gave him her hand, and with her quick elastic step went past the hall-porter and vanished into the carriage.

Her glance and the touch of her hand burnt him. He kissed the palm of his hand where she had touched it, and went home happy in the knowledge that in this one evening he had made more progress toward his aim than he had during the previous two months.

from *Resurrection*

And so the evening passed and night came. The doctor went to bed. Nekhlyudov's aunts had also retired; and he knew that Matryona Pavlovna was now with them in their bedroom, so that Katusha was sure to be alone in the maids' sitting-room. He again went out into the porch. It was dark, damp, and warm out of doors, and that white spring mist which drives away the last snow, or is caused by the thawing of the last snow, filled the air. From the river below the hill, about a hundred paces from the front door, came a strange sound. It was the ice breaking up. Nekhlyudov descended the steps and went to the window of the maids' room, stepping over the puddles on the patches of glazed snow. His heart was beating so fiercely in his breast that he seemed to hear it; his laboured breath came and went in a burst of long-drawn sighs. In the maids' room a small lamp was burning, and Katusha sat alone by the table looking thoughtfully in front of her. Nekhlyudov stood a long time without moving, and waited to see what she, not knowing that she was observed, would do. For a minute or two she did not move; then she lifted her eyes, smiled and shook her head as if chiding herself, then changed her pose and dropped both her arms on the table and again began gazing down before her. He stood and looked at her, involuntarily listening to the beating of his own heart and the strange sounds from the river. There on the river, beneath the white mist, the unceasing labour went on, and sounds as of something sobbing, cracking, dropping, being shattered to pieces, mingled with the thinking of the thin bits of ice as they broke against each other like glass.

There he stood, looking at Katusha's serious, suffering face, which betrayed the inner struggle of her soul, and he felt pity for her; but, strange though it may seem, this pity only increased his desire. Desire had taken entire possession of him.

He knocked at the window. She started as if she had received an electric shock, her whole body trembled, and a look of terror came into her face. Then she jumped up, approached the window, and brought her face close to the pane. The look of terror did not leave her face even when, holding her hands up to her eyes like blinkers and peering through the glass, she recognized him. Her face was unusually grave; he had never seen it so before. She returned his smile, but only in submission to him; there was no smile in her soul, only fear. He beckoned her with his hand to come out into the yard to him. But she shook her head and remained at the window. He brought his face close to the pane, and was going to call out to her, but at that moment she turned to the door. Evidently someone inside had called her. Nekhlyudov moved away from the window. The mist was so dense that five steps from the house the windows could not be seen, but the light from the lamp shone red and huge out of a shapeless black mass. And on the river the same strange sounds went on, sobbing and rustling and crackling and tinkling. Somewhere in the mist not far off, a cock crowed; another answered, and then others far in the village took up the cry, till the sound of the crowing blent into one, while all around was silent excepting the river. It was the second time the cocks crowed that night.

Nekhlyudov walked up and down behind the corner of the house, and once or twice stepped into a puddle. Then he again came up to the window. The lamp was still burning, and she was again sitting alone by the table as if uncertain what to do. He had hardly approached the window when she looked up. He tapped. Without looking who it was she at once ran out of the room, and he heard the outside door open with a snap. He waited for her near the side porch, and put his arms round her without saying a word. She clung to him, put up her face, and met his kiss with her lips. They were standing behind the corner of the side porch, on a place where the snow had all melted, and he was filled with tormenting, ungratified desire. Then the door again gave the same sort of snap and opened, and the voice of Matryona Pavlovna called out angrily "Katusha!"

She tore herself away from him and returned to the maids' room. He heard the latch click and then all was quiet. The red light disappeared and only the mist remained, and the bustle on the river went on. Nekhlyudov went up to the window, nobody was to be seen, he tapped but got no answer. He went back into the house by the front door, but could not sleep. He got up and went with bare feet along the passage to her door, next to Matryona Pavlovna's room. He heard Matryona Pavlovna snoring quietly, and was about to go on when she coughed and turned on her creaking bed, and his heart stopped, and he stood immovable for about five minutes. When all was quiet and she began to snore peacefully again, he went on, trying to step on the boards that did not creak, and came to Katusha's door. No sound was to be heard. She was probably awake, or else he would have heard her breathing. But as soon as he whispered "Katusha!" she jumped up and began to persuade him, as if angrily, to go away.

"What do you mean by it? What are you doing? Your aunts will hear." These were her words, but all her being was saying, "I am all thine." And it was this only that Nekhlyudov understood.

"Open! Let me in just for a moment! I implore you!" He hardly knew what he was saying.

She was silent; then he heard her hand feeling for the latch. The latch clicked, and he entered the room. He caught hold of her just as she was—in her coarse, stiff chemise, with her bare arms—lifted her, and carried her out.

"Oh, dear! What are you doing?" she whispered; but he, paying no heed to her words, carried her into his room.

"Oh don't; you mustn't! Let me go!" she said, clinging closer to him.

When she left him, trembling and silent, giving no answer to his words, he again went out into the porch and stood trying to understand the meaning of what had happened.

It was getting lighter. From the river below, the creaking and tinkling and sobbing of the breaking ice came still louder, and a gurgling sound could now also be heard. The mist had begun to sink, and from above it the waning moon dimly lit up something black and weird.

"What is the meaning of it all? Is it a great joy, or a great misfortune, that has befallen me?" he asked himself.

"It happens to everybody—everybody does it," he said to himself, and went to bed and to sleep.

❧ ❧

IVAN TURGENEV

from First Love

The days passed by. Zinaída grew more and more strange, more and more incomprehensible. One day I entered her house and found her sitting on a straw-bottomed chair, with her head pressed against the sharp edge of a table. She straightened up . . . her face was again all bathed in tears.

"Ah! It's you!"—she said, with a harsh grimace.—"Come hither."

I went up to her: she laid her hand on my head and, suddenly seizing me by the hair, began to pull it.

"It hurts" . . . I said at last.

"Ah! It hurts! And doesn't it hurt me? Doesn't it hurt me?"—she repeated.

"Aï!"—she suddenly cried, perceiving that she had pulled out a small tuft of my hair.—"What have I done? Poor M'sieu Voldemar!" She carefully straightened out the hairs she had plucked out, wound them round her finger, and twisted them into a ring.

"I will put your hair in my locket and wear it,"—she said, and tears glistened in her eyes.—"Perhaps that will comfort you a little . . . but now, good-bye."

I returned home and found an unpleasant state of things there. A scene was in progress between my father and my mother; she was upbraiding him for something or other, while he, according to his wont, was maintaining a cold, polite silence—and speedily went away. I could not hear what my mother was talking about, neither did I care to know: I remember only, that, at the conclusion of the scene, she ordered me to be called to her boudoir, and expressed herself with great dissatisfaction about my frequent visits at the house of the old Princess, who was, according to her assertions, *une femme capable de tout.* I kissed her hand (I always did that when I wanted to put an end to the conversation), and went off to my own room. Zinaída's tears had completely discomfited me; I positively did not know what to think, and was ready to cry myself: I was still a child, in spite of my sixteen years. I thought no more of Malévsky, although Byelovzóroff became more and more menacing every day, and glared at the shifty Count like a wolf at a sheep; but I was not thinking of anything or of anybody. I lost myself in conjectures and kept seeking isolated spots. I took a special fancy to the ruins of the hothouse. I could clamber up on the high wall, seat myself, and sit there such an unhappy, lonely, and sad youth that I felt sorry for myself—and how delightful those mournful sensations were, how I gloated over them! . . .

One day, I was sitting thus on the wall, gazing off into the distance and listening to the chiming of the bells . . . when suddenly something ran over me—not a breeze exactly, not a shiver, but something resembling a breath, the consciousness of some one's proximity. . . . I dropped my eyes. Below me, in a light grey gown, with a pink parasol on her shoulder, Zinaída was walking hastily along the road. She saw me, halted, and, pushing up the brim of her straw hat, raised her velvety eyes to mine.

"What are you doing there, on such a height?"—she asked me, with a strange sort of smile.—"There now,"—she went on,—"you are always declaring that you love me—jump down to me here on the road if you really do love me."

Before the words were well out of Zinaída's mouth I had flown down, exactly as though some one had given me a push from behind. The wall was about two fathoms high. I landed on the ground with my feet, but the shock was so violent that I could not retain my balance; I fell, and lost consciousness for a moment. When I came to myself I felt, without opening my eyes, that Zinaída was by my side.—"My dear boy,"—she was saying, as she bent over me—and tender anxiety was audible in her voice—"how couldst thou do that, how couldst thou obey? . . . I love thee . . . rise."

Her breast was heaving beside me, her hands were touching my head, and suddenly—what were my sensations then!—her soft, fresh lips began to cover my whole face with kisses . . . they touched my lips. . . . But at this point Zinaída probably divined from the expression of my face that I had already recovered consciousness, although I still did not open my eyes—and swiftly rising to her feet, she said:—"Come, get up, you rogue, you foolish fellow! Why do you lie there in the dust?"—I got up.

"Give me my parasol,"—said Zinaída.—"I have thrown it somewhere; and don't look at me like that . . . what nonsense is this? You are hurt? You have burned yourself with the nettles, I suppose. Don't look at me like that, I tell you. . . . Why, he understands nothing, he doesn't answer me,"—she added, as though speaking to herself. . . . "Go home, M'sieu Voldemar, brush yourself off, and don't dare to follow me—if you do I shall be very angry, and I shall never again . . ."

She did not finish her speech and walked briskly away, while I sat down by the roadside . . . my legs would not support me. The nettles had stung my hands, my back ached, and my head was reeling; but the sensation of beatitude which I then experienced has never since been repeated in my life. It hung like a sweet pain in all my limbs and broke out at last in rapturous leaps and exclamations. As a matter of fact, I was still a child.

ANTON CHEKHOV

The Kiss

On the evening of the twentieth of May, at eight o'clock, all six batteries of the N Artillery Brigade on their way to camp arrived at the village of Miestechky with the intention of spending the night.

The confusion was at its worst—some officers fussed about the guns, others in the church square arranged with the quartermaster—when from behind the church rode a civilian upon a most remarkable mount. The small, short-tailed bay with well-shaped neck progressed with a wobbly motion, all the time making dance-like movements with its legs as if someone were switching its hoofs. When he had drawn rein level with the officers the rider doffed his cap and said ceremoniously—

"His Excellency, General von Rabbek, whose house is close by, requests the honour of the officers' company at tea. . . ."

The horse shook its head, danced, and wobbled to the rear; its rider again took off his cap, and, turning his strange steed, disappeared behind the church.

"The devil take it!" was the general exclamation as the officers dispersed to their quarters. "We can hardly keep our eyes open, yet along comes this von Rabbek with his tea! I know that tea!"

The officers of the six batteries had lively memories of a past invitation. During recent manœuvres they had been asked, together with their Cossack comrades, to tea at the house of a local country gentleman, an officer in retirement, by title a Count; and this hearty, hospitable Count overwhelmed them with attentions, fed them to satiety, poured vodka down their throats, and made them stay the night. All this, of course, they enjoyed. The trouble was that the old soldier entertained his guests too well. He kept them up till daybreak while he poured forth tales of past adventures; he dragged them from room to room to point out valuable paintings, old engravings, and rare arms; he read them holograph letters from celebrated men. And the weary officers, bored to death, listened, gaped, yearned for their beds, and yawned cautiously in their sleeves, until at last when their host released them it was too late for sleep.

Was von Rabbek another old Count? It might easily be. But there was no neglecting his invitation. The officers washed and dressed, and set out for von Rabbek's house. At the church square they learnt that they must descend the hill to the river, and follow the bank till they reached the general's gardens, where they would find a path direct to the house. Or, if they chose to go up hill, they would reach the general's barns half a verst from Miestetchki. It was this route they chose.

"But who is this von Rabbek?" asked one. "The man who commanded the N Cavalry Division at Plevna?"

"No, that was not von Rabbek, but simply Rabbe—without the von."

"What glorious weather!"

At the first barn they came to, two roads diverged; one ran straight forward and faded in the dusk; the other turning to the right led to the general's house. As the officers drew near they talked less loudly. To right and left stretched rows of red-roofed brick barns, in aspect heavy and morose as the barracks of provincial towns. In front gleamed the lighted windows of von Rabbek's house.

"A good omen, gentlemen!" cried a young officer. "Our setter runs in advance. There is game ahead!"

On the face of Lieutenant Lobytko, the tall stout officer referred to, there was not one trace of hair though he was twenty-five years old. He was famed among comrades for the instinct which told him of the presence of women in the neighbourhood. On hearing his comrade's remark, he turned his head and said—

"Yes. There are women there. My instinct tells me."

A handsome, well-preserved man of sixty, in mufti, came to the hall door to greet his guests. It was von Rabbek. As he pressed their hands, he explained that though he was delighted to see them, he must beg pardon for not asking them to spend the night; as guests he already had his two sisters, their children, his brother, and several neighbours— in fact, he had not one spare room. And though he shook their hands and apologised and smiled, it was plain that he was not half as glad to see them as was last year's Count, and that he had invited them merely because good manners demanded it. The officers climbing the soft-carpeted steps and listening to their host understood this perfectly well; and realised that they carried into the house an atmosphere of intrusion and alarm. Would any man—they asked themselves—who had gathered his two sisters and their children, his brother and his neighbours, to celebrate, no doubt, some family festival, find pleasure in the invasion of nineteen officers whom he had never seen before?

A tall, elderly lady, with a good figure, and a long face with black eyebrows, who resembled closely the ex-Empress Eugenie, greeted them at the drawing-room door. Smiling courteously and with dignity, she affirmed that she was delighted to see the officers, and only regretted that she could not ask them to stay the night. But the courteous, dignified smile disappeared when she turned away, and it was quite plain that she had seen many officers in her day, that they caused not the slightest interest, and that she had invited them merely because an invitation was dictated by good breeding and by her position in the world.

In a big dining-room seated at a big table sat ten men and women, drinking tea. Behind them, veiled in cigar-smoke, stood several young men, among them one, red-whiskered and extremely thin, who spoke English loudly with a lisp. Through an open door the officers saw into a brightly lighted room with blue wall-paper.

"You are too many to introduce singly, gentlemen!" said the general loudly, with affected joviality. "Make one another's acquaintance, please—without formalities!"

The visitors, some with serious, even severe faces, some smiling constrainedly, all with a feeling of awkwardness, bowed, and took their seats at the table. Most awkward of all felt Staff-Captain Riabovich, a short, round-shouldered, spectacled officer, whiskered like a lynx. While his brother officers looked serious or smiled constrainedly, his face, his lynx whiskers, and his spectacles seemed to explain: "I am the most timid, modest, undistinguished officer in the whole brigade." For some time after he took his seat at the table he could not fix his attention on any single thing. Faces, dresses, the cut-glass cognac bottles, the steaming tumblers, the moulded cornices—all merged in a single, overwhelming sentiment which caused him intense fright and made him wish to hide his head. Like an inexperienced lecturer he saw everything before him, but could distinguish nothing, and was in fact the victim of what men of science diagnose as "psychical blindness."

But slowly conquering his diffidence, Riabovich began to distinguish and observe. As became a man both timid and unsocial, he remarked first of all the amazing temerity of his new friends. Van Rabbek, his wife, two elderly ladies, a girl in lilac, and the red-whiskered youth who, it appeared, was a young von Rabbek, sat down among the officers as unconcernedly as if they had held rehearsals, and at once plunged into various heated arguments in which they soon involved their guests. That artillerists have a much better time than cavalrymen or infantrymen was proved conclusively by the lilac girl, while von Rabbek and the elderly ladies affirmed the converse. The consternation became desultory. Ri-

abovich listened to the lilac girl fiercely debating themes she knew nothing about and took no interest in, and watched the insincere smiles
which appeared on and disappeared from her face.

While the von Rabbek family with amazing strategy inveigled their
guests into the dispute, they kept their eyes on every glass and mouth.
Had every one tea, was it sweet enough, why didn't one eat biscuits, was
another fond of cognac? And the longer Riabovich listened and looked,
the more pleased he was with this disingenuous, disciplined family.

After tea the guests repaired to the drawing-room. Instinct had not
cheated Lobytko. The room was packed with young women and girls,
and ere a minute had passed the setter-lieutenant stood beside a very
young, fair-haired girl in black, and, bending down as if resting on an invisible sword, shrugged his shoulders coquettishly. He was uttering, no
doubt, most unentertaining nonsense, for the fair girl looked indulgently
at his sated face, and exclaimed indifferently, "Indeed!" And this indifferent "Indeed!" might have quickly convinced the setter that he was on
a wrong scent.

Music began. As the notes of a mournful valse throbbed out of the
open window, through the heads of all flashed the feeling that outside
that window it was spring-time, a night of May. The air was odourous
of young poplar leaves, of roses and lilacs—and the valse and the spring
were sincere. Riabovich, with valse and cognac mingling tipsily in his
head, gazed at the window with a smile; then began to follow the movements of the women; and it seemed that the smell of roses, poplars, and
lilacs came not from the gardens outside, but from the women's faces and
dresses.

They began to dance. Young von Rabbek valsed twice round the
room with a very thin girl; and Lobytko, slipping on the parquetted
floor, went up to the girl in lilac, and was granted a dance. But Riabovich stood near the door with the wall-flowers, and looked silently on.
Amazed at the daring of men who in sight of a crowd could take unknown women by the waist, he tried in vain to picture himself doing the
same. A time had been when he envied his comrades their courage and
dash, suffered from painful heart-searchings, and was hurt by the knowledge that he was timid, round-shouldered, and undistinguished, that he
had lynx whiskers, and that his waist was much too long. But with years
he had grown reconciled to his own insignificance, and now looking at
the dancers and loud talkers, he felt no envy, but only mournful emotions.

At the first quadrille von Rabbek junior approached and invited two non-dancing officers to a game of billiards. The three left the room; and Riabovich who stood idle, and felt impelled to join in the general movement, followed. They passed the dining-room, traversed a narrow glazed corridor, and a room where three sleepy footmen jumped from a sofa with a start; and after walking, it seemed, through a whole houseful of rooms, entered a small billiard-room.

Von Rabbek and the two officers began their game. Riabovich, whose only game was cards, stood near the table and looked indifferently on, as the players, with unbuttoned coats, wielded their cues, moved about, joked, and shouted obscure technical terms. Riabovich was ignored, save when one of the players jostled him or caught his cue, and turning towards him said briefly, "Pardon!" so that before the game was over he was thoroughly bored, and impressed by a sense of his superfluity, resolved to return to the drawing-room, and turned away.

It was on the way back that his adventure took place. Before he had gone far he saw that he had missed the way. He remembered distinctly the room with the three sleepy footmen; and after passing through five or six rooms entirely vacant, he saw his mistake. Retracing his steps, he turned to the left, and found himself in an almost dark room which he had not seen before; and after hesitating a minute, he boldly opened the first door he saw, and found himself in complete darkness. Through a chink of the door in front peered a bright light; from afar throbbed the dulled music of a mournful mazurka. Here, as in the drawing-room, the windows were open wide, and the smell of poplars, lilacs, and roses flooded the air.

Riabovich paused in irresolution. For a moment all was still. Then came the sound of hasty footsteps; then, without any warning of what was to come, a dress rustled, a woman's breathless voice whispered "At last!" and two soft, scented, unmistakably womanly arms met round his neck, a warm cheek impinged on his, and he received a sounding kiss. But hardly had the kiss echoed through the silence when the unknown shrieked loudly, and fled away—as it seemed to Riabovich—in disgust. Riabovich himself nearly screamed, and rushed headlong towards the bright beam in the door-chink.

As he entered the drawing-room his heart beat violently, and his hands trembled so perceptibly that he clasped them behind his back. His first emotion was shame, as if every one in the room already knew that he had just been embraced and kissed. He retired into his shell, and looked fearfully around. But finding that hosts and guests were calmly dancing or talking, he regained courage, and surrendered himself to sensations experienced for the first time in life. The unexampled had happened. His neck, fresh from the embrace of two soft, scented arms, seemed anointed with oil; near his left moustache, where the kiss had fallen, trembled a slight, delightful chill, as from peppermint drops; and from head to foot he was soaked in new and extraordinary sensations, which continued to grow and grow.

He felt that he must dance, talk, run into the garden, laugh unrestrainedly. He forgot altogether that he was round-shouldered, undistinguished, lynx-whiskered, that he had an "indefinite exterior"—a description from the lips of a woman he had happened to overhear. As Madame von Rabbek passed him he smiled so broadly and graciously that she came up and looked at him questioningly.

"What a charming house you have!" he said, straightening his spectacles.

And Madame von Rabbek smiled back, said that the house still belonged to her father, and asked were his parents alive, how long he had been in the Army, and why he was so thin. After hearing his answers she departed. But though the conversation was over, he continued to smile benevolently, and think what charming people were his new acquaintances.

At supper Riabovich ate and drank mechanically what was put before him, heard not a word of the conversation, and devoted all his powers to the unravelling of his mysterious, romantic adventure. What was the explanation? It was plain that one of the girls, he reasoned, had arranged a meeting in the dark room, and after waiting some time in vain had, in her nervous tension, mistaken Riabovich for her hero. The mistake was likely enough, for on entering the dark room Riabovich had stopped irresolutely as if he, too, were waiting for someone. So far the mystery was explained.

"But which of them was it?" he asked, searching the women's faces. She certainly was young, for old women do not indulge in such romances. Secondly, she was not a servant. That was proved unmistakably by the rustle of her dress, the scent, the voice . . .

When at first he looked at the girl in lilac she pleased him; she had pretty shoulders and arms, a clever face, a charming voice. Riabovich piously prayed that it was she. But, smiling insincerely, she wrinkled her long nose, and that at once gave her an elderly air. So Riabovich turned his eyes on the blonde in black. The blonde was younger, simpler, sincerer; she had charming kiss-curls, and drank from her tumbler with inexpressible grace. Riabovich hoped it was she—but soon he noticed that her face was flat, and bent his eyes on her neighbour.

"It is a hopeless puzzle," he reflected. "If you take the arms and shoulders of the lilac girl, add the blonde's curls, and the eyes of the girl on Lobytko's left, then—"

He composed a portrait of all these charms, and had a clear vision of the girl who had kissed him. But she was nowhere to be seen.

Supper over, the visitors, sated and tipsy, bade their entertainers good-bye. Both host and hostess again apologised for not asking them to spend the night.

"I am very glad, very glad, gentlemen!" said the general, and this time seemed to speak sincerely, no doubt because speeding the parting guest is a kindlier office than welcoming him unwelcomed. "I am very glad indeed! I hope you will visit me on your way back. Without ceremony, please! Which way will you go? Up the hill? No, go down the hill and through the garden. That way is shorter."

The officers took his advice. After the noise and glaring illumination within doors, the garden seemed dark and still. Until they reached the wicket-gate all kept silence. Merry, half tipsy, and content, as they were, the night's obscurity and stillness inspired pensive thoughts. Through their brains, as through Riabovich's, sped probably the same question: "Will the time ever come when I, like von Rabbek, shall have a big house, a family, a garden, the chance of being gracious—even insincerely—to others, of making them sated, tipsy, and content?"

But once the garden lay behind them, all spoke at once, and burst into causeless laughter. The path they followed led straight to the river, and then ran beside it, winding around bushes, ravines, and overhanging willow-trees. The track was barely visible; the other bank was lost entirely in gloom. Sometimes the black water imaged stars, and this was the only indication of the river's speed. From beyond it sighed a drowsy snipe, and beside them in a bush, heedless of the crowd, a nightingale chanted loudly. The officers gathered in a group, and swayed the bush, but the nightingale continued his song.

"I like his cheek!" they echoed admiringly. "He doesn't care a kopeck! The old rogue!"

Near their journey's end the path turned up the hill, and joined the road not far from the church enclosure; and there the officers, breathless from climbing, sat on the grass and smoked. Across the river gleamed a dull red light, and for want of a subject they argued the problem, whether it was a bonfire, a window-light, or something else. Riabovich looked also at the light, and felt that it smiled and winked at him as if it knew about the kiss.

On reaching home, he undressed without delay, and lay upon his bed. He shared the cabin with Lobytko and a Lieutenant Marzliakov, a staid, silent little man, by repute highly cultivated, who took with him everywhere *The Messenger of Europe*, and read it eternally. Lobytko undressed, tramped impatiently from corner to corner, and sent his servant for beer. Merzliakov lay down, balanced the candle on his pillow, and hid his head behind *The Messenger of Europe*.

"Where is she now?" muttered Riabovich, looking at the soot-blacked ceiling.

His neck still seemed anointed with oil, near his mouth still trembled the speck of peppermint chill. Through his brain twinkled successively the shoulders and arms of the lilac girl, the kiss-curls and honest eyes of the girl in black, the waists, dresses, brooches. But though he tried his best to fix these vagrant images, they glimmered, winked, and dissolved; and as they faded finally into the vast black curtain which hangs before the closed eyes of all men, he began to hear hurried footsteps, the rustle of petticoats, the sound of a kiss. A strong, causeless joy possessed him. But as he surrendered himself to this joy, Lobytko's servant returned with the news that no beer was obtainable. The lieutenant resumed his impatient march up and down the room.

"The fellow's an idiot," he exclaimed, stopping first near Riabovich and then near Merzliakov. "Only the worst numbskull and blockhead can't get beer! *Canaille!*"

"Everyone knows there's no beer here," said Merzliakov, without lifting his eyes from *The Messenger of Europe*.

"You believe that!" exclaimed Lobytko. "Lord in heaven, drop me on the moon, and in five minutes I'll find both beer and women! I will find them myself! Call me a rascal if I don't!"

He dressed slowly, silently lighted a cigarette, and went out.

"Rabbek, Grabbek, Labbek," he muttered, stopping in the hall. "I won't go alone, devil take me! Riabovich, come for a walk! What?"

As he got no answer, he returned, undressed slowly, and lay down. Merzliakov sighed, dropped *The Messenger of Europe*, and put out the light. "Well?" muttered Lobytko, puffing his cigarette in the dark.

Riabovich pulled the bed-clothes up to his chin, curled himself into a roll, and strained his imagination to join the twinkling images into one coherent whole. But the vision fled him. He soon fell asleep, and his last impression was that he had been caressed and gladdened, that into his life had crept something strange, and indeed ridiculous, but uncommonly good and radiant. And this thought did not forsake him even in his dreams.

When he awoke the feeling of anointment and peppermint chill were gone. But joy, as on the night before, filled every vein. He looked entranced at the window-panes gilded by the rising sun, and listened to the noises outside. Someone spoke loudly under the very window. It was Lebedietsky, commander of his battery, who had just overtaken the brigade. He was talking to the sergeant-major, loudly, owing to lack of practice in soft speech.

"And what next?" he roared.

"During yesterday's shoeing, your honour, *Golubtchik* was pricked. The *feldscher* ordered clay and vinegar. And last night, your honour, mechanic Artemieff was drunk, and the lieutenant ordered him to be put on the limber of the reserve gun-carriage."

The sergeant-major added that Karpov had forgotten the tent-pegs and the new lanyards for the friction-tubes, and that the officers had spent the evening at General von Rabbek's. But here at the window appeared Lebedetzky's red-bearded face. He blinked his short-sighted eyes at the drowsy men in bed, and greeted them.

"Is everything all right?"

"The saddle wheeler galled his withers with the new yoke," answered Lobytko.

The commander sighed, mused a moment, and shouted—

"I am thinking of calling on Alexandra Yegorovna. I want to see her. Good-bye! I will catch you up before night."

Fifteen minutes later the brigade resumed its march. As he passed von Rabbek's barns Riabovich turned his head and looked at the house. The Venetian blinds were down; evidently all still slept. And among them slept she—she who had kissed him but a few hours before. He tried to visualise her asleep. He projected the bedroom window opened wide with green branches peering in, the freshness of the morning air, the smell of poplars, lilacs, and roses, the bed, a chair, the dress which rustled last night, a pair of tiny slippers, a ticking watch on the table— all these came to him clearly with every detail. But the features, the kind, sleepy smile—all, in short, that was essential and characteristic—fled his imagination as quicksilver flees the hand. When he had covered half a verst he again turned back. The yellow church, the house, gardens, and river were bathed in light. Imaging an azure sky, the green-banked river specked with silver sunshine flakes was inexpressibly fair; and, looking at Miestechky for the last time, Riabovich felt sad, as if parting forever with something very near and dear.

By the road before him stretched familiar, uninteresting scenes; to the right and left, fields of young rye and buckwheat with hopping rooks; in front, dust and the napes of human necks; behind, the same dust and faces. Ahead of the column marched four soldiers with swords—that was the advance guard. Next came the bandsmen. Advance guard and bandsmen, like mutes in a funeral procession, ignored the regulation intervals and marched too far ahead. Riabovich, with the first gun of Battery No. 5, could see four batteries ahead.

To a layman, the long, lumbering march of an artillery brigade is novel, interesting, inexplicable. It is hard to understand why a single gun needs so many men; why so many, such strangely harnessed horses are needed to drag it. But to Riabovich, a master of all these things, it was profoundly dull. He had learned years ago why a solid sergeant-major rides beside the officer in front of each battery; why the sergeant-major is called the *unosni,* and why the drivers of leaders and wheelers ride behind him. Riabovich knew why the near horses are called saddle-horses, and why the off horses are called led-horses—and all of this was interesting beyond words. On one of the wheelers rode a soldier still covered with yesterday's dust, and with a cumbersome, ridiculous guard on his right leg. But Riabovich, knowing the use of this leg-guard, found it in no way ridiculous. The drivers, mechanically and with occasional cries, flourished their whips. The guns in themselves were impressive. The limbers were packed with tarpaulin-covered sacks of oats; and the guns themselves, hung around with teapots and satchels, looked like harmless animals, guarded for some obscure reason by men and horses. In the lee of the gun tramped six gunners, swinging their arms; and behind each gun came more *unosniye,* leaders, wheelers; and yet more guns, each as ugly and uninspiring as the one in front. And as every one of the six batteries in the brigade had four guns, the procession stretched along the road at least half a verst. It ended with a wagon train, with which, its head bent in thought, walked the donkey Magar, brought from Turkey by a battery commander.

Dead to his surroundings, Riabovich marched onward, looking at the napes ahead or at the faces behind. Had it not been for last night's event, he would have been half asleep. But now he was absorbed in novel, entrancing thoughts. When the brigade set out that morning he had tried to argue that the kiss had no significance save as a trivial though mysterious adventure; that it was without real import; and that to think of it seriously was to behave himself absurdly. But logic soon flew away and surrendered him to his vivid imaginings. At times he saw himself in von Rabbek's dining-room, *tête-à-tête* with a composite being, formed of the girl in lilac and the blonde in black. At times he closed his eyes, and pictured himself with a different, this time quite an unknown, girl of cloudy feature; he spoke to her, caressed her, bent over her shoulder; he imagined war and parting . . . then reunion, the first supper together, children. . . .

"To the brakes!" rang the command as they topped the brow of each hill.

Riabovich also cried "To the brakes!" and each time dreaded that the cry would break the magic spell, and recall him to realities.

They passed a big country house. Riabovich looked across the fence into the garden, and saw a long path, straight as a ruler, carpeted with yellow sand, and shaded by young birches. In an ecstasy of enchantment, he pictured little feminine feet treading the yellow sand; and, in a flash, imagination restored the woman who had kissed him, the woman he had visualised after supper the night before. The image settled in his brain and never afterwards forsook him.

The spell reigned until midday, when a loud command came from the rear of the column.

"Attention! Eyes right! Officers!"

In a *calèche* drawn by a pair of white horses appeared the general of brigade. He stopped at the second battery, and called out something which no one understood. Up galloped several officers, among them Riabovich.

"Well, how goes it?" The general blinked his red eyes, and continued, "Are there any sick?"

Hearing the answer, the little skinny general mused a moment, turned to an officer, and said—

"The driver of your third-gun wheeler has taken off his leg-guard and hung it on the limber. *Canaille!* Punish him!"

Then raising his eyes to Riabovich, he added—

"And in your battery, I think, the harness is too loose."

Having made several other equally tiresome remarks, he looked at Lobytko, and laughed.

"Why do you look so downcast, Lieutenant Lobytko? You are sighing for Madame Lopukhov, eh? Gentlemen, he is pining for Madame Lopukhov!"

Madame Lopukhov was a tall, stout lady, long past forty. Being partial to big women, regardless of age, the general ascribed the same taste to his subordinates. The officers smiled respectfully; and the general, pleased that he had said something caustic and laughable, touched the coachman's back and saluted. The *calèche* whirled away.

"All this, though it seems to me impossible and unearthly, is in reality very commonplace," thought Riabovich, watching the clouds of dust raised by the general's carriage. "It is an everyday event, and within everyone's experience. . . . This old general, for instance, must have loved in his day; he is married now, and has children. Captain Wachter is also married, and his wife loves him, though he has an ugly red neck and no waist. . . . Salmanoff is coarse, and a typical Tartar, but he has had a romance ending in marriage. . . . I, like the rest, must go through it all sooner or later."

And the thought that he was an ordinary man, and that his life was ordinary, rejoiced and consoled him. He boldly visualised *her* and his happiness, and let his imagination run mad.

Towards evening the brigade ended its march. While the other officers sprawled in their tents, Riabovich, Merzliakov, and Lobytko sat around a packing-case and supped. Merzliakov ate slowly, and, resting *The Messenger of Europe* on his knees, read on steadily. Lobytko, chattering without cease, poured beer into his glass. But Riabovich, whose head was dizzy from uninterrupted daydreams, ate in silence. When he had drunk three glasses he felt tipsy and weak; and an overmastering impulse forced him to relate his adventure to his comrades.

"A most extraordinary thing happened to me at von Rabbek's," he began, doing his best to speak in an indifferent, ironical tone. "I was on my way, you understand, from the billiard-room. . . ."

And he attempted to give a very detailed history of the kiss. But in a minute he had told the whole story. In that minute he had exhausted every detail; and it seemed to him terrible that the story required such a short time. It ought, he felt, to have lasted all the night. As he finished, Lobytko, who as a liar himself believed in no one, laughed incredulously. Merzliakov frowned, and, with his eyes still glued to *The Messenger of Europe*, said indifferently—

"God knows who it was! She threw herself on your neck, you say, and didn't cry out! Some lunatic, I expect!"

"It must have been a lunatic," agreed Riabovich.

"I, too, have had adventures of that kind," began Lobytko, making a frightened face. "I was on my way to Kovno. I travelled second class. The carriage was packed, and I couldn't sleep. So I gave the guard a ruble, and he took my bag, and put me in a *coupé*. I lay down, and pulled my rug over me. It was pitch dark, you understand. Suddenly I felt some one tapping my shoulder and breathing in my face. I stretched out my hand, and felt an elbow. Then I opened my eyes. Imagine! A woman!

Coal-black eyes, lips red as good coral, nostrils breathing passion, breasts—buffers!"

"Draw it mild!" interrupted Merzliakov in his quiet voice. "I can believe about the breasts, but if it was pitch dark how could you see the lips?"

By laughing at Merzliakov's lack of understanding, Lobytko tried to shuffle out of the dilemma. The story annoyed Riabovich. He rose from the box, lay on his bed, and swore that he would never again take anyone into his confidence.

Life in camp passed without event. The days flew by, each like the one before. But on every one of these days Riabovich felt, thought, and acted as a man in love. When at daybreak his servant brought him cold water, and poured it over his head, it flashed at once into his half-awakened brain that something good and warm and caressing had crept into his life.

At night when his comrades talked of love and of women, he drew in his chair, and his face was the face of an old soldier who talks of battles in which he has taken part. And when the rowdy officers, led by setter Lobytko, made Don Juanesque raids upon the neighbouring "suburb," Riabovich, though he accompanied them, was morose and conscience-struck, and mentally asked *her* forgiveness. In free hours and sleepless nights, when his brain was obsessed by memories of childhood, of his father, his mother, of everything akin and dear, he remembered always Miestechky, the dancing horse, von Rabbek, von Rabbek's wife, so like the ex-Empress Eugenie, the dark room, the chink in the door.

On the thirty-first of August he left camp, this time not with the whole brigade but with only two batteries. As an exile returning to his native land, he was agitated and enthralled by daydreams. He longed passionately for the queer-looking horse, the church, the insincere von Rabbeks, the dark room; and that internal voice which cheats so often the love-lorn whispered an assurance that he should see *her* again. But doubt tortured him. How should he meet her? What must he say? Would she have forgotten the kiss? If it came to the worst—he consoled himself—if he never saw her again, he might walk once more through the dark room, and remember. . . .

Towards evening the white barns and well-known church rose on the horizon. Riabovich's heart beat wildly. He ignored the remark of an officer who rode by, he forgot the whole world, and he gazed greedily at the river glimmering afar, at the green roofs, at the dove-cote, over which fluttered birds, dyed golden by the setting sun.

As he rode towards the church, and heard again the quartermaster's raucous voice, he expected every second a horseman to appear from behind the fence and invite the officers to tea. . . . But the quartermaster ended his harangue, the officers hastened to the village, and no horseman appeared.

"When Rabbek hears from the peasants that we are back he will send for us," thought Riabovich. And so assured was he of this, that when he entered the hut he failed to understand why his comrades had lighted a candle, and why the servants were preparing the samovar.

A painful agitation oppressed him. He lay on his bed. A moment later he rose to look for the horseman. But no horseman was in sight. Again he lay down; again he rose; and this time, impelled by restlessness, went into the street, and walked towards the church. The square was dark and deserted. On the hill stood three silent soldiers. When they saw Riabovich they started and saluted, and he, returning their salute, began to descend the well-remembered path.

Beyond the stream, in a sky stained with purple, the moon slowly rose. Two chattering peasant women walked in a kitchen garden and pulled cabbage leaves; behind them their log cabins stood out black against the sky. The river bank was as it had been in May; the bushes were the same; things differed only in that the nightingale no longer sang, that it smelt no longer of poplars and young grass.

When he reached von Rabbek's garden Riabovich peered through the wicket-gate. Silence and darkness reigned. Save only the white birch trunks and patches of pathway, the whole garden merged in a black, impenetrable shade. Riabovich listened greedily, and gazed intent. For a quarter of an hour he loitered; then hearing no sound, and seeing no light, he walked wearily towards home.

He went down to the river. In front rose the general's bathing box; and white towels hung on the rail of the bridge. He climbed on to the bridge and stood still; then, for no reason whatever, touched a towel. It was clammy and cold. He looked down at the river which sped past swiftly, murmuring almost inaudibly against the bathing-box piles. Near the left bank glowed the moon's ruddy reflection, overrun by ripples which stretched it, tore it in two, and, it seemed, would sweep it away as twigs and shavings are swept.

"How stupid! How stupid!" thought Riabovich, watching the hurrying ripples. "How stupid everything is!"

Now that hope was dead, the history of the kiss, his impatience, his ardour, his vague aspirations and disillusion appeared in a clear light.

It no longer seemed strange that the general's horseman had not come, and that he would never again see *her* who had kissed him by accident instead of another. On the contrary, he felt, it would be strange if he did ever see her again. . . .

The water flew past him, whither and why no one knew. It had flown past in May; it had sped a stream into a great river; a river, into the sea; it had floated on high in mist and fallen again in rain; it might be, the water of May was again speeding past under Riabovich's eyes. For what purpose? Why?

And the whole world—life itself seemed to Riabovich an inscrutable, aimless mystification. . . . Raising his eyes from the stream and gazing at the sky, he recalled how Fate in the shape of an unknown woman had once caressed him; he recalled his summer fantasies and images—and his whole life seemed to him unnaturally thin and colourless and wretched. . . .

When he reached the cabin his comrades had disappeared. His servant informed him that all had set out to visit "General Fonrabbkin," who had sent a horseman to bring them. . . . For a moment Riabovich's heart thrilled with joy. But that joy he extinguished. He cast himself upon his bed, and wroth with his evil fate, as if he wished to spite it, ignored the invitation.

❦ ❦

ANATOLE FRANCE

from *The Crime of Sylvestre Bonnard*

It is strange that I should have lost my rest simply on account of a few old sheets of parchment; but it is unquestionably true. The poor man who has no desires possesses the greatest of riches; he possesses himself. The rich man who desires something is only a wretched slave. I am just such a slave. The sweetest pleasures—those of converse with someone of a delicate and well-balanced mind, or dining out with a friend—are insufficient to enable me to forget the manuscript which I know that I want, and have been wanting from the moment I knew of its existence. I feel the want of it by day and by night: I feel the want of it in all my joys and pains; I feel the want of it while at work or asleep.

I recall my desires as a child. How well I can now comprehend the intense wishes of my early years!

I can see once more, with astonishing vividness, a certain doll which, when I was eight years old, used to be displayed in the window of an ugly little shop of the Rue de la Seine. I cannot tell how it happened that this doll attracted me. I was very proud of being a boy; I despised little girls; and I longed impatiently for the day (which, alas! has come) when a strong white beard should bristle on my chin. I played at being a soldier; and, under the pretext of obtaining forage for my rocking-horse, I used to make sad havoc among the plants my poor mother used to keep on her windowsill. Manly amusements those, I should say! And, nevertheless, I was consumed with longing for a doll. Characters like Hercules have such weaknesses occasionally. Was the one I had fallen in love with at all beautiful? No. I can see her now. She had a splotch of vermilion on either cheek, short soft arms, horrible wooden hands, and long sprawling legs. Her flowered petticoat was fastened at the waist with two pins. Even now I can see the black heads of those two pins. It was a decidedly vulgar doll—smelt of the *faubourg*. I remember perfectly well that, even child as I was then, before I had put on my first pair of trousers, I was quite conscious in my own way that this doll lacked grace and style—that she was gross, that she was coarse. But I loved her in spite of that; I loved her just for that; I loved her only; I wanted her. My soldiers and my drums had become as nothing in my eyes. I ceased to stick sprigs of heliotrope and veronica into the mouth of my rocking-horse. That doll was all the world to me. I invented ruses worthy of a savage to oblige Virginie, my nurse, to take me by the little shop in the Rue de la Seine. I would press my nose against the window until my nurse had to take my arm and drag me away. "Monsieur Sylvestre, it is late, and your mamma will scold you." Monsieur Sylvestre in those days made very little of either scoldings or whippings. But his nurse lifted him up like a feather, and Monsieur Sylvestre yielded to force. In after-years, with age, he degenerated, and sometimes yielded to fear. But at that time he used to fear nothing.

I was unhappy. An unreasoning but irresistible shame prevented me from telling my mother about the object of my love. Thence all my sufferings. For many days that doll, incessantly present in fancy, danced before my eyes, stared at me fixedly, opened her arms to me, assuming in my imagination a sort of life which made her appear at once mysterious and weird, and thereby all the more charming and desirable.

Finally, one day—a day I shall never forget—my nurse took me to see my uncle, Captain Victor, who had invited me to breakfast. I admired my uncle a great deal, as much because he had fired the last French cartridge at Waterloo, as because he used to make with his own hands, at my mother's table, certain *chapons-à-l'ail,* which he afterwards put into the chicory-salad. I thought that was very fine! My Uncle Victor also inspired me with much respect by his frogged coat, and still more by his way of turning the whole house upside down from the moment he came into it. Even now I cannot tell just how he managed it, but I can affirm that whenever my Uncle Victor found himself in any assembly of twenty persons, it was impossible to see or to hear anybody but him. My excellent father, I have reason to believe, never shared my admiration for Uncle Victor, who used to sicken him with his pipe, gave him great thumps in the back by way of friendliness, and accused him of lacking energy. My mother, though always showing a sister's indulgence to the captain, sometimes advised him to fondle the brandy-bottle a little less frequently. But I had no part either in these repugnances or these re-proaches, and Uncle Victor inspired me with the purest enthusiasm. It was therefore with a feeling of pride that I entered into the little lodging-house where he lived, in the Rue Guénégaud. The entire breakfast, served on a small table close to the fire-place, consisted of porkmeats and con-fectionery.

The Captain stuffed me with cakes and pure wine. He told me of numberless injustices to which he had been a victim. He complained par-ticularly of the Bourbons; and as he neglected to tell me who the Bour-bons were, I got the idea—I can't tell how—that the Bourbons were horse-dealers established at Waterloo. The Captain, who never inter-rupted his talk except for the purpose of pouring out wine, furthermore made charges against a number of *morveux,* of *jeanfesses,* and "good-for-nothings" whom I did not know anything about, but whom I hated from the bottom of my heart. At dessert I thought I heard the Captain say my father was a man who could be led anywhere by the nose; but I am not quite sure that I understood him. I had a buzzing in my ears; and it seemed to me that the table was dancing.

My uncle put on his frogged coat, took his *chapeau tromblon,* and we descended to the street, which seemed to me singularly changed. It looked to me as if I had not been in it before for ever so long a time. Nevertheless, when we came to the Rue de la Seine, the idea of my doll suddenly returned to my mind and excited me in an extraordinary way. My head was on fire. I resolved upon a desperate expedient. We were passing before the window. She was there, behind the glass—with her red cheeks, and her flowered petticoat, and her long legs.

"Uncle," I said, with a great effort, "will you buy that doll for me?"

And I waited.

"Buy a doll for a boy—*sacrebleu!*" cried my uncle, in a voice of thunder. "Do you wish to dishonor yourself? And it is that old Mag there that you want! Well, I must compliment you, my young fellow! If you grow up with such tastes as that, you will never have any pleasure in life; and your comrades will call you a precious ninny. If you asked me for a sword or a gun, my boy, I would buy them for you with the last silver crown of my pension. But to buy a doll for you—a thousand thunders!—to disgrace you! Never in the world! Why, if I were ever to see you playing with a puppet rigged out like that, Monsieur, my sister's son, I would disown you for my nephew!"

On hearing these words, I felt my heart so wrung that nothing but pride—a diabolic pride—kept me from crying.

My uncle, suddenly calming down, returned to his ideas about the Bourbons; but I, still smarting from the blow of his indignation, felt an unspeakable shame. My resolve was quickly made. I promised myself never to disgrace myself—I firmly and forever renounced that red-cheeked doll.

❦ ❦

RICHARD BURTON

from *The Book of the Thousand Nights and a Night*

Shahrazad, to forestall her death, entrances her husband, the king, with a love story.

THE TALE OF AZIZ AND AZIZAH

My father was a wealthy merchant and Allah had vouchsafed him no other child than myself; but I had a cousin, Azizah hight, daughter of my paternal uncle and we twain were brought up in one house; for her father was dead and before his death, he had agreed with my father that I should marry her. So when I reached man's estate and she reached womanhood, they did not separate her from me or me from her, till at last my father spoke to my mother and said, "This very year we will draw up the contract of marriage between Aziz and Azizah." So having agreed upon this he betook himself to preparing provision for the wedding-feast. Still we ceased not to sleep on the same carpet knowing naught of the case, albeit she was more thoughtful, more intelligent and quicker-witted than I. Now when my father had made an end of his preparations, and naught remained for him but to write out the contract and for me but to consummate the marriage with my cousin, he appointed the wedding for a certain Friday, after public prayers; and, going round to his intimates among the merchants and others, he acquainted them with that, whilst my mother went forth and invited her women friends and summoned her kith and kin. When the Friday came, they cleaned the saloon and prepared for the guests and washed the marble floor; then they spread tapestry about our house and set out thereon what was needful, after they had hung its walls with cloth of gold. Now the folk had agreed to come to us after the Friday prayers; so my father went out and bade them make sweetmeats and sugared dishes, and there remained nothing to do but to draw up the contract. Then my mother sent me to the bath and sent after me a suit of new clothes of the richest; and, when I came out of the Hammam, I donned those habits which were so perfumed that as I went along, there exhaled from them a delicious fragrance scenting the wayside. I had designed to repair to the Cathedral-mosque, when I bethought me of one of my friends and returned in quest of him that he might be present at the writing of the contract; and quoth I to myself, "This matter will occupy me till near the time of congregational prayer." So I went on and entered a by-street which I had never before entered, perspiring profusely from the effects of the bath and the new clothes on my body; and the sweat streamed down whilst the scents of my dress were wafted abroad: I therefore sat me at the upper end of the street resting on a stone bench, after spreading under me an embroidered kerchief I had with me. The heat oppressed me more and more, making my forehead perspire and the drops trickled along my cheeks; but I could not wipe my face with my kerchief because it was dispread under me. I was about to take the skirt of my robe and wipe my cheeks with it, when unexpectedly there fell on me from above a white kerchief, softer to the touch than the morning breeze and pleasanter to the sight than healing to the diseased. I hent it in hand and raised my head to see whence it had fallen, when my eyes met the eyes of the lady who owned these gazelles.—And Shahrazad perceived the dawn of day and ceased saying her permitted say.

Now when it was the Hundred-and-thirteenth Night,

She said, It hath reached me, O auspicious King, that the youth continued to Taj al-Muluk:—So I raised my head to see whence this kerchief had fallen, when my eyes met those of the lady who owned these gazelles. And lo! she was looking out of a wicket in a lattice of brass and never saw my eyes a fairer than she; and in fine my tongue faileth to describe her beauty. When she caught sight of me looking at her, she put her forefinger into her mouth, then joined her middle finger and her witness-finger and laid them on her bosom, between her breasts; after which she drew in her head and closed the wicket-shutter and went her ways. Thereupon fire broke out in and was heaped upon my heart, and greater grew my smart; the one sight cost me a thousand sighs and I abode perplexed, for that I heard no word by her spoken, nor understood the meaning of her token. I looked at the window a second time, but found it shut and waited patiently till sundown, but sensed no sound and saw no one in view. So when I despaired of seeing her again, I rose from my place and taking up the handkerchief, opened it, when there breathed from it a scent of musk which caused me so great delight I became as one in Paradise. Then I spread it before me and out dropped from it a delicate little scroll; whereupon I opened the paper which was perfumed with a delicious perfume, and therein were writ these couplets:—

> I sent to him a scroll that bore my plaint of love,
>   Writ in fine delicate hand; for writing proves man's skill:
> Then quoth to me my friend, "Why is thy writing thus;
>   So fine, so thin-drawn 'tis to read unsuitable?"
> Quoth I, "For that I'm fine-drawn, wasted, waxed thin;
>   Thus lovers' writ should be, for so Love wills his will."

And after casting my eyes on the beauty of the kerchief, I saw upon one of its two borders the following couplets worked in with the needle:—

> His cheek-down writeth (O fair fall the goodly scribe!)
>   Two lines on table of his face in Rayhán-hand:
> O the wild marvel of the Moon when comes he forth!
>   And when he bends, O shame to every Willow-wand!

And on the opposite border these two couplets were traced:—

> His cheek-down writeth on his cheek with ambergris on pearl
>   Two lines, like jet on apple li'en, the goodliest design:
> Slaughter is in those languid eyne whene'er a glance they deal,
>   And drunkenness in either cheek and not in any wine.

When I read the poetry on the handkerchief the flames of love darted into my heart, and yearning and pining redoubled their smart. So I took the kerchief and the scroll and went home, knowing no means to win my wish, for that I was incapable of conducting love-affairs and inexperienced in interpreting hints and tokens. Nor did I reach my home ere the night was far spent and I found the daughter of my uncle sitting in tears. But as soon as she saw me she wiped away the drops and came up to me, and took off my walking dress and asked me the reason of my absence, saying, "All the folk, Emirs and notables and merchants and others, assembled in our house; and the Kazi and the witnesses were also present at the appointed time. They ate and tarried awhile sitting to await thine appearance for the writing of the contract; and, when they despaired of thy presence, they dispersed and went their ways. And indeed," she added, "thy father raged with exceeding wrath by reason of this, and swore that he would not celebrate our marriage save during the coming year, for that he hath spent on these festivities great store of money." And she ended by asking, "What hath befallen thee this day to make thee delay till now? And why hast thou allowed that to happen which happened because of thine absence?" Answered I, "O daughter of mine uncle, question me not concerning what hath befallen me." Then I told her all that had passed from beginning to end, and showed her the handkerchief. She took the scroll and read what was written therein; and tears ran down her cheeks and she repeated these cinquains:—

> Who saith that Love at first of free will came,
>   Say him:—Thou liest! Love be grief and grame:
> Yet shall such grame and grief entail no shame;
>   All annals teach us one thing and the same—
>   Good current coin clipt coin we may not clepe!

> An please thou, say there's pleasure in thy pain,
>   Find Fortune's playful gambols glad and fain:
> Or happy blessings in th' unhappy's bane,
>   That joy or grieve with equal might and main:—
>   'Twixt phrase and antiphrase I'm all a-heap!

> But he, withal, whose days are summer-bright,
>   Whom maids e'er greet with smiling lips' delight;
> Whom spicey breezes fan in every site
>   And wins whate'er he wills, that happy wight
>   White-blooded coward heart should never keep!

Then she asked me, "What said she, and what signs made she to thee?" I answered, "She uttered not a word, but put her forefinger in her mouth, then joining it to her middle finger, laid both fingers on her bosom and pointed to the ground. Thereupon she withdrew her head and shut the wicket; and after that I saw her no more. However, she took my heart with her, so I sat till sundown, expecting her again to look out of the window; but she did it not; and, when I despaired of her, I rose from my seat and came home. This is my history and I beg thee to help me in this my sore calamity." Upon this she raised her face to me and said, "O son of mine uncle, if thou soughtest my eye, I would tear it for thee from its eyelids, and perforce I cannot but aid thee to thy desire and aid her also to her desire; for she is whelmed in passion for thee even as thou for her." Asked I, "And what is the interpretation of her signs?";" and Az-izah answered, "As for the putting her finger in her mouth, it showed that thou art to her as her soul to her body and that she would bite into union with thee with her wisdom teeth. As for the kerchief, it betokeneth that her breath of life is bound up in thee. As for the placing her two fingers on her bosom between her breasts, its explanation is that she saith:—The sight of thee may dispel my grief. For know, O my cousin, that she loveth thee and she trusteth in thee. This is my interpretation of her signs and, could I come and go at will, I would bring thee and her together in shortest time, and curtain you both with my skirt."

❧ ☙

GUY DE MAUPASSANT

Love: Three Pages from a Sportsman's Book

I have just read among the general news in one of the papers a drama of passion. He killed her and then he killed himself, so he must have loved her. What matters He or She? Their love alone matters to me; and it does not interest me because it moves me or astonishes me, or because it soft-ens me or makes me think, but because it recalls to my mind a remem-brance of my youth; a strange recollection of a hunting adventure where Love appeared to me, as the Cross appeared to the early Christians, in the midst of the heavens.

    I was born with all the instincts and the senses of primitive man, tempered by the arguments and the restraints of a civilized being. I am passionately fond of shooting, yet the sight of the wounded animal, of the blood on its feathers and on my hands, affects my heart so as almost to make it stop.

That year the cold weather set in suddenly toward the end of autumn, and I was invited by one of my cousins, Karl de Rauville, to go with him and shoot ducks on the marshes, at daybreak.

My cousin was a jolly fellow of forty, with red hair, very stout and bearded, a country gentleman, an amiable semi-brute, of a happy disposition and endowed with that Gallic wit which makes even mediocrity agreeable. He lived in a house, half farmhouse, half château, situated in a broad valley through which a river ran. The hills right and left were covered with woods, old manorial woods where magnificent trees still remained, and where the rarest feathered game in that part of France was to be found. Eagles were shot there occasionally, and birds of passage, such as rarely venture into our over-populated part of the country, invariably lighted amid these giant oaks, as if they knew or recognized some little corner of a primeval forest which had remained there to serve them as a shelter during their short nocturnal halt.

In the valley there were large meadows watered by trenches and separated by hedges; then, further on, the river, which up to that point had been kept between banks, expanded into a vast marsh. That marsh was the best shooting ground I ever saw. It was my cousin's chief care, and he kept it as a preserve. Through the rushes that covered it, and made it rustling and rough, narrow passages had been cut, through which the flat-bottomed boats, impelled and steered by poles, passed along silently over dead water, brushing up against the reeds and making the swift fish take refuge in the weeds, and the wild fowl, with their pointed, black heads, dive suddenly.

I am passionately fond of the water: of the sea, though it is too vast, too full of movement, impossible to hold; of the rivers which are so beautiful, but which pass on, and flee away; and above all of the marshes, where the whole unknown existence of aquatic animals palpitates. The marsh is an entire world in itself on the world of earth—a different world, which has its own life, its settled inhabitants and its passing travelers, its voices, its noises, and above all its mystery. Nothing is more impressive, nothing more disquieting, more terrifying occasionally, than a fen. Why should a vague terror hang over these low plains covered with water? Is it the low rustling of the rushes, the strange will-o'-the-wisp lights, the silence which prevails on calm nights, the still mists which hang over the surface like a shroud; or is it the almost inaudible splashing, so slight and so gentle, yet sometimes more terrifying than the cannons of men or the thunders of the skies, which make these marshes resemble countries one has dreamed of, terrible countries holding an unknown and dangerous secret?

No, something else belongs to it—another mystery, profounder and graver, floats amid these thick mists, perhaps the mystery of the creation itself! For was it not in stagnant and muddy water, amid the heavy humidity of moist land under the heat of the sun, that the first germ of life pulsated and expanded to the day?

I arrived at my cousin's in the evening. It was freezing hard enough to split the stones.

During dinner, in the large room whose sideboards, walls, and ceiling were covered with stuffed birds, with wings extended or perched on branches to which they were nailed—hawks, herons, owls, nightjars, buzzards, tiercels, vultures, falcons—my cousin who, dressed in a sealskin jacket, himself resembled some strange animal from a cold country, told me what preparations he had made for that same night.

We were to start at half past three in the morning, so as to arrive at the place which he had chosen for our watching-place at about half past four. On that spot a hut had been built of lumps of ice, so as to shelter us somewhat from the trying wind which precedes daybreak, a wind so cold as to tear the flesh like a saw, cut it like the blade of a knife, prick it like a poisoned sting, twist it like a pair of pincers, and burn it like fire.

My cousin rubbed his hands: "I have never known such a frost," he said; "it is already twelve degrees below zero at six o'clock in the evening."

I threw myself on to my bed immediately after we had finished our meal, and went to sleep by the light of a bright fire burning in the grate.

At three o'clock he woke me. In my turn, I put on a sheepskin, and found my cousin Karl covered with a bearskin. After having each swallowed two cups of scalding coffee, followed by glasses of liqueur brandy, we started, accompanied by a gamekeeper and our dogs, Plongeon and Pierrot.

From the first moment that I got outside, I felt chilled to the very marrow. It was one of those nights on which the earth seems dead with cold. The frozen air becomes resisting and palpable, such pain does it cause; no breath of wind moves it, it is fixed and motionless; it bites you, pierces through you, dries you, kills the trees, the plants, the insects, the small birds themselves, who fall from the branches on to the hard ground, and become stiff themselves under the grip of the cold.

The moon, which was in her last quarter and was inclining all to one side, seemed fainting in the midst of space, so weak that she was unable to wane, forced to stay up yonder, seized and paralyzed by the severity of the weather. She shed a cold, mournful light over the world, that dying and wan light which she gives us every month, at the end of her period.

Karl and I walked side by side, our backs bent, our hands in our pockets and our guns under our arms. Our boots, which were wrapped in wool so that we might be able to walk without slipping on the frozen river, made no sound, and I looked at the white vapor which our dogs' breath made.

We were soon on the edge of the marsh, and entered one of the lanes of dry rushes which ran through the low forest.

Our elbows, which touched the long, ribbonlike leaves, left a slight noise behind us, and I was seized, as I had never been before, by the powerful and singular emotion which marshes cause in me. This one was dead, dead from cold, since we were walking on it, in the middle of its population of dried rushes.

Suddenly, at the turn of one of the lanes, I perceived the ice-hut which had been constructed to shelter us. I went in, and as we had nearly an hour to wait before the wandering birds would awake, I rolled myself up in my rug in order to try and get warm. Then, lying on my back, I began to look at the misshapen moon, which had four horns through the vaguely transparent walls of this polar house. But the frost of the frozen marshes, the cold of these walls, the cold from the firmament penetrated me so terribly that I began to cough. My cousin Karl became uneasy.

"No matter if we do not kill much today," he said: "I do not want you to catch cold; we will light a fire." And he told the gamekeeper to cut some rushes.

We made a pile in the middle of our hut, which had a hole in the middle of the roof to let out the smoke, and when the red flames rose up to the clear, crystal blocks they began to melt, gently, imperceptibly, as if they were sweating. Karl, who had remained outside, called out to me: "Come and look here!" I went out of the hut and remained struck with astonishment. Our hut, in the shape of a cone, looked like an enormous diamond with a heart of fire, which had been suddenly planted there in the midst of the frozen water of the marsh. And inside we saw two fantastic forms, those of our dogs, who were warming themselves at the fire.

But a peculiar cry, a lost, a wandering cry, passed over our heads, and the light from our hearth showed us the wild birds. Nothing moves one so much as the first clamor of a life which one does not see, which passes through the somber air so quickly and so far off, just before the first streak of a winter's day appears on the horizon. It seems to me, at this glacial hour of dawn, as if that passing cry which is carried away by the wings of a bird is the sigh of a soul from the world!

"Put out the fire," said Karl, "it is getting daylight."

The sky was, in fact, beginning to grow pale, and the flights of ducks made long, rapid streaks which were soon obliterated on the sky.

A stream of light burst out into the night; Karl had fired, and the two dogs ran forward.

And then, nearly every minute, now he, now I, aimed rapidly as soon as the shadow of a flying flock appeared above the rushes. And Pierrot and Plongeon, out of breath but happy, retrieved the bleeding birds, whose eyes still, occasionally, looked at us.

The sun had risen, and it was a bright day with a blue sky, and we were thinking of taking our departure, when two birds with extended necks and outstretched wings, glided rapidly over our heads. I fired, and one of them fell almost at my feet. It was a teal, with a silver breast, and then, in the blue space above me, I heard a voice, the voice of a bird. It was a short, repeated, heart-rending lament; and the bird, the little animal that had been spared began to turn round in the blue sky, over our heads, looking at its dead companion which I was holding in my hand.

Karl was on his knees, his gun to his shoulder watching it eagerly, until it should be within shot. "You have killed the duck," he said, "and the drake will not fly away."

He certainly did not fly away; he circled over our heads continually, and continued his cries. Never have any groans of suffering pained me so much as that desolate appeal, as that lamentable reproach of this poor bird which was lost in space.

Occasionally he took flight under the menace of the gun which followed his movements, and seemed ready to continue his flight alone, but as he could not make up his mind to this, he returned to find his mate.

"Leave her on the ground," Karl said to me, "he will come within shot by and by." And he did indeed come near us, careless of danger, infatuated by his animal love, by his affection for his mate, which I had just killed.

Karl fired, and it was as if somebody had cut the string which held the bird suspended. I saw something black descend, and I heard the noise of a fall among the rushes. And Pierrot brought it to me.

I put them—they were already cold—into the same game bag, and I returned to Paris the same evening.

❧ ☙

THOMAS HARDY

from *Under the Greenwood Tree*

"I'm afraid Dick's a lost man," said the tranter.

"What?—no!" said Mail, implying by his manner that it was a far commoner thing for his ears to report what was not said than that his judgment should be at fault.

"Ay," said the tranter, still looking at Dick's unconscious advance. "I don't at all like what I see! There's too many o' them looks out of the winder without noticing anything; too much shining of boots; too much peeping round corners; too much looking at the clock; telling about clever things she did till you be sick of it, and then upon a hint to that effect a horrible silence about her. I've walked the path once in my life and know the country, naibours; and Dick's a lost man!" The tranter turned a quarter round and smiled a smile of miserable satire at the rising new moon, which happened to catch his eye.

The others' looks became far too serious at this announcement to allow them to speak; and they still regarded Dick in the distance.

" 'Twas his mother's fault," the tranter continued, shaking his head two or three times, "in asking the young woman to our party last Christmas. When I eyed the blue frock and light heels o' the maid, I had my thoughts directly. 'God bless thee, Dicky my sonny,' I said to myself, 'there's a delusion for thee!' "

"They seemed to be rather distant in manner last Sunday, I thought?" said Mail tentatively, as became one who was not a member of the family.

"Ay, that's a part of the zickness. Distance belongs to it, slyness belongs to it, quarest things on earth belongs to it! There, 'tmay as well come early as late s'far as I know. The sooner begun, the sooner over; for come it will."

from *Tess of the D'Urbervilles*

Tess's heart ached. There was no concealing from herself the fact that she loved Angel Clare, perhaps all the more passionately from knowing that the others had also lost their hearts to him. There is contagion in this sentiment, especially among women. And yet that same hungry heart of hers compassionated her friends. Tess's honest nature had fought against this, but too feebly, and the natural result had followed.

"I will never stand in your way, nor in the way of either of you!" she declared to Retty that night in the bedroom (her tears running down). "I can't help this, my dear! I don't think marrying is in his mind at all; but if he were even to ask me I should refuse him, as I should refuse any man."

"Oh! would you? Why?" said wondering Retty.

"It cannot be! But I will be plain. Putting myself quite on one side, I don't think he will choose either of you."

"I have never expected it—thought of it!" moaned Retty. "But O! I wish I was dead!"

The poor child, torn by a feeling which she hardly understood, turned to the other two girls who came upstairs just then.

"We be friends with her again," she said to them. "She thinks no more of his choosing her than we do."

So the reserve went off, and they were confiding and warm.

"I don't seem to care what I do now," said Marian, whose mood was tuned to its lowest bass. "I was going to marry a dairyman at Stickleford, who's asked me twice; but—my soul—I would put an end to myself rather'n be his wife now! Why don't ye speak, Izz?"

"To confess, then," murmured Izz, "I made sure today that he was going to kiss me as he held me; and I lay still against his breast, hoping and hoping, and never moved at all. But he did not. I don't like biding here at Talbothays any longer! I shall go home."

The air of the sleeping-chamber seemed to palpitate with the hopeless passion of the girls. They writhed feverishly under the oppressiveness of an emotion thrust on them by cruel Nature's law—an emotion which they had neither expected nor desired. The incident of the day had fanned the flame that was burning the inside of their hearts out, and the torture was almost more than they could endure. The differences which distinguished them as individuals were abstracted by this passion, and each was but portion of one organism called sex.

❧ ❧

SARAH ORNE JEWETT

from *The Country of the Pointed Firs*

It seemed to me that there were peculiarities of character in the region of Dunnet Landing yet, but I did not like to interrupt.

"Yes," said Mrs. Todd after a moment of meditation, "there was certain a good many curiosities of human natur' in this neighborhood years ago. There was more energy then, and in some the energy took a singular turn. In these days the young folks is all copy-cats, 'fraid to death they won't be all just alike; as for the old folks, they pray for the advantage o' bein' a little different."

"I ain't heard of a copy-cat this great many years," said Mrs. Fosdick, laughing; " 'twas a favorite term o' my grandfather's. No, I wa'n't thinking o' those things, but of them strange straying creatur's that used to rove the country. You don't see them now, or the ones that used to hive away in their own houses with some strange notion or other."

I thought again of Captain Littlepage, but my companions were not reminded of his name; and there was brother William at Green Island, whom we all three knew.

"I was talking o' poor Joanna the other day. I hadn't thought of her for a great while," said Mrs. Fosdick abruptly. "Mis' Brayton an' I recalled her as we sat together sewing. She was one o' your peculiar persons, wa'-n't she? Speaking of such persons," she turned to explain to me, "there was a sort of a nun or hermit person lived out there for years all alone on Shell-heap Island. Miss Joanna Todd, her name was,—a cousin o' Almiry's late husband."

I expressed my interest, but as I glanced at Mrs. Todd I saw that she was confused by sudden affectionate feeling and unmistakable desire for reticence.

"I never want to hear Joanna laughed about," she said anxiously.

"Nor I," answered Mrs. Fosdick reassuringly. "She was crossed in love,—that was all the matter to begin with; but as I look back, I can see that Joanna was one doomed from the first to fall into a melancholy. She retired from the world for good an' all, though she was a well-off woman. All she wanted was to get away from folks; she thought she wasn't fit to live with anybody, and wanted to be free. Shell-heap Island come to her from her father, and first thing folks knew she'd gone off out there to live, and left word she didn't want no company. 'Twas a bad place to get to, unless the wind an' tide were just right; 'twas hard work to make a landing."

"What time of year was this?" I asked.

"Very late in the summer," said Mrs. Fosdick. "No, I never could laugh at Joanna, as some did. She set everything by the young man, an' they were going to marry in about a month, when he got bewitched with a girl 'way up the bay, and married her, and went off to Massachusetts. He wasn't well thought of,—there were those who thought Joanna's money was what had tempted him; but she'd given him her whole heart, an' she wa'n't so young as she had been. All her hopes were built on marryin', an' havin' a real home and somebody to look to; she acted just like a bird when its nest is spoilt. The day after she heard the news she was in dreadful woe, but the next she came to herself very quiet, and took the horse and wagon, and drove fourteen miles to the lawyer's, and signed a paper givin' her half of the farm to her brother. They never had got along very well together, but he didn't want to sign it, till she acted so distressed that he gave in. Edward Todd's wife was a good woman, who felt very bad indeed, and used every argument with Joanna; but Joanna took a poor old boat that had been her father's and lo'ded in a few things, and off she put all alone, with a good land breeze, right out to sea. Edward Todd ran down to the beach, an' stood there cryin' like a boy to see her go, but she was out o' hearin'. She never stepped foot on the mainland again long as she lived."

"How large an island is it? How did she manage in winter?" I asked.

"Perhaps thirty acres, rocks and all," answered Mrs. Todd, taking up the story gravely. "There can't be much of it that the salt spray don't fly over in storms. No, 'tis a dreadful small place to make a world of; it has a different look from any of the other islands, but there's a sheltered cove on the south side, with mud-flats across one end of it at low water where there's excellent clams, and the big shell-heap keeps some o' the wind off a little house her father took the trouble to build when he was a young man. They said there was an old house built o' logs there before that, with a kind of natural cellar in the rock under it. He used to stay out there days to a time, and anchor a little sloop he had, and dig clams to fill it, and sail up to Portland. They said the dealers always gave him an extra price, the clams were so noted. Joanna used to go out and stay with him. They were always great companions, so she knew just what 'twas out there. There was a few sheep that belonged to her brother an' her, but she bargained for him to come and get them on the edge o' cold weather. Yes, she desired him to come for the sheep; an' his wife thought perhaps Joanna'd return, but he said no, an' lo'ded the bo't with warm things an' what he thought she'd need through the winter. He come home with the sheep an' left the other things by the house, but she never so much as looked out o' the window. She done it for a penance. She must have wanted to see Edward by that time."

Mrs. Fosdick was fidgeting with eagerness to speak.

"Some thought the first cold snap would set her ashore, but she always remained," concluded Mrs. Todd soberly.

"Talk about the men not having any curiosity!" exclaimed Mrs. Fosdick scornfully. "Why, the waters round Shell-heap Island were white with sails all that fall. 'Twas never called no great of a fishin'-ground before. Many of 'em made excuse to go ashore to get water at the spring; but at last she spoke to a bo't-load, very dignified and calm, and said that she'd like it better if they'd make a practice of getting water to Black Island or somewheres else and leave her alone, except in case of accident or trouble. But there was one man who had always set everything by her from a boy. He'd have married her if the other hadn't come about an' spoilt his chance, and he used to get close to the island, before light, on his way out fishin', and throw a little bundle way up the green slope front o' the house. His sister told me she happened to see, the first time, what a pretty choice he made o' useful things that a woman would feel lost without. He stood off fishin', and could see them in the grass all day, though sometimes she'd come out and walk right by them. There was other bo'ts near, out after mackerel. But early next morning his present was gone. He didn't presume too much, but once he took her a nice firkin o' things he got up to Portland, and when spring come he landed her a hen and chickens in a nice little coop. There was a good many old friends had Joanna on their minds."

"Yes," said Mrs. Todd, losing her sad reserve in the growing sympathy of these reminiscences. "How everybody used to notice whether there was smoke out of the chimney! The Black Island folks could see her with their spy-glass, and if they'd ever missed getting some sign o' life they'd have sent notice to her folks. But after the first year or two Joanna was more and more forgotten as an every-day charge. Folks lived very simple in those days, you know," she continued, as Mrs. Fosdick's knitting was taking much thought at the moment. "I expect there was always plenty of driftwood thrown up, and a poor failin' patch of spruces covered all the north side of the island, so she always had something to burn. She was very fond of workin' in the garden ashore, and that first summer she began to till the little field out there, and raised a nice parcel o' potatoes. She could fish, o' course, and there was all her clams an' lobsters. You can always live well in any wild place by the sea when you'd starve to death up country, except 'twas berry time. Joanna had berries out there, blackberries at least, and there was a few herbs in case she needed them. Mullein in great quantities and a plant o' wormwood I remember seeing once when I stayed there, long before she fled out to Shell-heap. Yes, I recall the wormwood, which is always a planted herb, so there must have been folks there before the Todds' day. A growin' bush makes the best gravestone; I expect that wormwood always stood for somebody's solemn monument. Catnip, too, is a very endurin' herb about an old place."

"But what I want to know is what she did for other things," interrupted Mrs. Fosdick. "Almiry, what did she do for clothin' when she needed to replenish, or risin' for her bread, or the piece-bag that no woman can live long without?"

"Or company," suggested Mrs. Todd. "Joanna was one that loved her friends. There must have been a terrible sight o' long winter evenin's that first year."

"There was her hens," suggested Mrs. Fosdick, after reviewing the melancholy situation. "She never wanted the sheep after that first season. There wa'n't no proper pasture for sheep after the June grass was past, and she ascertained the fact and couldn't bear to see them suffer; but the chickens done well. I remember sailin' by one spring afternoon, an' seein' the coops out front o' the house in the sun. How long was it before you went out with the minister? You were the first ones that ever really got ashore to see Joanna."

I had been reflecting upon a state of society which admitted such personal freedom and a voluntary hermitage. There was something medieval in the behavior of poor Joanna todd under a disappointment of the heart. The two women had drawn closer together, and were talking on, quite unconscious of a listener.

"Poor Joanna!" said Mrs. Todd again, and sadly shook her head as if there were things one could not speak about.

"I called her a great fool," declared Mrs. Fosdick, with spirit, "but I pitied her then, and I pity her far more now. Some other minister would have been a great help to her,—one that preached self-forgetfulness and doin' for others to cure our own ills; but Parson Dimick was a vague person, well meanin', but very numb in his feelin's. I don't suppose at that troubled time Joanna could think of any way to mend her troubles except to run off and hide."

"Mother used to say she didn't see how Joanna lived without having nobody to do for, getting her own meals and tending her own poor self day in an' day out," said Mrs. Todd sorrowfully.

"There was the hens," repeated Mrs. Fosdick kindly. "I expect she soon came to makin' folks o' them. No, I never went to work to blame Joanna, as some did. She was full o' feeling, and her troubles hurt her more than she could bear. I see it all now as I couldn't when I was young."

ᏣᎦ ᏨᎤ

HENRY JAMES

from *Daisy Miller: A Study*

"I am afraid your habits are those of a flirt," said Winterbourne, gravely.

"Of course they are," she cried, giving him her little smiling stare again. "I'm a fearful, frightful flirt! Did you ever hear of a nice girl that was not? But I suppose you will tell me now that I am not a nice girl."

"You're a very nice girl, but I wish you would flirt with me, and me only," said Winterbourne.

"Ah! thank you, thank you very much; you are the last man I should think of flirting with. As I have had the pleasure of informing you, you are too stiff."

"You say that too often," said Winterbourne.

Daisy gave a delighted laugh. "If I could have the sweet hope of making you angry, I would say it again."

"Don't do that; when I am angry I'm stiffer than ever. But if you won't flirt with me, do cease at least to flirt with your friend at the piano; they don't understand that sort of thing here."

"I thought they understood nothing else!" exclaimed Daisy.

"Not in young unmarried women."

"It seems to me much more proper in young unmarried women than in old married ones," Daisy declared.

"Well," said Winterbourne, "when you deal with natives you must go by the custom of the place. Flirting is a purely American custom; it doesn't exist here. So when you show yourself in public with Mr. Giovanelli, and without your mother—"

"Gracious! poor mother!" interposed Daisy.

"Though you may be flirting, Mr. Giovanelli is not; he means something else."

"He isn't preaching, at any rate," said Daisy, with vivacity. "And if you want very much to know, we are neither of us flirting; we are too good friends for that; we are very intimate friends."

"Ah!" rejoined Winterbourne, "if you are in love with each other it is another affair."

She had allowed him up to this point to talk so frankly that he had no expectation of shocking her by this ejaculation; but she immediately got up, blushing visibly, and leaving him to exclaim mentally that little American flirts were the queerest creatures in the world.

❧ ❧

KATE CHOPIN

Caline

The sun was just far enough in the west to send inviting shadows. In the centre of a small field, and in the shade of a haystack which was there, a girl lay sleeping. She had slept long and soundly, when something awoke her as suddenly as if it had been a blow. She opened her eyes and stared a moment up in the cloudless sky. She yawned and stretched her long brown legs and arms, lazily. Then she arose, never minding the bits of straw that clung to her black hair, to her red bodice, and the blue cotonade skirt that did not reach her naked ankles.

The log cabin in which she dwelt with her parents was just outside the enclosure in which she had been sleeping. Beyond was a small clearing that did duty as a cotton field. All else was dense wood, except the long stretch that curved round the brow of the hill, and in which glittered the steel rails of the Texas and Pacific road.

When Caline emerged from the shadow she saw a long train of passenger coaches standing in view, where they must have stopped abruptly. It was that sudden stopping which had awakened her; for such a thing had not happened before within her recollection, and she looked stupid, at first, with astonishment. There seemed to be something wrong with the engine; and some of the passengers who dismounted went forward to investigate the trouble. Others came strolling along in the direction of the cabin, where Caline stood under an old gnarled mulberry tree, staring. Her father had halted his mule at the end of the cotton row, and stood staring also, leaning upon his plow.

There were ladies in the party. They walked awkwardly in their high-heeled boots over the rough, uneven ground, and held up their skirts mincingly. They twirled parasols over their shoulders, and laughed immoderately at the funny things which their masculine companions were saying.

They tried to talk to Caline, but could not understand the French patois with which she answered them.

One of the men—a pleasant-faced youngster—drew a sketch book from his pocket and began to make a picture of the girl. She stayed motionless, her hands behind her, and her wide eyes fixed earnestly upon him.

Before he had finished there was a summons from the train; and all went scampering hurriedly away. The engine screeched, it sent a few lazy puffs into the still air, and in another moment or two had vanished, bearing its human cargo with it.

Caline could not feel the same after that. She looked with new and strange interest upon the trains of cars that passed so swiftly back and forth across her vision, each day; and wondered whence these people came, and whither they were going.

Her mother and father could not tell her, except to say that they came form "loin là bas," and were going "Djieu sait é où."

One day she walked miles down the track to talk with the old flagman, who stayed down there by the big water tank. Yes, he knew. Those people came from the great cities in the north, and were going to the city in the south. He knew all about the city; it was a grand place. He had lived there once. His sister lived there now; and she would be glad enough to have so fine a girl as Caline to help her cook and scrub, and tend the babies. And he thought Caline might earn as much as five dollars a month, in the city.

So she went; in a new cotonade, and her Sunday shoes; with a sacredly guarded scrawl that the flagman sent to his sister.

The woman lived in a tiny, stuccoed house, with green blinds, and three wooden steps leading down to the banquette. There seemed to be hundreds like it along the street. Over the house tops loomed the tall masts of ships, and the hum of the French market could be heard on a still morning.

Caline was at first bewildered. She had to readjust all her preconceptions to fit the reality of it. The flagman's sister was a kind and gentle task-mistress. At the end of a week or two she wanted to know how the girl liked it all. Caline liked it very well, for it was pleasant, on Sunday afternoons, to stroll with the children under the great, solemn sugar sheds; or to sit upon the compressed cotton bales, watching the stately steamers, the graceful boats, and noisy little tugs that plied the waters of the Mississippi. And it filled her with agreeable excitement to go to the French market, where the handsome Gascon butchers were eager to present their compliments and little Sunday bouquets to the pretty Acadian girl; and to throw fistfuls of *lagniappe* into her basket.

When the woman asked her again after another week if she were still pleased, she was not so sure. And again when she questioned Caline the girl turned away, and went to sit behind the big, yellow cistern, to cry unobserved. For she knew now that it was not the great city and its crowds of people she had so eagerly sought; but the pleasant-faced boy, who had made her picture that day under the mulberry tree.

❧ ❧

WILLA CATHER

A Resurrection

"I contend that you ought to have set them house plants different, Margie, closer around the pulpit rail." Mrs. Skimmons retreated to the back of the church to take in the full effect of the decorations and give further directions to Margie. Mrs. Skimmons had a way of confining her services as chairman of the decorative committee to giving directions, and the benefit of her artistic eye.

Miss Margie good naturedly readjusted the "house plants" and asked, "How is that?"

"Well, it's some better," admitted Mrs. Skimmons, critically, "but I contend we ought to have had some evergreens, even if they do look like Christmas. And now that you've used them hy'cinths for the lamp brackets, what are you goin' to put on the little stand before the pulpit?"

"Martin Dempster promised to bring some Easter lilies up from Kansas City. I thought we'd put them there. He ought to be here pretty soon. I heard the train whistle in a bit ago."

"That's three times he's been to Kansas City this month. I don't see how he can afford it. Everybody knows the old ferry boat can't pay him very well, and he wasn't never much of a business man. It beats me how some people can fly high on nothing. There's his railroad fare and his expenses while he is there. I can't make out what he's doin' down there so much. More'n likely it's some girl or other he's goin' down the river after again. Now that you and your mother have brought up his baby for him, it would be just like Mart Dempster to go trapesin' off and marry some giddy thing and maybe fetch her up here for you to bring up, too. I can't never think he's acted right by you, Margie."

"So long as I'm satisfied, I can't see why it should trouble other people, Mrs. Skimmons."

"O, certainly not, if you are goin' to take offense. I meant well."

Margie turned her face away to avoid Mrs. Skimmons' scrutinizing gaze, and went on quietly with the decorations.

Miss Margie was no longer a girl. Most of the girls of her set who had frolicked and gone to school with her had married and moved away. Yet, though she had passed that dread meridian of thirty, and was the village schoolmistress to boot, she was not openly spoken of as an old maid. When a woman retains much of her beauty and youthful vigor the world, even the petty provincial world, feels a delicacy about applying to her that condemning title that when once adopted is so irrevocable. Then Miss Marjorie Pierson had belonged to one of the best families in the old days, before Brownville was shorn of its glory and importance by the railroad maneuvers that had left everybody poor. She had not always taught towheaded urchins for a living, but had once lived in a big house on the hill and gone to boarding school and driven her own phaeton, and entertained company from Omaha. These facts protected her somewhat.

She was a tall woman, finely, almost powerfully built and admirably developed. She carried herself with an erect pride that ill accorded with the humble position as the village schoolmistress. Her features were regular and well cut, but her face was comely chiefly because of her vivid coloring and her deeply set gray eyes, that were serious and frank like a man's. She was one of those women one sometimes sees, designed by nature in her more artistic moments, especially fashioned for all the fullness of life; for large experiences and the great world where a commanding personality is felt and valued, but condemned by circumstances to poverty, obscurity and all manner of pettiness. There are plenty of such women, who were made to ride in carriages and wear jewels and grace first nights at the opera, who, through some unaccountable blunder of stage management in this little *comédie humaine*, have the wrong parts assigned them, and cook for farm hands, or teach a country school like this one, or make gowns for ugly women and pad them into some semblance of shapeliness, while they themselves, who need no such artificial treatment, wear cast-offs; women who were made to rule, but who are doomed to serve. There are plenty of living masterpieces that are as completely lost to the world as the lost nine books of Sappho, or as the Grecian marbles that were broken under the barbarians' battle axes. The world is full of waste of this sort.

While Margie was arranging the "house plants" about the pulpit platform, and the other member of the committee was giving her the benefit of her advice, a man strode lazily into the church carrying a small traveling bag and a large pasteboard box.

"There you are, Miss Margie," he cried, throwing the box on the platform; and sitting down in the front pew he proceeded to fan himself with his soft felt hat.

"O, Martin, they are beautiful! They are the first things that have made me feel a bit like Easter."

"One of 'em is for you, Miss Margie, to wear tomorrow," said Martin bashfully. Then he hastened to add, "I feel more like it's Fourth of July than Easter. I'm right afraid of this weather, Mrs. Skimmons. It'll coax all the buds out on the fruit trees and then turn cold and nip 'em. And the buds'll just be silly enough to come out when they are asked. You've done well with your decorations, Mrs. Skimmons."

Mrs. Skimmons looked quizzically at Martin, puzzled by this unusual loquaciousness.

"Well, yes," she admitted, in a satisfied tone, "I think we've done right well considerin' this tryin' weather. I'm about prostrated with the heat myself. How are things goin' down in Kansas City? You must know a good deal about everything there, seein' you go down so much lately."

" 'Bout the same," replied Martin, in an uncommunicative tone which evidently offended Mrs. Skimmons.

"Well," remarked that lady briskly, "I guess I can't help you no more now, Margie. I've got to run home and see to them boys of mine. Mr. Dempster can probably help you finish." With this contemptuous use of his surname as a final thrust, Mrs. Skimmons departed.

Martin leaned back in the pew and watched Margie arranging the lilies. He was a big broad-chested fellow, who wore his broad shoulders carelessly and whose full muscular throat betrayed unusual physical strength. His face was simple and honest, bronzed by the weather, and with deep lines about the mild eyes that told that his simple life had not been altogether negative, and that he had not sojourned in this world for forty years without leaving a good deal of himself by the wayside.

"I didn't thank you for the lilies, Martin. It was very kind of you," said Margie, breaking the silence.

"O, that's all right. I just thought you'd like 'em," and he again relapsed into silence, his eyes following the sunny path of the first venturesome flies of the season that buzzed in and out of the open windows. Then his gaze strayed back to where the sunlight fell on Miss Margie and her lilies.

"The fact is, Miss Margie, I've got something to tell you. You know for a long time I've thought I'd like to quit the ferry and get somewhere where I'd have a chance to get ahead. There's no use trying to get ahead in Brownville, for there's nothing to get ahead of. Of late years I wanted to get a job on the lower Mississippi again, on a boat, you know. I've been going down to Kansas City lately to see some gentlemen who own boats down the river, and I've got a place at last, a first rate one that will pay well, and it looks like I could hold it as long as I want it."

Miss Margie looked up from the lilies she was holding and asked sharply, "Then you are going away, Martin?"

"Yes, and I'm going away this time so you won't never have to be ashamed of me for it."

"I ought to be glad on your account. You're right, there's nothing here for you, nor anybody else. But we'll miss you very much, Martin. There are so few of the old crowd left. Will you sell the ferry?"

"I don't just know about that. I'd kind of hate to sell the old ferry. You see I haven't got things planned out very clear yet. After all it's just the going away that matters most."

"Yes, it's just the going away that matters most," repeated Miss Margie slowly, while she watched something out of the window. "But of course you'll have to come back often to see Bobbie."

"Well, you see I was counting on taking Bobbie with me. He's about old enough now, and I don't think I could bear to be apart from him."

"You are not going to take Bobbie away from us, Martin?" cried Miss Margie in a tone of alarm.

"Why yes, Miss Margie. Of course I'll take him, and if you say so—"

"But I don't say so," cried Miss Margie in a tone of tremulous excitement. "He is not old enough, it would be cruel to take a bit of a child knocking around the world like that."

"I can't go without Bobbie. But, Miss Margie—"

"Martin," cried Miss Margie—she had risen to her feet now and stood facing him, her eyes full of gathering anger and her breast rising and falling perceptibly with her quick-drawn breathing—"Martin, you shall not take Bobbie away from me. He's more my child than yours, anyway. I've been through everything for him. When he was sick I walked the floor with him all night many a time and went with a headache to my work next morning. I've lived and worked and hoped just for him. And I've done it in the face of everything. Not a day passes but some old woman throws it in my face that I'm staying here drivelling my life out to take care of the child of the man who jilted me. I've borne all this because I loved him, because he is all my niggardly life has given me to love. My God! a woman must have something. Every woman's got to have. And I've given him everything, all that I'd starved and beat down and crucified in me. You brought him to me when he was a little wee baby, the only thing of your life you've ever given to mine. From the first time I felt his little cheek on mine I knew that a new life had come into me, and through another woman's weakness and selfishness I had at least one of the things which was mine by right. He was a helpless little baby, dependent on me for everything, and I loved him for just that. He needed my youth and strength and blood, and the very warmth of my body, and he was the only creature on earth who did. In spite of yourself you've given me half my womanhood and you shall not take it from me now. You shall not take it from me now!"

Martin heard her going, he heard the sob that broke as she reached the door but he did not stir from his seat or lift his bowed head. He sat staring at the sunlit spot in front of the pulpit where she had stood with the lilies in her hand, looking to him, somehow, despite her anger, like the pictures of the Holy woman who is always painted with lilies.

When the twilight began to fall and the shadows in the church grew dim he got up and went slowly down to the river toward the ferry boat. Back over the horseshoe-shaped gulch in which the town is built the sky was glorious with red splotches of sunset cloud just above the horizon. The big trees on the bluffs were tossing their arms restlessly in the breeze that blew up the river, and across on the level plains of the Missouri side the lights of the farm houses began to glow through the soft humid atmosphere of the April night. The smell of burning grass was everywhere, and the very air tasted of spring.

The boat hands had all gone to supper, and Martin sat down on the empty deck and lit his pipe. When he was perplexed or troubled he always went to the river. For the river means everything to Brownville folk; it has been at once their making and their undoing.

Brownville was not always the sleepy, deserted town that it is today, full of empty buildings and idle men and of boys growing up without aim or purpose. No, the town has had a history, a brief, sad little history which recalls the scathing epigram that Herr Heine once applied to M. Alfred de Musset; it is a young town with a brilliant past. It was the first town built on the Nebraska side of the river, and there, sheltered by the rugged bluffs and washed by the restless Missouri, a new state struggled into existence and proclaimed its right to be. Martin Dempster was the first child born on the Nebraska side, and he had seen the earth broken for the first grave. There, in Senator Tipton's big house on the hillside, when he was a very little boy, he had heard the first telegraph wire ever stretched across the Missouri click its first message that made the blood leap in all his boyish veins, "Westward the course of Empire takes it way."

In the days of his boyhood Brownville was the head of river navigation and the old steamboat trade. He had seen the time when a dozen river steamers used to tie up at the wharves at one time, and unload supplies for the wagon trains that went overland to Pikes Peak and Cherry Creek, that is Denver now. He had sat on the upper veranda of the old Marsh House and listened to the strange talk of the foreign potentates that the *Montana* and *Silver Heels* used to bring up the river and who stopped there on their way into the big game country. He had listened with them to the distant throbbing of the engines that once stirred the lonely sand-split waters of the old river, and watched the steamers swing around the bend at night, glittering with lights, with bands of music playing on their decks and the sparks from the smokestacks blowing back into the darkness. He had sat under the gigantic oak before the Lone Tree saloon and heard the teamsters of the wagon trains and the boat hands exchange stories of the mountains and alkali deserts for stories of the busy world and its doings, filling up the pauses in conversation with old frontier songs and the strumming of banjos. And he could remember only too well when the old *Hannibal* brought up the steel rails for the Union Pacific Railroad, the road that was to kill Brownville.

Brownville had happened because of the steamboat trade, and when the channel of the river had become so uncertain and capricious that navigation was impossible, Brownville became impossible too, and all the prosperity that the river had given it took back in its muddy arms again and swept away. And ever since, overcome by shame and remorse, it had been trying to commit suicide by burying itself in the sand. Every year the channel grows narrower and more treacherous and its waters more turbid. Perhaps it does not even remember any more how it used to hurry along into the great aorta of the continent, or the throb of the wheels of commerce that used to beat up the white foam on its dark waters, or how a certain old Indian chief desired to be buried sitting bolt upright upon the bluff that he might always watch the steamers go up and down the river.

So it was that the tide went out at Brownville, and the village became a little Pompeii buried in bonded indebtedness. The sturdy pioneers moved away and the "river rats" drifted in, a nondescript people who came up the river from nowhere, and bought up the big houses for a song, cut down the tall oaks and cedars in the yards for firewood, and plowed up the terraces for potato patches, and were content after the manner of their kind. The river gypsies are a peculiar people; like the Egyptians of old their lives are for and of the river. They each have their skiff and burn driftwood and subsist on catfish and play their banjos, and forget that the world moves—if they ever knew it. The river is the school and religion of these people.

And Martin Dempster was one of them. When most of the better people of the town moved away Martin remained loyal to the river. The feeling of near kinship with the river had always been in him, he was born with it. When he was a little boy he had continually run away from school, and when his father hunted for him he always found him about the river. River boys never take kindly to education; they are always hankering for the water. In summer its muddy coolness is irresistibly alluring, and in winter its frozen surface is equally so. The continual danger which attends its treacherous currents only adds to its enticing charm. They know the river in all its changes and fluctuations as a stock broker knows the markets.

When Martin was a boy his father owned a great deal of Brownville real estate and was considered a wealthy man. Town property was a marketable article in those days, though now no real estate ever sells in Brownville—except cemetery lots. But Martin never cared for business. The first ambition he was ever guilty of was that vague yearning which stirs in the breasts of all river boys, to go down the river sometime, clear down, as far as the river goes. Then, a little later, when he heard an old stump speaker who used to end all his oratorical flights with a figure about "rearing here in the Missouri Valley a monument as high as the thought of man," he had determined to be a great navigator and to bring glory and honor to the town of Brownville. And here he was, running the old ferry boat that was the last and meanest of all the flock of mighty river crafts. So it goes. When we are very little we all dream of driving a street car or wearing a policeman's star or keeping a peanut stand; and generally, after catching at the clouds a few times, we live to accomplish our juvenile ambitions more nearly than we ever realize.

When he was sixteen Martin had run away as cabin boy on the *Silver Heels*. Gradually he had risen to the pilot house on the same boat. People wondered why Marjorie Pierson should care for a fellow of that stamp, but the fact that she did care was no secret. Perhaps it was just because he was simple and unworldly and lived for what he liked best that she cared.

Martin's downfall dated back to the death of the steamboat trade at Brownville. His fate was curiously linked with that of his river. When the channel became so choked with sand that the steamers quit going up to Brownville, Martin went lower down the river, making his headquarters at St. Louis. And there the misfortune of his life befell him. There was a girl of French extraction, an Aimée de Mar, who lived down in the shipping district. She lived by her wits principally. She was just a wee mite of a thing, with brown hair that fluffed about her face and eyes that were large and soft like those of Guido's penitent Magdalen, and which utterly belied her. You would wonder how so small a person could make so much harm and trouble in the world. Not that she was naturally malignant or evil at all. She simply wanted the nice things of this world and was determined to have them, no matter who paid for them, and she enjoyed life with a frank sort of hedonism, quite regardless of what her pleasure might cost others. Martin was a young man who stood high in favor with the captains and boat owners and who seemed destined to rise. So Aimée concentrated all her energies to one end, and her project was not difficult of accomplishment under the circumstances. A wiser or worse man would have met her on her own ground and managed her easily enough. But Martin was slow at life as he had been at books, heady and loyal and foolish, the kind of man who pays for his follies right here in this world and who keeps his word if he walks alive into hell for it. The upshot of it was that, after writing

to Margie the hardest letter he ever wrote in his life, he married Aimée
de Mar.

Then followed those three years that had left deep lines in Martin's face and gray hairs over his temples. Once married Aimée did not
sing *"Toujours j'aimais!"* any more. She attired herself gorgeously in satins
and laces and perfumed herself heavily with *violettes de Parme* and spent her
days visiting her old friends of the milliners' and hairdressers' shops and
impressing them with her elegance. The evenings she would pass in a box
at some second-rate theatre, ordering ices brought to her between the
acts. When Martin was in town he was dragged willy-nilly through all
these absurdly vulgar performances, and when he was away matters
went even worse. This would continue until Martin's salary was exhausted, after which Aimée would languish at home in bitter resentment
against the way the world is run, and consoling herself with innumerable
cigarettes de Caporale until pay day. Then she would blossom forth in a new
outfit and the same program would be repeated. After running him
heavily into debt, by some foolish attempt at a flirtation with a man on
board his own boat, she drove Martin into a quarrel which resulted in a
fierce hand-to-hand scrimmage on board ship and was the cause of his
immediate discharge. In December, while he was hunting work, living
from hand to mouth and hiding from his creditors, his baby was born.
"As if," Aimée remarked, "the weather were not disagreeable enough
without that!"

In the spring, at Mardi-Gras time, Martin happened to be out of
town. Aimée was thoroughly weary of domesticity and poverty and of
being shut up in the house. She strained her credit for all it was worth
for one last time, and on the first night of the fête, though it was bitterly
cold, she donned an airy domino and ran away from her baby, and went
down the river in a steam launch, hung with colored lights and manned
by some gentlemen who were neither sober nor good boatmen. The
launch was overturned a mile below the Point, and three of the party
went to the bottom. Two days later poor little Aimée was picked up in
the river, the yellow and black velvet of her butterfly dress covered with
mud and slime, and her gay gauze wings frozen fast to her pretty shoulders.

So Martin spoke the truth when he said that everything that had
ever affected his life one way or the other was of the river. To him the
river stood for Providence, for fate.

Some of the saddest fables of ancient myth are of the fates of the
devotees of the River Gods. And the worship of the River Gods is by

no means dead. Martin had been a constant worshipper and a most faithful one, and here he was at forty, not so well off as when he began the world for himself at sixteen. But let no one dream that because the wages of the River God cannot be counted in coin or numbered in herds of cattle, that they are never paid. Its real wages are of the soul alone, and not visible to any man. To all who follow it faithfully, and not for gain but from inclination, the river gives a certain simpleness of life and freshness of feeling and receptiveness of mind not to be found among the money changers of the market place. It feeds his imagination and trains his eye, and gives him strength and courage. And it gives him something better than these, if aught can be better. It gives him, no matter how unlettered he may be, something of that intimate sympathy with inanimate nature that is the base of all poetry, something of that which the high-faced rocks of the gleaming Sicilian shore gave Theocritus.

Martin had come back to Brownville to live down the memory of his disgrace. He might have found a much easier task without going so far. Every day for six years he had met the reproachful eyes of his neighbors unflinchingly, and he knew that his mistake was neither condoned nor forgotten. Brownville people have nothing to do but to keep such memories perennially green. If he had been a coward he would have run away from this perpetual condemnation. But he had the quiet courage of all men who have wrestled hand to hand with the elements, and who have found out how big and terrible nature is. So he stayed.

Miss margie left the church with a stinging sense of shame at what she had said, and wondered if she were losing her mind. For the women who are cast in that tragic mould are always trying to be like their milder sisters, and are always flattering themselves that they have succeeded. And when some fine day the fire flames out they are more astonished and confounded than anyone else can be. Miss Margie walked rapidly through the dusty road, called by courtesy a street, and crossed the vacant building lots unmindful that her skirts were switching among the stalks of last year's golden rods and sunflowers. As she reached the door a little boy in much abbreviated trousers ran around the house from the back yard and threw his arms about her. She kissed him passionately and felt better. The child seemed to justify her in her own eyes. Then she led him in and began to get supper.

"Don't make my tea as strong as you did last night, Margie. It seems like you ought to know how to make it by this time," said the querulous invalid from the corner.

"All right, mother. Why mother, you worked my buttonholes in black silk instead of blue!"

"How was I to tell, with my eyes so bad? You ought to have laid it out for me. But there is always something wrong about everything I do," complained the old lady in an injured tone.

"No, there isn't, it was all my fault. You can work a better buttonhole than I can, any day."

"Well, in my time they used to say so," said Mrs. Pierson somewhat mollified.

Margie was practically burdened with the care of two children. Her mother was crippled with rheumatism, and only at rare intervals could "help about the house." She insisted on doing a little sewing for her daughter, but usually it had to come out and be done over again after she went to bed. With the housework and the monotonous grind of her work at school, Miss Margie had little time to think about her misfortunes, and so perhaps did not feel them as keenly as she would otherwise have done. It was a perplexing matter, too, to meet even the modest expenses of their small household with the salary paid a country teacher. She had never touched a penny of the money Martin paid for the child's board, but put it regularly in the bank for the boy's own use when he should need it.

After supper she put her mother to bed and then put on the red wrapper that she always wore in the evening hour that she had alone with Bobbie. The woman in one dies hard, and after she had ceased to dress for men the old persistent instinct made her wish to be attractive to the boy. She heard him say his "piece" that he was to recite at the Easter service tomorrow, and then sat down in the big rocking chair before the fire and Bobbie climbed up into her lap.

"Bobbie, I want to tell you a secret that we mustn't tell grandma yet. Your father is talking about taking you away."

"Away on the ferry boat?" his eyes glistened with excitement.

"No dear, away down the river; away from grandma and me for good."

"But I won't go away from you and grandma, Miss Margie. Don't you remember how I cried all night the time you were away?"

"Yes, Bobbie, I know, but you must always do what your father says. But you wouldn't like to go, would you?"

"Of course I wouldn't. There wouldn't be anybody to pick up chips, or go to the store, or take care of you and grandma, 'cause I'm the only boy you've got."

"Yes, Bobbie, that's just it, dear heart, you're the only boy I've got!"

And Miss Margie gathered him up in her arms and laid her hot cheek on his and fell to sobbing, holding him closer and closer.

Bobbie lay very still, not even complaining about the tears that wetted his face. But he wondered very much why anyone should cry who had not cut a finger or been stung by a wasp or trodden on a sand-burr. Poor little Bobbie, he had so much to learn! And while he was wondering he fell asleep, and Miss Margie undressed him and put him to bed.

During the five years since that night when Marjorie Pierson and her mother, in the very face of the village gossips, had gone to the train to meet Martin Dempster when he came back to Brownville, worn and weak with fever, and had taken his wailing little baby from his arms, giving it the first touch of womanly tenderness it had ever known, the two lonely women had grown to love it better than anything else in the world, better even than they loved each other. Marjorie had felt every ambition of her girlhood die out before the strength of the vital instinct which this child awakened and satisfied within her. She had told Martin in the church that afternoon that "a woman must have something." Of women of her kind this is certainly true. You can find them everywhere slaving for and loving other women's children. In this sorry haphazard world such women are often cut off from the natural outlet of what is within them; but they always make one. Sometimes it is an aged relative, sometimes an invalid sister, sometimes a waif from the streets no one else wants, sometimes it is only a dog. But there is something, always.

When the child was in his bed Miss Margie took up a bunch of examination papers and began looking through them. As she worked she heard a slow rapping at the door, a rap she knew well indeed, that had sent the blood to her cheeks one day. Now it only left them white.

She started and hesitated, but as the rap was repeated she rose and went to the door, setting her lips firmly.

"Good evening, Martin, come in," she said quietly. "Bobbie is in bed. I'm sorry."

Martin stood by the door and shook his head at the proffered chair. "I didn't come to see Bobbie, Margie. I came to finish what I began to say this afternoon when you cut me off. I know I'm slow spoken. It's always been like it was at school, when the teacher asked a question I knew as well as I knew my own name, but some other fellow'd get the answer out before me. I started to say this afternoon that if I took Bobbie to St. Louis I couldn't take him alone. There is somebody else I couldn't bear to be apart from, and I guess you've known who that is this many a year."

A painful blush overspread Miss Margie's face and she turned away and rested her arm on the mantel. "It is not like you to take advantage of what I said this afternoon when I was angry. I wouldn't have believed it of you. You have given me pain enough in years gone by without this—this that makes me sick and ashamed."

"Sick and ashamed? Why Margie, you must have known what I've been waiting in Brownville for all these years. Don't tell me I've waited too long. I've done my best to live it down. I haven't bothered you nor pestered you so folks could talk. I've just stayed and stuck it out till I could feel I was worthy. Not that I think I'm worthy now, Margie, but the time has come for me to go and I can't go alone."

He paused, but there was no answer. He took a step nearer. "Why Margie, you don't mean that you haven't known I've been loving you all the time till my heart's near burst in me? Many a night down on the old ferry I've told it over and over again to the river till even it seemed to understand. Why Margie, I've"—the note of fear caught in his throat and his voice broke and he stood looking helplessly at his boots.

Miss Margie still stood leaning on her elbow, her face from him. "You'd better have been telling it to me, Martin," she said bitterly.

"Why Margie, I couldn't till I got my place. I couldn't have married you here and had folks always throwing that other woman in your face."

"But if you had loved me you would have told me, Martin, you couldn't have helped that."

He caught her hand and bent over it, lifting it tenderly to his lips. "O Margie, I was ashamed, bitter ashamed! I couldn't forget that letter I had to write you once. And you might have had a hundred better men than me. I never was good enough for you to think of one minute. I wasn't clever nor ready spoken like you, just a tramp of a river rat who could somehow believe better in God because of you."

Margie felt herself going and made one last desperate stand. "Perhaps you've forgotten all you said in that letter, perhaps you've forgotten the shame it would bring to any woman. Would you like to see it? I have always kept it."

He dropped her hand.

"No, I don't want to see it and I've not forgot. I only know I'd rather have signed my soul away than written it. Maybe you're right and there are things a man can't live down—not in this world. Of course you can keep the boy. As you say he is more yours than mine, a thousand times more. I've never had anything I could call my own. It's always been like this and I ought to be used to it by this time. Some men are made that way. Good night, dear."

"O Martin, don't talk like that, you could have had me any day for the asking. But why didn't you speak before? I'm too old now!" Margie leaned closer to the mantel and the sobs shook her.

He looked at her for a moment in wonder, and, just as she turned to look for him, caught her in his arms. "I've always been slow spoken, Margie—I was ashamed—you were too good for me," he muttered between his kisses.

"Don't Martin, don't! That's all asleep in me and it must not come, it shan't come back! Let me go!" cried Margie breathlessly.

"O I'm not near through yet! I'm just just showing you how young you are—it's the quickest way," came Martin's answer muffled by the trimmings of her gown.

"O Martin, you may be slow spoken, but you're quick enough at some things," laughed Margie as she retreated to the window, struggling hard against the throb of reckless elation that arose in her. She felt as though some great force had been unlocked within her, great and terrible enough to rend her asunder, as when a brake snaps or a band slips and some ponderous machine grinds itself in pieces. It is not an easy thing, after a woman has shut the great natural hope out of her life, to open the flood gates and let the riotous, aching current come throbbing again through the shrunken channels, waking a thousand undreamed-of possibilities of pleasure and pain.

Martin followed her to the window and they stood together leaning against the deep casing while the spring wind blew in their faces, bearing with it the yearning groans of the river.

"We can kind of say goodbye to the old place tonight. We'll be going in a week or two now," he said nervously.

"I've wanted to get away from Brownville all my life, but now I'm someway afraid to think of going."

"How did that piece end we used to read at school, 'My chains and I—' Go on, you always remember such things."

"My very chains and I grew friends,
So much a long communion tends
To make us what we are. Even I
Regained my freedom with a sigh,"

quoted Margie softly.

"Yes, that's it. I'm counting on you taking some singing lessons again when we get down to St. Louis."

"Why I'm too old to take singing lessons now. I'm too old for everything. O Martin, I don't believe we've done right. I'm afraid of all this! It hurts me."

He put his arm about her tenderly and whispered: "Of course it does, darling. Don't you suppose it hurts the old river down there tonight when the spring floods are stirring up the old bottom and tearing a new channel through the sand? Don't you suppose it hurts the trees tonight when the sap is climbing up and up till it breaks through the bark and runs down their sides like blood? Of course it hurts."

"Oh Martin, when you talk like that it don't hurt any more."

Truly the service of the river has its wages and its recompense, though they are not seen of men. Just then the door opened and Bobby came stumbling sleepily across the floor, trailing his little night gown after him.

"It was so dark in there, and I'm scared of the river when it sounds so loud," he said, hiding his face in Margie's skirts.

Martin lifted him gently in his arms and said, "The water won't hurt you, my lad. My boy must never be afraid of the river."

And as he stood there listening to the angry grumble of the swollen waters, Martin asked their benediction on his happiness. For he knew that a river man may be happy only as the river wills.

❧ ❧

OSCAR WILDE

from *The Importance of Being Earnest*

Algernon [*speaking very rapidly*]: Cecily, ever since I first looked upon your wonderful and incomparable beauty, I have dared to love you wildly, passionately, devotedly, hopelessly.

Cecily: I don't think that you should tell me that you love me wildly, passionately, devotedly, hopelessly. Hopelessly doesn't seem to make much sense, does it?

Algernon: Cecily! . . .

. . . I don't care for anybody in the whole world but you. I love you, Cecily. You will marry me, won't you?

Cecily: You silly boy! Of course. Why, we have been engaged for the last three months.

Algernon: For the last three months?

Cecily: Yes, it will be exactly three months on Thursday.

Algernon: But how did we become engaged?

Cecily: Well, ever since dear Uncle Jack first confessed to us that he had a younger brother who was very wicked and bad, you, of course, have formed the chief topic of conversation between myself and Miss Prism. And, of course, a man who is much talked about is always very attractive. One feels there must be something in him, after all. I dare say it was foolish of me, but I fell in love with you. Ernest.

Algernon: Darling. And when was the engagement actually settled?

Cecily: On the 14th of February last. Worn out by your entire ignorance of my existence, I determined to end the matter one way or the other, and after a long struggle with myself I accepted you under this dear old tree here. The next day I bought this little ring in your name, and this is the little bangle with the true lovers' knot I promised you always to wear.

Algernon: Did I give you this? It's very pretty, isn't it?

Cecily: Yes, you've wonderfully good taste, Ernest. It's the excuse I've always given for your leading such a bad life. And this is the box in which I keep all your dear letters. [*Kneels at table, opens box, and produces letters tied up with blue ribbon.*]

Algernon: My letters! But, my own sweet Cecily, I have never written you any letters.

Cecily: You need hardly remind me of that, Ernest. I remember only too well that I was forced to write your letters for you. I wrote always three times a week, and sometimes oftener.

Algernon: Oh, do let me read them, Cecily?

Cecily: Oh, I couldn't possibly. They would make you far too conceited. [*Replaces box.*] The three you wrote me after I had broken off the engagement are so beautiful, and so badly spelled, that even now I can hardly read them without crying a little.

Algernon: But was our engagement ever broken off?

Cecily: Of course it was. On the 22nd of last March. You can see the entry if you like. [*Shows diary.*] "Today I broke off my engagement with Ernest. I feel it is better to do so. The weather still continues charming."

Algernon: But why on earth did you break it off? What had I done? I had done nothing at all. Cecily, I am very much hurt indeed to hear you broke it off. Particularly when the weather was so charming.

Cecily: It would hardly have been a really serious engagement if it hadn't been broken off at least once. But I forgave you before the week was out.

The Nightingale and the Rose

"She said that she would dance with me if I brought her red roses," cried the young Student; "but in all my garden there is no red rose."

From her nest in the holm-oak tree the Nightingale heard him, and she looked out through the leaves, and wondered.

"No red rose in all my garden!" he cried, and his beautiful eyes filled with tears. "Ah, on what little things does happiness depend! I have read all that the wise men have written, and all the secrets of philosophy are mine, yet for want of a red rose is my life made wretched."

"Here at last is a true lover," said the Nightingale. "Night after night have I sung to him, though I knew him not: night after night have I told his story to the stars, and now I see him. His hair is dark as the hyacinth-blossom, and his lips are red as the rose of his desire; but passion has made his face like pale ivory, and sorrow has set her seal upon his brow."

"The Prince gives a ball tomorrow night," murmured the young Student, "and my love will be of the company. If I bring her a red rose she will dance with me till dawn. If I bring her a red rose, I shall hold her in my arms, and she will lean her head upon my shoulder, and her hand will be clasped in mine. But there is no red rose in my garden, so I shall sit lonely, and she will pass me by. She will have no heed of me, and my heart will break."

"Here indeed is the true lover," said the Nightingale. "What I sing of, he suffers: what is joy to me, to him is pain. Surely Love is a wonderful thing. It is more precious than emeralds, and dearer than fine opals. Pearls and pomegranates cannot buy it, nor is it set forth in the marketplace. It may not be purchased of the merchants, nor can it be weighed out in the balance of gold."

"The musicians will sit in their gallery," said the young Student, "and play upon their stringed instruments, and my love will dance to the sound of the harp and the violin. She will dance so lightly that her feet will not touch the floor, and the courtiers in their gay dresses will throng round her. But with me she will not dance, for I have no red rose to give her"; and he flung himself down on the grass, and buried his face in his hands, and wept.

"Why is he weeping?" asked a little Green Lizard as he ran past him with his tail in the air.

"Why, indeed?" said a Butterfly, who was fluttering about after a sunbeam.

"Why, indeed?" whispered a Daisy to his neighbour, in a soft, low voice.

"He is weeping for a red rose," said the Nightingale.

"For a red rose!" they cried; "how very ridiculous!" and the little Lizard, who was something of a cynic, laughed outright.

But the Nightingale understood the secret of the Student's sorrow, and she sat silent in the oak-tree, and thought about the mystery of Love.

Suddenly she spread her brown wings for flight, and soared into the air. She passed through the grove like a shadow, and like a shadow she sailed across the garden.

In the centre of the grass-plot was standing a beautiful Rose-tree, and when she saw it, she flew over to it, and lit upon a spray.

"Give me a red rose," she cried, "and I will sing you my sweetest song."

But the Tree shook its head.

"My roses are white," it answered; "as white as the foam of the sea, and whiter than the snow upon the mountain. But go to my brother who grows round the old sun-dial, and perhaps he will give you what you want."

So the Nightingale flew over to the Rose-tree that was growing round the old sun-dial.

"Give me a red rose," she cried, "and I will sing you my sweetest song."

But the Tree shook its head.

"My roses are yellow," it answered; "as yellow as the hair of the mermaiden who sits upon an amber throne, and yellower than the daffodil that blooms in the meadow before the mower comes with his scythe. But go to my brother who grows beneath the Student's window, and perhaps he will give you what you want."

So the Nightingale flew over to the Rose-tree that was growing beneath the Student's window.

"Give me a red rose," she cried, "and I will sing you my sweetest song."

But the Tree shook its head.

"My roses are red," it answered; "as red as the feet of the dove, and redder than the great fans of coral that wave and wave in the ocean cavern. But the winter has chilled my veins, and the frost has nipped my buds, and the storm has broken my branches, and I shall have no roses at all this year."

"One red rose is all I want," cried the Nightingale. "Only one red rose! Is there any way by which I can get it?"

"There is a way," answered the Tree; "but it is so terrible that I dare not tell it to you."

"Tell it to me," said the Nightingale, "I am not afraid."

"If you want a red rose," said the Tree, "you must build it out of music by moonlight, and stain it with your own heart's-blood. You must sing to me with your breast against a thorn. All night long you must sing to me, and the thorn must pierce your heart, and your life-blood must flow into my veins, and become mine."

"Death is a great price to pay for a red rose," cried the Nightingale, "and Life is very dear to all. It is pleasant to sit in the green wood, and to watch the Sun in his chariot of gold, and the Moon in her chariot of pearl. Sweet is the scent of the hawthorn, and sweet are the bluebells that hide in the valley, and the heather that blows on the hill. Yet Love is better than Life, and what is the heart of a bird compared to the heart of a man?"

So she spread her brown wings for flight, and soared into the air. She swept over the garden like a shadow, and like a shadow she sailed through the grove.

The young Student was still lying on the grass, where she had left him, and the tears were not yet dry in his beautiful eyes.

"Be happy," cried the Nightingale, "be happy; you shall have your red rose. I will build it out of music by moonlight, and stain it with my own heart's-blood. All that I ask of you in return is that you will be a true lover, for Love is wiser than Philosophy, though she is wise, and mightier than Power, though he is mighty. Flame-coloured are his wings, and coloured like flame is his body. His lips are sweet as honey, and his breath is like frankincense."

The Student looked up from the grass, and listened, but he could not understand what the Nightingale was saying to him, for he only knew the things that are written down in books.

But the Oak-tree understood, and felt sad, for he was very fond of the little Nightingale who had built her nest in his branches.

"Sing me one last song," he whispered; "I shall feel very lonely when you are gone."

So the Nightingale sang to the Oak-tree, and her voice was like water bubbling from a silver jar.

When she had finished her song the Student got up, and pulled a notebook and a lead-pencil out of his pocket.

"She has form," he said to himself, as he walked away through the grove—"that cannot be denied her; but has she got feeling? I am afraid not. In fact, she is like most artists; she is all style, without any sincerity. She would not sacrifice herself for others. She thinks merely of music, and everybody knows that the arts are selfish. Still, it must be admitted that she has some beautiful notes in her voice. What a pity it is that they do not mean anything, or do any practical good." And he went into his room, and lay down on his little pallet-bed, and began to think of his love; and, after a time, he fell asleep.

And when the Moon shone in the heavens the Nightingale flew to the Rose-tree, and set her breast against the thorn. All night long she sang with her breast against the thorn, and the cold crystal Moon leaned down and listened. All night long she sang, and the thorn went deeper and deeper into her breast, and her life-blood ebbed away from her.

She sang first of the birth of love in the heart of a boy and a girl. And on the topmost spray of the Rose-tree there blossomed a marvellous rose, petal followed petal, as song followed song. Pale was it, at first, as the mist that hangs over the river—pale as the feet of the morning, and silver as the wings of the dawn. As the shadow of a rose in a mirror of silver, as the shadow of a rose in a water-pool, so was the rose that blossomed on the topmost spray of the Tree.

But the Tree cried to the Nightingale to press closer against the thorn. "Press closer, little Nightingale," cried the Tree, "or the Day will come before the rose is finished."

So the Nightingale pressed closer against the thorn, and louder and louder grew her song, for she sang of the birth of passion in the soul of a man and a maid.

And a delicate flush of pink came into the leaves of the rose, like the flush in the face of the bridegroom when he kisses the lips of the bride. But the thorn had not yet reached her heart, so the rose's heart remained white, for only a Nightingale's heart's-blood can crimson the heart of a rose.

And the Tree cried to the Nightingale to press closer against the thorn. "Press closer, little Nightingale," cried the Tree, "or the Day will come before the rose is finished."

So the Nightingale pressed closer against the thorn, and the thorn touched her heart, and a fierce pang of pain shot through her. Bitter, bitter was the pain, and wilder and wilder grew her song, for she sang of the Love that is perfected by Death, of the Love that dies not in the tomb.

And the marvellous rose became crimson, like the rose of the eastern sky. Crimson was the girdle of petals, and crimson as a ruby was the heart.

But the Nightingale's voice grew fainter, and her little wings began to beat, and a film came over her eyes. Fainter and fainter grew her song, and she felt something choking her in her throat.

Then she gave one last burst of music. The white Moon heard it, and she forgot the dawn, and lingered on in the sky. The red rose heard it, and it trembled all over with ecstasy, and opened its petals to the cold morning air. Echo bore it to her purple cavern in the hills, and woke the sleeping shepherds from their dreams. It floated through the reeds of the river, and they carried its message to the sea.

"Look, look! cried the Tree, "the rose is finished now"; but the Nightingale made no answer, for she was lying dead in the long grass, with the thorn in her heart.

And at noon the Student opened his window and looked out.

"Why, what a wonderful piece of luck!" he cried; "here is a red rose! I have never seen any rose like it in all my life. It is so beautiful that I am sure it has a long Latin name"; and he leaned down and plucked it.

Then he put on his hat, and ran up to the Professor's house with the rose in his hand.

The daughter of the Professor was sitting in the doorway winding blue silk on a reel, and her little dog was lying at her feet.

"You said that you would dance with me if I brought you a red rose," cried the Student. "Here is the reddest rose in all the world. You will wear it tonight next your heart, and as we dance together it will tell you how I love you."

But the girl frowned.

"I am afraid it will not go with my dress," she answered; "and, besides, the Chamberlain's nephew has sent me some real jewels, and everybody knows that jewels cost far more than flowers."

"Well, upon my word, you are very ungrateful," said the Student angrily; and he threw the rose into the street, where it fell into the gutter, and a cart-wheel went over it.

"Ungrateful!" said the girl. "I tell you what, you are very rude; and, after all, who are you? Only a Student. Why, I don't believe you have even got silver buckles to your shoes as the Chamberlain's nephew has"; and she got up from her chair and went into the house.

"What a silly thing Love is," said the Student as he walked away. "It is not half as useful as Logic, for it does not prove anything, and it is always telling one of things that are not going to happen, and making one believe things that are not true. In fact, it is quite unpractical, and, as in this age to be practical is everything, I shall go back to Philosophy and study Metaphysics."

So he returned to his room and pulled out a great dusty book, and began to read.

O. HENRY

The Gift of the Magi

One dollar and eighty-seven cents. That was all. And sixty cents of it was in pennies. Pennies saved one and two at a time by bulldozing the grocer and the vegetable man and the butcher until one's cheeks burned with the silent imputation of parsimony that such close dealing implied. Three times Della counted it. One dollar and eighty-seven cents. And the next day would be Christmas.

There was clearly nothing to do but flop down on the shabby little couch and howl. So Della did it. Which instigates the moral reflection that life is made up of sobs, sniffles, and smiles, with sniffles predominating.

While the mistress of the home is gradually subsiding from the first stage to the second, take a look at the home. A furnished flat at $8 per week. It did not exactly beggar description, but it certainly had that word on the lookout for the mendicancy squad.

In the vestibule below was a letter-box into which no letter would go, and an electric button from which no mortal finger could coax a ring. Also appertaining thereunto was a card bearing the name "Mr. James Dillingham Young."

The "Dillingham" had been flung to the breeze during a former period of prosperity when its possessor was being paid $30 per week. Now, when the income was shrunk to $20, the letters of "Dillingham" looked blurred, as though they were thinking seriously of contracting to a modest and unassuming D. But whenever Mr. James Dillingham Young came home and reached his flat above he was called "Jim" and greatly hugged by Mrs. James Dillingham Young, already introduced to you as Della. Which is all very good.

Della finished her cry and attended to her cheeks with the powder rag. She stood by the window and looked out dully at a gray cat walking a gray fence in a gray backyard. Tomorrow would be Christmas Day, and she had only $1.87 with which to buy Jim a present. She had been saving every penny she could for months, with this result. Twenty dollars a week doesn't go far. Expenses had been greater than she had calculated. They always are. Only $1.87 to buy a present for Jim. Her Jim. Many a happy hour she had spent planning for something nice for him. Something fine and rare and sterling—something just a little bit near to being worthy of the honor of being owned by Jim.

There was a pier-glass between the windows of the room. Perhaps you have seen a pier-glass in an $8 flat. A very thin and very agile person may, by observing his reflection in a rapid sequence of longitudinal strips, obtain a fairly accurate conception of his looks. Della, being slender, had mastered the art.

Suddenly she whirled from the window and stood before the glass. Her eyes were shining brilliantly, but her face had lost its color within twenty seconds. Rapidly she pulled down her hair and let it fall to its full length.

Now, there were two possessions of the James Dillingham Youngs in which they both took a mighty pride. One was Jim's gold watch that had been his father's and his grandfather's. The other was Della's hair. Had the Queen of Sheba lived in the flat across the airshaft, Della would have let her hair hang out the window some day to dry just to depreciate Her Majesty's jewels and gifts. Had King Solomon been the janitor, with all his treasures piled up in the basement, Jim would have pulled out his watch every time he passed, just to see him pluck at his beard from envy.

So now Della's beautiful hair fell about her rippling and shining like a cascade of brown waters. It reached below her knee and made itself almost a garment for her. And then she did it up again nervously and quickly. Once she faltered for a minute and stood still while a tear or two splashed on the worn red carpet.

On went her old brown jacket; on went her old brown hat. With a whirl of skirts and with the brilliant sparkle still in her eyes, she fluttered out the door and down the stairs to the street.

Where she stopped the sign read: "Mme. Sofronie. Hair Goods of All Kinds." One flight up Della ran, and collected herself, panting. Madame, large, too white, chilly, hardly looked the "Sofronie."

"Will you buy my hair?" asked Della.

"I buy hair," said Madame. "Take yer hat off and let's have a sight at the looks of it."

Down rippled the brown cascade.

"Twenty dollars," said Madame, lifting the mass with a practised hand.

"Give it to me quick," said Della.

Oh, and the next two hours tripped by on rosy wings. Forget the hashed metaphor. She was ransacking the stores for Jim's present.

She found it at last. It surely had been made for Jim and no one else. There was no other like it in any of the stores, and she had turned all of them inside out. It was a platinum fob chain simple and chaste in design, properly proclaiming its value by substance alone and not by meretricious ornamentation—as all good things should do. It was even worthy of The Watch. As soon as she saw it she knew that it must be Jim's. It was like him. Quietness and value—the description applied to both. Twenty-one dollars they took from her for it, and she hurried home with the 87 cents. With that chain on his watch Jim might be properly anxious about the time in any company. Grand as the watch was, he sometimes looked at it on the sly on account of the old leather strap that he used in place of a chain.

When Della reached home her intoxication gave way a little to prudence and reason. She got out her curling irons and lighted the gas and went to work repairing the ravages made by generosity added to love. Which is always a tremendous task, dear friends—a mammoth task.

Within forty minutes her head was covered with tiny, close-lying curls that made her look wonderfully like a truant schoolboy. She looked at her reflection in the mirror long, carefully, and critically.

"If Jim doesn't kill me," she said to herself, "before he takes a second look at me, he'll say I look like a Coney Island chorus girl. But what could I do—oh! what could I do with a dollar and eighty-seven cents?"

At 7 o'clock the coffee was made and the frying-pan was on the back of the stove hot and ready to cook the chops.

Jim was never late. Della doubled the fob chain in her hand and sat on the corner of the table near the door that he always entered. Then she heard his step on the stairway down on the first flight, and she turned white for just a moment. She had a habit of saying little silent prayers about the simplest everyday things, and now she whispered: "Please God, make him think I am still pretty."

The door opened and Jim stepped in and closed it. He looked thin and very serious. Poor fellow, he was only twenty-two—and to be burdened with a family! He needed a new overcoat and he was without gloves.

Jim stopped inside the door, as immovable as a setter at the scent of quail. His eyes were fixed upon Della, and there was an expression in them that she could not read, and it terrified her. It was not anger, nor surprise, nor disapproval, nor horror, nor any of the sentiments that she had been prepared for. He simply stared at her fixedly with that peculiar expression on his face.

Della wriggled off the table and went for him.

"Jim, darling," she cried, "don't look at me that way. I had my hair cut off and sold it because I couldn't have lived through Christmas without giving you a present. It'll grow out again—you won't mind, will you? I just had to do it. My hair grows awfully fast. Say 'Merry Christmas!' Jim, and let's be happy. You don't known what a nice—what a beautiful, nice gift I've got for you."

"You've cut off your hair?" asked Jim, laboriously, as if he had not arrived at that patent fact yet even after the hardest mental labor.

"Cut it off and sold it," said Della. "Don't you like me just as well, anyhow? I'm me without my hair, ain't I?"

Jim looked about the room curiously.

"You say your hair is gone?" he said, with an air almost of idiocy.

"You needn't look for it," said Della. "It's sold, I tell you—sold and gone, too. It's Christmas Eve, boy. Be good to me, for it went for you. Maybe the hairs of my head were numbered," she went on with a sudden serious sweetness, "but nobody could ever count my love for you. Shall I put the chops on, Jim?"

Out of his trance Jim seemed quickly to wake. He enfolded his Della. For ten seconds let us regard with discreet scrutiny some inconsequential object in the other direction. Eight dollars a week or a million a year—what is the difference? A mathematician or a wit would give you the wrong answer. The magi brought valuable gifts, but that was not among them. This dark assertion will be illuminated later on.

Jim drew a package from his overcoat pocket and threw it upon the table.

"Don't make any mistake, Dell," he said, "about me. I don't think there's anything in the way of a haircut or a shave or a shampoo that could make me like my girl any less. But if you'll unwrap that package you may see why you had me going a while at first."

White fingers and nimble tore at the string and paper. And then an ecstatic scream of joy; and then, alas! a quick feminine change to hysterical tears and wails, necessitating the immediate employment of all the comforting powers of the lord of the flat.

For there lay The Combs—the set of combs, side and back, that Della had worshipped for long in a Broadway window. Beautiful combs, pure tortoise shell, with jewelled rims—just the shade to wear in the beautiful vanished hair. They were expensive combs, she knew, and her heart had simply craved and yearned over them without the least hope of possession. And now, they were hers, but the tresses that should have adorned the coveted adornments were gone.

But she hugged them to her bosom, and at length she was able to look up with dim eyes and a smile and say: "My hair grows so fast, Jim!"

And then Della leaped up like a little singed cat and cried, "Oh, oh!"

Jim had not yet seen his beautiful present. She held it out to him eagerly upon her open palm. The dull precious metal seemed to flash with a reflection of her bright and ardent spirit.

"Isn't it a dandy, Jim? I hunted all over town to find it. You'll have to look at the time a hundred times a day now. Give me your watch. I want to see how it looks on it."

Instead of obeying, Jim tumbled down on the couch and put his hands under the back of his head and smiled.

"Dell," said he, "let's put our Christmas presents away and keep 'em a while. They're too nice to use just at present. I sold the watch to get the money to buy your combs. And now suppose you put the chops on."

The magi, as you know, were wise men—wonderfully wise men—who brought gifts to the Babe in the manger. They invented the art of giving Christmas presents. Being wise, their gifts were no doubt wise ones, possibly bearing the privilege of exchange in case of duplication. And here I have lamely related to you the uneventful chronicle of two foolish children in a flat who most unwisely sacrificed for each other the greatest treasures of their house. But in a last word to the wise of these days let it be said that of all who give gifts these two were the wisest. Of all who give and receive gifts, such as they are wisest. Everywhere they are wisest. They are the magi.

✺ ✺

EDITH WHARTON

from *Summer*

Charity's heart contracted. The first fall of night after a day of radiance often gave her a sense of hidden menace: it was like looking out over the world as it would be when love had gone from it. She wondered if some day she would sit in that same place and watch in vain for her lover. . . .

His bicycle-bell sounded down the lane, and in a minute she was at the gate and his eyes were laughing in hers. They walked back through the long grass, and pushed open the door behind the house. The room at first seemed quite dark and they had to grope their way in hand-in-hand. Through the window-frame the sky looked light by contrast, and above the black mass of asters in the earthen jar one white star glimmered like a moth.

"There was such a lot to do at the last minute," Harney was explaining, "and I had to drive down to Creston to meet someone who has come to stay with my cousin for the show."

He had his arms about her, and his kisses were in her hair and her lips. Under his touch things deep down in her struggled to the light and sprang up like flowers in sunshine. She twisted her fingers into his, and they sat down side by side on the improvised couch. She hardly heard his excuses for being late: in his absence a thousand doubts tormented her, but as soon as he appeared she ceased to wonder where he had come from, what had delayed him, who had kept him from her. It seemed as if the places he had been in, and the people he had been with, must cease to exist when he left them, just as her own life was suspended in his absence.

He continued, now, to talk to her volubly and gaily, deploring his lateness, grumbling at the demands on his time, and good-humouredly mimicking Miss Hatchard's benevolent agitation. "She hurried off Miles to ask Mr. Royall to speak at the Town Hall tomorrow: I didn't know till it was done." Charity was silent, and he added: "After all, perhaps it's just as well. No one else could have done it."

Charity made no answer: She did not care what part her guardian played in the morrow's ceremonies. Like all the other figures peopling her meagre world he had grown non-existent to her. She had even put off hating him.

"Tomorrow I shall only see you from far off," Harney continued. "But in the evening there'll be the dance in the Town Hall. Do you want me to promise not to dance with any other girl?"

Any other girl? Were there any others? She had forgotten even that peril, so enclosed did he and she seem in their secret world. Her heart gave a frightened jerk.

"Yes, promise."

He laughed and took her in his arms. "You goose—not even if they're hideous?"

He pushed the hair from her forehead, bending her face back, as his way was, and leaning over so that his head loomed black between her eyes and the paleness of the sky, in which the white star floated. . . .

❧

BRUNO SCHULZ

from *Sanatorium Under the Sign of the Hourglass*

A band is now playing every evening in the city park, and people on their spring outings fill the avenues. They walk up and down, pass one another, and meet again in symmetrical, continuously repeated patterns. The young men are wearing new spring hats and nonchalantly carrying gloves in their hands. Through the hedges and between the tree trunks the dresses of girls walking in parallel avenues glow. The girls walk in pairs, swinging their hips, strutting like swans under the foam of their ribbons and flounces; sometimes they land on garden seats, as if tired by the idle parade, and the bells of their flowered muslin skirts expand on the seats, like roses beginning to shed their petals. And then they disclose their crossed legs—white irresistibly expressive shapes—and the young men, passing them, grow speechless and pale, hit by the accuracy of the argument, completely convinced and conquered.

At a particular moment before dusk all the colors of the world become more beautiful than ever, festive, ardent yet sad. The park quickly fills with pink varnish, with shining lacquer that makes every other color glow deeper; and at the same time the beauty of the colors becomes too glaring and somewhat suspect. In another instant the thickets of the park strewn with young greenery, still naked and twiggy, fill with the pinkness of dusk, shot with coolness, spilling the indescribable sadness of things supremely beautiful but mortal.

Then the whole park becomes an enormous, silent orchestra, solemn and composed, waiting under the raised baton of the conductor for its music to ripen and rise; and over that potential, earnest symphony a quick theatrical dusk spreads suddenly as if brought down by the sounds swelling in the instruments. Above, the young greenness of the leaves is pierced by the tones of an invisible oriole, and at once everything turns somber, lonely, and late, like an evening forest.

A hardly perceptible breeze sails through the treetops, from which dry petals of cherry blossom fall in a shower. A tart scent drifts high under the dusky sky and floats like a premonition of death, and the first stars shed their tears like lilac blooms picked from pale, purple bushes.

It is then that a strange desperation grips the youths and young girls walking up and down and meeting at regular intervals. Each man transcends himself, becomes handsome and irresistible like a Don Juan, and his eyes express a murderous strength that chills a woman's heart. The girls' eyes sink deeper and reveal dark labyrinthine pools. Their pupils distend, open without resistance, and admit those conquerors who stare into their opaque darkness. Hidden paths of the park reveal themselves and lead to thickets, ever deeper and more rustling, in which they lose themselves, as in a backstage tangle of velvet curtains and secluded corners. And no one knows how they reach, through the coolness of these completely forgotten darkened gardens, the strange spots where darkness ferments and degenerates, and vegetation emits a smell like the sediment in long-forgotten wine barrels.

Wandering blindly in the dark plush of the gardens, the young people meet at last in an empty clearing, under the last purple glow of the setting sun, over a pond that has been growing muddy for years; on a rotting balustrade, somewhere at the back gate of the world, they find themselves again in pre-existence, a life long past, in attitudes of a distant age; they sob and plead, rise to promises never to be fulfilled, and, climbing up the steps of exaltation, reach summits and climaxes beyond which there is only death and the numbness of nameless delight.

Translated by Celina Wieniewska

❦ ❦

PHILIPPE THOBY-MARCELIN AND
PIERRE MARCELIN

from *The Beast of the Haitian Hills*

Straight and silent in her blue cotton print dress, an orange madras bound about her head, Irma left her parents' cabin where she had just made herself ready for her lover's visit.

The day declined softly. The olive-drab foliage, tinted violet for a moment in the pools of shadow, faded and became blurred into the deepening blackness. But the sky, where stars already began to glow, still dragged the pale green iridescent fringe of her robe across the slopes of the hills to the east.

The young girl went to seat herself on a big flat stone at the entrance of the courtyard like a squatting washerwoman, her legs spread wide, her skirt tucked between her thighs. Thus she awaited her fiance each evening—motionless, her gaze fixed and distant, sinking down into a profound, dreamlike reverie.

From time to time she would sigh to herself. Or a few words would escape from her moving lips.

"Little kitten!" she would murmur. Or simply, "Beloved of my heart."

Then the lines of her mouth would grow rigid and she would relapse into silence. It was a sort of incantation to hasten the arrival of the young man, and also an internal chant extolling him. She did these things mechanically, unaware of herself, thinking entirely of him. . . .

Ti-Charles, what a brave fellow he was! A real man in every way. . . .

Of course some people said he chased after the women; but was it his fault if at his slightest gesture they would throw themselves into his arms? Doesn't the proverb say that a good cock sings in all the chicken coops? The essential fact for Irma was that after these furtive liaisons her lover always returned completely to her, like an earthenware jug that one offers to any passerby who begs for a drink, but which he will not fail to give back as soon as his thirst is quenched. And so the girl shrugged disdainfully at gossipers.

Moreover, Ti-Charles did not conduct himself with her as do some suitors who drag things out, planning to celebrate Easter before fasting through Lent, and then slip away once their desire has been satisfied. Far from acting in this way, he had proposed to marry her right away; but Alcaeus, Irma's father, finding them too young to set up house, had postponed the marriage to the following year, around Christmas time.

This delay seemed interminable to the young woman. She must patiently wait eight long months more, and they already had waited so long! Irma would grind her teeth just thinking about it, and was irritated with her father, whose reasons she could not understand. She would willingly have dispensed with Alcaeus's consent and gone to live under the same roof with her lover, while awaiting the blessing of marriage, were it not for the respect she owed her father. And of course Ti-Charles would surely have judged such parental disrespect very improper. At least that is what she would say to herself to calm her fits of anger.

She was thus expressing only a feeble whim. At heart she was a fatalist and quickly submitted to the laws of fate. Apart from these twinges of revolt, she never impatiently desired anything which could not be achieved immediately. And so she was really content with Ti-Charles' regular visits and his chaste caresses. Whenever he took her in his arms, she would turn her thoughts back to the past, trying to live again the unforgettable instant when, matured by an exalting rapture, they had promised themselves to each other, and would thereby stifle her imperious desire for sexual contact.

What a surprise it had been for her! Having the same godfather as herself, Charles was, as they say, her baptismal brother. They had played together as little children, growing up side by side, and until they reached the age of puberty would go swimming naked in the spring along with all the other children of Musseau. After that, being her elder by three years, he had always treated her as a young girl. How could she have guessed that one fine day he would really fall in love with her?

It had happened all of a sudden the year before, at the Rara country festival during Holy Week. Aroused to a pitch of nervous excitement by the bamboo trumpets and the rhythm of a warrior's march which, at regular intervals, was punctuated by the low bellow of shining lambis seaconch shells, the strident notes of whistles and the crack of whips through four whole days and nights, the young people of Musseau wandered through the entire countryside together. They completed a wide circuit and joined in the festivities at Bourdon and all the other villages of the area. At each place they visited they were wined and dined. They sang and danced . . . danced . . . danced . . .

> "You've put our home too close to papa!
> You've built our cabin too near mama!
> Each time I wriggle papa hears me, oh! oh!
> And mama hears each sigh of love, oh! oh!"

That and a score of other folksongs they sang as they danced.

The dawn of Easter Monday broke fresh and clear, and all the countryside still vibrated with the Dionysian tumult of this springtime festival. The voices of the women, sharp and incisive as the first rays of the rising sun, pierced the deep chorus of male voices and rose high into the sky.

> "Calypso, you are a woman just like me;
> To you I tell what Sonson did to me.

I caressed Sonson,
I fondled Sonson,
I even went so far I nibbled Sonson!
When I begged Sonson something in return,
Sonson only snored the louder,
Sonson, he would not arise! . . ."

Irma's voice was the highest pitched, the most ardent. Giving her the cue, Ti-Charles for the first time looked at her as one will look at a woman he desires. His eyes were set and burning, but without the slightest sign of impertinence.

"You've put our home too close to papa!
You've built our cabin too near mama!
Each time I wriggle papa hears me, oh! oh!
And mama hears each sigh of love, oh! oh!"

When morning came they found themselves somehow alone on the road back to her home. They were troubled and silent, but inside themselves the sweetest and most intimate bonds were forged. Bidding her good-bye at the gate to her home, Ti-Charles looked away, and then said in a firm voice:
"Tomorrow I will write your father and mother. . . ."
She turned, and running like a woman possessed, rushed into the house, her heart pounding.

The letter had been drafted by Horace and he had recopied it in his most beautiful handwriting. The thick and thin strokes of the pen were traced with painstaking symmetry, on special paper with a border of fine, gilded imitation lacework and a letterhead decorated with a basket of blue forget-me-nots and two blue swallows. The contents of the letter were simple and unaffected:

Musseau, This 10 April 1936

To:
Master and Dame Alcaeus Jean-Baptiste and
Marie-Noel Dorleans.
Master and Dame,

I take up my pen in writing you this letter of request to ask you for the hand of your dear young daughter Irma whom I desire to take as my wife.

I trust this will meet with your most agreeable and welcome consent.
Please accept, Sir and Madam, my most distinguished salutations.

Signed:
Charles Metelus.

This letter had been solemnly delivered to the parents of the young woman by Horace. They were surprised and shocked by this request for their daughter's hand. They thought that Irma and Ti-Charles, having been held over the baptismal font by the same godfather, were obliged to consider themselves, before God and man, as brother and sister. Their marriage would therefore be nothing less than incest. Peasant customs had always decreed matters this way. But Horace, who was free of these superstitious beliefs, assured them that neither the Catholic religion nor the law agreed with them on this point. Nevertheless, they would not believe him.

"Irma is Ti-Charles' sister," Alcaeus repeated. "Therefore they cannot be married."

Horace was forced to bring them to Father Eusebius in order to convince them. The priest finally overcame their reluctance. . . .

Although she found it a delightful pastime to let these memories come to her mind again (or perhaps because it was so sweet) Irma felt that Ti-Charles was late in coming. Her impatience gradually increased to the point of real irritation. And, as though to displease her even more, he arrived very late that evening.

"What do you mean," she remarked dryly, "arriving at this hour of the night?"

"But it wasn't my fault," the young man replied, sitting on the ground close beside her. "Just as I was about to go out, a friend came to see me. It was Desilus himself."

"Couldn't you excuse yourself?"

"I really couldn't, dearest. He had to talk to me about a very serious matter."

"Ah, yes indeed, I understand," she retorted in a voice which hissed with rage. "Coming to see me isn't a serious matter at all, is it? It's only for your own amusement!"

Ti-Charles suppressed an angry retort.

"Irma! What you're saying isn't fair. And you know it very well!"

"How should I know if this friend of whom you speak wasn't a woman, one of those numerous young things who are always chasing around after you?"

Charles jumped up, furious. For once, indeed, his conscience was really clear! Something had already happened to irritate him, and now he let himself go!

"Since that's the way you feel about it," he said, "I think there's no further reason for me to come to visit you."

He pretended to be leaving. But, instantly alarmed, Irma held him back by the arm.

"What makes you so angry? Don't you see that I simply wanted to chide you a little for being late?"

She pleaded with him, trying to force a smile. Charles continued to sulk.

"Well, if that's the way you judge me . . ."

"Who says that I'm trying to judge you? . . . Come now, Ti-Charles, can't anyone joke with you any more?"

"Sure, Irma, sure they can. Especially you. But please understand, dearest, that it isn't good to say all the words that rise to your lips. Some of them can hurt. You can try hard to take them back afterwards, but the harm they've done remains. And that's why old people used to say that begging pardon does not heal wounds."

"So, dear, you are really angry with me?"

"No, Irma. You know very well that isn't possible . . ."

It was their very first quarrel. Seeing that it had now been dispelled, Irma tenderly and impulsively squeezed the hand of her fiancé, as young girls often do.

"Hush, Ti-Charles!" she whispered. "Let's forget such petty things. Sit down here beside me and tell me what your friend came to tell you. That must really have been serious, for you to keep me waiting."

"Yes, Irma, it was serious . . . It was very, very serious . . ."

He paused for a moment.

"It had to do with Bossuet. . . . Do you recall that horrible 'thing' he goes to visit in the Forban Gorge from time to time?"

"The Cigouave?" Irma asked, a strange uneasiness gripping her.

"Well, it was about the Cigouave, Irma . . . Desilus came to tell me that last night he heard the beast howling in Master Morin's courtyard."

"He heard it!" the girl groaned.

"Yes, he heard it. But that isn't all. Desilus, wanting to find out what was going on, got up without making a sound, opened the door a tiny crack, and there he saw the 'thing' which was leaping high in the air, turning somersaults, like a little kid. . . ."

"No, no, Ti-Charles! Enough!" she begged, closing her eyes with fear and leaning against him. "Enough, enough!"

"But what frightens you, Irma?" the young man asked. "The 'thing' certainly hasn't come for us. It has come for Master Morin."

"Yes, Ti-Charles, I know very well that it's after him. But wasn't it Bossuet who sent the Cigouave here? Then who knows for certain that it is only Master Morin that he is after? Hasn't he also got it in for you?"

The young man did not answer, even though the same foreboding had already crossed his mind. He got up to say goodnight.

"But you're not leaving already?" she said, a note of reproach in her voice.

"Yes, I'm going," he said.

He didn't want to add, for fear of upsetting her, that if he wished to return at this early hour it was to avoid the risk of meeting the Cigouave, which might happen if he lingered. She also felt this and did not try to hold him back, as she might have done under other conditions. But she insisted on walking part of the way with him. As they were in their last embrace before separating she suddenly felt an overwhelming need to give herself to him. It was not so much physical desire that drove her to it, but an obscure foreboding that perhaps never again would it be possible.

"Take me, Ti-Charles, take me!" she panted, her warm breath on his face, as she gripped him tightly around the neck and tried to draw him down to the earth.

Charles resisted and tried to break loose from her clinging arms. She arched her back, pressed her belly and thighs tightly against his body, pulling him down with all her strength. Her breath came in sharp, staccato gasps and her body quivered in every muscle. He soon gave in. His body followed hers softly down to the earth, and silently, without a cry, they merged their bodies until they were one.

Translated by Peter C. Rhodes

❧ ❧

THOMAS WOLFE

from *The Web and the Rock*

Autumn was kind to them, winter was long to them—but in April, late April, all the gold sang.

Spring came that year like magic and like music and like song. One day its breath was in the air, a haunting premonition of its spirit filled the hearts of men with its transforming loveliness, working its sudden and incredible sorcery upon grey streets, grey pavements, and on grey faceless tides of manswarm ciphers. It came like music faint and far, it came with triumph and a sound of singing in the air, with lutings of sweet bird cries at the break of day and the high, swift passing of a wing, and one day it was there upon the city streets with a strange, sudden cry of green, its sharp knife of wordless joy and pain.

Not the whole glory of the great plantation of the earth could have outdone the glory of the city streets that Spring. Neither the cry of great, green fields, nor the song of the hills, nor the glory of young birch trees bursting into life again along the banks of rivers, nor the oceans of bloom in the flowering orchards, the peach trees, the apple trees, the plum and cherry trees—not all of the singing and the gold of Spring, with April bursting from the earth in a million shouts of triumph, and the visible stride, the flowered feet of the Springtime as it came on across the earth, could have surpassed the wordless and poignant glory of a single tree in a city street that Spring. Monk had given up his tiny room in the dingy little hotel and had taken possession of the spacious floor in the old house on Waverly Place. There had been a moment's quarrel when he had said that from that time on he would pay the rent. She had objected that the place was hers, that she had found it— she wanted him to come, she would like to think of him as being there, it would make it seem more "theirs"—but she had been paying for it, and would continue, and it didn't matter. But he was adamant and said he woulnd't come at all unless he paid his way, and in the end she yielded.

And now each day he heard her step upon the stairs at noon. At noon, at high, sane, glorious noon, she came, the mistress of that big, disordered room, the one whose brisk, small step on the stairs outside his door woke a leaping jubilation in his heart. Her face was like a light and like a music in the light of noon: it was jolly, small, and tender, as delicate as a plum, and as rosy as a flower. It was young and good and full of health and delight; its sweetness, strength, and noble beauty could not be equaled anywhere on earth. He kissed it a thousand times because it was so good, so wholesome, and so radiant in its loveliness.

Everything about her sang out with hope and morning. Her face was full of a thousand shifting plays of life and jolly humor, as swift and merry as a child's, and yet had in it always, like shadows in the sun, all of the profound, brooding, and sorrowful depths of beauty.

Thus, when he heard her step upon the stairs at noon, her light knuckles briskly rapping at the door, her key turning in the lock, she brought the greatest health and joy to him that he had ever known. She came in like a cry of triumph, like a shout of music in the blood, like the deathless birdsong in the first light of the morning. She was the bringer of hope, the teller of good news. A hundred sights and magical colors which she had seen in the streets that morning, a dozen tales of life and work and business, sprang from her merry lips with the eager insistence of a child.

She got into the conduits of his blood, she began to sing and pulse through the vast inertia of his flesh, still heavied with great clots of sleep, until he sprang up with the goat cry in his throat, seized, engulfed, and devoured her, and felt there was nothing on earth he could not do, nothing on earth he could not conquer. She gave a tongue to all the exultant music of the Spring whose great pulsations trembled in the gold and sapphire singing of the air. Everything—the stick-candy whippings of a flag, the shout of a child, the smell of old, worn plankings in the sun, the heavy, oily, tarry exhalations of the Spring-warm streets, the thousand bobbing and weaving colors and the points of light upon the pavements, the smell of the markets, of fruits, flowers, vegetables, and loamy earth, and the heavy shattering *baugh* of a great ship as it left its wharf at noon on Saturday—was given intensity, structure, and a form of joy because of her.

She had never been as beautiful as she was that Spring, and sometimes it drove him almost mad to see her look so fresh and fair. Even before he heard her step upon the stair at noon he always knew that she was there. Sunken in sleep at twelve o'clock, drowned fathoms deep at noon in a strange, wakeful sleep, his consciousness of her was so great that he knew instantly the moment when she had entered the house, whether he heard a sound or not.

She seemed to be charged with all the good and joyful living of the earth as she stood there in the high light of noon. In all that was delicate in her little bones, her trim figure, slim ankles, full, swelling thighs, deep breast and straight, small shoulders, rose lips and flower face, and all the winking lights of her fine hair, jolliness, youth, and noble beauty—she seemed as rare, as rich, as high and grand a woman as any on earth could be. The first sight of her at noon always brought hope, confidence, belief, and sent through the huge inertia of his flesh, still drugged with the great anodyne of sleep, a tidal surge of invincible strength.

She would fling her arms around him and kiss him furiously, she would fling herself down beside him on his cot and cunningly insinuate herself into his side, presenting her happy, glowing little face insatiably to be kissed, covered, plastered with a thousand kisses. She was as fresh as morning, as tender as a plum, and so irresistible he felt he could devour her in an instant and entomb her in his flesh forever. And then, after an interval, she would rise and set briskly about the preparation of a meal for him.

There is no spectacle on earth more appealing than that of a beautiful woman in the act of cooking dinner for someone she loves. Thus the sight of Esther as, delicately flushed, she bent with the earnest devotion of religious ceremony above the food she was cooking for him, was enough to drive him mad with love and hunger.

In such a moment he could not restrain himself. He would get up and begin to pace the room in a madness of wordless ecstasy. He would lather his face for shaving, shave one side of it, and then begin to walk up and down the room again, singing, making strange noises in his throat, staring vacantly out of the window at a cat that crept along the ridges of the fence; he would pull books from the shelves, reading a line or page, sometimes reading her a passage from a poem as she cooked, and then forgetting the book, letting it fall upon the cot or on the floor, until the floor was covered with them. Then he would sit on the edge of the cot for minutes, staring stupidly and vacantly ahead, holding one sock in his hand. Then he would spring up again and begin to pace the room, shouting and singing, with a convulsion of energy surging through his body that could find no utterance and that ended only in a wild, goat-like cry of joy.

❦ ❦

ALICE ADAMS

Complicities

The young girl, Nan, who has come to stay with the Travises, Jay and Mary, on their farm in southern New Hampshire—Nan is so thin that when she goes swimming in the pond deep indentations show between her small ribs. Her finely downed cheeks are hollow, her eyes the enormous eyes of a famine victim, or perhaps a sufferer from some lengthy and wasting disease. It is for this, from a desire to "build her up," to put some flesh on those bones, that her parents have sent her to the Travises for the summer. Also, there is an unspoken wish to do good to Mary and Jay, who are known to be "up against it," as the phrase went.

This was all some time back, before any talk of eating disorders, and Nan's parents, a kindly small-town druggist and his wife, in western Pennsylvania, distant cousins of Mary Travis, do not think in terms of neurosis, rejections of love—although it does seem to them that Nan eats a fair amount and is still morbidly thin.

Nan, at thirteen, is a fairly silly, unnaturally devious, and potentially bright girl (highest IQ in the local eighth grade). She thinks she looks wonderful; she feels herself possessed of vast and thrilling secrets. How powerful she is! and how private; no one knows anything about her, re-ally, not even her lover. She does not use that word in thinking about Dr. Thurston, the minister whose babysitter she occasionally is; the man who is out of his mind, deranged with love for her, she says, and certainly he acts that way, following her everywhere in his car just to look at her as she walks home from school with friends, meeting her in that same car for rendezvous on the edge of town. Removing her clothes to cover her body with his mouth, kissing everywhere, breathing as though he might die.

Dr. Thurston (impossible to think of him as Bill, the name his fat wife uses) is one of Nan's secrets; the other is what she thinks of as "los-ing food," something she does in the bathroom with her fingers, after meals. Fingers down her throat, which if she has waited too long do not feel good. But it works, she can eat all she wants to and still have noth-ing on her bones but skin. Nothing to pinch, anywhere. "I adore your pale thin body," says Dr. Thurston. "I would never profane it."

Jay Travis is a failed painter; it is hard otherwise to make a sum of his life. Once a successful advertising man, he left his wife and married his assistant, Mary, and retired to the country to paint in a serious way, as he had always intended. Periodically he takes slides and sometimes canvases down to New York, but nothing has ever panned out, and they live mostly on the foolish articles that Mary writes (she knows they are foolish) for various "ladies' magazines." For editors who are old friends, from Mary's own single New York days.

Acerbic, melancholy, and exceptionally smart, Jay often feels that he may have been better off in a commercial venture at which he could constantly scoff; he fears that he is not doing well with this serious ded-

ication to his talents—"such as they are," as he himself would be the first
to add. And this has been an especially bad year for Jay; prostate surgery
in January ("Some New Year's present for a tired old cock" was his terrible joke) left him weak and further depressed. Nothing sold, and the
long wet spring wore on, and now they have this skinny nymphet in the
house, watching everything as fixedly as a cat.

What he truly loves, though, what Jay Travis literally adores is this
farm, this lovely hillside acre with its meadows and pond, its stands of
birches and hemlocks and Norway pines, its surrounding low stone
fence. And the falling-down red barn, with its population of busy, half-
tame cats, its bats and a family of owls. And he loves the house, low-
lying, weathered to silver, its long rooms smelling of apples and of
lavender. On a cane, which is half affectation, Jay paces his house and his
land; he inspects the fences (for what? he wonders, whatever could happen to a very old small stone fence?). He takes dishes of milk and tuna
out to the barn for the cats, and he squats there, hoping and watching
for some feline form of affection, or even notice.

He watches almost translucent Nan, as she walks gingerly across
the tender meadow grass and down to the pond in her childish skimpy
bathing suit—as, removing the towel from her shoulders, she shivers in
the summer morning air. Occasionally Jay goes into his studio, unveils
the canvas, and stares at it for a while.

Always, from his window, he is hoping for a sight of Mary, whom
he loves truly more than his land or his house, or his cats, or anything
in life that he can imagine.

Mary Travis, in early middle age (she is Jay's third wife; as she herself puts it, some men just never learn), is plump and beautiful and kind
and very restless. She doesn't move about a lot, as Jay always does, but she
sits and stares at books and windows, occasionally getting up to polish
something. She has found some wonderful lavender-smelling wax.

Or to cook. Mary likes to cook. What she serves up is in fact ex-
ceptional, great culinary triumphs, often. Even just for Jay, and recently
for Jay and Nan, she makes lovely foam-light soufflés, beautiful fresh vegetable terrines, and mysterious rich soups. And magnificent cakes; she is
perhaps at her best with cakes.

Having been told by Nan's parents, her cousins, of their worry over
their daughter's weight, Mary watches Nan's breakfast consumption of
blueberry muffins, her noontime intake of meat and cheese and fruit, her
adult-sized dinners. Pleased and flattered by this new consumer, Mary

feels her own views of her cooking confirmed (this is her not-so-secret vanity.) But then, further observing Nan, and with greater attention, she sees no change whatsoever in the almost transparent flesh stretched over those delicate ribs. And she notes too the alacrity with which Nan heads for the bathroom after each meal, a compulsion at first excused by murmurs about her dentist: "He's an absolute maniac about post-meal brushing."

Observant and wise, Mary thinks, Can that silly little bitch be making herself throw up? How entirely disgusting, not to mention the waste.

Though poor, the Travises are fond of giving parties, on Saturdays, generally. Around six in the evening people start to arrive in their shabby cars, seemingly from everywhere, bearing casseroles or bags of fruit, boxes of cookies. Or bottles: these parties involve an enormous number of bottles, Nan has observed. As she plans to say to her mother, they all drink like fish. An abstemious ghost, Nan hovers at the edges of these parties; she is often in white, as though to emphasize her difference.

They eat and they drink and they dance, these middle-aged hedonists.

They dance close together; mostly to old slow scratched records, old songs that Nan has barely heard of. Squinched down in an ancient leather chair with heavy book, in a barely lit corner of the living room, Nan, who is not really reading, looks up from time to time at whatever is going on—which is not much, usually.

Until the night that Mary sings.

More absorbed than usual in her reading (it is *Gone with the Wind*), Nan has come to what she thinks of as the good parts, Rhett kissing Scarlet. She looks up with surprise at the sound of the piano, which no one ever plays; someone is playing a song she knows, "Honeysuckle Rose," a favorite of her father's.

And then suddenly Mary is standing right there by the piano. And Mary is singing.

"Don't—need—sugar
You just have to touch my cup—"

She is singing and laughing, embarrassed, but still her voice is rich and confident and sexy—oh, so sexy! Mary is wearing a new blue dress, or maybe it's old. It is tight, some shiny material, stretched tight over those big breasts and hips. Nan, watching and listening ("—it's so sweet when you stir it up—"), experiences an extreme and nameless, incomprehensible disturbance. She feels like throwing up, or screaming, or maybe just grabbing up her knees so that her body is a tight-knit ball— and crying, crying there in the corner, in the semidark. Is this falling in love? Has she fallen in love with Mary? She thinks it is more that she wants to *be* Mary. She wants to be out there in the light, with everyone laughing and clapping. She wants to be singing, and *fat*. Oh, how wildly, suddenly, she yearns for flesh, her own flesh. Oh, fat!

"Were your other two wives as beautiful as Mary?"

None of your fucking business, is what Jay feels would have been the proper answer to this question. But Nan is only a child, he reminds himself. Also, she is their paying houseguest. And so he contents himself with saying, as vaguely as possible, "Not, not exactly."

They are walking very slowly around the edge of the pond in an August twilight, Jay with his cane and Nan in her tiny white shorts, a skin-tight T-shirt. He had not realized before that she had breasts—or does she? Those small protuberances look a little unreal, as though she had stuffed something into a tiny bra—and it comes to Jay, with the sureness of a vision, that she must have done exactly that; she stuffed her bra, but why? Why on earth? And why has she come out after him like this, interrupting his solitary stroll?

"Thin or fat?" this terrible child persists. "Your wives."

"Uh. On the plump side. I've always liked a little flesh."

But with great eagerness she has interrupted. "There's this man at home, you know? I babysit for him and his wife. He's a minister, can you believe it? And he is absolutely crazy about how thin I am. Just crazy! He follows me."

"Nan, you must avoid this man. Tell him to go away. Tell your father."

"Oh, I will. The very idea of him right now makes me—makes me want to throw up." Nan laughs immoderately at this disgusting remark.

"It's quite a puzzle," says Jay to Mary at dinner one night, about three weeks after that walk, that conversation with Nan. It is in fact the next-to-last night of Nan's visit, but she has gone to bed early, leaving Mary and Jay to finish what has been a celebratory feast: they are not so much celebrating her imminent departure (not explicitly, that is) but rather the fact that after years of professional drought, Jay's agent has sold a large painting, a landscape (in fact Jay's own landscape, the meadow and stand of trees next to his studio). Not only was the painting sold, there is also a commission for four more large landscapes. And that was their conversation at dinner: without Nan present, Jay was able to speak joyously of his good fortune, plans, and eagerness for work.

In terms of festivity, feasting, Mary quite outdid herself, with an oyster soufflé, and something that she calls her twenty-vegetable lamb stew, and an orange salad and a chocolate mousse. Nan, protesting fatigue, went off to bed before the mousse was served (I may come down for a little later on, will you save some for me, Mary?")—and it is this recent shift in Nan's eating habits that they now discuss, and that Jay has just described as a puzzle.

He continues, "I'd swear she's eating less now, and at the same time she's putting on some weight."

This has been expressed more or less as a question to Mary, which Mary accepts, but she only says, "I think I understand," and she smiles.

And then, simultaneously, they lose all interest in Nan; they turn to each other as though they had been separated for some time. They look at each other with a sort of pleased surprise—and then, because it strikes them funny, they begin to laugh.

"Shall we dance?" Jay is still laughing as she says this, but that is what they do; they put on some old Glenn Miller records, from their own era, and Jimmy Lunceford and Tommy Dorsey—and they dance. Laughing and dancing, very happy with each other, they end up necking on the sofa, exhaustedly, like kids.

And that is how Nan finds them, asleep on the sofa. Mary is snoring lightly as Jay, asleep, breathes heavily into her breast.

Giving them first a quick, disgusted look, Nan goes over to the cluttered table, which it does not occur to her to clear. There is a large, dissolving plate of chocolate mousse, all of which she spoons slowly into her mouth—ah, delicious! She will have to get the recipe for her mother, Nan thinks; they could have it at least once a week, which should mean two or three pounds right there.

Slipping back into bed without even brushing her teeth, Nan continues with what has been a waking dream, a plan: next summer, when she is sleek and fat—as fat as Mary is!—she will come back up here, and Jay will fall madly in love with her. He will follow her everywhere, the way Dr. Thurston used to do. But she will say no, no kissing even. You belong to Mary. And Mary, finding out what Nan has done, will say what a wonderful girl Nan is, how truly good, as well as beautiful, and fat.

And then Nan will leave, probably off with some boyfriend of her own by then, and Mary and Jay will mourn for her. Always. "If only Nan were with us again this summer," they will say, for years and years.

❦ ❦

KIM ADDONIZIO

Survivors

He and his lover were down to their last few T cells and arguing over who was going to die first. He wanted to be the first because he did not want to have to take care of his lover's parrot or deal with his lover's family, which would descend on their flat after the funeral, especially the father, who had been an Army major and had tried to beat his son's sexual orientation out of him with a belt on several occasions during adolescence; the mother, at least, would be kind but sorrowful, and secretly blame him, the survivor—he knew this from her letters, which his lover had read to him each week for the past seven years. He knew, too, that they all—father, mother, two older brothers—would disapprove of their flat, of the portrait of the two of them holding hands that a friend had painted and which hung over the bed, the Gay Freedom Day poster in the bathroom, all the absurd little knickknacks like the small plastic wind-up penis that hopped around on two feet; maybe, after his lover died, he would put some things away, maybe he would even take the parrot out of its cage and open the window so it could join the wild ones he'd heard of that nested in the palm trees on Dolores Street, a whole flock of bright tropical birds apparently thriving in spite of the chilly Bay Area weather—he would let it go, fly off, and he would be completely alone then; dear God, he thought, let me die first, don't let me survive him.

❦ ❦

ANTHONY CAPUTI

from *To Know the Wind Is Mortal*

Breakfast. Call it a ceremony. The altar is set with cruets of orange juice for Martha and prune juice for the colitic professor, heavy jars of granola and fibrous flakes, colorful mugs for decaffeinated coffee, cold skimmed milk for the cereal and coffee, and for the robust appetite the toaster stands ready to receive slim slices of whole wheat bread, like large, nut brown communion hosts. Martha has already had a tall glass of water, one of at least eight to be drunk in the course of the day. She sits looking out on the February garden that is not quite a garden but that could be if someone would in summer trim back the bushes and give just a little time to weeding. She is in profile and lost in thought. The sun strikes the wall behind her, backlighting a noble profile composed of strong, clean features and a fresh Anglo-Saxon cheek to delight a Van Dyck or a Gainsborough. He notices that she is wearing a new dressing gown, a blue quilted garment trimmed with a pale purple ghost of a flower. His mind opens it to the pink, somewhat pendulous form beneath. No, it is not the body of his dream the previous night, but it is his Martha. And she would still smell faintly of sleep.

"You have a new dressing gown."

"Mmm." Her eyes do not leave whatever has become the focus of her meditation. "Is it today you see Doctor Frankenheimer?"

A Martha maneuver this, slipping from the dressing gown, which he might expect to be asked if he liked, to his health. She's fanatic about good health and the diet, exercise, and inner poise that produce it. What he had not known initially was that the discipline required for it can also become a weapon.

"I see him at 2:30."

"Mmm." Her gaze returns to the garden.

In fact he has to admit that health—his, hers, and the world's—has produced the first tiny cracks in what friends on all sides have rejoiced in as a triumphant marriage. A polite, unacknowledged competition has developed between them with longevity as its prize. Does exercise, to be effective, have to be aerobic? She insists it does. And what qualifies as an equivalent for the water to be drunk each day? Absolutely nothing, she claims. And, by the way, who has the advantage in long-lived relatives?

Yet all this is only a minor leitmotif in the full exfoliation of their life together, a life often tender, serene, and by any measure happy.

"Have you any pain today?" she asks, looking squarely at him with gray-blue eyes. "I mean of course the colitis."

"How many times do I have to tell you it's not colitis. It's called Irritable Bowel Syndrome, or spastic colon, or spastic bowel. All such disgusting names that the initials IBS are used!"

"All right, IBS then. Good heavens!"

"Well, you must understand that what I'm seeing Frankenheimer about probably has nothing to do with that. As you know, they saw shadows in the x-rays last week—shadows that clearly have nothing to do with the IBS!"

"Strange that both occur in the same place."

"But they don't occur in the same place!"

"And what about the polyps? Weren't they . . . ?"

"What about the polyps? Look, what is this?"

"Calm down. I'm sure you're right. You'll know soon enough, in any case. I wouldn't be surprised if he forbade you red meat altogether."

The shaft of winter sunlight moves behind her and hits the white wall to frame her in dazzling chiaroscuro: for an instant her features wash out, and he thinks of Dolores Winnegar, the young wife of a new colleague in psychology. She had come to him about the dissertation she is writing for the University of Colorado, and he has agreed to counsel her. In tight jeans and a cotton blouse buttoned precariously to reveal the body of a slender girl, she had slouched in her chair, one long leg cocked over the other, and he had all he could do to keep a civil distance. He complimented her on her western boots and agreed with her that Restoration comedy was a fruitful subject for her. When she blinked her green eyes and asked why, he smiled that that would become clear as their work progressed. In that instant she not only joined the cast of females in his virtually nonstop reveries, she slipped into a starring role.

Yet a tightness grips his heart as he recognizes that some of the desire he now feels for Martha was born in that conversation with Dolores Winnegar. Not all, but enough to cause anguish. He has never been disloyal to Martha, certainly not in deed, and that, after all, is what counts. His reveries and divagations about women are his own and peculiar, he knows, but his behavior has always held to the highest standards. And yet somehow this cowgirl interested in Restoration comedy provokes a sharp quake in deep-laid foundations, and the felt vibrations worry him. The truth is he can't stop thinking about her, and he despises himself for thinking about *her* when he wants *Martha!* Not that he thinks himself above criticism. He knows better, knows that his flights of erotic fancy, whether about women he has loved or those who have merely shaken his equanimity, sometimes lead to imagined scenes he regrets. But he has never allowed his *de facto* affairs (he hates the frivolity of the word "affairs") to overlap.

There they are, in the chronology of his life as in the ferment of his consciousness, neatly distinct. Marion, his love in adolescence, barely kissed yet the source of volcanic imaginings, more a creature constructed than one he actually knew. Mrs. Frangipane, his former landlady, a widow, forlorn and eager to tell him all about it. She needed him, and he her. Then Margot, a graduate student his own age, wild with a worrisome seriousness. Three years of gaudy, stormy scenes, all highs and lows, followed by Mrs. Frangipane again. Then Shelley, a twenty-year-old when he was in his thirties, a student-groupie. It began in bad faith and ended in obsession. After that again Margot—the New York period— more madness, more extravagance. Then Elizabeth, an antidote to extravagance, beautiful with a ripe matronly balance. The parade could have ended there, but she wouldn't leave her husband. After Elizabeth again Shelley, a wife and mother by that time. Shelley would have left her husband. And, finally, Martha, found when his life seemed like a medieval romance in which the hero bounces from adventure to adventure, woman to woman, dragon to dragon, without anything to link them more than his own lack of focus. And yet even Martha may not be the end! Now there's Dolores Winnegar, who might have been the woman in the dream. But Marion to Martha is not very many. Not really—not for a man with fifty-eight years on his head. Six—in, let's say, forty years of testosterone and an ever-deepening acquaintance with dramatic literature? And Dolores is only possibly a new episode.

He resists a more complete summary, or a more definitive one. That is what he does for students with plays, novels, and poems. But life is not a complete narrative: it resembles one except that it still lacks episodes and, most notably, an ending. To live it one has to take it scene by scene, to be inside it yet conscious of its indeterminateness. While living it, it surely has episodes, episodes with what look like endings. But he has learned that these endings are not true endings. He can easily list the women he has loved and set them off chronologically, but in his present life he lives with all of them contemporaneously. No one of his affairs has actually ended!

These thoughts send a spiral of excitement through him. Martha is his fixed point in this current episode, and has been, to his joy, for nine years. Noble Martha, like a Renaissance duchess in her quilted dressing gown. He rises, takes another chair and places it next to hers, then sits and covers her hands with his own. She stiffens slightly and her eyes widen.

"Is anything wrong?"

"No, my darling, everything is right. I love it that you concern yourself with my humiliating problems."

" 'Humiliating?' How silly."

"Can't help it. I marvel that you put up with me and even profess to still love me now that you know everything about me."

She ponders for a moment. She has understood. "I doubt that I know everything."

"What more would you like to know? Ask me anything."

She smiles, frees her hand, and caresses his jaw. "Would you like to lie down for a bit before starting the day?"

He kisses her hand, and as she steps from her place, embraces her. She is stiff. But then her hand goes to the back of his neck as he holds her, and he senses a rush a joy. Walking to the bedroom, he knows she is consenting, not because she especially wants to, but because he needs her. And she may not understand how or why he needs her! Hence a large part of his joy consists in gratitude, not that he has begged and been gratified, but that once again she has revealed that generosity of true aristocrats. Dear, dear Martha.

NICHOLAS DELBANCO

from *Count Rumford: His Book*

Benjamin Thompson, Count Rumford, on the Nature of Order and Love

Let me take a single instance of the universal process: love. Love is widely construed to be a phenomenon of great consequence, as tending to define the interaction of the species—whether of child for parent, parent for child, partner for partner, master for slave. Romance is a principal topic in discourse and story and dream. Argument and hatred, too, may be viewed as the absence of love. Poets sing of it and playwrights put it on the stage and painters represent its practice; there are few topics as common and none, it may be, more so: the desire of two entities to commingle and conjoin is, one may fairly claim, a condition of existence as we know it, a *sine qua non.*

Yet who has studied that condition with microscope and rule? Who with telescope and caliper has charted its course and arrival; who can explain its origin or predict its course; who may measure this abstraction except by its effects? What we know of love, or think we know, has long been written down in manual and guide-book; the procedures and their etiquette have been minutely described. And it is of course a relatively simple matter to measure the physical *action* of love—the blush on cheek, the flush on brow, the upright nipple and distended member and, in pleasure's climacteric, the curled toe.

What will strike the curious observer as far more curious, however, is the order that such passion necessarily entails—the sequence, as it were, of stimulus and subsequent response. These are various and many: as numberless, it may be urged, as the forms of love itself. A partial catalogue must once again suffice:

Four partners at one time would seem, to the discerning practitioner, most satisfying. All else is superfluity. In this arrangement the mouth and hands and sexual organ each have their proper function and their place. Some subscribe further to the theory of the gratification of feet, as being yet another extremity, and that the plausible limit of partners in congress mounts therefore to six. But the attention wanders perforce; the perfect focus of engagement is diffused by sheer extension, and though one may commend a gallant for his acrobatics that is not the same as ardor: mere excess and consequent waste.

For reasons heretofore adduced, three partners may prove sufficient; this is according to taste. The rectangular arrangement is as satisfying and rather more symmetrical than the pentagonal; the triangular (two additional partners) may claim its adherents as well.

If we love without requital it is unrequited love. If we love in perfect harmony it is as an instrument tuned. If we love in disproportion it is comic where not sad—as when, say, a man plights his troth with a tree or woman vows fidelity forever to a crow. The old enamored of the young engender suspicion if wealthy, scorn if poor. The young enamored of the old and not of their possessions are few and far between. Brutality runs rampant in alley and kitchen and wood. Disinterest and debauched exhaustion and satiety must, too, be factored in; the Duc d'—, I am informed, had more mistresses than shoes, and of the latter he could claim three hundred pair. Fewer women would engage in sex if they might receive compliments standing; the soft flattery of courtship is best delivered prone.

But however strange or foolish the predicament of lovers seems to those untouched by Cupid's shaft, the stricken party to himself seems sane. It is this that Plato meant when speaking of the shadow self, and this the poet writes of when he wrote of scars *sans* wound. What does the suitor seek to find if not a sense of order; what do we in that lovelorn state require but requital, as of particles made whole? The numberless varieties of love in this regard look similar: there is a tremor of expectancy, imbalance seeking balance, unrest portending rest. All else is merely detail, divergence and diversity within the common ground. All else is fireless smoke.

E. L. Doctorow

Willi

One spring day I walked in the meadow behind the barn and felt rising around me the exhalations of the field, the moist sweetness of the grasses, and I imagined the earth's soul lifting to the warmth of the sun and mingling me in some divine embrace. There was such brilliant conviction in the colors of the golden hay meadow, the blue sky, that I could not help laughing. I threw myself down in the grass and spread my arms. I fell at once into a trance and yet remained incredibly aware, so that whatever I opened my eyes to look at I did not merely see but felt as its existence. Such states come naturally to children. I was resonant with the hum of the universe, I was made indistinguishable from the world in a great bonding of natural revelation. I saw the drowse of gnats weaving between the grasses and leaving infinitesimally fine threads of shimmering net, so highly textured that the breath of the soil below lifted it in gentle billows. Minute crawling life on the stalks of hay made colossal odyssey, journeys of a lifetime, before my eyes. Yet there was no thought of miracle, of the miracle of microscopic sentience. The scale of the universe was not pertinent, and the smallest indications of energy were in proportion to the sun, which lay like an Egyptian eye between the stalks, and lit them as it lights the earth, by halves. The hay had fallen under me so that my own body's outline was patterned on the field, the outspread legs and arms, the fingers, and I was aware of my being as the arbitrary shape of an agency that had chosen to make me in this manner as a means of communicating with me. The very idea of a head and limbs and a body was substantive only as an act of communication, and I felt myself in the prickle of the flattened grass, and the sense of imposition was now enormous, a prodding, a lifting of this part of the world that was for some reason my momentary responsibility, that was giving me possession of itself. And I rose and seemed to ride on the planes of the sun, which I felt in fine striations, alternated with thin lines of the earth's moist essences. And invisibled by my revelation, I reached the barn and examined the face of it, standing with my face in the painted whiteness of its glare as a dog or a cat stands nose to a door until someone comes and lets it out. And I moved along the white barn wall, sidestepping until I came to the window which was a simple square without glass, and could only be felt by the geometrical coolness of its volume of inner air, for it was black within. And there I stood, as if in the mouth of a vacuum, and felt the insubstantial being of the sun meadow pulled past me into the barn, like a torrential implosion of light into darkness and life into death, and I myself too disintegrated in that force and was sucked like the chaff of the field in that roaring. Yet I stood where I was. And in quite normal spatial relationship with my surroundings felt the sun's quiet warmth on my back and the coolness of the cool barn on my face. And the windy universal roar in my ears had narrowed and refined itself to a recognizable frequency, that of a woman's pulsating song in the act of love, the gasp and note and gasp and note of an ecstatic score. I listened. And pressed upon by the sun, as if it were a hand on the back of my neck, I moved my face into the portal of the cool darkness, and no longer blinded by the sunlight, my eyes saw on the straw and in the dung my mother, denuded, in a pose of utmost degradation, a body, a reddened headless body, the head enshrouded in her clothing, everything turned inside out, as if blown out by the wind, all order, truth, and reason, and this defiled mama played violently upon and being made to sing her defilement. How can I describe what I felt! I felt I deserved to see this! I felt it was my triumph, but I felt monstrously betrayed. I felt drained suddenly of the strength to stand. I turned my back and slid down the wall to a sitting position under the window. My heart in my chest banged in sickened measure of her cries. I wanted to kill him, this killer of my mother who was killing her. I wanted to leap through the window and drive a pitchfork into his back, but I wanted him to be killing her, I wanted him to be killing her for me. I wanted to be him. I lay on the ground, and with my arms over my head and my hands clasped and my ankles locked, I rolled down the slope behind the barn, through the grass and the crop of hay. I flattened the hay like a mechanical cylinder of irrepressible force rolling fast and faster over rocks, through rivulets, across furrows and over hummocks of the uneven imperfect flawed irregular earth, the sun flashing in my closed eyes in diurnal emergency, as if time and the planet had gone out of control. As it has. (I am recalling these things now, a man older than my father when he died, and to whom a woman of my mother's age when all this happened is a young woman barely half my age. What an incredible achievement of fantasy is the scientific mind! We posit an empirical world, yet how can I be here at this desk in this room—and not be here? If memory is a matter of the stimulation of so many cells of the brain, the greater the stimulus—remorse, the recognition of fate—the more powerfully complete becomes the sensation of the memory until there is transfer, as in a time machine, and the memory is in the ontological sense another reality.) Papa, I see you now in the universe of your own making. I walk the polished floorboards of your house and seat myself at your dining table. I feel the tassels of the tablecloth on the tops of my bare knees. The light of the candelabra shines on your smiling mouth of big teeth. I notice the bulge of your neck produced by your shirt collar. Your pink scalp is visible through the close-cropped German-style haircut. I see your head raised in conversation and your white plump hand of consummate gesture making its point to your wife at the other end of the table. Mama is so attentive. The candle flame burns in her eyes and I imagine the fever there, but she is quite calm and seriously engrossed by what you say. Her long neck, very white, is hung with a thin chain from which depends on the darkness of her modest dress a cream-colored cameo, the carved profile of another fine lady of another time. In her neck a soft slow pulse beats. Her small hands are folded and the bones of her wrists emerge from the touch of lace at her cuffs. She is smiling at you in your loving proprietorship, proud of you, pleased to be yours, and the mistress of this house, and the mother of this boy. Of my tutor across the table from me who idly twirls the stem of his wineglass and glances at her, she is barely aware. Her eyes are for her husband. I think now Papa her feelings in this moment are sincere. I know now each moment has its belief and what we call treachery is the belief of each moment, the wish for it to be as it seems to be. It is possible in joy to love the person you have betrayed and to be refreshed in your love for him, it is entirely possible. Love renews all faces and customs and ideals and leaves the bars of the prison shining. But how could a boy know that? I ran to my room and waited for someone to follow me. Whoever dared to enter my room, I would attack—would pummel. I wanted it to be her, I wanted her to come to me, to hug me and to hold my head and kiss me on the lips as she liked to do, I wanted her to make those wordless sounds of comfort as she held me to her when I was hurt or unhappy, and when she did that I would beat her with my fists, beat her to the floor, and see her raise her hands helplessly in terror as I beat her and kicked her and jumped upon her and drove the breath from her body. But it was my tutor who, sometime later, opened the door, looked in with his hand upon the knob, smiled, said a few words, and wished me good night. He closed the door and I heard him walk up the steps to the next floor, where he had his rooms. Ledig was his name. He was a Christian. I had looked but could not find in his face any sign of smugness or leering pride or cruelty. There was nothing coarse about him, nothing that could possibly give me offense. He was barely twenty. I even thought I saw in his eyes a measure of torment. He was habitually melancholic anyway, and during my lessons his mind often wandered and he would gaze out the window and sigh. He was as much a schoolboy as his pupil. So there was every reason to refrain from judgment, to let time pass, to think, to gain understanding. Nobody knew that I knew. I had that choice. But did I? They had made my position intolerable. I was given double vision, the kind that comes with a terrible blow. I found I could not have anything to do with my kind sweet considerate mother. I found I could not bear the gentle pedagogics of my tutor. How, in that rural isolation, could I be expected to go on? I had no friends, I was not permitted to play with the children of the peasants who worked for us. I had only this trinity of Mother and Tutor and Father, this unholy trinity of deception and ignorance who had excommunicated me from my life at the age of thirteen. This of course in the calendar of traditional Judaism is the year a boy enjoys his initiation into manhood.

Meanwhile my father was going about the triumph of his life, running a farm according to the most modern principles of scientific management, astonishing his peasants and angering the other farmers in the region with his success. The sun brought up his crops, the Galician Agricultural Society gave him an award for the quality of his milk, and he lived in the state of abiding satisfaction given to individuals who are more than a match for the life they have chosen for themselves. I had incorporated him into the universe of giant powers that I, a boy, experienced in the changes of the seasons. I watched bulls bred to cows, watched mares foal, I saw life come from the egg and the multiplicative wonders of mudholes and ponds, the jell and slime of life shimmering in gravid expectation. Everywhere I looked, life sprang from something not life, insects unfolded from sacs on the surface of still waters and were instantly on the prowl for their dinner, everything that came into being knew at once what to do and did it unastonished that it was what it was, unimpressed by where it was, the great earth heaving up its bloodied newborns from every pore, every cell, bearing the variousness of itself from every conceivable substance which it contained in itself, sprouting life that flew or waved in the wind or blew from the mountains or stuck to the damp black underside of rocks, or swam or suckled or bellowed or silently separated in two. I placed my father in all of this as the owner and manager. He lived in the universe of giant powers by understanding it and making it serve him, using the daily sun for his crops and breeding what naturally bred, and so I distinguished him in it as the god-eye in the kingdom, the intelligence that brought order and gave everything its value. He loved me and I can still feel my pleasure in making him laugh, and I might not be deceiving myself when I remember the feel on my infant hand of his unshaved cheek, the winy smell of his breath, the tobacco smoke in his thick wavy hair, or his mock-wondering look of foolish happiness during our play together. He had close-set eyes, the color of dark grapes, that opened wide in our games. He would laugh like a horse and show large white teeth. He was a strong man, stocky and powerful—the constitution I inherited—and he had emerged as an orphan from the alleys of cosmopolitan eastern Europe, like Darwin's amphibians from the sea, and made himself a landowner, a husband and father. He was a Jew who spoke no Yiddish and a farmer raised in the city. I was not allowed to play with village children, or to go to their crude schools. We lived alone, isolated on our estate, neither Jew nor Christian, neither friend nor petitioner of the Austro-Hungarians, but in the pride of the self-constructed self. To this day I don't know how he arranged it or what hungering rage had caused him to deny every classification society imposes and to live as an anomaly, tied to no past in a world which, as it happened, had no future. But I am in awe that he did it. Because he stood up in his life he was exposed to the swords of Mongol horsemen, the scythes of peasants in revolution, the lowered brows of monstrous bankers and the cruciform gestures of prelates. His arrogance threatened him with the cumulative power of all of European history which was ready to take his head, nail it to a pole and turn him into one of the scarecrows in his fields, arms held stiffly out toward life. But when the moment came for this transformation, it was accomplished quite easily, by a word from his son. I was the agency of his downfall. Ancestry and myth, culture, history and time were ironically composed in the shape of his own boy.

I watched her for several days. I remembered the rash of passion on her flesh. I was so ashamed of myself that I felt continuously ill, and it was the vaguest, most diffuse nausea, nausea of the blood, nausea of the bone. In bed at night I found it difficult breathing, and terrible waves of fever broke over me and left me parched in my terror. I couldn't purge from my mind the image of her overthrown body, the broad whitenesses, her shoed feet in the air; I made her scream ecstatically every night in my dreams and awoke one dawn in my own sap. That was the crisis that toppled me, for in fear of being found out by the maid and by my mother, for fear of being found out by them all as the archcriminal of my dreams, I ran to him, I went to him for absolution, I confessed and put myself at his mercy. Papa, I said. He was down by the kennels mating a pair of vizslas. He used this breed to hunt. He had rigged some sort of harness for the bitch so that she could not bolt, a kind of pillory, and she was putting up a terrible howl, and though her tail showed her amenable, she moved her rump away from the proddings of the erect male, who mounted and pumped and missed and mounted again and couldn't hold her still. My father was banging the fist of his right hand into the palm of his left. Put it to her, he shouted, come on, get it in there, give it to her. Then the male had success and the mating began, the female standing there quietly now, sweat dripping off her chops, an occasional groan escaping from her. And then the male came, and stood front paws on her back, his tongue lolling as he panted, and they waited as dogs do for the detumescence. My father knelt beside them and soothed them with quiet words. Good dogs, he said, good dogs. You must guard them at this time, he said to me, they try to uncouple too early and hurt themselves. Papa, I said. He turned and looked at me over his shoulder as he knelt beside the dogs, and I saw his happiness, and the glory of him in his workpants tucked into a black pair of riding boots and his shirt open at the collar and the black hair of his chest curled as high as the throat, and I said, Papa, they should be named Mama and Ledig. And then I turned so quickly I do not even remember his face changing, I did not even wait to see if he understood me, I turned and ran, but I am sure of this—he never called after me.

There was a sun room in our house, a kind of conservatory with a glass outer wall and slanted ceiling of green glass framed in steel. It was a very luxurious appointment in that region, and it was my mother's favorite place to be. She had filled it with plants and books, and she liked to lie on a chaise in this room and read and smoke cigarettes. I found her there, as I knew I would, and I gazed at her with wonder and fascination because I knew her fate. She was incredibly beautiful, with her dark hair parted in the center and tied behind her in a bun, and her small hands, and the lovely fullness of her chin, the indications under her chin of some fattening, like a quality of indolence in her character. But a man would not dwell on this as on her neck, so lovely and slim, or the high modestly dressed bosom. A man would not want to see signs of the future. Since she was my mother it had never occurred to me how many years younger she was than my father. He had married her out of the gymnasium; she was the eldest of four daughters and her parents had been eager to settle her in prosperous welfare, which is what a mature man offers. It is not that the parents are unaware of the erotic component for the man in this sort of marriage. They are fully aware of it. Rectitude, propriety, are always very practical. I gazed at her in wonder and awe. I blushed. What? she said. She put her book down and smiled and held out her arms. What, Willi, what is it? I fell into her arms and began to sob and she held me and my tears wet the dark dress she wore. She held my head and whispered, What, Willi, what did you do to yourself, poor Willi? Then, aware that my sobs had become breathless and hysterical, she held me at arm's length—tears and snot were dribbling from me—and her eyes widened in genuine alarm.

That night I heard from the bedroom the shocking exciting sounds of her undoing. I have heard such terrible sounds of blows upon a body in Berlin after the war, Freikorps hoodlums in the streets attacking whores they had dragged from the brothel and tearing the clothes from their bodies and beating them to the cobblestones. I sat up in bed, hardly able to breathe, terrified, but feeling undeniable arousal. Give it to her, I muttered, banging my fist in my palm. Give it to her. But then I could bear it no longer and ran into their room and stood between them, lifting my screaming mother from the bed, holding her in my arms, shouting at my father to stop, to stop. But he reached around me and grabbed her hair with one hand and punched her face with the other. I was enraged, I pushed her back and jumped at him, pummeling him, shouting that I would kill him. This was in Galicia in the year 1910. All of it was to be destroyed anyway, even without me.

❧ ❧

LAMAR HERRIN

from *The Lies Boys Tell*

The second he awoke he thought, We're going across. He couldn't smell the water, not with *his* nose, and with so many heat-emitting semis accompanying them he never caught a trace of its chill. Plus the fact, he lay now with his head toward the rear of the van and the distance he felt from the front and the three people sitting there was enormous. Still, he knew they were crossing the Mississippi. The van began to rise, its tire-pitch to sharpen, there was an instant's release, and then it was as if they had begun a long suspended leap between halves of a continent. That was how it felt to him. He weighed nothing. His weight came back to him only if he moved. But motionless, unaffected by gravity and undiscovered by his pain, he felt they might sail on like this forever.

He thought he'd earned it. For years—at Quincy and at Hannibal and at Cairo—he'd had to cross the Mississippi on a ferry, and what he remembered best from those frequently pre-dawn crossings was not the chill of the water, rank and fierce enough to take off the top of your head, or the broad glistening back of the river itself, but the weight, the incredible sense of weight of those ferries loaded with trucks and cars, and their slow plodding progress toward a light on the far shore. This was in payment for that—if he lay still. Then not even lying still did any good. With a feverish start his pain returned. The van touched down bumpily on the Illinois shore. He came fully awake then, and realized he did not know where they were, whether they'd crossed at Chester or Cape Giradeau or farther south at Cairo.

He opened his eyes. Jeff sat between his mother and father, the bright blonde of his hair turning from one to the other like a beacon. Ed had wanted to be able to see them—it was the reason he'd turned himself around on the mattress, which Connie had now provided with a form-fitting sheet, plus slips for the pillows. But he hadn't wanted to hear them, to *overhear* them, and he couldn't make out what Jeff was saying now. He was obviously excited, and in his presence his parents were subdued. Even if Ed hadn't known their histories he would have had to judge them a family forced into place. Instead of propping an elbow on the window Larry drove with both hands squarely on the wheel, at intervals flexing the tension out of his neck. Connie was turned slightly inward in her seat, and gave the impression of not having spoken for some time. Her hair looked healthy only in patches—or perhaps it had been poorly cut—and Larry's was thinning not only on the crown but down the back. Age seemed to be overtaking them as they sat there. Jeff saw it too and swiveled back and forth between his mother and father as if he were watching people harden into statues before his eyes. And it was true, age did that. He could have told them: from now on till the end of your life, every day will be a race between the age that hardens you in your isolated ways and your love. But he didn't. He'd feel like a hypocrite talking about love, and hypocrisy was not good for his pain. Nor was shame. Still . . . he loved his wife, his younger son and daughter, he loved his older son and his loving ex-daughter-in-law, his grandson, all his grandchildren, it was like a spiral with an ever-widening reach, his love, but there at the funneled-down point he was a champion of his isolated ways, and he was afraid. . . .

Of what? He didn't know. He couldn't say. It was as if he were thinking in pictures. That spiral he saw was like a radio signal we transmit into the night, like the bell of a great horn. We might blow out with a full expanse of lungs, we might send out our signal all the days of our life, for there was nothing out there to impede us. Sooner or later, though, we would reach a point when our breath failed us and that great spiraling transmission began to wind back on itself. We might marvel then at how far and wide our love had ranged. We might applaud our capacity for love, never remembering it was fear that had powered us on. Fear, we might choose to forget, was sometimes responsible for superhuman feats. But we couldn't deceive ourselves forever. The winding down would wind us back to knowledge: we loved because we were afraid and we were afraid because we were alone and the greatest lovers were those with the most terrible fear of their loneliness. But even as we learned the truth about ourselves that spiral continued to unwind until we were back where we started, alone again with no breath left in our fear.

He was not used to visions or illuminations of this sort, and as this one was given to him it was taken away, leaving him with the sight of his estranged son and daughter-in-law at the other end of the van, their son dividing his attention between them. He'd been told at the start that he couldn't play his tapes while his grandfather was asleep, and afraid now that Jeff would turn back and find him awake, Ed closed his eyes. He had no one then. But isn't that where we all started, he asked himself, alone in the dark? And as we reached out in our lonely need to find people to love, did we ever really open our eyes? And didn't we *create* people instead, blind to who they might otherwise become? Larry, for instance. He loved Larry both as a father and husband created in his own image, and as a homebreaker, an outcast, a rebel, a vagrant, a bum. Connie he'd wanted to give back to Larry for his own good, but he thought he saw now that he was putting his work off on her. Everything was coming in glimpses, he couldn't be sure. And the logic he followed was as tenuous as the afterimage of his vision. But as long as it held he realized this son he'd fathered—fathered twice, once in physical fact and again as a misbegotten object of his love—he'd left unfinished, and maybe that was the real reason he had asked Larry to come out on this trip, so that he could finish with him while there was still time.

He came to a stop and a blurring-out there. How could he finish anything in the state he was in? And if Larry was a creation of his who begged to be recreated, what did he need to fix in himself first before he tried again? And what was he talking about anyway? He was a dying man, there was nothing to fix because everything was coming apart. And anyway, anyway, wasn't he going crazy? A moment ago didn't he think he was flying?

And there were others to consider. Did he really believe he could clear his mind of everybody else he had lovingly installed out on the whorls of that spiral while he dedicated his last breath and ounce of strength to Larry? They wouldn't stay away. On the influx that always followed that efflux he could already feel them pouring back in. And how many of them, when he looked closely, might also be unfinished, incomplete?

He lay still, either awake or half asleep and dreaming, and in a succession of luminous scenes the others began to appear to him. Some he hadn't thought about in years. There was Harry Conklin, a childhood playmate he'd smoked his first cigarette with at the age of ten; Will Farley, a man he regularly joined for morning coffee until his son had been killed in Vietnam; old Ralph Lickerson, a deacon in the church like him, with whom he'd passed the collection plate; Mabel Stuart and her husband Carl, but mainly Mabel, who on a giddy New Year's Eve had told him solemnly she'd go to Alaska with him if he wasn't already married to her best friend; the long sallow-faced girl, whose name was gone, to whom he'd lost his virginity on a Tuesday night because that was the day written on the slip of paper he'd picked out of Kip Mobley's hat; golfing buddies, foursomes passing by him like small migrating herds attended by their caddies, Skeet and Bob Barley and Hawk Wilson and the Rabbi and Jimmy Paul Willard and Raymer and Cochise, a mixture of ages and places and handicaps, men of a swaggering sort of banter he had not really gotten to know; Pete Richie, his caddy, a quiet boy whom Ed had given a job delivering orders until he'd had to fire him for petty theft; his own father, his mother, his brother Randell and his sisters Louise and Emma; and then in a consanguineous rush that seemed to crowd the remaining air out of his lungs, his other son, his daughter and his wife.

They came to mourn him, and behind the mask of that mourning to take him to task. Nell was sweet about it; while Sylvia and Russ exchanged cold words under their breath, Nell whispered, "Daddy . . . Daddy," in a beseeching tone that evoked for him a moment in the woods across from their house, until Chris Simmons had bought the property and built on it. She was asking him to go back there with her again, just as she'd chosen him before to console her. When her little Missie had died of distemper Nell had picked out the burial site and sworn him to secrecy: *he* was to hold her hand, tell her about dog heaven, assure her that Missie would always be waiting for her there—*he*, and no one else. From scrap lumber in the garage he'd built a small coffin, and she in misshapen letters had painted "Missie" on top. She'd left the small patty-cake prints of her hands in the mounded dirt over Missie's grave. He'd grieved for her, a sensation as sad and pleasurable as any he'd ever known. Then he'd forgotten about it. But she had remembered and was asking him now to take her back, whispering, "Daddy . . . Daddy" so close to his ear her voice was like the sound of a conch.

He should have known better. Out of the whorls of that spiraling conch, or out of the whorls of his inner ear, he heard other voices now, sweet like his daughter's, and accusing like hers, "Hey, Pop," and still quieter, a summons to memory, "Ed"—and he tried not to listen. But that was like trying not to feel pain, like directing your attention elsewhere while pain burned through your tissues with the finest of flames.

Russ, in his loyal and methodical way, had moments he too wanted to relive, words of advice he wanted to reconfirm, questions he wanted to ask concerning the business, treacherous doubts he wanted his father to allay—about the life they had chosen, about the lastingness of its values, about responsibility and honor and love, of course, and the chances of staying sane. What could Ed say? The doubts were real, permanent and deep; he pictured his second son as a once-solid block of wood and the doubts as cracks. His fault, he knew—these were cracks *he'd* fathered. Everything he'd once loved he'd fathered, and everybody. When did it stop? A man fathered, it seemed, the second he ceased to be a child, and kept on until his breath rattled in his lungs like peas in a gourd. Crawling off to die he'd fathered. A man was a fecundating fool. When did it stop? "Ed," she said, and he'd told her, Let's wait, we're in no hurry, and she said, "Ed," her voice quiet and full with an impersonal sort of resonance, and he'd said, There's no future in this job, let's wait at least till I get something that'll take us from one year to the next, and "Ed," as if that name itself possessed some delectable power for her which if she repeated it long enough would engender the child they'd waited eight years to have. "Ed . . . Ed . . . Ed . . ."

Then he'd gotten the job, they'd made a downpayment on a house and moved in, and it was in every corner of that childless house, the sound of his name. When he'd finally given in it was like slipping unsheathed into the oil-rich waters of life, an intoxicating and disorienting immersion, and he'd understood: past the accidents of face and figure, height and width, cheerful or sullen disposition, she was this mothering space and he this fathering muscle, soon to be converted into light. "Ed," she said, an admonishment now, and he turned away from her as though from a mind-deranging dilemma, for hadn't he fathered her too? Fourteen she'd been, not when they'd married but when she'd been born to him—and hadn't he coached her up through the years? Freshman, sophomore, junior, senior, and hadn't she graduated as his bride? Then to father her into motherhood at once, then to somehow grandfather himself and come crawling to death there on their marriage bed—No! It was too much to ask! "Ed." No, he would not do it! "Ed." He would not!

"Ed . . ." she insisted in a long musical moan, and it didn't matter that he distrusted her, that all the wiles in the world found a home in her voice, because he was doing it again, she had somehow enlivened him to it, motored as though by this van he was rising up into that measureless mothering space, he had felt that instant's release and as the tire-pitch sharpened had begun to take that long leap, as though between halves of a continent. . . .

Cold fear seized him then, arresting his leap. I am dying, he said, and opened his eyes. His grandson was staring at him intently, too intent to realize in that first second that his grandfather was now looking back at him. Ed thought, I'm not dying, not yet, we're going back, we're crossing back over the Mississippi. Why's that? Why have they decided to do that?

Ed said, "Why are we going back over the Mississippi, Larry?"

"It's the Ohio, Dad," his son answered, but gently and gravely, as though it were an embarrassing secret they shared.

Then it was Jeff's turn. "You said when Granddad woke up. . . ."

❦ ❦

EDWARD HOWER

Miriamu and the King

On Independence night, the African Star Uhuru Bar was packed with celebrators.

"Every man in the village was in my bed tonight," Adija said. Adija and Salome were barmaids at the African Star. "Every man but the one I want."

"The whites are staying in their houses this night," Salome said.

"He'll come. You'll see." Adija lay on her side next to Salome. "He's not fearing me. I'm only half-African, anyway."

Adija's back was pale, pale brown in the glow of the lantern. Her bones stood out beneath her skin. Tiny ridges rippled up her spine. Salome's eyes hurt to look at them. She pulled the blanket up over Adija. "Are you very sore?" she asked.

Adija was rubbing oil into her crotch. She pretended not to hear. "You see that picture of the king?" she asked, pointing at the wall.

Salome looked. Adija's crazy collection. If you stick people to the wall with pins, Adija had explained, they can't move about or shout at you or behave badly. They just have to keep smiling. You can think they're trying to please you with their smiles. Salome searched for the picture of the king. Elvis Presley leered at her. Satchmo flashed his teeth. A fridge gaped, a television stared. Queen Elizabeth smiled at a procession of schoolchildren waving their Union Jacks. The country's cabinet ministers stood beside their new houses and motorcars. They were smiling.

There was the newspaper photograph of Adija's white man. He was standing on an airport runway with the other missionary teachers from America. Beside the photograph was a color picture of the king. He was sitting on his throne beneath a crown that looked too heavy for his delicate, brown face. "I found it," Salome said.

"Beneath it is the picture of Rita Tushingham. The one in the school uniform."

"It's not a school uniform. It's a servant's uniform."

"It's a school uniform," Adija said. "You want to hear the story, or don't you?"

"One of your stories." Salome laughed. "Yes, go ahead. It'll distract me."

"Miriamu was a poor schoolgirl," Adija began. She raised her hands as she spoke, in the manner of the Arab fishermen who lived in her home village on the coast, and told the following story.

The other schoolgirls mocked her, because she was poor. The men in her town called her a slut, because her father was an Arab trader. Her mother beat her, because she failed her examinations at school. But Miriamu was always happy.

One day all the schoolgirls went to the palace of the king to shout their praises and wave their flags at him. The king had a beautiful big palace. It had four rondavels at the corners, with roofs of woven palm leaves, and high white walls between the rondavels. It was finer than the finest mosque in the city. The king stood on the wall and looked down at the schoolgirls. He was very bored with these parades of school-children. He was not feeling happy that day, because he had not been out of the palace in a long time. But when he saw Miriamu he smiled. He said: "Here is the most beautiful girl in my kingdom. She is the one I am going to marry."

He sent his ministers to discover who the beautiful girl was.

"Her name is Miriamu," said the Minister for Commerce.

"But she is too ignorant. She is thin and her skin is a strange, pale color," said the Minister for Home Affairs.

"She is not good enough to marry a king. You must marry a girl of a royal caste," said the Minister for Information, Tourism, and Wildlife.

"I am the king," said the king.

"If you marry her," said all the ministers together, "we will plot a coup to overthrow you."

"Really, I think she is good enough," said the king.

The ministers all whispered together. "If you wish to marry her, we will have to test her," said the Minister for Education. "We will have to see if she is worthy to live among us at the palace."

"All right," said the king. "But mind you don't harm her."

"No, no. We won't," said the ministers.

They sent a messenger to fetch Miriamu. "You see that mountain," said the Minister for Education. "There is a cross at the top of it. You just have to bring it to us. The king wants it badly, but he can't leave the palace. When you bring it back, then you can marry him."

"All right," said Miriamu.

But Miriamu was very unhappy. The mountain was very high, higher even than Kilimanjaro, and its top was covered with snow. She walked along the beach, kicking the coconuts at her feet. She looked up at the mountain and wept. She knew that the ministers wanted to kill her with their test. They didn't want the king to have any women, be-cause they thought he would neglect his duties if he had any. But Miri-amu did not want to disappoint the king, so she started up the mountain.

The first night she thought she would freeze to death. She had on only her school uniform. Already there was much snow on the ground. But then she saw a hut. It had white walls like the palace, and a tile roof like her school.

The door of the hut opened. There stood a fierce-looking man. His eyes were flashing on and off, like the signboards of the city. They flashed blue and brown, blue and brown. His hair flashed too, as if there were lightning in it. It flashed yellow and black and red, and sometimes it vanished altogether and the man's skull flashed out at her in different colors. The man had a great bulge in the front of his trousers. It looked like a sack full of snakes. The bulge moved in and out as his eyes flashed. He was a witch, and Miriamu was fearing him very much.

"*Karibu,* Miriamu. Come in out of the snow," said the witch, smiling.

Miriamu was trembling, but she stepped inside. The witch gave her some beer. As he drank, he boasted of all the things he owned and all the things he knew. Miriamu decided to flatter him. What else could she do?

"Your Bata shoes are very smart," she said. "And that suit you're wearing—you must have ordered it all the way from England. I'm sure you are very clever from watching that handsome television. What a beautiful fridge you have—look how it shines!"

The witch was very pleased with her flattery. He continued boasting about all the places he had visited and all the things he knew. Miriamu listened carefully, for she thought he might tell her the secret of how to get to the top of the mountain.

But soon he passed out from drinking too much beer. Miriamu was disappointed. She decided to continue her journey. But when she tried the door, she found that it was locked. All the doors and windows were locked. She could not get out. The house was dark and dirty. She watched the television for a while, and listened carefully to all the programs. But when the national anthem was played and the station shut down for the night, Miriamu had still not learned any useful secrets.

She was hungry. So she went to the fridge and opened it. Then she jumped back. For a *jinni* flew out of the fridge. It was tall and looked like a jellyfish, trailing a cloak of icicles.

"I am the *Jinni* of the Fridge," said the *jinni.* "Ask me a wish, and I shall grant it."

Miriamu was frightened. She began to weep. She told the *jinni* her sad story.

The *jinni* took pity on her, and said: "All right, here is what you must do. When my master wakes, you must give him more beer. Then you must open up his trousers. There you will find a sack of many-colored snakes. You will be fearing them very much, but they will not harm you. Take this tablet, and the snakes will not harm you."

And the *jinni* gave Miriamu an aspirin.

"Take hold of the snakes and push them into all the holes of your body until the snakes are tired and go to sleep. Then my master will be sleepy, as well. Tell him he is very wise. But say that there is one thing you are sure he doesn't know. And that is: how to drive a Land Rover.

"He will say: 'Yes, I know even that!' But you must keep doubting him, until he tells you all the things necessary for driving a Land Rover. Give him more beer, then. He will go to sleep.

"Now, on his watch chain you will find a silver key and a golden key. The silver key is for unlocking the door of his hut, and the golden key is for starting the Land Rover. The Land Rover is in the yard. You can drive it to the top of the mountain and down again. Here is some petrol for you."

And the *jinni* waved his hand. The beer in the fridge turned into tins of petrol.

"Good luck," said the *jinni*. "Now please close the fridge, before I melt like ice cream."

Miriamu did all that she was bidden. After the witch had gone to sleep again, she unlocked the door with the silver key and started up the Land Rover with the golden key. Then she drove the Land Rover to the top of the mountain. The road was very winding, but Miriamu didn't get stuck in any ditch, because she knew all the things necessary for driving a Land Rover.

The cross was high on the highest peak of the mountain. She drove backwards up to the peak. When the back of the Land Rover hit the rock where the cross stood, the cross fell into the back of the Land Rover. The cross was of gold, and heavier than the heaviest stone. But the Land Rover was very strong. It carried Miriamu and the cross all the way to the bottom of the mountain.

The ministers were surprised to see Miriamu driving along the beach toward the palace. They thought she had died on the mountain. Also, they had never seen a woman driving a Land Rover before. The king was pleased with the cross. He put it in his garden among the palm trees and flowering bushes. The king had many motorcars—Ford Zephyrs and Wolseleys and even a Mercedes. But he didn't have any Land Rover. So he was overjoyed when Miriamu gave it to him.

"The story's not over," Adija said, sitting up in bed. "Where are you going?"

"I'm cold." Salome went to the charcoal brazier where she had warmed her maize-meal supper. She blew on the coals, but got only a faceful of ashes for her trouble; the coals had gone out. The lantern, too, was dimming, and there was no more kerosene. Outside in the street, a woman shrieked. It was the kind of sound a woman makes when a man is teasing her too roughly: at first loud laughter, then a panicky cry. A dog barked. Someone slammed a door. Cursing, Salome took down the army greatcoat she wore when it rained. She spread it over her on the bed. When she offered to share it with Adija, Adija shook her head.

"You're the one who's usually shivering," Salome said.

"As long as I'm awake, the room's warm enough with the lantern lit." Adija took two cigarettes from her pack, lit them, and handed one to Salome. "You want me to go on with the story?"

"Sure. It's better than freezing in silence."

Adija puffed on her cigarette a few times, and then continued:

The king was very pleased with Miriamu and her gifts. "You see, the girl is clever," he said to his ministers. "She is worthy to be my bride. Summon all the chiefs in my kingdom for my wedding!"

"Just a minute," said the Minister for Defense. "*Bado kidogo,* if you please."

The king waited.

The ministers all whispered together. Then the Minister for Education said to the king: "All right, she has brought gifts for you. But what of us? If she doesn't bring gifts for us, we will plot a coup to overthrow you."

"My army is strong," said the king. "I'll take my chances. Let the drummers drum from all the hilltops for my wedding!"

"No, no!" pleaded Miriamu to the king. "They will kill you if we are married now. Let me first get some gifts for them."

"All right," said the king. "But hurry up. I have not had any women for many years, and I am lonely."

Miriamu asked the ministers: "Do you want some lovely Bata shoes and English suits and televisions and fridges? I know where I can get some for you."

The ministers all whispered together again. Then they all shook their heads. "What we want are some pearls from the ocean. Just go to the ocean and fetch some for us," said the Minister for Foreign Affairs.

"But I can't swim," cried Miriamu.

"You don't have to swim," said the Minister for Transportation. "Just go down to the Nyara Beach Hotel and hire a boat to take you to the reef. On the reef you will find a hole."

"It isn't a very deep hole," said the Minister for Finance, chuckling.

"You can reach in and gather up the pearls," said the Minister for Education. Really, that Minister for Education was the wickedest of the lot. "We will be waiting for you on the verandah."

So Miriamu drove down to the Nyara Beach Hotel in her Land Rover and hired an outrigger canoe. The boatman poled her out to the reef. The ministers waved to her from the verandah. They were laughing as they waved.

Miriamu was weeping with fear, for the water was crashing against the reef. But finally she found the hole. It was a deep, dark hole, not a shallow one as the minister had told her. She was cursing those ministers very much. She knelt down and reached her hand into the hole, though, for she could see the pearls shining up at her out of the water.

As soon as her hand touched the water, something grabbed her. She was pulled down, down into the hole. Seaweeds slid across her face. She thought surely she would drown. But then she got pulled into a cave. There was air in the cave. The air smelled foul and it was dim, but Miriamu could breathe it. She looked around, to see what had pulled her down into the water.

It was an octopus that had pulled her down into the water. It must be a witch, thought Miriamu, because it is as strange-looking, in its way, as the man on the mountain. It was black as the underbelly of a cooking pot. Its eyes were full of flames, like the flames that leap out of the end of a rifle. Its arms were very long and strong. At the end of each arm was a weapon. The octopus had knives and spears and *pangas* and rifles and pistols and Sten guns and even bombs. It waved the weapons all at once at Miriamu and its eyes glowed red.

Miriamu was fearing this witch very much. But now she was more clever than before. She told it: "Look how powerful your weapons are! I think that pistol can shoot very straight. That Sten gun, I think it must make a fearsome noise. Can you slice off a man's head with that *panga?* I think so!"

Miriamu was gasping for breath as she spoke, for the octopus was wrapping its arms around her tight. She thought that she would be crushed in the arms of the octopus. But it was pleased that Miriamu was admiring its weapons. It gave Miriamu a small knife to look at.

Now Miriamu remembered what she had learned on the mountain. When the octopus let go of the knife, Miriamu pushed the end of its arm into her vagina. She put another arm into her anus, and another into her mouth, and soon weapons were falling all over the floor of the cave. Miriamu was feeling very happy, for the octopus was holding her gently now.

When the last of its arms went limp, the octopus opened its mouth. Inside its mouth was a basket full of shining pearls. Miriamu reached in and took out the basket. She looked down into the basket to admire the pearls. When she looked up, the octopus was gone. In its place was a beautiful woman.

The woman was lying asleep on the floor of the cave. Miriamu rushed to her and woke her. The woman sat up, rubbing her eyes. She was very happy to greet Miriamu.

"*Salaama*," said the beautiful woman. "Why have you come to this reef?"

Miriamu told her the story of the king and the ministers and the pearls.

"Listen," said the woman, "those ministers are just going to trick you. I know them. They are the ones who bewitched me into the shape of an octopus many years ago. I will return with you. We will bring my weapons and kill them."

"All right," said Miriamu. "But what if the boatman refuses to carry us?"

"Don't worry. I will give him some pearls," said the woman.

So Miriamu and the woman went back to shore with a boat full of weapons. The ministers were still sitting on the verandah. They were drinking brandy and laughing. But when they saw the boat, they stopped laughing.

As soon as the boat touched the beach, the woman attacked the verandah. The ministers tried to run away, but they were too fat to run fast. The woman threw a bomb, and half the ministers were blown up. They lay bleeding all over the verandah.

Then the woman shot all the rest of the ministers with the Sten gun. They were lying on the floor of the verandah. Their organs were splattered on the walls. They were moaning and cursing and clutching their fat bellies. They all bled to death.

The manager of the Nyara Beach Hotel was very unhappy. "What am I going to do with all these dead bodies on my verandah?" he asked.

"Here, take some pearls," said the woman. And the manager was quiet.

Miriamu and the woman drove to the palace in the Land Rover. The people came out into the streets to see them. They were cheering and waving their flags at them. They were happy that the wicked ministers had been killed. Even the palm trees were happy on that day. They were waving their leaves over Miriamu and the woman as the Land Rover drove through the streets of the city.

The king was overjoyed to see Miriamu. He embraced her.

"This is my friend," said Miriamu, and she showed the woman to the king. "She killed all the ministers."

"My ministers are dead?" shouted the king. *"Eii!* This is the best news in many years!" And he greeted the woman in a very friendly way.

"Well, I will be going back to my cave now," said the woman.

"No, no! You must stay!" said the king. "You can come to my wedding. Afterwards, you can live in the palace with us. I will make you brigadier of my army."

"All right," said the woman.

The king summoned all the chiefs in the kingdom. He ordered his drummers to drum from all the hilltops for his wedding. He caused the palace to be decorated with flowers of many colors. The sun shone bright on the day of the wedding. As the king and Miriamu walked together into the chapel, the palm trees lifted their leaves toward Heaven.

After the wedding ceremony, the king and his bride had a big party. All the king's friends were there. Queen Elizabeth was there. Elvis Presley was there, and Shashi Kapoor and Pearl Bailey and Miriam Makeba and Pélé and Satchmo and Cliff Richard and the Shadows, and all the famous film stars. Miriamu and the king and the woman sat at the biggest table. They were not drinking beer, they were drinking palm wine and Bee Hive Brandy and Gilbey's Gin. They were not eating maize-meal porridge, they were eating roasted goat and sheep and prawn curry and coconuts and paw-paw and fish cooked in palm wine. They got very drunk and fat.

Miriamu and the king and the woman stood on the wall of the palace. The people cheered and waved their flags at them. Even the schoolgirls who used to mock Miriamu were cheering. Even the men who used to abuse Miriamu were cheering. Even Miriamu's mother, who used to beat her, was cheering. But now they were cheering only because they were fearing Miriamu.

"Shall I tell the army to chase them away?" the woman asked Miriamu.

"All right," said Miriamu. "Tell the army to chase them into the ocean."

The army chased them into the ocean and they drowned.

Then Miriamu and the king and the woman ate and drank some more. Even the king got drunk. Even Miriamu got fat. Everyone was very happy on that day.

"And that," Adija said, "is the story of Miriamu and the king."

"And the woman," Salome said.

"Yes."

Adija rolled over on her back. Her breasts were flat on her chest, her nipples cold and hard in the chill air. "Was the story good?"

Salome laughed. "I think so. Are you sure you made it up?"

"Of course! You've never heard it before, have you?"

"Yes and no," Salome said. "I have and I haven't."

"Look!—" Adija pointed up at the ceiling. A tiny lizard was running upside down along the corrugated tin. It scurried back and forth, then disappeared under the edge of the roof. "It was gray, in that shadow," Adija said. "This afternoon it was orange."

"I don't like lizards. My people say they crawl into your head while you're sleeping and eat your brain."

"I don't believe in witchcraft," Adija said. "I like them."

"You would." Salome shivered. "You're a witch yourself, you know. You've crawled into my brain and now I'm stuck with you."

Adija giggled. She pressed her cheek against Salome's broad shoulder and closed her eyes.

Salome let the lantern burn down. As the globe became sooty, the light shrank down the walls, flickering. Still, it seemed to provide some warmth in the room. Light and shadow flickered on Adija's pictures, making the faces indistinguishable, just a wall of glossy squares. Adija pushed closer to Salome beneath the blanket to absorb more of her warmth. Her mouth opened, and soon she was snoring softly.

A car engine roared in the street. Some men shouted and banged on the door of the bar, wanting one last drink. Salome heard them cursing. Tires squealed, the engine roared again. Headlight beams shot through the window, flashed along the walls, then vanished. The smell of dust billowed through the room. Salome reached underneath the bed. Her hand found the handle of her *panga*, and she gripped it tight.

Another car engine approached, this one from the opposite direction. It sounded noisy enough to be a Land Rover, but Salome knew the car, the teacher's tinny old Morris. Footsteps crunched in the dirt outside the room; there was a soft knock on the door.

"What do you want?"

"It's Billy," the voice whispered. "Is Adija there?"

"Adija's sleeping. She is celebrating Independence tonight."

The footsteps crunched in place. "All right. I'll be back tomorrow."

I know you will, Salome thought. You'll all be back. But not tonight.

She pulled the blanket up tighter around Adija's shoulders. Then she lay very still. The shadows flickered down the wall, as if trying to lap up what little warmth was left in the room.

꧁ ꧂

WILLIAM KENNEDY

from *Ironweed*

"Buy a flower, sir?" she asked Francis.

"Why not? How much?"

"Just a quarter."

"Give us one."

He fished a quarter out of his pants and pinned the gardenia on Helen's lapel with a pin the girl handed him. "It's been a while since I bought you flowers," he said. "You gonna sing up there for us, you gotta put on the dog a little."

Helen leaned over and kissed Francis on the mouth, which always made him blush when she did it in public. She was always a first-rate heller between the sheets, when there was sheets, when there was somethin' to do between them.

"Francis always bought me flowers," she said. "He'd get money and first thing he'd do was buy me a dozen roses, or a white orchid even. He didn't care what he did with the money as long as I got my flowers first. You did that for me, didn't you, Fran?"

"Sure did," said Francis, but he could not remember buying an orchid, didn't know what orchids looked like.

"We were lovebirds," Helen said to Oscar, who was smiling at the spectacle of bum love at his bar. "We had a beautiful apartment up on Hamilton Street. We had all the dishes anybody'd ever need. We had a sofa and a big bed and sheets and pillowcases. There wasn't anything we didn't have, isn't that right, Fran?"

"That's right," Francis said, trying to remember the place.

"We had flowerpots full of geraniums that we kept alive all winter long. Francis loved geraniums. And we had an icebox crammed full of food. We ate so well, both of us had to go on a diet. That was such a wonderful time."

"When was that?" Pee Wee asked. "I didn't know you ever stayed anyplace that long."

"What long?"

"I don't know. Months musta been if you had an apartment."

"I was here awhile, six weeks maybe, once."

"Oh we had it much longer than that," Helen said.

"Helen knows," Francis said. "She remembers. I can't call one day different from another."

"It was the drink," Helen said. "Francis wouldn't stop drinking and then we couldn't pay the rent and we had to give up our pillowcases and our dishes. It was Haviland china, the very best you could buy. When you buy, buy the best, my father taught me. We had solid mahogany chairs and my beautiful upright piano my brother had been keeping. He didn't want to give it up, it was so nice, but it was mine. Paderewski played on it once when he was in Albany in nineteen-oh-nine. I sang all my songs on it."

"She played pretty fancy piano," Francis said. "That's no joke. Why don't you sing us a song, Helen?"

"Oh I guess I will."

"What's your pleasure?" Oscar asked.

"I don't know. 'In the Good Old Summertime,' maybe."

"Right time to sing it," Francis said, "now that we're freezin' our ass out there."

"On second thought," said Helen, "I want to sing one for Francis for buying me that flower. Does your friend know 'He's Me Pal,' or 'My Man'?"

"You hear that, Joe?"

"I hear," said Joe the piano man, and he played a few bars of the chorus of "He's Me Pal" as Helen smiled and stood and walked to the stage with an aplomb and grace befitting her reentry into the world of music, the world she should never have left, oh why ever did you leave it,

Helen? She climbed the three steps to the platform, drawn upward by familiar chords that now seemed to her to have always evoked joy, chords not from this one song but from an era of songs, thirty, forty years of songs that celebrated the splendors of love, and loyalty, and friendship, and family, and country, and the natural world. Frivolous Sal was a wild sort of devil, but wasn't she dead on the level too? Mary was a great pal, heaven-sent on Christmas morning, and love lingers on for her. The new-mown hay, the silvery moon, the home fires burning, these were sanctuaries of Helen's spirit, songs whose like she had sung from her earliest days, songs that endured for her as long as the classics she had committed to memory so indelibly in her youth, for they spoke to her, not abstractly of the aesthetic peaks of the art she had once hoped to master, but directly, simply, about the everyday currency of the heart and soul. The pale moon will shine on the twining of our hearts. My heart is stolen, lover dear, so please don't let us part. Oh love, sweet love, oh burning love—the songs told her—you are mine, I am yours, forever and a day. You spoiled the girl I used to be, my hope has gone away. Send me away with a smile, but remember: you're turning off the sunshine of my life.

Love.

A flood tide of pity rose in Helen's breast. Francis, oh sad man, was her last great love, but he wasn't her only one. Helen has had a lifetime of sadnesses with her lovers. Her first true love kept her in his fierce embrace for years, but then he loosened that embrace and let her slide down and down until the hope within her died. Hopeless Helen, that's who she was when she met Francis. And as she stepped up to the microphone on the stage of The Gilded Cage, hearing the piano behind her, Helen was a living explosion of unbearable memory and indomitable joy.

And she wasn't a bit nervous either, thank you, for she was a professional who had never let the public intimidate her when she sang in a church, or at musicales, or at weddings, or at Woolworth's when she sold song sheets, or even on the radio with that audience all over the city every night. Oscar Reo, you're not the only one who sang for Americans over the airwaves. Helen had her day and she isn't a bit nervous.

But she is . . . all right, yes, she is . . . a girl enveloped by private confusion, for she feels the rising of joy and sorrow simultaneously and she cannot say whether one or the other will take her over during the next few moments.

"What's Helen's last name?" Oscar asked.

"Archer," Francis said. "Helen Archer."

"Hey," said Rudy, "how come you told me she didn't have a last name?"

"Because it don't matter what anybody tells you," Francis said. "Now shut up and listen."

"A real old-time trouper now," said Oscar into the bar mike, "will give us a song or two for your pleasure, lovely Miss Helen Archer."

And then Helen, still wearing that black rag of a coat rather than expose the even more tattered blouse and skirt that she wore beneath it, standing on her spindle legs with her tumorous belly butting the metal stand of the microphone and giving her the look of a woman five months pregnant, casting boldly before the audience this image of womanly disaster and fully aware of the dimensions of this image, Helen then tugged stylishly at her beret, adjusting it forward over one eye. She gripped the microphone with a sureness that postponed her disaster, at least until the end of this tune, and sang then "He's Me Pal," a ditty really, short and snappy, sang it with exuberance and wit, with a tilt of the head, a roll of the eyes, a twist of the wrist that suggested the proud virtues. Sure, he's dead tough, she sang, but his love ain't no bluff. Wouldn't he share his last dollar with her? Hey, no millionaire will ever grab Helen. She'd rather have her pal with his fifteen a week. Oh Francis, if you only made just fifteen a week.

If you only.

The applause was full and long and gave Helen strength to begin "My Man," Fanny Brice's wonderful torch, and Helen Morgan's too. Two Helens. Oh Helen, you were on the radio, but where did it take you? What fate was it that kept you from the great heights that were yours by right of talent and education? You were born to be a star, so many said it. But it was others who went on to the heights and you were left behind to grow bitter. How you learned to envy those who rose when you did not, those who never deserved it, had no talent, no training. There was Carla, from high school, who could not even carry a tune but who made a movie with Eddie Cantor, and there was Edna, ever so briefly from Woolworth's, who sang in a Broadway show by Cole Porter because she learned how to wiggle her fanny. But ah, sweetness was Helen's, for Carla went off a cliff in an automobile, and Edna sliced her wrists and bled her life away in her lover's bathtub, and Helen laughed last. Helen is singing on a stage this very minute and just listen to the voice she's left with after all her troubles. Look at those well-dressed people out there hanging on her every note.

Helen closed her eyes and felt tears forcing their way out and could not say whether she was blissfully happy or fatally sad. At some point it all came together and didn't make much difference anyway, for sad or happy, happy or sad, life didn't change for Helen. Oh, her man, how much she loves you. You can't imagine. Poor girl, all despair now. If she went away she'd come back on her knees. Some day. She's yours. Forevermore.

Oh thunder! Thunderous applause! And the elegant people are standing for Helen, when last did that happen? More, more, more, they yell, and she is crying so desperately now for happiness, or is it for loss, that it makes Francis and Pee Wee cry too. And even though people are calling for more, more, more, Helen steps delicately back down the three platform steps and walks proudly over to Francis with her head in the air and her face impossibly wet, and she kisses him on the cheek so all will know that this is the man she was talking about, in case you didn't notice when we came in together. This is the man.

By god that was great, Francis says. You're better'n anybody.

Helen, says Oscar, that was first-rate. You want a singing job here, you come round tomorrow and I'll see the boss puts you on the payroll. That's a grand voice you've got there, lady. A grand voice.

Oh thank you all, says Helen, thank you all so very kindly. It is so pleasant to be appreciated for your God-given talent and for your excellent training and for your natural presence. Oh I do thank you, and I shall come again to sing for you, you may be sure.

Helen closed her eyes and felt tears beginning to force their way out and could not say whether she was blissfully happy or devastatingly sad. Some odd-looking people were applauding politely, but others were staring at her with sullen faces. If they're sullen, then obviously they didn't think much of your renditions, Helen. Helen steps delicately back down the three steps, comes over to Francis, and keeps her head erect as he leans over and pecks her cheek.

"Mighty nice, old gal," he says.

"Not bad at all," Oscar says. "You'll have to do it again sometime."

Helen closed her eyes and felt tears forcing their way out and knew life didn't change. If she went away she'd come back on her knees. It is so pleasant to be appreciated.

Helen, you are like a blackbird, when the sun comes out for a little while. Helen, you are like a blackbird made sassy by the sun. But what will happen to you when the sun goes down again?

I do thank you.

And I shall come again to sing for you.

Oh sassy blackbird! Oh!

❦❦

MILAN KUNDERA

from *The Book of Laughter and Forgetting*

WHAT IS *LITOST*?

Litost is a Czech word with no exact translation into any other language. It designates a feeling as infinite as an open accordion, a feeling that is the synthesis of many others: grief, sympathy, remorse, and an indefinable longing. The first syllable, which is long and stressed, sounds like the wail of an abandoned dog.

Under certain circumstances, however, it can have a very narrow meaning, a meaning as definite, precise, and sharp as a well-honed cutting edge. I have never found an equivalent in other languages for this sense of the word either, though I do not see how anyone can understand the human soul without it.

Let me give an example. One day the student went swimming with his girlfriend. She was a top-notch athlete; he could barely keep afloat. He had trouble holding his breath underwater, and was forced to thrash his way forward, jerking his head back and forth above the surface. The girl was crazy about him and tactfully kept to his speed. But as their swim was coming to an end, she felt the need to give her sporting instincts free rein, and sprinted to the other shore. The student tried to pick up his tempo too, but swallowed many mouthfuls of water. He felt humiliated, exposed for the weakling he was; he felt the resentment, the special sorrow which can only be called *litost*. He recalled his sickly childhood— no physical exercise, no friends, nothing but Mama's ever-watchful eye— and sank into utter, all-encompassing despair. On their way back to the city they took a shortcut through the fields. He did not say a word. He was wounded, crestfallen; he felt an irresistible desire to beat her. "What's wrong with you?" she asked him, and he went into a tirade about how the undertow on the other side of the river was very dangerous and he had told her not to swim over there and she could have drowned—then he slapped her face. The girl burst out crying, and when he saw the tears running down her face, he took pity on her and put his arms around her, and his *litost* melted into thin air.

Or take an instance from the student's childhood: the violin lessons that were forced on him. He was not particularly gifted, and his teacher would stop him and point out his mistakes in a cold, unbearable voice. It humiliated him, he felt like crying. But instead of trying to play in tune and make fewer mistakes, he would make mistakes on purpose. As the teacher's voice became more and more unbearable, enraged, he would sink deeper and deeper into his bitterness, his *litost.*

Well then, what is *litost?*

Litost is a state of torment caused by a sudden insight into one's own miserable self.

One of the standard remedies for personal misery is love. The recipient of an absolute love cannot be miserable. All his faults are redeemed by love's magic eyes, which make even uncoordinated thrashing and a head jerking back and forth above the water look charming.

The absolute quality of love is actually a desire for absolute identification. We want the woman we love to swim as slowly as we do; we want her to have no past of her own to look back on happily. But as soon as the illusion of absolute identity falls apart (the girl looks back happily on her past or picks up speed), love turns into a permanent source of that great torment we call *litost.*

Anyone with broad experience in the general imperfectability of mankind is fairly well protected against its excesses. He accepts insights into his own miserable self as ordinary and uninteresting. *Litost,* in other words, is characteristic of immaturity. It is one of the ornaments of youth.

Litost works like a two-stroke motor. First comes a feeling of torment, then the desire for revenge. The goal of revenge is to make one's partner look as miserable as oneself. The man can't swim, but the woman cries when slapped. It makes them feel equal and keeps their love alive.

Since revenge can never reveal its true motivation (the student can't tell the girl he slapped her because she swam too fast), it must plead false ones. In other words, *litost* is unthinkable without a kind of passionate hypocrisy: the young man proclaims he was frantic at the thought of his girl drowning, and the child plays agonizingly off-key, feigning hopeless ineptitude.

I was originally going to call this chapter *Who Is the Student?* But even if it now deals with the emotion I call *litost,* it still is very much about the student as well. In fact, the student represents *litost* incarnate. No wonder the girl he was in love with finally left him. There is nothing particularly pleasant about having your face slapped for knowing how to swim.

The butcher's wife from his hometown entered his life in the form of a giant-sized bandage ready-made for his wounds. She admired him, worshiped him. When he talked to her about Schopenhauer, she never tried to make her own independent personality felt by raising objections (as did the girlfriend of inglorious memory); and when she looked at him, he was so moved by her emotion he seemed to see tears welling up in her eyes. We must also bear in mind that he had not made love since breaking up with his girlfriend.

Translated by Michael Henry Heim

ALISON LURIE

Something Borrowed, Something Blue

In the end, it was the perfect wedding, though there were problems at the start—and a near-disaster at the end, but I'll get to that. The main problem was, where to have the ceremony? My parents are in the foreign service, and they were posted to India at the time, and Mark's were in California. So we decided to get married at Corinth University, where he was teaching in the law school. Then it turned out that Mark had a conference in Canada two weeks before the date we'd chosen, and I was involved in a tax case my firm was handling. Who was going to arrange everything?

But then Cleo Wolf, who ran the Dean's office, volunteered to help. It would be a piece of cake for her, she said, because she'd planned so many law school events. She got reservations for the chapel, and for the sit-down brunch at the College Inn afterwards, and she knew the best caterers and photographers and musicians, what to ask for and how much they should charge.

I was really grateful, because Cleo was not only a super administrator, she had style. Even when she was dressed for the office, in a quiet beige Armani-type suit and cream silk shirt, she looked amazingly elegant, and madly sexy. She reminded me of those models who wear designer clothes in magazines, only she was older of course; maybe ten years older than me. Mom said after they met that Cleo looked as if she'd been round the garden a few times, but back then that didn't bother me; it gave me confidence.

Cleo thought of everything. When my wedding dress was delivered she reminded me that I needed something old, something borrowed and something blue to wear with it. I had Grandmom's pearl necklace and drop earrings, but nothing borrowed or blue. So Cleo lent me this really spectacular slip: heavy flame-blue satin, smooth as ice, edged with a wide band of blue lace. If you had the right accessories, it could have gone to a fancy restaurant or disco. I was almost afraid to wear Cleo's slip; but she insisted I must, for luck. I didn't notice then that she never said whose luck or what kind.

When I got home that evening I tried the slip on. I was taller than she, but it fitted perfectly. Then I looked in the mirror. I'd wondered sometimes what it would be like to be Cleo, somebody that wherever you went, men turned around to stare. Now I could sort of see how it would be. The built-in push-up bra gave me cleavage for the first time in my life, and my skin had a kind of tea-rose glow. I bent over and shook my hair out the way I'd seen Cleo do once in the law school washroom, and widened my eyes and mouth the way she did when she listened to men, and all of a sudden I looked different: confident and sophisticated and sexy.

But what was strange was that I didn't only look different, I felt different. I'd lived all over the world with Mom and Dad, but I wasn't actually very experienced. I used to worry that I might be undersexed compared to Mark, and when he really got to know me he would be disappointed, though he'd be too polite ever to say so. Now I felt that I was a beautiful, passionate woman, and that the world and everything in it was there for my pleasure. I wondered if that was how Cleo felt all the time. Then I hung the slip in the closet and kind of forgot about it for the next few weeks, because I had so much to do.

At the wedding rehearsal I was pretty nervous, worrying about where people would sit and whether I would trip coming up the aisle, and a whole slew of other dumb things. Even though Mark was right there, I didn't think of sex once, not seriously anyhow.

But on the wedding day it was all I could think of. As soon as I put on Cleo's slip it was just like before: I felt beautiful and erotically charged. As I got into my dress and veil the slither of the different silks and satins and laces on my skin was like the caresses of invisible lovers. When I brushed my hair sparks seemed to fly from it, and the lipstick on my mouth felt like a slow kiss. And everything in the room suddenly looked sexy. I ran my hand over the polished blonde oak of my chest of drawers, and it was like touching a man's body. It was the same in the limo when Mom handed me my bouquet, all delicate lace and sprays of lily of the valley and miniature roses the colour of double cream, like the softest flesh; I had this crazy impulse to rub it over my face and breasts.

Everybody said how beautiful I looked, which of course they always say to brides, but I knew they were telling the truth. And what was weird, they all looked beautiful to me too, sexually beautiful. I realized that not only was I excited about getting married, I was on some kind of sensual high. And it didn't stop when we got to the chapel. Coming up the aisle I wanted to touch and embrace people. Then I glanced at the minister and even though I'd thought him very ordinary-looking the day before, he seemed awfully attractive, and I wondered what he would be like in bed. Then I thought, How can I be wondering this now, in the middle of my wedding, am I crazy or wicked?

But then I saw Mark standing there, and he was the most desirable man in the whole world. I wanted to kiss him passionately right then, before the minister said we could.

At the reception afterwards it was the same, only more so. It was as if I were in love not only with Mark, but with everyone and everything—the food, the flowers, the curtains and table-cloths. I kept kissing and embracing people in this very warm, well, hot way. You can see it in the wedding photos: I look kind of over the top with sexual charge. There's one where I'm licking icing off Mark's fingers that's practically pornographic, and in a couple of the others I'm all over him. I told myself it was the champagne; I'd never had so much champagne, anyhow not so early in the day.

Cleo was at the party, of course, and I thanked her for everything and said how great her slip was and how sexy it made me feel. I thought it must have some secret power, I told her. Her face got a kind of tight expression, and she gave me a funny little smile and said, "Oh yes, I'm sure it does."

Then I went up to change in my parents' room at the College Inn. My bridesmaid Marylou, and Mark's sister Viola, who was the matron of honour, came along to help me. I was still on this crazy high, and I had the impulse to wrap myself around them and rub up against them: my best and oldest friend Marylou whom I loved so much, and Viola who looked so much like Mark, both of them so tall and fair and curly-haired.

As she lifted off my wedding-dress Viola saw the borrowed blue slip for the first time, and she said, 'Wow! Where did you get that?'

So I told her Cleo Wolf had lent it to me, wasn't it wonderful, wasn't that sweet of her. Viola must have had a lot of champagne too, probably, because she said, "Well, I guess she figured her slip could get married to Mark, even if she couldn't."

I stared at Viola and asked what she meant by that. She looked embarrassed and tried to take it back, but Marylou and I wouldn't let her, and finally she admitted that Mark had had what she called a "brief relationship" with Cleo before I knew him.

I just stood there, with one white satin pump off and one on. I thought that probably Mark had seen Cleo's slip before. And then I realized that if I hadn't found out about their Brief Relationship, that evening in our hotel when I let him slowly take off my travelling clothes, he would see it again. He would remember it, and he would remember Cleo wearing it; but naturally he wouldn't say anything, and that silent lie would be the beginning of our marriage.

I dragged the thing off as if it were poisoned; and all of a sudden I felt as if I'd come up from underwater in an overheated pool. Marylou and Viola and everything else in the room looked normal again: attractive, but not like characters and props in a soft-porn flick. I had the impulse to destroy Cleo's slip, or maybe cut it into little pieces and mail it back. I wanted her to know that even if she'd given me some bad memories, she hadn't got away with the surprise she'd planned for Mark.

But then I thought no, I wouldn't say anything. I would keep Cleo guessing. And I would keep her slip for a while, because you never know when something with powers like that might come in handy for someone.

❧ ❧

JEANNE MACKIN

from *The Wise and Foolish Virgins*

It is easy at all times to create a scandal in Philadelphia, Maggie wrote, many sad years after her arrival there.

What a city she chose for her first and only love affair! Did she really believe she could win over those blue-blooded, stiff-backed matrons of prim, snobby Philadelphia, those harpy guardians of her beloved . . . she, a coarse farm girl who performs in public with her feet bare and white ankles flashing, and speaks to ghosts?

She is sixteen. Doors are still opening for her. None have yet been slammed in her face. There's a first time for everything, her father has warned.

The love affair has been written about by several historians; the details are there, the dates, the tokens, the first meeting, first quarrel, first mention of Dr. Kane's so-very-respectable family. This affair will be the stuff of Victorian melodrama. Like Maggie herself, if it hadn't actually happened, someone would have invented it.

Maggie is no longer a straight and skinny farmgirl. Her chest and hips swell and curve; her waist is stylishly pinched. When she's not performing, she wears her thick, dark hair parted in the middle and pulled back on either side of her face, like glistening blackbird plumage; for the seances that thick, lustrous hair hangs loose all the way to her hips. Her black eyes are large and shining. Her red mouth is full. She is beautiful, but not in the approved way. In one of those dreadful dime novels Victorian booksellers kept in the back room, she would be the femme fatale, the wrong woman for the right man, the Veiled Lady who must go over the cliff, or to Havana, or to the insane asylum, so that the true lovers can finally be happy together. Maggie is not the right type for a happy ending.

She seems a bit young for such sinister passion. There is still innocence in those dark eyes. She has not been kissed or even touched by anyone other than her mother and sisters. But according to Victorian standards, she is fruit ready for the harvest. Edgar Allan Poe fell in love with his cousin, Virginia, when she was eleven years old; in many households, daughters were engaged by the age of thirteen, and the average New York City prostitute of the times began walking the streets at the age fourteen. Childhood was short in the 1850s; Maggie's is about to end.

She's ready. Leah has kept her shut up in hotel rooms and apartments for much of the past three years. But even though Maggie couldn't go to the world, the world came to her, in the form of clients. Like a king indoctrinated by hand-picked and narrow-minded ministers, like a sultan cultivated in the hothouse climate of a harem, she has received an education of sorts. Observant of those ladies who called on her and came for sittings, she knows how to crook her little finger over her teacup, smile with closed lips rather than laugh aloud, keep her voice low, shed tears on demand, swoon. She knows the styles being worn in Paris and the names of journalists in all major American cities. She can say please and thank you and do come again (but no more than that) in four languages. She knows that *artistes* (always pronounced the French way) and intellectuals favor abolition, while the capitalists condone the continuance of slavery, even if they don't say so in so many words. She knows that a lady never slurps the tea out of her saucer, that the tricky long *A* should be pronounced in one syllable, not the two used in upstate New York, that limbs should be crossed only at the ankles, never the knees.

In fact, in the Union Hotel suite in Philadelphia, in the stormy autumn of 1852, she is curled up on the sofa in the parlor, frowning over a German grammar. She chews the tip of her pen and grimaces, determined to master this language of fashionable ladies.

This wet and dreary morning, this moment, is the closest Maggie will come to happiness. Years after, she will look back at this instant in time and see that this was where her destiny offered a forked and treacherous path. Which one to take? It is the kind of moment that leads to regrets and bitterness, though of course one can't know it at the time. The moment slides through time as easily as the ones that go before and after, yet it is different. A single proton can live for tens of billions and billions of years, almost as long as a regret.

Maggie, though she is grimacing, is happy. Elder Sister Leah, she of the pinching, slapping hands, is gone, only Mother is here and Mother doesn't want her daughter to be a performing monkey, as greedy Leah does. There are no more sittings scheduled three or four times a day, every day but Sunday. Maggie sits for her clients once a day at most, just enough to keep the hotel bill and seamstress and hairdresser paid. And, there is money in the bank. Not as much as there should be. Leah took more than her share. But tucked inside Maggie's new lavender lace reticule is a little book with hand-written entries, and they add up to a sum that makes Maggie smile when she thinks of it. She never has to go back to Hydesville, to the farm house, to Father, again. She is safe. From what, she isn't certain, but that is what she will think when she looks back at this moment: I was safe, then.

A single knock, and this serene moment landslides into history.

Dr. Elisha Kent Kane, though prone to impatience, is a gentleman. He knocks softly and waits for the maid to answer the door, he does not batter it with his fist and even throw it open himself as some clients, too eager to talk with the dear departed, do. This alone makes Maggie look up from her dog-eared grammar book. Curiosity enlarges her already large eyes. She is still chewing on her pen, still curled on the sofa, long legs tucked under frothing skirts and petticoats. Her young body tenses with expectancy. Did she somehow see his arrival in a vision? Why did she rent the bridal suite of the hotel, as we know she did?

This is how Mr. Elisha Kane sees Maggie: childish, perplexed, just emerging from the chrysalis of innocence, an exotic butterfly waiting to be named, a land waiting to be claimed, a virgin ready to be taken.

He has come because he is curious. He wants to meet this impostor, this liar, this fraud from New York who claims to speak with the dead. Philadelphia is speaking of her—in lowered voices, and with a disapproving wag of the head, certainly, but speaking nonetheless—and he wants to see with his own eyes this virago of tricks, this monster of female wiles and deceit.

Kane, thirty-two years old, wealthy, well-bred, handsome, already famous as a naval surgeon and Arctic explorer, is not without ego. For the past week, this feminine upstart from upstate has had more column space in the Philadelphia papers than he has.

The maid opens the door wider. Dr. Kane blushes, stammers, backs away into the hall, thinking he has knocked at the wrong suite. This room, with the young virgin on the sofa with her school book, the old mother in the rocking chair, the polite and silent women guests sitting on assorted chairs (Maggie is rarely alone, even when alone, so popular is she) looks like a morning tea party, not the expected den of iniquity.

"No, no," says Mrs. Fox. "This is Margaret Fox, my Maggie. This is the party for which you seek," she says trying to sound elegant and instead sounding foolish.

It is too late. He has seen Maggie. She has seen him. He comes into the parlor. The door is closed behind him.

This is what Maggie sees, what she knows from reading the papers: a man blessed with physical beauty, wealth and virtue . . . but not good health. Elisha Kane is tall but too thin and pale despite his strenuous outdoor life. He has had several attacks of rheumatic fever, which have left him with little regard for mortality. At any moment, without warning, his ravaged heart could stop beating. He has defied rather than pampered that heart, circling the world and contracting and recovering from the diseases of travelers—malaria, typhus, dysentery, scurvy—with a bravado that stronger men envy.

He has sailed to the mysterious Arctic, searching for (and not finding) Sir John Franklin, who disappeared without a trace into that frozen wilderness seven years ago. He has slept in a tent, sled dogs packed beside him for warmth, on the cold whiteness of Beechey Island and seen the building-tall pinnacle of ice that marks the entrance to Baffin Bay.

Kane is feverish with ambition. The Victorians were obsessed with discovering two opposing secrets of the earth: the source of the Amazon, and absolute north. Kane has chosen to explore not the fetid tropics with their rain forests and obscene lusciousness, but the frozen pole from whence all flows south. But first, because he is a gentleman and gentleman do such things, he must find and rescue Sir John. Even now his secretary is recopying a letter to the Secretary of the Navy, John Kennedy, asking for funds, permission, support for another expedition. His stay in Philadelphia was meant to be a short one.

Moreover, his fifteen-year-old brother has just died, and Elisha Kane is in mourning. There is a black band on the calling card he has handed Mrs. Fox, a black band rimming his kid gloves. He pulls off the gloves because the room seems excessively warm, as women's rooms often do, especially to a man who has pitched camp on glaciers and icebergs.

Suddenly, seeing that virgin on the sofa looking up at him with those deep, dark eyes, he doesn't know what to do with his hands. The maid has taken his hat and cane so he can't fidget with those. He sits bolt upright on the offered chair and puts his hands over his knees. The girl is looking at them. He is proud of his hands. They are long-fingered, elegant, strong. He blushes again, feeling suddenly as exposed as if he were naked, because of the way she is looking at his hands. He already wants to stroke her dark, lustrous hair, that dewy forehead.

Dr. Kane, at this moment, has an agreement with another young woman, a woman selected by his mother, a woman who fits nicely into a drawing room, who is attractive yet does not attract attention, who is pretty but not seductive, who can say much more than please and thank you in several languages. This young woman will be disappointed by him in the very near future. The word *jilted* will never be used, for both parties come from good families, but jilted she will be.

Do Maggie and Kane talk on this first morning, or simply devour each other with their eyes? Does he tell her that icebergs remind him of Greek architecture, that he has seen icebergs as large as the Parthenon? Does he tell her that frostbitten fingertips turn black, as if they have been burnt rather than frozen, thus proving once again that opposites are, in fact, the same thing?

Perhaps Maggie says something like, "I see, sir, you are mourning. Your brother has died."

He, with no little sarcasm: "Have your spirit guides told you this?"

Maggie: "No, sir, the papers, and the sorrow in your eyes. You loved him, and love does not evidence itself only in the supernatural."

Maggie plays none of her tricks on Elisha Kane. He is not a believer. He is not a dupe. He hates spiritualism and spiritualists. He hates Maggie. And he cannot stay away from her. True north is buried in her heart, her secret thoughts. Her little white body will become his new destination.

After that first visit, he comes to the bridal suite of the Union Hotel twice, thrice a week. He sends Maggie gifts, and takes her riding in his cousin's carriage. He is careful to stir no hint of gossip, to give no proof of bad behavior. The gifts are first presented to Mrs. Fox who decides to accept or reject them in her daughter's name. (She accepts everything, even the expensive gold necklace she should have refused.) The carriage is open, and Maggie never leaves the hotel unescorted. Kane never visits the bridal suite without another friend in tow, to protect what is left of Maggie's name and reputation.

Elisha Kent Kane is a man of passion and of quick decisions, a man who finds life bearable only if it has direction, a course, a mission. Sir John Franklin would or would not be found and that would end that mission. He would need another, and beautiful, wayward Maggie is the perfect challenge. Kane has already decided that Maggie will be his wife.

There will be conditions, of course.

❧ ❧

ROBERT MORGAN

from *The Truest Pleasure*

The work in the sun and the sunburn acted like a spur to our lovemaking. It was as if the heat of July and August stored up in our veins and skin as a fever to be quenched by love in the hours of darkness. Never had I seemed to need less sleep. After he got home each evening, milked and washed and had supper, Tom counted the money he had made. The coins shined like little flames and faces on the hearth. The bills crackled as he smoothed them in booklets. Afterwards he put the money in the cigar box.

As he counted the money, we talked about what we needed to buy for winter, for the children and for the place. Jewel would start school that fall, and needed new clothes. "You have to dress your girls nicer than boys," Tom said.

As soon as the children was asleep Tom and me went to bed ourselves. Pa was reading in the kitchen, and we tried not to disturb him. When Locke come on furlough for a week he slept on the couch and we tried to be careful not to bother him as we giggled in the dark and tried to keep the bed from creaking.

It was as if we was not ourselves some nights, but bigger and more powerful, more perfect, as we would want to be. The day had been a long delay and build-up of fever toward the summer night. And it felt like we couldn't do anything wrong. Every place we touched was right, and every pause was right. Everything we did in the dark led to something new and better.

As a girl I would not have thought a man of forty was capable of such exertions, or a woman of thirty-four for that matter. At moments of joy I felt this was what all the feeling of my life had been tending toward, including my shouting and dancing at meetings. It was all just a preparation for this.

But I put such thoughts out of mind for they was blasphemous. I may have felt them, but I didn't want to think them, least of all to say them. Long as I didn't put my feelings in words they was innocent. Kept at the edge of thought they couldn't hurt.

And I told myself lovemaking was also worship and praise. I told myself it was through love we take part in God's creation.

I remember one night in August special. We had picked beans in the far end of the bottom and Tom sold them by the bushel to women in the village. I reckon he had made more than ten dollars. But on the way home the axle of the wagon broke. I don't know why it broke. Maybe the extra hauling had wore it out. Tom had stuck in a sapling to hold up the wheel till he got home. The new axle would cost ten dollars, so the day had been wasted, he felt.

Now I have noticed that loving is best when you're feeling real good, or sometimes when you're feeling a little bad. If you're feeling a mite low you resist lovemaking at first, and then it comes like a blessing. And your body takes over and reminds you of things you had forgot. The body has its own wisdom and its own will, and sometimes it knows what you need most.

That night I saw Tom needed to be cheered up. I took a full bath in the tub in the bedroom, and made myself rosy and soft. I put on powder and rubbed on cologne. By the time I had finished Tom had already gone to bed. I knowed he was tired, and when you want to forget some loss or bad news nothing is as comforting as sleep. In fact, I think he might already have been asleep when I put out the lamp and got in bed.

But as I slipped under the covers I could feel him waking. First, it was the way he stirred and was quiet in his breathing. Then he pushed against me a little, just enough to show it was intended. It's strange how much a little pressure tells you.

Well I won't go into detail. Folks got no right to hear what married couples do. But it was a time I never forgot. The katydids was out, loud in the woods beyond the orchard. And there was crickets in the yard, meadow moles with their mellow note. After the heat of the day the house was cracking and knocking.

But I soon forgot the sounds in the dark. Time got big and magnified. The dark was lit with purple fires. I could feel colors through my fingertips and through every place I touched.

And we had so much time. Every instant was stretched out, and stretched further. Our bodies was big as landscapes and mountains and we had all the time in the world to climb and cross them. There was no hurry, never had been. There was years for a kiss.

It was also like a patient waiting. We was in no hurry because we knowed something would be give to us. I thought about the beans we had picked that day, and how beans get hard when they are ready to pick. You could pick beans just by the feel of them. With your fingers you could tell the pulses in a bean, and then count the beans into a basket.

I thought of Solomon again. "I *am* my beloved's, and his desire *is* toward me," I whispered. The words seemed perfect in the dark. "I *am* a wall, and my breasts are like towers: then was I in his eyes as one that found favor," I said.

We did some things new that night. Don't matter exactly what, but they was new to us. It was like we found out more things about each other. I guess it was like climbing way up a beautiful mountain past ridges and hollers. Laboring up a slope you think you are almost at the top, but when you get there see it is a false peak, and the real summit is higher and further.

The smells of the body are thrilling, the scent of armpits and sweat on skin. The skin has its own savors and salts. It is the salt of memory and wit and laughter. There is the salt that wakes you up, and salt like the taste of rocks deep in the ground.

"Tom," I said. I had never been one to talk much while making love. Before, it had felt better to be hushed. "Tom," I said again, "This is the best thing, ain't it?"

He didn't say anything. He was waiting for me to say more.

"Tom," I said, "we won't never know anything this real."

It was like the dark was smoothing out in contours of pasture hills and deep valleys lined with fur and velvet.

"I can see where the sky touches the ground," I said, "and it's smooth as milk."

There was rivers of sparks in the soil and they swirled through the dark and spread in wind to the end of the earth. It was a warm Nile flooding out of soil, lifting higher and higher.

"This is the place," I said, "ain't it?"

Tom still didn't say anything. He was waiting for me to go on. He never liked to waste a single word. It was for me to say things to him.

"This is the place it all starts," I said. "This is the place of creation."

And then in the dark I could see Tom's face. I don't know how I did in the pitch dark. Maybe there was heat lightning, or maybe a meteor outside. But I saw Tom's face, and his eyes was looking right into mine, like he saw what I was thinking and feeling. He could see and feel any part of me. Even if he laid still he could feel every inch of me that was moving.

"Tom!" I said. And then I knowed my talking made another kind of sense. It wasn't daylight talk with its words and sentences. It was a higher kind of talk. And it come to me I was speaking in tongues. It was the first time I had spoke in tongues outside a service. I didn't know what I was saying, but I saw what was visited upon me was a gift. "Tom!" I said, and my mouth flew like a bird and my tongue soared. I gripped and sung out and didn't hardly know what I was doing. I was on a long journey that went on and on over banks and gullies, valleys and mountains of flowers. The whole world was coming to us in the dark.

And then I saw what we had been going toward. Everything swung around like compass needles pointing in the same direction. It was in the eye of a dove setting high on a tree at the mountaintop. The eye was still as a puddle with no wind. It was still at the center of the whirl and clutter of things.

"This is what was meant," I said.

Tom still didn't say anything.

"This is really the place," I said. "Ain't it?"

"Yeah," Tom said. It was all he said, but it was enough.

❧ ❧

BRADFORD MORROW

from *The Almanac Branch*

The limbs groaned and gave tonight and here he was up in the tree again, naked except for his origami hat made of newspaper, ship-shaped, and she wondered how he lived in that wild cherry tree without freezing or starving—he never once ate the food she laid out in its branches for him, the warm chicken giblets in the tinfoil tray, the lamb chop she took from the kitchen—she knew that the cherries were inedible. Desmond had bird's balance in his body now, but he wasn't hungry. When she told him to eat, he stared at her and screwed his face into the most quizzical look. He didn't understand anymore what eating was. Tails flashing like plumes, the squirrels who bounded over from other trees were first to get to the pieces of bread she put out using long sticks lashed together. What the squirrels didn't want the starlings and jays carried away in their beaks.

Desmond watched her through the rippled old glass. You could see through him, but he wasn't a ghost. He was like an image superimposed in a film upon another image—that was how he looked; solid and palpable and real, but, well, a little translucent. For her part, she assumed that out there in the snow-tipped branches of his tree he felt sympathetic pains toward her suffering, but she wondered sometimes how could a person in his position—he must have powers, surely, living where he lived—sit by like an idle sovereign, while her face disappeared in those coffee-glitter lights, leaving a doughnut in the mirror, and nothing more, no eyes, no lips, no face.

Somehow, though she never told him in so many words of her feelings, he had changed. His attentions were not tendered in a way she might have wanted. She knew that tonight he would come to her, having been distant, unapproachable, and would burn clean through the glass, burn clear into her forehead, in a way the lights in the old ailanthus had never done.

Desmond bided his time until his sister—her skin flushed with megrim, her hair damp, her head dully pounding—was drowsy. Djuna locked, as always, the double-sash window, and while Grace could hardly stand she crept from the bureau mirror to the window, eyes closed against the icicle lights, and turned the latch. She wanted him to realize that even though she didn't know if he would come in or not, she was waiting. She looked at him across the night glass and thought she saw him nod. Sensing that if she didn't stand at the window and invite him he was more likely to join her, she went back to bed, and curled into a chrysalis of expectancy. He had developed an indefinable, contrary personality, had Desmond, and she knew that this was all she could do.

She waited for what seemed a very long time. A fluttery and scant breeze—where from?—cooled her forehead. And then he drifted, was the word, drifted rather than leaped or even flew from the branch where he lived, to the sill of the window.

The window drew up quietly, or seemed to. Had the breeze come from there? The light people had never been able to do that. As he came closer, she wondered how it must be for one who is used to living in a tree, the leafy-in-summer, barren-in-winter cherry tree, to be inside her room. She had read about the flying fish, and other beasts whose needs and habits took them from one world into another (what were we to make of the earthbound caterpillar destined to flutter away into the air with its painted wings?)—and what was Desmond's sense of coming from there to here? She would have asked him, but she knew that he wouldn't understand the question.

Grace opened her eyes and studied him as he knelt beside her, saw the details of his face, fine hair between his narrow eyebrows, the fanning wrinkles at the corners of his eyes, wrinkles that were more common in a man much older than he must have been. His boldness was unexpected. After brushing aside the comforter and sheets, he carried her from her bed and placed her on the old prayer rug by the dying fire, then raised her hips off the floor, pulled her pajama bottoms down to her ankles, rolled her over. At first she trembled pleasantly to the feel of the wool against her belly. When he ran the stiff bristles of the coal broom over her buttocks Grace's megrim crimped just like it was made of foil or curtain cloth and sprang right out of the side of her head, and she felt liberated all of a sudden from its dry, idiotic pain. She dared not move. The andirons stood like sentinels over her, smiling and knowing, and the poker and shovel and log forks she could see were instruments any of which might find their way into his hands. Inasmuch as they might, she knew that they ought to, in a way, ought to because she felt it was she who must atone for what happened; and since everything in life is first the discovery of balance versus imbalance, second the understanding of how absolution may come to pass, third the will to sacrifice—she knew he would never do anything to her that would be unmerciful. He had found balance she knew just by the way he was able to walk the branches of the tree like some seasoned acrobat. He had found understanding, she could just tell, by the way he'd carried her, and touched her, and by how he had seemed somehow to become a man, unlike the boy under the osprey nest who knew nothing. She was willing to sacrifice whatever he might want her to sacrifice, and knew that he wouldn't want something that she wouldn't happily be able to give him. He would never punish her, as such. This was a thought not made of words or intelligence, rather like a sensation that she kept before her as the boy spanked her with the coal brush, rather methodically, while at the same time caressing her cheek with his free hand. She kissed his hand and her pillow (how had she been moved back into her bed?) not caring which was which but just rejoicing in being able to touch him again and be touched by him. As she kissed, her experience became concentrated at the base of her spine. It was warm.

She tried to stiffen, to show him that she was confused. He must have known. There was a smell of mayonnaise, yes that was exactly what the air had come to smell like then, which she attempted to wipe off her mouth onto the sheets. It was as if she'd fallen into a cactus plant like the ones they had found on the dunes, yellow and barbed to protect themselves from animals that were thirsty and would like to eat their green flesh, and Desmond began to work his mouth along her lower spine and her thighs, which were spread apart as far as he could make them give. He was kissing her through what seemed like impossible curves, and she bit her knuckle so as not to scream out, which she both wanted and didn't want to do. To steady herself, she hooked one knee over the side of the bed. Was this what was supposed to happen? she thought, and made the thought travel through her back down into her pelvis, and spread through her buttocks, all over her flesh, through her naked pubis, and again, as the thought traveled the thought itself knew there was no fact of Grace but for the dense, magnetic scent of apricot and Desmond and mayonnaise, all of it mingling into something delicious, into which he sank his tongue, his mouth, his face and, ultimately, his whole head, which she understood to be . . . well it had to be impossible, for he would have had to open her up between her legs in a way that they just wouldn't be able to be opened, to fit his precious head there, but it seemed so simple and not the result of such violence that he was moving in and out of her slowly, deliberately, and when she thought what it meant, thought of her brother's head, the delicate brain tissue (she had seen brains once, in a restaurant, and watched Faw spoon it, it was like burnt tapioca, into his mouth, unable to eat her own food as she was so overwhelmed by what he was dining on, what it once had been) cradled within his bone-bowl, his cranium, and thought of his soft ears, the silken hair that now was running damp with her, and wet with the oil of forgiveness, it became concrete and imaginable, and therefore familiar, and she gave herself over to it as not just a possibility but what was happening to her, the magnificent wisdom of what she had needed to have happen to her, and sensed new clear distinctions such as the grit of his tongue passing over her, again, and having her, again, and her control was gone, she was moaning and heaving and she didn't care whether Djuna or Berg or Faw or Mother or all of them came rushing into the room to find her with Desmond there on her bed, crazy with the pleasure of being bold, and just as the scream rose into her throat he stopped and rested his soaked face in the small of her back.

Between her legs she ached like fire under bellows and prong. He clutched her tightly, kissed her hair, chewed—even roughly—at her temple and on down her cheek. What happened then would prevent her from ever understanding the nature of Desmond's love for her, because what appeared to happen to her after this delay was that her head in a fever was gently knocked into the mattress, and he hardened over her, binding her hands with his, raging with his mouth over her shoulder and down her neck, until her megrim was abstracted so that she could shove back, with him and at him, and when he felt her moving at him and with him and against him he entered, except that now she was on her back and he was under her, his arms wrapped around her chest, his ankles wrapped around and over her ankles.

Lights like crystals started up on the ceiling. Their sharpness seemed to have nothing in common with the bite of Desmond's hips and thighs. They were measured, she soon realized, against the beat of her own heart. Once she understood this her eyes and throat began to hurt, as did her fingers, her neck, and before long her whole body. She carried on, forward, thrusting by herself. Desmond somehow had maneuvered himself out from underneath her and stood beside her on the bed and burst into light over her face and breasts and belly. The room was full of the apricot scent, and Grace, breathing hard, began to worry again that the smell would escape the room, creep under the door, to give her away here at the height of their freedom, bring the others who loved her into the room from without and bring her to some kind of new shame and with it an absence of freedom.

But it didn't happen. Desmond, again himself, was already out on the ledge, and back into the tree.

The window was ajar. The house was silent. The wind buffeted the branches in the cherry tree, and the waves knocked as ever on the stones. The sheets and blankets on her bed were mussed with their extraordinary perfume—a perfume that reminded her then of her mother's potpourri—and she pulled them, and the perfume they gave off, back over her against the fresh chill in the room. This was how the ravishments began.

STEPHEN F. POLESKIE

Love and Janus Zyvka

Fall on the whole is a savage season, its winds and disturbances and atmospheric conditions favor an existence which is precarious at best, a time when ghosts and spirits traditionally walk the earth. It was fall when the professor and his wife came to our small college from Prague, just after the Soviet tanks had rolled into their native city.

A well-liked professor of art history, Janus Zyvka often brought his classes to The Ornamental Garden nearby. His students would laugh, joke; but the garden, with its taxus bushes shaped to the human forms of Seurat's painting "A Sunday Afternoon on the Island of La Grande Jatte" never failed to incite their interest.

Now I come to the garden alone, I no longer teach at the college. I come often, at times when no one will be here. Lecturing to these motionless topiary figures, cut from a painting in France, and translated in yew to the middle of America, serves a need in me that has not died with my dismissal.

"Love is the forgotten theme of the Modern Era," I proclaimed to my class; "Today's artists and writers give us depictions of sex and passion, but they do not concern themselves with love, it is as if they have not experienced what it means to love. It is because love must come from the heart, inside, not a kind of postmodern academic theory that can be learned, but a feeling that must be ignited like a flame."

Then my own lost love was rekindled.

She was not an especially pretty girl, but not unattractive. I had agreed to give her a tutorial.

Berenice was also the name of my beloved wife, who had died three years ago while giving birth. Suddenly alone, overcome by grief, I dropped out of life and buried myself in my writing and teaching.

Each time Berenice comes to my office for her appointment, her long dark hair, nose too angular by American standards, and the way she carries her slender figure, all remind me of my dead wife. Was even her name more than a coincidence? I could not deny to you that although she was much younger than I, and a student, I was hopelessly in love with her.

Proceeding cautiously, I invite Berenice for a coffee, next a drink, a week later for dinner. Summer came, and she did not go home, but stayed in town to waitress at a restaurant. This glorious season filled with romance and happiness for both of us. I made love to her, a closure of my fidelity to a dead wife. Under clear summer skies, glorious sunsets, Berenice and I would sit in The Ornamental Garden, our own secret place, talking and holding hands; ready for all the joys, and all the risks, our love could bring.

Her mother and stepfather learned of our relationship from one of Berenice's friends. Without speaking to their daughter or to me, the parents sent off letters to the college president, the provost, and all the other names listed in the catalog that seemed to them to be of any importance. Against the pleadings of Berenice, they hired a lawyer, and brought a sexual harassment lawsuit against me, bombarding the local newspapers and television with accusations, statements, and interviews. I am publicly referred to as a "rapist" and a "pervert." Convicted in the popular media, I am asked to resign. Berenice's parents transfer her to another school. An injunction forbids me from having contact with her.

Janus Zyvka sits alone among the topiary talking to his usual friends: the man with the top hat, the woman with the umbrella holding the child's hand, the reclining man with a pipe. He speaks to these green figures in private; he can act differently now, say all sorts of things; act silly, express heretical ideas, repeat himself, bad-mouth his former colleagues, shout out loud.

The erstwhile professor remembers the summer two lovers sat among the yew figures each telling the other of their past failures, and their hopes and dreams.

Janus spoke of the books he planned to write, and of his dead wife and the child they never had. "I was there when she died, I was supposed to be assisting at a birth . . . and two hearts just stopped . . . no one knew why . . . they just stopped."

Berenice talked of her father, missing in Vietnam, his death was never clearly established, but her mother grew tired of waiting and remarried. Her stepfather had sexually exploited her as a child—she told, but her mother had not wanted to believe her. "He made me play games that he would make up . . . like filling station, where he put his nozzle in my gas tank . . . and stick shift . . . and suck the lollipop. . . ."

Over the next year, Janus comes to The Ornamental Garden almost daily; it forms one corner of the rectangle that has become his life, the other three angles being his small apartment, the local library, and a Hamburger Hut where he now works as a night manager.

Unexpectedly a letter arrives from Berenice; her roommate is coming to the college for an interview, she would come along for the ride. She wanted to see him if he did her; no one must know, they would meet in The Ornamental Garden.

Midday, the sun has not yet gained enough strength to warm the garden, even the lengthy shadows are only a dull gray. The air is crisp with fall, a scent that makes the quondam teacher nostalgic for the start of a new school year. Janus expects the garden will be empty, but there is someone there; no matter, he has become comfortable being with people again.

Thirty miles away a young woman dies when the car she is a passenger in stalls at a railroad crossing and is crushed by a train. The driver, on her way to the college for an interview, is thrown free.

Janus stands to the side, not wanting to intrude. The woman in the garden turns and walks toward him; although she has changed a great deal, is changing, Janus recognizes her, her dark hair, the way she carries her slender body.

Seeing him, Berenice stops and smiles, she takes Janus's hand in hers; her hand is cold. She lifts his hand to her cold lips, but her kiss is warm. Janus wraps his arms around her, holds her close, dizzy with the excitement of seeing her again. He has no words to describe this new love. The misfortune of his life with both Berenices was that nothing ever succeeded, nothing ever reached a definite conclusion. Gestures hung in the air, and moments were prematurely exhausted; intentions, projects, and anticipations became impotent and empty. Now both Berenices are one. Janus and Berenice no longer feel threatened by the possibilities of their fulfillment, or shaken by the nearness of their new reality.

Eyes on the ground, as if they dare not look up in order to remain anchored in the present, the yew people begin to move about. Green men, green women, green dogs, a green monkey off its leash, each proceeding as if guided by some cosmic plan. Impatiently avoiding one another, their comings and goings, meetings and passings, suddenly create a gap. A view opens on a stretch of schizoid sky, puffs of cloud moving ever lower toward the distant horizon, the perspective opening onto the depths of the day. In the distance thunder can be heard, the yew people increase their pace, the sounds seeming to give urgency to their activities as they dance in the gusts of wind.

After a brief space of time, the tide of movement slows, and begins to ebb. The crazy green excitement scatters, an imitative character returns to the garden. All chiaroscuro gone, the colors are bright, flat; no longer the illusion of an afternoon, but a man and a woman in the eternity of an afternoon. Janus and Berenice join the citizens of La Grande Jatte standing there, forever in love, forever together.

Scratching for an embellishment to an accident story, a local reporter attempts to contact Janus for a statement about the student he once loved, but is unable to find him. His landlord says it appears as if Janus Zyvka has gone away suddenly: "I checked his apartment and all his things are still there, although I haven't seen him for several days now. . . . I have seen his car though, out by The Ornamental Garden . . . it looks like he's abandoned it there."

"Do you believe that love can be like the sun; omnipresent and perpetual?" Janus Zyvka once asked his class.

᳝᳝ ᳝᳝

JOANNA SCOTT

from *The Manikin*

White spruce kindling for their fire. Red pine needles for their bed. Even in midsummer the nights were chilly and they had no blankets, only the clothes on their backs. They would embrace for warmth as much as for love, and they'd sleep with their legs braided together, but still they'd wake up shivering. "Hop to, hop to," she'd say to him, pulling him to his feet, and as quickly as possible they'd stir the fire to uncover the warm embers, add tinder, and puff and puff until the flames rose.

Every morning they'd follow the creek upstream for a half mile to the waterfall. By July the cascade over the far edge of the grotto had dried to a trickle, a faucet's worth of water that made the moss shimmer, but the pool was still deep enough to cover their heads when they stood on the bottom. In one of the curved granite walls, about ten feet above the pool, a rectangular opening had been carved, probably by Indians, though for what original purpose they could never figure out, since the hole was too high up the sheer wall to explore. Birds used it now—bitterns that darted in and out like flies.

They ate wild plums and blackberries and whatever fish they could catch with their hands. Once when she was hungry she said, "I'll eat you!" and sank her teeth into his arm. She'd only meant to play, but she managed to break the skin and draw a bit of blood. He had great fun teasing her for it.

They both knew they'd have to move on when the weather turned. For weeks on end they'd take off their clothes in the morning and put them on at night—in the warm, mottled sunlight, they went naked. They vowed to stone to death anyone unlucky enough to wander into their paradise.

Tucked between two boulders at one edge of the pool was a sandy strip about three feet wide and six feet long. After they bathed they'd fall onto the sand and they'd kiss and dandle. When he grew hard he'd find his way into her body. Years later, he can recall the sensation of water dripping from her hair onto his chest. And the smell of tannin everywhere. He remembers the sharpness of her ribs and the salty taste of her nipples. He remembers the tiny cracks in her lips. He remembers thinking, This isn't happening. *He remembers her vividly. The dream of her. Sap beneath their fingernails. The shock of cold as they plunged together into the pool. The shadowy water.*

Such places exist, even though they seem to belong more to the imagination than to the world. The grotto and waterfall are hidden at the bottom of Firethorn Mountain's western slope, just beyond the boundary of the Craxton estate. The place is real, and everything else is possible. Junket probably will grow old; he will always remember loving Peg Griswood, though never making love. They'd swum in the grotto—the Devil's Cauldron, as Lore had named it. As children, they'd swum naked on dusty summer afternoons and stained their lips with the juice of wild berries. The little beach would have made a perfect bed, though it serves this purpose only in Junket's fantasy, which he tries to disguise as memory.

Junket thinks he loves Peg a little less each day. But then at night, his mind turns toward the future that has always included Peg. Sometimes he wonders whether it is even love he feels or the passion born from intense friendship. For three quarters of his life they have been like brother and sister, at ease with each other and fiercely loyal. But neither can pretend to continue this affection anymore—Junket hardly blames Peg for wanting better. He's just a scrubby, raffish yokel who can't add fractions. He understands that time usually dulls even the most mystical pain, and he can comfort himself during the day by ignoring Peg, but when he lies in the darkness, his love threatens to drive him mad if it is not satisfied. A mad old hermit with his beard tangled in his toes—this will be Junket. No, he will be nothing without Peg. It's as though he's been following her farther and farther into a forest, and now she has disappeared, leaving him to fend for himself. She has judged him capable, self-sufficient. Not at all. He's inept on his own. The idea of solitude fills him more with terror than with pride these days. So he indulges the desire that he should be forbidding himself, tries to twist it into hindsight. He will love Peg in a future memory. He will remember loving her.

So far the winter has been like any other, perhaps harsher than most, which suits Junket just fine. He dreads spring and its erratic thaws and rain and waxy green shoots that smell like rotting meat. And summer. How can he bear to live through a whole summer?

During the day he splits logs and transports wood from the shed to the house, he carries buckets full of kitchen slops, he helps his father skin and gut his game, all the while remaining within view of the Manikin, just in case Peg is watching from her third-floor window. He wants her to see that he isn't thinking about her. But night after night he thinks about her plenty, succeeds in calming himself only after he has indulged the fantasy of loving Peg. He should be loving her less. He'd wanted to leave the Manikin in order to forget her. Now he doesn't want to leave at all, since as long as he is near Peg Griswood he can pretend to ignore her.

Rarely do children of Junket's age commit themselves to failed love with such relentlessness—ordinarily, adolescence diverts emotions, mending through sheer distraction. But Junket loves with the fervor of a much younger child, convinced that this love is necessary, that Peg had incited him to depend upon her and then abandoned him. He falls more deeply into love, into an unreal future, and denies himself the chance of any future at all.

If he can't have Peg he wants to remain at the edge of childhood, no older, no more separate from Peg than he already is, and then to swoop forward to some distant point beyond life. He wants to linger and then leave the world. In this sense he is vastly different from his father, who refuses to let even the most monstrous changes overwhelm him. Lore is a great believer in stasis and accepts change by convincing himself that he must conform to the patterns of nature. He is the kind of man who, in the face of devastating loss, will quietly and efficiently rebuild his life.

Junket doesn't have enough of a life to rebuild. When he lies awake at night thinking of Peg, of his expectations, of the empty future, it feels like slow suicide.

AMY TAN

from *The Hundred Secret Senses*

Soon Yiban and Miss Banner were spending many long hours together. Mostly they spoke in English, so I had to ask Miss Banner what they said. Oh, she told me, nothing very important: their life in America, their life in China, what was different, what was better. I felt jealous, knowing she and I had never talked about these not very important things.

"What is better?" I asked.

She frowned and searched her mind. I guessed she was trying to decide which of the many Chinese things she loved should be mentioned first. "Chinese people are more polite," she said, then thought some more. "Not so greedy."

I waited for her to continue. I was sure she would say that China was more beautiful, that our thinking was better, our people more refined. But she did not say these things. "Is there anything better in America?" I asked.

She thought a little bit. "Oh . . . comfort and cleanliness, stores and schools, walkways and roadways, houses and beds, candies and cakes, games and toys, tea parties and birthdays, oh, and big loud parades, lovely picnics on the grass, rowing a boat, putting a flower in your hat, wearing pretty dresses, reading books, and writing letters to friends. . . ." On and on she went, until I felt myself growing small and dirty, ugly, dumb, and poor. Often I have not liked my situation. But this was the first time I had this feeling of not liking myself. I was sick with envy— not for the American things she mentioned, but that she could tell Yiban what she missed and he could understand her old desires. He belonged to her in ways that I could not.

"Miss Banner," I asked her, "you feel something for Yiban Johnson, ah?"

"Feel? Yes, perhaps. But just as a friend, though not as good a friend as you. Oh! And not with the feeling between a man and woman—no, no, *no!* After all, he's Chinese, well, not completely, but half, which is almost worse. . . . Well, in our country, an American woman can't possibly. . . . What I mean is, such romantic friendships would *never* be allowed."

I smiled, all my worries put to rest.

Then, for no reason, she began to criticize Yiban Johnson. "I must tell you, though, he's awfully serious! No sense of humor! So gloomy about the future. China is in trouble, he says, soon even Changmian will not be safe. And when I try to cheer him up, tease him a little, he won't laugh. . . ." For the rest of the afternoon, she criticized him, mentioning all his tiny faults and the ways she could change them. She had so many complaints about him that I knew she liked him better than she said. *Not just a friend.*

The next week, I watched them sitting in the courtyard. I saw how he learned to laugh. I heard the excited voices of boy-girl teasing. I knew something was growing in Miss Banner's heart, because I had to ask many questions to find out what it was.

I'll tell you something, Libby-ah. What Miss Banner and Yiban had between them was love as great and constant as the sky. She told me this. She said, "I have known many kinds of love before, never this. With my mother and brothers, it was tragic love, the kind that leaves you aching with wonder over what you might have received but did not. With my father, I had uncertain love. I loved him, but I don't know if he loved me. With my former sweethearts, I had selfish love. They gave me only enough to take back what they wanted from me.

"Now I am content," Miss Banner said. "With Yiban, I love and am loved, fully and freely, nothing expected, more than enough received. I am like a falling star who has finally found her place next to another in a lovely constellation, where we will sparkle in the heavens forever."

I was happy for Miss Banner, sad for myself. Here she was, speaking of her greatest joy, and I did not understand what her words meant. I wondered if this kind of love came from her American sense of importance and had led to conclusions that were different from mine. Or maybe this love was like an illness—many foreigners became sick at the slightest heat or cold. Her skin was now often flushed, her eyes shiny and big. She was forgetful of time passing. "Oh, is it that late already?" she often said. She was also clumsy and needed Yiban to steady her as she walked. Her voice changed too, became high and childlike. And at night she moaned. Many long hours she moaned. I worried that she had caught malaria fever. But in the morning, she was always fine.

Don't laugh, Libby-ah. I had never seen this kind of love in the open before. Pastor and Mrs. Amen were not like this. The boys and girls of my old village never acted like this, not in front of other people, at least. That would have been shameful—showing you care more for your sweetheart than for all your family, living and dead.

I thought that her love was another one of her American luxuries, something Chinese people could not afford. For many hours each day, she and Yiban talked, their heads bent together like two flowers reaching for the same sun. Even though they spoke in English, I could see that she would start a thought and he would finish it. Then he would speak, stare at her, and misplace his mind, and she would find the words that he had lost. At times, their voices became low and soft, then lower and softer, and they would touch hands. They needed the heat of their skin to match the warmth of their hearts. They looked at the world in the courtyard—the holy bush, a leaf on the bush, a moth on the leaf, the moth he put in her palm. They wondered over this moth as though it were a new creature on earth, an immortal sage in disguise. And I could see that this life she carefully held was like the love she would always protect, never let come to harm.

By watching all these things, I learned about romance. And soon, I too had my own little courtship—you remember Zeng, the one-eared peddler? He was a nice man, not bad-looking, even with one ear. Not too old. But I ask you: How much exciting romance can you have talking about cracked jars and duck eggs?

Well, one day Zeng came to me as usual with another jar. I told him, "No more jars. I have no eggs to cure, none to give you."

"Take the jar anyway," he said. "Give me an egg next week."

"Next week I still won't have any to give you. That fake American general stole the Jesus Worshippers' money. We have only enough food to last until the next boat from Canton comes with Western money."

The next week Zeng returned and brought me the same jar. Only this time, it was filled with rice. So heavy with feelings! Was this love? Is love rice in a jar, no need to give back an egg?

I took the jar. I didn't say, Thank you, what a kind man you are, someday I'll pay you back. I was like—how do you say it?—*a diplomat.* "- Zeng-ah," I called as he started to leave. "Why are your clothes always so dirty? Look at all those grease spots on your elbows! Tomorrow you bring your clothes here, I'll wash them for you. If you're going to court me, at least you should look clean."

You see? I knew how to do romance too.

JOHN VERNON

from *All for Love: Baby Doe and Silver Dollar*

Last in the pile was a cable to Haw from Mr. Reed in Boston. As she read it, her heart drained.

> Have secured mortgage on Tabor Block and Grand Opera Block for $350,000 with the two blocks as security. Five years at 6%, 10% at maturity if principal unpaid. Reply requested.

She balled it up and threw it to the floor. She retrieved it and carefully flattened it out and placed it on the table and kicked the table over. Where was Haw when she needed him? In Gunnison, with his pistol. He'd discussed this with her, mortgaging the Tabor block, but she never thought he'd really do it. Better to sell the copper fields in Texas!

All at once she felt herself moving very cautiously. She stood up with prudence, settled back on the sofa so as not to crush the cushions. Dear God in heaven, don't let Haw get hurt. She pictured him swaggering down a wooden sidewalk. Don't let him go inspect any new mines or ride on a horse or get into a poker game. And if we're not married in your eyes, God—let Harvey and Augusta die. Let them expire of natural causes, or have an accident. I'll make six novenas, I'll send Father Guida enough money to take the whole parish to Jerusalem. I won't go myself, though, because I'm not worthy. I may be a sinner, but I've never hurt a soul. I'll let a dog bite me and offer it up. . . .

She lay back on the sofa thinking bad thoughts; for example, strewing broken glass in Mrs. Senator Teller's cake batter. She closed her eyes and with her fingers plugged her ears. She breathed through the hollow flutes of her nose. Children stamped. Somewhere in the distance a muffled chorus chanted Latin. When she squeezed her eyes, clouds rubbed her eardrums. Was someone in the house? Someone walking down the hallway, pushing doors open, searching for her? Her eyes flew open.

The room looked perfectly still and empty. But the softened afternoon light was a cheat. It claim-jumped dreams. Well, let him mortgage the blocks. Haw did business the way he made love, he never said what it was he really wanted. She had to guess. He was due home today, this afternoon. She wouldn't mention the cable. Let him find it himself, let him bring it up. Nobody these days ever owned things anyway. Banks did, and boards. Slowly and deeply, like uncoiling snakes, her bowels opened up, her milk ducts loosened, her blood sank inside her. Let the house of cards collapse.

She'd read rumors in the paper that he was courting insolvency. Haw always laughed them off. Together, they'd planned the expansion of his empire. If it never stopped expanding it never could collapse. They sank a million dollars into the Overland Broadgauge Railroad Company, which hadn't, nonetheless, yet laid a tie. They bought patent rights to the cyanide process of extracting gold; purchased new mines in New Mexico, Arizona, Nevada, and Texas; and bought grazing rights to a half-million acres in southern Colorado. The bank in Gunnison, stockyards in Chicago, hotels, glassworks, steam companies, telephone systems—futures, options, patents, stocks. Haw'd recently scouted the Chihuahua region in Mexico and they'd bought three mines there. It was his notion that the nouveau riche of America required vast reservoirs of mahogany to panel their new mansions, so for a million dollars they'd purchased two hundred square miles of forest in Honduras, plus a grant of mineral rights for an additional hundred and fifty square miles. They planned steamship and rail lines, logging operations, sawmills, lumber towns. For weeks, they pored over maps of their property. Baby saw herself visiting this kingdom in her Queen of the Night dress, with the fringe of silver crescents and stars, and the jeweled waist-girdle in the shape of a serpent. Natives would carry her canopied chair past fruits and birds of fantastic shapes and colors, beneath towering trees with umbrella leaves flapping, past slimy bark thin and green as frogskin which, if you cut it, oozed jeweled yellow resin. Spiders large as kittens clung to bananas, blossoms splashed foreheads, six-fingered hands waved. Vegetable life arranged in profusion staged anatomy lessons around her. Nothing stank. Buckets of slime and moss manured sweet dreams. Perfumed galls burst. . . .

She squirmed on the couch, touching her throat. She dug her fuzzy buttocks into the cushions. The first time Haw ever fumbled to enter her, his sperm snaked reluctantly out against her thigh. It hesitated, pumping as though weakly attempting to suck itself back, then he detumesced and slumped, sound asleep on the bed.

After that, things improved. Her tender, forgiving nature helped, also her complicated lust. She could tell he liked innocence, so she conjured its devices, and learned to play the novice, but with accidental pinches and squeals. She increased his gratitude. She made him conquer her. Each night began with every hair in place, Baby laced up and rouged and eyeblacked, but ended with her beneath him—or on top—whipping her hair back and forth and snarling; it seemed to excite him. Lust had to be imagined first, apparently. You pictured yourself in every conceivable posture of degradation and victory: against the wall, battering the headboard, splayed across pillows. Then, to actually do what you imagined doubled the pleasure, by giving it body. What delicious stratagems. . . .

Haw also learned to play the beast, with coaxing. He became a bull thrashing above her. With drooling muzzle and popping eyes, his enormous head bellowed and roared. He covered her face with his hot smelly breath, his spawl rained upon her, his bristles, raw and stiff, scraped her tender skin. The noise he made shook the bed and rattled the windows and broke her open, then his bull head and horns lashed back and forth with consummate fury and he blanketed her face with his great heavy tongue. His skin smelled of urine. Not from having leaked; he bathed regularly now, often four times a day. She could smell it *through* the skin, as though it ran in his veins.

He liked to lie in bed upstairs and call for her to come. *Baby, I'm ready!* She pictured him, hairy and large, like a hippo. No, hippos were hairless. Maybe a bear struck by lightning, say, temporarily disabled, thrown on his back—tongue hanging out—*Baaaby!* His smell, his dirt, his growl, what else? Even four baths a day weren't enough to deodorize his skin, tarnished and pungent like the leather on a saddle—like copper and salt. Billy Bush had smelled of cheap Macassar oil and some sort of immigrant minty lamb sauce. Haw's breath smelled of American grease. He smelled like good dirt. His coarse hair tickled. His growl, his big round pillowy flesh. . . . He never trimmed the long claws on his fingers, which sliced her poor shoulders. His wide mouth cracked his big face in two.

She'd gone moist below. She longed for his body. She thought of it all day and they did it every night, when he was home. He was always twice as large when he was with her. She was small and he was big. Was her chin too fat? Inside herself, she still felt like a little girl. With his length and girth and years—fifty-six now—sometimes it became a triumph for Haw just to climb on top of his wife. In her hands, he felt powerful and adept—and he was! Even token passion worked, she knew. It was true what Nealie said; men acknowledged the inferiority of their sex by the pride they took in beholding gratified women beneath them.

But he couldn't touch her secrets. He was short and thick, not long and deep. His balls, like baskets of fruit, hung below. The crack of his ass was the Great Divide, the Grand Canyon. His donkey gasp and honk when he finished. . . . Often she was left still gazing down the maw of unthinkable things, the bloody toothless mouth. Pack my fudge, Haw, don't churn my butter. Sometimes he just went on and on forever, leaving her behind, and she cried out, he'd abandoned her. Wait for me, Daddy! He'd crossed a hill up ahead, but when she breeched the top what did she see, she saw a mean wolf. Crouched, fangs exposed, he sprang for her throat. . . .

They were copies, she and Haw, reproductions of the real Baby Doe and Horace Tabor, floating in a heaven shaped like the Tabor Grand.

"Baaaby!" He was home! Haw had come home. "Baby, I'm ready!" She stood. She rushed upstairs. When had he arrived?

❧ ☙

PAUL WEST

from *Life with Swan*

Astonishing to me, but commonplace to her, she played both violin and guitar, taking her proficiency at both as something easy and natural as breathing. Perhaps she played so well, with educated brio, because music dangled and was dandled on the fringe of poetry. As a child she had swung on the doorknobs of rooms, improvising poems above what she regarded as appalling depths. Asking her to demonstrate this on the doors of the not very sturdy house I rented was asking for trouble, but I did so, and she mimicked it, clasping the knobs hard but without abandoning her body to its weight. She heaved to and fro, smiling as I envied her agility (after all, as an imminent graduate who had not yet fulfilled her phys. ed. requirement, she was obliged to play squash and to swim). When I attempted the same feat, or even its diffident simulation, the knob tore out of the panel with a grating crunch and fell to the floor. End of games. For once I had amused her, I who usually made her wince or look away, what with my Celtic temper and so on. The music that really bonded us together, though, was not that which she played, even if it induced in me an ecstasy of direct address, like a poem dedicated to me or a prolonged, unpercussive kiss. During those long boozy nights we listened to, mainly, Shostakovich and Vaughan Williams, some Hindemith and Brahms: not what you might call daring fodder. I was advancing, however, and she got me into Scriabin and some other composers right for my outlandish tastes. Set for incessant repeat, the record player ground on through the night and she lay there on the rug like a small factory in my arms, nodding and rocking, sometimes dozing, but ever-present in the meniscus of sleep or the pericardium of delight; I had only to stir my incompetent bulk (once that of a professional jock), twice her weight and twice her age, and she would stir, peer at weakening night or triumphant dawn and ask if we needed breakfast.

About the same time as we sprawled on the rug, listening to the scratchy 78's I had managed to bring with me from Canada, we evolved special ways of talking to each other. Affectopaths was a word we liked to say. We agreed that each was the other's child: she had had no upbringing to speak of, I had had almost no adult manhood. When we lay on the floor in the direct sun intensified by glass, we called it *spanieling*. I was in the presence of that ineffable miracle, a young woman in full flower, delighted to be where she was, and in fact belated in this state, coming into it from the last stages of puberty. That distant and obscure marriage of hers had been a mere kindergarten bauble, erased by one sunset or a good bubble bath, and she had reverted to whom she had been before it, before *before*. It was all new like one of those books of blank pages the beauty of whose binding readies you for something more velvet than a vacancy. She was growing up with appetitive innocence before my eyes, almost as if she had been entrusted to me by some beneficent force wafting at random through the universe, at last able to bring her justice and love. Or so I thought. But no one applauds the tenor for clearing his throat, or the soprano for gargling. We blundered about in joyful unanimity, she making many more concessions than I. *Victim of the Molecule* she called her first book, unpublished, alas, but now she had moved along and the molecule was her patron saint. She thought about the planets all day and wrote copious odes to them, deleting as many lines as not. She was inspired.

One day around Christmas, we were absentmindedly helping ourselves to a box of candycanes, red and white sugar sticks supposedly evocative of Christmas shepherds' crooks. These were wrapped in the softest, most clinging form of cellophane that clung to your fingers long after you had finished sucking and licking. Was it surface tension or some weak electrical force that made the pieces of cellophane cling thus?

As you seized hold, it bonded to the seizing hand, and on and on, which meant that, so long as you tried to free your hand of it, it clung. It sounded almost like a pejorative account of love that, where you least expected it, held fast, reminding you with a faint stroke that it was there, attached in the least demanding way. Wherever I thought my Swan was not, she was, and I found my merest yearnings being intercepted by a mood of genial anticipation. I was swathed in the tenderest of linings, invisibly wrapped up, as never in many years. Our affectopathy was working well, keeping us warm and calm, yet without, I thought, any assist from shepherds tending sheep, unless we were sheep ourselves. A timely image, to be sure, it told us we had reached a plateau of sorts on which to repine and spaniel: one we had no doubt earned, scaled up in a coiled transparency of our own devising. We had been reborn and like dumb, dazzled animals were licking away the fragments of birth-sac, maybe even eating them, the peppermint of salvation.

Predictably the poet and the novelist invented special ways of talking to each other, from an early word "flaff," which meant pointlessness raised to exponential maximum, to "mrok," which denoted a plaintive cry often uttered when one of us was alone in the house, just hoping with that cry to find the other. People we concocted included two pedantic Frenchmen, devised to liven up the sound of English: Auguste Mrok (descendant of *mrok*) and Jean-Louis Grandquel. We avoided developing their attributes; they were just names to say at inappropriate moments. Hand became *handle*, of course, and breakfast *breaklefast*, mouthwash *mousewash*, and lens *lensness*. Not major deformations, these, they revealed our affection for words as we found them, but nonetheless evinced our desire to leave a little mark on them, as with *shelbst* for self, *schluffy* for sleep, and *Carsonienses* for the Carson Show. One especially fond reference we abbreviated to A.C.H.M., often written "Achmed," commemorating the tiniest mouse we had ever seen, in a botanical garden in St. Louis: A Certain Harvest Mouse, a phrase we would sometimes emit simultaneously, to the dismay of others. Sometimes *pi* was trout (we never eat trout) and sometimes *I*, or *HB*, was rabbit. Our intimate bestiary also included stuffed animals from panther to pregnant sheep (sheep with lamb), many lions and seals. Our totemism gave us a private world as secret as that of Cockney rhyming slang, but also a new angle on the world we wrote about, which was that of other folk. Quite often, in carpet slippers, she walked on top of my feet as I padded slowly backward and we let out a noise we had linked to the roseate spoonbill exquisitely depicted in water colors in the laboratory waiting room at the local hospital:

clack-clack-clack-clack, we went, together being a bird that stepped in and out of tidal pools. Anyone overhearing this racket seemed dismayed, whereas anyone catching a glimpse of a kiss imposed on the corner of the mouth followed by the phrase "Consider yourself wrenned" was merely mystified, having observed a first wren-kiss. The wren, a perky hostile little bird that skimmed like a military support jet over lawns and gardens, appealed to us because we also knew of a high-wing monoplane (actually a converted Cessna) called a Wren which had hen's teeth on top of its wings and could take off *across* a runway, so efficient were its slow-flight qualities, though we had heard it was almost impossible to get out of a spin. One of our Christmas songs went like this, never overheard until now:

> Khyber Khyber Khyber Pass,
> If you want a splendiferous Christlemas,
> Get on to your most secret self
> That enigmatic red elf,
> Who in the night so quietly spoken
> May bring you an extra token.
> There's one big thing about a Khyber:
> You can't outwit or bribe her.
> Be nice to her ad infinitum
> And you may receive an extra item.
> Until next year, just be your shelbst
> And await the renaissance of that red elf.

Untidy, incoherent, and unworked-upon, this doggerel vented our seasonal exuberance of spirit, and you would have to know that, of all present-givers and -wrappers, Swan is the supremest, working throughout the year to find and wrap gifts of flawless appropriateness for her closest friends, from chocolate alligators to exquisitely crafted tiny suitcases that hold visiting cards in leather. Reconnoitering the stores wherever her work takes her, she doesn't so much shop for Christmas as reexamine the world of phenomena in case there is something she might have missed. Her glistening browns, which have scrutinized Amazon rain forest and the ice massifs of Antarctica, are just as much at home at Henri Bendel's and Saks. She is fascinated by human inventiveness, so she pores over counters, asks countless questions, calls manufacturers, writes to catalogue compilers, and ends up with something unheard of, later on making her loved ones gasp at the ingenuity and resolve that have gone into the gifts. My favorite among my own, I think, is still the pen-sized microscope that lets me squinny even as I am traveling, although a certain purple bathrobe held my affection long after it developed holes and tears: it was my first gift from her, handed me like a prize after an especially arduous trip from Europe. Truly, her gifts are benisons to make the recipients feel a little bit out of this world, almost as if a faith healer tapped them. I would have expected no less from the inventor of the rhyming riddle that sometimes goes, assuming the form of a spurious question: "How many islets does a broncheyelet on Pontius Pilate's islet—?" The answer is always "Three." Other words topple into this dire puzzle, from *pilot* to *Bali Hilet*, without changing the answer.

Early on, her tenderness for life astounded me, I who had grown up among a rough crowd and gone on to a crowd of genteel ruffians in which I at last learned how to assert myself "like a man," which was to say with astute brutishness. Swan revered life for its utter mysteriousness in everyone she met, discerning even in me the sensitive novelist behind the brusque façade and willing to coax me out into the open, be less cerebral and more emotional, most of all in my work. This calling, as I regard it, has seen her through many crises, but the unique miracle of her days has been the way she grew up whole and harmless during such an awful childhood, ever alert to discern in people their potential and then to have them achieve it. An enabler from the outset, she swallowed the misery of many, listening to them and counselling as if she had never had anything but a gentle, pensive upbringing. It was like having faith in atoms, over and above the ills to which people's personalities were heir. Her view of others was unconventionally religious, as if compassion were a reflex and had only to be shown to people to have them willing to accept it. Never mawkish about this, she recognized its presence in her, yet only when forced, told that she had this selfless gift inherited not from her parents but from members of the family she never knew about. Or, harassed young, she deduced its necessity from circumstances, born the custodian of some bright impetus easily lost and wasted. All this went on in her mind before she was twenty, but I saw it in action as she took charge of me, urged me to quit drinking, to desist from pondering violence (its historical version, anyway). What interested me most was the difference between historical and ontological trauma: what happened to you, born when you were, and what was the quality of your existence from peristalsis to heartbeat whether or not you were at that instant subject to historical forces. She never approved of this distinction, but she took much pleasure in citing it to make me squirm, so I assumed a piece of her enjoyed it and thought it had merit. I wondered about the person who, to test the distinction, lived an entire life indoors, was never bombed, arrested, mugged, or called for jury duty: the Indoor Person attuned to her/his seeping, gurgling body. I was always after the bodily resonance of people, wondering if they knew what their existence was like. Yet there was this other side to us both; we worked hard at being phrasemakers, doing our best never to do what had already been done, but then resorted to extravagant verbal fun in order to unwind, embracing the silly, harping on the frivolous and the trivial, just to give the mind a sedative waltz. When we drove, she sang Childe ballads in a peerless croon I shall hear and love to my dying day, and I reciprocated with initially improvised songs (or Latin-American-style *piropos* of extravagant praise) that soon became permanent formulas, as much part of an outing as her Childe ballads:

> She has a more than silky smile,
> With eyes like dark brown chocolate drops
> Into which we plun—n—g—ge
> And Cliffs of Dover whiteness to her teeth,
> Above and beneath.

As long as I live, I will chew on the guilt of not having responded to her tenderness with something similar. She was in many ways an open book, vulnerable and tempting like a sunny ample valley witnessed from an icy upland, almost a Ganges delta seen from the Matterhorn. I exaggerate, but the simile reveals my chagrin. I could have done better, recognizing that, when she uttered the word "harsh" (her mild complaint when I said something tactless or wounding), she was giving me all kinds of chances. A precious experiment in life had been placed in my hands, and I was not, sometimes, showing even the tact of a market gardener. She who had suffered so much had this extraordinary honorable gentility to her, something worth adoring instead of being taken for granted as a humbled adjustment. It was no use saying I was not myself; I was. And who knows what self one is from day to day, year to year, rather than a mess of psychotic confetti? No, she was regal, serene, lavishly young, and here she was unwilling to run away without in the least trying to reform me, as if I were the worst-done-by specimen on the planet, worthier of rest and rehabilitation than she herself. I wince when I think how kind and understanding I could have been to her instead of reading her work with a bark. What I told her about style was correct, I imagine, but the bower of bliss deserved a nicer tutor. Only much later did I realize she had all along the mentality of the healer: the wounded surgeon. A superb poet, she had all the makings of psychiatry, learned in the raw in the woods of night.

In no time, but of course only over months, we evolved a game or sport that had me dozing and purring in my habitual solitary fantasy, sometimes heaving a haunch or flailing a paw in unwitting unconscious exertion, merely to stretch, no signal intended. Remember how a sleeping house will creak and snap, at deep play with itself? I would pretend to awaken, then go back to sleep with a contented snarl, having noticed nothing, certainly not the presence of the nude with the black mane. On I slept, with a slight quiver and a half-cough, but with no eye opening. After more rasps and a purr rather more vociferous than usual, I would open an eye, then another, as unable to see as a newborn, but working myself up gradually into a quasi-paroxysm. During this, Swan lay there paralyzed with mock-panic, waiting the full gaze of the monster she was lying with, even as he felt around with an arm and a paw without trying hard, however, to see anything because he knew nothing was there. But, as I became a fraction more aware of my surroundings, I opened an eye wider, ostentatiously looking away from my companion, who now pretended to shudder with fear, knowing the instant of discovery was at hand. I protracted the wake-up process a few seconds more, now adding a moan and a slight impending roar to my vocal act, and then, suddenly, my eyes opened wide, I saw the other creature stranded there and, even as she screamed, I roared and seized her for the prolonged kiss we ended with.

Time and again we talked about how seriously we were taking our affair whereas all else struck us as trivial buffoonery. This was no doubt arrogant on our part, but we could not rid ourselves of the notion that we were the only serious people in town. Or was it that, within their shells of silliness, all the others were every bit as serious as we were and had serious thoughts about themselves? And did they find us as silly as we found them? No, it could not be: their vapidity began on the outside and went right through, you could tell that a mile off. How came it then that we had been singled out for this exercise in intense, undeviating, rhapsodic, mutual, unprecedented infatuation? What had we done right, and when? Thinking along these lines was akin to behaving like the needlewoman who, repairing an old shirt, scratches an itchy eye with a scissors in hand and thus cuts her eye open without thinking. We could injure ourselves, each other, by being so abstracted from the world at large, by calling each other "Buns" and "Cuddleskin" in high-camp euphoria. There was some danger, wasn't there, in so abstruse a love. We felt Chaucerian, at once frivolous and dead serious, each watching the other watch him or her self. It was like being in a pavane or in a sedan chair. There was no weather, no time. There was no furniture beyond flesh and bone. There was no sun, no ice, no vegetation.

It struck me then that up to now I had spent little time kissing; oh, there had been the usual connections, of course, but relatively little of that tender holding and inhaling without which love in life is a mere scamper. Swan and I spent hour upon hour with our faces close together, appointed to wear out proximity as an hypnotic device. In this way we discovered an almost visceral quietness related to a peace that, certainly passing all human understanding, supplied a fragrant bank on which to rest, as in some old poems and plays. There was a gift of mutual immersion I had never known before, requiring no training and no motive, but only the sublime sink into liquid homage. This sounds grandiose, but it was humble and uncontrived, possibly the natural condition of the soul, with, in its modern incarnation, huge petals from some unimaginable amaryllis piled high on horizontal eyelids, several inches deep, then a foot, then six feet, twenty, a hundred, all the way into the sky, a towering skyscraper of petals, undulating and flexing but never falling, there for the wind to bend. Some such experience in which acute vulnerability met singular physics. In a word, we held together, in all the versions of that phrase, coming to a halt in life, surrendering all volition like a flag catching fire and slowly blowing away to all points. The key to such experience, of course, was how our awareness of it fed back into the experience itself: perceived, it became different, but the difference fed into the original, not merely disarming us, quite ridding us of any self-consciousness about perception, but also inviting us into a further and presumably infinite prolongation of what was happening. Always perceived, and ever changing, it could never exhaust itself or us, but went on metamorphosing as in the creation of Nature itself, becoming—here my imagination has to grapple with unprecedented concepts—planetary, alkaline, juridical, spherically geometric, anally complete. It would no more go into words than into lips, this ravishing sotto voce union that might have wafted from the entanglement of two aliens on the run, all veils and cube roots, unseeable and incapable of being addressed. One flails around in the hinterland of any such experience, always trying to banish crude approximations: being converted into an angel, lifted off Earth into weightless sublimity, dying without ever believing it and with a brain alive enough to worry. If only we had had some ready-made handle other than "love," but we did not and hence were condemned— some condemnation!—to the choked suburb of definitions, where the tumult of defining haunted each word in every language. All the same, we had a hint, a glimpse, a tang of infinity, at least as far as humans may know it, and we surrendered to it as if we knew what it was other than chaos yawning wide, wider, yawn without end. That all this could come from four lips touched in a mood akin to weariness (delight enervates) astounded us and kept us quiet when we might well have replighted our troth noisily.

Our dealings with each other in those days were buoyant and euphoric; nothing, we thought, would go amiss, and even being parted was a merely temporary snag that would sweeten reunion. We waltzed from mood to mood, capping each with a smartass line, her best one being something at once musical, lugubrious, and witty in a predatory way: "After many a summer dies the *Schwann*." My own best is hardly worth reporting, but we did manage to score verbal victories over vicissitude (and to alliterate as well!) without exerting our brains too much. It was the phase of an affair when no one heeds colds, but plunges willy-nilly into the cold climate of a partner's viruses, heedless of drip, cough, and sneeze. Indeed, there was something intimately voluptuous about infecting each other with invisible life forms, almost as if we had taken too much to heart Donne's bracing poem about the flea. Prudence in these matters would come later, when the first flush had yielded to the second flush, and so on until love had become a well-tended castle with a portcullis and all kinds of prophylactic taboos. Depression, sadness, however, we passed from one to the other with connoisseurs' casualness, having ample reason to feel low. Parting was not death, as the tradition had it, but a form of premature loneliness that mechanical means such as the telephone could not quite dispatch. There was nothing like murmuring in each other's ears, with the possibility of instant replay if something sounded bad. The speed of response was paramount. We wanted to be more efficient, almost capable of mind-reading, impatient with the conventional means of colloquial exchange. Presumably Paolo and Francesca, stuck in hell, drove each other out of his or her mind by merely conversing, such were the memories of the ecstasy in which they had adulterously begun. One of their penalties was not to want to talk with each other ever again: nothing with the lascivious dripping pink tongue at all. We had decided to nuke them, but they kept intruding into our thoughts, which was perhaps what Dante intended;

he had meant to inject into all spontaneous amour the desperate chance of love in excess, for which you entered the second circle. Surely, we thought, no amount of intense marital love got you skewered, it was only adultery that got you into trouble. After all, the boredom of the uxorious was legendary; surely nobody would enter the second circle for *too much* marital devotion. It was hard to tell, but we strengthened our conviction that no theologian should come near our obeisances, whether accomplished with a lubricant or with a frozen lip fresh from winter's clamp.

Even packing took us apart, though we did it only a few hundred yards apart. She had her stuff and I had mine, and she was abandoning her now virtually unused apartment, given over to Catherine and their cats. The day came and went, neither of us able to speak, but she was soon sending me little packets of Dino cigarillos disguised as socks and hankies, at least on the green customs slip. My mother and I watched TV westerns and reminisced about the old days, which didn't seem very distant to me. Letters reminded me what gorgeous, emphatic, cuneiform handwriting she had, and I discovered that, especially when apart, one can develop a fixation on somebody's penmanship, each whorl and curlicue embodying a caress. Most people's handwriting left me cold, and in the dark as well (I a poor decipherer), but hers blazed forth from the paper often in royal blue, an unmistakable network of signs and symbols that sang across space and tweaked the tail of time. I kept all her candid, generous letters, reading and rereading them with a fanatic's thoroughness, hunting an innuendo I had missed, or parallels only now calling out to each other in bewitching reciprocity. Her writing was much like her poetry: Nerudian frontal pageantry, saying "I am very much right here behind it." Some folk got so little of themselves into their handwriting that they wrote in order to vanish before their own eyes, allowing no space in their o's and e's and a's, flattening everything as if penmanship were camouflage. Well, *her* boldly drawn letters loomed large in two dimensions, each commensurate with the others, and the overall effect was of a lovingly inscribed tablet. If this was the conduit of poetic thinking, then she honored it, fusing elegance with substantiality, telling the reader there was more here than met the eye—if only you would go back over the lines, you would discover implicit treasures galore, all for you.

HILMA WOLITZER

Sundays

Howard is the beauty in this family. Even the mirrors in our apartment are hung at his eye level. I don't mind. What's wrong with a little role reversal, anyway? What's so bad about a male sex object, for a change? That ability to sprout hair like dark fountains, the flat tapering planes of their buttocks and hips, and oh, those *hands*, and erections pointing the way to bed like road markers.

Besides, I have my own good points, not the least of them my disposition. Sunny, radiant, I wake with the same dumb abundance of hope every day. The bed always seems too small to contain both me and that expansion of joy.

It's only Thursday or Sunday. It's only my own flesh, pale and sleep-creased and smelling like bread near my rooting nose. Nothing special has happened, for which I am grateful. Anything might happen, for which I am expectant and tremblingly ready.

On the other hand, Howard is depressed, hiding in the bedclothes, moaning in his dream. Even without opening my eyes, I can feel the shape of his mood beside me. Then my eyes do open. Ta da! Another gorgeous day! Just what I expected. The clock hums, electric, containing its impulse to tick, the wallpaper repeats itself around the room, and Howard burrows into his pillow, refusing to come to terms with the dangers of consciousness.

My hand is as warm and as heavy as a baby's head, and I lay it against his neck, palm up. If I let him sleep, he would do it for hours and hours. That's depression.

Years ago, my mother woke me with a song about a bird on a windowsill and about sunshine and flowers and the glorious feeling of being alive that had nothing in the world to do with the sad still life of a school lunch and the reluctant walk in brown oxfords, one foot and then the other, for six blocks. It had nothing to do with that waxed ballroom of a gymnasium and the terrible voice of the whistle that demanded agility and grace where there were only clumsy confusion and an enormous desire to be the other girl on the other team, the one leaping in memory toward baskets and dangling ropes.

I didn't want to get up, either—at least not until I had grown out of it, grown away from teachers, grown out of that thin body in an undershirt and lisle stockings and garter belt abrasive on white hipbones. I would get up when I was good and ready, when it was all over and I could have large breasts and easy friendships.

Howard blames his depression on real things in his real life because he doesn't believe in the unconscious. At parties where all the believers talk about the interpretation of dreams, about wish fulfillment and surrogate symbols, Howard covers his mouth with one hand and mutters, "Bullshit!"

Is he depressed because his parents didn't want him to be born, because his mother actually hoisted his father in her arms every morning for a month, hoping to bring on that elusive period? Not a chance!

Is he sad because his sister was smarter in school, or at least more successful, or because she seduced him to the point of action and then squealed? Never!

He is depressed, he says, because it starts to rain when he's at a ball game and the men pulling the tarpaulin over the infield seem to be covering a grave. He is sad, he says, because his boss is a prick and the kid living upstairs roller-skates in the kitchen.

Ah, Howard. My hand is awake now, buzzing with blood, and it kneads the flesh of his neck and then his back, works down through the warm tunnel of bedclothes until it finds his hand and squeezes hard. "It's a gorgeous day, lover! Hey, kiddo, wake up and I'll tell you something."

Howard opens his eyes, but they are glazed and without focus. "Huhhnn?"

"Do you know what?" Searching my head for therapeutic news.

His vision finds the room, the morning light, his whole life. His eyes close again.

"Howard. It's Sunday, the day of rest. The paper is outside, thick and juicy, hot off the press. I'll make waffles and sausages for breakfast. Do you want to go for a drive in the country?"

"Oh, for Christ's sake, will you leave me alone! I want to sleep."

"Sleep? Sweetheart, you'll sleep enough when you're dead."

I see *that* idea roll behind his eyelids. Death. What next?

The children whisper like lovers in the other bedroom.

"Come on, sleepyhead, get up. We'll visit model homes. We'll look in the paper for some new ones." I pat him on the buttocks, a loving but fraternal gesture, a manager sending his favorite man into the game.

Why am I so happy? It must be the triumph of the human spirit over genetics and environment. I know the same bad things Howard knows. I have my ups and downs, traumas, ecstasies. Maybe this happiness is only a dirty trick, another of life's big come-ons. I might end up the kind who can't ride on escalators or sit in chairs that don't have arms. Who knows?

But in the meantime I sing as I whip up waffle batter, pour golden juice into golden glasses, while Howard sits in a chair dropping pages of the *Times* like leaves from a deciduous tree.

I sing songs from the Forties, thinking there's nothing in this life like the comfort of your own nostalgia. I sing *Ferry-Boat Serenade,* I sing *Hut-Sut Rallson on the Riller-ah.* The waffles stick to the iron. "Don't sit under the apple tree with anyone else but me," I warn Howard, willing the waffle and coffee smells into the living room where he sits like an inmate in the wintry garden of a small sanitorium.

"BREAKFAST IS READY!" I have the healthy bellow of a short-order cook.

He shuffles in, still convalescing from his childhood.

The children come in too, his jewels, his treasures. They climb his legs to reach the table, to scratch themselves on his morning beard. Daddy, my Daddy, and he runs his hands over them, a blind man trying to memorize their bones. The teakettle sings, the sun crashes in through the window, and my heart will not be swindled.

"What's the matter, Howie? If something is bothering you, *talk* about it."

He smiles, that calculated, ironic smile, and I think that we hardly talk about anything that matters.

I waited all my life to become a woman, damn it, to sit in a kitchen and say grown-up things to the man facing me, words that would float like vapor over the heads of the children. Don't I remember that language from my own green days, code words in Yiddish and pig latin, and a secret but clearly sexual jargon that made my mother laugh and filled me with a dark and trembling longing and rage?

Ix-nay, the *id*-kay.

Now I want to talk over the heads of *my* children, in the modern language of the cinema. There are thousands of words they wouldn't understand and would never remember, except for the rhythm and the mystery.

Fellatio. Howard. *Vasectomy.*

He rattles the Real Estate section and slowly turns the pages.

"Well, did you find a development for us? Find one with a really inspired name this time."

I try so hard to encourage him. Looking at model homes has become a standard treatment for Howard's depression. For some reason we believe the long drive out of the city, the ordered march through unlived-in rooms, restores him. Not that *we* want to live in the suburbs. How we laugh and poke one another at the roped-off bedrooms hung in velvet drapery, the plastic chickens roosting in warm refrigerators. The thing is, places like that confirm our belief in our own choices. We're *safe* here in the city, in our tower among towers. Flyspecks, so to speak, in the population.

On other days, we've gone to Crestwood Estates, Seaside Manor (miles from any sea), to Tall Oaks and Sweet Pines, to Châteaux Printemps, and Chalets-on-the-Sound.

But the pickings are slim now. All the worthwhile land has been gobbled up by speculators, and those tall oaks and sweet pines fallen to bulldozers. There are hardly any developments left for our sad Sundays. The smart money is in garden apartments and condominiums, cities without skylines. Maybe later, when we are older, we'll visit the Happy Haven and the Golden Years Retreat, to purge whatever comes with mortality and the final vision.

But now Howard is trying. "Here's one," he says. *"Doncastle Greens. Only fifty minutes from the heart of Manhattan. Live like a king on a commoner's budget."*

"Let me see!" I rush to his side, ready for conspiracy. "Hey, listen to this. *Come on down today and choose either a twenty-one-inch color TV or a deluxe dishwasher, as a bonus, absolutely free!* Howie, what do you choose?"

But Howard chooses silence, will not be cajoled so easily, so early in his depression.

I hide the dishes under a veil of suds and we all get dressed. The children are too young to care where we are going, as long as they can ride in the car, the baby steering crazily in her car seat and Jason contemplating the landscape and the faces of other small boys poised at the windows of other cars.

The car radio sputters news and music and frantic advice. It is understood that Howard will drive there and I will drive back.

He sits forward, bent over the wheel, as if visibility is poor and the traffic hazardous. In fact, it's a marvelous, clear day and the traffic is moving without hesitation past all the exits, past the green signs and the abandoned wrecks like modern sculpture at roadside, past dead dogs, their brilliant innards squeezed out onto the divider.

Jason points, always astounded at the first corpse, but we are past

it before he can speak. It occurs to me that everywhere here there are families holding dangling leashes and collars, walking through the yards of
their neighborhoods, calling, Lucky! Lucky! and then listening for that
answering bark that will not come. Poor Lucky, deader than a doornail,
flatter than a bath mat.

I watch Howard, that gorgeous nose so often seen in profile, that
crisp gangster's hair, and his ear, unspeakably vulnerable, waxen and con-
voluted.

And then we are there. Doncastle Greens is a new one for us. The
builder obviously dreamed of moats and grazing sheep. Model No. I,
The Shropshire, recalls at once gloomy castles and thatched cottages,
Richard III and Miss Marple. Other cars are already parked under the
colored banners when we pull in.

The first step is always the brochure, wonderfully new and smelly
with printer's ink. The motif is British, of course, and there are taprooms
and libraries as opposed to the dens and funrooms of Crestwood Estates,
les salons et les chambres de Châteaux Printemps.

Quelle savvy!

The builder's agent is young and balding, busy sticking little flags
into promised lots on a huge map behind his desk. He calls us folks.
"Good to see you, folks!" Every once in a while he rubs his hands together as if selling homes makes one cold. During his spiel I try to catch
Howard's eye, but Howard pretends to be listening. What an actor!

We move in a slow line through Model I, behind an elderly couple. I know we've seen them before, at Tall Oaks perhaps, but there are
no greetings exchanged. They'll never buy, of course, and I wonder about
their motives, which are probably more devious than ours.

Some of the people, I can see, are really buyers. One wife holds her
husband's hand as if they are entering consecrated premises.

I poke Howard, just below the heart, a bully's semaphore. I can talk
without moving my lips. "White brocade couch on bowlegs," I mutter.
"Definitely velvet carpeting." I wait, but Howard is grudging.

"Plastic-covered lampshades," he offers, finally.

I urge him on. "Crossed rifles over the fireplace. Thriving plastic
dracaena in the entrance." I snicker, roll my eyes, do a little soft shoe.

But Howard isn't playing. He is leaning against the braided ropes
that keep us from muddying the floor of the drawing room, and he
looks like a man at the prow of a ship.

"Howard?" Tentative. Nervous.

"You know, kiddo, it's not really that bad," he says.

"Do you mean the *house?*"

Howard doesn't answer. The older man takes a tape measure from his pocket and lays it against the dark molding. Then he writes something into a little black notebook.

The buyers breathe on our necks, staring at their future. "Oh, *Ronnie,*" she says, an exhalation like the first chords of a hymn. I would not be surprised if she kneels now or makes some other mysterious or religious gesture.

"One of these days," Howard says, "*pow,* one of us will be knocked on the head in that crazy city. Raped. Strangled."

"Howie. . . ."

"And do we have adequate bookshelves? You know I have no room for my books."

The oak bookshelves before us hold all the volumes, A through Z, of the *American Household Encyclopedia.*

The old man measures the doorframe and writes again in his book. Perhaps he will turn around soon and measure us, recording his findings in a feathery hand.

Jason and another boy discover one another and stare like mirrors. What would happen if we took the wrong one home, bathed him and gave him Frosted Flakes, kissed him and left the night-light on until he forgot everything else and adjusted? The baby draws on her pacifier and dreamily pats my hair.

Everyone else has passed us and Howard is still in the same doorway. I pull on his sleeve. "The baby is getting heavy."

He takes her from me and she nuzzles his cheek with her perfect head.

We proceed slowly to the master bathroom, the one with the dual vanities and a magazine rack embossed with a Colonial eagle.

"Howie, will you look at this. His and *hers.*"

He doesn't answer.

We go into the bedroom itself, where ghosts of dead queens rest on the carved bed. "Mortgages. Cesspools. Community living." I face him across the bed and hiss the words at him, but he does not even wince. He looks sleepy and relaxed. I walk around the bed and put my arm through his. "Maybe we ought to join Marriage Encounter, after all. Maybe we look in the wrong places for our happiness, Howard."

He pats my hand, distracted but solicitous. I walk behind him now, a tourist following a guide. At the olde breakfast nooke, I want to sit him down and explain that I am terrified of change, that the city is my hideout and my freedom, that one of us might take a lover, or worse.

But I am silent in the pantry, in the wine cellar and the vestibule, and we are finished with the tour of the house, evicted before occupation. We stand under the fluttering banners and watch the serious buyers reenter the builder's trailer. Howard shifts the baby from arm to arm as if she interferes with his concentration. Finally, he passes her to me without speaking. He puts his hands into his pockets and he has that dreaming look on his face.

"*I'll* drive back," I say, as if this weren't preordained.

There is more traffic now, and halfway home we slow to observe the remains of an accident. Some car has jumped the guardrail and there is a fine icing of shattered glass on the road.

"Do you *see?*" I say, not sure of my moral.

But Howard is asleep, his head tilted against the headrest. At home, I can see that he's coming out of it. He is interested in dinner, in the children's bath. He stands behind me at the sink and he has an erection.

Later, in bed again, I get on top, for the artificial respiration I must give. His mouth opens to receive my tongue, a communion wafer. I rise above him, astounded at the luminosity of my skin in the half-light.

Howard smiles, handsome, damp with pleasure, yes, with *happiness*, his ghosts mugged and banished from this room.

"Are you happy?" I must know, restorer of faith, giver of life. "Are you happy?"

And even as I wait for his answer, my own ghosts enter, stand solemn at the foot of the bed, thin girls in undershirts, jealous and watchful, whispering in some grown-up language I can never understand.

POETRY

Charm to Quell a Rival

From out of the earth I dig this plant, an herb of most effectual
    power,
Wherewith one quells the rival wife and gains the husband for oneself.
Auspicious, with expanded leaves, sent by the gods, victorious plant,
Blow thou the rival wife away, and make my husband only mine.
Stronger am I, O Stronger one, yea, mightier than the mightier;
And she who is my rival wife is lower than the lowest dames.
Her very name I utter not: she takes no pleasure in this man.
Far into distance most remote drive we the rival wife away.
I am the conqueror, and thou, thou also art victorious:
As victory attends us both we will subdue my fellow-wife.
I have gained thee for vanquisher, have grasped thee with a stronger
    spell.
As a cow hastens to her calf, so let thy spirit speed to me, hasten like
    water on its way.

ANONYMOUS, EGYPTIAN

Stand Fast, O My Heart

It fleeth away, my heart, quickly,
When I recall my love of thee,
Nor suffereth me to walk in human wise,
But is affrighted from its place

It suffereth me not to don a tunic,
Nor to attire myself with my fan.
I put not paint upon mine eyes,
Nor anoint myself at all.
Bide not, but get thee home,
Saith it to me as often as I recall him.
Act not the fool, O my heart;
Wherefore playest thou the madman?
Sit calm, until thy brother come to thee.
Let not the folk say concerning me,
A woman distraught with love.
Stand fast as often as thou recallest him,
O my heart, and do not flee.

ANONYMOUS, EGYPTIAN

from *The Crossing*

My God, my lotus, my love
the north wind is blowing.
How pleasant to reach the river!
    breath
    flower . . .
My heart longs to go down
to bathe before you
to show you my loveliness
in a tunic of expensive
royal linen, drenched
in oil, my hair
braided in plaits like reeds.
I'll enter the river with you
and come out carrying
a red fish for you
splendid in my fingers.
I'll offer it to you
as I behold your beauty.
O my hero, my love,
come and behold me.

❧ ❧

THE BIBLE

from *The Song of Solomon*

I am the rose of Sharon, and the lily of the valleys.
    As the lily among thorns, so is my love among the daughters.
    As the apple tree among the trees of the wood, so is my beloved
        among the sons. I sat down under his shadow with great delight,
        and his fruit was sweet to my taste.
    He brought me to the banqueting house, and his banner over me
        was love.
    Stay me with flagons, comfort me with apples: for I am sick of
        love.
    His left hand is under my head, and his right hand doth embrace
        me.
    I charge you, O ye daughters of Jerusalem, by the roes, and by the
        hinds of the field, that ye stir not up, nor awake my love, till the
        please.
    The voice of my beloved! behold, he cometh leaping upon the
        mountains, skipping upon the hills.
    My beloved is like a roe or a young hart: behold, he standeth
        behind our wall, he looketh forth at the windows, showing
        himself through the lattice.
    My beloved spake, and said unto me, Rise up, my love, my fair one,
        and come away.
    For, lo, the winter is past, the rain is over and gone;
    The flowers appear on the earth; the time of the singing of birds is
        come, and the voice of the turtle is heard in our land:
    The fig tree putteth forth her green figs, and the vines with the
        tender grape give a good smell. Arise, my love, my fair one, and
        come away.
    O my dove, that art in the clefts of the rock, in the secret places of
        the stairs, let me see thy countenance, let me hear thy voice; for
        sweet is thy voice, and thy countenance is comely.
    Take us the foxes, the little foxes, that spoil the vines: for our vines
        have tender grapes.
    My beloved is mine, and I am his: he feedeth among the lilies.
    Until the day break, and the shadows flee away, turn, my beloved,

and be thou like a roe or a young hart upon the mountains of Bether.

❧ ❧

ONO NO YOSHIKI

My Love

My love
Is like the grasses
Hidden in the deep mountain:
Though its abundance increases,
There is none that knows.

❧ ❧

TS'AO CHIH

Sorrow, in Seven

A bright moon illumines the high building
With shimmering rays, just dancing back and forth.
Upstairs is an anxious minded woman,
Sadly sighing with endless sorrow.
I venture to ask who the sighing one is?
I am a wanderer's wife, she says.
My lord went off more than ten years ago,
While I have remained here always alone.
My lord is like dust on a clear road;
I am like mud in turbid water.
Floating, sinking, each in different circumstances;
When shall we reunite in harmony?
Would that I were the southwest wind,
To hurry off to the bosom of my lord.
If the bosom of my lord be not open to me,
Where can my poor self find refuge?

Drifting Duckweed

Drifting duckweed floats on the clear water
Blown by the wind east and west.
Hair done up, I bade farewell to my parents,
To come to be my lord's mate.
Respectful and careful morning and night,
Without cause I got your accusations and blame.
In the past I was favoured with love and kindness,
In harmony and joy like harp and lute.
Why do you now reject me,
And separate us like east-star and west-star?
Dogwood itself has fragrance,
But not like the cassia and orchid;
Though you can love a new woman
It will be nothing like your old happiness.
Passing clouds return in time;
Shall, by chance, your love return?
Unsatisfied, unsatisfied, I look to the sky and sigh;
To what shall my anxious heart appeal?
The sun and moon stay not always in the same place;
Man's life is as insignificant as an overnight stay.
A sad wind comes and enters my breast;
Tears drop like falling dew.
I'll open this box and make some clothes,
Cut and sew the glossy silk and plain silk.

TU FU

Restless Night

As bamboo chill drifts into the bedroom,
Moonlight fills every corner of our
Garden. Heavy dew beads and trickles.
Stars suddenly there, sparse, next aren't.
Fireflies in dark flight flash. Waking
Waterbirds begin calling, one to another.

All things caught between shield and sword,
All grief empty, the clear night passes.

⁂

LIU HSIAO-WEI

For My Wife

A charming girl, full of dejected love,
Weaves plain silk as autumn sounds stir.
Passing the yarn-guide her bracelet jade trembles,
Pressing the shears her belt pearls tinkle.
Warp so fine threatens to jam the shuttle,
Woof snaps, she's cross the silk is too thin.
Grapevine begins to look finished,
Mandarin ducks have yet to emerge.

Under cloudy ridge-poles all the weavers stroll,
Silk windows open to each other.
Through window grilles float eyebrow whispers,
From silk to light come smiling eyes.
Blurred, screened by thinnest silk,
Yet clearly glimpsed cosmetic flower:
Sweetheart lotus roots studded with jade,
Loveknot flowers strung with jewels,
Her red gown fastened at the back,
Gold pins slant toward her sidecurls.
From the loom top hangs gay braid,
From the loom's side cascade strings of pearls.
Green silk threads draw in the pivot's crouching hare,
Yellow gold encircles the pulley's Lulu knob.
Rich tints dart from her skirt hem,
Scented gloss glistens on her lips.
One-hundred-city barons ask after her,
Five-horse teams paw the ground before her.

There is only me in my bedroom,
Faithful to past love, not seeking new amours.

In dreams weeping soaks my flowery pillow,
Waking tears drench my silk kerchief.
Sleeping alone is so hard for me,
My double quilt still feels cold.
Even more I desire your skin's marbrous warmth,
More than ever long for horizontal pleasures.

❦ ❦

KAMAL UD-DIN

O Love, Thy Hair!

O love, thy hair! thy locks of night and musk!
The very wind therein doth lose his way,
While in the perfumed darkness he would stray;
And my heart, too, is lost in scented dusk.

Thy crescent brows irradiate the night;
Love, of thy lips and tresses give thou me—
Thy breast is like a restless, heaving sea;
Thine eyes are stars of sorrow and delight.

Yet grieve not that I grieve, Soul of the Sea—
What is my heart that thou shouldst comfort it
With wine or song, with smile or dance or wit?
Dust of thy threshold is enough for me.

❦ ❦

SOPHOCLES

from *Antigone*

CHORUS: Love, never foiled in fight!
           Warrior Love, that on Wealth workest havoc!
           Love, who in ambush of young maid's soft cheek
           All night keep'st watch!—Thou roamest over seas:
           In lonely forest homes thou harbourest.

Who may avoid thee? None!
Moral, Immortal,
All are o'erthrown by thee, all feel thy frenzy.

Lightly thou draw'st awry
Righteous minds into wrong to their ruin.
Thou this unkindly quarrel hast inflamed
'Tween kindred men.—Triumphantly prevails
The heart-compelling eye of winsome bride,
Compeer of mighty Law
Thronèd, commanding.
Madly thou mockest men, dread Aphrodite.

HOMER

from *The Odyssey*

CALYPSO BIDS ULYSSES DEPART

Even a god could not help being charmed with such a lovely spot, so Mercury stood still and looked at it; but when he had admired it sufficiently he went inside the cave.

Calypso knew him at once—for the gods all know each other, no matter how far they live from one another—but Ulysses was not within; he was on the sea-shore as usual, looking out upon the barren ocean with tears in his eyes, groaning and breaking his heart for sorrow. Calypso gave Mercury a seat and said, "Why have you come to see me, Mercury—honoured, and ever welcome—for you do not visit me often? Say what you want; I will do it for you at once if I can, and if it can be done at all; but come inside, and let me set refreshment before you."

As she spoke she drew a table loaded with ambrosia beside him and mixed him some red nectar, so Mercury ate and drank till he had had enough, and then said:—

"We are speaking god and goddess to one another, and you ask me why I have come here, and I will tell you truly as you would have me do. Jove sent me; it was no doing of mine; who could possibly want to come all this way over the sea where there are no cities full of people to offer me sacrifices or choice hecatombs? Nevertheless I had to come, for none of us other gods can cross Jove, nor transgress his orders. He says that you have here the most ill-starred of all those who fought nine years before the city of King Priam and sailed home in the tenth year after having sacked it. On their way home they sinned against Minerva, who raised both wind and waves against them, so that all his brave companions perished, and he alone was carried hither by wind and tide. Jove says that you are to let this man go at once, for it is decreed that he shall not perish here, far from his own people, but shall return to his house and country and see his friends again."

Calypso trembled with rage when she heard this, "You gods," she exclaimed, "ought to be ashamed of yourselves. You are always jealous, and hate seeing a goddess take a fancy to a mortal man, and live with him in open matrimony. So when rosy-fingered Dawn made love to Orion, you precious gods were all of you furious till Diana went and killed him in Ortygia. So again when Ceres fell in love with Jason, and yielded to him in a thrice-ploughed fallow field, Jove came to hear of it before so very long and killed Jason with his thunderbolts. And now you are angry with me too because I have a man here. I found the poor creature sitting all alone astride of a keel, for Jove had struck his ship with lightning and sunk it in mid ocean, so that all his crew were drowned, while he himself was driven by wind and waves on to my island. I got fond of him and cherished him, and had set my heart on making him immortal, so that he should never grow old all his days; still I cannot cross Jove, nor bring his counsels to nothing; therefore, if he insists upon it, let the man go beyond the seas again; but I cannot send him anywhere myself for I have neither ships nor men who can take him. Nevertheless I will readily give him such advice, in all good faith, as will be likely to bring him safely to his own country."

"Then send him away," said Mercury, "or Jove will be angry with you and punish you."

ULYSSES RETURNS TO PENELOPE

"I will say what I think will be best," answered Ulysses. "First wash and put your shirts on; tell the maids also to go to their own room and dress; Phemins shall then strike up a dance tune on his lyre, so that if people outside hear, or any of the neighbours, or someone going along the street, happens to notice it, they may think there is a wedding in the house, and no rumours about the death of the suitors will get about in the town, before we can escape to the woods upon my own land. Once there, we will settle which of the courses heaven vouchsafes us shall seem wisest."

Thus did he speak, and they did even as he had said. First they washed and put their shirts on, while the women got ready. Then Phemius took his lyre and set them all longing for sweet song and stately dance. The house re-echoed with the sound of men and women dancing, and the people outside said, "I suppose the queen has been getting married at last. She ought to be ashamed of herself for not continuing to protect her husband's property until he comes home."

This was what they said, but they did not know what it was that had been happening. The upper servant Eurynome washed and anointed Ulysses in his own house and gave him a shirt and cloak, while Minerva made him look taller and stronger than before; she also made the hair grow thick on the top of his head, and flow down in curls like hyacinth blossoms; she glorified him about the head and shoulders just as a skillful workman who has studied art of all kinds under Vulcan or Minerva—and his work is full of beauty—enriches a piece of silver plate by gilding it. He came from the bath looking like one of the immortals, and sat down opposite his wife on the seat he had left. "My dear," said he, "heaven has endowed you with a heart more unyielding than woman ever yet had. No other woman could bear to keep away from her husband when he had come back to her after twenty years of absence, and after having gone through so much. But come, nurse, get a bed ready for me; I will sleep alone, for this woman has a heart as hard as iron."

"My dear," answered Penelope, "I have no wish to set myself up, nor to depreciate you; but I am not struck by your appearance, for I very well remember what kind of a man you were when you set sail from Ithaca. Nevertheless, Euryclea, take his bed outside the bed chamber that he himself built. Bring the bed outside this room, and put bedding upon it with fleeces, good coverlets, and blankets."

She said this to try him, but Ulysses was very angry and said, "Wife, I am much displeased at what you have just been saying. Who has been taking my bed from the place in which I left it? He must have found it a hard task, no matter how skilled a workman he was, unless some god came and helped him to shift it. There is no man living, however strong and in his prime, who could move it from its place, for it is a marvellous curiosity which I made with my very own hands. There was a young olive growing within the precincts of the house, in full vigour, and about as thick as a bearing-post. I built my room round this with strong walls of stone and a roof to cover them, and I made the doors strong and well-fitting. Then I cut off the top boughs of the olive tree and left the stump standing. This I dressed roughly from the root up-wards and then worked with carpenter's tools well and skillfully, straight-ening my work by drawing a line on the wood, and making it into a bed-prop. I then bored a hole down the middle, and made it the centre-post of my bed, at which I worked till I had finished it, inlaying it with gold and silver; after this I stretched a hide of crimson leather from one side of it to the other. So you see I know all about it, and I desire to learn whether it is still there, or whether anyone has been removing it by cut-ting down the olive tree at its roots."

When she heard the sure proofs Ulysses now gave her, she fairly broke down. She flew weeping to his side, flung her arms about his neck, and kissed him, "Do not be angry with me Ulysses," she cried, "you, who are the wisest of mankind. We have suffered, both of us. Heaven has denied us the happiness of spending our youth, and of growing old, together; do not then be aggrieved or take it amiss that I did not embrace you thus as soon as I saw you. I have been shuddering all the time through fear that someone might come here and deceive me with a lying story; for there are many very wicked people going about. Jove's daughter Helen would never have yielded herself to a man from a foreign country, if she had known that the sons of Achæans would come after her and bring her back. Heaven put it in her heart to do wrong, and she gave no thought to that sin, which has been the source of all our sor-rows. Now, however, that you have convinced me by showing that you know all about our bed (which no human being has ever seen but you and I and a single maidservant, the daughter of Actor, who was given me by my father on my marriage, and who keeps the doors of our room), hard of belief though I have been I can mistrust no longer."

Then Ulysses in his turn melted, and wept as he clasped his dear and faithful wife to his bosom. As the sight of land is welcome to men who are swimming towards the shore, when Neptune has wrecked their ship with the fury of his winds and waves; a few alone reach the land, and these, covered with brine, are thankful when they find themselves on firm ground and out of danger—even so was her husband welcome to her as she looked upon him, and she could not tear her two fair arms from about his neck. Indeed they would have gone on indulging their sorrow till rosy-fingered morn appeared, had not Minerva determined otherwise, and held night back in the far west, while she would not suffer Dawn to leave Oceanus, nor to yoke the two steeds Lampus and Phaethon that bear her onward to break the day upon mankind.

At last, however, Ulysses said, "Wife, we have not yet reached the end of our troubles. I have an unknown amount of toil still to undergo. It is long and difficult, but I must go through with it, for thus the shade of Teiresias prophecied concerning me, on the day when I went down into Hades to ask about my return and that of my companions. But now let us go to bed, that we may lie down and enjoy the blessed boon of sleep."

Translated by Samuel Butler

LUCRETIUS

The Posture

Of like importance is the posture too,
In which the genial feat of Love we do:
For as the Females of the four foot kind,
Receive the leapings of their Males behind;
So the good Wives, with loins uplifted high,
And leaning on their hands and fruitful stroke may try:
For in that posture will they best conceive;
Not when supinely laid they frisk and heave;
For active motions only break the blow,
And more of Strumpets than of Wives they show;
When answering stroke with stroke, the mingled liquors flow.
Endearments eager, and too brisk a bound,
Throws off the Plow-share from the furrow'd ground.
But common Harlots in conjunction heave,
Because 'tis less their business to conceive
Than to delight, and to provoke the deed;
A trick which honest Wives but little need.
Nor is it from the Gods, or Cupids dart,
That many a homely Woman takes the heart;
But Wives well humour'd, dutiful, and chaste,
And clean, will hold their wandring Husbands fast,
Such are the links of Love, and such a Love will last.
For what remains, long habitude, and use,
Will kindness in domestick Bands produce:

For Custome will a strong impression leave;
Hard bodies, which the lightest stroke receive,
In length of time, will moulder and decay,
And stones with drops of rain are wash'd away.

Translated by John Dryden

❧ ❧

VIRGIL

from *The Aeneid*

BOOK IV: DIDO BURNS FOR AENEAS

With these words she fanned into flame the queen's love-enkindled heart, put hope in her wavering mind, and loosed the bonds of shame. First they visit the shrines and sue for peace at every altar; duly they slay chosen sheep to Ceres the law-giver, to Phoebus and father Lyaeus, before all to Juno, guardian of wedlock bonds. Dido herself, matchless in beauty, with cup in hand, pours libation midway between the horns of a white heifer, or in presence of the gods moves slowly to the rich altars, and solemnizes the day with gifts, then, gazing into the opened breasts of victims, consults the quivering entrails. Ah, blind souls of seers! Of what avail are vows or shrines to one wild with love? All the while the flame devours her tender heart-strings, and deep in her breast lives the silent wound. Unhappy Dido burns, and through the city wanders in frenzy—even as a hind, smitten by an arrow, which, all unwary, amid the Cretan woods, a shepherd hunting with darts has pierced from afar, leaving in her the winged steel, unknowing: she in flight ranges the Dictaean woods and glades, but fast to her side clings the deadly shaft. Now through the city's midst she leads with her Aeneas, and displays her Sidonian wealth and the city built; she essays to speak and stops with the word half-spoken. Now, as day wanes, she seeks that same banquet, again madly craves to hear the sorrows of Ilium and again hangs on the speaker's lips. Then when all have gone their ways, and in turn the dim moon sinks her light, and the setting stars invite sleep, alone she mourns in the empty hall, and falls on the couch he has left. Though absent, each from each, she hears him, she sees him, or, captivated by his father's look, she holds Ascanius on her lap, if so she may beguile a passion beyond all utterance. No longer rise the towers begun, no longer do the youth exercise in arms, or toil at havens or bulwarks for safety in war; the works are broken off and idle—huge threatening walls and the engine uptowering to heaven.

Soon as the loved wife of Jove saw that she was held in a passion so fatal, and that her good name was now no bar to her frenzy, the daughter of Saturn accosts Venus thus: "Splendid indeed is the praise and rich the spoils ye win, thou and thy boy; mighty and glorious is the power divine, if one woman is subdued by the guile of two gods! Nay, it escapes me not how, in fear of our city, thou hast held in suspicion the homes of high Carthage. But what shall be the end? or how far goes all this contest now? Why work we not rather an enduring peace and a plighted wedlock? What thou didst seek with all thy heart thou hast; Dido is on fire with love and has drawn the madness through her veins. Let us then rule this people jointly with equal sovereignty; let her serve a Phrygian husband and yield her Tyrians to thy hand as dowry!"

To her—for she knew that with feigned purpose she had spoken, to turn the empire from Italy to Libya's coasts—Venus thus began in reply: "Who so mad as to refuse such terms, or choose rather to strive with thee in war, if only Fortune favour the fulfilment of thy word? But the Fates send me adrift, uncertain whether Jupiter wills that there be one city for the Tyrians and the wanderers from Troy, or approves the blending of peoples and the league of union. Thou art his wife; thou mayest probe his heart with entreaty. Go on; I will follow!"

Then queenly Juno thus replied: "With me shall rest that task. Now in what way the present purpose can be achieved, hearken and I will explain in brief. Aeneas and unhappy Dido plan to go a-hunting together in the forest, soon as tomorrow's sun shows his rising and with his rays unveils the world. On them, while the hunters run to and fro and gird the glades with nets, I will pour down from above a black rain mingled with hail, and wake the whole welkin with thunder. The company shall scatter and be veiled in gloom of night; to the same cave shall come Dido and the Trojan chief. I will be there and, if certain of thy goodwill, will link them in sure wedlock, sealing her for his own; this shall be their bridal!" Yielding to her suit, the Cytherean gave assent and smiled at the guile discovered.

Meanwhile Dawn rose and left the ocean. When sunlight has burst forth, there issues from the gates a chosen band of youth; with meshed nets, toils, broad-pointed hunting-spears, there stream forth Massylian horsemen and their strong, keen-scented hounds. As the queen lingers in her bower, the Punic princes await her at the doorway; her prancing steed stands brilliant in purple and gold, and fiercely champs the foaming bit. At last she comes forth, attended by a mighty throng, and clad in a Sidonian robe with embroidered border. Her quiver is of gold, her tresses are knotted into gold, golden is the buckle to clasp her purple cloak. With her pace a Phrygian train and joyous Iülus. Aeneas himself, goodly beyond all others, advances to join her and unites his band with hers. As when Apollo quits Lycia, his winter home, and the streams of Xanthus, to visit his mother's Delos, and renews the dance, while mingling about his altars Cretans and Dryopes and painted Agathyrsians raise their voices—he himself treads the Cynthian ridges, and with soft leafage shapes and binds his flowing locks, braiding it with golden diadem; the shafts rattle on his shoulders: so no less lightly than he went Aeneas, such beauty shines forth from his noble face! When they came to the mountain heights and pathless lairs, lo! wild goats dislodged from the rocky peaks ran down the ridges; in another part stags scurry across the open moors and amid clouds of dust mass their bands in flight, as they leave the hills behind. But in the midst of the valleys the young Ascanius glories in his fiery steed, galloping past now these, now those, and prays that amid the timorous herds a foaming boar may be granted to his vows or a tawny lion come down from the mountain.

Meanwhile in the sky begins the turmoil of a wild uproar; rain follows, mingled with hail. The scattered Tyrian train and the Trojan youth, with the Dardan grandson of Venus, in their fear seek shelter here and there over the fields; torrents rush down from the heights. To the same cave come Dido and the Trojan chief. Primal Earth and nuptial Juno give the sign; fires flashed in Heaven, the witness to their bridal, and on the mountain-top screamed the Nymphs. That day was the first day of death, that first the cause of woe. For no more is Dido swayed by fair show or fair fame, no more does she dream of a secret love: she calls it marriage and with that name veils her sin!

Forthwith Rumour runs through Libya's great cities—Rumour of all evils the most swift.

Translated by H. Rushton Fairclough

Love and the Creatures

Thus every creature, and of every kind,
The secret joys of sweet coition find:
Not only man's imperial race; but they

That wing the liquid air, or swim the sea,
Or haunt the desert, rush into the flame:
For love is lord of all; and is in all the same.
'Tis with this rage, the mother lion stung,
Scours o're the plain; regardless of her young:
Demanding rites of love, she sternly stalks;
And hunts her lover in his lonely walks.
　　'Tis then the shapeless bear his den forsakes;
In woods and fields a wild destruction makes.
Boars whet their tusks; to battle tygers move;
Enrag'd with hunger, more enrag'd with love.
Then woe to him, that in the desert land
Of Lybia travels, o're the burning sand.
The stallion snuffs the well-known scent afar;
And snorts and trembles for the distant mare:
Nor bitts nor bridles, can his rage restrain;
And rugged rocks are interpos'd in vain:
He makes his way o're mountains, and contemns
Unruly torrents, and unforded streams.
The bristled boar, who feels the pleasing wound,
New grinds his arming tusks, and digs the ground.
The sleepy leacher shuts his little eyes;
About his churning chaps the frothy bubbles rise:
He rubs his sides against a tree; prepares
And hardens both his shoulders for the wars.

Translated by John Dryden

❧ ❧

PETRONIUS

Doing, a Filthy Pleasure Is, and Short

Doing, a filthy pleasure is, and short;
And done, we straight repent us of the sport:
Let us not then rush blindly on unto it,
Like lustfull beasts, that only know to do it:
For lust will languish, and that heat decay,
But thus, thus, keeping endless Holy-day,

Let us together closely lie, and kiss,
There is no labour, nor so shame in this;
This hath pleas'd, doth please, and long will please; never
Can this decay, but is beginning ever.

Translated by Ben Jonson

OVID

To His Mistress
Whose husband is invited to a feast with them. The poet instructs her how to behave her-
self in his company

Your husband will be with us at the treat;
May that be the last supper he shall eat.
And am poor I, a guest invited there,
Only to see, while he may touch the Fair?
To see you kiss and hug your nauseous Lord,
While his lewd hand descends below the board?
Now wonder not that Hippodamia's charms,
At such a sight, the Centaurs urged to arms;
That in a rage they threw their cups aside,
Assailed the bridegroom, and would force the bride.
I am not half a horse (I would I were):
Yet hardly can from you my hands forbear.
Take then my counsel; which, observed, may be
Of some importance both to you and me.
Be sure to come before your man be there;
There's nothing can be done; but come howe'er.
Sit next him (that belongs to decency);
But tread upon my foot in passing by.
Read in my looks what silently they speak,
And slyly, with your eyes, your answer make.
My lifted eyebrow shall declare my pain;
My right-hand to his fellow shall complain;
And on the back a letter shall design;
Besides a note that shall be writ in wine.
Whene'er you think upon our last embrace,

With your forefinger gently touch your face.
If any word of mine offend my dear,
Pull, with your hand, the velvet of your ear.
If you are pleased with what I do or say,
Handle your rings, or with your fingers play.
As suppliants use at altars, hold the board,
Whene'er you wish the Devil may take your Lord.
When he fills for you, never touch the cup;
But bid th' officious cuckold drink it up.
The waiter on those services employ.
Drink you, and I will snatch it from the boy:
Watching the part where your sweet mouth hath been,
And thence, with eager lips, will suck it in.
If he, with clownish manners, thinks it fit
To taste, and offer you the nasty bit,
Reject his greasy kindness, and restore
Th' unsavory morsel he had chewed before.
Nor let his arms embrace your neck, nor rest
Your tender cheek upon his hairy breast.
Let not his hand within your bosom stray,
And rudely with your pretty bubbies play.
But above all, let him no kiss receive;
That's an offence I never can forgive.
Do not, O do not that sweet mouth resign,
Lest I rise up in arms, and cry, 'Tis mine.
I shall thrust in betwixt, and avoid of fear
The manifest adulterer will appear.
These things are plain to sight; but more I doubt
What you conceal beneath your petticoat.
Take not his leg between your tender thighs,
Nor, with your hand, provoke my foe to rise.
How many love-inventions I deplore,
Which I, myself, have practised all before!
How oft have I been forced the robe to lift
In company to make a homely shift
For a bare bout, ill huddled o'er in haste,
While o'er my side the Fair her mantle cast.
You to your husband shall not be so kind;
But, lest you should, your mantle leave behind.
Encourage him to tope; but kiss him not,

Nor mix one drop of water in his pot.
If he be fuddled well, and snores apace
Then we may take advice from Time and Place.
When all depart, when compliments are loud,
Be sure to mix among the thickest crowd.
There I will be, and there we cannot miss,
Perhaps to grubble, or at least to kiss.
Alas, what length of labour I employ,
Just to secure a short and transcient joy!
For night must part us; and when night is come,
Tucked underneath his arms he leads you home.
He locks you in; I follow to the door,
His fortune envy, and my own deplore.
He kisses you, he more than kisses too;
Th' outrageous cuckold thinks it all his due.
But, add not to his joy, by your consent,
And let it not be given, but only lent.
Return no kiss, nor move in any sort;
Make it a dull and a malignant sport.
Had I my wish, he should no pleasure take,
But slubber o'er your business for my sake.
And what e'er Fortune shall this night befall,
Coax me tomorrow, by forswearing all.

Translated by John Dryden

Elegy 5

In summer's heat and mid-time of the day
To rest my limbs upon a bed I lay,
One window shut, the other open stood,
Which gave such light, as twinkles in a wood,
Like twilight glimpse at setting of the sun,
Or night being past, and yet not day begun.
Such light to shamefast maidens must be shown,
Where they must sport, and seem to be unknown.
Then came Corinna in a long loose gown,
Her white neck hid with tresses hanging down:

Resembling fair Semiramis going to bed
Or Lays of a thousand wooers sped.
I snatched her gown, being thin, the harm was small,
Yet strived she to be covered there withal.
And striving thus as one that would be cast,
Betrayed herself, and yielded at the last.
Stark naked as she stood before mine eye,
Not one wen in her body could I spy.
What arms and shoulders did I touch and see,
How apt her breasts were to be pressed by me.
How smooth a belly under her waist saw I?
How large a leg, and what a lusty thigh?
To leave the rest, all liked me passing well,
I clinged her naked body, down she fell,
Judge you the rest, being tired she bade me kiss.
Jove send me more such afternoons as this.

CATULLUS

Let Us Live and Love

My sweetest Lesbia, let us live and love;
And though the sager sort our deeds reprove,
Let us not weigh them. Heaven's great lamps do dive
Into their west, and straight again revive;
But, soon as once set is our little light,
Then must we sleep one ever-during night.

If all would lead their lives in love like me,
Then bloody swords and armor should not be;
No drum nor trumpet peaceful sleeps should move,
Unless alarm came from the camp of love.
But fools do live and waste their little light,
And seek with pain their ever-during night.

When timely death my life and fortune ends,
Let not my hearse be vexed with mourning friends;

But let all lovers rich in triumph come,
And with sweet pastime grace my happy tomb.
And, Lesbia, close up thou my little light,
And crown with love my ever-during night.

Translated and adapted by Thomas Campion

❧ ❧

SAPPHO

Sonnet XXVII

Oh! ye bright Stars! that on the Ebon fields
 Of Heav'n's empire, trembling seems to stand;
 'Till rosy morn unlocks her portal bland,
Where the proud Sun his fiery banner wields!
To flames, less fierce than mine, your lustre yields,
 And pow'rs more strong my countless tears command;
 Love strikes the feeling heart with ruthless hand,
And only spares the breast which dullness shields!
 Since, then, capricious nature but bestows
The fine affections of the soul, to prove
 A keener sense of desolating woes,
Far, far from me the empty boast remove;
 If bliss from coldness, pain from passion flows,
Ah! who would wish to feel, or learn to love?

❧ ❧

PETRARCH

Sonnet CCXXIV

If a loving belief, an artless heart,
A soft abandon, a courteous desire,
If honest wishes which a pure fire start,
An endless erring through a blind empire,
If on my forehead every thought revealed,

Or in some words broken as soon as heard,
And now by fear and now by shame repealed,
If in violet and love my face interred,
If holding someone else more than self dear,
Ever weeping and sighing without rest,
Feeding on grief, on anger and torment,
If burning when away and freezing near,
Are the causes why loving I am distressed,
Yours the sin, Lady, mine the punishment.

HAFIZ

Ode 147

Beauty alone will not account for her;
No single attribute her charm explains;
Though each be named, beyond it glimmers she,
Strangely distinct, mysteriously fair:
Hers this, this hers, and this—yet she remains.
Wonderful are her locks—she is not there;
Her body a spirit is—it is not she;
Her waist the compass of a silken thread;
Her mouth a ruby—but it is not she:
Say all of her, yet hast thou nothing said.
Surely the beauty of houri or of fay
A fashion of beauty is—but to my eye
Her way of beauty is beauty's only way

Unto this spring, sweet rose, pray draw anigh;
Sweet water 'tis—my tears—to water thee.

Thine eye, ah! what an arrow! thine eyebrow,
How strong a bow! and what an archer thou!
Ah! what a target hast thou made of me.

Love's secret verily no one man knows,
Though each in lore of loving deems him wise;
Love's like a meadow all aflower with spring,

But in the shadow autumn waiting lies,
And the wise bird is half afraid to sing—
A vanished song unto a vanished rose.

HAFIZ, a power strange to touch the heart
Of late hath stolen subtly in thy song,
Through thy firm reed unwonted pathos blows;
Her praise it is, and no new touch of art,
That gives this grace of tears unto thy song.

Ode 173

All the long night we talked of your long hair:
The hollow listening hours rolled darkly by,
The solemn world beneath the steady stars
To morning moved, sleep-walking up the sky;
Only in Shiraz in the realm of Fars
The dark night long kept open one bright eye—
'Twas where we sat up talking of your hair.

Each one of us, though wounded and far spent,
With arrowed eyelash sticking in his heart,
Still longed to see that bow your eyebrow bent,
And speeding yet another poisoned dart.
For 'tis so many days since we have heard
News of you, that our hearts grew faint with fear;
But now at last the East Wind brings us word:
Ah! blame him not—we had such need to hear.

Ere you were born love was not; through you fell
The bitter curse of beauty on the world—
Yes! it was all that hair upon your head;
Amid its crafty convolutions curled
All the dark arts of beauty lie in wait;
For even I, before I came to tread
That darkling way, among the saints did dwell,
And full of grace and safety was my state.

Open your tunic: I would lay my head
Upon your heart—ah! deep within your side

Silence and shelter sweet I ever found;
Else must I seek them in the grave instead.
When HAFIZ sleeps indeed beneath the ground,
Visit his grave—it was for you he died.

ELIZABETH I

On Monsieur's Departure

I grieve and dare not show my discontent,
I love and yet am forced to seem to hate,
I do, yet dare not say I ever meant,
I seem stark mute but inwardly do prate.
I am and not, I freeze and yet am burned,
Since from myself another self I turned.

My care is like my shadow in the sun,
Follows me flying, flies when I pursue it,
Stands and lies by me, doth what I have done.
His too familiar care doth make me rue it.
No means I find to rid him from my breast,
Till by the end of things it be supprest.

Some gentler passion slide into my mind,
For I am soft and made of melting snow;
Or be more cruel, love, and so be kind.
Let me or float or sink, be high or low.
Or let me live with some more sweet content,
Or die and so forget what love ere meant.

WILLIAM SHAKESPEARE

"My mistress' eyes are nothing like the sun"

My mistress' eyes are nothing like the sun;
Coral is far more red than her lips' red:

If snow be white, why then her breasts are dun;
If hairs be wires, black wires grow on her head.
I have seen roses demasked, red and white,
But no such roses see I in her cheeks;
And in some perfumes is there more delight
Than in the breath that from my mistress reeks.
I love to hear her speak; yet well I know
That music hath a far more pleasing sound:
I grant I never saw a goddess go,
My mistress, when she walks, treads on the ground:
   And yet, by heaven, I think my love as rare
   As any she belied with false compare.

"When my love swears that she is made of truth"

When my love swears that she is made of truth,
I do believe her, though I know she lies,
That she might think me some untutored youth,
Unlearnéd in the world's false subtleties.
Thus vainly thinking that she thinks me young,
Although she knows my days are past the best,
Simply I credit her false-speaking tongue:
On both sides thus is simple truth suppressed.
But wherefore says she not she is unjust?
And wherefore say not I that I am old?
O, love's best habit is in seeming trust,
And age in love loves not to have years told.
   Therefore I lie with her and she with me,
   And in our faults by lies we flattered be.

"Shall I compare thee to a summer's day?"

Shall I compare thee to a summer's day?
Thou art more lovely and more temperate:
Rough winds do shake the darling buds of May,
And summer's lease hath all too short a date:
Sometime too hot the eye of heaven shines,

And often is his gold complexion dimmed;
And every fair from fair sometime declines,
By chance, or nature's changing course untrimmed;
But thy eternal summer shall not fade,
Nor lose possession of that fair thou owest,
Nor shall death brag thou wanderest in his shade,
When in eternal lines to time thou growest;
    So long as men can breathe, or eyes can see,
    So long lives this, and this gives life to thee.

"When in disgrace with fortune and men's eyes"

When in disgrace with fortune and men's eyes,
I all alone beweep my outcast state,
And trouble deaf heaven with my bootless cries,
And look upon myself, and curse my fate,
Wishing me like to one more rich in hope,
Featured like him, like him with friends possess'd,
Desiring this man's art and that man's scope,
With what I most enjoy contented least;
Yet in these thoughts myself almost despising,
Haply I think on thee, and then my state,
Like to the lark at break of day arising
From sullen earth, sings hymns at heaven's gate;
    For thy sweet love remember'd such wealth brings
    That then I scorn to change my state with kings.

"Let me not to the marriage of true minds"

Let me not to the marriage of true minds
Admit impediments. Love is not love
Which alters when it alteration finds,
Or bends with the remover to remove.
Oh, no! it is an ever-fixed mark
That looks on tempests and is never shaken;
It is the star to every wandering bark,

Whose worth's unknown, although his height be taken.
Love's not Time's fool, though rosy lips and cheeks
Within his bending sickle's compass come;
Love alters not with his brief hours and weeks,
But bears it out even to the edge of doom.
   If this be error and upon me proved,
   I never writ, nor no man ever loved.

from *Antony and Cleopatra*

   Enobarus . . . The barge she sat in, like a burnish'd throne,
Burn'd on the water. The poop was beaten gold;
Purple the sails, and so perfumed that
The winds were love-sick with them; the oars were silver,
Which to the tune of flutes kept stroke, and made
The water which they beat to follow faster,
As amorous of their strokes. For her own person,
It beggar'd all description. She did lie
In her pavilion, cloth-of-gold, of tissue,
O'erpicturing that Venus where we see
The fancy out-work nature. On each side her
Stood pretty dimpled boys, like smiling Cupids,
With divers-colour'd fans, whose wind did seem
To glow the delicate cheeks which they did cool,
And what they undid did.
   Agrippa   O, rare for Antony!
   Enobarbus   Her gentlewomen, like the Nereides,
So many mermaids, tended her i' th' eyes,
And made their bends adornings. At the helm
A seeming mermaid steers. The silken tackle
Swell with the touches of those flower-soft hands
That yarely frame the office. From the barge
A strange invisible perfume hits the sense
Of the adjacent wharfs. The city cast
Her people out upon her; and Antony,
Enthron'd i' th' market-place, did sit alone,
Whistling to th' air; which, but for vacancy,
Had gone to gaze on Cleopatra too,

And made a gap in nature.
    Agrippa   Rare Egyptian!
    Enobarbus   Upon her landing, Antony sent to her,
Invited her to supper. She replied
It should be better he became her guest;
Which she entreated. Our courteous Antony,
Whom ne'er the word of 'No' woman heard speak,
Being barber'd ten times o'er, goes to the feast,
And for his ordinary pays his heart
For what his eyes eat only.

from *The Merchant of Venice*

    Lorenzo   The moon shines bright. In such a night as this,
When the sweet wind did gently kiss the trees,
And they did make no noise—in such a night,
Troilus methinks mounted the Troyan walls,
And sigh'd his soul toward the Grecian tents,
Where Cressid lay that night.
    Jessica   In such a night
Did Thisby fearfully o'ertrip the dew,
And saw the lion's shadow ere himself,
And ran dismayed away.
    Lorenzo   In such a night
Stood Dido with a willow in her hand
Upon the wild sea-banks, and waft her love
To come again to Carthage.
    Jessica   In such a night
Medea gathered the enchanted herbs
That did renew old Æson.
    Lorenzo   In such a night
Did Jessica steal from the wealthy Jew,
And with an unthrift love did run from Venice
As far as Belmont.
    Jessica   In such a night
Did young Lorenzo swear he lov'd her well,
Stealing her soul with many vows of faith,
And ne'er a true one.

Lorenzo   In such a night
Did pretty Jessica, like a little shrew,
Slander her love, and he forgave it her.

from *Romeo and Juliet*

Romeo   But soft, what light through yonder window breaks!
It is the east, and Juliet is the sun!
Arise, fair sun, and kill the envious moon,
Who is already sick and pale with grief,
That thou, her maid, art far more fair than she.
Be not her maid, since she is envious;
Her vestal livery is but sick and green,
And none but fools do wear it; cast it off.
    [*Enter Juliet aloft*]
It is my lady, O, it is my love;
O that she knew she were!
She speaks, yet she says nothing. What of that?
Her eye discourses; I will answer it.
I am too bold. 'Tis not to me she speaks:
Two of the fairest stars in all the heaven,
Having some business, do entreat her eyes
To twinkle in their spheres till they return.
What if her eyes were there, they in her head?—
The brightness of her cheek would shame those stars
As daylight doth a lamp; her eye in heaven
Would through the airy region stream so bright
That birds would sing and think it were not night.
See how she leans her cheek upon her hand:
O! that I were a glove upon that hand,
That I might touch that cheek.
    Juliet   Ay me!
    Romeo [*aside*]   She speaks.
O, speak again, bright angel; for thou art
As glorious to this night, being o'er my head,
As is a wingèd messenger of heaven
Unto the white upturnèd wond'ring eyes
Of mortals that fall back to gaze on him

When he bestrides the lazy-passing clouds,
And sails upon the bosom of the air.
 Juliet [*not knowing Romeo hears her*]
O Romeo, Romeo, wherefore art thou Romeo?
Deny thy father and refuse thy name,
Or if thou wilt not, be but sworn my love,
And I'll no longer be a Capulet.
 Romeo [*aside*]
Shall I hear more, or shall I speak at this?
 Juliet 'Tis but thy name that is my enemy;
Thou art thyself, though not a Montague.
What's Montague? It is nor hand, nor foot,
Nor arm, nor face, nor any other part
Belonging to a man. O! be some other name:
What's in a name? That which we call a rose
By any other word would smell as sweet;
So Romeo would, were he not Romeo called,
Retain that dear perfection which he owes
Without that title. Romeo, doff thy name;
And for thy name—which is no part of thee,
Take all myself.

BEN JONSON

Drink to Me Only with Thine Eyes

Drink to me only with thine eyes,
 And I will pledge with mine;
Or leave a kiss but in the cup
 And I'll not look for wine.
The thirst that from the soul doth rise
 Doth ask a drink divine;
But might I of Jove's nectar sup,
 I would not change for thine.

I sent thee late a rosy wreath,
 Not so much honoring thee
As giving it a hope that there

It could not withered be;
But thou thereon didst only breathe
     And sent'st it back to me;
Since when it grows, and smells, I swear,
     Not of itself but thee!

❧ ❧

CLEMENT ROBINSON

Greensleeves

Alas, my love, you do me wrong
     To cast me off discourteously;
And I have lovéd you so long,
     Delighting in your company.

Greensleeves was all my joy,
     Greensleeves was my delight:
Greensleeves was my heart of gold,
     And who but Lady Greensleeves.

I have been ready at your hand
     To grant whatever you would crave;
I have both wagéd life and land,
     Your love and good will for to have.

Greensleeves was all my joy, &c.

I bought thee kerchiefs for thy head,
     That were wrought fine and gallantly;
I kept thee both at board and bed,
     Which cost my purse well favoredly.

Greensleeves was all my joy, &c.

Thy crimson stockings all of silk,
     With gold all wrought above the knee;
Thy pumps as white as is the milk,
     And yet thou wouldst not love me.

Greensleeves was all my joy, &c.

My gayest gelding I thee gave,
   To ride wherever likéd thee;
No lady ever was so brave,
   And yet thou wouldst not love me.

Greensleeves was all my joy, &c.

Thou couldst desire no earthly thing,
   But still thou hadst it readily;
Thy music still to play and sing;
   And yet thou wouldst not love me.

Greensleeves was all my joy, &c.

Greensleeves, now farewell, adieu;
   God I pray to prosper thee;
For I am still thy lover true;
   Come once again and love me.

Greensleeves was all my joy,
   Greensleeves was my delight;
Greensleeves was my heart of gold,
   And who but Lady Greensleeves.

✺ ✺

JOHN DONNE

The Flea

   Mark but this flea, and mark in this,
How little that which deny'st me is;
Me it sucked first, and now sucks thee,
And in this flea, our two bloods mingled be;
Confess it, this cannot be said
A sin, or shame, or loss of maidenhead,
     Yet this enjoys before it woo,

And pampered swells with one blood made of two,
And this, alas, is more than we would do.

Oh stay, three lives in one flea spare,
Where we almost, nay more than married are:
This flea is you and I, and this
Our marriage bed, and marriage temple is;
Though parents grudge, and you, we're met,
And cloistered in these living walls of jet.
  Though use make thee apt to kill me,
  Let not to this, self murder added be,
  And sacrilege, three sins in killing three.

Cruel and sudden, hast thou since
Purpled thy nail, in blood of innocence?
In what could this flea guilty be,
Except in that drop which it sucked from thee?
Yet thou triumph'st, and say'st that thou
Find'st not thyself, nor me the weaker now;
  'Tis true, then learn how false, fears be;
  Just so much honour, when thou yield'st to me,
  Will waste, as this flea's death took life from thee.

The Sun Rising

  Busy old fool, unruly Sun,
   Why dost thou thus,
Through windows and through curtains call on us?
Must to thy motions lovers' seasons run?
  Saucy pedantic wretch, go chide
  Late school-boys, and sour 'prentices,
 Go tell court-huntsmen that the King will ride,
  Call country ants to harvest offices;
Love, all alike, no season knows, nor clime,
Nor hours, days, months, which are the rags of time.

  Thy beams, so reverend and strong
   Why shouldst thou think?

I could eclipse and cloud them with a wink,
But that I would not lose her sight so long:
  If her eyes have not blinded thine,
  Look, and tomorrow late tell me,
 Whether both the Indias of spice and mine
 Be where thou left'st them, or lie here with me.
Ask for those kings whom thou saw'st yesterday,
And thou shalt hear, 'All here in one bed lay.'

  She's all States, and all Princes I;
  Nothing else is.
Princes do but play us; compared to this,
All honour's mimic; all wealth alchemy.
  Thou, Sun, art half as happy as we,
  In that the world's contracted thus;
 Thine age asks ease, and since thy duties be
 To warm the world, that's done in warming us.
Shine here to us, and thou art everywhere;
This bed thy centre is, these walls thy sphere.

Song

Go and catch a falling star,
 Get with child a mandrake root,
Tell me where all past years are,
 Or who cleft the Devil's foot,
Teach me to hear mermaids singing,
Or to keep off envy's stinging,
  And find
  What wind
Serves to advance an honest mind.

If thou beest born to strange sights,
 Things invisible to see,
Ride ten thousand days and nights,
 Till age snow white hairs on thee,
Thou, when thou return'st, wilt tell me
All strange wonders that befell thee,

And swear
No where
Lives a woman true, and fair.

If thou find'st one, let me know,
   Such a pilgrimage were sweet;
Yet do not, I would not go,
   Though at next door we might meet;
Though she were true when you met her,
And last till you write your letter,
      Yet she
      Will be
False, ere I come, to two, or three.

The Ecstasy

Where, like a pillow on a bed,
   A pregnant bank swelled up, to rest
The violet's reclining head,
   Sat we two, one another's best,
Our hands were firmly cemented
   With a fast balm, which thence did spring;
Our eye-beams twisted, and did thread
   Our eyes upon one double string;
So to entergraft our hands, as yet
   Was all our means to make us one,
And pictures on our eyes to get
   Was all our propagation.
As 'twixt two equal armies, Fate
   Suspends uncertain victory,
Our souls (which to advance their state
   Were gone out) hung 'twixt her and me.
And whilst our souls negotiate there,
   We like sepulchral statues lay;
All day the same our postures were,
   And we said nothing all the day.
If any, so by love refined
   That he soul's language understood,

And by good love were grown all mind,
    Within convenient distance stood,
He (though he knew not which soul spake,
    Because both meant, both spake the same)
Might thence a new concoction take,
    And part far purer than he came.
This ecstasy doth unperplex
    (We said) and tell us what we love,
We see by this, it was not sex,
    We see, we saw not what did move:
But as all several souls contain
    Mixture of things, they know not what,
Love these mixed souls doth mix again,
    And makes both one, each this and that.
A single violet transplant,
    The strength, the colour, and the size,
(All which before was poor and scant)
    Redoubles still, and multiplies.
When love with one another so
    Interinanimates two souls,
That abler soul, which thence doth flow,
    Defects of loneliness controls.
We then, who are this new soul, know
    Of what we are composed, and made,
For the atomies of which we grow
    Are souls, whom no change can invade.
But, O alas! so long, so far
    Our bodies why do we forbear?
They are ours, though they are not we; we are
    The intelligences, they the sphere.
We owe them thanks, because they thus
    Did us, to us, at first convey,
Yielded their forces, sense, to us,
    Nor are dross to us, but allay.
On man heaven's influence works not so,
    But that it first imprints the air;
So soul into the soul may flow,
    Though it to body first repair.
As our blood labours to beget
    Spirits, as like souls as it can;

Because such fingers need to knit
    That subtle knot, which makes us man;
So must pure lovers' souls descend
    To affections, and to faculties,
Which sense may reach and apprehend,
    Else a great Prince in prison lies.
To our bodies turn we then, that so
    Weak men on love revealed may look;
Love's mysteries in souls do grow,
    But yet the body is his book.
And if some lover, such as we,
    Have heard this dialogue of one,
Let him still mark us, he shall see
    Small change, when we're to bodies gone.

ANONYMOUS, SCOTTISH

Barbara Allen

All in the merry month of May,
    When green buds they were swelling,
Young Jemmy Grove on his death-bed lay
    For love of Barbara Allen.

He sent his man unto her then,
    To the town where she was dwelling:
"O haste and come to my master dear,
    If your name be Barbara Allen."

Slowly, slowly she rose up,
    And she came where he was lying;
And when she drew the curtain by,
    Says, "Young man, I think you're dying."

"O it's I am sick, and very, very sick,
    And it's all for Barbara Allen."
"O the better for me you'll never be,
    Tho' your heart's blood were a-spilling!

"O do you not mind, young man," she says,
　"When the red wine you were filling,
That you made the healths go round and round,
　And slighted Barbara Allen?"

He turned his face unto the wall,
　And death with him was dealing:
"Adieu, adieu, my dear friends all;
　Be kind to Barbara Allen."

As she was walking o'er the fields,
　She heard the dead-bell knelling;
And every toll the dead-bell struck,
　Cried, "Woe to Barbara Allen!"

"O mother, mother, make my bed,
　To lay me down in sorrow.
My love has died for me today,
　I'll die for him tomorrow."

JOHN GAY

To a Young Lady, with Some Lampreys

With lovers 'twas of old the fashion
By presents to convey their passion;
No matter what the gift they sent,
The Lady saw that love was meant.
Fair *Atalanta*, as a favour,
Took the boar's head her Hero gave her;
Nor could the bristly thing affront her,
'Twas a fit present from a hunter.
When Squires send woodcocks to the dame,
It serves to show their absent flame:
Some by a snip of woven hair,
In posied lockets bribe the fair;
How many mercenary matches
Have sprung from Di'mond-rings and watches!

But hold—a ring, a watch, a locket,
Would drain at once a Poet's pocket;
He should send songs that cost him nought,
Nor ev'n he prodigal of thought.
    Why then send Lampreys? fye, for shame!
'Twill set a virgin's blood on flame.
This to fifteen a proper gift!
It might lend sixty-five a lift.
    I know your maiden Aunt will scold,
And think my present somewhat bold.
I see her lift her hands and eyes.
    "What eat it, Niece? eat *Spanish* flies!
Lamprey's a most immodest diet:
You'll neither wake nor sleep in quiet.
Should I tonight eat Sago cream,
'Twould make me blush to tell my dream;
If I eat Lobster, 'tis so warming,
That ev'ry man I see looks charming;
Wherefore had not the filthy fellow
Laid *Rochester* upon your pillow?
I vow and swear, I think the present
Had been as modest and as decent.
    Who has her virtue in her power?
Each day has its unguarded hour;
Always in danger of undoing,
A prawn, a shrimp may prove our ruin!
    The shepherdess, who lives on salad,
To cool her youth, controls her palate;
Should *Dian's* maids turn liqu'rish livers,
And of huge lampreys rob the rivers,
Then all beside each glade and Visto,
You'd see Nymphs lying like *Calisto.*
    The man who meant to heat your blood,
Needs not himself such vicious food—"
    In this, I own, your Aunt is clear,
I sent you what I well might spare:
For when I see you, (without joking)
Your eyes, lips, breasts, are so provoking,
They set my heart more cock-a-hoop,
Than could whole seas of craw-fish soup.

ANDREW MARVELL

To His Coy Mistress

Had we but world enough, and time,
This coyness, lady, were no crime.
We would sit down, and think which way
To walk, and pass our long love's day.
Thou by the Indian Ganges' side
Shouldst rubies find: I by the tide
Of Humber would complain. I would
Love you ten years before the flood,
And you should, if you please, refuse
Till the conversion of the Jews;
My vegetable love should grow
Vaster than empires and more slow;
An hundred years should go to praise
Thine eyes, and on thy forehead gaze;
Two hundred to adore each breast,
But thirty thousand to the rest;
An age at least to every part,
And the last age should show your heart.
For, lady, you deserve this state;
Nor would I love at lower rate.

But at my back I always hear
Time's wingéd chariot hurrying near;
And yonder all before us lie
Deserts of vast eternity.
Thy beauty shall no more be found,
Nor in thy marble vault shall sound
My echoing song; then worms shall try
That long preserved virginity;
And your quaint honor turn to dust,
And into ashes all my lust:
The grave's a fine and private place,
But none, I think, do there embrace.

Now therefore, while the youthful hue
Sits on thy skin like morning dew,
And while thy willing soul transpires
At every pore with instant fires,
Now let us sport us while we may,
And now, like amorous birds of prey,
Rather at once our time devour
Than languish in his slow-chapped power
Let us roll all our strength and all
Our sweetness up into one ball,
And tear our pleasures with rough strife
Through the iron gates of life:
Thus, though we cannot make our sun
Stand still, yet we will make him run.

The Definition of Love

My love is of a birth as rare
As 'tis for object strange and high;
It was begotten by Despair
Upon Impossibility.

Magnanimous Despair alone
Could show me so divine a thing
Where feeble Hope could ne'er have flown,
But vainly flapp'd its tinsel wing.

And yet I quickly might arrive
Where my extended soul is fixt,
But Fate does iron wedges drive,
And always crowds itself betwixt.

For Fate with jealous eye does see
Two perfect loves, nor lets them close;
Their union would her ruin be,
And her tyrannic pow'r depose.

And therefore her decrees of steel
Us as the distant poles have plac'd,
(Though love's whole world on us doth wheel)
Not by themselves to be embrac'd;

Unless the giddy heaven fall,
And earth some new convulsion tear;
And, us to join, the world should all
Be cramp'd into a planisphere.

As lines, so loves oblique may well
Themselves in every angle greet;
But ours so truly parallel,
Though infinite, can never meet.

Therefore the love which us doth bind,
But Fate so enviously debars,
Is the conjunction of the mind,
And opposition of the stars.

WILLIAM CARTWRIGHT

No Platonic Love

Tell me no more of minds embracing minds,
    And hearts exchang'd for hearts;
That spirits spirits meet, as winds do winds,
    And mix their subt'lest parts;
That two unbodied essences may kiss,
And then like Angels, twist and feel one Bliss.

I was that silly thing that once was wrought
    To practise this thin love;
I climb'd from sex to soul, from soul to thought;
    But thinking there to move,
Headlong I rolled from thought to soul, and then
From soul I lighted at the sex again.

As some strict down-looked men pretend to fast,
    Who yet in closets eat;
So lovers who profess they spirits taste,
    Feed yet on grosser meat;
'know they boast they souls to souls convey,
Howe'r they meet, the body is the way.

Come, I will undeceive thee, they that tread
    Those vain aerial ways,
Are like young heirs and alchemists misled
    To waste their wealth and days,
For searching thus to be forever rich,
They only find a med'cine for the itch.

ROBERT HERRICK

The Vine

I dreamed this mortal part of mine
Was metamorphosed to a vine;
Which crawling one and every way,
Enthralled my dainty Lucia.
Methought, her long small legs and thighs
I with my tendrils did surprise;
Her belly, buttocks, and her waist
By now soft nervelets were embraced:
About her head I writhing hung,
And with rich clusters (hid among
The leaves) her temples I behung
So that my Lucia seemed to me
Young Bacchus ravished by his tree.
My curls about her neck did crawl,
And arms and hands they did enthral:
So that she could not freely stir,
(All parts there made one prisoner).
But when I crept with leaves to hide
Those parts, which maids keep unespied,

Such fleeting pleasures there I took,
That with the fancy I awoke;
And found (Ah me!) this flesh of mine
More like a stock, than like a vine.

Kisses Loathsome

I abhor the slimy kiss,
(Which to me most loathsome is).
Those lips please me which are placed
Close, but not too strictly laced:
Yeilding I would have them; yet
Not a wimbling Tongue admit:
What should poking-sticks make there,
When the ruffle is set elsewhere?

To the Virgins, to Make Much of Time

Gather ye rosebuds while ye may,
   Old Time is still a-flying:
And this same flower that smiles today
   Tomorrow will be dying.

The glorious lamp of heaven, the sun,
   The higher he's a-getting,
The sooner will his race be run,
   And nearer he's to setting.

That age is best which is the first,
   When youth and blood are warmer;
But being spent, the worse, and worst
   Times still succeed the former.

Then be not coy, but use your time,
   And while ye may, go marry:
For having lost but once your prime,
   You may forever tarry.

Upon Julia's Clothes

Whenas in silks my Julia goes,
Then, then, methinks, how sweetly flows
That liquefaction of her clothes.

Next, when I cast mine eyes, and see
That brave vibration each way free,
O how that glittering taketh me!

Delight in Disorder

A sweet disorder in the dress
Kindles in clothes a wantonness:
A lawn about the shoulders thrown
Into a fine distractiòn;
An erring lace, which here and there
Enthralls the crimson stomacher;
A cuff neglectful, and thereby
Ribbands to flow confusedly;
A winning wave (deserving note)
In the tempestuous petticoat;
A careless shoe-string, in whose tie
I see a wild civility;
Do more bewitch me, than when art
Is too precise in every part.

Be My Mistress Short or Tall

Be my mistress short or tall
And distorted therewithall
Be she likewise one of those
That an acre hath of nose
Be her teeth ill hung or set
And her grinders black as jet
Be her cheeks so shallow too

As to show her tongue wag through
Hath she thin hair, hath she none
She's to me a paragon.

JOHN CLARE

First Love

I ne'er was struck before that hour
    With love so sudden and so sweet,
Her face it bloomed like a sweet flower
    And stole my heart away complete.

My face turned pale as deadly pale,
    My legs refused to walk away,
And when she looked, what could I ail?
    My life and all seemed turned to clay.

And then my blood rushed to my face
    And took my eyesight quite away,
The trees and bushes round the place
    Seemed midnight at noonday.
I could not see a single thing,
    Words from my eyes did start—
They spoke as chords do from the string,
    And blood burnt round my heart.

Are flowers the winter's choice?
    Is love's bed always snow?
She seemed to hear my silent voice,
    Not love's appeals to know.
I never saw so sweet a face
    As that I stood before.
My heart has left its dwelling-place
    And can return no more.

JOHN MILTON

from *Paradise Lost*

Love refines
The thoughts, and heart enlarges, hath his seat
In reason, and is judicious, is the scale
By which to heavenly love thou mayest ascend.

ABRAHAM COWLEY

from *Anacreon*

A mighty pain to love it is,
And 'tis a pain that pain to miss;
But of all pains, the greatest pain,
It is to love, but love in vain.

THOMAS CAREW

Mediocrity in Love Rejected

Give me more love, or more disdain;
The torrid or the frozen zone
Bring equal ease unto my pain;
The temperate affords me none:
Either extreme, of love or hate,
Is sweeter than a calm estate.

Give me a storm, if it be love,
Like Danaë in that golden shower,
I swim in pleasure; if it prove
Disdain, that torrent will devour

My vulture hopes; and he's possessed
Of heaven that's from hell released.
Then crown my joys, or cure my pain;
Give me love or more disdain.

Fear Not, Dear Love

Fear not, dear love, that I'll reveal
Those hours of pleasure we both steal;
No eye shall see, nor yet the sun
Descry what thou and I have done.

No ear shall hear our love, but we
Silent as the night will be;
The god of love himself, whose dart
Did first wound mine and then thy heart,

Shall never know, that we can tell,
What sweets in stol'n embraces dwell.
This only means may find it out,
If, when I die, physicians doubt

What caused my death, and there to view
Of all their judgments which was true,
Rip up my heart. Oh! then, I fear,
The world will see thy picture there.

THOMAS WYATT

They Flee from Me

They flee from me, that sometime did me seek,
With naked foot stalking in my chamber.
I have seen them, gentle, tame, and meek,
That now are wild, and do not remember

That sometime they put themselves in danger
To take bread at my hand; and now they range,
Busily seeking with a continual change.

Thanked be Fortune it hath been otherwise,
Twenty times better; but once in special,
In thin array, after a pleasant guise,
When her loose gown from her shoulders did fall,
And she me caught in her arms long and small,
And therewith I sweetly did me kiss
And softly said, "Dear heart, how like you this?"

It was no dream, I lay broad waking.
But all is turned, thorough my gentleness,
Into a strange fashion of forsaking;
And I have leave to go, of her goodness,
And she also to use newfangleness.
But since that I so kindly am served,
I fain would know what she hath deserved.

❦ ❦

SIR PHILIP SIDNEY

Heart Exchange

My true love hath my heart, and I have his,
By just exchange, one for the other giv'n:
I hold his dear, and mine he cannot miss:
There never was a bargain better driv'n.

His heart in me keeps me and him in one,
My heart in him his thoughts and senses guides:
He loves my heart, for once it was his own:
I cherish his, because in me it bides.

His heart his wound received from my sight:
My heart was wounded with his wounded heart.
For as from me on him his hurt did light:

So still me thought in me his heart did smart.
　　Both equal hurt, in his change sought our bliss:
　　My true Love hath my heart, and I have his.

CHRISTOPHER MARLOWE

The Passionate Shepherd to His Love

Come live with me and be my love,
And we will all the pleasures prove
That valleys, groves, hills, and fields,
Woods, or steepy mountain yields.

And we will sit upon the rocks,
Seeing the shepherds feed their flocks,
By shallow rivers to whose falls
Melodious birds sing madrigals.

And I will make thee beds of roses
And a thousand fragrant posies,
A cap of flowers, and a kirtle
Embroidered all with leaves of myrtle;

A gown made of the finest wool
Which from our pretty lambs we pull;
Fair lined slippers for the cold,
With buckles of the purest gold;

A belt of straw and ivy buds,
With coral clasps and amber studs:
And if these pleasures may thee move,
Come live with me, and be my love.

The shepherds' swains shall dance and sing
For thy delight each May morning:
If these delights thy mind may move,
Then live with me and be my love.

SIR WALTER RALEGH

The Nymph's Reply to the Shepherd

If all the world and love were young,
And truth in every shepherd's tongue,
These pretty pleasures might me move
To live with thee and be thy love.

Time drives the flocks from field to fold
When rivers rage and rocks grow cold,
And Philomel becometh dumb;
The rest complains of cares to come.

The flowers do fade, and wanton fields
To wayward winter reckoning yields;
A honey tongue, a heart of gall,
Is fancy's spring, but sorrow's fall.

Thy gowns, thy shoes, thy beds of roses,
Thy cap, thy kirtle, and thy posies
Soon break, soon wither, soon forgotten—
In folly ripe, in reason rotten.

Thy belt of straw and ivy buds,
Thy coral clasps and amber studs,
All these in me no means can move
To come to thee and be thy love.

But could youth last and love still breed,
Had joys no date nor age no need,
Then these delights my mind might move
To live with thee and be thy love.

GEORGE HERBERT

Love

Love bade me welcome, yet my soul drew back,
    Guilty of dust and sin.
But quick-eye'd Love, observing me grow slack
    From my first entrance in,
Drew nearer to me, sweetly questioning
    If I lack'd anything.

"A guest," I answer'd, "worthy to be here";
    Love said, "You shall be he."
"I, the unkind, the ungrateful? ah my dear,
    I cannot look on thee."
Love took my hand and smiling did reply,
    "Who made the eyes but I?"

"Truth, Lord, but I have marr'd them; let my shame
    Go where it doth deserve."
"And know you not," says Love, "who bore the blame?"
    "My dear, then I will serve."
"You must sit down," says Love, "and taste my meat."
    So I did sit and eat.

JOHN WILMOT, SECOND EARL OF ROCHESTER

Written in a Lady's Prayer Book

Fling this useless book away,
And presume no more to pray.
Heaven is just, and can bestow
Mercy on none but those that mercy show.
With a proud heart maliciously inclined

Not to increase, but to subdue mankind,
In vain you vex the gods with your petition;
Without repentance and sincere contrition,
You're in a reprobate condition,
Phyllis, to calm the angry powers
And save my soul as well as yours,
Relieve poor mortals from despair,
And justify the gods that made you fair;
And in those bright and charming eyes
Let pity first appear, then love,
That we by easy steps may rise
Through all the joys on earth to those above.

The Imperfect Enjoyment

Naked she lay, clasped in my longing arms,
I filled with love, and she all over charms;
Both equally inspired with eager fire,
Melting through kindness, flaming in desire.
With arms, legs, lips, close clinging to embrace,
She clips me to her breast and sucks me to her face.
Her nimble tongue, Love's lesser lightning, played
Within my mouth, and to my thoughts conveyed
Swift orders that I should prepare to throw
The all-dissolving thunderbolt below.
My fluttering soul, sprung with the pointed kiss,
Hangs hovering o'er her balmy brinks of bliss
But whilst her busy hand would guide that part
Which should convey my soul up to her heart,
In liquid raptures I dissolve all o'er,
Melt into sperm, and spend at every pore.
A touch from any part of her had done't—
Her hand, her foot, her very look's a cunt.

   Smiling, she chides in a kind murmuring noise
And from her body wipes the clammy joys,
When with a thousand kisses wandering o'er
My panting bosom, "Is there then no more?"

She cries. "All this to love and rapture's due;
Must we not pay a debt to pleasure, too?"

But I, the most forlorn, lost man alive
To show my wished obedience vainly strive.
I sigh, alas!, and kiss—but cannot swive.
Eager desires confound my first intent,
Succeeding shame does more success prevent,
And rage at last confirms me impotent.
Even her fair hand, which might bid heat return
To frozen age, and make cold hermits burn,
Applied to my dead cinder warms no more
Than fire to ashes could past flames restore.
Trembling, confused, despairing, limber, dry,
A wishing, weak, unmoving lump I lie.
This dart of love whose piercing point, oft tried,
With virgin blood ten thousand maids has dyed,
Which nature still directed with such art
That it through every cunt reached every heart
(Stiffly resolved, 'twould carelessly invade
Woman or man, nor aught its fury stayed—
Where'er it pierced, a cunt it found or made)
Now languid lies in this unhappy hour
Shrunk up and sapless like a withered flower.

Thou treacherous, base deserter of my flame,
False to my passion, fatal to my fame,
Through what mistaken magic dost thou prove
So true to lewdness, so untrue to love?
What oyster-cinder-beggar-common whore
Didst thou e'er fail in all thy life before?
When vice, disease and scandal lead the way
With what officious haste dost thou obey!
Like a rude, roaring hector in the streets
Who scuffles, cuffs and jostles all he meets,
But if his King or country claim his aid
The rake-hell villain shrinks and hides his head;
Even so thy brutal valour is displayed,
Breaks every stew, does each small whore invade,
But when great Love the onset does command,

Base recreant to thy prince, thou darest not stand.
Worse part of me, and henceforth hated most,
Through all the town a common fucking post
On whom each whore relieves her tingling cunt
As hogs on gates do rub themselves and grunt:
Mayst thou to ravenous cankers be a prey,
Or in consuming weepings waste away;
May stranguary and stone thy days attend,
Mayst thou ne'er piss who didst refuse to spend
When all my joys did on false thee depend.
And may ten thousand abler pricks agree
To do the wronged Corinna right for thee.

ANNE BRADSTREET

To My Dear and Loving Husband

If ever two were one then surely we.
If ever man were loved by wife, then thee;
If ever wife were happy in a man,
Compare with me, ye women, if you can.
I prize thy love more than whole mines of gold
Or all the riches that the East doth hold.
My love is such that rivers cannot quench,
Nor aught but love from thee give recompense.
Thy love is such I can no way repay,
The heavens reward thee manifold, I pray.
Then while we live, in love let's so perservere
That when we live no more, we may live ever.

JOHN KEATS

Modern Love

And what is love? It is a doll dress'd up
For idleness to cosset, nurse, and dandle;

A thing of soft misnomers, so divine
That silly youth doth think to make itself
Divine by loving, and so goes on
Yawning and doting a whole summer long,
Till Miss's comb is made a pearl tiara,
And common Wellingtons turn Romeo boots;
Then Cleopatra lives at number seven,
And Antony resides in Brunswick Square.
Fools! if some passions high have warm'd the world,
If Queens and Soldiers have play'd deep for hearts,
It is no reason why such agonies
Should be more common than the growth of weeds.
Fools! make me whole again that weighty pearl
The Queen of Egypt melted, and I'll say
That ye may love in spite of beaver hats.

"I cry your mercy"

I cry your mercy—pity—love!—aye, love!
    Merciful love that tantalizes not,
One-thoughted, never-wandering, guileless love,
    Unmasked, and being seen—without a blot!
O! let me have thee whole,—all—all—be mine!
    That shape, that fairness, that sweet minor zest
Of love, your kiss,—those hands, those eyes divine,
    That warm, white, lucent, million-pleasured breast,—

Yourself—your soul—in pity give me all,
    Withhold no atom's atom or I die,
Or living on perhaps, your wretched thrall,
    Forget, in the mist of idle misery,
Life's purposes,—the palate of my mind
Losing its gust, and my ambition blind!

LORD BYRON

She Walks in Beauty

She walks in beauty, like the night
   Of cloudless climes and starry skies;
And all that's best of dark and bright
   Meet in her aspect and her eyes:
Thus mellowed to that tender light
   Which heaven to gaudy day denies.

One shade the more, one ray the less,
   Had half impaired the nameless grace
Which waves in every raven tress,
   Or softly lightens o'er her face;
Where thoughts serenely sweet express
   How pure, how dear their dwelling place.

And on that cheek, and o'er that brow,
   So soft, so calm, yet eloquent,
The smiles that win, the tints that glow,
   But tell of days in goodness spent,
A mind at peace with all below,
   A heart whose love is innocent!

When We Two Parted

When we two parted
   In silence and tears,
Half broken-hearted
   To sever for years,
Pale grew thy cheek and cold,
   Colder thy kiss;
Truly that hour foretold
   Sorrow to this.

The dew of the morning
   Sunk chill on my brow—
It felt like the warning
   Of what I feel now.
Thy vows are all broken,
   And light is thy fame;
I hear thy name spoken,
   And share in its shame.

They name thee before me,
   A knell to mine ear;
A shudder comes o'er me—
   Why wert thou so dear?
They know not I knew thee,
   Who knew thee too well:—
Long, long shall I rue thee,
   Too deeply to tell.

In secret we met—
   In silence I grieve
That thy heart could forget,
   Thy spirit deceive.
If I should meet thee
   After long years,
How should I greet thee?—
   With silence and tears.

We'll Go No More A-Roving

So we'll go no more a-roving
   So late into the night,
Though the heart be still as loving,
   And the moon be still as bright.

For the sword outwears its sheath,
   And the soul wears out the breast,
And the heart must pause to breathe,
   And love itself have rest.

Though the night was made for loving,
    And the day returns too soon,
Yet we'll go no more a-roving
    By the light of the moon.

·❦ ❦·

PERCY BYSSHE SHELLEY

Love's Philosophy

The fountains mingle with the river
    And the rivers with the Ocean,
The winds of Heaven mix forever
    With a sweet emotion;
Nothing in the world is single;
    All things by a law divine
In one spirit meet and mingle.
    Why not I with thine?—

See the mountains kiss high Heaven
    And the waves clasp one another;
No sister-flower would be forgiven
    If it disdained its brother;
And the sunlight clasps the earth
    And the moonbeams kiss the sea:
What is all this sweet work worth
    If thou kiss not me?

·❦ ❦·

WILLIAM BLAKE

Song

My silks and fine array,
My smiles and languish'd air,
By love are driv'n away;
And mournful lean Despair

Brings me yew to deck my grave;
Such end true lovers have.

His face is fair as heav'n
When springing buds unfold;
O why to him was't giv'n
Whose heart is wintry cold?
His breast is love's all-worshipp'd tomb,
Where all love's pilgrims come.

Bring me an axe and spade,
Bring me a winding sheet;
When I my grave have made
Let winds and tempests beat:
Then down I'll lie as cold as clay.
True love doth pass away!

❧ ❧

A. C. SWINBURNE

Before Parting

A month or twain to live on honeycomb
Is pleasant; but one tires of scented time,
Cold sweet recurrence of accepted rhyme,
And that strong purple under juice and foam
Where the wine's heart has burst;
Nor feel the latter kisses like the first.

Once yet, this poor one time; I will not pray
Even to change the bitterness of it,
The bitter taste ensuring on the sweet,
To make your tears fall where your soft hair lay
All blurred and heavy in some perfumed wise
Over my face and eyes.

And yet who knows what end the scythèd wheat
Makes of its foolish poppies' mouths of red?

These were not sown, these are not harvested,
They grow a month and are cast under feet
And none has care thereof,
As none has care of a divided love.

I know each shadow of your lips by rote,
Each change of love in eyelids and eyebrows;
The fashion of fair temples tremulous
With tender blood, and colour of your throat;
I know not how love is gone out of this,
Seeing that all was his.

Love's likeness there endures upon all these:
But out of these one shall not gather love.
Day hath not strength nor the night shade enough
To make love whole and fill his lips with ease,
As some bee-builded cell
Feels at filled lips the heavy honey swell.

I know not how this last month leaves your hair
Less full of purple colour and hid spice,
And that luxurious trouble of closed eyes
Is mixed with meaner shadow and waste care;
And love, kissed out by pleasure, seems not yet
Worth patience to regret.

MATTHEW ARNOLD

Dover Beach

The sea is calm tonight,
The tide is full, the moon lies fair
Upon the straits;—on the French coast the light
Gleams and is gone; the cliffs of England stand,
Glimmering and vast, out in the tranquil bay.
Come to the window, sweet is the night-air!

Only, from the long line of spray
Where the sea meets the moon-blanched land,
Listen! you hear the grating roar
Of pebbles which the waves draw back, and fling,
At their return, up the high strand,
Begin, and cease, and then again begin,
With tremulous cadence slow, and bring
The eternal note of sadness in.

Sophocles long ago
Heard it on the Aegean, and it brought
Into his mind the turbid ebb and flow
Of human misery; we
Find also in the sound a thought,
Hearing it by this distant northern sea.

The Sea of Faith
Was once, too, at the full, and round earth's shore
Lay like the folds of a bright girdle furled.
But now I only hear
Its melancholy, long, withdrawing roar,
Retreating, to the breath
Of the night-wind, down the vast edges drear
And naked shingles of the world.

Ah, love, let us be true
To one another! for the world, which seems
To lie before us like a land of dreams,
So various, so beautiful, so new,
Hath really neither joy, nor love, nor light,
Nor certitude, nor peace, nor help for pain;
And we are here as on a darkling plain
Swept with confused alarms of struggle and flight,
Where ignorant armies clash by night.

SAMUEL TAYLOR COLERIDGE

Desire

Where true Love burns Desire is Love's pure flame;
It is the reflex of our earthly frame,
That takes its meaning from the nobler part,
And but translates the language of the heart.

Love

All thoughts, all passions, all delights,
Whatever stirs this mortal frame,
All are but ministers of Love,
    And feed his sacred flame.

Oft in my waking dreams do I
Live o'er again that happy hour,
When midway on the mount I lay,
    Beside the ruin'd tower.

The moonshine, stealing o'er the scene,
Had blended with the lights of eve;
And she was there, my hope, my joy,
    My own dear Genevieve!

She lean'd against the armèd man,
The statue of the armèd Knight;
She stood and listen'd to my lay,
    Amid the lingering light. . . .

She half enclosed me with her arms,
She press'd me with a meek embrace;
And bending back her head, look'd up,
    And gazed upon my face.

'Twas partly love, and partly fear,
And partly 'twas a bashful art,
That I might rather feel, than see,
   The swelling of her heart.

I calm'd her fears, and she was calm,
And told her love with virgin pride;
And so I won my Genevieve,
   My bright and beauteous Bride.

ALFRED, LORD TENNYSON

Summer Night

   Now sleeps the crimson petal, now the white;
Nor waves the cypress in the palace walk;
Nor winks the gold fin in the porphyry font:
The firefly wakens: waken thou with me.

   Now droops the milk-white peacock like a ghost,
And like a ghost she glimmers on to me.

   Now lies the Earth all Danaë to the stars,
And all thy heart lies open unto me.

   Now slides the silent meteor on, and leaves
A shining furrow, as thy thoughts in me.

   Now folds the lily all her sweetness up,
And slips into the bosom of the lake:
So fold thyself, my dearest, thou, and slip
Into my bosom and be lost in me.

WILLIAM WORDSWORTH

Perfect Woman

She was a phantom of delight
When first she gleam'd upon my sight;
A lovely apparition, sent
To be a moment's ornament;
Her eyes as stars of twilight fair;
Like twilight's, too, her dusky hair;
But all things else about her drawn
From May-time and the cheerful dawn;
A dancing shape, an image gay,
To haunt, to startle, and waylay.

I saw her upon nearer view,
A Spirit, yet a Woman too!
Her household motions light and free,
And steps of virgin liberty;
A countenance in which did meet
Sweet records, promises as sweet;
A creature not too bright or good
For human nature's daily food;
For transient sorrows, simple wiles,
Praise, blame, love, kisses, tears, and smiles.

And now I see with eye serene
The very pulse of the machine;
A being breathing thoughtful breath,   ·
A traveller between life and death;
The reason firm, the temperate will,
Endurance, foresight, strength, and skill;
A perfect Woman, nobly plann'd,
To warn, to comfort, and command;
And yet a Spirit still, and bright
With something of angelic light.

The Cottager to Her Infant

The days are cold, the nights are long,
The north-wind sings a doleful song;
Then hush again upon my breast;
All merry things are now at rest,
    Save thee, my pretty Love!

The kitten sleeps upon the hearth,
The crickets long have ceased their mirth;
There's nothing stirring in the house
Save one *wee*, hungry, nibbling mouse,
    Then why so busy thou?

Nay! start not at that sparkling light;
'Tis but the moon that shines so bright
On the window pane bedropped with rain:
Then little Darling! sleep again,
    And wake when it is day.

ROBERT BURNS

Ye Flowery Banks

Ye flowery banks o' bonnie Doon,
How can ye bloom so fair?
How can ye chant, ye little birds,
And I so full o' care?

Thou'll break my heart, thou bonnie bird,
That sings upon the bough;
Thou minds me o' the happy days,
When my false love was true.

Thou'll break my heart, thou bonnie bird,
That sings beside thy mate;
For so I sat, and so I sang,
And knew not o' my fate.

Oft have I rov'd by bonnie Doon
To see the wood-bine twine,
And every bird sang o' its love,
And so did I o' mine.

Wi' lightsome heart I pulled a rose
From off its thorny tree;
And my false lover stole my rose
But left the thorn wi' me.

Sweet Afton

Flow gently, sweet Afton! among thy green braes,
Flow gently, I'll sing thee a song in thy praise;
My Mary's asleep by thy murmuring stream,
Flow gently, sweet Afton, disturb not her dream.

Thou stock-dove whose echo resounds through the glen,
Ye wild whistling blackbirds in yon thorny den,
Thou green-crested lapwing, thy screaming forbear,
I charge you, disturb not my slumbering fair.

How lofty, sweet Afton, thy neighboring hills,
Far marked with the courses of clear, winding rills;
There daily I wander as noon rises high,
My flocks and my Mary's sweet cot in my eye.

How pleasant thy banks and green valleys below,
Where, wild in the woodlands, the primroses blow;
There oft, as mild ev'ning weeps over the lea,
The sweet-scented birk shades my Mary and me.

Thy crystal stream, Afton, how lovely it glides,
And winds by the cot where my Mary resides;
How wanton thy waters her snowy feet lave,
As, gathering sweet flowerets, she stems thy clear wave.

Flow gently, sweet Afton, among thy green braes,
Flow gently, sweet river, the theme of my lays;
My Mary's asleep by thy murmuring stream,
Flow gently, sweet Afton, disturb not her dream.

EDGAR ALLAN POE

To Helen

Helen, thy beauty is to me
　　Like those Nicèan barks of yore
That gently, o'er a perfumed sea,
　　The weary way-worn wanderer bore
　　To his own native shore.

On desperate seas long wont to roam,
　　Thy hyacinth hair, thy classic face,
Thy Naiad airs have brought me home
　　To the glory that was Greece,
And the grandeur that was Rome.

Lo, in yon brilliant window-niche
　　How statue-like I see thee stand,
　　The agate lamp within thy hand,
Ah! Psyche, from the regions which
　　Are holy land!

Annabel Lee

It was many and many a year ago,
　　In a kingdom by the sea,
That a maiden there lived whom you may know
　　By the name of Annabel Lee;—
And this maiden she lived with no other thought
　　Than to love and be loved by me.

She was a child and *I* was a child,
   In this kingdom by the sea,
But we loved with a love that was more than love—
   I and my Annabel Lee—
With a love that the wingéd seraphs of Heaven
   Coveted her and me.

And this was the reason that, long ago,
   In this kingdom by the sea,
A wind blew out of a cloud by night
   Chilling my Annabel Lee;
So that her highborn kinsmen came
   And bore her away from me,
To shut her up in a sepulchre
   In this kingdom by the sea.

The angels, not half so happy in Heaven,
   Went envying her and me:—
Yes! that was the reason (as all men know,
   In this kingdom by the sea)
That the wind came out of a cloud, chilling
   And killing my Annabel Lee.

But our love it was stronger by far than the love
   Of those who were older than we—
   Of many far wiser than we—
And neither the angels in Heaven above
   Nor the demons down under the sea,
Can ever dissever my soul from the soul
   Of the beautiful Annabel Lee:—

For the moon never beams without bringing me dreams
   Of the beautiful Annabel Lee;
And the stars never rise but I see the bright eyes
   Of the beautiful Annabel Lee;
And so, all the night-tide, I lie down by the side
Of my darling, my darling, my life and my bride,
   In her sepulchre there by the sea—
   In her tomb by the side of the sea.

EMILY DICKINSON

"My life closed twice"

My life closed twice before its close—
It yet remains to see
If Immortality unveil
A third event to me

So huge, so hopeless to conceive,
As these that twice befell.
Parting is all we know of heaven,
And all we need of hell.

"I cannot live with You"

I cannot live with You—
It would be Life—
And Life is over there—
Behind the Shelf

The Sexton keeps the Key to—
Putting up
Our Life—His Porcelain—
Like a Cup—

Discarded of the Housewife—
Quaint—or Broke—
A newer Sevres pleases—
Old Ones crack—

I could not die—with You—
For One must wait
To shut the Other's Gaze down—
You—could not—

And I—Could I stand by
And see You—freeze—
Without my Right of Frost—
Death's privilege?

Nor could I rise—with You—
Because Your Face
Would put out Jesus'—
That New Grace

Glow plain—and foreign
On my homesick Eye—
Except that You than He
Shone closer by—

They'd judge Us—How—
For You—served Heaven—You know,
Or sought to—
I could not—

Because You saturated Sight—
And I had no more Eyes
For sordid excellence
As Paradise

And were You lost, I would be—
Though My Name
Rang loudest
On the Heavenly fame—

And were You—saved—
And I—condemned to be
Where you were not—
That self—were Hell to Me—

So We must meet apart—
You there—I—here—
With just the Door ajar
That Oceans are—and Prayer—
And that Pale Sustenance—
Despair—

"Wild Nights"

Wild Nights—Wild Nights!
Were I with thee
Wild Nights should be
Our luxury!

Futile—the Winds—
To a Heart in port—
Done with the Compass—
Done with the chart!

Rowing in Eden—
Ah, the Sea!
Might I but moor—Tonight—
In Thee!

"It's such a little thing to weep—"

It's such a little thing to weep—
So short a thing to sigh—
And yet—by Trades—the size of *these*
We men and women die!

"The Rose did caper"

The Rose did caper on her cheek—
Her Bodice rose and fell—
Her pretty speech—like drunken men—
Did stagger pitiful—

Her fingers fumbled at her work—
Her needle would not go—
What ailed so smart a little Maid—
It puzzled me to know—

Till opposite—I spied a cheek
That bore *another* Rose—
Just opposite—Another speech
That like the Drunkard goes—

A Vest that like her Bodice, danced—
To the immortal tune—

Till those two troubled—little Clocks
Ticked softly into one.

❦ ❦

HO XUAN HUONG

On Sharing a Husband

Screw the fate that makes you share a man.
One cuddles under cotton blankets; the other's cold.
Every now and then, well, maybe or maybe not,
once or twice a month, oh, it's like nothing.
You try to stick to it like a fly on rice
but the rice is rotten. You work like a servant,
but without pay. If I had known how it would go
I surely would have lived alone.

Translated by John Balaban

Translator's Note: Ho Xuan Huong was a *vo le*, a concubine, or wife of second rank. Poor families like hers (impoverished from her father's early death) could not provide dowries and so had little prospect of securing proper marriages for their daughters. The wealthy, on the other hand, practiced polygamy, the king being permitted 126 wives in 6 different categories, while even a student could have "five concubines, seven wives." Thus many women *circa* 1800 could choose only between living alone or becoming a concubine and risking the indignities in this poem. Sometimes, however, the arrangements worked out, as in HXH's marriage to the Prefect of Vinh-Tuong, whom she seems to have both admired and loved. Her second "marriage" to a mandarin (ridiculed in his funeral lament as Mr. Frog) was an evident disaster. "Screw," above, is the best I could do for *chem cha*, an untranslatable curse meaning, literally, "cut father."

❧ ❧

ELIZABETH BARRETT BROWNING

How Do I Love Thee?

How do I love thee? Let me count the ways.
I love thee to the depth and breadth and height
My soul can reach, when feeling out of sight
For the ends of Being and ideal Grace.
I love thee to the level of everyday's
Most quiet need, by sun and candlelight.
I love thee freely, as men strive for Right;
I love thee purely, as they turn from praise.
I love thee with the passion put to use
In my old griefs, and with my childhood's faith.
I love thee with a love I seemed to lose—
With my lost saints,—I love thee with the breath,
Smiles, tears, of all my life!—and, if God choose,
I shall but love thee better after death.

Sonnets from the Portuguese, XIII

And wilt thou have me fashion into speech
The love I bear thee, finding words enough,
And hold the torch out, while the winds are rough,
Between our faces, to cast light on each?—
I drop it at thy feet. I cannot teach
My hand to hold my spirit so far off
From myself—me—that I should bring thee proof
In words, of love hid in me out of reach.
Nay, let the silence of my womanhood
Commend my woman-love to thy belief,—
Seeing that I stand unwon, however wooed,
And rend the garment of my life, in brief,

By a most dauntless, voiceless fortitude,
Lest one touch of this heart convey its grief.

❧❧

ROBERT BROWNING

Meeting at Night

The grey sea and the long black land;
And the yellow half-moon large and low;
And the startled little waves that leap
In fiery ringlets from their sleep,
As I gain the cove with pushing prow,
And quench its speed i' the slushy sand.

Then a mile of warm sea-scented beach;
Three fields to cross till a farm appears;
A tap at the pane, the quick sharp scratch
And blue spurt of a lighted match,
And a voice less loud, through its joys and fears,
Than the two hearts beating each to each!

The Lost Mistress

All's over, then: does truth sound bitter
    As one at first believes?
Hark, 'tis the sparrows' good-night twitter
    About your cottage eaves!

And the leaf-buds on the vine are woolly,
    I noticed that, to-day;
One day more bursts them open fully
    —You know the red turns grey.

Tomorrow we meet the same then, dearest?
    May I take your hand in mine?
Mere friends are we,—well, friends the merest
    Keep much that I'll resign:

For each glance of that eye so bright and black,
    Though I keep with heart's endeavour,—
Your voice, when you wish the snowdrops back,
    Though it stay in my soul for ever!—

Yet I will but say what mere friends say,
    Or only a thought stronger;
I will hold your hand but as long as all may,
    Or so very little longer!

❦ ❦

OSCAR WILDE

In the Gold Room

A Harmony.
    Her ivory hands on the ivory keys
        Strayed in a fitful fantasy,
    Like the silver gleam when the poplar trees
        Rustle their pale leaves listlessly,
    Or the drifting foam of a restless sea
        When the waves show their teeth in the flying breeze.
    Her gold hair fell on the wall of gold
        Like the delicate gossamer tangles spun
    On the burnished disk of the marigold,
        Or the sunflower turning to meet the sun
        When the gloom of the jealous night is done,
    And the spear of the lily is aureoled.
    And her sweet red lips on these lips of mine
        Burned like the ruby fire set
    In the swinging lamp of a crimson shrine,
        Or the bleeding wounds of the pomegranate,
        Or the heart of the lotus drenched and wet
    With the spilt-out blood of the rose-red wine.

❧❧

GERARD MANLEY HOPKINS

At the Wedding March

God with honour hang your head,
Groom, and grace you, bride, your bed
With lissome scions, sweet scions,
Out of hallowed bodies bred.
Each be other's comfort kind:
Deep, deeper than divined,
Divine charity, dear charity,
Fast you ever, fast bind.
Then let the March tread our ears:
I to him turn with tears
Who to wedlock, his wonder wedlock,
Deals triumph and immortal years.

❧❧

RALPH WALDO EMERSON

Give All to Love

Give all to love;
Obey thy heart;
Friends, kindred, days,

Estate, good-fame,
Plans, credit and the Muse,
—Nothing refuse.

'Tis a brave master;
Let it have scope:
Follow it utterly,

Hope beyond hope:
High and more high
It dives into noon,

With wing unspent,
Untold intent;
But it is a god,

Knows its own path
And the outlets of the sky.
It was never for the mean;

It requireth courage stout.
Souls above doubt,
Valor unbending,

It will reward,—
They shall return
More than they were,

And ever ascending.
Leave all for love;
Yet, hear me, yet,

One word more thy heart behoved,
One pulse more of firm endeavor,
—Keep thee today,

Tomorrow, forever,
Free as an Arab
Of thy beloved.

Cling with life to the maid;
But when the surprise,
First vague shadow of surmise

Flits across her bosom young,
Of a joy apart from thee,
Free be she, fancy-free;
Nor thou detain her vesture's hem,

Nor the palest rose she flung
From her summer diadem.
Though thou loved her as thyself,

As a self of purer clay,
Though her parting dims the day,
Stealing grace from all alive;

Heartily know,
When half-gods go,
The gods arrive.

❧ ❦

WALT WHITMAN

Press Close Bare-Bosom'd Night

Press close bare-bosom'd night—press close magnetic nourishing
    night!
Night of south winds—night of the large few stars!
Still nodding night—mad naked summer night.

Smile O voluptuous cool-breath'd earth!
Earth of the slumbering and liquid trees!
Earth of departed sunset—earth of the mountains misty-topt!
Earth of the vitreous pour of the full moon just tinged with blue!
Earth of shine and dark mottling the tide of the river!
Earth of the limpid gray of clouds brighter and clearer for my sake!
Far-swooping elbow'd earth—rich apple-blossom'd earth!
Smile, for your lover comes.

Prodigal, you have given me love—therefore I to you give love!
O unspeakable passionate love.

From Pent-up, Aching Rivers

From pent-up, aching rivers;
From that of myself, without which I were nothing;
From what I am determined to make illustrious, even if I stand sole
    among men;
From my own voice resonant—singing the phallus,

Singing the song of procreation,
Singing the need of superb children, and therein superb grown people,
Singing the muscular urge and the blending,
Singing the bedfellow's song, (O resistless yearning!
O for any and each, the body correlative attracting!
O for you, whoever you are, your correlative body! O it, more than all
    else, you delighting!)
—From the hungry gnaw that eats me night and day;
From native moments—from bashful pains—singing them;
Singing something yet unfound, though I have diligently sought it,
    many a long year,
Singing the true song of the Soul, fitful, at random;
Singing what, to the Soul, entirely redeemed her, the faithful one, even
    the prostitute, who detained me when I went to the city;
Singing the song of prostitutes;
Renascent with grossest Nature, or among animals;
Of that—of them, and what goes with them, my poems informing;
Of the smell of apples and lemons—of the pairing of birds,
Of the wet of woods—of the lapping of waves,
Of the mad pushes of waves upon the land—I them chanting;
The overture lightly sounding—the strain anticipating;
The welcome nearness—the sight of the perfect body;
The swimmer swimming naked in the bath, or motionless on his back
    lying and floating;
The female form approaching—I, pensive, love-flesh tremulous,
    aching;
The divine list, for myself or you, or for any one, making;
The face—the limbs—the index from head to foot, and what it
    arouses;
The mystic deliria—the madness amorous—the utter abandonment;
(Hark close, and still, what I now whisper to you,
I love you—O you entirely possess me,
O I wish that you and I escape from the rest, and go utterly off—O
    free and lawless,
Two hawks in the air—two fishes swimming in the sea not more
    lawless than we;)
—The furious storm through me careering—I passionately trembling;
The oath of the inseparableness of two together—of the woman that
    loves me, and whom I love more than my life—that oath
    swearing;
(O I willingly stake all, for you!

O let me be lost, if it must be so!

O you and I—what is it to us what the rest do or think?

What is all else to us? only that we enjoy each other, and exhaust each
     other, if it must be so:)

—From the master—the pilot I yield the vessel to;

The general commanding me, commanding all—from him permission
     taking;

From time the programme hastening, (I have loitered too long, as it
     is;)

From sex—From the warp and from the woof;

(To talk to the perfect girl who understands me,

To waft to her these from my own lips—to effuse them from my own
     body;)

From privacy—from frequent repinings alone;

From plenty of persons near, and yet the right person not near;

From the soft sliding of hands over me, and thrusting of fingers
     through my hair and beard;

From the long sustained kiss upon the mouth or bosom;

From the close pressure that makes me or any man drunk, fainting
     with excess;

From what the divine husband knows—from the work of fatherhood;

From exultation, victory, and relief—from the bedfellow's embrace in
     the night;

From the act-poems of eyes, hands, hips, and bosoms,

From the cling of the trembling arm,

From the bending curve and the clinch,

From side by side, the pliant coverlid off-throwing,

From the one so unwilling to have me leave—and me just as unwilling
     to leave,

(Yet a moment, O tender waiter, and I return;)

—From the hour of shining stars and dropping dews,

From the night, a moment, I, emerging, flitting out,

Celebrate you, act divine—and you, children prepared for,

And you, stalwart loins.

When I Heard at the Close of the Day

When I heard at the close of the day how my name had been received
     with plaudits in the capitol, still it was not a happy night for me
     that followed,

And else when I caroused, or when my plans were accomplished, still I
    was not happy,
But the day when I rose at dawn from the bed of perfect health,
    refreshed, singing, inhaling the ripe breath of autumn,
When I saw the full moon in the west grow pale and disappear in the
    morning light,
When I wandered alone over the beach, and undressing bathed,
    laughing with the cool waters, and saw the sun rise,
And when I thought how my dear friend my lover was on his way
    coming, O then I was happy,
O then each breath tasted sweeter, and all that day my food nourished
    me more, and the beautiful day passed well,
And the next came with equal joy, and with the next at evening came
    my friend,
And that night while all was still I heard the waters roll slowly
    continually up the shores,
I heard the hissing rustle of the liquid and sands as directed to me
    whispering to congratulate me,
For the one I love most lay sleeping by me under the same cover in the
    cool night,
In the stillness in the autumn moonbeams his face was inclined toward
    me,
And his arm lay lightly around my breast—and that night I was
    happy.

We Two Boys Together Clinging

We two boys together clinging,
One the other never leaving,
Up and down the roads going, North and South excursions making,
Power enjoying, elbows stretching, fingers clutching,
Armed and fearless, eating, drinking, sleeping, loving,
No law less than ourselves owning, sailing, soldiering, thieving,
    threatening,
Misers, menials, priests alarming, air breathing, water drinking, on the
    turf or the sea-beach dancing,
Cities wrenching, ease scorning, statues mocking, feebleness chasing,
Fulfilling our foray.

THOMAS HARDY

Neutral Tones

We stood by a pond that winter day,
And the sun was white, as though chidden of God,
And a few leaves lay on the starving sod;
   They had fallen from an ash, and were gray.

Your eyes on me were as eyes that rove
Over tedious riddles solved years ago;
And some words played between us to and fro
   On which lost the more by our love.

The smile on your mouth was the deadest thing
Alive enough to have strength to die;
And a grin of bitterness swept thereby
   Like an ominous bird a-wing. . . .

Since then, keen lessons that love deceives,
And wrings with wrong, have shaped to me
Your face, and the God-curst sun, and a tree,
   And a pond edged with grayish leaves.

LEIGH HUNT

Jenny Kissed Me

Jenny kissed me when we met,
Jumping from the chair she sat in;
Time, you thief, who love to get
Sweets into your list, put that in!
Say I'm weary, say I'm sad,
Say that health and wealth have missed me,
Say I'm growing old, but add,
Jenny kissed me.

E. E. CUMMINGS

i like my body when it is with your

i like my body when it is with your
body.   It is so quite new a thing.
Muscles better and nerves more.
i like your body.   i like what it does,
i like its hows.   i like to feel the spine
of your body and its bones,and the trembling
-firm-smooth ness and which i will
again and again and again
kiss,   i like kissing this and that of you,
i like,slowly stroking the,shocking fuzz
of your electric fur,and what-is-it comes
over parting flesh. . . . And eyes big love-crumbs,

and possibly i like the thrill

of under me you so quite new

somewhere i have never travelled,gladly beyond

somewhere i have never travelled,gladly beyond
any experience,your eyes have their silence:
in your most frail gesture are things which enclose me,
or which i cannot touch because they are too near

your slightest look easily will unclose me
though i have closed myself as fingers,
you open always petal by petal myself as Spring opens
(touching skilfully,mysteriously)her first rose

or if your wish be to close me,i and
my life will shut very beautifully,suddenly,
as when the heart of this flower imagines
the snow carefully everywhere descending;

nothing which we are to perceive in this world equals
the power of your intense fragility:whose texture
compels me with the colour of its countries,
rendering death and forever with each breathing

(i do not know what it is about you that closes
and opens;only something in me understands
the voice of your eyes is deeper than all roses)
nobody,not even the rain,has such small hands

love's function is to fabricate unknownness

love's function is to fabricate unknownness

(known being wishless;but love,all of wishing)
though life's lived wrongsideout,sameness chokes oneness
truth is confused with fact,fish boast of fishing

and men are caught by worms(love may not care
if time totters,light droops,all measures bend
nor marvel if a thought should weigh a star
—dreads dying least;and less,that death should end)

how lucky lovers are(whose selves abide
under whatever shall discovered be)
whose ignorant each breathing dares to hide
more than most fabulous wisdom fears to see

(who laugh and cry)who dream,create and kill
while the whole moves;and every part stands still:

the mind is its own beautiful prisoner

the mind is its own beautiful prisoner.
Mine looked long at the sticky moon
opening in dusk her new wings

then decently hanged himself,one afternoon.

The last thing he saw was you
naked amid unnaked things,

your flesh,a succinct wandlike animal,
a little strolling with the futile purr
of blood;your sex squeaked like a billiard-cue
chalking itself,as not to make an error,
with twists spontaneously methodical.
He suddenly tasted worms windows and roses

he laughed,and closed his eyes as a girl closes
her left hand upon a mirror.

SAMUEL BECKETT

Cascando

I

why not merely the despaired of
occasion of
wordshed

is it not better abort than be barren

the hours after you are gone are so leaden
they will always start dragging too soon
the grapples clawing blindly the bed of want
bringing up the bones the old loves
sockets filled once with eyes like yours
all always is it better too soon than never
the black want splashing their faces
saying again nine days never floated the loved
nor nine months
nor nine lives

2

saying again
if you do not teach me I shall not learn
saying again there is a last
even of last times
last times of begging
last times of loving
of knowing not knowing pretending
a last even of last times of saying
if you do not love me I shall not be loved
if I do not love you I shall not love

the churn of stale words in the heart again
love love love thud of the old plunger
pestling the unalterable
whey of words

terrified again
of not loving
of loving and not you
of being loved and not by you
of knowing not knowing pretending
pretending

I and all the others that will love you
if they love you

3

unless they love you

✺✺

WILLIAM BUTLER YEATS

A Drinking Song

Wine comes in at the mouth
And love comes in at the eye;

That's all we know for truth
Before we grow old and die.
I lift the glass to my mouth,
I look at you, and I sigh.

When You Are Old

When you are old and gray and full of sleep,
And nodding by the fire, take down this book,
And slowly read, and dream of the soft look
Your eyes had once, and of their shadows deep;

How many loved your moments of glad grace,
And loved your beauty with love false or true,
But one man loved the pilgrim soul in you,
And loved the sorrows of your changing face;

And bending down beside the glowing bars,
Murmur, a little sadly, how Love fled
And paced upon the mountains overhead
And hid his face amid a crowd of stars.

❧ ☙

JAMES WRIGHT

A Blessing

Just off the highway to Rochester, Minnesota,
Twilight bounds softly forth on the grass.
And the eyes of those two Indian ponies
Darken with kindness.
They have come gladly out of the willows
To welcome my friend and me.
We step over the barbed wire into the pasture
Where they have been grazing all day, alone.
They ripple tensely, they can hardly contain their happiness
That we have come.

They bow shyly as wet swans. They love each other.
There is no loneliness like theirs.
At home once more,
They begin munching the young tufts of spring in the darkness.
I would like to hold the slenderer one in my arms,
For she has walked over to me
And nuzzled my left hand.
She is black and white,
Her mane falls wild on her forehead,
And the light breeze moves me to caress her long ear
That is delicate as the skin over a girl's wrist.
Suddenly I realize
That if I stepped out of my body I would break
Into blossom.

To the Muse

It is all right. All they do
Is go in by dividing
One rib from another. I wouldn't
Lie to you. It hurts
Like nothing I know. All they do
Is burn their way in with a wire.
It forks in and out a little like the tongue
Of that frightened garter snake we caught
At Cloverfield, you and me, Jenny
So long ago.

I would lie to you
If I could.
But the only way I can get you to come up
Out of the suckhole, the south face
Of the Powhatan pit, is to tell you
What you know:

You come up after dark, you poise alone
With me on the shore.
I lead you back to this world.

Three lady doctors in Wheeling open
Their offices at night.
I don't have to call them, they are always there.
But they only have to put the knife once
Under your breast.
Then they hang their contraption.
And you bear it.

It's awkward a while. Still, it lets you
Walk about on tiptoe if you don't
Jiggle the needle.
It might stab your heart, you see.
The blade hangs in your lung and the tube
Keeps it draining.
That way they only have to stab you
Once. Oh Jenny,
I wish to God I had made this world, this scurvy
And disastrous place. I
Didn't, I can't bear it
Either, I don't blame you, sleeping down there
Face down in the unbelievable silk of spring,
Muse of black sand,
Alone.

I don't blame you, I know
The place where you lie.
I admit everything. But look at me.
How can I live without you?
Come up to me, love,
Out of the river, or I will
Come down to you.

❧ ☙

JOHN BERRYMAN

from *The Dream Songs*

4

Filling her compact & delicious body
with chicken páprika, she glanced at me
twice.

Fainting with interest, I hungered back
and only the fact of her husband & four other people
kept me from springing on her

or falling at her little feet and crying
"You are the hottest one for years of night
Henry's dazed eyes
have enjoyed, Brilliance." I advanced upon
(despairing) my spumoni.—Sir Bones: is stuffed,
de world, wif feeding girls.

—Black hair, complexion Latin, jewelled eyes
downcast . . . The slob beside her   feasts . . . What wonders is
she sitting on, over there?
The restaurant buzzes. She might as well be on Mars.
Where did it all go wrong? There ought to be a law against Henry.
—Mr. Bones: there is.

STEPHEN SPENDER

Daybreak

At dawn she lay with her profile at that angle
Which, when she sleeps, seems the carved face of an angel.
Her hair a harp, the hand of a breeze follows
And plays, against the white cloud of the pillows.
Then, in a flush of rose, she woke, and her eyes that opened
Swam in blue through her rose flesh that dawned.
From her dew of lips, the drop of one word
Fell like the first of fountains: murmured
"Darling," upon my ears the song of the first bird.

"My dream becomes my dream," she said, "come true.
I waken from you to my dream of you."
Oh, my own wakened dream then dared assume
The audacity of her sleep. Our dreams
Poured into each other's arms, like streams.

EDNA ST. VINCENT MILLAY

"What lips my lips have kissed"

What lips my lips have kissed, and where, and why,
I have forgotten, and what arms have lain
Under my head till morning; but the rain
Is full of ghosts tonight, that tap and sigh
Upon the glass and listen for reply,
And in my heart there stirs a quiet pain
For unremembered lads that not again
Will turn to me at midnight with a cry.
Thus in the winter stands the lonely tree,
Nor knows what birds have vanished one by one,
Yet knows its boughs more silent than before:
I cannot say what loves have come and gone,
I only know that summer sang in me
A little while, that in me sings no more.

"Love is not all"

Love is not all: it is not meat nor drink
Nor slumber nor a roof against the rain;
Nor yet a floating spar to men that sink
And rise and sink and rise and sink again;
Love can not fill the thickened lung with breath,
Nor clean the blood, nor set the fractured bone;
Yet many a man is making friends with death
Even as I speak, for lack of love alone.
It well may be that in a difficult hour,
Pinned down by pain and moaning for release,
Or nagged by want past resolution's power,
I might be driven to sell your love for peace,
Or trade the memory of this night for food.
It well may be. I do not think I would.

KENNETH FEARING

Love 20¢ the First Quarter Mile

All right. I may have lied to you and about you, and made a few
    pronouncements a bit too sweeping, perhaps, and possibly
    forgotten to tag the bases here or there,
And damned your extravagance, and maligned your tastes, and libeled
    your relatives, and slandered a few of your friends,
O.K.,
    Nevertheless, come back.

Come home. I will agree to forget the statements that you issued so
    copiously to the neighbors and the press,
And you will forget that figment of your imagination, the blonde from
    Detroit;
I will agree that your lady friend who lives above us is not crazy, bats,
    nutty as they come, but on the contrary rather bright,
And you will concede that poor old Steinberg is neither a drunk, nor a
    swindler, but simply a guy, on the eccentric side, trying to get
    along.
(Are you listening, you bitch, and have you got this straight?)

Because I forgive you, yes, for everything.
I forgive you for being beautiful and generous and wise,
I forgive you, to put it simply, for being alive, and pardon you, in
    short, for being you.

Because tonight you are in my hair and eyes,
And every street light that our taxi passes shows me you again, still
    you,
And because tonight all other nights are black, all other hours are cold
    and far away, and now, this minute, the stars are very near and
    bright

Come back. We will have a celebration to end all celebrations.
We will invite the undertaker who lives beneath us, and a couple of
    boys from the office, and some other friends.

And Steinberg, who is off the wagon, and that insane woman who
    lives upstairs, and a few reporters, if anything should break.

W. H. AUDEN

"Lay your sleeping head, my love"

Lay your sleeping head, my love,
Human on my faithless arm;
Time and fevers burn away
Individual beauty from
Thoughtful children, and the grave
Proves the child ephemeral:
But in my arms till break of day
Let the living creature lie,
Mortal, guilty, but to me
The entirely beautiful.

Soul and body have no bounds:
To lovers as they lie upon
Her tolerant enchanted slope
In their ordinary swoon,
Grave the vision Venus sends
Of supernatural sympathy,
Universal love and hope;
While an abstract insight wakes
Among the glaciers and the rocks
The hermit's sensual ecstasy.

Certainty, fidelity
On the stroke of midnight pass
Like vibrations of a bell
And fashionable madmen raise
Their pedantic boring cry;
Every farthing of the cost,
All the dreaded cards foretell,
Shall be paid, but from this night

Not a whisper, not a thought,
Not a kiss nor look be lost.

Beauty, midnight, vision dies:
Let the winds of dawn that blow
Softly round your dreaming head
Such a day of sweetness show
Eye and knocking heart may bless,
Find the mortal world enough;
Noons of dryness see you fed
By the involuntary powers,
Nights of insult let you pass
Watched by every human love.

T. S. ELIOT

A Dedication to My Wife

To whom I owe the leaping delight
That quickens my senses in our wakingtime
And the rhythm that governs the repose of our sleepingtime,
    The breathing in unison

Of lovers whose bodies smell of each other
Who think the same thoughts without need of speech
And babble the same speech without need of meaning.

No peevish winter wind shall chill
No sullen tropic sun shall wither
The roses in the rose-garden which is ours and ours only

But this dedication is for others to read:
These are private words addressed to you in public.

DYLAN THOMAS

If I Were Tickled by the Rub of Love

If I were tickled by the rub of love,
A rooking girl who stole me for her side,
Broke through her straws, breaking my bandaged string,
If the red tickle as the cattle calve
Still set to scratch a laughter from my lung,
I would not fear the apple nor the flood
Nor the bad blood of spring.

Shall it be male or female? say the cells,
And drop the plum like fire from the flesh.
If I were tickled by the hatching hair,
The winging bone that sprouted in the heels,
The itch of man upon the baby's thigh,
I would not fear the gallows nor the axe
Nor the crossed sticks of war.

Shall it be male or female? say the fingers
That chalk the walls with green girls and their men.
I would not fear the muscling-in of love
If I were tickled by the urchin hungers
Rehearsing heat upon a raw-edged nerve.
I would not fear the devil in the loin
Nor the outspoken grave.

If I were tickled by the lovers' rub
That wipes away not crow's-foot nor the lock
Of sick old manhood on the fallen jaws,
Time and the crabs and the sweethearting crib
Would leave me cold as butter for the flies,
The sea of scums could drown me as it broke
Dead on the sweethearts' toes.

This world is half the devil's and my own,
Daft with the drug that's smoking in a girl

And curling round the bud that forks her eye.
An old man's shank one-marrowed with my bone,
And all the herrings smelling in the sea,
I sit and watch the worm beneath my nail
Wearing the quick away.

And that's the rub, the only rub that tickles.
The knobbly ape that swings along his sex
From damp love-darkness and the nurse's twist
Can never raise the midnight of a chuckle,
Nor when he finds a beauty in the breast
Of lover, mother, lovers, or his six
Feet in the rubbing dust.

And what's the rub? Death's feather on the nerve?
Your mouth, my love, the thistle in the kiss?
My Jack of Christ born thorny on the tree?
The words of death are dryer than his stiff,
My wordy wounds are printed with your hair.
I would be tickled by the rub that is:
Man be my metaphor.

✤ ✤

ROBINSON JEFFERS

Granddaughter

And here's a portrait of my granddaughter Una
When she was two years old: a remarkable painter,
A perfect likeness; nothing tricky nor modernist,
Nothing of the artist fudging his art into the picture,
But simple and true. She stands in a glade of trees with a still inlet
Of blue ocean behind her. Thus exactly she looked then,
A forgotten flower in her hand, those great blue eyes
Asking and wondering.
                        Now she is five years old
And found herself. She does not ask any more but commands,
Sweet and fierce-tempered; that light red hair of hers

Is the fuse for explosions. When she is eighteen
I'll not be here. I hope she will find her natural elements,
Laughter and violence; and in her quiet times
The beauty of things—the beauty of transhuman things,
Without which we are all lost. I hope she will find
Powerful protection and a man like a hawk to cover her.

GEORGE BARKER

To My Mother

Most near, most dear, most loved and most far,
Under the window where I often found her
Sitting as huge as Asia, seismic with laughter,
Gin and chicken helpless in her Irish hand,
Irresistible as Rabelais, but most tender for
The lame dogs and hurt birds that surround her,—
She is a procession no one can follow after
But be like a little dog following a brass band.

She will not glance up at the bomber, or condescend
To drop her gin and scuttle to a cellar,
But lean on the mahogany table like a mountain
Whom only faith can move, and so I send
O all my faith and all my love to tell her
That she will move from mourning into morning.

JOHN CIARDI

Men Marry What They Need

Men marry what they need. I marry you,
morning by morning, day by day, night by night,
and every marriage makes this marriage new.

In the broken name of heaven, in the light
that shatters granite, by the spitting shore,
in air that leaps and wobbles like a kite,

I marry you from time and a great door
is shut and stays shut against wind, sea, stone,
sunburst, and heavenfall. And home once more

inside our walls of skin and struts of bone,
man-woman, woman-man, and each the other,
I marry you by all dark and all dawn

and have my laugh at death. Why should I bother
the flies about me? Let them buzz and do.
Men marry their queen, their daughter, or their mother

by hidden names, but that thin buzz whines through:
where reasons are no reason, cause is true.
Men marry what they need. I marry you.

THEODORE ROETHKE

I Knew a Woman

I knew a woman, lovely in her bones,
When small birds sighed, she would sigh back at them;
Ah, when she moved, she moved more ways than one:
The shapes a bright container can contain!
Of her choice virtues only gods should speak,
Or English poets who grew up on Greek
(I'd have them sing in chorus, cheek to cheek).

How well her wishes went! She stroked my chin,
She taught me Turn, and Counter-turn, and Stand;
She taught me Touch, that undulant white skin;
I nibbled meekly from her proffered hand;
She was the sickle; I, poor I, the rake,

Coming behind her for her pretty sake
(But what prodigious mowing we did make).

Love likes a gander, and adores a goose:
Her full lips pursed, the errant note to seize;
She played it quick, she played it light and loose;
My eyes, they dazzled at her flowing knees;
Her several parts could keep a pure repose,
Or one hip quiver with a mobile nose
(She moved in circles, and those circles moved).

Let seed be grass, and grass turn into hay:
I'm martyr to a motion not my own;
What's freedom for? To know eternity.
I swear she cast a shadow white as stone.
But who would count eternity in days?
These old bones live to learn her wanton ways:
(I measure time by how a body sways).

PHYLLIS MCGINLEY

Launcelot with Bicycle

Her window looks upon the lane.
From it, anonymous and shy,
Twice daily she can see him plain,
Wheeling heroic by.
She droops her cheek against the pane
And gives a little sigh.

Above him maples at their bloom
Shake April pollen down like stars
While he goes whistling past her room
Toward unimagined wars,
A tennis visor for his plume,
Scornful of handlebars.

And, counting over in her mind
His favors, gleaned like windfall fruit
(A morning when he spoke her kind,
An afterschool salute,
A number that she helped him find,
Once, for his paper route),

Sadly she twists a stubby braid
And closer to the casement leans—
A wistful and a lily maid
In moccasins and jeans,
Despairing from the seventh grade
To match his lordly teens.

And so she grieves in Astolat
(Where other girls have grieved the same)
For being young and therefore not
Sufficient to his fame—
Who will by summer have forgot
Grief, April, and his name.

❧ ❧

A. E. HOUSMAN

When I Was One-and-Twenty

When I was one-and-twenty
I heard a wise man say,
"Give crowns and pounds and guineas
But not your heart away;
Give pearls away and rubies
But keep your fancy free."
But I was one-and-twenty,
No use to talk to me.

When I was one-and-twenty
I heard him say again,
"The heart out of the bosom

Was never given in vain;
'Tis paid with sighs a-plenty
And sold for endless rue."
And I am two-and-twenty,
And oh, 'tis true, 'tis true!

✥ ✥

ANNE SEXTON

The Ballad of the Lonely Masturbator

The end of the affair is always death.
She's my workshop. Slippery eye,
out of the tribe of myself my breath
finds you gone. I horrify
those who stand by. I am fed.
At night, alone, I marry the bed.

Finger to finger, now she's mine.
She's not too far. She's my encounter.
I beat her like a bell. I recline
in the bower where you used to mount her.
You borrowed me on the flowered spread.
At night, alone, I marry the bed.

Take for instance this night, my love,
that every single couple puts together
with a joint overturning, beneath, above,
the abundant two on sponge and feather,
kneeling and pushing, head to head.
At night alone, I marry the bed.

I break out of my body this way,
an annoying miracle. Could I
put the dream market on display?
I am spread out. I crucify.
My *little plum* is what you said.
At night, alone, I marry the bed.

Then my black-eyed rival came.
The lady of water, rising on the beach,
a piano at her fingertips, shame
on her lips and a flute's speech.
And I was the knock-kneed broom instead.
At night, alone, I marry the bed.

She took you the way a woman takes
a bargain dress of the rack
and I broke the way a stone breaks.
I give back your books and fishing tack.
Today's paper says that you are wed.
At night, alone, I marry the bed.

The boys and girls are one tonight.
They unbutton blouses. They unzip flies.
They take off shoes. They turn off the light.
The glimmering creatures are full of lies.
They are eating each other. They are overfed.
At night, alone, I marry the bed.

✦ ✦

SARA TEASDALE

Barter

Life has loveliness to sell,
All beautiful and splendid things,
Blue waves whitened on a cliff,
Soaring fire that sways and sings,
And children's faces looking up,
Holding wonder like a cup.
Life has loveliness to sell
Music like a curve of gold,
Scent of pine trees in the rain,
Eyes that love you, arms that hold,
And for your spirit's still delight,
Holy thoughts that star the night.

Spend all you have for loveliness,
Buy it and never count the cost;
For one white singing hour of peace
Count many a year of strife well lost,
And for a breath of ecstacy
Give all you have been, or could be.

❦ ❦

MAY SWENSON

In Love Made Visible

In love are we made visible

As in a magic bath
are unpeeled
to the sharp pit
so long concealed

With love's alertness
we recognize
the soundless whimper
of the soul
behind the eyes
A shaft opens
and the timid thing
at last leaps to surface
with full-spread wing

The fingertips of love discover
more than the body's smoothness
They uncover a hidden conduit
for the transfusion
of empathies that circumvent
the mind's intrusion

In love are we set free
Objective bone
and flesh no longer insulate us

to ourselves alone
We are released
and flow into each other's cup
Our two frail vials pierced
drink each other up

❧ ❧

RICHARD WILBUR

For C.

After the clash of elevator gates
And the long sinking, she emerges where,
A slight thing in the morning's crosstown glare,
She looks up toward the window where he waits,
Then in a fleeting taxi joins the rest
Of the huge traffic bound forever west.

On such grand scale do lovers say goodbye—
Even this other pair whose high romance
Had only the duration of a dance,
And who, now taking leave with stricken eye,
See each in each a whole new life forgone.
For them, above the darkling clubhouse lawn,

Bright Perseids flash and crumble; while for these
Who part now on the dock, weighed down by grief
And baggage, yet with something like relief,
It takes three thousand miles of knitting seas
To cancel out their crossing, and unmake
The amorous rough and tumble of their wake.

We are denied, my love, their fine tristesse
And bittersweet regrets, and cannot share
The frequent vistas of their large despair,
Where love and all are swept to nothingness;
Still, there's a certain scope in that long love
Which constant spirits are the keepers of,

And which, though taken to be tame and staid,
Is a wild sostenuto of the heart,
A passion joined to courtesy and art
Which has the quality of something made,
Like a good fiddle, like the rose's scent,
Like a rose window or the firmament.

The Writer

In her room at the prow of the house
Where light breaks, and the windows are tossed with linden,
My daughter is writing a story.

I pause in the stairwell, hearing
From her shut door a commotion of typewriter-keys
Like a chain hauled over a gunwale.

Young as she is, the stuff
Of her life is a great cargo, and some of it heavy:
I wish her a lucky passage.

But now it is she who pauses,
As if to reject my thought and its easy figure.
A stillness greatens, in which

The whole house seems to be thinking,
And then she is at it again with a bunched clamor
Of strokes, and again is silent.

I remember the dazed starling
Which was trapped in that very room, two years ago;
How we stole in, lifted a sash

And retreated, not to affright it;
And how for a helpless hour, through the crack of the door,
We watched the sleek, wild, dark

And iridescent creature
Batter against the brilliance, drop like a glove
To the hard floor, or the desk-top,

And wait then, humped and bloody,
For the wits to try it again; and how our spirits
Rose when, suddenly sure,

It lifted off from a chair-back,
Beating a smooth course for the right window
And clearing the sill of the world.

It is always a matter, my darling,
Of life or death, as I had forgotten. I wish
What I wished you before, but harder.

MARK STRAND

Our Masterpiece Is the Private Life

I

Is there something down by the water keeping itself from us,
Some shy event, some secret of the light that falls upon the deep,
Some source of sorrow that does not wish to be discovered yet?

Our happiness says we should not care, that desire
Could cast its rainbows over the coarse porcelain of the world's skin
And with its measures fill the air. Why look for more?

Why not in the brightness of this weather allow ourselves to be
Astonished by the music and the privilege of our passing?

II

And now, my love, while the advocates of awfulness and sorrow
Push their dripping barge up and down the beach, let's eat
Our brill, and sip this beautiful white Beaune.

True, the light is artificial, and we are not well-dressed.
So what. We like it here. We like the bullocks in the field next door,
We like the sound of wind passing over grass. The way you speak,

In that low voice, our late night disclosures . . . why live
For anything else? Our masterpiece is the private life.

III

Standing on the quay between the Roving Swan and the Star
       Emaculate,
Breathing the night air as the moment of pleasure taken
In pleasure vanishing seems to grow, its self-soiling

Beauty, which can only be what it was, sustaining itself
A little longer in its going, I think of our own smooth passage
Through the graded partitions, the crises that bleed

Into the ordinary, leaving us a little more tired each time,
A little more distant from the experiences, which, in the old days,
Held us captive for hours. The drive along the winding road

Back to the house, the sea pounding against the cliffs,
The glass of whiskey on the table, the open book, the questions,
All the day's rewards waiting at the doors of sleep. . . .

The Coming of Light

Even this late it happens:
the coming of love, the coming of light.
You wake, and the candles are lit as if by themselves,
Stars gather, dreams pour into your pillows,
sending up warm bouquets of air.
Even this late the bones of the body shine
and tomorrow's dust flares into breath.

MAXINE KUMIN

We Are

Love, we are a small pond.
In us yellow frogs take the sun.
Their legs hang down. Their thighs open
like the legs of the littlest children.
On our skin waterbugs suggest incision
but leave no marks of their strokes.
Touching is like that. And what touch evokes.

Just here the blackest berries fatten
over the pond of our being.
It is a rich month for putting up weeds.
They jut like the jaws of Hapsburg kings.
Tomorrow they will drop their blood
as the milkweed bursts its cotton
leaving dry thorns and tight seeds.

Meanwhile even knowing
that time comes down to shut the door
—headstrong, righteous, time hard at the bone
with ice and one thing more—
we teem, we overgrow. The shelf
is tropic still. Even knowing
that none of us can catch up with himself

we are making a run
for it. Love, we are making a run.

Relearning the Language of April

Where this man walks his fences
the willows do pliés with green laces,
eyelashes fly from the white plums,
the gaunt elms begin to open their frames.

When he passes, lithe with morning,
the terriers, rump-deep in a chuckhole,
boom out to follow,
the squirrels chirrup like cardinals.

Five prick-eared ponies
lift from their serious chewing.
The doomed cattle, wearing
intelligent smiles, turn.

For miles around, the plowed fields
release a sweet rancidness
warm as sperm.

I lie in the fat lap of noon
overhearing the doves' complaint.
Far off, a stutter of geese raise alarms.

Once more, Body, Old Paint,
how could you trick me like this
in spring's blowzy arms?

❧ ☙

JAMES TATE

My Felisberto

My felisberto is handsomer than your mergotroid,
although, admittedly, your mergotroid may be the wiser of the two.
Whereas your mergotroid never winces or quails,
my felisberto is a titan of inconsistencies.
For a night of wit and danger and temptation
my felisberto would be the obvious choice.
However, at dawn or dusk when serenity is desired
your mergotroid cannot be ignored.
Merely to sit near it in the garden
and watch the fabrications of the world swirl by,
the deep-sea's bathymetry wash your eyes,

not to mention the little fawns of the forest
and their flip-floppy gymnastics, ah, for this
and so much more your mergotroid is infinitely preferable.
But there is a place for darkness and obscurity
without which life can sometimes seem too much,
too frivolous and too profound simultaneously,
and that is when my felisberto is needed,
is longed for and loved, and then the sun can rise again.
The bee and the hummingbird drink of the world,
and your mergotroid elaborates the silent concert
that is always and always about to begin.

A Dangerous Adventure

The woman I love is typing in a nearby room.
Clippity clippity clippity clippity, then silence.
She's thinking, like a jaguar, or a dagger.
Words but more than words. Currents, hairpin
turns. It's scary but exciting. It's like dancing
on a precipice or sleeping under a waterfall.
She doesn't know the way home but she's running
and leaping over chasms in the earth, and she's singing too,
in a foreign language she's never heard spoken.
But the melody is one I've known all my life.
As a child I hummed it when I dreamed of her,
when I calculated the thousands of accidents it would take
to find her. And now her several rivers
are tossing up ancient maps with military strategies
traced in nearly invisible ink. She's typing, typing
in hot pursuit, a delirium possesses her,
she falls, gets up, shakes herself. A reverie
chases her through a forest, clippity clippity.
Then silence. Perhaps aphasia, or dysphasia.
She's a blind mystic who hasn't spoken in seven years.
She's walking backwards across a jumbo desert.
This is one of her more difficult passages.
A very obscure god peaks at her from the corner of a mirage.
And I think, that's my baby, come on baby,

you're in the homestretch now. But she won't
come home. She's hang gliding over a volcano
and has no use for the old ritual of "dinner."

PHILIP APPLEMAN

A Priest Forever

The first time?
So long ago—that brown-eyed boy . . .
How can I say this, your Reverences,
so you'll understand? Maybe
it was the tilt of his pretty neck
when he pondered the mysteries—Grace,
the Trinity—the way his lower lip
curled like a petal, the way . . .
But *you* know what I mean—down
from your high pulpits and into the dirty streets—
you know there are some provocations
the good Lord made no sinew
strong enough to resist. Think
of David and Jonathan, snarled forever
in a tender web as tough as twine—
like that, maybe—like being driven
by flames, deep in the places we hide,
renounce, deny . . .

No, Monsignor, try to understand—
if your inquest here is meant
to "evaluate" me again, then
you have to feel that fever in the loins
when a child's face looks up
from the wafer-thin body of Christ, innocent
eyes flooding with wonder. You have to see
that the Lord, the good Lord,
has willed something beyond commandments,
beyond dogma, beyond law or custom,
something—irresistible . . .

All right—the first time—
of course I remember.
It was a smoldering August afternoon,
the hottest day in the history
of this whole state, and there
in the cobweb aftermath
of too many questions—what is mortal sin,
what are the dangers to chastity?—alone,
almost alone in the church, after
my little pupils had all run off
to baseball, ice cream, whatever,
he lingered on, in the dim vestry . . .

Well, if you insist, I did ask him
to stay—because,
after all those catechism lessons, there was still
one urgent question hanging
in the clammy air,
and inch by inch, among the ghostly chasubles,
we found ourselves edging closer to it.
Somehow, then, my anointed hand was blessing
his brown hair, one finger ordained to touch
the petal of that lower lip. And there
in that sweaty room—dear Jesus, how I still
feel the heat—I . . . We . . .

Yes, of course—the others. All
the others . . . But after the first time,
how do you tell them apart?
Let's see—there was a blue-eyed kid
with an angel's tongue—what was his name?
And a cherub with golden hair, who
used his indifference like a tease, and . . .
Sixty-eight of them, did you say? All
testifying to . . .

What? I? "Ruined their lives"?
Wait a minute, let's get this straight—
my passion *gave* them a life, gave them
something rich and ripe in their green youth,

something to measure all intimate flesh against,
forever. After that,
they ruined their own lives, maybe.
But with me they were full of a love
firmer than anything their meager years
had ever tasted . . .

Love, you heard me—you
with all your degrees, your tight mouths,
your clinical jargon, don't tell me
you've never had a movement below your belt
that wasn't intestinal. Listen,
this is not in Aquinas,
not in our learned encyclicals. But
there's a force that moves in our marrow,
that slithered there, long before
theology—something with ape in it,
something with the squirm of snakes,
the thrust of rams. And whatever it is,
it knows what it wants . . .

Ah—your glittering eyes
show me you understand. And your ramrod backs
tell me you'll never admit it.
But I'm not alone here, am I?
We're in this together, the same old
celibate fix—"It's better
to marry than to burn," our little
inside joke. And it all comes down
to one poor sinner in a straight-back chair
entertaining a dozen sanctimonious . . .

That word is for the record, Monsignor.
Remember the last time we met like this—
how I pleaded time, place, circumstance,
mitigating niceties, anything but the truth.
And how you enjoyed flaying me then—
you nailed me to lust like a rugged cross,
brushed aside my passion, turned your back
on my word made flesh, hoping

that no more boyish voices
would speak its name to daylight . . .

Yes, Reverends, I learned
a little something then, in all that
groveling—learned that whatever
the meek may wangle in this life,
whatever skimpy joy they manage
to snuggle up to at night, one thing
is as certain as graveyards—the meek
will never, in any shy season,
inherit the earth.
So excuse me if I don't
bob and duck this time.
You have your job to do, go ahead,
throw me to the wolves
and pay off my little lovers—
plaintiffs, have it your way—
hush them up with a million bucks
in widows' pennies. Not a bad price
for all that ecstasy . . .

Oh, I know where I'm headed—
to "therapy," as we always say,
a little paid vacation
with others who loved not wisely
but too young—and also, of course,
with the usual slew of dehydrating
whiskey priests. But don't forget
than when they say I'm "recovered" again,
they'll send me off to another parish,
with more of those little lambs—a priest,
after all, is a priest forever.
Meanwhile, as I bide my time,
and count my beads, and hum to myself
those luscious songs of Solomon,
what I'll be thinking about—
rely on this. Your Reverences—
what I'll be thinking about
is that brown-eyed boy

with the graceful neck, and the lower lip
that curled like a petal.

Crystal Anniversary

Deep in a glassy ball, the future looks
Impacted, overdue, a thing that ticks
And dings with promise, but will not happen; we,
Meanwhile, tick-and-dinging through the glow
Of one more married morning, mind the clock
Of age, fading slowly into black-
On-white biographies. The crimson bird
You welcomed sunrise with, and somehow scared,
Has skirred off, blazing, to a hazy past. Still,
It's all there, deep in the glassy ball,
The past as future: you and that morning flash
Of wings bore anniversaries, a rush
Of visions—you, golden on a far-off beach
Sand-silver—anniversary of such
An earlier you, ringed with the flickering churn
Of antique fountains—anniversary again
Of you, you, dazzling in the fever of love
And smiling on those nights we'd hardly move,
But stand for hours, deep in crystal flakes
Of bundled, quiet winter, touching cheeks.
It wasn't then our worst, or yet our best:
It was the first.

❧ ❧

MARJORIE APPLEMAN

Love

She kissed him, pissing.
I love you, she said,
be careful when you leave.
The trickle paused: you

be careful, too.
Back in bed,
love, she thought,
remembering gray whiskers
mixed with the black.
Love, she whispered,
hearing the trickle
warm and
healthy.
Love,
still going strong.

Another Beginning

A sunrise siren wakes
my cold clock, sparrows
sound alarm, digits freeze
the moment you take wing.
Grounded, I feel your dark
absence, fall back to nightmare,
keeping you close:

> on the wrong side of the glass
> she sees him swim a surf of ice
> cradles his head above the snow
> her sigh his breath
> you are life   love
> watches him watch her float
> out of white recovery clouded
> in bandages lids closed looks
> through blue liquid deep into
> iris brown wanting his touch her
> skin his mouth her lips knowing
> he knows eyes open hears

his call? birdsong?
Gone. A plane roars fear
through a salt sky. The telephone

blurs, not ready to ring you in safe.
I know you think of me
when I'm not there, tasting
worry in your coffee cup. You know
the name I say to fill
an empty room, words as old
as spring, not prayer but
a human promise held
against time.
It's all beginnings with us.

JOHN UPDIKE

Report of Health

I

I am alone tonight.
The wrong I have done you
sits like a sore beneath my thumb,
burns like a boil on my heart's left side.
I am unwell.

My viscera, long clenched in love of you,
have undergone a detested relaxation.

There is, within, a ghostly maze
of phantom tubes and nodules where
those citizens, our passions, flit; and here,
like sunlight passing from a pattern of streets,
I feel your bright love leaving.

II

Another night. Today I am told,
dear friend, by another,
you seem happy and well.
Nothing could hurt me more.

How dare you be happy, you,
shaped so precisely for me,
my cup and my mirror—
how dare you disdain to betray,
by some disarray of your hair,
my being torn from you?

I would rather believe
that you knew your friend would come to me,
and so seemed well—
"not a hair / out of place"—
like an actress blindly hurling a pose
into the fascinated darkness.

As for me, you are still the eyes of the air.
I travel from point to point in your presence.
Each unattended gesture hopes to catch your eye.

III

I may not write again. My voice
goes nowhere. Dear friend,
don't let me heal. Don't
worry, I am well.
I am happy
to dwell in a world whose Hell I will:

the doorway hints at your ghost
and a tiger pounces on my heart;
the lilac bush is a devil
inviting me into your hair.

DONALD JUSTICE

Women in Love

It always comes, and when it comes they know.
To will it is enough to bring them there.
The knack is this, to fasten and not let go.

Their limbs are charmed; they cannot stay or go.
Desire is limbo—they're unhappy there.
It always comes, and when it comes they know.

Their choice of hells would be the one they know.
Dante describes it, the wind circling there.
The knack is this, to fasten and not let go.

The wind carries them where they want to go,
Yet it seems cruel to strangers passing there.
It always comes, and when it comes they know
The knack is this, to fasten and not let go.

On an Anniversary

Thirty years and more go by
In the blinking of an eye,
    And you are still the same
As when first you took my name.

Much the same blush now as then
Glimmers through the peach-pale skin.
    Time (but as with a glove)
Lightly touches you, my love.

Stand with me a minute still
While night climbs our little hill.
    Below, the lights of cars
Move, and overhead the stars.

The estranging years that come,
Come and go, and we are home.
    Time joins us as a friend,
And the evening has no end.

PHILIP LEVINE

In the Dark

In the last light of a summer day facing the Canadian shore
we watched from the island as night sifted into the river,
blackening the still surface. An ore boat passed soundlessly
trailing a tiny wake that folded in upon itself with a sigh,
unless that sigh was hers or mine. In the darkness it's hard
to tell who is listening and who is speaking. St. Augustine
claimed we made love in the dark—though he did not write
"made love"—because we were ashamed to do it in the sight
of anything, although I suppose God could see in the dark, having
at least as good eyesight as a cat. Our cat Nellie used to like
to watch my wife and me at love, but she was not a creature
who generalized and of all things she liked best a happy household.
"God loves a happy giver," I read in the Abyssinian chapel
on top of the Holy Sepulcher, which suggests the old saint
had no idea what he was talking about, but in the darkness
it's not easy to tell who is talking and who listening, who giving,
who taking, who praying, who cursing. Even then, watching
from the island, I thought that making love was a form of prayer.
You got down on your knees, if you were a boy, and prepared
    yourself
for whatever the future held in store, and no matter how firm
your plans without the power of another power you were lost.
It's so dark back then I can't tell what I'm thinking, although
I haven't placed my hand on Millie's shoulder for nothing,
nor have I turned my face toward Millie's merely to catch
a reflection of the darkness in her wide, hazel eyes, cat eyes
I called them then. Millie sighs, the ore boat passes silently
to disappear into a future that's still mysterious, I take a breath,
the deepest breath of my life, and knowing the generations of stars
are watching from above, I go down on my knees in prayer.

February 14th

Awakening at dawn thirty-
six years ago, I see
the lifting of her eyelids
welcome me home. I can
recall her long arms en-
circling me, and I reach
out until the moment slides
into all the forgotten hours.
All the rest of our lives
the tree outside that window
groans in the wind. In other
rooms we'll hear other houses
mutter and won't care, and
go on hearing and not
caring until our names
merge with the wind. One
room, bare, uncurtained,
in a city long ago lost,
goes with us into the wide
measureless light. A tune
goes with us too. Hear
it in the little weirs
collecting winter waters,
in the drops of frozen rain
ticking from the eaves to
pool in the tiny valleys
of their making. Six weeks,
and the wide world is green

ANTHONY HECHT

A Birthday Poem

June 22, 1976

Like a small cloud, like a little hovering ghost
    Without substance or edges,

Like a crowd of numbered dots in a sick child's puzzle,
   A loose community of midges
Sways in the carven shafts of noon that coast
Down through the summer trees in a golden dazzle.

Intent upon such tiny copter flights,
    The eye adjusts its focus
To those billowings about ten feet away,
   That hazy, woven hocus-pocus
Or shell game of the air, whose casual sleights
Leave us unable certainly to say

What lies behind it, or what sets it off
    With fine diminishings,
Like the pale towns Mantegna chose to place
  Beyond the thieves and King of Kings:
Those domes, theatres and temples, clear enough
On that mid-afternoon of our disgrace.

And we know at once it would take an act of will
    Plus a firm, inquiring squint
To ignore those drunken motes and concentrate
   On the blurred, unfathomed background tint
Of deep sea-green Holbein employed to fill
The space behind his ministers of state,

As if one range slyly obscured the other.
    As, in the main, it does.
All of our Flemish distances disclose
   A clarity that never was:
Dwarf pilgrims in the green faubourgs of Mother
And Son, stunted cathedrals, shrunken cows.

It's the same with Time. Looked at *sub specie*
    Aeternitatis, from
The snow-line of some Ararat of years,
   Scholars remark those kingdoms come
To nothing, to grief, without the least display
Of anything so underbred as tears,

And with their Zeiss binoculars descry
    Verduns and Waterloos,
The man-made mushroom's deathly overplus,
    Caesars and heretics and Jews
Gone down in blood, without batting an eye,
As if all history were deciduous.

It's when we come to shift the gears of tense
    That suddenly we note
A curious excitement of the heart
    And slight catch in the throat:——
When, for example, from the confluence
That bears all things away I set apart

The inexpressible lineaments of your face,
    Both as I know it now,
By heart, by sight, by reverent touch and study,
    And as it once was years ago,
Back in some inaccessible time and place,
Fixed in the vanished camera of somebody.

You are four years old here in this photograph.
    You are turned out in style,
In a pair of bright red sneakers, a birthday gift.
    You are looking down at them with a smile
Of pride and admiration, half
Wonder and half joy, at the right and the left.

The picture is black and white, mere light and shade.
    Even the sneakers' red
Has washed away in acids. A voice is spent,
    Echoing down the ages in my head:
What is your substance, whereof are you made,
That millions of strange shadows on you tend?

O my most dear, I know the live imprint
    Of that smile of gratitude,
Know it more perfectly than any book.
    It brims upon the world, a mood
Of love, a mode of gladness without stint.
O that I may be worthy of that look.

Peripeteia

Of course, the familiar rustling of programs,
My hair mussed from behind by a grand gesture
Of mink. A little craning about to see
If anyone I know is in the audience,
And, as the house fills up,
A mild relief that no one there knows me.
A certain amount of getting up and down
From my aisle seat to let the others in.
Then my eyes wander briefly over the cast,
Management, stand-ins, make-up men, designers,
Perfume and liquor ads, and rise prayerlike
To the false heaven of rosetted lights,
The stucco lyres and emblems of high art
That promise, with crude Broadway honesty,
Something less than perfection:
Two bulbs are missing and Apollo's bored.

And then the cool, drawn-out anticipation,
Not of the play itself, but the false dusk
And equally false night when the houselights
Obey some planetary rheostat
And bring a stillness on. It is that stillness
I wait for.
              Before it comes,
Whether we like it or not, we are a crowd,
Foul-breathed, gum-chewing, fat with arrogance,
Passion, opinion, and appetite for blood.
But in that instant, which the mind protracts,
From dim to dark before the curtain rises,
Each of us is miraculously alone
In calm, invulnerable isolation,
Neither a neighbor nor a fellow but,
As at the beginning and end, a single soul,
With all the sweet and sour of loneliness.
I, as a connoisseur of loneliness,
Savor it richly, and set it down
In an endless umber landscape, a stubble field
Under a lilac, electric, storm-flushed sky,
Where, in companionship with worthless stones,

Mica-flecked, or at best some rusty quartz,
I stood in childhood, waiting for things to mend.
A useful discipline, perhaps. One that might lead
To solitary, self-denying work
That issues in something harmless, like a poem,
Governed by laws that stand for other laws,
Both of which aim, through kindred disciplines,
At the soul's knowledge and habiliment.
In any case, in a self-granted freedom,
The mind, lone regent of itself, prolongs
The dark and silence; mirrors itself, delights
In consciousness of consciousness, alone,
Sufficient, nimble, touched with a small grace.

Then, as it must at last, the curtain rises,
The play begins. Something by Shakespeare.
Framed in the arched proscenium, it seems
A dream, neither better nor worse
Than whatever I shall dream after I rise
With hat and coat, go home to bed, and dream.
If anything, more limited, more strict—
No one will fly or turn into a moose.
But acceptable, like a dream, because remote,
And there is, after all, a pretty girl.
Perhaps tonight she'll figure in the cast
I summon to my slumber and control
In vast arenas, limitless space, and time
That yield and sway in soft Einsteinian tides.
Who is she? Sylvia? Amelia Earhart?
Some creature that appears and disappears
From life, from reverie, a fugitive of dreams?
There on the stage, with awkward grace, the actors,
Beautifully costumed in Renaissance brocade,
Perform their duties, even as I must mine,
Though not, as I am, always free to smile.

Something is happening. Some consternation.
Are the knives out? Is someone's life in danger?
And can the magic cloak and book protect?
One has, of course, real confidence in Shakespeare.

And I relax in my plush seat, convinced
That prompt as dawn and genuine as a toothache
The dream will be accomplished, provisionally true
As anything else one cares to think about.
The players are aghast. Can it be the villain,
The outrageous drunks, plotting the coup d'état,
Are slyer than we thought? Or we more innocent?
Can it be that poems lie? As in a dream,
Leaving a stunned and gap-mouthed Ferdinand,
Father and faery pageant, she, even she,
Miraculous Miranda, steps from the stage,
Moves up the aisle to my seat, where she stops,
Smiles gently, seriously, and takes my hand
And leads me out of the theatre, into a night
As luminous as noon, more deeply real,
Simply because of her hand, than any dream
Shakespeare or I or anyone ever dreamed.

GARRETT KAORU HONGO

A Restless Night

for Cynthia

The night surrounds me in a dark grey fog.
I feel its chill even under my *futon*.
The *tatami* underneath stiffens my spine.
I am tense and rise to snap on the light,
Set her photographs out before me on the floor.
I take out the old cardboard *hana* cards
My grandfather gave me and pretend she is here
To play this game of old men and young lovers.

The cards show me prints of the wooden sailboat
Piled up to its masts with cherry blossoms.
Young Prince Genji dips his umbrella
To acknowledge the small orange frog

Playing among pine boughs by the river.
The crane of a thousand days
Considers the swollen red sun of dusk.
Brown ducks fly in a triad over a charred field.

I deal the cards first to her picture,
Smiling as a breeze ruffles through her long hair.
I draw the full moon into my hand
And we go through the plays quickly.
The animal pictures come to me:
A golden-haired yearling buck, butterflies
Flickering around a cluster of peonies.
She takes the red rice bowl, chrysanthemums,
Green stalks of rice plants, and maple leaves
Blazing like filaments of dawn in a basket.

The game is over too soon.
I feel the chill of night
Clench into a fine mist,
Low on the ground outside.
At my window, I see the stars go out.
I pour myself a cup of wine.
Alone again, I drink with the moon.

WENDELL BERRY

The Country of Marriage

I.
I dream of you walking at night along the streams
of the country of my birth, warm blooms and the nightsongs
of birds opening around you as you walk.
You are holding in your body the dark seed of my sleep.

2.
This comes after silence. Was it something I said
that bound me to you, some mere promise

or, worse, the fear of loneliness and death?
A man lost in the woods in the dark, I stood
still and said nothing. And then there rose in me,
like the earth's empowering brew rising
in root and branch, the words of a dream of you
I did not know I had dreamed. I was a wanderer
who feels the solace of his native land
under his feet again and moving in his blood.
I went on, blind and faithful. Where I stepped
my track was there to steady me. It was no abyss
that lay before me, but only the level ground.

3.
Sometimes our life reminds me
of a forest in which there is a graceful clearing
and in that opening a house,
an orchard and garden,
comfortable shades, and flowers
red and yellow in the sun, a pattern
made in the light for the light to return to.
The forest is mostly dark, its ways
to be made anew day after day, the dark
richer than the light and more blessed,
provided we stay brave
enough to keep on going in.

4.
How many times have I come to you out of my head
with joy, if ever a man was,
for to approach you I have given up the light
and all directions. I come to you
lost, wholly trusting as a man who goes
into the forest unarmed. It is as though I descend
slowly earthward out of the air. I rest in peace
in you, when I arrive at last.

5.
Our bond is no little economy based on the exchange
of my love and work for yours, so much for so much
of an expendable fund. We don't know what its limits are—

that puts it in the dark. We are more together
than we know, how else could we keep on discovering
we are more together than we thought?
You are the known way leading always to the unknown,
and you are the known place to which the unknown is always
leading me back. More blessed in you than I know,
I possess nothing worthy to give you, nothing
not belittled by my saying that I possess it.
Even an hour of love is a moral predicament, a blessing
a man may be hard up to be worthy of. He can only
accept it, as a plant accepts from all the bounty of the light
enough to live, and then accepts the dark,
passing unencumbered back to the earth, as I
have fallen time and again from the great strength
of my desire, helpless, into your arms.

6.
What I am learning to give you is my death
to set you free of me, and me from myself
into the dark and the new light. Like the water
of a deep stream, love is always too much. We
did not make it. Though we drink till we burst
we cannot have it all, or want it all.
In its abundance it survives our thirst.
In the evening we come down to the shore
to drink our fill, and sleep, while it
flows through the regions of the dark.
It does not hold us, except we keep returning
to its rich waters thirsty. We enter,
willing to die, into the commonwealth of its joy.

7.
I give you what is unbounded, passing from dark to dark,
containing darkness: a night of rain, an early morning.
I give you the life I have let live for love of you:
a clump of orange-blooming weeds beside the road,
the young orchard waiting in the snow, our own life
that we have planted in this ground, as I
have planted mine in you. I give you my love for all
beautiful and honest women that you gather to yourself

again and again, and satisfy—and this poem,
no more mine than any man's who has loved a woman.

Air and Fire

From my wife and household and fields
that I have so carefully come to in my time
I enter the craziness of travel,
the reckless elements of air and fire.
Having risen up from my native land,
I find myself smiled at by beautiful women,
making me long for a whole life
to devote to each one, making love to her
in some house, in some way of sleeping
and waking I would make only for her.
And all over the country I find myself
falling in love with houses, woods, and farms
that I will never set foot in.
My eyes go wandering through America,
two wayfaring brothers, resting in silence
against the forbidden gates. O what if
an angel came to me, and said,
"Go free of what you have done. Take
what you want." The atoms of blood
and brain and bone strain apart
at the thought. What I am is the way home.
Like rest after a sleepless night,
my old love comes on me in midair.

SIV CEDERING

Country Music

You say you like whales, and I surface, spout
toward the heavens, flip my tail and listen
for your strange song. "Beluga—Beluga!"

I wallow in delight with everything that's large
about me, wanting to be larger beside you,
to tumble, touched everywhere, as if by water,
the waves billowing from such leviathan playing.

You say you love flamenco dancers, and
my swayed back arches, my waist grows slender,
my buttocks firm, and nothing is hidden
in the tight red dress that flares like a fuchsia
around my insistently stamping feet: "Now! Now!"
—the quickening heartbeat of my petulant desire.
My head is high, my eyes cast behind the fan
that opens and closes my face to entice you.

You say you wanted to marry a Chippewa princess
when you were eight, and I tell about the doeskin
dress I bought from a trader in a motel room
in Colorado. Its bleached skins are soft and
fringed, the bead work complex. It waits
in my attic. I have not felt I have the right
to wear it, but now I want to put it on and go
to the mountain where you want to marry me.

Oh, middle age is sweet. I can with confidence say
I know almost as much about love as I did
when I was seven and serenaded the beautiful
blue-eyed boy from under his balcony, while dancing
the hula, under the midnight sun of the Arctic.
Yes, I knew about love—I knew what to do!
You laugh. We laugh, rolling in the billow of
the bed, to poise ourselves in that formal dance,

before we are done and sink into the sigh
of a promise as true as the one we have made
to the land. Not having found the language yet
for everything that opens inside me,
I speak of the internal loaves and fishes
that divide themselves like cells, the thousand hands
that reach for you, the thousand eyes that see you
in each unfolding miracle of this world.

For I would go westward with you, riding
on one horse, if we had only one, or walking,
if we had none. Meanwhile I part my hair
in the back and braid two even braids. I cultivate
the perfect rose, not knowing when
I might need to bite the stem, to quench the scream.

I swim out beyond the crashing breakers and dive deep
into the flickering light, listening for a larger song.

Ukiyo-E

What explanation is given for the phosphorus light
That you, as boy, went out to catch
When summer dusk turned to night?
You caught the fireflies, put them in a jar,
Careful to let in some air,
Then you fed them dandelions, unsure
Of what such small and fleeting things
Need, and when
Their light grew dim, you
   Let them go.

There is no explanation for the fire
That burns in our bodies
Or the desire that grows, again and again,
So that we must move toward each other
In the dark.
We have no wings.
We are ordinary people, doing ordinary things.
The story can be told on rice paper.
There is a lantern, a mountain, whatever
   We can remember.

Hiroshige's landscape is so soft.
What child, woman, would not want to go out
Into that dark, and be caught,
And caught again, by you?

I want these pictures of the floating world
To go on, but when
The light begins to dim, catch me.
Give me whatever a child imagines
To keep me aglow, then
   Let me go.

Crossing the Sound by Ferry One Night During the Gulf War

Leaving the book of love poems beside you,
I go out on deck. Lights of oil refineries
glide by, submarines in dry dock, buoys.
Not able to align the inside with the outside,
I climb the metal stairs for a better view.

In the stern, the frayed flag
snaps the wind and the wake North,
where the Pole Star swings the Cup of the Bear
like a boy betting his little sister
the upside-down bucket won't spill.

No longer believing a star falls
when somebody dies, I still look for the three
in Orion's belt, his sword, the dogs at his feet,
the almost invisible arc of his bow, and follow
his aim past the V-shaped face of the Bull

to the wound. On separate coasts,
my parents are sinking into silence.
A stroke has made it difficult for my brother
to speak. Soon only my sister and I will be left
talking long distance.

Thinking I could slip unheard
over the railing, I lean against the bin
of life jackets, and like a child
who knows the story by heart,
I make my way across the heavens,

mouthing the names Lyre, Pegasus, Swan,
while their stories mingle with my own,
my children's. From a plane,
this ferry crossing the Sound
would look like a star falling slowly

from constellation to constellation.
You look up as I enter the lit room.
"I was worried," you say. I touch you
and pick up the book, where
a man and a woman

learn to love
growing old.

WILLIAM MEREDITH

The Ghosts of the House

Enabling love, roof of this drafty hutch
of children and friends and pets, and chiefly of the dear
one asleep beside me now, the warm body-house
I sack like a Hun nightly in your service,
take care of the haunts who stay with us here.

In a little space for a long while they've walked,
wakeful when we sleep, averting their sad glance
when we're clumsy with one another, they look
at something we can't look at yet, they creak the boards
beside the bed we creak, in some hard durance.

And if we're weary at night, what must they be?
Bed them like us at last under your roof.
You who have sternly set all lovers to walk
the hallways of the world-hutch for a lucky while,
speaking good of our short durance here,

wishing our sibling spirits nothing but good,
let them see these chambers once with the daylight eyes
you lend to lovers for our mortal time.
Or change some loveless stalker into me
before my bone-house clatters into lime.

Poem

The swans on the river, a great
flotilla in the afternoon sun
in October again.

In a fantasy, Yeats saw himself appear
to Maud Gonne as a swan,
his plumage fanning his desire.

One October at Coole Park
he counted fifty-nine wild swans.
He flushed them into a legend.

Lover by lover is how he said they flew,
but one of them must have been without a mate.
Why did he not observe that?

We talk about Zeus and Leda and Yeats
as if they were real people, we identify constellations
as if they were drawn there on the night.

Cygnus and Castor & Pollux
are only ways of looking at
scatterings of starry matter,

a god putting on swan-flesh
to enter a mortal girl
is only a way of looking at love-trouble.

The violence and calm of these big fowl!
When I am not with you
I am always the fifty-ninth.

Crossing Over

> *It was now early spring, and the river was swollen and turbulent; great cakes of floating ice were swinging heavily to and fro in the turbid waters. Owing to a peculiar form of the shore, on the Kentucky side, the land bending far out into the water, the ice had been lodged and detained in great quantities, and the narrow channel which swept round the bend was full of ice, piled one cake over another, thus forming a temporary barrier to the descending ice, which lodged, and formed a great undulating raft. . . . Eliza stood, for a moment, contemplating this unfavorable aspect of things.*
>
> Uncle Tom's Cabin (Chapter VII, "The Mother's Struggle")/Harriet Beecher Stowe

That's what love is like. The whole river
is melting. We skim along in great peril,

having to move faster than ice goes under
and still find foothold in the soft floe.

We are one another's floe. Each displaces the weight
of his own need. I am fat as a bloodhound,

hold me up. I won't hurt you. Though I bay,
I would swim with you on my back until the cold

seeped into my heart. We are committed, we
are going across this river willy-nilly.

No one, black or white, is free in Kentucky,
old gravity owns everybody. We're weighty.

I contemplate this unfavorable aspect of things.
Where is something solid? Only you and me.

Has anyone ever been to Ohio?
Do the people there stand firmly on icebergs?

Here all we have is love, a great undulating
raft, melting steadily. We go out on it

anyhow. I love you, I love this fool's walk.
The thing we have to learn is how to walk light.

✥ ✥

RICHARD HARTEIS

Einsteinian Love

"I'm thirty-six,"
you said at seventy-seven.
"I'm thirty-six,"
I said at forty-nine.
"You're fourteen," you said.
"You're thirty-six," I said.
We work it out somehow,
over the years, this lovely
mysterious mathematics
whereby we divide our age
and meet each other at the
fulcrum moment of who we are:

there we damn well are,
seeing through stone,
as the brother says,
prisoners of love and time
out of ourselves
infinity equalling zero
an abiding Mobius strip
of friendship
forward and back
my dear, my dear.

Winter Lesson

For Mackie

There were nights the snow began as powder
dusting the ceramic bulldog on the step

until by morning he wore a white bowler
or was buried altogether. Others,
these gentle fields became moonscape,
a polished crust thick enough to
hold a man without snowshoes. Clear then,
with brittle stars and a freeze so deep
the earth seemed finally irreparable—
you would die if you went too far from home.

Often I lay like a spoiled hibernating bear
after too many nightcaps or excesses
sure the cold would numb me to death, when
the cave grew warmer somehow with dreams of
plump fish hiding in the rainbows of spring streams.

Once I actually woke and stumbled down to
catch you in your father's woolen bathrobe
feeding logs into the wood stove, a dream too.
You could have been counting thousand dollar bills
or preparing the first martini of the day.

Twice a night throughout winter and just before
dawn smashed through the the kitchen and required
breakfast, you danced this ritual. Sometimes I came down
to smoked ham and eggs over light and remembered to
complain how cold I'd been and how your odd movements
wakened me in the night. The heat I accepted like air.

Now I sit in the same woolen robe
wondering how soon the light will come, and
if these logs will hold till then. You,
can't take the stairs as well anymore. Your
circulation's poor. Sometimes you shake a little
in your sleep. I hold you tighter till it's over
or I stoke the fire. I know the ritual like a
well-trained dancing bear. More than habit though,
sometimes the tenderness I come to as I watch you
curl into the warmth of your sleep feels like perfect
instinct, like slapping the wet air to hook a rainbow.

Star Trek III

The fantasy spaceman
returning from death
greets his captain
gingerly: "Jim?"

Spock's Vulcan father explains
that only time will tell
if the priestess' magic
will bring him totally back.
Instead of "the end"
the film's last frames promise,
"the adventure continues."

I want to cry a little:
I grew up on these heroes—
to be as good as Kirk . . .

But life is a little closer now.
We watch the film together
and I explain the plot
the way one would talk to someone
trapped under ice. My manuals say
I musn't convey anxiety.

I remember the day after
weeks at your bedside when
you said my name finally.

You were IN there,
KNEW me.

The same shock the cardiac nurse
felt the year before when she
randomly took the tape from
your sweet eyes and they flew open
as she called your name.

We've been in a few
tight spots lately.

All these months.
My loneliness deepens.
I cry in private
when you forget my name.

Still, you love me clearly,
whoever I am.

The adventure continues.

❦ ❦

GALWAY KINNELL

Telephoning in Mexican Sunlight

Talking with my beloved in New York
I stood at the outdoor public telephone
in Mexican sunlight, in my purple shirt.
Someone had called it a man/woman
shirt. The phrase irked me. But then
I remembered that Rainer Maria
Rilke, who until he was seven wore
dresses and had long yellow hair,
wrote that the girl he almost was
"made her bed in my ear" and "slept me the world."
I thought, OK this shirt will clothe the other in me.
As we fell into long-distance love talk
a squeaky chittering started up all around,
and every few seconds came a sudden loud
buzzing. I half expected to find
the insulation on the telephone line
laid open under the pressure of our talk
leaking low-frequency noises.
But a few yards away a dozen hummingbirds,
gorgets going drab or blazing
according as the sun struck them,
stood on their tail rudders in a circle
around my head, transfixed
by the flower-likeness of the shirt.

And perhaps also by a flush rising into my face,
for a word—one with a thick sound,
as if a porous vowel had sat soaking up
saliva while waiting to get spoken,
possibly the name of some flower
that hummingbirds love, perhaps
"honeysuckle" or "hollyhock"
or "phlox"—just then shocked me
with its suddenness, and this time
apparently did burst the insulation,
letting the word sound in the open
where all could hear, for these tiny, irascible,
nectar-addicted puritans jumped back
all at once, fast, as if the air gasped.

Rapture

I can feel she has got out of bed.
That means it is seven A.M.
I have been lying with eyes shut,
thinking, or possibly dreaming,
of how she might look if, at breakfast,
I spoke about the hidden place in her
which, to me, is like a soprano's tremolo,
and right then, over toast and bramble jelly,
if such things are possible, she came.
I imagine she would show it while trying to conceal it.
I imagine her hair would fall about her face
and she would become apparently downcast,
as she does at a concert when she is moved.
The hypnopompic play passes, and I open my eyes
and there she is, next to the bed,
bending to a low drawer, picking over
various small smooth black, white,
and pink items of underwear. She bends
so low her back runs parallel to the earth,
but there is no sway in it, there is little burden, the day has hardly
    begun.

The two mounds of muscles for walking, leaping, lovemaking,
lift toward the east—what can I say?
Simile is useless; there is nothing like them on earth.
Her breasts fall full; the nipples
are deep pink in the glare shining up through the iron bars
of the gate under the earth where those who could not love
press, wanting to be born again.
I reach out and take her wrist
and she falls back into bed and at once starts unbuttoning my
    pajamas.
Later, when I open my eyes, there she is again,
rummaging in the same low drawer.
The clock shows eight. Hmmm.
With huge, silent effort of great,
mounded muscles the earth has been turning.
She takes a piece of silken cloth
from the drawer and stands up. Under the falls
of hair her face has become quiet and downcast,
as if she will be, all day among strangers,
looking down inside herself at our rapture.

CHARLES SIMIC

Marked Playing Cards

I took my TV and bass fiddle to the pawnshop.
Then I had my car stolen and everything in it.
This morning I'm down to a windbreaker and house slippers,
But I feel cheerful, even though it's snowing.
This proves she loves me, I said to the crowd
Waiting for the bus. They were afraid to look my way.

I let myself be reduced to rags, I explained.
I marked playing cards to cheat against myself.
All my life I kept raising the stakes, knowing
That each new loss assured me of her complete love.
(The bus was late, so they had to hear the rest.)

I told them that I never met her, but that I was certain
She has a premonition of my existence,
As I do of hers. Perhaps this is the moment
She comes along and recognizes me standing here?

Because my mind was busy with our first kiss,
I didn't hear the bus arrive and leave.
High over the roofs, the sky was already clearing.
I still had the greasy cards in my pocket.
With my bad luck, I surmised, she was due by nightfall.
Shuffling through the snow and shivering,
I was ready to bet the rest of my clothes on her.

At the Cookout

The wives of my friends
Have the air
Of having shared a secret.
Their eyes are lowered
But when we ask them
What for?
They only glance at each other
And smile,
Which only increases our desire
To know . . .

Something they did
Long ago,
Heedless of the consequences,
That left
Such a lingering sweetness?

Is that the explanation
For the way
They rest their chins
In the palms of their hands,
Their eyes closed
In the summer heat?

Come tell us,
Or give us a hint.
Trace a word or just a single letter
In the wine
Spilled on the table.

No reply. Both of them
Lovey-dovey
With the waning sunlight
And the evening breeze
On their faces.
The husbands drinking
And saying nothing,
Dazed and mystified as they are
By their wives' power
To give
And take away happiness,
As if their heads
Were crawling with snakes.

LINDA HOGAN

The Origins of Corn

This is the female corn.
This is the male.
These are the wild skirts flying
and here is the sweet dark daughter
that passed between those
who were currents of each other's love.
She sleeps
in milky sweetness. She is the stranger
that comes from a remote land, another time
where sky and earth are lovers always
for the first time each day,
where crops begin to stand
amid brown dry husks, to rise straight

and certain as old people with yellowed hair
who carry medicines,
the corn song,
the hot barefoot dance
that burns your feet
but you can't stop
trading gifts
with the land,
putting your love in the ground
so that after the long sleep of seeds
all things will grow
and the plants who climb into this world
will find it green and alive.

Nothing

Nothing sings in our bodies
like breath in a flute.
It dwells in the drum.
I hear it now
that slow beat
like when a voice said to the dark,
let there be light,
let there be ocean
and blue fish
born of nothing
and they were there.
I turn back to bed,
The man there is breathing.
I touch him
with hands already owned by another world.
Look, they are desert,
they are rust. They have washed the dead.
They have washed the just born.
They are open.
They offer nothing.
Take it.
Take nothing from me.

There is still a little life
left inside this body,
a little wildness here
and mercy
and it is the emptiness
we love, touch, enter in one another
and try to fill.

❧ ❧

LAURENCE GOLDSTEIN

Aubade

"Cascade is my favorite word," she said
and drew the blinds.
Sunlight smashed through the windows
gouging my eyes. I smiled.
"Mine is tundra; the sound is palpable as flesh."
"My flesh?" her voice soothed in the sun's malaise.
I cuddled my pillow, wondering
what poetry would simulate her flesh.
At the bathroom door she turned
and asked, was I happy?
I said yes.

Eros in Long Beach

Where I see the marooned Pike
of the Navy's withdrawal,
no longer charismatic tars or hidalgos
casting silver onto the games of chance,
but vagrants who
shuffle by in worn jeans and t-shirts,
stir balloons with badly-thrown darts
or heave basketballs to win a pink tiger

she sees The Petrified Man,
his skin bulging with knots,
nearly arboral like the maids of Ovid's book,
greased by sweat from his bald dome down.
"Knock on my leg,
feel the vibration in my skull!"
he exclaimed to a trembling child
who now relives his words with the same salt chill.

She touches my hand. At once
his less-than-ghostly quick
stiffens within me, a source of her craving,
location of sensual undertones
more pungent than
hummingbird stabs of the tattoo
or vomit-smell where the Rotor
turns its barrel of riff-raff at dizzy speed.

In such places I look for
passionate history,
the incognitos a wife illuminates,
unlikely grails at the psyche's core.

Two lives have I
so long as I inwardly collect
the resonance of her world,
gather like a bag lady these souvenirs.

I comfort her with kisses.
I've learned one thing: learning
is more accidental than the order of words,
is a wound the mind reopens by force.
I walk that Pike
like a revenant seeking blood,
a guest in her ruthless Eden
where love for me was made possible by terror.

JORIE GRAHAM

Studies in Secrecy

The secret we don't know we're trying to find, the thing *un-*
                       seen,
is it ironic? is it a sign of anything?—raw
               vertigo
the suction-point of which we now are trying to feed
                   our lives
into—the point devoid of ancestry, the bullioned point,
                 so sleek,
dwindling yet increasingly aswarm,
the chittering of manyness in it as it is made to
                  clot
into a thrumming singleness—the secret—the place where the words
                       twist—
we are looking for it everywhere—
we look on my breast, we try the nipple,
we look in the gaiety of your fingertips, the curriculum
                  of caresses
twisting and windy in the architecture of
             my neck, my
open mouth—we look in your mouth—
we look, quick, into the-day-before-yesterday—we look
                   away—
we look again into your violent mouth,
into the edifice of your whisper, into the dwindling oxygen
                 we eat,
inhaling, exhaling—
we look into the glassy eyes we have between us—
we try not to shift, we stare,
there seems to be an enclosure in there, maybe a struck
                note, an hypothesis,
we look in each other's hair
as in ripe shrubs bearing and withering,
we feel time glide through the room, between our legs,

round through our glance—we think we can look in the walled-up
                                            thoughts—
we let our nights get tangled, we try to stare—
if something happens—the phone rings, a cigarette is lit,
maybe a massacre, maybe in spring the curtain
blossoms—gossamer—we look in there—
then we go back to the green-eyed heat, and stare,
beating on the icy film between each thing, knocking, tapping,
                                        to see what's happening,
"the wasteland grows; woe to him hiding wastelands
                            within" (*The Portable*
Nietzsche—Viking '54—we look in there),
also look in "Alas, the time is coming when
man will no longer shoot the arrow of his longing
beyond man"—"the string of his bow has forgotten
to whir"—it is a haze—the radio's
                on, the automated
churchbells ring—we start the matter up again, we cry, we finger
the folds—we open our lips—we bite our necks—
don't make me explain, one wing of it is soot, one wing
                        of it is blood,
we lick it, we nibble aimlessly, not so much tired as
increasingly ignorant—the minutes barbed now—the
blue streak where we hear a siren louder now,
our shoulders glistening, our backs greasy with hope,
foraging now (we try the book again) (we try putting things
                            in each other
to see how much room)("the earth has become smaller
                        and on it hop
the last men") so that we have to start
saying the words again (the last men live longest)—
I love you I say—poor secret, did you need us?
did you need us to find you?—
(live longest—*we have invented happiness,* they say)—
I love you, you say, rising among the motes, the spores—
and *forever and forever* like a sleeve we slide the hissing secret in—
the golden-headed, the upthrown—have invented *happiness* say the
    last men—
and blink.

MONA VAN DUYN

Late Loving

> "What Christ was saying, what he meant [in the story of Mary and Martha] was that the pleasures of that hair, that ointment, must be taken. Because the accidents of death would deprive us soon enough. We must not deprive ourselves, our loved ones, of the luxury of our extravagant affections. We must not try to second-guess death by refusing to love the ones we loved. . . ."
>
> Mary Gordon, *Final Payments*

If in my mind I marry you every year
it is to calm an extravagance of love
with dousing custom, for it flames up fierce
and wild whenever I forget that we live
in double rooms whose temperature's controlled
by matrimony's turned-down thermostat.
I need the mnemonics, now that we are old,
of oath and law in re-memorizing that.
Our dogs are dead, our child never came true.
I might use up, in my weak-mindedness,
the whole human supply of warmth on you
before I could think of others and digress.
"Love" is finding the familiar dear.
"In love" is to be taken by surprise.
Over, in the shifty face you wear,
and over, in the assessments of your eyes,
you change, and with new sweet or barbed word
find out new entrances to my inmost nerve.
When you stand at the stove it's I who am most stirred.
When you finish work I rest without reserve.
Daytimes, sometimes, our three-legged race seems slow.
Squabbling onward, we chafe from being so near.
But all night long we lie like crescents of Velcro,
turning together till we re-adhere.
Since you, with longer stride and better vision,
more clearly see the finish line, I stoke

my hurrying self, to keep it in condition,
with light and life-renouncing meals of smoke.
As when a collector scoops two Monarchs in
at once, whose fresh flights to and from each other
are netted down, so in vows I re-imagine
I re-invoke what keeps us stale together.
What you try to give is more than I want to receive,
yet each month when you pick up scissors for our appointment
and my cut hair falls and covers your feet I believe
that the house is filled again with the odor of ointment.

Earth Tremors Felt in Missouri

The quake last night was nothing personal,
you told me this morning. I think one always wonders,
unless, of course, something is visible: tremors
that take us, private and willy-nilly, are usual.

But the earth said last night that what I feel,
you feel; what secretly moves you, moves me.
One small, sensuous catastrophe
makes inklings letters, spelled in a worldly tremble.

The earth, with others on it, turns in its course
as we turn toward each other, less than ourselves, gross,
mindless, more than we were. Pebbles, we swell
to planets, nearing the universal roll,
in our conceit even comprehending the sun,
whose bright ordeal leaves cool men woebegone.

W. S. MERWIN

Late Spring

Coming into the high room again after years
after oceans and shadows of hills and the sounds of lies
after losses and feet on stairs

after looking and mistakes and forgetting
turning there thinking to find
no one except those I knew
finally I saw you
sitting in white
already waiting

you of whom I had heard
with my own ears since the beginning
for whom more than once
I had opened the door
believing you were not far

Before Us

You were there all the time and I saw only
the days the air
the nights the moon changing
cars passing and faces at windows
the windows
the rain the leaves the years
words on pages telling of something else
wind in a mirror

everything begins so late after all
when the solitaires have already gone
and the doves of Tanna
when the Laughing Owls have
long been followed by question marks
and honeycreepers and the brown
bears of Atlas
the white wolf and the sea mink have not been seen
by anyone living

we wake so late after many dreams
it is clear
when the lake has vanished
the shepherds have left the shielings

grandparents have dissolved with their memories
dictionaries are full of graves
most of the rivers are lethal
we thought we were younger
through all those ages of knowing nothing
and there you are
at last after such fallings away and voyages
beside me in the dawning

we wake together and the world is here in its dew
you are here and the morning is whole
finally the light is young
because it is here it is not like anything
how could it have taken you so long to appear
bloom of air tenderness of leaves
where were you when the lies were voting
and the fingers believed faces on money
where were we when the smoke washed us
and the hours cracked as they rang
where was I when we passed each other
on the same streets
and travelled by the same panes to the same stations

now we have only the age that is left
to be together
the brief air the vanishing green
ordure in office tourists on the headland
the last hours of the sea
now we have only the words we remember
to say to each other
only the morning of your eyes and the day
of our faces to be together
only the time of our hands with its vexed
motor and the note
of the thrush on the guava branch in the shining rain
for the rest of our lives

RICHARD HOWARD

L'Invitation au Voyage

Wandering with you the shore
That parallels our river
   Like a second thought.
Singular and sad I wore
The habit of a lover
   Almost inside out.

Night in its black behaving
Muffled every lamp and dyed
   The wooly season,
Pig-iron boats were leaving
For the lake, slowly the loud
   Bridges had risen:

A landscape for the lonely
Or the lewd, as you observed,
   When of a sudden
Something steep and with only
Momentary warning moved
   Out of the hidden

Harbor. It was a dark boat
And *Cytherea* it said
   Low on the long bow.
"A cabin for two," cried out
A voice, and I saw a head
   That I thought I knew—

"Fifteen days to the Island:
We sail tonight with the tide!"
   I remember now,
Turning, how your face went blind.

   Moved but unmoving, I
   Sit here and stare your sleep

Out of countenance. My
Crude hopes crumble to a heap
     As retrospectively
     I sift what I would keep
Of all such savored, severed fellowship:

     Tall in my mind stands one
     (I seldom heard him speak)
     Whose only lifelong work
Was burnishing the boyhood on
     His face; and one whose look
     I know, though I have known
No likes of him: unlikely guest, he's gone

     (Our neighborly disgrace)
     Without a proper name;
     Here's one I had for whom
No second act, or try, or time
     Was real; another whose
     Fortunes went up in flames—
His ghost, among the ghosts, in ashes goes.

     But let the darkness fall
     Politely on them all:
     The past must have an end.
Your dreaming body and my mind
     Alone at last contend.
     Courageously I send
My thought against you while your mute limbs loll

     At enviable ease.
     You lie without surprise
     Beside me as I wait
For clues: the file is incomplete.
     Who is it that you meet
     When your round shoulders rise
And shed your hands like dead leaves on the sheet?

     You sigh and smile and seem
     Released. I ask you where

You've been. What is the home
You visit while in exile here?
    As if you couldn't care
    Less (your record is clear)
You answer in a trance, "I never dream."

The Lover Showeth Wherefore He Is Abandoned of the Beloved He Sometime
Enjoyed, Even in Sleep

    Tonight (the moonless kind
    That Judith might have spent
    In Holofernes' tent
Until her ravished victim found
    His final ravishment)
    The many come to mind
Who lately came and, coming, later went,

    Taking a way you must
    Soon take yourself, I trust,
    While by the brazen laws
That league diversion with disgust
    Those others plead their cause
    Elsewhere, to the applause
I lavished best when they deserved it least.

    I lean now on your bed
    And trace a pulsing vein
    That proves you are not dead:
Dividing us, that other Red
    Sea dandles you within
    Its tides until you deign
To wake and make the sea divide again.

    Each of us peers into
    Mirrors for what is true
    About the rest: mostly
We spend our spare time in the blue
    Movies of memory.

We are blind seeing, see
Blind, and find our way the way moles do.
    The river sighed in its bed
        And although a few

    Gulls were loud in their abuse
    You did not once look up. When
        To their obloquy
    No protest was made, I chose
    To learn what I've always known:
        We shall never go.

❧ ❧

HEATHER McHUGH

Dry Time

Killed, the sand
didn't give. All waves
went dead: your border
crossed itself.

I couldn't tell or tear
us apart. In the absence
of hourglasses
meanwhiles

piled up, swells of the
dispellable. Even the diamond
shed no oil, not a drop
to delight the drilltip.

*

Partners having come
unwelded (blasted by nuclear
family life) we went
a long

way back,
as far as Abacus (empire
of rook and stork). We roused
some dowsers

from a timeless doze, we had them
scatter Onan's
nanoseconds
everywhere: in particles, the clearest

solitudes could be broadcast. At last
you kissed me, I could die in waves again, and one
good lick of quick-
sand took. . . .

Untitled

There is much unsaid, though the edges of the said
so long and so
perversely have
attracted me. And even now
how can I tell
what old unbearabilities of mind in animal amount

to my drive to seize you, you who have
become my being's being,
owner than myself? Parmenides' muse
(Dike the indicator, Dike the just)
insists no part is more existent
than another, no part less; and yet

there SEEMS to be less being in a self
than in another: self is least
the seeable, in self's esteem; one's sense of it
a sixth, at most, whereas one's senses of another
billow full and five. . . . YOU I can feel

all ways: I run an eye on your leg,
look a foot in your eye. In you
I am very advanced: I see the end
of my own inwardness. But if I turn

to me, the second splits. There's instantaneous
adjustment—surface slid in place: I face someone who's always
facing back, or inside-out, or rightside-down;

someone who saw me first, and fixed herself;
someone whose other faces I know nothing of.
If for a moment she were clearly
visible to me, I think

I'd fall forever, out of love.

❧❧

ROBERT PINSKY

The Time of Year, the Time of Day

One way I need you, the way I come to need
Our custom of speech, or need this other custom
Of speech in lines, is to alleviate
The weather, the time of year, the time of day.

I mean for instance the way the dusk in late
Winter or early spring recalls adolescence:
The pity of my comical unease
And vague depression on the long walk home

From the grim school through washed-out extra daylight
And the yellow light that waited in kitchen windows,
Daydreaming victories on the long parades
Of artificial brick and bare hydrangea.

But how cold in retrospect the afternoon
And evening even in July could seem,
Cold heralding that now those very hours
Are on the way, the very hours which one

Had better use, which may be what it is
About the time of year and the time of day,
Their burden of a promise but a promise
Limited, that sends folk huddling to their bodies

Or kitchens as colonizers of the day
And of the year, rough settlers who throughout
The stunning winter couple in a fury
To fill the brown width of their tillable plains.

The Want Bone

The tongue of the waves tolled in the earth's bell.
Blue rippled and soaked in the fire of blue.
The dried mouthbones of a shark in the hot swale
Gaped on nothing but sand on either side.

The bone tasted of nothing and smelled of nothing,
A scalded toothless harp, uncrushed, unstrung.
The joined arcs made the shape of birth and craving
And the welded-open shape kept mouthing O.

Ossified cords held the corners together
In groined spirals pleated like a summer dress.
But where was the limber grin, the gash of pleasure?
Infinitesimal mouths bore it away,

The beach scrubbed and etched and pickled it clean.
But O I love you it sings, my little my country
My food my parent my child I want you my own
My flower my fin my life my lightness my O.

❧ ☙

LINDA PASTAN

Wildflowers

You gave me dandelions.
They took our lawn

by squatters' rights—
round suns rising
in April, soft moons
blowing away in June.
You gave me lady slippers,
bloodroot, milkweed,
trillium whose secret number
the children you gave me
tell. In the hierarchy
of flowers, the wild
rise on their stems
for naming.
Call them weeds.
I pick them as I
picked you,
for their fierce,
unruly joy.

Late Love Songs

I. CLERESTORY

Because, like the sun,
happiness can blind
when stared at
with the naked eye,
I have learned
to avert my face
partway

from certain
pleasures. They flood
the body anyhow,
as sunlight floods
our clerestory window
this morning, and lights
the entire room.

2. MARCH HAIKU

White petals, not snow,
fall improbably down on
our winter picnic.

3. FLOODPLAIN

In this strange spring—
cherry and dogwood blossoms overlapped
for the first time, forsythia
like electric lights left on too long—
I am as overwrought as the colors
in this garden, a floodplain
of feeling after the long rains
of April, the hours of weeping
over nothing, as the trout lilies
with their spotted, oval leaves
take hold everywhere.

4. ENVOI

In this brief space I try
to say goodbye, sitting
at your empty desk where,
if forty years have made us
one flesh, your pen
will recognize my hand
as my hand knows the touch
of yours in dark theaters,
in all the dark places.

꿏 ꙫ

DAVID WAGONER

At the Mouth of a Creek

This creek, as old as rain, flows past our fire
And, after a riffle and a broadening rush

On a spillway of gray-green stones, enters a river.
Evening without clouds under the hemlocks,
And the level sun is winnowing around us
In stems and stalks a thicket of gold light.
I've watched you stare at the incessantly
Changeable downheaval of a current
Ending as it began. Though it may alter
Quick moment by still moment like your eyes,
It stays translucent down to its wild bed.

Love, it was always you who brought me here,
Who came here with me, though I seemed alone,
Who stayed with me as the osprey turned above us
And we called the salmon home and the wren whispered
The almost silent song no one may hear
Without a change of mind, and it was you
Who burned with me that hour in the melting snow.
You had no name at first, no face, no voice,
But you became yourself in the real air
Beside me as our coupled imaginations,
Transfixed by the play of light, discovered us.

I've come to the creek's mouth and found you again.
Always before, my raw-edged restlessness
Took us away too soon. So let's lie down
And fill the night with our two shuddering hearts.
We have in us the same dust as these stones
Covered with golden algae and water moss
Like *dura mater.* The scattering of ashes
After our fire may bring us morning knowledge
At last to light our frail, permanent love.

A Woman Photographing Holsteins

Her slender body moves among the herd
On the grassy dike as surely as the sun
Goes down, as slowly
As they themselves can move one hoof at a time.

Their level spines are taller than she is,
Each flank a different country,
Islands of milk at nightfall, black-and-white
Deliberations of complete fulfillment.

She steps around the high gates of their thighs.
Their ears swivel,
And she takes in their deeply, broodingly
Contemplative profiles staring straight at her.

One bolts, but stops, having forgotten why.
The dewlap quivers. The veins
Of the udder pulse. As round, as large as her lens,
The eyes turn to the salt marsh and the sea.

She follows, kneels to focus, and with the gaze
Of the goddesses of meadows
The two of them wait there in the last of the light,
A horned moon rising. Then she rises too
And, smiling, comes my way, led by her shadow
Into my arms. We hum as if in clover.

🙶 🙷

LONNIE BALABAN

The Poet's Wife Sends Him a Poem

Snow piles up these lonely nights.
This winter you are gone.
Knee-deep, February drifts choke
the railroad bed we walked in summer
edged by daisies and black-eyed susans.

From the woods Rangers drag out deer.
Ribs poke through their rusty coats.
The Rangers say "no forage." Too much snow.
The coldest winter in our century.

Fitting that we should be apart.
Powerful winds and hibernation of the soul.
Like the deer pawing for bark, I peel away
the crust of my own heart, pumping these days
in a white expanse, frozen every dawn,
as snow falls where we walked together.

❧ ☙

JOHN BALABAN

His Reply

> *Sweetest love, I do not go*
> *For weariness of thee. . . .*
>
>   —John Donne

Let's say that I was called away
summoned by a voice I heard first as a boy
when belly down on the cool bank
I looked in the wrinkling water
at skeeters sculling tiny oars,
at a crayfish wading through willow roots
unraveling under clear ripples.
I was so still a woodthrush supped beside me.
So quiet, I dwelt with spotted newts.

"Come" is all that voice has ever said,
wet with ferns and mossy logs
with catbird cry and frog croak.
And when I followed I was always happy
reading delight in signatures of fish,
in moth glyphs scribbled beneath elm bark,
even though lonely; as now, for you.

What calls me away shall call me home.
I knew your voice before we met.
These journeys out, are journeys back.
Let's say my travels tend towards you.

LOUIS SIMPSON

Birch

Birch tree, you remind me
Of a room filled with breathing,
The sway and whisper of love.

She slips off her shoes;
Unzips her skirt; arms raised,
Unclasps an earring, and the other.

Just so the sallow trunk
Divides, and the branches
Are pale and smooth.

Dvonya

In the town of Odessa
there is a garden
and Dvonya is there,
Dvonya whom I love
though I have never been in Odessa.

I love her black hair, and eyes
as green as a salad
that you gather in August
between the roots of alder,
her skin with an odor of wildflowers.

We understand each other perfectly.
We are cousins twice removed.
In the garden we drink our tea,
discussing the plays of Chekhov
as evening falls and the lights begin to twinkle.

But this is only a dream.
I am not there
with my citified speech,
and the old woman is not there
peering between the curtains.

We are only phantoms, bits of ash,
like yesterday's newspaper
or the smoke of chimneys.
All that passed long ago
on a summer night in Odessa.

❧ ❧

JOHN HOLLANDER

Heat of Snow

> *Anne par jeu me jecta de la neige*
>
> —Clément Marot

When she, laughing, plastered a snowball on me,
all the crisp, white, sherbety cold we both were
waiting for seemed suddenly to have melted;
      somehow, her shoulders

fell against my own as the thing hit both of
us at once, and then as we fell together
on the high, soft drift that the sun made bright we
      burned, oh we burned, but

not because such sunlight was any warmer
than the glaring ice on the pond beyond us,
forcing us to squint as we sat and shivered
      later together

when we thought how even inside the snow there
blazed such warmth; how nothing was colder now than
our informing flame; and, if ice perhaps might
      cool it a little,

then how painful, blinding, the prospect toward the
shimmering pond where, lifeless, the ice awaited
first our shielded gaze, then our tired march and
                    final arrival.

White Above Green

High on this whitest place,
Towering into the wild,
Green wind in which we turn,
Our eyes burn. Your face
Is a wide mind—my own—
With mild hair blown
Over the sky your eyes
Turn to, while mine trace
Descents of towers lower
Than ours: plunged, yearning
For shaded lawns (those mild
Green minds no winds burn)
Turning slowly below
The blowing on our windy heights.

Minds are whitened, our hands
Grown even now in green
Confusions among wild,
Shaded places: as if sand
From a wide, far, white beach
Lying like a felled tower
Among green dunes, blowing
Into our widening eyes
Burned not at all, but turned
Our tongues to grass, our minds
To fiery, white unknowns
While our wide hearts, our whirling
Hearts, confused, were burning.

Wide, wide are the high places!

PHYLLIS JANOWITZ

Fisherman's Wife

By the side of the lake where last summer
the drowned man was hooked, the lilacs,

pale silver, filigreed, weighted
with perfume, tremble without concern.
In their rented bungalows the lake

dwellers, equally indifferent
wait for warmer weather, the drowning
forgotten that last summer supplied

a suitable object for the passion
no one would admit to. Not I—not you.
Blue lake, two people, the air blurred

between them. Sinkers tied like bells,
wrists and ankles, sinkers around
my waist. I was not alone

when I prepared for the sounding
and not alone when I went under.
They pulled up one, they pulled up two

stone blue, wound with fish-line and reeds.
I coughed and shook the water from
my ears, painted two bloody moons

on my cheeks—you, gasping, a great
blotchy fish, wanted only to stay
at the bottom, steeped in that brackish

pond, me, hooked in your arms, sun snaking
the surface, no shadows between us.

Reunion with Jake at Still Pond Creek

We are becoming martyrs to our spirits,
you and I. Every time I see you,
you are thinner, listless, eating less.
You have given up breakfast and dinner,
sometimes indulging in a lettuce leaf
at noon. I know you aim to disappear.
What we both want is sensation without
shame or fear. And now I am bored
by sex, washing my hair, my clothes,
the bathroom scarred with drying underwear.
The time a body takes. The waste. Forests
of Kleenex. Six ibis for an acre of grain.
The pull of gravity shrinking us, drying
out the tissues of the brain. Bodiless
we could go anywhere. For how could we
transgress? To fly with no fear of falling,
no planes, schedules; no one inspecting our
baggage, dirty socks spilling from plastic
sacks, condoms, Tampax, the ungraceful
reminders our bodies insist on. I'm afraid
this flesh will always be too solid for us,
Jake. Your cigarettes reveal that. I take
up smoking when we are together. We eye
each other through the clouds we make.

NICHOLAS CHRISTOPHER

Rice Wine

From a long bottle with a curved neck
she poured it on her feet when we began
our journey on the white road to the sea,

past the broken statues of horses lining the fields,
their eye sockets brimming with starlight
that slid like tears down their cheeks.

No one had told us how far we had to travel.
Or warned us about the hazards of that country:
crows with human voices that continued

our conversation when we lapsed into silence;
trees without roots that followed in our wake;
stones warm as blood that pulsed in our hands;

fire-colored vines that hissed to life
when the rain fell, and mountains so steep
the boulders tumbled down their faces night and day.

And then there were the muddy rivers
that snaked back on themselves,
so in a single week we might ford the same one

a dozen times, always finding the current faster
and the bank more slippery, until finally we arrived
at our destination, overhanging the sea on crumbling terraces:

a city busy with people and animals we never saw;
with a single stone building that had reproduced
itself millions of times along an enormous grid;

with parks whose concentric paths never connected,
and streets of powdered stone that flickered like canals;
a city in which we had anticipated slaking our thirst

only to be told the wells were dry;
from which we had hoped to embark by ship
until we found it possessed no harbor;

a city filled with vacant hotels where only by bribing
a string of clerks could we secure a room,
without a bed, or even glass in the windows,

where, at nightfall, while moonlight rushed
from the gutters, we heard those crows
complete the conversation we had long ago abandoned.

Then she poured us each a tumbler of rice wine
from that same bottle we had carried
with us all those months but never touched,

and in the darkness across the sea
like a match head a distant point flared to life:
a place we would never reach now,

where our names were being recorded
in a burning ledger and our images etched—
with terrible precision—in sand ground from mirrors.

Sleep

for Constance

In this blue room, behind salt-streaked shutters, my wife sleeps,
the corner of the pillowcase beside her lips fluttering.
A spider is suspended from the ceiling fan,
and on the beach storm winds are lashing the breakers.

Today a cluster of black birds alighted, squawking, in a tree
dotted with red flowers beneath which I was sleeping.

Close by, the waves were sliding in through sheets of light,
and in the clouds a blue room appeared, identical to this room
in which I wind my way to sleep each night watching that spider spin.

Over the coast of this island, far from any continent, Antares,
the red star at the heart of Scorpio, is glowing brightly.

At dawn my wife will tell me how she saw that star from out at sea,
like a drop of blood in the night sky, as she tried to steady
her tossing skiff and return to shore, where loud birds
filled a solitary tree beside which I stood, waving her in.

DIANE ACKERMAN

Beija-Flor
     (Hummingbird)

When you kiss me, moths flutter in my mouth;
when you kiss me, leaf-cutting ants lift up
their small burdens and carry them along
corridors of scent; when you kiss me,
caymans slither down wet banks in moonlight,
jaws yawning open, eyes bright red lasers;
when you kiss me, my tiny fist conceals
the bleached skull of a sloth; when you kiss me,
the waters wed in my ribs, dark and pale
rivers exchange their potions—she gives him
love's power, he gives her love's lure;
when you kiss me, my heart, surfacing, steals
a small breath like a pink river dolphin;
when you kiss me, the rain falls thick as rubber,
sunset pours molasses down my spine
and, in my hips, the green wings of the jungle flutter;
when you kiss me, blooms explode like land mines
in trees loud with monkey muttering
and the kazooistry of birds; when you kiss me,
my flesh sambas like an iguana; when you kiss me,
the river-mirror reflects an unknown land,
eyes glitter in the foliage, ships pass
like traveling miracle plays, and coca sets
brush fires in my veins; when you kiss me,
the river wraps its wet thighs around a bend;
when you kiss me, my tongue unfolds its wings
and flies through shadows as a leaf-nosed bat,
a ventriloquist of the twilight shore
which hurls its voice against the tender world
and aches to hear its echo rushing back;
when you kiss me, anthuria send up
small telescopes, the vine-clad trees wear
pantaloons, a reasonably evitable moon

rises among a signature of clouds,
the sky fills with the pandemonium
of swamp monkeys, the aerial slither
and looping confetti of butterflies;
when you kiss me, time's caravan pauses
to sip from the rich tropic of the heart,
find shade in the oasis of a touch,
bathe in Nature carnal, mute and radiant;
you find me there trembling and overawed;
for, when you kiss me, I become the all
you love: a peddler on your luminous river,
whose salted-fish are words, daughter
of a dolphin; when you kiss me, I smell
of night-blooming orchids; when you kiss me,
my mouth softens into scarlet feathers—
an ibis with curved bill and small dark smile;
when you kiss me, jaguars lope through my knees;
when you kiss me, my lips quiver like bronze
violets; oh, when you kiss me. . . .

Ode to the Alien

    Beast, I've known you
in all love's countries, in a baby's face
   knotted like walnut meat,
      in the crippled obbligato
   of a polio-stricken friend,
in my father's eyes
   pouchy as two marsupials,
      in the grizzly radiance
of a winter sunset, in my lover's arm
   veined like the Blue Ridge Mountains.
To me, you are beautiful
      until proven ugly.

    Anyway, I'm no cosmic royalty
either, but a bastard of matter
   descended from countless rapes

and invasions
of cell upon cell upon cell.
I crawled out of slime;
I swung through the jungles
of Madagascar;
I drew wildebeest on the caves at Lascaux;
I lived a grim life
hunting peccary and maize
in some godforsaken mudhole in the veldt.

I may squeal
from the pointy terror of a wasp,
or shun the breezy rhetoric
of a fire;
but, whatever your form, gait, or healing,
you are no beast to me,
I who am less than a heart-flutter
from the brute,
I who have been beastly so long.
Like me, you are that pool
of quicksilver in the mist,
fluid, shimmery, fleeing, called life.

And life, full of pratfall and poise,
life where a bit of frost
one morning can turn barbed wire
into a string of stars,
life aromatic with red-hot pizazz
drumming ha-cha-cha
through every blurt, nub, sag,
pang, twitch, war, bloom of it,
life as unlikely as a pelican, or a thunderclap,
life's our tour of duty
on our far-flung planets,
our cage, our dole, our reverie.

Have you arts?
Do waves dash over your brain
like tide along a rocky coast?
Does your moon slide

into the night's back pocket,
    just full when it begins to wane,
and all joy seems interim?
    Are you flummoxed by that millpond,
deep within the atom, rippling out to every star?
    Even if your blood is quarried,
I pray you well,
    and hope my prayer your tonic.

    I sit at my desk now
        like a tiny proprietor,
a cottage industry in every cell.
    Diversity is my middle name.
My blood runs laps;
    I doubt yours does,
        but we share an abstract fever
            called thought,
    a common swelter of a sun.
So, Beast, pause a moment,
        you are welcome here.
    I am life, and life loves life.

Zoë

Ultimate immigrant,
who passed through the Ellis Island
of your mother's hips,
with a name slit loose
from its dialect of cell and bone:
welcome to the citadel of our lives.
We listened for the hoofbeats
(your heart) for nine months
and then your mother nearly died,
hospitably, to give you light.

Like an Hawaiian princess,
you are carried everywhere,
on a litter, in a carriage,
by the arabesque of one's arm.

Your feet have never touched ground.
You, who can't even roll over
when you want, creamy little tyrant,
control the lives of all around you.

Sound leaps from your face
and your ribs quake
each time the downy world chafes.
Last week, you first smiled
because grownups acted silly.
Things elude you, but you can grasp
absurdity already.

By mistake, you suck your wrist
instead of Mother's nipple.
We laugh. With your operatic cries,
and Michelin-man pudge,
and seepages from below.
and eyes alert as twin deer,
you have no sense of self whatever.

Zoë Klein, goddaughter
with a hybrid name,
living in the soft new crook
of your mother's arm,
with a face like a Dalai Lama's
or a small Neanderthal's,
born out of a dream by two,
you live a dream by halves now:
slumbrous, milky-breathed.

In time, love will answer questions
you didn't raise. A belled marvel,
the cat of your inquiry, will stalk
through a world brighter
and more plural than you guess,
where a baby's fingerprints,
loopy weather systems, one for each tip,
will leave you spellbound

that matter could come to this.

ROBERT BLY

Listening to the Köln Concert

After we had loved each other intently,
we heard notes tumbling together,
in late winter, and we heard ice
falling from the ends of twigs.

The notes abandon so much as they move.
They are the food not eaten, the comfort
not taken, the lies not spoken.
The music is my attention to you.

And when the music came again,
later in the day, I saw tears in your eyes.
I saw you turn your face away
so that the others would not see.

When men and women come together,
how much they have to abandon! Wrens
make their nests of fancy threads
and string ends, animals

abandon all their money each year.
What is that men and women leave?
Harder than wrens' doing, they have
to abandon their longing for the perfect.

The inner nest not made by instinct
will never be quite round,
and each has to enter the nest
made by the other imperfect bird.

A Third Body

A man and a woman sit near each other, and they do not long
at this moment to be older, or younger, nor born

in any other nation, or time, or place.
They are content to be where they are, talking or not-talking.
Their breaths together feed someone whom we do not know.
The man sees the way his fingers move;
he sees her hands close around a book she hands to him.
They obey a third body that they share in common.
They have made a promise to love that body.
Age may come, parting may come, death will come.
A man and a woman sit near each other;
as they breathe they feed someone we do not know,
someone we know of, whom we have never seen.

ERICA JONG

Sentient

Awake at four
with the old brain beating
its fast tatoo—
I want, I want—
I think of love,
of the hot scramble
of limbs in darkness;

of the mind
pulsing its secrets
in metaphor;
of synapses firing
need, longing, love;
of the body
with its midnight hungers;

of the mind
caught between dream and waking,
wondering what it is,
self-creating always;

of god,
whatever *she* is
asking the questions:
who are you anyway
and *how did you get here*
and *what is the distance*
between two stars,
between two brain cells.
between two lovers

here in the rosy
pink-ringed dark
when all the birds—
sentient in their own way
as we—
are on the verge
of wakefulness
and song.

We Learned

>   *the decorum of fire . . .*

>   —Pablo Neruda

We learned the decorum of fire,
the flame's curious symmetry,
the blue heat at the center of the thighs,
the flickering red of the hips,
& the tallow gold of the breasts
lit from within
by the lantern in the ribs.

You tear yourself out of me
like a branch that longs to be grafted
onto a fruit tree,
peach & pear

crossed with each other,
fig & banana served on one plate,
the leaf & the luminous snail
that clings to it.

We learned that the tearing
could be a joining,
that the fire's flickering
could be a kindling,
that the old decorum of love—
to die into the poem,
leaving the lover lonely with her pen—
was all an ancient lie.

So we banished the evil eye:
you have to be unhappy to create;
you have to let love die before it writes;
you have to lose the joy to have the poem—
& we re-wrote our lives with fire.

See this manuscript covered
with flesh-colored words?
It was written in invisible ink
& held up to our flame.

The words darkened on the page
as we sank into each other.

We are ink & blood
& all things that make stains.
We turn each other golden as we turn,
browning each other's skins like suns.

Hold me up to the light;
you will see poems.

Hold me in the dark;
you will see light.

WILLIAM MATTHEWS

Cooking for C.

For her candor, salt.
For her independence,
oil and water not mixing.

For her scepticism I have pried
from each of forty shrimp a blue
filament of shrimpshit.

To honor her spry laugh
and light-giving smile,
I have taken a luridly purple
and cello-shaped eggplant
and diced it and simmered it
in broth with Vidalia onions
and turmeric and cumin and ground
coriander seeds for a cold cream soup.

Because the days are long and hot
and her schedule is clamorous,
I have made her a salad of couscous
and mint and plum tomatoes and olive oil.

For the daily gift of her intelligence,
a wand of bread, a fresh baguette.

For her hungers, food.
For her company, pleased thanks.

The Cloister

The last light of a July evening drained
into the streets below. My love and I had hard
things to say and hear and we sat over
wine, faltering, picking our words carefully.

The afternoon before I had lain across
my bed and my cat leapt up to lie
alongside me, purring and slowly
growing dozey. By this ritual I can

clear some clutter from my baroque brain.
And into that brief vacancy the image
of a horse cantered, coming straight to me,
and I knew it brought hard talk and hurt

and fear. How did we do? A medium job,
which is well above average. But because
she had opened her heart to me as far
as she did, I saw her fierce privacy,

like a gnarled, luxuriant tree all hung
with disappointments, and I knew
that to love her I must love the tree
and the nothing it cares for me.

❧ ☙

JOYCE CAROL OATES

Public Love

Listen, they are applauding.
The tops of their skulls—
cautious half-dollar-sized holes—
are showing through the earth.
The worm-fine soil about them
is agitated; we are doing well.

My love, we are on exhibit.
There is nothing private
in the senses.
Falling upon me you make me delicate,
a universal woman!
Others have done these things before.

A man like you has fallen
in an avalanche of love upon me
or upon someone like me.
Others have done these things before.
Most of them are now dead.

We rise suddenly as if called by name,
we have only been playing dead.
Where are our names? Who has seen us?
We are fine-grained and sweet and mild
now as apples, innocent of our bodies.

I think it is all those dead
lives in you I love,
dead men grown to roots
solid and loving in the earth,
holding down a new universe.
All the good husbands!
There is nothing deadly in their deaths.
Their golf-ball-sized eyes admire us.
We are loving in pantomime.

You / Your

you must be imagining walls:
my arms brush against them

your eyes are small hazy suns
        with the look of being blind
drawing me up to
day

if you were to turn me lightly
        inside out
I would become the fixed center
of the famous universe

CAROLYN KIZER

The Light

To wake embedded in warm weight of limbs
Never till now so wholly in repose,
Then to detach your body, strand by strand
From his; but slumbering, murmurous a moment
He confidently drowns again. His arms
Gather you closer, stirring to take leave,
The birds' hushed rapture ushering the dawn.
But hesitate before you break his bonds:

Suspend this moment, see beyond the hour
His form, so tenderly alone and calm,
Yet clinging to that sensual catacomb
Where we embrace eternally in last night.
You rational marvel! As if will were all,
As if this image could be kept or doomed
By what you choose. While still he hems you round
His closed eye holds you faster than your sight.

The Gift

Gift of another day!
To hold in velvet glove
This heavy force of love,
Of you alive in me.

Gift of another noon,
Its crest of tenderness:
In touching we converse,
Thrill in our joy-spent bones.

Gift, as the light declines
Of her reviving powers.
You drench me in new wines.
I fill my hands with flowers.

Gift of another moon,
The perfect O of love
For your single arrow, bowman,
Feather and shaft and eye,

Before we are drawn away
Back into the cold
Scald of the world again
Let us rest, hold, stay.

❧ ❧

Rod Jellema

Because I Never Learned the Names of Flowers

it is moonlight and white where
I slink away from my cat-quiet blue rubber truck
and motion myself to back it up to your ear.
I peel back the doors of the van and begin
to hushload into your sleep
the whole damn botanical cargo of Spring.

Sleeper, I whisk you
Trivia and Illium, Sweet Peristalsis, Flowering Delirium.

Sprigs of Purple Persiflage and Lovers' Leap, slips
of Hysteria stick in my hair. I gather clumps of Timex,
handfuls of Buttertongues, Belly buttons, and Bluelets.

I come with Trailing Nebula, I come with Late-Blooming
Paradox, with Creeping Pyromania, Pink Apoplex,
and Climbing Solar Plexis,

whispering: Needlenose,
Juice Cup, Godstem, Nexus, Sex-us, Condominium.

Note to Marina Marquez of El Paso, Who Sublet My Apartment for the Summer

We miss each other by just an eyelash.
We never met, and yet this place
is still your home before it drifts back home
to being mine. The shelf that's empty
of scotch keeps the smoke of tequilla,
a Flamenco album sidles up to Mahler's Eighth.
I surprised the tortillas and hot chili peppers
you left in our freezer
as I put in a bag of potatoes.

I tiptoe when thinking the hairpin under the bed.
This morning in the shower, my third day back,
through steam I noticed again
the gleam of a single dark pubic hair.
Sometimes I listen hard, At night
in the vaguely foreign country of my bed
I lie very still, I breathe it deep.
I write you nowhere, afraid you will
startle away too soon if I dare to tell you
I miss you and wish you would stay.

ALBERT GOLDBARTH

Seriema Song

The flamingo delouses its belly with the easy speed
of a power lawn trimmer. The osprey; the emu; the kiwi. . . .
In a glass-paned cage labeled *Toucan / Lemur,*
two new arrivals—red-legged seriema, says a docent—
stalk their confines, querulous and
frantic. One jabs adamantly at a strew of mulch
and feather-molt over the damp ground, and the other,
with a fierce determination better sized to the gorilla

than this shin-high bristled bird, uptussles
a fake plant from its anchorage and then
using its beak as a pliers and hammerclaw, single-mindedly
labors until it frees a formerly-hidden square
of wire screen—a jailbreak, we think, then see
the seriema repeatedly lift the mesh in its beak
and slam it at the ground, again, again, a motion
something like the beating of a fire with a blanket,
and we realize they're attempting to build a nest
in this alien habitat, the seriema expects
this scarf-large square of screen to break apart
eventually into useable shreds. Again. Again.
Each swing and its connection jolts the bird
like live electrodes. Again. The goddam wire screen.
Again. We leave to watch the August heat
curl up inside the lioness's yawn, then turn
to blue lace over the seals' pool, then stand
foursquare to meet the rhino's
lumbrous run head-on. When we return
the bird's still fighting the wire screen.
That night you turn to me: "I bet
it's *still* beating that screen at the ground."
Lifting it overhead like a professional wrestler
raising an opponent and whomping him
onto the mat. We laugh. We sleep
and the seriema's hitting the screen at the ground.
We wake, we quarrel, and that stupid,
faithful bird is hitting the screen at the ground.
We strive to make the marriage work. We stray
but return to the job of keeping its seams together,
rivet, needle-and-thread. We sweat
and the seriema rises and falls like an oil-well pump,
we dream, we fling ourselves against our dreams,
and the seriema's not done. We lift our fists
to God against the background of that bird. We
watch the news, and sleeplessly turn in the pit
of the news, and enter another day of effort
and salary, effort and the tiny painful
glitches in our friendships, effort and upkeep,
a day made of patchwork and glues, and the bird

is whipping its wire screen against the planet, tireless,
sapbrained, necessary bird, we fret
and it's still at its toil, we soften the abrasive
grain of our love, and it's still at its passionate
task, we're ageing and the seriema, the universe
and the seriema, the face in the mirror,
it's night, its velvet covering us again
and that bird.

The Two Parts of the Day Are,

first: I'm driving home when BOOMER cuts me off
with a tidily-clipped illegal left at Central & Oliver.
The Age of Lizards, the Age of Mammals, and now the Age
of Vanity Plates. AGNESJ appears from out of a cloud
of briquette-gray exhaust, and GRANNY, and KSSMYA.
A blonde woman in a t-shirt proclaiming her NATE'S
is piling her car trunk with monogrammed luggage, E;
her keychain flashes out DICK. It's depressing. And

second: Skyler greets me with the news that north
on Woodward, someone rode around the blocks this morning
shooting down people at random—pedestrians,
other drivers, nine in all who won't be coming home today
or ever. He was found with a bomb, an axe, and a beheaded
goose in his back seat. Nine people. Now they're just
the names being grieved in a few raw throats in this city;
on this planet; through the flux called Outer Space. The third

part of the day isn't day at all. It's night; and everywhere,
in the least of its creakings and beetle-jaws,
in the infinite zip of lepton and of quark
through what we like to think is "sky" but is burning and
emptiness, emptiness and burning . . . the night is saying
itself, in its language. I can't sleep. The moon makes silver
lace of my wife's unsheeted shoulder. And: SKYLER, I'm
whispering suddenly, like a 15-year-old at the fresh cement

—at the air, at the dark, at the thin lunar light,
at whatever of this world might read me.

❧ ❧

PATTIANN ROGERS

Love Song

It's all right, together with me tonight,
How your whole body trembles exactly like the locust
Establishing its dry-cymbal quivering
Even in the farthest branch-tip leaves
Of the tree in which it screams.

Lying next to me, it's all right how similar
You become to the red deer in its agitated pacing
On the open plains by the sea, in its sidling
Haunch against haunch, in the final mastery
of its mounting.

And it's all right, in those moments,
How you possess the same single-minded madness
of the opened wood poppy circling and circling,
The same wild strength of its golden eye.

It's true. You're no better
Than the determined boar snorgling and rooting,
No better than the ridiculous, ruffled drumming
Of the prairie chicken, no better
Than the explosion of the milkweed pod
Spilling the white furl of the moon deep
In the midnight field. You're completely
Indistinguishable from the enraged sand myrtle
Absurd in its scarlet spread on the rocky bluffs.

But it's all right. Don't you know
This is precisely what I seek, mad myself
To envelop every last drupe and pearl-dropped ovule,

Every nip and cry and needle-fine boring, every drooping,
Spore-rich tassel of oak flower, all the whistling,
Wing-beating, heavy-tipped matings of an entire prairie
Of grasses, every wafted, moaning seed hook
You can possibly manage to bring to me,
That this is exactly what I contrive to take into my arms
With you, again and again.

The Hummingbird: A Seduction

If I were a female hummingbird perched still
And quiet on an upper myrtle branch
In the spring afternoon and if you were a male
Alone in the whole heavens before me, having parted
Yourself, for me, from cedar top and honeysuckle stem
And earth down, your body hovering in midair
Far away from jewelweed, thistle and bee balm;

And if I watched how you fell, plummeting before me,
And how you rose again and fell, with such mastery
That I believed for a moment *you* were the sky
And the red-marked bird diving inside your circumference
Was just the physical revelation of the light's
Most perfect desire;

And if I saw your sweeping and sucking
Performance of swirling egg and semen in the air,
The weaving, twisting vision of red petal
And nectar and soaring rump, the rush of your wing
In its grand confusion of arcing and splitting
Created completely out of nothing just for me,

Then when you came down to me, I would call you
My own spinning bloom of ruby sage, my funnelling
Storm of sunlit sperm and pollen, my only breathless
Piece of scarlet sky, and I would bless the base
Of each of your feathers and touch the tine
Of string muscles binding your wings and taste
The odor of your glistening oils and hunt

The honey in your crimson flare
And I would take you and take you and take you
Deep into any kind of nest you ever wanted.

❧ ☙

MARVIN BELL

The Last Thing I Say

to a thirteen-year-old sleeping,
tone of an angel, breath of a soft wing,
I say through an upright dark space
as I narrow it pulling the door
sleepily to let the words go surely into
the bedroom until I close them in
for good, a nightwatchman's-worth
of grace and a promise for morning
not so far from some God's first notion
that the world be an image by first light
so much better than pictures of hope
drawn by firelight in ashes,
so much clearer too, a young person
wanting to be a man might draw one finger
along an edge of this world and it
would slice a mouth there
to speak blood and then should he put that wound
into the mouth of his face,
he will be kissed there and taste
the salt of his father as he lowers
himself from his son's high bedroom
in the heaven of his image of
a small part of himself and sweet dreams.

Sounds of the Resurrected Dead Man's Footsteps #9

1. BRACELET, THIMBLE AND HOOF

I'll give myself an hour, I said, and then it was over.
Or a minute, I said, to think.

It was already too late.
I had my Bacchanalian hoof in my mouth.
I had ten thimbles for fingers, clams for hands, you know the way they
    say it.
They say, He was all thumbs, and heck yes.
Middle of summer, patch of snow—inside me, I mean.
Can't see the summer for the snow, they say.
Was I wearing a bracelet or handcuffs, I can't remember.
I could feel the ground reshaping itself under my feet.

2. SOUP, TOAST AND ELBOW

I married my shy mistress, the one who made two eggs, bacon and
    toast.
No bull, thirty-six years now.
I opened many a sticky door with my elbow, my hip and my noggin.
I made alphabet soup of whatever I tried to say.
She was the one whose ego couldn't be held hostage, not for a minute.
She slowed down the earth so I could regain my footing.
We have dined on soup and toast, and often I lean on my elbow
    philosophically, but it's really to keep my mouth shut.
She takes me to see the stars and the lightning.
She can sit for hours watching the fireflies showing off in the dark.

ROALD HOFFMANN

How It Grows

Where the creek bed turns
the paired redwoods' roots
lift rock, surface inter-
twined to wrestle each
other back underground.
Sloughing off big brown
slates of bark, seedlings
given to the wind, they've

long shared this wet earth.
Look up, love, look to
all that up-thrust, which
couldn't rise, and wouldn't
withstand the wind, but
for these twisted roots
hard-won common ground.

❧ ☙

GERALD STERN

Both of Them Were Sixty-five

ordinarily I wouldn't be introducing Aaron Copland to Ida Stern
nor be there to watch him bow ever so slightly
and appreciate her beauty—in spite of things—and see
him take in her white powder and her heavy rouge.

nor see her in her girlish role, a little bit
haughty, maybe a little flirtatious, her wisdom
something else from what I knew, a kind of
pact between them—in spite of things—and during

the second part I wouldn't have half leaned back
in those rocking theatre chairs and smile my smile
as I did then at my newly discovered mother
nor listen, as it were, almost for the first time

to his pure sounds, and watch her listen, and smile
her victory smile—in spite of things—nor see them
pass beside each other and see him bow
again, so skinny beside her, he who wore

white knickers in 1925 and grey
ribbed socks. If he were in Pittsburgh in 1920
they could have danced together after the basketball
and eaten later at Dan Givanni's and talked

for an hour or two on Vine Street, Beryl listening
with one eye open, a blue, and made some plan,
in spite of things, for another Friday of Saturday,
and he would have smiled at her music, though most respectfully,

especially the Caruso, and even listen
to the voice and the window rattling, one of my fathers
certainly, though Ida is dead, and Copland
never taught me stickball and never painted

quarter notes and eighth notes inside my crib
and never walked with her down Fifth Avenue
and through the arcade on Liberty and never
rented a room at the Roosevelt as I did

in 1948, and carry bricks
inside a suitcase for the room clerk's sake. I
was thirty-nine when they met and I was starting
to spread my gloom; she was with her powder

and her perfume hanging on to the nearer side,
as I am now. There would be a Greek ship captain,
a financier, a Turkish Jew, and a loving
hillbilly she met at the Moose, but none

would be like him, in spite of things, nor would there
be a spring like that one was, a bursting
you can't imagine, a marriage canopy shaking,
a fiddle to match, a fire—and candles—burning.

June First

for Abigail Thomas

Some blossoms are so white and luscious, when they
hold their long thin hands up you strip them for love
and scatter them on the ground as you walk;

and some birds look at you as if there were no
great line drawn between their lives and yours,
as if you drank together from the same cement;

and some pods spin in the wind as if you would not pick
them up gingerly to see if they had wings
and then would not break them open to see what made them
fall, to study their visceras.

I touch you as I would the sawdust in the eaves
or the crazy buttercups in the middle of the mulepath
or the frightening foil
jumping and leaping in front of the oily grackles;

and I touch you as I touch the grass, my body falls down on the
        ground
and I pull at the roots as I watch you in the limbs
bending down to avoid the red blossoms,
hiding in the leaves,
reaching up like the tallest dryad,
your curved arms and your jeweled fingers
waving slowly again in the hot sun.

❧ ☙

DONALD HALL

Weeds and Peonies

Your peonies burst out, white as snow squalls,
with red flecks at their shaggy centers,
in your border of prodigies by the porch.
I carry one magnanimous blossom inside
to float in a glass bowl, as you used to do.

Ordinary happiness, remembered in sorrow,
blows like snow into the abandoned garden
overcoming the daisies. Your blue coat
vanishes down Pond Road into imagined snowflakes
with Gus at your side, his great tail swinging,

but you will not return, tired and satisfied,
and grief's repeated particles suffuse the air—
like the dog yipping through the entire night,
or the cat stretching awake, then curling
as if to dream of her mother's milky nipples.

A raccoon dislodges a geranium from its pot.
Flowers, roots, and dirt lie upended
in the back garden, where lilies begin
their daily excursions above stone walls
in the season of old roses. I pace beside weeds

and snowy peonies, staring at Mount Kearsarge
where you climbed wearing purple hiking boots.
"Hurry back. Be careful, climbing down."
Your peonies lean their vast heads westward
as if they might topple. Some topple.

Gold

Pale gold of the walls, gold
of the centers of daisies, yellow roses
pressing from a clear bowl. All day
we lay on the bed, my hand
stroking the deep
gold of your thighs and your back.
We slept and woke
entering the golden room together,
lay down in it breathing
quickly, then
slowly again,
caressing and dozing, your hand sleepily
touching my hair now.

We made in those days
tiny identical rooms inside our bodies
which the men who uncover our graves
will find in a thousand years,
shining and whole.

RITA DOVE

His Shirt

does not show his
true colors. Ice-

blue and of stuff
so common

anyone
could have bought it,

his shirt
is known only

to me, and only
at certain times

of the day.
At dawn

it is a flag
in the middle

of a square
waiting to catch

chill light.
Unbuttoned, it's

a sail surprised
by boundless joy.

In candlelight at turns
a penitent's

scarf or beggar's
fleece, his shirt is

inapproachable.
It is the very shape

and tint
of desire

and could be mistaken
for something quite

fragile and
ordinary.

❧ ☙

JILL BIALOSKY

Without

Why does the woman lay her head so far
against her shoulder, why the still smile?
Her blouse only covers one of her breasts
and her plump arms are milky white.
Perhaps she has just made love, dressed,
and moved to the red chair after her lover
has left. Her hands are placed
over her crotch but it is not pain that draws
her face, or if so, pain cut small by pleasure.
In the hour after she held on to him the way
she must have been held as a young girl
before she had begun to bleed.
Already one side of her face is darkening.
Later she might cut her yellow hair.
She is without her lover and her father
is far away. Her face is the halves of a heart.

GARY SNYDER
Cross-Legg'd

> *for Carole*

Cross-legg'd under the low tent roof,
dim light, dinner done,

drinking tea. We live
in dry old west

lift shirts bare skin
lean   touch lips—

old touches.
Love made, poems, makyngs,

always new, same stuff
life after life,

as though Milarepa
four times built a tower of stone

like each time was the first.
Our love is mixed with

rocks and streams,
a heartbeat, a breath, a gaze

makes place in the dizzy eddy.
Living this old clear way

—a sizzle of ash and embers.
Scratchy breeze on the tent fly

one sip tea, hunch on bones,
We two be here   what comes.

DAVID IGNATOW

The Men You've Loved

The men you've loved are one man.
The women I've known are one woman:
I hold your hand and look
into your face with love, in peace.
We lie down together
and nothing matters
but making each of us
the first and the last.

The Principle

Make no mistake, you cannot take
my love without accepting my body,
and you cannot accept my body
without a claim to all that I am
and shall be always, that which
has determined me from the beginning,
in the branches of the rain,
in the blood of animals and trees.
As you take me in your arms,
you are making love to all the world
that I am.

JOHN GILL

6/16/94

I'm so ripe I could drop
from the Tree of Heaven
at the slightest breeze

Your warm breath in my ear
could do it

or my nipples lightly brushed
by your hand

to say nothing of moist kisses
and other soul-sinking delights
generating intensity unbearably . . .

until the roots heave and the Tree
keels over
kicking up dust and bringing
the World as we knew it
down with us.

❦ ❦

LOUISE GLÜCK

The White Lilies

As a man and woman make
a garden between them like
a bed of stars, here
they linger in the summer evening
and the evening turns
cold with their terror: it
could all end, it is capable
of devastation. All, all
can be lost, through scented air
the narrow columns
uselessly rising, and beyond,
a churning sea of poppies—

Hush, beloved. It doesn't matter to me
how many summers I live to return:
this one summer we have entered eternity.
I felt your two hands
bury me to release its splendor.

Happiness

A man and woman lie on a white bed.
It is morning. I think
Soon they will waken.
On the bedside table is a vase
of lilies; sunlight
pools in their throats.
I watch him turn to her
as though to speak her name
but silently, deep in her mouth—
At the window ledge,
once, twice,
a bird calls.
And then she stirs; her body
fills with his breath.

I open my eyes; you are watching me.
Almost over this room
the sun is gliding.
Look at your face, you say,
holding your own close to me
to make a mirror.
How calm you are. And the burning wheel
passes gently over us.

🙿🙽

DARA WIER

Dreamland

It's not really enough
to want and to believe
because you've said it:
these aren't the sturdy ribs of pigs
I'm eating, these are the ribs of flamingos.
The Gulf is rarely crystal blue,
it is the Gulf of Mexico,
full of oil and bananas, important

to shipping, balmy and warm.
Lay back your hungry ears,
be reckless as a sponge is.
There's a bucket and it's glass
on the bottom so you see
right where you're falling
the sauce is so sweet, maybe
too sweet you think
it's the kind of sauce
that loves to drench the meat.
Your desire is indefatigable,
it oils the pattern
of your white shirt's fabric.
It's impossible to stop yourself.
You want to rub the sauce
on your chest. You want to eat
your shirt in public.
You want to be able and careful,
you want to keep your balance
but there's someone sculling
the boat that's carrying you
and your bucket and waiting
for you is the entire
crew of Greek sailors
who are tired themselves
after so long without surprises,
nothing but the buckets and buckets
of the puzzles of science, more
valuable as they pass from hand
to hand, as their futures sharpen
like stakes driven up beyond the needs
and pleasures of the real living bodies
stacking up on the deck. The poor sailors
will have to stomp the living sauce
under their bare and beautiful feet.
Vulcan bathed with a sponge. Venus
must have touched that sponge
one sailor thinks
as he kicks up his feet
another sailor picks up the drift

and sails into the clear blue
Gulf air. The whole deck shines,
the ribs of the sailors
are the polished ribs
of flamingos in flight,
inexhaustible and light, durable,
light and inexhaustible.

Nude Descending a Staircase

We're made to
    exclude and be
        excluded. How much

    the cubists make
        that plain
presenting their plans

        for our omniscience,
our science of the everything-all-
        at-once.

        So this is why
    innocence isn't bliss
and even

    isn't ignorance even
but a kind
    of slight

insult—cold, delicious
    soup served up
        with silver forks

    on a wet, freezing evening.
        Though we remain
permeable,

not skintight,
not shutdown
　　and not set in stone.

Our eternal shopping lists
　　flap on
the breezy line, long

and thick, dirty with data,
　　lists of demographics
　　　　full

of the telephone ringing,
　　out of time
like a baby crying,

calming, calm
then startled
　　into more cries

that can't be calmed
　　by smooth talk
　　　　or sweet song

or the body's
　　longing answer,
come here to me, come here.

❧ ❧

JOHN ASHBERY

Just Walking Around

What name do I have for you?
Certainly there is no name for you
In the sense that the stars have names
That somehow fit them. Just walking around,

An object of curiosity to some,
But you are too preoccupied
By the secret smudge in the back of your soul
To say much, and wander around,

Smiling to yourself and others.
It gets to be kind of lonely
But at the same time off-putting,
Counterproductive, as you realize once again

That the longest way is the most efficient way,
The one that looped among islands, and
You always seemed to be traveling in a circle.
And now that the end is near

The segments of the trip swing open like an orange.
There is light in there, and mystery and food.
Come see it. Come not for me but it.
But if I am still there, grant that we may see each other.

A Blessing in Disguise

Yes, they are alive and can have those colors,
But I, in my soul, am alive too.
I feel I must sing and dance, to tell
Of this in a way, that knowing you may be drawn to me.

And I sing amid despair and isolation
Of the chance to know you, to sing of me
Which are you. You see,
You hold me up to the light in a way

I should never have expected, or suspected, perhaps
Because you always tell me I am you,
And right. The great spruces loom.
I am yours to die with, to desire.

I cannot ever think of me, I desire you
For a room in which the chairs ever
Have their backs turned to the light
Inflicted on the stones and paths, the real trees

That seem to shine at me through a lattice toward you.
If the wild light of this January day is true
I pledge me to be truthful unto you
Whom I cannot ever stop remembering.

Remembering to forgive. Remember to pass beyond you into the
        day
On the wings of the secret you will never know.
Taking me from myself, in the path
Which the pastel girth of the day has assigned to me.

I prefer "you" in the plural, I want "you,"
You must come to me all golden and pale
Like the dew and the air.
And then I start getting this feeling of exaltation.

꘎꘎

AGHA SHAHID ALI

Ghazal

for Hayden Carruth

The Belovéd will leave you behind from the start.
Light is difficult: one must be blind from the start.

You begin to feel better when the clocks are set back?
Child of northern darkness—so defined from the start.

Between two snow-heavy boughs, perhaps a bright star?
Or in one sparkling many stars combined from the start.

Solomon's throne was a toy, his Judgment mere talk—
Only our sins must be enshrined from the start.

Poet, tell me again how the white heron rises.
For the spirit, they say, is confined from the start.

To *What is mind?* we swiftly answer *O, no matter!*
Those who know matter never mind from the start.

Will the middle class give up its white devotions?
Feed their infants cayenne and tamarind from the start!

I am mere dust. The desert hides itself in me.
Against me the ocean has reclined from the start.

Who but Satan can know God's sorrow in heaven?
God longs for the lover He undermined from the start.

"But I / am here in this real life / that I was given. . . ."
To what else should we be resigned from the start?

You have dwelt at the root of a scream forever—
The Forever Shahid's countersigned from the start.

❧ ☙

JOSEPHINE JACOBSEN

The Edge

The edge? The edge is:
lie by the breath you cannot
do without; while
the breather sleeps.

Precious, subtle, that air
comes, goes, comes.
The heart propels it. It has
its thousands of hours, but

it will not last as long
as the sun, the moon's subservient
tides. It will stop, go back
to the great air's surround.

But now, subtle, precious,
regular as tide and sun
it moves in the warm body, lifts
the chest, says yes.

Listen to it, through the night.
If you wish to know the extent
to which you are vulnerable
only listen.

This is called the breath
of life. But it continues
saving your life
through the dark,

since this engine that drives your joy
is unrenounceable.
Listen, listen. Say, Love, love,
breathe so, breathe so.

The Wind in the Sunporch

The chinese windchimes
stir
suddenly thin glass rings on thin glass
great leaves
nod
sideways sideways petals stir
to let it pass
clang-cling it plays.

My ribs lift up and
fall

my parted lips could dance a feather
under my palms both
your shoulder-blades fall and
lift
together with that huge light breath.

It Is the Season

    when we learn
or do not learn
to say goodbye. . . .

The crone leaves that, as green
virgins, opened themselves
to sun, creak at our feet

and all farewells return
to crowd the air:
say, Chinese lovers by a bridge,

with crows and a waterfall;
he will cross
the bridge, the crows fly;

children who told each other
secrets, and will not speak
next summer.

Some speech of parting
mentions God, as in
a Dieu, Adios,

commending what cannot
be kept
to permanence.

There is nothing of north
unknown, as the dark
comes earlier. The birds

take their lives in their wings
for the cruel trip.
All farewells are rehearsals.

Darling, the sun rose
later today.
Summer, summer

is what we had.
Say nothing yet.
Prepare.

ESSAYS

A Father's Advice to His Daughter, from the Aztec Codices

Here you are, my little girl, my necklace of precious stones, my plumage, my human creation, born of me. You are my blood, my color, my image.

Now listen, understand. You are alive, you have been born; Our Lord, the Master of the Close and the Near, the maker of people, the inventor of men, has sent you to earth.

Now that you begin to look around you, be aware. Here it is like this: there is no happiness, no pleasure. There is heartache, worry, fatigue. Here spring up and grow suffering and distress.

Here on earth is the place of much wailing, the place where our strength is worn out, where we are well acquainted with bitterness and discouragement. A wind blows, sharp as obsidian it slides over us.

They say truly that we are burned by the force of the sun and the wind. This is the place where one almost perishes of thirst and hunger. This is the way it is here on earth.

Listen well, my child, my little girl. There is no place of well-being on the earth, there is no happiness, no pleasure. They say that the earth is the place of painful pleasure, of grievous happiness.

The elders have always said: "So that we should not go round always moaning, that we should not be filled with sadness, the Lord has given us laughter, sleep, food, our strength and fortitude, and finally the act of love."

All this sweetens life on earth so that we are not always moaning. But even though it be true that there is only suffering and this is the way things are on earth, even so, should we always be afraid? Should we always be fearful? Must we live weeping?

PLATO

from *Phaedrus*

"Everyone sees that love is a desire, and we know also that non-lovers desire the beautiful and good. Now in what way is the lover to be distinguished from the non-lover? Let us note that in every one of us there are two guiding and ruling principles which lead us whither they will; one is the natural desire of pleasure, the other is an acquired opinion which is in search of the best; and these two are sometimes in harmony and then again at war, and sometimes the one, sometimes the other conquers. When opinion conquers, and by the help of reason leads us to the best, the conquering principle is called temperance; but when desire, which is devoid of reason, rules in us and drags us to pleasure, that power of misrule is called excess. . . . Now to him who is not in his right senses that is agreeable which is not opposed to him, but that which is equal or superior is hateful to him, and therefore the lover will not brook any superiority or equality on the part of his beloved; he is always employed in reducing him to inferiority. And the ignorant is the inferior of the wise, the coward of the brave, the slow of speech of the speaker, the dull of the clever. These are the sort of natural and inherent defects in the mind of the beloved which enhance the delight of the lover, and there are acquired defects which he must produce in him, or he will be deprived of his fleeting joy. And therefore he can not help being jealous, and will debar him from the advantages of society which would make a man of him, and especially from that society which would make a man of him, and especially from that society which would have given him wisdom. That is to say, he will be compelled to banish from him divine philosophy, in his excessive fear lest he should come to be despised in his eyes; and there is no greater injury which he can inflict on him than this. Moreover, he will contrive that he shall be wholly ignorant, and in everything dependent on himself; he is to be the delight of his lover's heart, and a curse to himself. Verily, a lover is a profitable guardian and associate for him in all that relates to his mind.

* * *

Ten thousand years must elapse before the soul can return to the place from whence she came, for she can not grow her wings in less; only the soul of a philosopher, guileless and true, or the soul of a lover, who is not without philosophy, may acquire wings in the third recurring period of a thousand years: and if they choose this life three times in succession, then they have their wings given them, and go away at the end of three thousand years.

*   *   *

But of beauty, I repeat again that we saw her there shining in company with the celestial forms; and coming to earth we find her here too, shining in clearness through the clearest aperture of sense. For sight is the keenest of our bodily senses; though not by that is wisdom seen, for her loveliness would have been transporting if there had been a visible image of her, and this is true of the loveliness of the other ideas as well. But beauty only has this portion, that she is at once the loveliest and also the most apparent. Now he who has not been lately initiated or who has become corrupted, is not easily carried out of this world to the sight of absolute beauty in the other; he looks only at that which has the name of beauty in this world, and instead of being awed at the sight of her, like a brutish beast he rushes on to enjoy and beget; he takes wantonness to his bosom, and is not afraid or ashamed of pursuing pleasure in violation of nature. But he whose initiation is recent, and who has been the spectator of many glories in the other world, is amazed when he sees any one having a god-like face or form, which is the expression or imitation of divine beauty; and at first a shudder runs through him, and some "misgiving" of a former world steals over him; then looking upon the face of his beloved as of a god he reverences him, and if he were not afraid of being thought a downright madman, he would sacrifice to his beloved as to the image of a god; then as he gazes on him there is a sort of reaction, and the shudder naturally passes into an unusual heat and perspiration; for, as he receives the effluence of beauty through the eyes, the wing moistens and he warms. And as he warms, the parts out of which the wing grew, and which had been hitherto closed and rigid, and had prevented the wing from shooting forth are melted, and as nourishment streams upon him, the lower end of the wing begins to swell and grow from the root upwards, extending under the whole soul—for once the whole was winged. Now during this process the whole soul is in a state of effervescence and irritation, like the state of irritation and pain in the gums at the time of cutting teeth; in like manner the soul when beginning to grow wings has inflammation and pains and ticklings, and when looking at the beauty of youth she receives the sensible warm traction of particles which flow towards her, therefore called attraction (ιμεροζ), and is refreshed and warmed by them, and then she ceases from her pain with joy. But when she is separated and her moisture fails, then the orifices of the passages out of which the wing shoots dry up and close, and intercept the germ of the wing; which, being shut up within in company with desire, throbbing as with the pulsations of an artery, pricks the aperture which is nearest, until at length the entire soul is pierced and maddened and pained, and at the recollection of beauty is again delighted. And from both of them together the soul is oppressed at the strangeness of her condition, and is in a great strait and excitement, and in her madness can neither sleep by night nor abide in her place by day. And wherever she thinks that she will behold the beautiful one, thither in her desire she runs. And when she has seen him, and drunk rivers of desire, her constraint is loosened, and she is refreshed, and has no more pangs and pains; and this is the sweetest of all pleasures at the time, and is the reason why the soul of the lover never forsakes his beautiful one, whom he esteems above all; he has forgotten his mother and brethren and companions, and he thinks nothing of the neglect and loss of his property; and as to the rules and proprieties of life, on which he formerly prided himself, he now despises them, and is ready to sleep and serve, wherever he is allowed, as near as he can to his beautiful one who is not only the object of his worship, but the only physician who can heal him in his extreme agony. And this state, my dear imaginary youth, is by men called love, and among the gods has a name which you, in your simplicity, may be inclined to mock; there are two lines in honor of love in the Homeric Apocrypha in which the name occurs. One of them is rather outrageous, and is not quite metrical; they are as follow:—

> Mortals call him Eros (love),
> But the immortals call him Pteros (fluttering dove),
> Because fluttering of wings is a necessity to him.

You may believe this or not as you like. At any rate the loves of lovers and their causes are such as I have described.

＊　＊　＊

Now the lover who is the attendant of Zeus is better able to bear the winged god, and can endure a heavier burden; but the attendants and companions of Ares, when under the influence of love, if they fancy that they have been at all wronged, are ready to kill and put an end to themselves and their beloved. And in like manner he who follows in the train of any other god honors him, and imitates him as far as he is able while the impression lasts; and this is his way of life and the manner of his behavior to his beloved and to every other in the first period of his earthly existence. Every one chooses the object of his affections according to his character, and this he makes his god, and fashions and adorns as a sort of image which he is to fall down and worship. The followers of Zeus desire that their beloved should have a soul like him; and, therefore, they seek some philosophical and imperial nature, and when they have found him and loved him, they do all they can to create such a nature in him, and if they have no experience hitherto, they learn of any one who can teach them, and themselves follow in the same way. And they have the less difficulty in finding the nature of their own god in themselves, because they have been compelled to gaze intensely on him; their recollection clings to him, and they become possessed by him, and receive his character and ways, as far as man can participate in God. These they attribute to the beloved, and they love him all the more, and if they draw inspiration from Zeus, like the Bacchic Nymphs, they pour this out upon him in order to make him as like their god as possible. But those who are the followers of Hera seek a royal love, and when they have found him they do the same with him; and in like manner the followers of Apollo, and of every other god walking in the ways of their god, seek a love who is to be like their god, and when they have found him, they themselves imitate their god, and persuade their love to do the same, and bring him into harmony with the form and ways of the god as far as they can; for they have no feelings of envy or mean enmity towards their beloved, but they do their utmost to create in him the greatest likeness of themselves and the god whom they honor. And the desire of the lover, if effected, and the initiation of which I speak into the mysteries of true love, is thus fair and blissful to the beloved when he is chosen by the lover who is driven mad by love.

ARISTOTLE

from *Ethica Nicomachea*

The kinds of friendship may perhaps be cleared up if we first come to know the object of love. For not everything seems to be loved but only the lovable, and this is good, pleasant, or useful; but it would seem to be that by which some good or pleasure is produced that is useful, so that it is the good and the pleasant that are lovable as ends. Do men love, then, *the* good, or what is good for *them?* These sometimes clash. So too with regard to the pleasant. Now it is thought that each loves what is good for himself, and that the good is without qualification lovable, and what is good for each man is lovable for him; but each man loves not what is good for him but what seems good. This however will make no difference; we shall just have to say that this is "that which seems lovable." Now there are three grounds on which people love; of the love of lifeless objects we do not use the word "friendship"; for it is not mutual love, nor is there a wishing of good to the other (for it would surely be ridiculous to wish wine well; if one wishes anything for it, it is that it may keep, so that one may have it oneself); but to a friend we say we ought to wish what is good for his sake. But to those who thus wish good we ascribe only goodwill, if the wish is not reciprocated; goodwill when it *is* reciprocal being friendship. Or must we add "when it is recognized"? For many people have goodwill to those whom they have not seen but judge to be good or useful; and one of these might return this feeling. These people seem to bear goodwill to each other; but how could one call them friends when they do not know their mutual feelings? To be friends, then, they must be mutually recognized as bearing goodwill and wishing well to each other for one of the aforesaid reasons.

Now these reasons differ from each other in kind; so, therefore, do the corresponding forms of love and friendship. There are therefore three kinds of friendship, equal in number to the things that are lovable; for with respect to each there is a mutual and recognized love, and those who love each other wish well to each other in that respect in which they love one another. Now those who love each other for their utility do not love each other for themselves but in virtue of some good which they get from each other. So too with those who love for the sake of pleasure; it is not for their character that men love ready-witted people, but because they find them pleasant. Therefore those who love for the sake of utility love for the sake of what is good for *themselves,* and those who love for the sake of pleasure do so for the sake of what is pleasant to *themselves,* and not in so far as the other is the person loved but in so far as he is useful or pleasant. And thus these friendships are only incidental; for it is not as being the man he is that the loved person is loved, but as providing some good or pleasure. Such friendships, then, are easily dissolved, if the parties do not remain like themselves;

for if the one party is no longer pleasant or useful the other ceases to love him.

* * *

Most people seem, owing to ambition, to wish to be loved rather than to love; which is why most men love flattery; for the flatterer is a friend in an inferior position, or pretends to be such and to love more than he is loved; and being loved seems to be akin to being honoured, and this is what most people aim at. But it seems to be not for its own sake that people choose honour, but incidentally. For most people enjoy being honoured by those in positions of authority because of their hopes (for they think that if they want anything they will get it from them; and therefore they delight in honour as a token of favour to come); while those who desire honour from good men, and men who know, are aiming at confirming their own opinion of themselves; they delight in honour, therefore, because they believe in their own goodness on the strength of the judgement of those who speak about them. In being loved, on the other hand, people delight for its own sake; whence it would seem to be better than being honoured, and friendship to be desirable in itself. But it seems to lie in loving rather than in being loved, as is indicated by the delight mothers take in loving; for some mothers hand over their children to be brought up, and so long as they know their fate they love them and do not seek to be loved in return (if they cannot have both), but seem to be satisfied if they see them prospering; and they themselves love their children even if these owing to their ignorance give them nothing of a mother's due. Now since friendship depends more on loving, and it is those who love their friends that are praised, loving seems to be the characteristic virtue of friends, so that it is only those in whom this is found in due measure that are lasting friends, and only their friendship that endures. . . .

Further, love is like activity, being loved like passivity; and loving and its concomitants are attributes of those who are the more active.

Again, all men love more what they have won by labour; e.g. those who have made their money love it more than those who have inherited it; and to be well treated seems to involve no labour, while to treat others well is a laborious task. These are the reasons, too, why mothers are fonder of their children than fathers; bringing them into the world costs them more pains, and they know better that the children are their own. This last point, too, would seem to apply to benefactors.

The question is also debated, whether a man should love himself most, or some one else. People criticize those who love themselves most, and call them self-lovers, using this as an epithet of disgrace, and a bad man seems to do everything for his own sake, and the more so the more wicked he is—and so men reproach him, for instance, with doing nothing of his own accord—while the good man acts for honour's sake, and the more so the better he is, and acts for his friend's sake, and sacrifices his own interest.

But the facts clash with these arguments, and this is not surprising. For men say that one ought to love best one's best friend, and a man's best friend is one who wishes well to the object of his wish for his sake, even if no one is to know of it; and these attributes are found most of all in a man's attitude towards himself, and so are all the other attributes by which a friend is defined; for, as we have said, it is from this relation that all the characteristics of friendship have extended to our neighbours. All the proverbs, too, agree with this, e.g., "a single soul," and "what friends have is common property," and "friendship is equality," and "charity begins at home"; for all these marks will be found most in a man's relation to himself; he is his own best friend and therefore ought to love himself best.

Translated by W. D. Ross

THE BIBLE

PROVERBS 30. 18–19
There be three things which are too wonderful for me, yea, four which I know not: The way of an eagle in the air; the way of a serpent upon a rock; the way of a ship in the sea; and the way of a man with a maid.

CORINTHIANS 13
Though I speak with the tongues of men and of angels, and have not love, I am become as sounding brass, or a tinkling cymbal. And though I have the gift of prophecy, and understand all mysteries, and all knowledge; and though I have all faith, so that I could remove mountains, and have not love, I am nothing. And though I bestow all my goods to feed the poor, and though I give my body to be burned, and have not love, it

profiteth me nothing. Love suffereth long, and is kind; love envieth not; love vaunteth not itself, is not puffed up. Doth not behave itself unseemly, seeketh not her own, is not easily provoked, thinketh no evil; rejoiceth not in iniquity but rejoiceth in the truth; beareth all things, believeth all things, hopeth all things, endureth all things.

SENECA

On Grief for Lost Friends

You have buried one whom you loved; look about for someone to love. It is better to replace your friend than to weep for him. What I am about to add is, I know, a very hackneyed remark, but I shall not omit it simply because it is a common phrase: A man ends his grief by the mere passing of time, even if he has not ended it of his own accord. But the most shameful cure for sorrow, in the case of a sensible man, is to grow weary of sorrowing. I should prefer you to abandon grief, rather than have grief abandon you; and you should stop grieving as soon as possible, since, even if you wish to do so, it is impossible to keep it up for a long time. Our forefathers have enacted that, in the case of women, a year should be the limit for mourning; not that they needed to mourn for so long, but that they should mourn no longer. In the case of men, no rules are laid down, because to mourn at all is not regarded as honourable. For all that, what woman can you show me, of all the pathetic females that could scarcely be dragged away from the funeral-pile or torn from the corpse, whose tears have lasted a whole month? Nothing becomes offensive so quickly as grief; when fresh, it finds someone to console it and attracts one or another to itself; but after becoming chronic, it is ridiculed, and rightly. For it is either assumed or foolish.

He who writes these words to you is no other than I, who wept so excessively for my dear friend Annaeus Serenus that, in spite of my wishes, I must be included among the examples of men who have been overcome by grief. Today, however, I condemn this act of mine, and I understand that the reason why I lamented so greatly was chiefly that I had never imagined it possible for his death to precede mine. The only thought which occurred to my mind was that he was the younger, and much younger, too,—as if the Fates kept to the order of our ages!

Therefore let us continually think as much about our own mortality as about that of all those we love. In former days I ought to have said: "My friend Serenus is younger than I; but what does that matter? He would naturally die after me, but he may precede me." It was just because I did not do this that I was unprepared when Fortune dealt me the sudden blow. Now is the time for you to reflect, not only that all things are mortal, but also that their mortality is subject to no fixed law. Whatever can happen at any time can happen today. Let us therefore reflect, my beloved Lucilius, that we shall soon come to the goal which this friend, to our own sorrow, has reached. And perhaps, if only the tale told by wise men is true and there is a bourne to welcome us, then he whom we think we have lost has only been sent on ahead. Farewell.

PLUTARCH

from *The Lives of the Noble Grecians and Romans*

from ANTONY

Such being his temper, the last and crowning mischief that could befall him came in the love of Cleopatra, to awaken and kindle to fury passions that as yet lay still and dormant in his nature, and to stifle and finally corrupt any elements that yet made resistance in him of goodness and a sound judgment. He fell into the snare thus. When making preparation for the Parthian war, he sent to command her to make her personal appearance in Cilicia, to answer an accusation, that she had given great assistance, in the late wars, to Cassius. Dellius, who was sent on this message, had no sooner seen her face, and remarked her adroitness and subtlety in speech, but he felt convinced that Antony would not so much as think of giving any molestation to a woman like this; on the contrary, she would be the first in favour with him. So he set himself at once to pay his court to the Egyptian, and gave her his advice, "to go," in the Homeric style, to Cilicia, "in her best attire," and bade her fear nothing from Antony, the gentlest and kindest of soldiers. She had some faith in the words of Dellius, but more in her own attractions; which, having formerly recommended her to Cæsar and the young Cnæus Pompey, she did not doubt might prove yet more successful with Antony. Their acquaintance was with her when a girl, young and ignorant of the world, but she was to meet Antony in the time of life when women's beauty is most splendid, and their intellects are in full maturity. She made great preparation for her journey, of money, gifts, and ornaments of value, such as so wealthy a kingdom might afford, but she brought with her her surest hopes in her own magic arts and charms.

She received several letters, both from Antony and from his friends, to summon her, but she took no account of these orders; and at last, as if in mockery of them, she came sailing up the river Cydnus, in a barge with gilded stern and outspread sails of purple, while oars of silver beat time to the music of flutes and fifes and harps. She herself lay all along under a canopy of cloth of gold, dressed as Venus in a picture and beautiful young boys, like painted Cupids, stood on each side to fan her. Her maids were dressed like sea nymphs and graces, some steering at the rudder, some working at the ropes. The perfumes diffused themselves from the vessel to the shore, which was covered with multitudes, part following the galley up the river on either bank, part running out of the city to see the sight. The market-place was quite emptied, and Antony at last was left alone sitting upon the tribunal; while the word went through all the multitude, that Venus was come to feast with Bacchus, for the common good of Asia. On her arrival, Antony sent to invite her to supper. She thought it fitter he should come to her; so, willing to show his good-humour and courtesy, he complied, and went. He found the preparations to receive him magnificent beyond expression, but nothing so admirable as the great number of lights; for on a sudden there was let down altogether so great a number of branches with lights in them so ingeniously disposed, some in squares, and some in circles, that the whole thing was a spectacle that has seldom been equalled for beauty.

The next day, Antony invited her to supper, and was very desirous to outdo her as well in magnificence as contrivance; but he found he was altogether beaten in both, and was so well convinced of it that he was himself the first to jest and mock at his poverty of wit and his rustic awkwardness. She, perceiving that his raillery was broad and gross, and savoured more of the soldier than the courtier, rejoined in the same taste, and fell into it at once, without any sort of reluctance or reserve. For her actual beauty, it is said, was not in itself so remarkable that none could be compared with her, or that no one could see her without being struck by it, but the contact of her presence, if you lived with her, was irresistible; the attraction of her person, joining with the charm of her conversation, and the character that attended all she said or did, was something bewitching. It was a pleasure merely to hear the sound of her voice, with which, like an instrument of many strings, she could pass from one language to another; so that there were few of the barbarian nations that she answered by an interpreter; to most of them she spoke herself, as to the Æthiopians, Troglodytes, Hebrews, Arabians, Syrians, Medes, Parthians, and many others, whose language she had learnt; which was all the more surprising because most of the kings, her predecessors, scarcely gave themselves the trouble to acquire the Egyptian tongue, and several of them quite abandoned the Macedonian.

Antony was so captivated by her that, while Fulvia his wife maintained his quarrels in Rome against Cæsar by actual force of arms, and the Parthian troops, commanded by Labienus (the king's generals having made him commander-in-chief), were assembled in Mesopotamia, and ready to enter Syria, he could yet suffer himself to be carried away by her to Alexandria, there to keep holiday, like a boy, in play and diversion. . . .

✳   ✳   ✳

To return to Cleopatra; Plato admits four sorts of flattery, but she had a thousand. Were Antony serious or disposed to mirth, she had at any moment some new delight or charm to meet his wishes; at every turn she was upon him, and let him escape her neither by day nor by night. She played at dice with him, drank with him, hunted with him; and when he exercised in arms, she was there to see. At night she would go rambling with him to disturb and torment people at their doors and windows, dressed like a servant-woman, for Antony also went in servant's disguise, and from these expeditions he often came home very scurvily answered, and sometimes even beaten severely, though most people guessed who it was. However, the Alexandrians in general liked it all well enough, and joined good-humouredly and kindly in his frolic and play, saying they were much obliged to Antony for acting his tragic parts at Rome, and keeping his comedy for them. It would be trifling without end to be particular in his follies, but his fishing must not be forgotten. He went out one day to angle with Cleopatra, and, being so unfortunate as to catch nothing in the presence of his mistress, he gave secret orders to the fishermen to dive under water, and put fishes that had been already taken upon his hooks; and these he drew so fast that the Egyptian perceived it. But, feigning great admiration, she told everybody how dexterous Antony was, and invited them next day to come and see him again. So, when a number of them had come on board the fishing-boats, as soon as he had let down his hook, one of her servants was beforehand with his divers, and fixed upon his hook a salted fish from Pontus. Antony, feeling his line give, drew up the prey, and when, as may be imagined, great laughter ensued, "Leave," said Cleopatra, "the fishing-rod, general, to us poor sovereigns of Pharos and Canopus; your game is cities, provinces, and kingdoms."

Whilst he was thus diverting himself and engaged in this boy's play, two despatches arrived; one from Rome, that his brother Lucius and his wife Fulvia, after many quarrels among themselves, had joined in war against Cæsar, and having lost all, had fled out of Italy; the other bringing little better news, that Labienus, at the head of the Parthians, was overruning Asia, from Euphrates and Syria as far as Lydia and Ionia. So, scarcely at last rousing himself from sleep, and shaking off the fumes of wine, he set out to attack the Parthians, and went as far as Phœnicia; but, upon the receipt of lamentable letters from Fulvia, turned his course with two hundred ships to Italy. And, in his way, receiving such of his friends as fled from Italy, he was given to understand that Fulvia was the sole cause of the war, a woman of a restless spirit and very bold, and withal her hopes were that commotions in Italy would force Antony from Cleopatra. . . .

Translated by John Dryden

❧ ❧

VATSYAYANA

from *The Kama Sutra*

The span of human life is about one hundred years, and during this time a man must practice Dharma (obedience to Holy Scriptures), Artha (acquisition of lands, cattle, riches, friends and proficiency in the arts) and Kama (enjoyment of material things through the senses), in such a way that his whole existence achieves a perfect balance. . . .

A man who practices Dharma, Artha and Kama tastes happiness— both in this life and the next. People usually practice only those things that do not compromise the future and which do not harm their welfare. Any act which ultimately leads to the practice of Dharma, Artha and Kama, united or separately, should be encouraged. But the prudent man will refrain from the performance of any acts which will lead to the fulfillment of one of these principles at the expense of the other two. . . .

The basic definition of Kama is the special contact between the sensory organ and its object, and the resulting pleasure is known as Kama. Kama is taught by the Kama Sutras (verses of desire) and by experience.

from THE LIFE OF THE CITIZEN
The evening should begin with song. Then the head of the household should retire to his perfumed chamber with a friend and await the arrival of the woman who loves him, who may send him a messenger or who may come herself to find him. When she finally arrives, the head of the house and his friend should welcome her and pass the hours of the evening in amusing conversation until desire slowly comes upon them. Then the lord of the house should dismiss his friend and so fulfill his last duty of the day.

THE DIFFERENT KINDS OF LOVE
Scholars define four kinds of love:
    1. Love that results from the execution, constant and continued, of a certain act is known as Love acquired through Constant Practice and Habit. For example, the love of sexual intercourse, the love of alcohol, gambling and sports.
    2. Love that is felt for things out of the ordinary, and which is entirely based on the imagination or intellect, is called Love as the result of Imagination. For example, the love certain men or women feel for oral intercourse, and the love everyone feels for kisses, caresses, etc.
    3. Love that is completely reciprocal and sincere, and when each one sees in the other the complement of himself, is known as Love as the result of Faith.
    4. Love as a result of the Perception of Exterior Objects is known to everyone, as the sight of a beautiful woman has moved more poets to verse, and lovers to madness than any other form of love.

THE KINDS OF EMBRACES
The embrace is the bodily contact which reflects the joy of a man and woman united in love.
    The old writings state that there are four kinds of embrace:
    1. When a man, feeling the hard bite of desire, touches a woman's body with his own (generally using some pretext or excuse, for this is the

most elementary of all bodily contacts), it is known as the Embrace of Touch.

2. If, in some secluded room, a woman bends down to pick something up, and in doing so her breasts gently pierce her lover's body and are at once seized by him—it is known as the Embrace of Penetration.

These two forms of bodily contact are used only by lovers who are not yet sure of their mutual feelings and intentions.

3. When two lovers slowly walk together down some quiet shaded garden gently rubbing their bodies, one against the other, it is known as the Embrace of Friction.

4. But when one presses his body strongly and passionately against that of his lover it is known as the Embrace of Pressure.

These last two are used by those who have already succumbed to the arrows of Kama, and who are willing to float together on the stormy sea of desire.

❦ ❦

BOETHIUS

from *The Consolation of Philosophy*

Now what should I speak of bodily pleasures, the desire of which is full of anxiety, and the enjoying of them breeds repentance? How many diseases, how intolerable griefs bring they forth in the bodies of their possessors, as it were the fruits of their own wickedness! I know not what sweetness their beginnings have, but whosoever will remember his lusts shall understand that the end of pleasure is sadness.

> All pleasure hath this property,
> She woundeth those who have her most.
> And, like unto the angry bee
> Who hath her pleasant honey lost,
> She flies away with nimble wing
> And in our hearts doth leave her sting.

HUGH OF SAINT VICTOR

from Of the Nature of Love

We daily drop some word respecting love lest, if we do not heed it, its fire perhaps should kindle in our hearts and burst into a flame, whose property is either to consume or purify a thing entire. For all that is good derives from it, and from it every evil comes. A single spring of love, welling up within us, pours itself out in two streams. The one is the love of the world, cupidity; the other the love of God, charity. The heart of man is in fact the ground from which, when inclination guides it towards outward things, there breaks that which we call cupidity; although, when its desire moves it towards that which is within, its name is charity.

There are, then, two streams that issue from the fount of love, cupidity and charity. And cupidity is the root of every evil, and charity the root of every good. So all that is good derives from it, and from it every evil comes. Whatever it may be, then, it is a great force in us, and everything in us derives from it, for this is why it is love.

But what is love, and how great? What is love, and whence? The Word of God also discusses this. Is not this a subject rather for those who commonly debase love and decency? See how many there are who gladly take up the question of its mysteries, and how few who are not ashamed to discuss it in public! What, then, are we thinking of? Perhaps in an excess of wantonness we wear a harlot's face, since we are not ashamed to compose something in writing about love, though these are matters that even the shameless are sometimes unable to express in words without a blush. Yet it is one thing to delve into vice in order to root it out, and another to incite to what is vicious, that truth and virtue be not loved. Our purpose is to probe and seek that we may know and—when we know—avoid that into which some others go that they may know and, knowing, may indulge therein—namely, what it is in us that divides our desires in so many ways and leads our hearts in different directions.

Now we find that this thing is nothing else but love which, as a single movement of the heart, is of its nature one and single, yet is divided in its act. When it moves inordinately—that is, whither it should not—it is called cupidity; but, when it is rightly ordered, it is termed charity. How, then, can we define this movement of the heart that we call love?

It will be worth our while to look more closely at this movement from which, when it is evil, so many ills proceed and, when it is good, so many blessings come, lest to some extent it should elude us and remain unknown and consequently unavoided when it is evil and, when it is good, unsought and undiscovered. Let us, therefore, go into this matter of its definition and think about it; for the object of our inquiry is a hidden matter, and the deeper it lies, the more it controls the heart in either direction.

Love, then, appears to be, and is, the attachment of any heart to anything, for any reason, whether it be desire or joy in its fruition, hastening towards it by desire, tranquil in its enjoyment. Here lies your good, O heart of man, here also is your evil; for, if good you be, your good can have no other source; nor can your evil, if it is evil that you are, except in that you love that which is good rightly or wrongly, as the case may be. For everything that exists is good; but, when that which is good is wrongly loved, the thing in itself is good, but the love of it is bad. So it is not the lover, nor what he loves, nor the love wherewith he loves it that is evil; but it is the fact that he loves it wrongly that is altogether evil. Only set charity in order, then, and there is no evil left.

It is our desire, if only we be equal to the task, to persuade you of an important fact. Almighty God, who lacks for nothing because He is Himself the supreme and true Good, He who can neither receive increase from another, since all things come from Him, nor suffer a personal loss that could cause Him to fail, since in Him all things live unchangeably, this God created the rational spirit by no necessity but out of love alone, in order to bestow on it a share in His own blessedness. That it might, moreover, be fitted to enjoy such bliss, He put love in it, a certain spiritual sense of taste, as it were, to relish inward sweetness, so that through that very love it might savour the happiness of its true joy and cleave to it with unwearying desire.

By love, then, God has joined the rational creature to Himself, so that by ever holding fast to Him it might as it were by its affection suck, by its desire drink, and by its joy possess in Him the good that would make it happy. Suck, little bee, suck and drink the sweetness of thy Sweet that passes telling! Plunge in and take thy fill, for He can never fail unless you first grow weary. So cleave to Him, abide in Him, receive Him and have joy of Him. If appetite be everlasting, everlasting too shall be the blessedness. Let us no longer be ashamed or regretful for having spoken about love. Let us not be regretful where there is such profit; where there is such loveliness, let us not be ashamed.

ANDREAS CAPELLANUS

from *The Art of Courtly Love*

Every attempt of a lover tends toward the enjoyment of the embraces
of her whom he loves; he thinks about it continually, for he hopes that
with her he may fulfill all the mandates of love—that is, those things
which we find in treatises on the subject. Therefore in the sight of a
lover nothing can be compared to the act of love, and a true lover
would rather be deprived of all his money and of everything that the
human mind can imagine as indispensable to life rather than be without love, either hoped for or attained. For what under heaven can a man
possess or own for which he would undergo so many perils as we continually see lovers submit to of their own free will? We see them despise
death and fear no threats, scatter their wealth abroad and come to great
poverty. Yet a wise lover does not throw away wealth as a prodigal
spender usually does, but he plans his expenditures from the beginning
in accordance with the size of his patrimony; for when a man comes
to poverty and want he begins to go along with his face downcast and
to be tortured by many thoughts, and all joyousness leaves him. And
when that goes, melancholy comes straightway to take its place, and
wrath claims a place in him; so he begins to act in a changed manner
toward his beloved and to appear frightful to her, and the things that
cause love to increase begin to fail. Therefore love begins to grow less,
for love is always either decreasing or increasing. I know from my own
experience that when poverty comes in, the things that nourished love
begin to leave, because "poverty has nothing with which to feed its
love."

WHERE LOVE GETS ITS NAME

Love gets its name (*amor*) from the word for hook (*amus*), which means
"to capture" or "to be captured," for he who is in love is captured in the
chains of desire and wishes to capture someone else with his hook. Just
as a skillful fisherman tries to attract fishes by his bait and to capture
them on his crooked hook, so the man who is a captive of love tries to
attract another person by his allurements and exerts all his efforts to
unite two different hearts with an intangible bond, or if they are already
united he tries to keep them so forever.

How Love, When It Has Been Acquired, May Be Kept

Now since we have already said enough about acquiring love, it is not unfitting that we should next see and describe how this love may be retained after it has once been acquired. The man who wants to keep his love affair for a long time untroubled should above all things be careful not to let it be known to any outsider, but should keep it hidden from everybody; because when a number of people begin to get wind of such an affair, it ceases to develop naturally and even loses what progress it has already made. Furthermore a lover ought to appear to his beloved wise in every respect and restrained in his conduct, and he should do nothing disagreeable that might annoy her. Moreover every man is bound, in time of need, to come to the aid of his beloved, both by sympathizing with her in all her troubles and by acceding to all her reasonable desires. Even if he knows sometimes that what she wants is not so reasonable, he should be prepared to agree to it after he has asked her to reconsider. And if inadvertently he should do something improper that offends her, let him straightway confess with downcast face that he has done wrong, and let him give the excuse that he lost his temper or make some other suitable explanation that will fit the case. And every man ought to be sparing of praise of his beloved when he is among other men; he should not talk about her often or at great length, and he should not spend a great deal of time in places where she is. When he is with other men, if he meets her in a group of women, he should not try to communicate with her by signs, but should treat her almost like a stranger, lest some person spying on their love might have opportunity to spread malicious gossip. Lovers should not even nod to each other unless they are sure that nobody is watching them. Every man should also wear things that his beloved likes and pay a reasonable amount of attention to his appearance—not too much because excessive care for one's looks is distasteful to everybody and leads people to despise the good looks that one has. If the lover is lavish in giving, that helps him retain a love he has acquired, for all lovers ought to despise all worldly riches and should give alms to those who have need of them. Nothing is considered more praiseworthy in a lover than to be known to be generous, and no matter how worthy a man may be otherwise, avarice degrades him, while many faults are excused if one has the virtue of liberality. Also, if the lover is one who is fitted to be a warrior, he should see to it that his courage is apparent to everybody, for it detracts very much from the good character of a man if he is timid in a fight. A lover should always offer his services and obedience freely to every lady, and he ought to root out all his pride and be very humble. He ought to give a good deal of attention to acting toward all in such fashion that no one may be sorry to call to mind his good deeds or have reason to censure anything he has done. Then, too, he must keep in mind the general rule that lovers must not neglect anything that good manners demand or good breeding suggests, but they should be very careful to do everything of this sort. Love may also be retained by indulging in the sweet and delightful solaces of the flesh, but only in such manner and in such number that they may never seem wearisome to the loved one. Let the lover strive to practice gracefully and manfully any act or mannerism which he has noticed is pleasing to his beloved. A clerk should not, of course, affect the manners or the dress of the laity, for no one is likely to please his beloved, if she is a wise woman, by wearing strange clothing or by practicing manners that do not suit his status. Furthermore a lover should make every attempt to be constantly in the company of good men and to avoid completely the society of the wicked. For association with the vulgar makes a lover who joins them a thing of contempt to his beloved.

What we have said about retaining love you should understand as referring to a lover of either sex. There are doubtless many other things which may be useful in retaining love that a wide-awake diligent lover may discover for himself.

HOW A LOVE, ONCE CONSUMMATED, MAY BE INCREASED
We shall attempt to show you in a few words how love may be increased after it has been consummated. Now in the first place it is said to increase if the lovers see each other rarely and with difficulty; for the greater the difficulty of exchanging solaces, the more do the desire for them and the feeling of love increase. Love increases, too, if one of the lovers shows that he is angry at the other; for the lover falls at once into a great fear that this feeling which has arisen in his beloved may last forever. Love increases, likewise, if one of the lovers feels real jealousy, which is called, in fact, the nurse of love. Even if he does not suffer from real jealousy, but from a shameful suspicion, still by virtue of this his love always increases and grows more powerful. What constitutes real jealousy and what shameful suspicion you can easily see in the discussion between the man of the higher nobility and the noblewoman. Love increases, too, if it happens to last after it has been made public; ordinarily it does not last, but begins to fail just as soon as it is revealed. Again, if one of the lovers dreams about the other, that gives rise to love, or if love already exists it increases it. So, too, if you know that someone is trying to win your

beloved away from you, that will no doubt increase your love and you will begin to feel more affection for her. I will go further and say that even though you know perfectly well that some other man is enjoying the embraces of your beloved, this will make you begin to value her solaces all the more. . . .

꧁ ꧂

MICHEL DE MONTAIGNE

That Our Desires Are Increased by Difficulty

There is no reason but hath another contrary unto it, saith the wisest party of Philosophers. I did erewhile ruminate upon this notable saying, which an ancient writer allegeth for the contempt of life. No good can bring us any pleasure, except that, against whose losse we are prepared: *In æquo est, dolor amissæ rei, et timor amittendæ.* "Sorrow for a thing lost, and fear of losing it, are on an even ground." Meaning to gain thereby, that the fruition of life cannot perfectly be pleasing unto us, if we stand in any fear to lose it. A man might nevertheles say on the contrary part, that we embrace and clasp this good so much the harder, and with more affection, as we perceive it to be less sure, and fear it should be taken from us. For, it is manifestly found, that as fire is roused up by the assistance of cold, even so our will is whetted on by that which doth resist it.

> *Si nunquam Danaen habuisset ahenea turris,*
> *Non esset Danae de Iove facta parens.*

> If Danae had not been clos'd in brazen Tower,
> love had not clos'd with Danae in golden shower.

And that there is nothing so naturally opposite to our taste, as satiety, which comes from ease and facility, nor nothing that so much sharpeneth it as rareness and difficulty. *Omnium rerum voluptas ipso quo debet fugare periculo crescit.* "The delight of all things encreaseth by the danger, whereby it rather should terrify them that affect it."

> *Galla nega; satiatur amor, nisi gaudia torquent.*

> Good wench, deny, my love is cloied,
> Unless joys grieve, before enjoyed.

To keep love in breath and longing, Lycurgus ordained, that the married men of Lacedemonia might never converse with their wives, but by stealth, and that it should be as great an imputation and shame to find them laid together, as if they were found lying with others. The difficulty of assignations or matches appointed, the danger of being surprised, and the shame of ensuing tomorrow,

> —*et languor, et silentium,*
> *Et latere petitus imo spiritus.*

> And whispering voice, and languishment,
> And breath in sighs from deepe sides sent,

are the things that give relish and tartness to the sauce. How many most laciviously-pleasant sports, proceed from modest and shamefast manner of speech, of the daliances and workes of love? Even voluptuousness seeks to provoke and stir itself up by smarting. It is much sweeter when it itcheth, and endeared when it gauleth. The courtesan Flora was wont to say, that she never lay with Pompey, but she made him carry away the marks of her teeth.

> *Quod petiere, premunt arctè, faciúntque dolorem*
> *Corporis, et dentes inlidunt sæpe labellis:*
> *Et stimuli subsunt, qui instigant lædere id ipsum*
> *Quodcumque est, rabies unde illi germina surgunt.*

So goės it every where: Rarenesse and difficulty giveth esteem unto things. Those of Marca d'Ancona in Italy, make their vows, and go on pilgrimage rather unto Iames in Galicia, and those of Galicia rather unto our Lady of Loreto. In the Country of Liege, they make more account of the Baths of Luca; and they of Tuscany esteem the Baths of Spawe more than their own: In Rome the Fence-schools are ever full of Frenchmen, when few Romans come unto them. Great Cato, as well as any else, was even cloied and distasted with his wife, so long as she was his own, but when another man's, then wished he for her, and would fain have licked his fingers at her. I have heretofore put forth an old stallion to soil, who before did no sooner see or smell a mare, but was so lusty, that no man could rule him, nor no ground hold him; ease and facility, to come to his own when he list, hath presently quailed his stomach, and so cloyed him, that he is weary of them: But toward strange mares, and the first that passeth by his pasture, there is no hoe with him, but suddenly he returns to his old wonted neighings, and furious heat. Our appetite doth condemn and pass over what he hath in his free choice and own possession, to run after and pursue what he hath not.

> *Transuolat in medio posita, et fugientia captat.*

> It over flies what open lies,
> Pursuing only that which flies.

To forbid us any thing, is the ready way to make us long for it.

> —*nisi tu servare puellam*
> *Incipis, incipiet desinere esse mea.*

> If you begin not your wench to enshrine,
> She will begin to leave off to be mine.

And to leave it altogether to our will, is but to breed dislike and contempt in us; So that to want, and to have store, breedeth one self same inconvenience.

> *Tibi quod super est, mihi quod desit, dolet.*

> You grieve because you have to much;
> It grieve's me that I have none such.

Wishing and enjoying trouble us both alike. The rigor of a mistress is irksome, but ease and facility (to say true) much more; forasmuch as discontent and vexation proceed of the estimation we have of the thing desired, which sharpen love, and set it afire: Whereas Satiety begets distaste: It is a dull, blunt, weary, and drowzy passion.

> *Siqua volet regnare diu, contemnat amantem.*

> If any list long to bear sway,
> Scorn she her lover, ere she play.

> —*contemnite amantes,*
> *Sic hodie veniet, siqua negavit heri.*

Lovers, your lovers scorn, condemn, delude, deride;
So will she come today, that yesterday denied.

Why did Poppea devise to mask the beauties of her face, but to endear
them to her lovers? Why are those beauties veiled down to the heels,
which all desire to show, which all wish to see? Why do they cover with
so many lets, one over another, those parts, where chiefly consisteth our
pleasure and theirs? And to what purpose serve those baricadoes, and ver-
dugalles, wherewith our women arm their flanks, but to allure our appetite, and inveigle us to them by putting us off?

Et fugit ad salices, et se cupit ante videri.

She to the willows runs to hide,
Yet gladly would she first be spied.

Interdum tunica duxit operta moram.

She cover'd with her coat in play,
Did sometime make a short delay.

Whereto serves this maiden-like bashfulness, this wilfull quaintness, this
severe countenance, this seeming ignorance of those things, which they
know better than ourselves, that go about to instruct them, but to en-
crease a desire, and endear a longing in us, to vanquish, to gourmandize,
and at our pleasure, to dispose all this squeamish ceremony, and all these
peevish obstacles? For, it is not only a delight, but a glory to besot and
debauch this dainty and nice sweetness, and this infantine bashfullness,
and to subject a marble and stern gravity to the mercy of our flame. It
is a glory (say they) to triumph over modesty, chastity and temperance:
and who dissuadeth Ladies from these parts, betrayeth both them and
himself. It is to be supposed, that their heart yerneth for fear, that the
sound of our words woundeth the purity of their ears, for which they
hate us, and with a forced constraint, agree to withstand our importunity. Beauty with all her might, hath not wherewith to give a taste of herself without these interpositions. See in Italy, where most, and of the
finest beauty is to be sold, how it is forced to seek other strange means
and subtle devices, arts and tricks, to yield herself pleasing and acceptable: and yet in good sooth, do what it can, being venal and common, it
remaineth feeble and is even languishing. Even as in virtue, of two equal

effects, we hold that the fairest, and worthiest, wherein are proposed more lets, and which affordeth greater hazards. It is an effect of Gods providence, to suffer his holy Church to be vexed and turmoiled as we see, with so many troubles and storms, to rouse, and awaken by this opposition and strife the godly and religious souls, and raise them from out a lethal security and stupified slumber, wherein so long tranquillity had plunged them. If we shall counterpoise the loss we have had, by the number of those that have strayed out of the right way, and the profit that acrueth unto us, by having taken heart of grace, and by reason of combat raised our zeal, and forces; I wot not whether the profit doth surmount the loss. We thought to tie the bond of our marriages the faster, by removing all means to dissolve them; but by how much faster, that of constraint hath been tied, so much more hath that of our will and affection been slacked and loosed: Whereas on the contrary side, that, which so long time held marriages in honour and safety in Rome, was the liberty to break them who list. They kept their wives the better, forsomuch as they might leave them; and when divorces might freely be had, there past five hundred years and more, before any would ever make use of them.

Quod licet, ingratum est, quod non licet, acrius urit.

What we may do, doth little please:
It wormes us more, that hath less ease.

To this purpose might the opinion of an ancient writer be adjoined; that torments do rather encourage vices, than suppress them; that they beget not a care of well-doing, which is the work of reason and discipline, but only a care not to be surprised in doing evil.

Latius excisæ pestis contagia serpunt.

Th' infection of the plague nigh spent
And rooted out, yet further went.

I wot not whether it be true, but this I know by experience, that policy was never found to be reformed that way. The order and regiment of manners dependeth of some other mean. The Greek stories make mention of the Agrippians, neighbouring upon Scithia, who live without any rod or staff of offence, where not only no man undertakes to buckle with any other man, but whosoever can but save himself, there (by reason of their virtue and sanctity of life) is as it were in a Sanctuary: And no man dares so much as touch him. Many have recourse to them, to attone and take up quarrels and differences, which arise amongst men elsewhere. There is a Nation, where the enclosures of gardens and fields they intend to keep several, are made with a seely twine of cotton, which amongst them is found to be more safe and fast, then are our ditches and hedges. *Furem signata sollicitant, Aperta effractarius præterit.* "Things sealed up solicit a thief to break them open: Whereas a common burglar will pass by quietly things that lie open." Amongst other means, ease and facility doth haply cover and fence my house from the violence of civil wars: Enclosure and fencing draw on the enterprise; and distrust, the offence; I have abated and weakened the soldiers design, by taking hazard and all means of military glory from their exploit, which is wont to serve them for a title, and stead them for an excuse. What is performed courageously, at what time justice lieth dead, and law hath not her due course, is ever done honorably. I yield them the conquest of my house dastardly and trecherous. It is never shut to any that knocketh. It hath no other guardian or provision but a porter, as an ancient custom, and used ceremony, who serveth not so much to defend my gate, as to offer it more decently and courteously to all comers. I have nor watch nor sentinel, but what the stars keep for me. That gentleman is much to blame, who makes a show to stand upon his guard, except he be very strong indeed. Who so is open on one side, is so everywhere. Our forefathers never dreamed on building of frontier towns or castles.

The means to assail (I mean without battery, and troops of armed men) and to surprise our houses increase daily beyond the means of guarding or defending. Mens' wits are generally exasperated and whetted on that way. An invasion concerneth all, the defense none but the rich. Mine was sufficiently strong, according to the times when it was made. I have since added nothing unto it that way; and I would fear the strength of it should turn against my self. Seeing a peaceable time will require we shall unfortify them. It is dangerous not to be able to recover them again, and it is hard for one to be assured of them. For, concerning intestine broils, your own servant may be of that faction you stand in fear of. And where religion serveth for a pretence, even alliances and consanguinity become mistrustfull under colour of justice. Common rents cannot entertain our private garrisons. They should all be consumed. We have not wherewith, nor are we able to do it, without our apparent ruin, or more incommodiously, and therewithall injuriously, without the common peoples destruction. The state of my loss should not be much worse. And if you chance to be a loser, your own friends are readier to accuse your improvidence and unhediness then to moan you, and excuse your ignorance and carelessness, concerning the offices belonging to your profession. That so many strongly-guarded houses have been lost, whereas mine continueth still, makes me suspect they were overthrown only because they were so dilligently guarded. It is that which affordeth a desire, and ministreth a pretense to the assailant. All guards bear a show of war; which if God be so pleased may light upon me. But so it is, I will never call for it. It is my sanctuary or retreat to rest myself from wars. I endeavour to free this corner from the public storm, as I do another corner in my soul. Our war may change form, and multiply and diversify how and as long as it list; but for myself I never stir. Amongst so many barricaded and armed houses, none but myself (as far as I know) of my quality, hath merely trusted the protection of his unto the heavens: For I never removed neither plate, nor hangings, nor my evidences. I will neither fear, nor save myself by halves. If a full acknowledgement purchaseth the favour of God, it shall last me forever unto the end: If not, I have continued long enough, to make my continuance remarkable, and worthy the registering. What? Is not thirty years a goodly time?

✺ ✺

JOHANNES SECUNDUS

from *The Kisses*

WHY HE WRITES WANTONLY

Do you ask why I fill all my books with wanton poems? I do it to repel dull grammarians. If I sang the warlike exploits of magnanimous Cæsar, or the pious deeds of holy men, what a load of notes, what corrections of the text, I should have to endure! What a torment I should become for little boys! But now that moist kisses are my theme, and the lusty blood tingles at my prurient verses, let me be read by the youth who hopes to please his virgin mistress, by the gentle girl who longs to please her new-made spouse, and by every sprightly brother poet who loves voluptuous ease and mirth. But stand aloof from these frolic joys, ye sour pedants, and keep off your injurious hands, that no boy, whipped and crying on account of my amorous fancies, may wish the earth to press hard upon my bones.

You ask why thus I sport in wanton strains;
Why Love, in every verse, luxuriant reigns?
Because I would not have dull pedants cumber
My light effusions with their learned lumber.
If lives of sainted men inspired my lays,
Or if I sang heroic Cæsar's praise,
What notes (oppressive weight!) must I endure;
What comments, obvious readings to obscure;
What tedious stuff conceived by addled brains,
To boys the certain cause of future pains!
But while on Kisses I employ my song,
Kisses, or moist or dry, or short or long;
Me, summon the unmarried youth to aid;
Me, bent on joy, the newly-married maid;
Me, the gay bard, whom lighter studies please,
Wisely indulging in delicious ease.
But from these sports, sour scholiasts, abstain!
These never with unhallow'd hands profane!
Nor turn to grief, what we to mirth design;
Lest, punish'd for some soft perverted line.
Wrong'd innocence, with tears unjustly shed,
Wish the cold earth lie heavy on my head!

KISS II

"Give me one little kiss," I said, "sweet girl!" You laid your delicious lips on mine, and then, like one who has trod on a snake and starts back in terror, you snatched your mouth away. Light of my eyes, this is not what one should call giving a kiss; it is only giving a piteous craving for a kiss.

"One little kiss, sweet maid!" I cry—
    And round my neck your arms you twine!
Your luscious lips of crimson dye
    With rapturous haste encounter mine.

But quick those lips my lips forsake,
    With wanton, tantalizing jest;
So starts some rustic from the snake
    Beneath his heedless footstep prest.

Is this to grant the wish'd-for kiss?—
　　Ah! no, my love—'tis but to fire
The bosom with a transient bliss,
　　Inflaming unallay'd desire.

It is not kisses Neæra gives, it is nectar, it is fragrant breath-dews, it is nard, and thyme, and cinnamon, and honey such as the bees gather on the brows of Hymettus or in the Attic rose-thickets, and store in osier hives. If many such are given me to devour, I shall soon become immortal and partake of the banquets of the great gods. Be sparing then of such gifts, or become a goddess with me, Neæra. Without you I care not for the tables of the celestials, not though the gods and goddesses would depose Jove, and force me to rule over the sunny realms.

Kiss X

The pleasure I derive from kisses is not limited to any particular kind; when you join your moist lips to mine, moist kisses delight me. Nor are dry kisses without their charms; many a time they send a thrilling flush through the frame. Pleasant too it is to lay kisses on wanton eyes, and punish the authors of our pain; or to revel all over a cheek, or a neck, or snowy shoulders, or a snowy bosom, and cover cheek and neck, and white shoulders and bosom, with black marks; or with eager lips to such a tremulous tongue, and to mingle breath with joined mouths, and transfuse two souls, each into the other's body, whilst Love lies swooning with ecstasy. Welcome to me the kiss, whether short or long, whether with lips that lightly touch or that cling close together, whether you give it me, light of my life, or I give it you. But never give me back such kisses as you receive, but let each vary the delight in different ways. And let whichever of us shall first be at fault for a change of method, hear and obey this sentence with downcast eyes: As many sweet kisses as have been previously given on both sides, so many shall the delinquent give singly to the other, and in as many ways.

On the soft neck, or blooming cheek exprest,
On the white shoulder, or still whiter breast.
'Twixt yielding lips, in every thrilling kiss,
To dart the trembling tongue—what matchless bliss!
Inhaling sweet each other's mingling breath,
While Love lies gasping in the arms of Death!
While soul with soul in ecstasy unites,

Intranced, impassion'd, with the fond delights,
From thee received, or given to thee, my love!
Alike to me those kisses grateful prove;
The kiss that's rapid, or prolong'd with art,
The fierce, the gentle, equal joys impart:
But mark—be all my kisses, beauteous maid!
With diff'rent kisses from thy lips repaid;
Then varying raptures shall from either flow,
As varying kisses either shall bestow:
And let the first, who with an unchanged kiss
Shall cease to thus diversify the bliss,
Observe with looks in meek submission dress'd
That law, by which this forfeiture's express'd:
"As many kisses as each lover gave,
As each might in return again receive;
So many kisses, from the vanquish'd side
The victor claims, so many ways applied."

KISS XIII

Faint and languid from the sweet conflict, I lay, my love, with my arm upon your neck. My breath, all wasted in my parching mouth, could yield my heart no refreshment. Already I had Styx before my eyes, and the sunless realms, and old Charon's lurid boat; when you breathed on my dry lips a deep-fetched moist kiss, a kiss that brought me back from the Stygian vale, and left the old ferryman without a freight. I was wrong: he did not go back with an empty boat, for my shade went with him to the sad regions of the dead. Part of your soul, my life! lives in this body, and upholds my frame; but impatient to return to its original command, it strives fretfully to make its way out by secret issues; and unless you cherish it with your loved breath, it will presently desert my fainting frame. Come then, glue your lips to mine, and let one breath continually animate us both; until, when age shall have wearied but not sated our passionate hearts, one single life shall quit our two bodies.

EPITHALAMIUM

The hour is come with the ordained changes of the heavens, the sweet voluptuous hour; hour for fondlings, mirth, and laughter; hour for sweet dalliance, and sport, and whispers; hour for kisses and for enjoyment equal to that of Jupiter and the great gods; hour than which none happier could be granted by the holy goddess of Gnidos; nor by him who roams the world with his quiver, mingling delicious joys with sorrows, the glittering golden-winged Cupid; nor by the sister-spouse of the great thunderer; nor by the flower-decked dweller on the tuneful rock, Hymen, who snatches blooming maids from their mothers' close embrace, and clasps them in the bridegroom's eager arms. O happy youth! happy maid!

Happy bridegroom! the object of thy ardent desire now rests within thy arms, a maid blessed with heavenly beauty, such as might content great Venus, or Juno, or helmeted Pallas born of Jove's divine brain, should they resolve to go again together to the shady valleys of green Ida; beauty decked with which any one of the three would, by the decision of any judge, victoriously bear back the golden apple to the skies. O happy youth! happy maid!

Happy bride! the object of thy ardent desire, a youth of excelling beauty, soon stretched beside thee in the blissful bed, will clasp thy neck in his arms; the youth who, smitten by those rosy lips, those snowy breasts, that sunny hair, and vanquished by those expressive eyes, has long been devoured by a secret flame, and ever chides the slow-paced sun, and ever invokes the tardy-coming moon. O happy youth! happy maid!

Forbear your wishes, hot bridegroom; cease your sighs and complaints: the sweet time is hurrying on; gentle Venus has heard the prayers of her votaries. Cynthius hides his face, and plunging into the Iberean Sea, makes way for his night-travelling sister; and Hesperus, the leader of the golden host, of all stars that shine the dearest to lovers, lifts his head and glitters in the sky. O happy youth! happy maid!

Soon will the virgin enter the chamber, whence, bridegroom, let her not depart a virgin. Soon the virgin laid between the snowy sheets, and covered with ingenuous blushes, will long for and tremble at your approach. Perhaps too her cheeks will be wet with tears, and she will sigh and lament; but you will come without delay, and put an end to plaints, and sighs, and tears, drying her eyes with your lips, and making a sweet murmuring take the place of her complainings. O happy youth! happy maid!

When then the happy bed receives the fair limbs of the beautiful virgin, (limbs disposed to soft slumber,) and when you too laid in bed, are exalted by blessed Dione above purpled kings and Jove himself, soon stirred with due fervour, you will address yourself to pretty-phrased disputes and tender strife; boldly planting here and there prosperous standards of bloodless war, laying many kisses on her neck, many on her cheeks, more on her lips, more on her eyes. She will resist and will call you "naughty," and say "enough" with a trembling voice, and will stop your forward lips with her hand, and push away your forward hand. O night thrice blest, and more!

Let her resist strenuously; let her resist: the tender loves like to be fed by resistance; resistance will redouble your ardour and give you new vigour for the conflict. Pass your lustful hand nimbly over her white neck, over that breast that vies in hue with ivory, over her smooth thighs and her belly, and the parts which are next to both, and give her as many kisses as there are shining stars in heaven. O four times blessed night!

And fail not to utter phrases of endearment, and all sorts of touching words, and murmurings sweet as those which the leaves utter to the gentle zephyr, or the dove, or the aged swan emits with dying bill; until, overcome by the potent arrows and the secret fire of the winged boy, and growing by degrees less and less coy, she shall lay aside her blushing bashfulness, yielding her neck to your clasping arms, and folding her arms round yours. O four times blessed night!

Then, then you will take delicious kisses, not snatched hastily, but lingering, close, and varied. Then the maid will venture in her turn on similar dalliance, and putting her half-open mouth to yours, which she now allows you to keep unclosed, she will enchant your glowing soul with the rapturous excitement of her fragrant breath. Soon growing bolder, she will utter sweeter words of endearment, will put forth her fingers with more freedom, and will practise more wanton toying. O too, too blest night!

Then stand to your arms; then Venus and Cupid call to arms; then charge and deal pleasing wounds; nimbly wield the spear, whose frequent thrusts are guided by the raging hand not of the sister but the mistress of Mars, of Venus, who always delights in new blood. Let your laborious flanks have no rest, nor your active hips, until panting, exhausted, with languid limbs, both shall be bathed in twofold exudations. O too, too blest night!

Toil thus to the full of your desires, and spend long days and nights in unstinted dalliance, and soon produce sweet children, and children's children in long succession, a little throng to soothe your age, relieve your pains in sickness, cherish you in your infirm years, and lay you in the grave with filial piety. O happy youth! happy maid!

COUNT BALDESAR CASTIGLIONE

from *The Book of the Courtier*

—Then messer Federico said:

"My lord Magnifico, you discourse of this matter as if everyone who pays court to women must needs speak lies and seek to deceive them: if the which were true, I should say that your teachings were sound; but if this cavalier who is speaking loves truly and feels that passion which sometimes so sorely afflicts the human heart, do you not consider in what pain, in what calamity and mortal anguish you put him by insisting that the lady shall never believe anything he says on this subject? Ought his supplications, tears, and many other signs to go for naught? Have a care, my lord Magnifico, lest it be thought that besides the natural cruelty which many of these ladies have in them, you are teaching them still more."

The Magnifico replied:

"I spoke not of him who loves, but of him who entertains with amourous talk, wherein one of the most necessary conditions is that words shall never be lacking. But just as true lovers have glowing hearts, so they have cold tongues, with broken speech and sudden silence; wherefore perhaps it would not be a false assumption to say: 'Who loves much, speaks little.' Yet as to this I believe no certain rule can be given, because of the diversity of men's habits; nor could I say anything more than that the Lady must be very cautious, and always bear in mind that men can declare their love with much less danger than women can."

—Then my lord Gaspar said, laughing:

"Would you not, my lord Magnifico, have this admirable Lady of yours love in return even when she knows that she is loved truly? For if the Courtier were not loved in return, it is not conceivable that he should go on loving her; and thus she would lose many advantages, and especially that service and reverence with which lovers honour and almost adore the virtue of their beloved."

"As to that," replied the Magnifico, "I do not wish to give advice; but I do say that I think love, as you understand it, is proper only for unmarried women; for when this love cannot end in marriage, the lady must always find in it that remorse and sting which things illicit give her, and run risk of staining that reputation for chastity which is so important to her."

Then messer Federico replied, laughing:

"This opinion of yours, my lord Magnifico, seems to me very austere, and I think you have learned it from some preacher—one of those who rebuke women for loving laymen, in order to have themselves the better part therein. And methinks you impose too hard a rule on married women, for many of them are to be found whose husbands bear them the greatest hatred without cause, and affront them grievously, sometimes by loving other women, sometimes by causing them all the annoyances possible to devise; some against their will are married by their fathers to old men, infirm, loathsome and disgusting, who make them live in continual misery. If such women were allowed to be divorced and separated from those with whom they are ill mated, perhaps it would not be fitting for them to love any but their husbands; but when, either by enmity of the stars or by unfitness of temperament or by other accident, it happens that the marriage bed, which ought to be a nest of concord and of love, is strewn by the accursed infernal fury with the seed of its venom, which then brings forth anger, suspicion and the stinging thorns of hatred to torment those unhappy souls cruelly bound by an unbreakable chain until death,—why are you unwilling that the woman should be allowed to seek some refuge from the heavy lash, and to bestow on others that which is not only spurned but hated by her husband? I am quite of the opinion that those who have suitable husbands and are loved by them, ought not to do them wrong; but the others wrong themselves by not loving those who love them."

"Nay," replied the Magnifico, "they wrong themselves by loving others than their husbands. Still, since not to love is often beyond our power, if this mischance shall happen to the Court Lady (that her husband's hate or another's love brings her to love), I would have her yield her lover nothing but her spirit; nor ever let her show him any clear sign of love (either by words or by gestures or by any other means) by which he may be sure of it."

Then messer Roberto da Bari said, laughing:

"I appeal from this judgment of yours, my lord Magnifico, and think I shall have many with me; but since you will teach married women this rusticity, so to speak, do you wish also to have the unmarried equally cruel and discourteous?—and complaisant to their lovers in nothing whatever?"

"If my Court Lady be unmarried," replied my lord Magnifico, "and must love, I wish her to love someone whom she can marry; nor shall I account it an errour if she shows him some sign of love: as to which matter I wish to teach her one universal rule in a few words, to the end that she may with little pains be able to bear it in mind; and this is, let her show him who loves her every token of love except such as may imbue her lover's mind with the hope of obtaining something wanton from her. And it is necessary to give great heed to this, for it is an errour committed by countless women, who commonly desire nothing more than to be beautiful: and since to have many lovers seems to them proof of their beauty, they take every pains to get as many as they can. Thus they are often carried into reckless behaviour, and forsaking that temperate modesty which so becomes them, they employ certain pert looks with scurrile words and acts full of immodesty, thinking that they are gladly seen and listened to for this and that by such ways they make themselves loved: which is false; for the demonstrations that are made to them spring from desire excited by a belief in their willingness, not from love. Wherefore I wish that my Court Lady may not by wanton behaviour seem to offer herself to anyone who wants her and to do her best to lure the eyes and appetite of all who look upon her, but that by her merits and virtuous conduct, by her loveliness, by her grace, she may imbue the mind of all who see her with that true love which is due to all things lovable, and with that respect which always deprives him of hope who thinks of any wantonness.

Thomas Dekker

from *The Bachelor's Banquet*

It is the natural inclination of a young gallant, in the pleasant prime and flower of his flourishing youth, being fresh, lusty, jocond, to take no other care, but to employ his money to buy gay presents for pretty Lasses, to frame his green wits in penning love ditties, his voice to sing them sweetly, his wandering eyes to gaze on the fairest dames, and his wanton thoughts to plot means for the speedy accomplishment of his wished desires, according to the compass of his estate. And albeit his parents or some other of his kindred do perhaps furnish him with necessary maintenance, so that he wants nothing, but lives in all ease and delight, yet cannot this content him, or satisfy his unexperienced mind: for although he doth daily see many married men, first lapt in lobbes pownd [held in love's pound], wanting former liberty, and compassed round in a cage of many cares, yet notwithstanding being overruled by self-will, and blinded by folly: he supposes them therein to have the fullness of their delight, because they have so near them the Image of content, *Venus* star gloriously blazing upon them, I mean a dainty fair wife, bravely attired, whose apparel perhaps is not yet paid for, (howsoever to draw their husbands into a fool's paradise) they make him believe that their father or mother have of their cost and bounty afforded it. This lusty youth (as I earst said) seeing them already in this maze of bitter sweetness, he goes round about, turmoiling himself in seeking an entrance, and takes such pains to find his own pain, that in the end, in he gets, when for the haste he makes, to have a taste of these supposed delicates, he hath no leisure to think, or no care to provide those things that are hereunto requisite. The jolly yonker being thus gotten in, doth for a time swim in delight, and hath no desire at all to wind himself out again, till time and use, which makes all things more familiar and less pleasing, do qualify this humor.

FRANCIS BACON

The Myth of Cupid

The particulars related by the poets of Cupid, or Love, do not properly agree to the same person; yet they differ only so far, that if the confusion of persons be rejected, the correspondence may hold. They say, that Love was the most ancient of all the gods, and existed before everything else, except Chaos, which is held coeval therewith. But for Chaos, the ancients never paid divine honours, nor gave the title of a god thereto. Love is represented absolutely without progenitor, excepting only that he is said to have proceeded from the egg of Nox; but that himself begot the gods, and all things else, on Chaos. His attributes are four, viz.: 1, perpetual infancy; 2, blindness; 3, nakedness; and 4, archery.

There was also another Cupid, or Love, the youngest son of the gods, born of Venus; and upon him the attributes of the elder are transferred with some degree of correspondence.

This fable points out, and enters, the cradle of nature. Love seems to be the appetite, or incentive, of the primitive matter; or, to speak more distinctly, the natural motion, or moving principle, of the original corpuscles, or atoms; this being the most ancient and only power that made and wrought all things out of matter. It is absolutely without parent, that is, without cause; for causes are as parents to effects; but this power of efficacy could have no natural cause; for, excepting God, nothing was before it; and therefore it could have no efficient in nature. And as nothing is more inward with nature, it can neither be a genius nor a form; and, therefore, whatever it is, it must be somewhat positive, though inexpressible. And if it were possible to conceive its modus and process, yet it could not be known from its cause, as being, next to God, the cause of causes, and itself without a cause. And perhaps we are not to hope that the modus of it should fall or be comprehended, under human inquiry. Whence it is properly feigned to be the egg of Nox, or laid in the dark.

The divine philosopher declares that "God has made everything beautiful in its season: and has given over the world to our disputes and inquiries: but that man cannot find out the work which God has wrought, from its beginning to its end." Thus the summary or collective law of nature, or the principle of love, impressed by God upon the original particles of all things, so as to make them attack each other and come together, by the repetition and multiplication whereof all the variety in the universe is produced, can scarce possibly find full admittance into the thoughts of men, though some faint notion may be had thereof. The Greek philosophy is subtile, and busied in discovering the material principles of things, but negligent and languid in discovering the principles of motion, in which the energy and efficacy of every operation consists. And here the Greek philosophers seem perfectly blind and childish: for the opinion of the Peripatetics, as to the stimulus of matter, by privation, is little more than words, or rather sound than signification. And they who refer it to God, though they do well therein, yet they do it by a start, and not by proper degrees of assent; for doubtless there is one summary, or capital law, in which nature meets subordinate to God, viz., the law mentioned in the passage above quoted from Solomon; or the work which God has wrought from its beginning to its end.

Democritus, who further considered this subject having first supposed an atom, or corpuscle, or some dimension or figure, attributed thereto an appetite, desire, or first motion simply, and another comparatively, imagining that in all things properly tended to the centre of the world; those containing more matter falling faster to the centre, and thereby removing, and in the shock driving away, such as held less. But this is a slender conceit, and regards too few particulars; for neither the revolutions of the celestial bodies, nor the contractions and expansion of things, can be reduced to this principle. And for the opinion of Epicurus, as to the declination and fortuitous agitation of atoms, this only brings the matter back again to a trifle, and wraps it up in ignorance and night.

Cupid is elegantly drawn a perpetual child; for compounds are larger things, and have their periods of age; but the first seeds or atoms of bodies are small, and remain in a perpetual infant state.

He is again just represented as naked; as all compounds may properly be said to be dressed and clothed, or to assume a personage; whence nothing remains truly naked, but the original particles of things.

The blindness of Cupid contains a deep allegory; for this same Cupid, Love, or appetite of the world, seems to have very little foresight, but directs his steps and motions conformably to what he finds next him, as blind men do when they feel out their way; which rends the divine and overruling Providence and foresight the more surprising; as by a certain steady law, it brings such a beautiful order and regularity of things out of what seems extremely casual, void of design, and, as it were, really blind.

The last attribute of Cupid is archery, viz., a virtue of power operating at a distance; for everything that operates at a distance may seem, as it were, to dart, or shoot with arrows. And whoever allows of atoms and vacuity, necessarily supposes that the virtue of atoms operates at a distance; for without this operation, no motion could be excited, on account of the vacuum interposing, but all things would remain sluggish and unmoved.

As to the other Cupid, he is properly said to be the youngest son of the gods, as his power could not take place before the formation of the species, or particular bodies. The description given us of him transfers the allegory to morality, though he still retains some resemblance with the ancient Cupid; for as Venus universally excites the affection of association and the desire of procreation, her son Cupid applies the affection of individuals; so that the general disposition proceeds from Venus, the more close sympathy from Cupid. The former depends upon a near approximation of causes, but the latter upon deeper, more necessitating, and uncontrollable principles, as if they proceeded from the ancient Cupid, on whom all exquisite sympathies depend.

Of Love

The stage is more beholding to love than the life of man; for as to the stage, love is ever matter of comedies, and now and then of tragedies; but

in life it doth much mischief, sometimes like a siren, sometimes like a
fury. You may observe, that amongst all the great and worthy persons
(whereof the memory remaineth, either ancient or recent), there is not
one that hath been transported to the mad degree of love; which shows
that great spirits and great business do keep out this weak passion. You
must except, nevertheless, Marcus Antonius, the half-partner of the empire of Rome, and Appius Claudius, the decemvir and lawgiver; whereof
the former was indeed a voluptuous man, and inordinate, but the latter
was an austere and wise man: and therefore it seems (though rarely) that
love can find entrance, not only in an open heart, but also into a heart
well fortified, if watch be not well kept. It is a poor saying of Epicurus,
"Satis magnum alter alteri theatrum sumus,"—as if a Man, made for the
contemplation of heaven, and all noble objects, should do nothing but
kneel before a little idol, and make himself a subject, though not of the
mouth (as beasts are), yet of the eye, which was given him for higher purposes.

   It is a strange thing to note the excess of this passion, and how it
braves the nature and value of things, by this, that the speaking in a perpetual hyperbole is comely in nothing but in love; neither is it merely in
the phrase; for whereas it hath been well said, "That the arch flatterer,
with whom all the petty flatterers have intelligence, is a man's self," certainly the lover is more; for there was never a proud man thought so absurdly well of himself as the lover doth of the person loved; and
therefore it was well said, "That it is impossible to love and be wise."
Neither doth this weakness appear to others only, and not to the party
loved, but to the loved most of all, except the love be reciprocal; for it is
a true rule, that love is ever rewarded either with the reciprocal, or with
an inward or secret contempt; by how much more then, men ought to beware of this passion, which loseth not only other things, but itself. As
for the other losses, the poet's relation doth well figure them: "That he
that preferreth Helena, quitted the gifts of Juno and Pallas," for whosoever esteemeth too much of amorous affection, quitteth both riches and
wisdom. This passion hath its floods in the very times of weakness,
which are great prosperity and great adversity; though this latter has
been less observed; both which times kindle love, and make it more fer-
vent, and therefore show it to be the child of folly. They do best who, if
they cannot but admit love, yet make it keep quarter, and sever it wholly
from their serious affairs and actions of life; for if it check once with
business, it troubleth men's fortunes, and maketh men that they can no
ways be true to their own ends. I know not how, but martial men are

given to love: I think it is, but as they are given to wine; for perils commonly ask to be paid in pleasures. There is in Man's nature a secret inclination and motion towards love of others, which, if it be not spent upon some one or a few, doth naturally spread itself towards many, and maketh men become humane and charitable, as it is seen sometimes in friars. Nuptial love maketh mankind; friendly love perfecteth it; but wanton love corrupteth and embaseth it.

SIR THOMAS OVERBURY

An Amorist

Is a man blasted or planet-strooken, and is the dog that leads blind Cupid; when he is at the best his fashion exceeds the worth of his weight. He is never without verses and musk confects, and sighs to the hazard of his buttons. His eyes are all white, either to wear the livery of his mistress's complection or to keep Cupid from hitting the black. He fights with passion, and loseth much of his blood by his weapon; dreams, thence his paleness. His arms are carelessly used, as if their best use was nothing but embracements. He is untrussed, unbuttoned, and ungartered, not out of carelessness, but care; his farthest end being but going to bed. Sometimes he wraps his petition in neatness, but he goeth not alone; for then he makes some other quality moralize his affection, and his trimness is the grace of that grace. Her favor lifts him up as the sun moisture; when he disfavors, unable to hold that happiness, it falls down in tears. His fingers are his orators, and he expresseth much of himself upon some instrument. He answers not, or not to the purpose, and no marvel, for he is not at home. He scotcheth time with dancing with his mistress, taking up of her glove, and wearing her feather; he is confined to her color, and dares not pass out of the circuit of her memory. His imagination is a fool, and it goeth in a pied coat of red and white. Shortly, he is translated out of a man into folly; his imagination is the glass of lust, and himself the traitor to his own discretion.

Robert Burton

from *The Anatomy of Melancholy*

You have heard how this tyrant Love rageth with brute beasts and spirits; now let us consider what passions it causeth amongst men.

How it tickles the hearts of mortal men I am almost afraid to relate, amazed, and ashamed, it hath wrought such stupendous and prodigious effects, such foul offences. Love indeed (I may not deny) first united provinces, built cities, and by a perpetual generation makes and preserves mankind, propagates the Church; but if it rage, it is no more Love, but burning Lust, a Disease, Phrensy, Madness, Hell. It is no virtuous habit this, but a vehement perturbation of the mind, a monster of nature, wit, and art. It subverts kingdoms, overthrows cities, towns, families; mars corrupts, and makes a massacre of men; thunder and lightning, wars, fires, plagues, have not done that mischief to mankind, as this burning lust, this brutish passion. Let Sodom and Gomorrah, Troy and I know not how many cities bear record.

Notwithstanding they know these and many such miseries, threats, tortures, will surely come upon them, yet either out of their own weakness, a depraved nature, or love's tyranny, which so furiously rageth, they suffer themselves to be led like an ox to the slaughter. . . .

Symptoms of Love Melancholy are either of body or mind; of body, paleness, leanness, dryness, etc. Love causeth leanness, makes hollow eyes, dryness, symptoms of this disease, to go smiling to themselves, or acting as if they saw or heard some delectable object. They pine away, and look ill with waking cares, sighs, with groans, griefs, sadness, dullness, want of appetite, etc. A reason for all this is that the liver does not perform his part, nor turns the aliment into blood as it ought; and for that cause the members are weak for want of sustenance, they are lean and pine, as the herbs of my garden do this month of May, for want of rain. The Green-sickness therefore often happeneth to young women. . . .

Many such symptoms there are of the body to discern lovers by. Can a man, sayeth Solomon, carry fire in his bosom and not burn?

But the best conjectures are taken from such symptoms as appear when they (the lovers) are both present; all their speeches, amorous glances, actions, lascivious gestures, will betray them, they cannot contain themselves, but that they will be still kissing.

Every poet is full of such catalogues of love symptoms, but fear and sorrow may justly challenge the chief place. Love is full of fear, anxiety, doubt, care, peevishness, suspicion, it turns a man into a woman. . . .

A lover that hath as it were lost himself through impotency, impatience, must be called home as a traveller by music, feasting, good wine, if need be, to drunkenness itself, which many so commend for the easing of the mind, all kinds of sports and merriments, to see fair pictures, hangings, buildings, pleasant fields, orchards, gardens, groves, fishing, hunting, to hear merry tales and pleasant discourse, to use exercise till he sweat, that new spirits may succeed, of by some vehement affection or contrary passion, to be diverted till he be fully weaned from anger, suspicion, cares, fears, and habituated into another course. . . .

. . . for love extended is mere madness.

❧ ❧

JOHN DONNE

That Women Ought to Paint

Foulness is *Lothsome:* can that be so which helps it? who forbids his beloved to gird in her waste? to mend by shooing her uneven lameness? to burnish her teeth? or to perfume her breath? yet that the *Face* be more precisely regarded, it concerns more: For as open confessing sinners are always punished, but the wary and concealing offenders without witness do it also without punishment; so the secret parts needs the less respect; but of the *Face*, discovered to all Examinations and surveys, there is not too nice a Jealousy. Nor doth it only draw the busy Eyes, but it is subject to the divinest touch of all, to *kissing*, the strange and mystical union of souls. If she should prostitute her self to a more unworthy man than thy self, how earnestly and justly wouldst thou exclaim, that for want of this easier and ready way of repairing, to betray her body to ruin and deformity (the tyrannous *Ravishers*, and sodain *Deflowerers* of all women) what a heinous adultery is it! What thou lovest in her *face* is *colour*, and *painting* gives that, but thou hatest it, not because it is, but because thou knowest it. Fool, whom ignorance makes happy, the Stars, the Sun, the Sky whom thou admirest, alas, have no *colour*, but are fair, because they seem to be coloured: If this seeming will not satisfy thee in her, thou hast good assurance of her *colour,* when thou seest her *lay* it on. If her *face* be *painted* on a Board or Wall, thou wilt love it, and the Board, and the Wall: Canst thou loath it then when it speaks, smiles, and kisses, because it is *painted?* Are we not more delighted with seeing Birds, Fruits, and Beasts *painted* than we are with Naturals? And do we not with pleasure behold the *painted* shape of Monsters and Devils, whom true, we durst not regard? We repair the ruins of our houses, but first cold tempests warn us of it, and bites us through it; we mend the wrack and stains of our Apparel, but first our eyes, and other bodies are offended; but by this providence of Women, this is prevented. If in *Kissing* or *breathing* upon her, the *painting* fall off, thou art angry; wilt thou be so, if it stick on? Thou didst love her; if thou beginnest to hate her, then 'tis because she is not *painted.* If thou wilt say now, thou didst hate her before, thou didst hate her and love her together. Be constant in something, and love her who shews her great *love* to thee, in taking this pains to seem *lovely* to thee.

❧ ☙

SIR RICHARD STEELE

Conversations on Marriage

> —*Properat cursu*
> *Vita citato.*—
>
> *Senec. Trag.*

With speedy step life posts away.

I this morning did myself the honour to visit lady Lizard, and took my chair at the tea-table, at the upper end of which that graceful woman, with her daughters about her, appeared to me with greater dignity than ever any figure, either of Venus attended by the Graces, Diana with her nymphs, or any other celestial who owes her being to poetry.

The discourse we had there, none being present but our own family, consisted of private matters, which tended to the establishment of these young ladies in the world. My lady, I observed, had a mind to make mention of the proposal to Mrs. Jane, of which she is very fond, and I as much avoided, as being equally against it; but it is by no means proper the young ladies should observe we ever dissent; therefore I turned the discourse, by saying, "It was time enough to think of marrying a young lady, who was but three and twenty, ten years hence." The whole table was alarmed at the assertion, and the Sparkler scalded her fingers, by leaning suddenly forward to look in my face: but my business at present, was to make my court to the mother; therefore, without regarding the resentment in the looks of the children, "Madam," said I, "there is a petulant and hasty manner practised in this age, in hurrying away the life of woman, and confining the grace and principal action of it to those years wherein reason and discretion are most feeble, humour and passion most powerful. From the time a young woman of quality has first appeared in the drawing-room, raised a whisper and curiosity of the men about her, had her health drunk in gay companies, and been distinguished at public assemblies: I say, madam, if within three or four years of her first appearance in town, she is not disposed of, her beauty is grown familiar, her eyes are disarmed, and we seldom after hear her mentioned but with indifference. What doubles my grief on this occasion is, that the more discreetly the lady behaves herself, the sooner is her glory extinguished. Now, Madam, if merit had a greater weight in our thoughts, when we form to ourselves agreeable characters of women, men would think, in making their choices, of such as would take care of, as well as supply children for, the nursery. It was not thus in the illustrious days of good queen Elizabeth. I was this morning turning over a folio, called, The Complete Ambassador, consisting chiefly of letters from Lord Burleigh, Earl of Leicester, and Sir Thomas Smith. Sir Thomas writes a letter to Sir Francis Walsingham, full of learned gallantry, wherein you may observe he promises himself the French king's brother, who, it seems, was but a cold lover, would be quickened by seeing the queen in person, who was then in the thirty-ninth year of her age. A certain sobriety in thoughts, words, and action, which was the praise of that age, kept the fire of love alive; and it burnt so equally, that it warmed and preserved, without tormenting and consuming our beings. The letter I mentioned is as follows:

'To the Right Worshipful Mr. Francis Walsingham,
Ambassador, resident in France.

'Sir,
'I am sorry that so good a matter should, upon so nice a point, be deferred We may say that the lover will do little,

if he will not take the pains once to see his love; but she must first say yea, before he see her, or she him; twenty ways might be devised why he might come over and be welcome, and possibly do more in an hour than he may in two years. *Cupido ille qui vincit omnia, in oculis insidel, et ex oculis ejaculatur, et in oculis utriusque videndo non solum, ut ait poëta, fœmina virum, sed vir fœminam;* "That powerful being Cupid, who conquers all things, resides in the eyes, he sends out all his darts from the eyes: by throwing glances at the eyes, according to the poet, not only the woman captivates the man, but also the man the woman." What force, I pray you, can hearsay, and "I think, and I trust," do in comparison of that *cùm præsens præsentem tuetur et alloquitur, et, furore forsitan amoris ductus, amplectitur,* when they face to face see and converse with each other, and the lover in an ecstasy not to be commanded, snatches an embrace, and saith to himself, and openly that she may hear, *Teneone te mea, an etiamnum somno volunt fœminæ videri cogi ad id quod maximum cupiunt?* "Are you in my arms, my fair one, or do we both dream, and will women even in their sleep seem forced to what they most desire?" If we be cold, it is our part, besides the person, the sex requireth it. Why are you cold? Is it not a young man's part to be bold, courageous, and to adventure? If he should have, he should have but *honorificam repulsam;* even a repulse here is glorious: the worst that can be said of him is but as of Phaëton, *Quam si non tenuit magnis tamen excidit ausis:* "though he could not command the chariot of the sun, his fall from it was illustrious." So far as I conceive, *Hæc est sola nostra anchora, hæc jacenda est nobis alea;* "this is our only anchor, this die must be thrown." In our instability, *Unum momentum est uno momento perfectum factum, ac dictum stabilitatem facere potest;* "one lucky moment would crown and fix all." This, or else nothing is to be looked for but continual dalliance and doubtfulness, so far as I can see.

'Your assured friend,
'Thomas Smith.'

'From Killingworth, Aug. 22, 1572.'

Though my lady was in very good humour, upon the insinuation that, according to the Elizabeth scheme, she was but just advanced above the character of a girl; I found the rest of the company as much disheartened, that they were still but mere girls. I went on, therefore, to attribute the immature marriages which are solemnized in our days to the importunity of the men, which made it impossible for young ladies to remain virgins so long as they wished, from their own inclinations, and the freedom of a single life.

There is no time of our life, under what character soever, in which men can wholly divest themselves of an ambition to be in the favour of women. Cardan, a grave philosopher and physician, confesses, in one of his chapters, that though he had suffered poverty, repulses, calumnies, and a long series of afflictions, he never was thoroughly dejected, and impatient of life itself, but under a calamity which he suffered from the beginning of his twenty-first, to the end of his thirtieth year. He tells us, that the raillery he suffered from others, and the contempt which he had of himself, were afflictions beyond expression. I mention this only as an argument extorted from this good and grave man, to support my opinion of the irresistible power of women. He adds, in the same chapter, that there are ten thousand afflictions and disasters attend the passion itself; that an idle word, imprudently repeated by a fair woman, and vast expenses to support her folly and vanity, every day reduce men to poverty and death; but he makes them of little consideration to the miserable and insignificant condition of being incapable of their favour.

I make no manner of difficulty of professing I am not surprised that the author has expressed himself after this manner, with relation to love: the heroic chastity so frequently professed by humourists of the fair sex, generally ends in an unworthy choice, after having overlooked overtures to their advantage It is for this reason that I would endeavour to direct, and not pretend to eradicate, the inclinations of the sexes to each other. Daily experience shows us, that the most rude rustic grows humane as soon as he is inspired by this passion; it gives a new grace to our manners, a new dignity to our minds, a new visage to our persons. Whether we are inclined to liberal arts, to arms, or address in our exercise, our improvement is hastened by a particular object whom we would please. Cheerfulness, gentleness, fortitude, liberality, magnificence, and all the virtues which adorn men, which inspire heroes, are most conspicuous in lovers. I speak of love as when such as are in this company are the objects of it, who can bestow upon their husbands, if they follow their excellent mother, all its joys, without any of its anxieties.

BENJAMIN FRANKLIN

Advising a Young Man as to the Selection of a Mistress

To * * * *   [Philadelphia,] 25 June, 1745.
My Dear Friend:

I know of no medicine fit to diminish the violent natural inclinations you mention; and if I did, I think I should not communicate it to you. Marriage is the proper remedy. It is the most natural state of man, and therefore the state in which you are most likely to find solid happiness. Your reasons against entering into it at present appear to me not well founded. The circumstantial advantages you have in view by postponing it, are not only uncertain, but they are small in comparison with that of the thing itself, the being married and settled. It is the man and woman united that make the complete human being. Separate, she wants his force of body and strength of reason; he, her softness, sensibility and acute discernment. Together they are more likely to succeed in the world. A single man has not nearly the value he would have in the state of union. He is an incomplete animal. He resembles the odd half of a pair of scissors. If you get a prudent, healthy wife, your industry in your profession, with her good economy, will be a fortune sufficient.

But if you will not take this counsel and persist in thinking a commerce with the sex inevitable, then I repeat my former advice, that in all your amours you should prefer old women to young ones.

You call this a paradox and demand my reasons. They are these:

1. Because they have more knowledge of the world, and their minds are better stored with observations, their conversation is more improving, and more lastingly agreeable.

2. Because when women cease to be handsome they study to be good. To maintain their influence over men, they supply the diminution of beauty by an augmention of utility. They learn to do a thousand services small and great, and are the most tender and useful of friends when you are sick. Thus they continue amiable. And hence there is hardly such a thing to be found as an old woman who is not a good woman.

3. Because there is no hazard of children, which irregularly produced may be attended with much inconvenience.

4. Because through more experience they are more prudent and discreet in conducting an intrigue to prevent suspicion. The commerce with

them is therefore safer with regard to your reputation. And with regard to theirs, if the affair should happen to be known, considerate people might be rather inclined to excuse an old woman, who would kindly take care of a young man, form his manners by her good counsels, and prevent his ruining his health and fortune among mercenary prostitutes.

5. Because in every animal that walks upright, the deficiency of the fluids that fill the muscles appears first in the highest part. The face first grows lank and wrinkled; then the neck; then the breast and arms; the lower parts continuing to the last as plump as ever: so that covering all above with a basket, and regarding only what is below the girdle, it is impossible of two women to know an old one from a young one. And as in the dark all cats are grey, the pleasure of corporal enjoyment with an old woman is at least equal, and frequently superior; every knack being, by practice, capable of improvement.

6. Because the sin is less. The debauching a virgin may be her ruin, and make her for life unhappy.

7. Because the compunction is less. The having made a young girl miserable may give you frequent bitter reflection; none of which can attend the making an old woman happy.

8thy & lastly. They are so grateful!!

Thus much for my paradox. But still I advise you to marry directly; being sincerely

Your affectionate Friend,
Benjamin Franklin

Joseph Addison

History of the Lover's Leap

> As if with sports my suff'rings I could ease;
> Or by my pains the god of love appease.
>
> Dryden

I shall in this paper discharge myself of the promise I have made to the public, by obliging them with a translation of the little Greek manuscript, which is said to have been a piece of those records that were preserved in the temple of Apollo upon the promontory of Leucate. It is a short history of the Lover's Leap, and is inscribed, An account of persons, male and female, who offered up their vows in the temple of the Pythian Apollo in the forty-sixth Olympiad, and leaped from the promontory of Leucate into the Ionian Sea, in order to cure themselves of the passion of love.

This account is very dry in many parts, as only mentioning the name of the lover who leaped, the person he leaped for, and relating, in short, that he was either cured, or killed, or maimed, by the fall. It indeed gives the names of so many who died by it, that it would have looked like a Bill of Mortality, had I translated it at full length; I have therefore made an abridgement of it, and only extracted such particular passages as have something extraordinary, either in the case or in the cure, or in the fate of the person who is mentioned in it. After this short preface, take the account as follows:—

Battus, the son of Menaleas the Sicilian, leaped for Bombyca, the musician: got rid of his passion with the loss of his right leg and arm, which were broken in the fall.

Melissa, in love with Daphnis: very much bruised, but escaped with life.

Cynisca, the wife of Æschines, being in love with Lycus; and Æschines, her husband, being in love with Eurilla, which had made this married couple very uneasy to one another for several years: both the husband and the wife took the leap by consent; they both of them escaped, and have lived very happily together ever since.

Larissa, a virgin of Thessaly, deserted by Plexippus, after a courtship of three years: she stood upon the brow of the promontory for some time, and having thrown down a ring, a bracelet, and a little picture, with other presents which she had received from Plexippus, she threw herself into the sea, and was taken up alive.

N. B. Larissa, before she leaped, made an offering of a silver cupid in the temple of Apollo.

Simætha, in love with Daphnis, the Myndian, perished in the fall.

Charixus, the brother of Sappho, in love with Rhodope the courtesan, having spent his whole estate upon her, was advised by his sister to leap in the beginning of his amour, but would not hearken to her till he was reduced to his last talent; being forsaken by Rhodope, at length resolved to take the leap: perished in it.

Aridæus, a beautiful youth of Epirus, in love with Praxinoe, the wife of Thespis; escaped without damage, saving only that two of his fore-teeth were struck out and his nose a little flatted.

Cleora a widow of Ephesus, being inconsolable for the death of

her husband, was resolved to take this leap in order to get rid of her passion for his memory; but, being arrived at the promontory, she there met
with Dymmachus, the Milesian, and after a short conversation with him,
laid aside the thoughts of her leap, and married him in the temple of
Apollo.

N. B. Her widow's weeds are still to be seen hanging up in the western corner of the temple.

Olphis, the fisherman, having received a box on the ear from
Thestylis the day before, and being determined to have no more to do
with her, leaped, and escaped with life.

Atalanta, an old maid, whose cruelty had several years before driven two or three despairing lovers to this leap; being now in the fifty-fifth
year of her age, and in love with an officer of Sparta, broke her neck in
the fall.

Hipparchus, being passionately fond of his own wife, who was
enamoured of Bathyllus, leaped and died of his fall: upon which his wife
married her gallant.

Tettyx, the dancing master, in love with Olympia, an Athenian
matron, threw himself from the rock with great agility, but was crippled
in the fall.

Diagoras, the usurer, in love with his cook-maid; he peeped several
times over the precipice, but his heart misgiving him, he went back, and
married her that evening.

Cinædus, after having entered his own name in the Pythian records,
being asked the name of the person whom he leaped for, and being
ashamed to discover it, he was set aside, and not suffered to leap.

Eunica, a maid of Paphos, aged nineteen, in love with Eurybates:
hurt in the fall, but recovered.

N. B. This was her second time of leaping.

Hesperus, a young man of Tarentum, in love with his master's
daughter: drowned, the boats not coming in soon enough to his relief.

Sappho, the Lesbian, in love with Phaon, arrived at the temple of
Apollo habited like a bride, in garments as white as snow. She wore a garland of myrtle on her head, and carried in her hand the little musical instrument of her own invention. After having sung a hymn to Apollo, she
hung up her garland on one side of his altar and her harp on the other.
She then tucked up her vestments like a Spartan virgin, and amidst thousands of spectators, who were anxious for her safety and offered up
vows for her deliverance, marched directly forwards to the utmost summit of the promontory, where, after having repeated a stanza of her

own verses, which we could not hear, she threw herself off the rock with such an intrepidity as was never before observed in any who had attempted that dangerous leap. Many who were present related, that they saw her fall into the sea, from whence she never rose again; though there were others who affirmed that she never came to the bottom of her leap, but that she was changed into a swan as she fell, and that they saw her hovering in the air under that shape. But whether or no the whiteness and fluttering of her garments might not deceive those who looked upon her, or whether she might not really be metamorphosed into that musical and melancholy bird, is still a doubt among the Lesbians.

Alcæus, the famous lyric poet, who had for some time been passionately in love with Sappho, arrived at the promontory of the Leucate that very evening, in order to take the leap upon her account; but hearing that Sappho had been there before him, and that her body could be nowhere found, he very generously lamented her fall, and is said to have written his hundred and twenty-fifth ode upon that occasion.

Leaped in this olympiad

Males	124
Females	126
	250

Cured

Males	51
Females	69
	120

❧ ☙

GEORGE COLMAN AND BONNEL THORNTON

On Superstitions in Love

> *Necte tribus nodis ternos, Amarylli, colores:*
> *Necte, Amarylli, modò, et Veneris, dic, vincula necto.*
> *Ducite ab urbe domum, mea carmina, ducite Daphnim.*
> *Limus ut hic durescit, et hæc ut cera liquescit,*
> *Uno eodemque igni; sic nostro Daphnis amore.*

Virg. Ecl. viii. 77.

Three colours weave in three-fold knots, and cry,
"In three-fold bond this true-love's knot I tie."
As the same fire makes hard this cake of clay,
In which this waxen image melts away,
Thus, God of Love, be my true shepherd's breast
Soft to my flame, but hard to all the rest.
Ye songs, spells, philters, amulets, and charms!
Bring, quickly bring, my Daphnis to my arms.

The idle superstitions of the vulgar are no where so conspicuous as in the affairs of love. When a raw girl's brain is once turned with a sweetheart, she converts every trifling accident of her life into a good or bad omen, and makes every thing conspire to strengthen her in so pleasing a delusion. Virgil represents Dido, as soon as she has contracted her fatal passion for Æneas, as going to the priests to have her fortune told. In like manner, the lovesick girl runs to the cunning-man, or crosses the gipsy's hand with her last sixpence, to know when she shall be married, how many children she shall have, and whether she shall be happy with her husband. She also consults the cards, and finds out her lover in the knave of hearts. She learns how to interpret dreams, and every night furnishes her with meditations for the next day. If she happens to bring out any thing in conversation which another person was about to say, she comforts herself that she shall be married first; and if she tumbles as she is running up stairs, imagines she shall go to church with her sweetheart before the week is at an end. But if, in the course of their amour, she gives the dear man her hair wove in a true-lover's knot, or breaks a crooked ninepence with him, she thinks herself assured of his inviolable fidelity.

It would puzzle the most profound antiquary to discover, what could give birth to the strange notions cherished by fond nymphs and swains. The god of love has more superstitious votaries, and is worshipped with more unaccountable rites, than any fabulous deity whatever. Nothing, indeed, is so whimsical as the imagination of a person in love. The dying shepherd carves the name of his mistress on the trees, while the fond maid knits him a pair of garters with an amorous posy: and both look on what they do as a kind of charm to secure the affection of the other. A lover will rejoice to give his mistress a bracelet or a top-knot, and she perhaps will take pleasure in working him a pair of ruffles. These they will regard as the soft bonds of love; but neither would, on any account, run the risk of cutting love by giving or receiving such a present as a knife or a pair of scissors. But to wear the picture of the beloved object constantly near the heart, is universally accounted a most excellent and never-failing preservative of affection.

Some few years ago there was publicly advertised, among the other extraordinary medicines whose wonderful qualities are daily related in the last page of our newspapers, a most efficacious love-powder; by which a despairing lover might create affection in the bosom of the most cruel mistress. Lovers have, indeed, always been fond of enchantment. Shakespeare has represented Othello as accused of winning his Desdemona by "conjuration and mighty magic"; and Theocritus and Virgil have both introduced women into their pastorals, using charms and incantations to recover the affections of their sweethearts. In a word, talismans, genii, witches, fairies, and all the instruments of magic and enchantment were first discovered by lovers, and employed in the business of love.

But I never had a thorough insight into all this amorous sorcery till I received the following letter, which was sent me from the country a day or two after Valentine's day; and I make no doubt, but all true lovers most religiously performed the previous rites mentioned by my correspondent.

"To Mr. Town.

"Dear Sir,
"You must know I am in love with a very clever man, a Londoner; and as I want to know whether it is my fortune to have him, I have tried all the tricks I can hear of for that purpose. I have seen him several times in coffee-grounds with a sword by his side; and he was once at the bottom of a tea-cup in a coach and six with two footmen behind it. I got up last May morning, and went into the fields to hear the cuckoo: and when I pulled off my left shoe, I found a hair in it exactly the same colour with his. But I shall never forget what I did last Midsummer-eve. I and my two sisters tried the Dumb Cake together: you must know, two must make it, two bake it, two break it; and the third put it under each of their pillows, but you must not speak a word all the time, and then you will dream of the man you are to have. This we did; and to be sure I did nothing all night but dream of Mr. Blossom. The same night, exactly at twelve o'clock, I sowed hemp-seed in our back yard, and said to myself, 'Hempseed I sow, Hempseed I hoe, and he that is my true love come after me and mow.' Will you believe me? I looked back, and saw him behind me, as plain as eyes could see him. After that, I took a clean shift, and turned it, and hung it upon the back of a chair; and very likely my sweetheart would have come and turned it right again, for I heard his

step, but I was frightened, and could not help speaking, which broke the charm. I likewise stuck up two Midsummer men, one for myself and one for him. Now if his had died away, we should never have come together; but I assure you his blowed and turned to mine. Our maid Betty tells me, that if I go backwards, without speaking a word, into the garden upon Midsummer-eve, and gather a rose, and keep it in a clean sheet of paper, without looking at it till Christmas-day, it will be as fresh as in June; and if I then stick it in my bosom, he that is to be my husband will come and take it out. If I am not married before the time come about again, I will certainly do it; and only mind if Mr. Blossom is not the man.

"I have tried a great many other fancies, and they have all turned out right. Whenever I go to lie in a strange bed, I always tie my garter nine times round the bed-post, and knit nine knots in it, and say to myself, 'This knot I knit, this knot I tie, to see my love as he goes by, in his apparel and array, as he walks in every day.' I did so last holidays at my uncle's, and to be sure I saw Mr. Blossom draw my curtains, and tuck up the clothes at my bed's feet. Cousin Debby was married a little while ago, and she sent me a piece of bride-cake to put under my pillow; and I had the sweetest dream—I thought we were going to be married together. I have, many is the time, taken great pains to pare an apple whole, and afterwards flung the peel over my head; and it always falls in the shape of the first letter of his surname or Christian name. I am sure Mr. Blossom loves me, because I stuck two of the kernels upon my forehead, while I thought upon him and the lubberly squire my papa wants me to have: Mr. Blossom's kernel stuck on, but the other dropped off directly.

"Last Friday, Mr. Town, was Valentine's day; and I'll tell you what I did the night before. I got five bay-leaves, and pinned four of them to the four corners of my pillow, and the fifth to the middle; and then, if I dreamed of my sweetheart, Betty said we should be married before the year was out. But, to make it more sure, I boiled an egg hard, and took out the yolk, and filled it up with salt: and when I went to bed, eat it shell and all, without speaking or drinking after it, and this was to have the same effect with the bay-leaves. We also wrote our lovers' names upon bits of paper, and rolled them up in clay, and put them into water; and the first that rose up was to be our Valentine. Would you think it? Mr. Blossom was my man; and I lay abed, and shut my eyes all the morning, till he came to our house; for I would not have seen another man before him for all the world.

"Dear Mr. Town, if you know any other ways to try our fortune by, do put them in your paper. My mamma laughs at us, and says there is nothing in them; but I am sure there is, for several misses at our boarding-school have tried them, and they have all happened true: and I am sure my own sister Hetty, who died just before Christmas, stood in the church-porch last Midsummer eve to see all that were to die that year in our parish; and she saw her own apparition.

> "*Your humble servant,*
> "*Arabella Whimsey.*"

❧ ☙

VOLTAIRE (FRANÇOIS-MARIE AROUET)

from *A Philosophical Dictionary*

LOVE

There are so many kinds of love, that in order to define it, we scarcely know which to direct our attention to. Some boldly apply the name of "love" to a caprice of a few days, a connection without attachment, passion without affection, the affectations of cicisbeism, a cold usage, a romantic fancy, a taste speedily followed by a distaste. They apply the name to a thousand chimeras.

Should any philosophers be inclined profoundly to investigate a subject in itself so little philosophical, they may recur to the banquet of Plato, in which Socrates, the decent and honorable lover of Alcibiades and Agathon, converses with them on the metaphysics of love.

Lucretius speaks of it more as a natural philosopher; and Virgil follows the example of Lucretius. "*Amor omnibus idem.*" [Love is the same for everyone.]

It is the embroidery of imagination on the stuff of nature. If you wish to form an idea of love, look at the sparrows in your garden; behold your doves; contemplate the bull when introduced to the heifer; look at that powerful and spirited horse which two of your grooms are conducting to the mare that quietly awaits him, and is evidently pleased at his approach; observe the flashing of his eyes, notice the strength and loudness of his neighings, the boundings, the curvetings, the ears erect, the mouth opening with convulsive gaspings, the distended nostrils, the breath of fire, the raised and waving mane, and the impetuous movement with which he rushes towards the object which nature has destined for him; do not, however, be jealous of his happiness; but reflect on the advantages of the human species; they afford ample compensation in love for all those which nature has conferred on mere animals—strength, beauty, lightness, and rapidity.

There are some classes, however, even of animals totally unacquainted with sexual association. Fishes are destitute of this enjoyment. The female deposits her millions of eggs on the slime of the waters, and the male that meets them passes over them and communicates the vital principle, never consorting with, or perhaps even perceiving the female to whom they belong.

The greater part of those animals which copulate are sensible of the enjoyment only by a single sense; and when appetite is satisfied, the whole is over. No animal, besides man, is acquainted with embraces; his whole frame is susceptible; his lips particularly experience a delight which never wearies, and which is exclusively the portion of his species; finally, he can surrender himself at all seasons to the endearments of love, while mere animals possess only limited periods. If you reflect on these high pre-eminences, you will readily join in the earl of Rochester's remark, that love would impel a whole nation of atheists to worship the divinity.

As men have been endowed with the talent of perfecting whatever nature has bestowed upon them, they have accordingly perfected the gift of love. Cleanliness, personal attention, and regard to health render the frame more sensitive, and consequently increase its capacity of gratification. All the other amiable and valuable sentiments enter afterwards into that of love, like the metals which amalgamate with gold; friendship and esteem readily fly to its support; and talents both of body and of mind are new and strengthening bonds.

Nam facit ipsa suis interdum femina factis,
Morigerisque modis, et mundo corpore cultu
Ut facile insuescat secum vir degere vitam.

—Lucretius, iv, 1275.

Self-love, above all, draws closer all these various ties. Men pride themselves in the choice they have made; and the numberless illusions that crowd around constitute the ornament of the work, of which the foundation is so firmly laid by nature.

Such are the advantages possessed by man above the various tribes of animals. But, if he enjoys delights of which they are ignorant, how many vexations and disgusts, on the other hand, is he exposed to, from which they are free! The most dreadful of these is occasioned by nature's having poisoned the pleasures of love and sources of life over three-quarters of the world by a terrible disease, to which man alone is subject; nor is it with this pestilence as with various other maladies, which are the natural consequences of excess. It was not introduced into the world by debauchery. The Phrynes and Laises, the Floras and Messalinas, were never attacked by it. It originated in islands where mankind dwelt together in innocence, and has thence been spread throughout the Old World.

If nature could in any instance be accused of despising her own work, thwarting her own plan, and counteracting her own views, it would be in this detestable scourge which has polluted the earth with horror and shame. And can this, then, be the best of all possible worlds? What! if Cæsar and Antony and Octavius never had this disease, was it not possible to prevent Francis the First from dying of it? No, it is said; things were so ordered all for the best; I am disposed to believe it; but it is unfortunate for those to whom Rabelais has dedicated his book.

Erotic philosophers have frequently discussed the question, whether Héloïse could truly love Abelard after he became a monk and mutilated? One of these states much wronged the other.

Be comforted, however, Abelard, you were really beloved; imagination comes in aid of the heart. Men feel a pleasure in remaining at table, although they can no longer eat. Is it love? is it simply recollection? is it friendship? It is a something compounded of all these. It is a confused feeling, resembling the fantastic passions which the dead retained in the Elysian Fields. The heroes who while living had shone in the chariot races, guided imaginary chariots after death. Héloïse lived with you on illusions and supplements. She sometimes caressed you, and with so much the more pleasure as, after vowing at Paraclet that she would love you no more, her caresses were become more precious to her in proportion as they had become more culpable. A woman can never form a passion for a eunuch; but she may retain her passion for her lover after his becoming one, if he still remains amiable.

The case is different with respect to a lover grown old in the service; the external appearance is no longer the same; wrinkles affright, grizzly eyebrows repel, decaying teeth disgust, infirmities drive away; all that can be done or expected is to have the virtue of being a patient and kind nurse, and bearing with the man that was once beloved, all which amounts to—burying the dead.

᭢᭢

SAMUEL TAYLOR COLERIDGE

Passion and Order

Perhaps there is no more sure criterion of refinement in moral character, of the purity of intellectual intention, and of the deep conviction
and perfect sense of what our own nature really is in all its combinations,
than the different definitions different men would give of love. I will not
detain you by stating the various known definitions, some of which it
may be better not to repeat: I will rather give you one of my own, which,
I apprehend, is equally free from the extravagance of pretended Platonism (which, like other things which super-moralise, is sure to demoralise)
and from its grosser opposite.

Consider myself and my fellow-men as a sort of link between
heaven and earth, being composed of body and soul, with power to reason and to will, and with that perpetual aspiration which tells us that this
is ours for a while, but it is not ourselves; considering man, I say, in this
two-fold character yet united in one person, I conceive that there can be
no correct definition of love which does not correspond with our being,
and with that subordination of one part to another which constitutes our
perfection. I would say therefore that—

"Love is a desire of the whole being to be united to some thing,
or some being, felt necessary to its completeness, by the most perfect
means that nature permits, and reason dictates."

It is inevitable to every noble mind, whether man or woman, to feel
itself, of itself, imperfect and insufficient, not as an animal only, but as
a moral being. How wonderfully, then, has Providence contrived for us,
by making that which is necessary to us a step in our exaltation to a
higher and nobler state! The Creator has ordained that one should possess qualities which the other has not, and the union of both is the most
complete ideal of human character. In everything the blending of the
similar with the dissimilar is the secret of all pure delight. Who shall dare
to stand alone, and vaunt himself, in himself, sufficient? In poetry it is
the blending of passion with order that constitutes perfection: this is still
more the case in morals, and more than all in the exclusive attachment
of the sexes.

True it is, that the world and its business may be carried on without marriage; but it is so evident that Providence intended man (the
only animal of all climates, and whose reason is preeminent over in-

stinct) to be the master of the world, that marriage, or the knitting together of society by the tenderest, yet firmest ties, seems ordained to render him capable of maintaining his superiority over the brute creation.
Man alone has been privileged to clothe himself, and to do all things so
as to make him, as it were, a secondary creator of himself, and of his own
happiness or misery: in this, as in all, the image of the Deity is impressed upon him.

Providence, then, has not left us to prudence only; for the power
of calculation, which prudence implies, cannot have existed, but in a state
which pre-supposes marriage. If God has done this, shall we suppose that
he has given us no moral sense, no yearning, which is something more
than animal, to secure that, without which man might form a herd, but
could not be a society? The very idea seems to breathe absurdity.

From this union arise the paternal, filial, brotherly and sisterly relations of life; and every state is but a family magnified. All the operations of mind, in short, all that distinguishes us from brutes, originate
in the more perfect state of domestic life.—One infallible criterion in
forming an opinion of a man is the reverence in which he holds women.
Plato has said, that in this way we rise from sensuality to affection, from
affection to love, and from love to the pure intellectual delight by which
we become worthy to conceive that infinite in ourselves, without which
it is impossible for man to believe in a God. In a word, the grandest and
most delightful of all promises has been expressed to us by this practical state—our marriage with the Redeemer of mankind.

I might safely appeal to every man who hears me, who in youth has
been accustomed to abandon himself to his animal passions, whether
when he first really fell in love, the earliest symptom was not a complete
change in his manners, a contempt and a hatred of himself for having
excused his conduct by asserting that he acted according to the dictates
of nature, that his vices were the inevitable consequences of youth, and
that his passions at that period of life could not be conquered? The
surest friend of chastity is love: it leads us, not to sink the mind in the
body, but to draw up the body to the mind—the immortal part of our
nature. See how contrasted in this respect are some portions of the
works of writers, whom I need not name, with other portions of the
same works: the ebullitions of comic humour have at times, by a lamentable confusion, been made the means of debasing our nature, while
at other times, even in the same volume, we are happy to notice the utmost purity, such as the purity of love, which above all other qualities
renders us most pure and lovely.

Love is not, like hunger, a mere selfish appetite: it is an associative quality. The hungry savage is nothing but an animal, thinking only of the satisfaction of his stomach: what is the first effect of love, but to associate the feeling with every object in nature? the trees whisper, the roses exhale their perfumes, the nightingales sing, nay the very skies smile in unison with the feeling of true and pure love. It gives to every object in nature a power of the heart, without which it would indeed be spiritless.

CHARLES LAMB

A Bachelor's Complaint of the Behavior of Married People

As a single man, I have spent a good deal of my time in noting down the infirmities of Married People, to console myself for those superior pleasures, which they tell me I have lost by remaining as I am.

I cannot say that the quarrels of men and their wives ever made any great impression upon me, or had much tendency to strengthen in those anti-social resolution, which I took up long ago upon more substantial considerations. What oftenest offends me at the houses of married persons where I visit, is an error of quite a different description;—it is that they are too loving.

Not too loving neither: that does not explain my meaning. Besides, why should that offend me? The very act of separating themselves from the rest of the world, to have the fuller enjoyment of each other's society, implies that they prefer one another to all the world.

But what I complain of is, that they carry this preference so undisguisedly, they perk it up in the faces of us single people so shamelessly, you cannot be in their company a moment without being made to feel, by some indirect hint or open avowal, that *you* are not the object of this preference. Now there are some things which give no offence, while implied or taken for granted merely; but expressed, there is much offence in them. If a man were to accost the first homely-featured or plain-dressed young woman of his acquaintance, and tell her bluntly, that she was not handsome or rich enough for him, and he could not marry her, he would deserve to be kicked for his ill manners; yet no less is implied in the fact, that having access and opportunity of putting the question to her, he has never yet thought fit to do it. The young woman understands this as clearly as if it were put into words; but no reasonable

young woman would think of making this the ground of a quarrel. Just
as little right have a married couple to tell me by speeches, and looks that
are scarce less plain than speeches, that I am not the happy man,—the
lady's choice. It is enough that I know I am not: I do not want this perpetual reminding.

The display of superior knowledge or riches may be made sufficiently mortifying; but these admit of a palliative. The knowledge which
is brought out to insult me, may accidentally improve me; and in the rich
man's houses and pictures,—his parks and gardens, I have a temporary
usufruct at least. But the display of married happiness has none of these
palliatives: it is throughout pure, unrecompensed, unqualified insult.

Marriage by its best title is a monopoly, and not of the least invidious sort. It is the cunning of most possessors of any exclusive privilege to keep their advantage as much out of sight as possible, that their
less favoured neighbours, seeing little of the benefit, may the less be disposed to question the right. But these married monopolists thrust the
most obnoxious part of their patent into our faces.

Nothing is to me more distasteful than that entire complacency
and satisfaction which beam in the countenances of a new-married couple,—in that of the lady particularly: it tells you, that her lot is disposed
of in this world: that *you* can have no hopes of her. It is true, I have none:
nor wishes either, perhaps; but this is one of those truths which ought,
as I said before, to be taken for granted, not expressed.

The excessive airs which those people give themselves, founded on
the ignorance of us unmarried people, would be more offensive if they
were less irrational. We will allow them to understand the mysteries belonging to their own craft better than we, who have not had the happiness to be made free of the company: but their arrogance is not content
within these limits. If a single person presume to offer his opinion in
their presence, though upon the most indifferent subject, he is immediately silenced as an incompetent person. Nay, a young married lady of
my acquaintance, who, the best of the jest was, had not changed her condition above a fortnight before, in a question on which I had the misfortune to differ from her, respecting the properest mode of breeding
oysters for the London market, had the assurance to ask with a sneer,
how such an old Bachelor as I could pretend to know anything about
such matters!

But what I have spoken of hitherto is nothing to the airs these creatures give themselves when they come, as they generally do, to have children. When I consider how little of a rarity children are,—that every

street and blind alley swarms with them,—that the poorest people commonly have them in most abundance,—that there are few marriages that are not blest with at least one of these bargains,—how often they turn out ill, and defeat the fond hopes of their parents, taking to vicious courses, which end in poverty, disgrace, the gallows etc.—I cannot for my life tell what cause for pride there can possibly be in having them. If they were young phœnixes, indeed, that were born but one in a year, there might be a pretext. But when they are so common—

I do not advert to the insolent merit which they assume with their husbands on these occasions. Let *them* look to that. But why *we*, who are not their natural-born subjects, should be expected to bring our spices, myrrh, and incense,—our tribute and homage of admiration,—I do not see.

"Like as the arrows in the hand of the giant, even so are the young children": so says the excellent office in our Prayer-book appointed for the churching of women. "Happy is the man that hath his quiver full of them": So say I; but then don't let him discharge his quiver upon us that are weaponless:—let them be arrows, but not to gall and stick us. I have generally observed that these arrows are double-headed: they have two forks, to be sure to hit with one or the other. As for instance, where you come into a house which is full of children, if you happen to take no notice of them (you are thinking of something else, perhaps, and turn a deaf ear to their innocent caresses), you are set down as untractable, morose, a hater of children. On the other hand, if you find them more than usually engaging,—if you are taken with their pretty manners, and set about in earnest to romp and play with them, some pretext or other is sure to be found for sending them out of the room; they are too noisy or boisterous, or Mr. —— does not like children. With one or other of these folks the arrow is sure to hit you.

I could forgive their jealousy, and dispense with toying with their brats, if it gives them any pain; but I think it unreasonable to be called upon to *love* them, where I see no occasion,—to love a whole family, perhaps eight, nine, or ten, indiscriminately,—to love all the pretty dears, because children are so engaging!

I know there is a proverb, "Love me, love my dog": that is always so very practicable, particularly if the dog be set upon you to tease you or snap at you in sport. But a dog, or a lesser thing—any inanimate substance, as a keepsake, a watch or a ring, a tree, or the place where we last parted when my friend went away upon a long absence, I can make shift to love, because I love him, and anything that reminds me of him; provided it be in its nature indifferent, and apt to receive whatever hue fancy can give it. But children have a real character, and an essential being of themselves: they are amiable or unamiable *per se;* I must love or hate them as I see cause for either in their qualities. A child's nature is too serious a thing to admit of its being regarded as a mere appendage to another being, and to be loved or hated accordingly: they stand with me upon their own stock, as much as men and women do. Oh! but you will say, sure it is an attractive age,—there is something in the tender years of infancy that of itself charms us? This is the very reason why I am more nice about them. I know that a sweet child is the sweetest thing in nature, not even excepting the delicate creatures which bear them; but the prettier the kind of a thing is, the more desirable it is that it should be pretty of its kind. One daisy differs not much from another in glory; but a violet should look and smell the daintiest.—I was always rather squeamish in my women and children.

But this is not the worst: one must be admitted into their familiarity at least, before they can complain of inattention. It implies visits, and some kind of intercourse. But if the husband be a man with whom you have lived on a friendly footing before marriage—if you did not come in on the wife's side—if you did not sneak into the house in her train, but were an old friend in fast habits of intimacy before their courtship was so much as thought on,—look about you—your tenure is precarious—before a twelvemonth shall roll over your head, you shall find your old friend gradually grow cool and altered towards you, and at last seek opportunities of breaking with you. I have scarce a married friend of my acquaintance, upon whose firm faith I can rely, whose friendship did not commence *after the period of his marriage.* With some limitations, they can endure that; but that the good man should have dared to enter into a solemn league of friendship in which they were not consulted, though it happened before they knew him,—before they that are now man and wife ever met,—this is intolerable to them. Every long friendship, every old authentic intimacy, must be brought into their office to be new stamped with their currency, as a sovereign prince calls in the good old money that was coined in some reign before he was born or thought of, to be new marked and minted with the stamp of his authority, before he will let it pass current in the world. You may guess what luck generally befalls such a rusty piece of metal as I am in these *new mintings.*

Innumerable are the ways which they take to insult and worm you out of their husband's confidence. Laughing at all you say with a kind of wonder, as if you were a queer kind of fellow that said good things, *but an oddity,* is one of the ways;—they have a particular kind of stare for the purpose;—till at last the husband, who used to defer to your judgment, and would pass over some excrescences of understanding and manner for the sake of a general vein of observation (not quite vulgar) which he perceived in you, begins to suspect whether you are not altogether a humourist,—a fellow well enough to have consorted with in his bachelor days, but not quite so proper to be introduced to ladies. This may be called the staring way; and is that which has oftenest been put in practice against me.

Then there is the exaggerating way, or the way of irony; that is, where they find you an object of especial regard with their husband, who is not so easily to be shaken from the lasting attachment founded on esteem which he has conceived towards you, by never qualified exaggerations to cry up all that you say or do, till the good man, who understands well enough that it is all done in compliment to him, grows weary of the debt of gratitude which is due to so much candour, and by relaxing a little on his part, and taking down a peg or two in his enthusiasm, sinks at length to the kindly level of moderate esteem—that "decent affection and complacent kindness" toward you, where she herself can join in sympathy with him without much stretch and violence to her sincerity.

Another way (for the ways they have to accomplish so desirable a purpose are infinite) is, with a kind of innocent simplicity, continually to mistake what it was which first made their husband fond of you. If an esteem for something excellent in your moral character was that which riveted the chain which she is to break, upon any imaginary discovery of a want of poignancy in your conversation, she will cry, "I thought, my dear, you described your friend, Mr. ——, as a great wit?" If, on the other hand, it was for some supposed charm in your conversation that he first grew to like you, and was content for this to overlook some trifling irregularities in your moral deportment, upon the first notice of any of these she as readily exclaims, "This, my dear, is your good Mr. —— !" One good lady whom I took the liberty of expostulating with for not showing me quite so much respect as I thought due to her husband's old friend, had the candour to confess to me that she had often heard Mr. —— speak of me before marriage, and that she had conceived a great desire to be acquainted with me, but that the sight of me had very much disappointed her expectations; for from her husband's representations of me, she had formed a notion that she was to see a fine, tall, officer-like-looking man (I use her very words), the very reverse of which proved to be the truth. This was candid; and I had the civility not to ask her in return, how she came to pitch upon a stand of personal accomplishments for her husband's friends which differed so much from his own; for my

friend's dimensions as near as possible approximate to mine; he standing five feet five in his shoes, in which I have the advantage of him by
about half an inch; and he no more than myself exhibiting any indications of a martial character in his air or countenance.

These are some of the mortifications which I have encountered in
the absurd attempt to visit at their houses. To enumerate them all would
be a vain endeavour; I shall therefore just glance at the very common impropriety of which married ladies are guilty,—of treating us as if we
were their husbands, and *vice versa*. I mean, when they use us with familiarity, and their husbands with ceremony. *Testacea*, for instance, kept me
the other night two or three hours beyond my usual time of supping,
while she was fretting because Mr. —— did not come, till the oysters
were all spoiled, rather than she would be guilty of the impoliteness of
touching one in his absence. This was reversing the point of good manners: for ceremony is an invention to take off the uneasy feeling which
we derive from knowing ourselves to be less the object of love and esteem with a fellow-creature than some other person is. It endeavours to
make up, by superior attentions in little points, for that invidious preference which it is forced to deny in the greater. Had *Testacea* kept the oysters back for me, and withstood her husband's importunities to go to
supper, she would have acted according to the strict rules of propriety.
I know no ceremony that ladies are bound to observe to their husbands,
beyond the point of a modest behaviour and decorum: therefore I must
protest against the vicarious gluttony of *Cerasia*, who at her own table sent
away a dish of Morellas, which I was applying to with great good-will,
to her husband at the other end of the table, and recommended a plate
of less extraordinary gooseberries to my unwedded palate in their stead.
Neither can I excuse the wanton affront of ——

But I am weary of stringing up all my married acquaintances by
Roman denominations. Let them amend and change their manners, or I
promise to record the full-length English of their names, to the terror
of all such desperate offenders in future.

❧ ☙

PERCY BYSSHE SHELLEY

Love Is a Powerful Attraction

What is love? Ask him who lives, what is life? ask him who adores, what
is God?

    I know not the internal constitution of other men, nor even thine, whom I now address. I see that in some external attributes they resemble me, but when, misled by that appearance, I have thought to appeal to something in common, and unburthen my inmost soul to them, I have found my language misunderstood, like one in a distant and savage land. The more opportunities they have afforded me for experience, the wider has appeared the interval between us, and to a greater distance have the points of sympathy been withdrawn. With a spirit ill fitted to sustain such proof, trembling and feeble through its tenderness, I have everywhere sought sympathy and have found only repulse and disappointment.

    Thou demandest what is love? It is that powerful attraction towards all that we conceive, or fear, or hope beyond ourselves, when we find within our own thoughts the chasm of an insufficient void, and seek to awaken in all things that are, a community with what we experience within ourselves. If we reason, we would be understood; if we imagine, we would that the airy children of our brain were born anew within another's; if we feel, we would that another's nerves should vibrate to our own, that the beams of their eyes should kindle at once and mix and melt into our own, that lips of motionless ice should not reply to lips quivering and burning with the heart's best blood. This is Love. This is the bond and the sanction which connects not only man with man, but with everything which exists. We are born into the world, and there is something within us, from the instant that we live, that more and more thirsts after its likeness. It is probably in correspondence with this law that the infant drains milk from the bosom of its mother; this propensity develops itself with the development of our nature. We dimly see within our intellectual nature a minimum as it were of our entire self, yet deprived of all that we condemn or despise, the ideal prototype of everything excellent or lovely that we are capable of conceiving as belonging to the nature of man. Not only the portrait of our external being, but an assemblage of the minutest particles of which our nature is composed; a mirror whose surface reflects only the forms of purity and brightness; a soul within our soul that describes a circle around its proper paradise, which pain, and sorrow, and evil dare not overleap. To this we eagerly refer all sensations, thirsting that they should resemble or correspond with it. The discovery of its antitype; the meeting with an understanding capable of clearly estimating our own; and imagination which should enter into and seize upon the subtle and delicate peculiarities which we have delighted to cherish and unfold in secret; with a frame whose nerves, like the chords of two exquisite lyres, strung to the accompaniment of one delightful voice, vibrate with the vibrations of our own; and of a combination of all these in such proportion as the type within demands; this is the invisible and unattainable point to which Love tends. . . .

꧁ ꧂

Washington Irving

The Broken Heart

> I never heard
> Of any true affection, but 'twas nipt
> With care, that, like the caterpillar, eats
> The leaves of the spring's sweetest book, the rose.
>
> Middleton.

It is a common practice with those who have outlived the susceptibility of early feeling, or have been brought up in the gay heartlessness of dissipated life, to laugh at all love stories, and to treat the tales of romantic passion as mere fictions of novelists and poets. My observations on human nature have induced me to think otherwise. They have convinced me that, however the surface of the character may be chilled and frozen by the cares of the world, or cultivated into mere smiles by the arts of society, still there are dormant fires lurking in the depths of the coldest bosom, which, when once enkindled, become impetuous, and are sometimes desolating in their effects. Indeed, I am a true believer in the blind deity, and go to the full extent of his doctrines. Shall I confess it?—I believe in broken hearts, and the possibility of dying of disappointed love! I do not, however, consider it a malady often fatal to my own sex; but I firmly believe that it withers down many a lovely woman into an early grave.

Man is the creature of interest and ambition. His nature leads him forth into the struggle and bustle of the world. Love is but the embellishment of his early life, or a song piped in the intervals of the acts. He seeks for fame, for fortune, for space in the world's thought and dominion over his fellow-men. But a woman's whole life is a history of the affections. The heart is her world: it is there her ambition strives for empire; it is there her avarice seeks for hidden treasures. She sends forth her sympathies on adventure; she embarks her whole soul in the traffic of affection; and if shipwrecked, her case is hopeless, for it is a bankruptcy of the heart.

To a man, the disappointment of love may occasion some bitter pangs; it wounds some feelings of tenderness, it blasts some prospects of felicity; but he is an active being—he may dissipate his thoughts in the whirl of varied occupation, he may plunge into the tide of pleasure; or, if the scene of disappointment be too full of painful associations, he can shift his abode at will, and taking, as it were, the wings of the morning, can "fly to the uttermost parts of the earth, and be at rest."

But woman's is comparatively a fixed, a secluded, and meditative life. She is more the companion of her own thoughts and feelings; and if they are turned to ministers of sorrow, where shall she look for consolation? Her lot is to be wooed and won; and if unhappy in her love, her heart is like some fortress that has been captured and sacked and abandoned and left desolate.

How many bright eyes grow dim, how many soft cheeks grow pale, how many lovely forms fade away into the tomb, and none can tell the cause that blighted their loveliness! As the dove will clasp its wings to its side, and cover and conceal the arrow that is preying on its vitals, so is it the nature of woman to hide from the world the pangs of wounded affection. The love of a delicate female is always shy and silent. Even when fortunate, she scarcely breathes it to herself; but when otherwise, she buries it in the recesses of her bosom, and there lets it cower and brood among the ruins of her peace. With her, the desire of the heart has failed—the great charm of existence is at an end. She neglects all the cheerful exercises which gladden the spirits, quicken the pulses, and send the tide of life in healthful currents through the veins. Her rest is broken—the sweet refreshment of sleep is poisoned by melancholy dreams—"dry sorrow drinks her blood," until her enfeebled frame sinks under the slightest external injury. Look for her after a little while, and you find friendship weeping over her untimely grave, and wondering that one who but lately glowed with all the radiance of health and beauty should so speedily be brought down to "darkness and the worm." You will be told of some wintry chill, some casual indisposition, that laid her low; but no one knows of the mental malady which previously sapped her strength, and made her so easy a prey to the spoiler.

She is like some tender tree, the pride and beauty of the grove, graceful in its form, bright in its foliage, but with the worm preying at its heart. We find it suddenly withering, when it should be most fresh and luxuriant. We see it drooping its branches to the earth, and shedding leaf by leaf, until, wasted and perished away, it falls even in the stillness of the forest; and as we muse over the beautiful ruin, we strive in vain to recollect the blast of thunderbolt that could have smitten it with decay.

I have seen many instances of women running to waste and self-neglect, and disappearing gradually from the earth, almost as if they had been exhaled to heaven, and have repeatedly fancied that I could trace their deaths through the various declensions of consumption, cold, debility, languor, melancholy, until I reached the first symptom of disappointed love. But an instance of the kind was lately told to me; the circumstances are well known in the country where they happened, and I shall but give them in the manner in which they were related.

Every one must recollect the tragical story of young E———, the Irish patriot; it was too touching to be soon forgotten. During the troubles in Ireland he was tried, condemned, and executed, on a charge of treason. His fate made a deep impression on public sympathy. He was so young, so intelligent, so generous, so brave—so everything that we are apt to like in a young man. His conduct under trial, too, was so lofty and intrepid. The noble indignation with which he repelled the charge of treason against his country, the eloquent vindication of his name, and his pathetic appeal to posterity in the hopeless hour of condemnation,—all these entered deeply into every generous bosom, and even his enemies lamented the stern policy that dictated his execution.

But there was one heart whose anguish it would be impossible to describe. In happier days and fairer fortunes he had won the affections of a beautiful and interesting girl, the daughter of a late celebrated Irish barrister. She loved him with the disinterested fervor of a woman's first and early love. When every worldly maxim arrayed itself against him; when, blasted in fortune, and disgrace and danger darkened around his name, she loved him the more ardently for his very sufferings. If, then, his fate could awaken the sympathy even of his foes, what must have been the agony of her whose whole soul was occupied by his image? Let those tell who have had the portals of the tomb suddenly closed between them and the being they most loved on earth—who have sat at its threshold, as one shut out in a cold and lonely world, whence all that was most lovely and loving had departed.

But then the horrors of such a grave!—so frightful, so dishonored! There was nothing for memory to dwell on that could soothe the pang of separation—none of those tender, though melancholy circumstances which endear the parting scene—nothing to melt sorrow into those blessed tears, sent like the dews of heaven, to revive the heart in the parting hour of anguish.

To render her widowed situation more desolate, she had incurred her father's displeasure by her unfortunate attachment, and was an exile from the paternal roof. But could the sympathy and kind offices of friends have reached a spirit so shocked and driven in by horror, she would have experienced no want of consolation, for the Irish are a people of quick and generous sensibilities. The most delicate and cherishing attentions were paid her by families of wealth and distinction. She was led into society, and they tried by all kinds of occupation and amusement to dissipate her grief and wean her from the tragical story of her loves. But it was all in vain. There are some strokes of calamity which scathe and scorch the soul—which penetrate to the vital seat of happiness, and blast it, never again to put forth bud or blossom. She never objected to frequent the haunts of pleasure, but was as much alone there as in the depths of solitude, walking about in a sad revery, apparently unconscious of the world around her. She carried with her an inward woe that mocked at all the blandishments of friendship, and "heeded not the song of the charmer, charm he never so wisely."

The person who told me her story had seen her at a masquerade. There can be no exhibition of far-gone wretchedness more striking and painful than to meet it in such a scene—to find it wandering like a spectre, lonely and joyless, where all around is gay—to see it dressed out in the trappings of mirth, and looking so wan and woe-begone, as if it had tried in vain to cheat the poor heart into momentary forgetfulness of sorrow. After strolling through the splendid rooms and giddy crowd with an air of utter abstraction, she sat herself down on the steps of an orchestra, and, looking about for some time with a vacant air, that showed her insensibility to the garish scene, she began, with the capriciousness of a sickly heart, to warble a little plaintive air. She had an exquisite voice; but on this occasion it was so simple, so touching, it breathed forth such a soul of wretchedness—that she drew a crowd, mute and silent, around her and melted every one into tears.

The story of one so true and tender could not but excite great interest in a country remarkable for enthusiasm. It completely won the heart of a brave officer, who paid his addresses to her, and thought that one so true to the dead could not but prove affectionate to the living. She declined his attentions, for her thoughts were irrevocably engrossed by the memory of her former lover. He, however, persisted in his suit. He solicited not her tenderness, but her esteem. He was assisted by her conviction of his worth, and her sense of her own destitute and dependent situation, for she was existing on the kindness of friends. In a word, he at length succeeded in gaining her hand, though with the solemn assurance that her heart was unalterably another's.

He took her with him to Sicily, hoping that a change of scene might wear out the remembrance of early woes. She was an amiable and exemplary wife, and made an effort to be a happy one; but nothing could cure the silent and devouring melancholy that had entered into her very soul. She wasted away in a slow, but hopeless decline, and at length sunk into the grave, the victim of a broken heart.

It was on her that Moore, the distinguished Irish poet, composed the following lines:—

> She is far from the land where her young hero sleeps
>   And lovers around her are sighing:
> But coldly she turns from their gaze, and weeps,
>   For her heart in his grave is lying.
>
> She sings the wild song of her dear native plains,
>   Every note which he loved awaking—
> Ah! little they think, who delight in her strains,
>   How the heart of the minstrel is breaking!
>
> He had lived for his love—for his country he died,
>   They were all that to life had entwined him—
> Nor soon shall the tears of his country be dried,
>   Nor long will his love stay behind him!
>
> Oh! make her a grave where the sunbeams rest,
>   When they promise a glorious morrow;
> They'll shine o'er her sleep, like a smile from the west,
>   From her own loved island of sorrow!

STENDHAL (MARIE HENRI BEYLE)

from *Of Love*

Even a very small degree of hope is enough to cause the birth of love.

Hope may subsequently cease after two or three days, but love is born nonetheless.

For lovers who are decisive, bold and impulsive and have an imagination developed by the misfortunes of life, the degree of hope may be smaller.

Hope may even die completely without killing love.

If the lover has had misfortunes, if he has a nature that is tender and thoughtful, if he is no longer interested in other women, if he has a lively admiration for the one woman who stirs him, then more ordinary pleasures will not distract him from the second crystallization of love. He would rather dream of the uncertain chance of one day pleasing his beloved than receive from common women all they might offer him.

To put a stop to this, it is necessary for his beloved to kill his hope in the cruelest manner, holding him up to public contempt so that he may never again face people.

The birth of love permits much longer intervals between these stages, but it needs greater, more sustained hope for people who are cold and cautious, and for those who have passed their first youth.

What ensures the perseverance of love is the second crystallization, during which one realizes at every moment that one must love or die. How, with this conviction always present in one's thoughts and made habit through months of love, could one bear even the thought of ceasing to love?

This evening I discovered that music, when it is perfect, affects the heart in the same way as does the presence of the beloved; that is to say, it provides the most rapturous joy to be found on earth. . . . The lover who is in favor with his mistress is enthralled by the famous duet in *Armida e Rinaldo* by Rossini, who paints so clearly those little doubts of happy love and the delicious moments that follow reconciliations. . . . I dare not say all that I feel about this; Northerners would think me mad.

Translated by Jeanne Mackin

꧁꧂

WILLIAM HAZLITT

from *Liber Amoris*

UNALTERED LOVE

Love is not love that alteration finds:
Oh no! it is an ever-fixed mark,
That looks on tempests and is never shaken.

Shall I not love her for herself alone, in spite of fickleness and folly? To love her for her regard to me, is not to love her, but myself. She has robbed me of herself: shall she also rob me of my love of her? Did I not live on her smile? Is it less sweet because it is withdrawn from me? Did I not adore her every grace? Does she bend less enchantingly, because she has turned from me to another? Is my love then in the power of fortune, or of her caprice? No, I will have it lasting as it is pure; and I will make a Goddess of her, and build a temple to her in my heart, and worship her on indestructible altars, and raise statues to her: and my homage shall be unblemished as her unrivalled symmetry of form; and when that fails, the memory of it shall survive; and my bosom shall be proof to scorn, as hers has been to pity; and I will pursue her with an unrelenting love, and sue to be her slave, and tend her steps without notice and without reward; and serve her living, and mourn for her when dead. And thus my love will have shown itself superior to her hate; and I shall triumph and then die. This is my idea of the only true and heroic love! Such is mine for her.

PERFECT LOVE

Perfect love has this advantage in it, that it leaves the possessor of it nothing farther to desire. There is one object (at least) in which the soul finds absolute content, for which it seeks to live, or dares to die. The heart has as it were filled up the moulds of the imagination. The truth of passion keeps pace with and outvies the extravagance of mere language. There are no words so fine, no flattery so soft, that there is not a sentiment beyond them, that it is impossible to express, at the bottom of the heart where true love is. What idle sounds the common phrases, *adorable creature, angel, divinity*, are! What a proud reflection it is to have a feeling answering to all these, rooted in the breast, unalterable, unutterable, to which all other feelings are light and vain! Perfect love reposes on the object of its choice, like the halcyon on the wave; and the air of heaven is around it.

❧ ❧

RALPH WALDO EMERSON

Love

Every promise of the soul has innumerable fulfilments; each of its joys ripens into a new want. Nature, uncontainable, flowing, forelooking, in the first sentiment of kindness anticipates already a benevolence which shall lose all particular regards in its general light. The introduction to this felicity is in a private and tender relation of one to one, which is the enchantment of human life; which, like a certain divine rage and enthusiasm, seizes on man at one period, and works a revolution in his mind and body; unites him to his race, pledges him to the domestic and civic relations, carries him with new sympathy into nature, enhances the power of the senses, opens the imagination, adds to his character heroic and sacred attributes, establishes marriage, and gives permanence to human society.

The natural association of the sentiment of love with the heyday of the blood seems to require, that in order to portray it in vivid tints, which every youth and maid should confess to be true to their throbbing experience, one must not be too old. The delicious fancies of youth reject the least savour of a mature philosophy, as chilling with age and pedantry their purple bloom. And, therefore, I know I incur the imputation of unnecessary hardness and stoicism from those who compose the Court and Parliament of Love. But from these formidable censors I shall appeal to my seniors. For it is to be considered that this passion of which we speak, though it begin with the young, yet forsakes not the old, or rather suffers no one who is truly its servant to grow old, but makes the aged participators of it, not less than the tender maiden, though in a different and nobler sort. For it is a fire that, kindling its first embers in the narrow nook of a private bosom, caught from a wandering spark out of another private heart, glows and enlarges until it warms and beams upon multitudes of men and women, upon the universal heart of all, and so lights up the whole world and all nature with its generous flames. It matters not, therefore, whether we attempt to describe the passion at twenty, at thirty, or at eighty years. He who paints it at the first period will lose some of its later, he who paints it at the last, some of its earlier traits. Only it is to be hoped that, by patience and the Muses' aid, we may attain to that inward view of the law, which shall describe a truth ever young and beautiful, so central that it shall commend itself to the eye, at whatever angle beholden.

And the first condition is, that we must leave a too close and lingering adherence to facts, and study the sentiment as it appeared in hope and not in history. For each man sees his own life defaced and disfigured, as the life of man is not, to his imagination. Each man sees over his own experience a certain stain of error, whilst that of other men looks fair and ideal. Let any man go back to those delicious relations which make the beauty of his life, which have given him sincerest instruction and nourishment, he will shrink and moan. Alas! I know not why, but infinite compunctions embitter in mature life the remembrances of budding joy, and cover every beloved name. Everything is beautiful seen from the point of the intellect, or as truth. But all is sour, if seen as experience. Details are melancholy; the plan is seemly and noble. In the actual world—the painful kingdom of time and place—dwell care, and canker, and fear. With thought, with the ideal, is immortal hilarity, the rose of joy. Round it all the Muses sing. But grief cleaves to names, and persons, and the partial interests of today and yesterday.

The strong bent of nature is seen in the proportion which this topic of personal relations usurps in the conversation of society. What do we wish to know of any worthy person so much, as how he has sped in the history of this sentiment? What books in the circulating libraries circulate? How we glow over these novels of passion, when the story is told with any spark of truth and nature! And what fastens attention, in the intercourse of life, like any passage betraying affection between two parties? Perhaps we never saw them before, and never shall meet them again. But we see them exchange a glance, or betray a deep emotion, and we are no longer strangers. We understand them, and take the warmest interest in the development of the romance. All mankind love a lover. The earliest demonstrations of complacency and kindness are nature's most winning pictures. It is the dawn of civility and grace in the coarse and rustic. The rude village boy teases the girls about the school-house door;—but today he comes running into the entry, and meets one fair child disposing her satchel; he holds her books to help her, and instantly it seems to him as if she removed herself from him infinitely, and was a sacred precinct. Among the throng of girls he runs rudely enough, but one alone distances him; and these two little neighbours, that were so close just now, have learned to respect each other's personality. Or who can avert his eyes from the engaging, half-artful, half-artless ways of school-girls who go into the country shops to buy a skein of silk or a sheet of paper, and talk half an hour about nothing with the broad-faced, good-natured shop-boy. In the village they are on a perfect equality, which love delights in, and without any coquetry the happy, affectionate nature of woman flows out in this pretty gossip. The girls may have little beauty, yet plainly do they establish between them and the good boy the most agreeable, confiding relations, what with their fun and their earnest, about Edgar, and Jonas, and Almira, and who was invited to the party, and who danced at the dancing-school, and when the singing-school would begin, and other nothings concerning which the parties cooed. By and by that boy wants a wife, and very truly and heartily will he know where to find a sincere and sweet mate, without any risk such as Milton deplores as incident to scholars and great men.

I have been told that in some public discourses of mine my reverence for the intellect has made me unjustly cold to the personal relations. But now I almost shrink at the remembrance of such disparaging words. For persons are love's world, and the coldest philosopher cannot recount the debt of the young soul wandering here in nature to the power of love, without being tempted to unsay, as treasonable to nature, aught derogatory to the social instincts. For, though the celestial rapture falling out of heaven seizes only upon those of tender age, and although a beauty overpowering all analysis or comparison, and putting us quite beside ourselves, we can seldom see after thirty years, yet the remembrance of these visions outlasts all other remembrances, and is a wreath of flowers on the oldest brows. But here is a strange fact; it may seem to many men, in revising their experience, that they have no fairer page in their life's book than the delicious memory of some passages wherein affection contrived to give a witchcraft surpassing the deep attraction of its own truth to a parcel of accidental and trivial circumstances. In looking backward, they may find that several things which were not the charm have more reality to this groping memory than the charm itself which embalmed them. But be our experience in particulars what it may, no man ever forgot the visitations of that power to his heart and brain, which created all things new; which was the dawn in him of music, poetry, and art; which made the face of nature radiant with purple light, the morning and the night varied enchantments; when a single tone of one voice could make the heart bound, and the most trivial circumstance associated with one form is put in the amber of memory; when he became all eye when one was present, and all memory when one was gone; when the youth becomes a watcher of windows, and studious of a glove, a veil, a ribbon, or the wheels of a carriage; when no place is too solitary, and none too silent, for him who has richer company and sweeter conversation in his new thoughts, than any old friends, though best and purest, can give him; for the figures, the motions, the words of the beloved object are not like other images written in water, but, as Plutarch said, "enamelled in fire," and make the study of midnight.

> Thou art not gone being gone, where'er thou art,
> Thou leav'st in him thy watchful eyes, in him thy loving heart.

In the noon and the afternoon of life we still throb at the recollection of days when happiness was not happy enough, but must be drugged with the relish of pain and fear; for he touched the secret of the matter, who said of love,—

All other pleasures are not worth its pains;

and when the day was not long enough, but the night, too, must be consumed in keen recollections; when the head boiled all night on the pillow with the generous deed it resolved on; when the moonlight was a pleasing fever, and the stars were letters, and the flowers ciphers, and the air was coined into song; when all business seemed an impertinence, and all the men and women running to and fro in the streets, mere pictures.

The passion rebuilds the world for the youth. It makes all things alive and significant. Nature grows conscious. Every bird on the boughs of the tree sings now to his heart and soul. The notes are almost articulate. The clouds have faces as he looks on them. The trees of the forest, the waving grass, and the peeping flowers have grown intelligent; and he almost fears to trust them with the secret which they seem to invite. Yet nature soothes and sympathizes. In the green solitude he finds a dearer home than with men.

Fountain-heads and pathless groves,
Places which pale passion loves,
Moonlight walks, when all the fowls
Are safely housed, save bats and owls,
A midnight bell, a passing groan,—
These are the sounds we feed upon.

Behold there in the wood the fine madman! He is a palace of sweet sounds and sights; he dilates; he is twice a man; he walks with arms akimbo; he soliloquizes; he accosts the grass and the trees; he feels the blood of the violet, the clover, and the lily in his veins; and he talks with the brook that wets his foot.

The heats that have opened his perceptions of natural beauty have made him love music and verse. It is a fact often observed, that men have written good verses under the inspiration of passion, who cannot write well under any other circumstances.

The like force has the passion over all his nature. It expands the sentiment; it makes the clown gentle, and gives the coward heart. Into the most pitiful and abject it will infuse a heart and courage to defy the world, so only it have the countenance of the beloved object. In giving him to another, it still more gives him to himself. He is a new man, with new perceptions, new and keener purposes, and a religious solemnity of character and aims. He does not longer appertain to his family and society; *he* is somewhat; *he* is a person; *he* is a soul.

And here let us examine a little nearer the nature of that influence which is thus potent over the human youth. Beauty, whose revelation to man we now celebrate, welcome as the sun wherever it pleases to shine, which pleases everybody with it and with themselves, seems sufficient to itself. The lover cannot paint his maiden to his fancy poor and solitary. Like a tree in flower, so much soft, budding, informing loveliness is society for itself, and she teaches his eye why Beauty was pictured with Loves and Graces attending her steps. Her existence makes the world rich. Though she extrudes all other persons from his attention as cheap and unworthy, she indemnifies him by carrying out her own being into somewhat impersonal, large, mundane, so that the maiden stands to him for a representative of all select things and virtues. For that reason, the lover never sees personal resemblances in his mistress to her kindred or to others. His friends find in her a likeness to her mother, or her sisters, or to persons not of her blood. The lover sees no resemblance except to summer evenings and diamond mornings, to rainbows and the song of birds.

The ancients called beauty the flowering of virtue. Who can analyze the nameless charm which glances from one and another face and form? We are touched with emotions of tenderness and complacency, but we cannot find whereat this dainty emotion, this wandering gleam, points. It is destroyed for the imagination by any attempt to refer it to organization. Nor does it point to any relations of friendship or love known and described in society, but, as it seems to me, to a quite other and unattainable sphere, to relations of transcendent delicacy and sweetness, to what roses and violets hint and foreshow. We cannot approach beauty. Its nature is like opaline doves'-neck lustres, hovering and evanescent. Herein it resembles the most excellent things, which all have this rainbow character, defying all attempts at appropriation and use. What else did Jean Paul Richter signify, when he said to music, "Away! away! thou speakest to me of things which in all my endless life I have not found, and shall not find." The same fluency may be observed in every work of the plastic arts. The statue is then beautiful when it begins to be incomprehensible, when it is passing out of criticism, and can no longer be defined by compass and measuring-wand, but demands an active imagination to go with it, and to say what it is in the act of doing. The god or hero of the sculptor is always represented in a transition *from* that which is representable to the senses, *to* that which is not. Then first it ceases to be a stone. The same remark holds of painting. And of poetry, the success is not attained when it lulls and satisfies, but when it astonishes and fires us with new endeavours after the unattainable. Concerning it, Landor inquires "whether it is not to be referred to some purer state of sensation and existence."

In like manner, personal beauty is then first charming and itself, when it dissatisfies us with any end; when it becomes a story without an end; when it suggests gleams and visions, and not earthly satisfactions; when it makes the beholder feel his unworthiness; when he cannot feel his right to it, though he were Cæsar; he cannot feel more right to it than to the firmament and the splendors of a sunset.

Hence arose the saying, "If I love you, what is that to you?" We say so, because we feel that what we love is not in your will, but above it. It is not you, but your radiance. It is that which you know not in yourself, and can never know.

This agrees well with that high philosophy of Beauty which the ancient writers delighted in; for they said that the soul of man, embodied here on earth, went roaming up and down in quest of that other world of its own, out of which it came into this, but was soon stupefied by the light of the natural sun, and unable to see any other objects than those of this world, which are but shadows of real things. Therefore, the Deity sends the glory of youth before the soul, that it may avail itself of beautiful bodies as aids to its recollection of the celestial good and fair; and the man beholding such a person in the female sex runs to her, and finds the highest joy in contemplating the form, movement, and intelligence of this person, because it suggests to him the presence of that which indeed is within the beauty, and the cause of the beauty.

If, however, from too much conversing with material objects, the soul was gross, and misplaced its satisfaction in the body, it reaped nothing but sorrow; body being unable to fulfil the promise which beauty holds out; but if, accepting the hint of these visions and suggestions which beauty makes to his mind, the soul passes through the body, and falls to admire strokes of character, and the lovers contemplate one another in their discourses and their actions, then they pass to the true palace of beauty, more and more inflame their love of it, and by this love extinguishing the base affection, as the sun puts out the fire by shining on the hearth, they become pure and hallowed. By conversation with that which is in itself excellent, magnanimous, lowly, and just, the lover comes to a warmer love of these nobilities, and a quicker apprehension of them. Then he passes from loving them in one to loving them in all, and so is the one beautiful soul only the door through which he enters to the society of all true and pure souls. In the particular society of his mate, he attains a clearer sight of any spot, any taint, which her beauty has contracted from this world, and is able to point it out, and this with mutual joy that they are now able, without offence, to indicate blemishes and hindrances in each other, and give to each all help and comfort in curing the same. And, beholding in many souls the traits of the divine beauty, and separating in each soul that which is divine from the taint which it has contracted in the world, the lover ascends to the highest beauty, to the love and knowledge of the Divinity, by steps on this ladder of created souls.

Somewhat like this have the truly wise told us of love in all ages. The doctrine is not old, nor is it new. If Plato, Plutarch, and Apuleius taught it, so have Petrarch, Angelo, and Milton. It awaits a truer unfolding in opposition and rebuke to that subterranean prudence which presides at marriages with words that take hold of the upper world, whilst one eye is prowling in the cellar, so that its gravest discourse has a savor of hams and powdering-tubs. Worst, when this sensualism intrudes into the education of young women, and withers the hope and affection of human nature by teaching that marriage signifies nothing but a housewife's thrift, and that woman's life has no other aim.

But this dream of love, though beautiful, is only one scene in our play. In the procession of the soul from within outward, it enlarges its circles ever, like the pebble thrown into the pond, or the light proceeding from an orb. The rays of the soul alight first on things nearest, on every utensil and toy, on nurses and domestics, on the house, and yard, and passengers, on the circle of household acquaintance, on politics, and geography, and history. But things are ever grouping themselves according to higher or more interior laws. Neighbourhood, size, numbers, habits, persons, lose by degrees their power over us. Cause and effect, real affinities, the longing for harmony between the soul and the circumstance, the progressive, idealizing instinct, predominate later, and the step backward from the higher to the lower relations is impossible. Thus even love, which is the deification of persons, must become more impersonal every day. Of this at first it gives no hint. Little think the youth and maiden who are glancing at each other across crowded rooms, with eyes so full of mutual intelligence, of the precious fruit long hereafter to proceed from this new, quite external stimulus. The work of vegetation begins first in the irritability of the bark and leaf-buds. From exchanging glances, they advance to acts of courtesy, of gallantry, then to fiery passion, to plighting troth, and marriage. Passion beholds its object as a perfect unit. The soul is wholly embodied, and the body is wholly ensouled.

> Her pure and eloquent blood
> Spoke in her cheeks, and so distinctly wrought,
> That one might almost say her body thought.

Romeo, if dead, should be cut up into little stars to make the heavens fine. Life, with this pair, has no other aim, asks no more, than Juliet,—than Romeo. Night, day, studies, talents, kingdoms, religion, are all contained in this form full of soul, in this soul which is all form. The lovers delight in endearments, in avowals of love, in comparisons of their regards. When alone, they solace themselves with the remembered image of the other. Does that other see the same star, the same melting cloud, read the same book, feel the same emotion, that now delight me? They try and weigh their affection, and, adding up costly advantages, friends, opportunities, properties, exult in discovering that willingly, joyfully, they would give all as a ransom for the beautiful, the beloved head, not one hair of which shall be harmed. But the lot of humanity is on these children. Danger, sorrow, and pain arrive to them, as to all. Love prays. It makes covenants with Eternal Power in behalf of this dear mate. The union which is thus effected, and which adds a new value to every atom in nature, for it transmutes every thread throughout the whole web of relation into a golden ray, and bathes the soul in a new and sweeter element, is yet a temporary state. Not always can flowers, pearls, poetry, protestations, nor even home in another heart, content the awful soul that dwells in clay. It arouses itself at last from these endearments, as toys, and puts on the harness, and aspires to vast and universal aims. The soul which is in the soul of each, craving a perfect beatitude, detects incongruities, defects, and disproportion in the behaviour of the other. Hence arise surprise, expostulation, and pain. Yet that which drew them to each other was signs of loveliness, signs of virtue; and these virtues are there, however eclipsed. They appear and reappear, and continue to attract; but the regard changes, quits the sign, and attaches to the substance. This repairs the wounded affection. Meantime, as life wears on, it proves a game of permutation and combination of all possible positions of the parties, to employ all the resources of each, and acquaint each with the strength and weakness of the other. For it is the nature and end of this relation, that they should represent the human race to each other. All that is in the world, which is or ought to be known, is cunningly wrought into the texture of man, of woman.

> The person love does to us fit,
> Like manna, has the taste of all in it.

The world rolls; the circumstances vary every hour. The angels that inhabit this temple of the body appear at the windows, and the gnomes and vices also. By all the virtues they are united. If there be virtue, all the vices are known as such; they confess and flee. Their once flaming regard is sobered by time in either breast, and, losing in violence what it gains in extent, it becomes a thorough good understanding. They resign each other, without complaint, to the good offices which man and woman are severally appointed to discharge in time, and exchange the passion which once could not lose sight of its object, for a cheerful, disengaged furtherance, whether present or absent, of each other's designs. At last they discover that all which at first drew them together,—those once sacred features, that magical play of charms,—was deciduous, had a prospective end, like the scaffolding by which the house was built; and the purification of the intellect and the heart, from year to year, is the real marriage, foreseen and prepared from the first, and wholly above their consciousness. Looking at these aims with which two persons, a man and a woman, so variously and correlatively gifted, are shut up in one house to spend in the nuptial society forty or fifty years, I do not wonder at the emphasis with which the heart prophesies this crisis from early infancy, at the profuse beauty with which the instincts deck the nuptial bower, and nature, and intellect, and art emulate each other in the gifts and the melody they bring to the epithalamium.

Thus are we put in training for a love which knows not sex, nor person, nor partiality, but which seeks virtue and wisdom everywhere, to the end of increasing virtue and wisdom. We are by nature observers, and thereby learners. That is our permanent state. But we are often made to feel that our affections are but tents of a night. Though slowly and with pain, the objects of the affections change, as the objects of thought do. There are moments when the affections rule and absorb the man, and make his happiness dependent on a person or persons. But in health the mind is presently seen again,—its overarching vault, bright with galaxies of immutable lights, and the warm loves and fears that swept over us as clouds, must lose their finite character and blend with God, to attain their own perfection. But we need not fear that we can lose anything by the progress of the soul. The soul may be trusted to the end. That which is so beautiful and attractive as these relations must be succeeded and supplanted only by what is more beautiful, and so on forever.

❧ ❧

ROBERT LOUIS STEVENSON

On Falling in Love

"Lord, what fools these mortals be!"

—*A Midsummer-Night's Dream*

There is only one event in life which really astonishes a man and startles him out of his prepared opinions. Everything else befalls him very much as he expected. Event succeeds to event, with an agreeable variety indeed, but with little that is either startling or intense; they form together no more than a sort of background, or running accompaniment to the man's own reflections; and he falls naturally into a cool, curious, and smiling habit of mind, and builds himself up in a conception of life which expects tomorrow to be after the pattern of today and yesterday. He may be accustomed to the vagaries of his friends and acquaintances under the influence of love. He may sometimes look forward to it for himself with an incomprehensible expectation. But it is a subject in which neither intuition nor the behaviour of others will help the philosopher to the truth. There is probably nothing rightly thought or rightly written on this matter of love that is not a piece of the person's experience. I remember an anecdote of a well-known French theorist, who was debating a point eagerly in his *cénacle*. It was objected against him that he had never experienced love. Whereupon he arose, left the society, and made it a point not to return to it until he considered that he had supplied the defect. "Now," he remarked, on entering, "now I am in a position to continue the discussion." Perhaps he had not penetrated very deeply into the subject after all; but the story indicates right thinking, and may serve as an apologue to readers of this essay.

When at last the scales fall from his eyes, it is not without something of the nature of dismay that the man finds himself in such changed conditions. He has to deal with commanding emotions instead of the easy dislikes and preferences in which he has hitherto passed his days; and he recognises capabilities for pain and pleasure of which he had not yet suspected the existence. Falling in love is the one illogical adventure, the one thing of which we are tempted to think as supernatural, in our trite and reasonable world. The effect is out of all proportion with the cause. Two persons, neither of them, it may be, very amiable or very beautiful, meet, speak a little, and look a little into each other's eyes. That has been done a dozen or so of times in the experience of either with no great result. But on this occasion all is different. They fall at once into that state in which another person becomes to us the very gist and centrepoint of God's creation, and demolishes our laborious theories with a smile; in which our ideas are so bound up with the one master-thought that even the trivial cares of our own person become so many acts of devotion, and the love of life itself is translated into a wish to remain in the same world with so precious and desirable a fellow-creature. And all the while their acquaintances look on in stupor, and ask each other, with almost passionate emphasis, what so-and-so can see in that woman, or such-an-one in that man? I am sure, gentlemen, I cannot tell you. For my part, I cannot think what the women mean. It might be very well, if the Apollo Belvedere should suddenly glow all over into life, and step forward from the pedestal with that godlike air of his. But of the misbegotten changelings who call themselves men, and prate intolerably over dinner-tables, I never saw one who seemed worthy to inspire love—no, nor read of any, except Leonardo da Vinci, and perhaps Goethe in his youth. About women I entertain a somewhat different opinion; but there, I have the misfortune to be a man.

There are many matters in which you may waylay Destiny, and bid him stand and deliver. Hard work, high thinking, adventurous excitement, and a great deal more that forms a part of this or the other person's spiritual bill of fare, are within the reach of almost anyone who can dare a little and be patient. But it is by no means in the way of everyone to fall in love. You know the difficulty Shakespeare was put into when Queen Elizabeth asked him to show Falstaff in love. I do not believe that Henry Fielding was ever in love. Scott, if it were not for a passage or two in *Rob Roy*, would give me very much the same effect. These are great names and (what is more to the purpose) strong, healthy, highstrung, and generous natures, of whom the reverse might have been expected. As for the innumerable army of anemic and tailorish persons who occupy the face of this planet with so much propriety, it is palpably absurd to imagine them in any such situation as a love-affair. A wet rag goes safely by the fire; and if a man is blind, he cannot expect to be much impressed by romantic scenery. Apart from all this, many lovable people miss each other in the world, or meet under some unfavourable star. There is the nice and critical moment of declaration to be got over. From timidity or lack of opportunity a good half of possible love cases never get so far, and at least another quarter do there cease and determine. A very adroit person, to be sure, manages to prepare the way and out with his declaration in the nick of time. And then there is a fine solid sort of man, who goes on from snub to snub; and if he has to declare forty times, will continue imperturbably declaring, amid the astonished consideration of men and angels, until he has a favourable answer. I daresay, if one were a woman, one would like to marry a man who was capable of doing this, but not quite one who had done so. It is just a little bit abject, and somehow just a little bit gross; and marriages in which one of the parties has been thus battered into consent scarcely form agreeable subjects for meditation. Love should run out to meet love with open arms. Indeed, the ideal story is that of two people who go into love step for step, with a fluttered consciousness, like a pair of children venturing together into a dark room. From the first moment when they see each other, with a pang of curiosity, through stage after stage of growing pleasure and embarrassment, they can read the expression of their own trouble in each other's eyes. There is here no declaration properly so called; the feeling is so plainly shared, that as soon as the man knows what it is in his own heart, he is sure of what it is in the woman's.

This simple accident of falling in love is as beneficial as it is astonishing. It arrests the petrifying influence of years, disproves cold-blooded and cynical conclusions, and awakens dormant sensibilities. Hitherto the man had found it a good policy to disbelieve the existence of any enjoyment which was out of his reach; and thus he turned his back upon the strong, sunny parts of nature, and accustomed himself to look exclusively on what was common and dull. He accepted a prose ideal, let himself go blind of many sympathies by disuse; and if he were young and witty, or beautiful, wilfully forewent these advantages. He joined himself to the following of what, in the old mythology of love, was prettily called *nonchaloir*; and in an odd mixture of feelings, a fling of self-respect, a preference for selfish liberty, and a great dash of that fear with which honest people regard serious interests, kept himself back from the straightforward course of life among certain selected activities. And now, all of a sudden, he is unhorsed, like St. Paul, from his infidel affectation. His heart, which has been ticking accurate seconds for the last year, gives a bound and begins to beat high and irregularly in his breast. It seems as if he had never heard or felt or seen until that moment; and by the report of his memory, he must have lived his past life between sleep or waking, or with the preoccupied attention of a brown study. He is practically incommoded by the generosity of his feelings, smiles much when he is alone, and develops a habit of looking rather blankly upon the moon and stars. But it is not at all within the province of a prose essayist to give a picture of this hyperbolical frame of mind; and the thing has been done already, and that to admiration. In *Adelaide*, in Tennyson's *Maud*, and in some of Heine's songs, you get the absolute expression of this midsummer spirit. Romeo and Juliet were very much in love; although they tell me some German critics are of a different opinion, probably the same who would have us think Mercutio a dull fellow. Poor Antony was in love, and no mistake. That lay figure Marius, in *Les Misérables*, is also a genuine case in his own way, and worth observation. A good many of George Sand's people are thoroughly in love; and so are a good many of George Meredith's. Altogether, there is plenty to read on the subject. If the root of the matter be in him, and if he has the requisite chords to set in vibration, a young man may occasionally enter, with the key of art, into that land of Beulah which is upon the borders of Heaven and within sight of the City of Love. There let him sit awhile to hatch delightful hopes and perilous illusions.

One thing that accompanies the passion in its first blush is certainly difficult to explain. It comes (I do not quite see how) that from having a very supreme sense of pleasure in all parts of life—in lying down to sleep, in waking, in motion, in breathing, in continuing to be— the lover begins to regard his happiness as beneficial for the rest of the world and highly meritorious in himself. Our race has never been able contentedly to suppose that the noise of its wars, conducted by a few young gentlemen in a corner of an inconsiderable star, does not re-echo among the courts of Heaven with quite a formidable effect. In much the same taste, when people find a great to-do in their own breasts, they imagine it must have some influence in their neighbourhood. The presence of the two lovers is so enchanting to each other that it seems as if it must be the best thing possible for everybody else. They are half inclined to fancy it is because of them and their love that the sky is blue and the sun shines. And certainly the weather is usually fine while people are courting. . . . In point of fact, although the happy man feels very kindly towards others of his own sex, there is apt to be something too much of the magnifico in his demeanour. If people grow presuming and self-important over such matters as a dukedom or the Holy See, they will scarcely support the dizziest elevation in life without some suspicion of a strut; and the dizziest elevation is to love and be loved in return. Consequently, accepted lovers are a trifle condescending in their address to other men. An overweening sense of the passion and importance of life hardly conduces to simplicity of manner. To women, they feel very nobly, very purely, and very generously, as if they were so many Joan-of-Arc's; but this does not come out in their behaviour; and they treat them to Grandisonian airs marked with a suspicion of fatuity. I am not quite certain that women do not like this sort of thing; but really, after having bemused myself over *Daniel Deronda,* I have given up trying to understand what they like.

If it did nothing else, this sublime and ridiculous superstition, that the pleasure of the pair is somehow blessed to others, and everybody is made happier in their happiness, would serve at least to keep love generous and great-hearted. Nor is it quite a baseless superstition after all. Other lovers are hugely interested. They strike the nicest balance between pity and approval, when they see people aping the greatness of their own sentiments. It is an understood thing in the play that while the young gentlefolk are courting on the terrace, a rough flirtation is being carried on, and a light, trivial sort of love is growing up, between the footman and the singing chambermaid. As people are generally cast for the leading parts in their own imaginations, the reader can apply the parallel to real life without much chance of going wrong. In short, they are quite sure this other love-affair is not so deep-seated as their own, but they like dearly to see it going forward. And love, considered as a spectacle, must have attractions for many who are not of the confraternity. The sentimental old maid is a commonplace of the novelists; and he must be rather a poor sort of human being, to be sure, who can look on at this pretty madness without indulgence and sympathy. For nature commends itself to people with a most insinuating art; the busiest is now and again arrested by a great sunset; and you may be as pacific or as cold-blooded as you will, but you cannot help some emotion when you read of well-disputed battles, or meet a pair of lovers in the lane.

Certainly, whatever it may be with regard to the world at large, this idea of beneficent pleasure is true as between the sweethearts. To do good and communicate is the lover's grand intention. It is the happiness of the other that makes his own most intense gratification. It is not possible to disentangle the different emotions, the pride, humility, pity, and passion, which are excited by a look of happy love or an unexpected caress. To make one's self beautiful, to dress the hair, to excel in talk, to do anything and all things that puff out the character and attributes and make them imposing in the eyes of others, is not only to magnify one's self, but to offer the most delicate homage at the same time. And it is in this latter intention that they are done by lovers; for the essence of love is kindness; and indeed it may be best defined as passionate kindness: kindness, so to speak, run mad and become importunate and violent. Vanity in a merely personal sense exists no longer. The lover takes a perilous pleasure in privately displaying his weak points and having them, one after another, accepted and condoned. He wishes to be assured that he is not loved for this or that good quality, but for himself, or something as like himself as he can contrive to set forward. For, although it may have been a very difficult thing to paint the marriage of Cana, or write the fourth act of *Antony and Cleopatra*, there is a more difficult piece of art before every one in this world who cares to set about explaining his own character to others. Words and acts are easily wrenched from their true significance; and they are all the language we have to come and go upon. A pitiful job we make of it, as a rule. For better or worse, people mistake our meaning and take our emotions at a wrong valuation. And generally we rest pretty content with our failures; we are content to be misapprehended by cackling flirts; but when once a man is moonstruck with this affection of love, he makes it a point of honour to clear such dubieties away. He cannot have the Best of her Sex misled upon a point of this importance; and his pride revolts at being loved in a mistake.

He discovers a great reluctance to return on former periods of his life. To all that has not been shared with her, rights and duties, bygone fortunes and dispositions, he can look back only by a difficult and repugnant effort of the will. That he should have wasted some years in ignorance of what alone was really important, that he may have entertained the thought of other women with any show of complacency, is a burthen almost too heavy for his self-respect. But it is the thought of another past that rankles in his spirit like a poisoned wound. That he himself made a fashion of being alive in the bald, beggarly days before a certain meeting, is deplorable enough in all good conscience. But that She should have permitted herself the same liberty seems inconsistent with a Divine providence.

A great many people run down jealousy, on the score that it is an artificial feeling, as well as practically inconvenient. This is scarcely fair; for the feeling on which it merely attends, like an ill-humoured courtier, is itself artificial in exactly the same sense and to the same degree. I suppose what is meant by that objection is that jealousy has not always been a character of man; formed no part of that very modest kit of sentiments with which he is supposed to have begun the world; but waited to make its appearance in better days and among richer natures. And this is equally true of love, and friendship, and love of country, and delight in what they call the beauties of nature, and most other things worth having. Love, in particular, will not endure any historical scrutiny: to all who have fallen across it, it is one of the most incontestable facts in the world; but if you begin to ask what it was in other periods and countries, in Greece for instance, the strangest doubts begin to spring up, and everything seems so vague and changing that a dream is logical in comparison. Jealousy, at any rate, is one of the consequences of love; you may like it or not, at pleasure; but there it is.

It is not exactly jealousy, however, that we feel when we reflect on the past of those we love. A bundle of letters found after years of happy union creates no sense of insecurity in the present; and yet it will pain a man sharply. The two people entertain no vulgar doubt of each other: but this preexistence of both occurs to the mind as something indelicate. To be altogether right, they should have had twin birth together, at the same moment with the feeling that unites them. Then indeed it would be simple and perfect and without reserve or afterthought. Then they would understand each other with a fullness impossible otherwise. There would be no barrier between them of associations that cannot be imparted. They would be led into none of those comparisons that send the blood back to the heart. And they would know that there had been no time lost, and they had been together as much as was possible. For besides terror for the separation that must follow some time or other in the future, men feel anger, and something like remorse, when they think of that other separation which endured until they met. Someone has written that love makes people believe in immortality, because there seems not to be room enough in life for so great a tenderness, and it is inconceivable that the most masterful of our emotions should have no more than the spare moments of a few years. Indeed, it seems strange; but if we call to mind analogies, we can hardly regard it as impossible.

"The blind bow-boy," who smiles upon us from the end of terraces in old Dutch gardens, laughingly hails his bird-bolts among a fleeting generation. But for as fast as ever he shoots, the game dissolves and disappears into eternity from under his falling arrows; this one is gone ere he is struck; the other has but time to make one gesture and give one passionate cry; and they are all the things of a moment. When the generation is gone, when the play is over, when the thirty years' panorama has been withdrawn in tatters from the stage of the world, we may ask what has become of these great, weighty, and undying loves, and the sweethearts who despised mortal conditions in a fine credulity; and they can only show us a few songs in a bygone taste, a few actions worth remembering, and a few children who have retained some happy stamp from the disposition of their parents.

๙๏ ๏๛

THOMAS BULFINCH

from *Age of Fable*

CUPID AND PSYCHE

A certain king and queen had three daughters. The charms of the two elder were more than common, but the beauty of the youngest was so wonderful that the poverty of language is unable to express its due praise. The fame of her beauty was so great that strangers from neighbouring countries came in crowds to enjoy the sight, and looked on her with amazement, paying her that homage which is due only to Venus herself. In fact Venus found her altars deserted, while men turned their devotion to this young virgin. As she passed along, the people sang her praises, and strewed her way with chaplets and flowers.

This perversion of homage due only to the immortal powers to the exaltation of a mortal gave great offence to the real Venus. Shaking her ambrosial locks with indignation, she exclaimed, "Am I then to be eclipsed in my honours by a mortal girl? In vain then did that royal shepherd, whose judgment was approved by Jove himself, give me the palm of beauty over my illustrious rivals, Pallas and Juno. But she shall not so quietly usurp my honours. I will give her cause to repent of so unlawful a beauty."

Thereupon she calls her winged son Cupid, mischievous enough in his own nature, and rouses and provokes him yet more by her complaints. She points out Psyche to him and says, "My dear son, punish that contumacious beauty; give thy mother a revenge as sweet as her injuries are great; infuse into the bosom of that haughty girl a passion for some low, mean, unworthy being, so that she may reap a mortification as great as her present exultation and triumph."

Cupid prepared to obey the commands of his mother. There are two fountains in Venus's garden, one of sweet waters, the other of bitter. Cupid filled two amber vases, one from each fountain, and suspending them from the top of his quiver, hastened to the chamber of Psyche, whom he found asleep. He shed a few drops from the bitter fountain over her lips, though the sight of her almost moved him to pity; then touched her side with the point of his arrow. At the touch she awoke, and opened eyes upon Cupid (himself invisible), which so startled him that in his confusion he wounded himself with his own arrow. Heedless of his wound, his whole thought now was to repair the mischief he had done, and he poured the balmy drops of joy over all her silken ringlets.

Psyche, henceforth frowned upon by Venus, derived no benefit from all her charms. True, all eyes were cast eagerly upon her, and every mouth spoke her praises; but neither king, royal youth, nor plebeian presented himself to demand her in marriage. Her two elder sisters of moderate charms had now long been married to two royal princes; but Psyche, in her lonely apartment, deplored her solitude, sick of that beauty which, while it procured abundance of flattery, had failed to awaken love.

Her parents, afraid that they had unwittingly incurred the anger of the gods, consulted the oracle of Apollo, and received this answer: "The virgin is destined for the bride of no mortal lover. Her future husband awaits her on the top of the mountain. He is a monster whom neither gods nor men can resist."

This dreadful decree of the oracle filled all the people with dismay, and her parents abandoned themselves to grief. But Psyche said, "Why, my dear parents, do you now lament me? You should rather have grieved when the people showered upon me undeserved honours, and with one voice called me a Venus. I now perceive that I am a victim to that name. I submit. Lead me to that rock to which my unhappy fate has destined me." Accordingly, all things being prepared, the royal maid took her place in the procession, which more resembled a funeral than a nuptial pomp, and with her parents, amid the lamentations of the people, ascended the mountain, on the summit of which they left her alone, and with sorrowful hearts returned home.

While Psyche stood on the ridge of the mountain, panting with fear and with eyes full of tears, the gentle Zephyr raised her from the earth and bore her with an easy motion into a flowery dale. By degrees her mind became composed, and she laid herself down on the grassy bank to sleep. When she awoke refreshed with sleep, she looked round and beheld near by a pleasant grove of tall and stately trees. She entered it, and in the midst discovered a fountain, sending forth clear and crystal waters, and fast by, a magnificent palace whose august front impressed the spectator that it was not the work of mortal hands, but the happy retreat of some god. Drawn by admiration and wonder, she approached the building and ventured to enter. Every object she met filled her with pleasure and amazement. Golden pillars supported the vaulted roof, and the walls were enriched with carvings and paintings representing beasts of the chase and rural scenes, adapted to delight the eye of the beholder. Proceeding onward, she perceived that besides the apartments of state there were others filled with all manner of treasures, and beautiful and precious productions of nature and art.

While her eyes were thus occupied, a voice addressed her, though she saw no one, uttering these words: "Sovereign lady, all that you see is yours. We whose voices you hear are your servants and shall obey all your commands with our utmost care and diligence. Retire, therefore, to your chamber and repose on your bed of down, and when you see fit repair to the bath. Supper awaits you in the adjoining alcove when it pleases you to take your seat there."

Psyche gave ear to the admonitions of her vocal attendants, and after repose and the refreshment of the bath, seated herself in the alcove, where a table immediately presented itself, without any visible aid from waiters or servants, and covered with the greatest delicacies of food and the most nectareous wines. Her ears too were feasted with music from invisible performers; of whom one sang, another played on the lute, and all closed in the wonderful harmony of a full chorus.

She had not yet seen her destined husband. He came only in the hours of darkness and fled before the dawn of morning, but his accents were full of love, and inspired a like passion in her. She often begged him to stay and let her behold him, but he would not consent. On the contrary he charged her to make no attempt to see him, for it was his pleasure, for the best of reasons, to keep concealed. "Why should you wish to behold me?" he said; "have you any doubt of my love? have you any wish ungratified? If you saw me, perhaps you would fear me, perhaps adore me, but all I ask of you is to love me. I would rather you would love me as an equal than adore me as a god."

This reasoning somewhat quieted Psyche for a time, and while the novelty lasted she felt quite happy. But at length the thought of her parents, left in ignorance of her fate, and of her sisters, precluded from sharing with her the delights of her situation, preyed on her mind and made her begin to feel her palace as but a splendid prison. When her husband came one night, she told him her distress, and at last drew from him an unwilling consent that her sisters should be brought to see her.

So, calling Zephyr, she acquainted him with her husband's commands, and he, promptly obedient, soon brought them across the mountain down to their sister's valley. They embraced her and she returned their caresses. "Come," said Psyche, "enter with me my house and refresh yourselves with whatever your sister has to offer." Then taking their hands she led them into her golden palace, and committed them to the care of her numerous train of attendant voices, to refresh them in her baths and at her table, and to show them all her treasures. The view of these celestial delights caused envy to enter their bosoms, at seeing their young sister possessed of such state and splendour, so much exceeding their own.

They asked her numberless questions, among others what sort of a person her husband was. Psyche replied that he was a beautiful youth, who generally spent the daytime in hunting upon the mountains. The sisters, not satisfied with this reply, soon made her confess that she had never seen him. Then they proceeded to fill her bosom with dark suspicions. "Call to mind," they said, "the Pythian oracle that declared you destined to marry a direful and tremendous monster. The inhabitants of this valley say that your husband is a terrible and monstrous serpent, who nourishes you for a while with dainties that he may by and by devour you. Take our advice. Provide yourself with a lamp and a sharp knife; put them in concealment that your husband may not discover them, and when he is sound asleep, slip out of bed, bring forth your lamp, and see for yourself whether what they say is true or not. If it is, hesitate not to cut off the monster's head, and thereby recover your liberty."

Psyche resisted these persuasions as well as she could, but they did not fail to have their effect on her mind, and when her sisters were gone, their words and her own curiosity were too strong for her to resist. So she prepared her lamp and a sharp knife, and hid them out of sight of her husband. When he had fallen into his first sleep, she silently rose and uncovering her lamp beheld not a hideous monster, but the most beautiful and charming of the gods, with his golden ringlets wandering over his snowy neck and crimson cheek, with two dewy wings on his shoulders, whiter than snow, and with shining feathers like the tender blossoms of spring. As she leaned the lamp over to have a nearer view of his face a drop of burning oil fell on the shoulder of the god, startled with which he opened his eyes and fixed them full upon her; then, without saying one word, he spread his white wings and flew out of the window. Psyche, in vain endeavouring to follow him, fell from the window to the ground. Cupid, beholding her as she lay in the dust, stopped his flight for an instant and said, "O foolish Psyche, is it thus you repay my love? After having disobeyed my mother's commands and made you my wife, will you think me a monster and cut off my head? But go; return to your sisters, whose advice you seem to think preferable to mine. I inflict no other punishment on you than to leave you for ever. Love cannot dwell with suspicion." So saying, he fled away, leaving poor Psyche prostrate on the ground, filling the place with mournful lamentations.

When she had recovered some degree of composure she looked around her, but the palace and gardens had vanished, and she found herself in the open field not far from the city where her sisters dwelt. She repaired thither and told them the whole story of her misfortunes, at which, pretending to grieve, those spiteful creatures inwardly rejoiced. "For now," said they, "he will perhaps choose one of us." With this idea, without saying a word of her intentions, each of them rose early the next morning and ascended the mountain, and having reached the top, called upon Zephyr to receive her and bear her to his lord; then leaping up, and not being sustained by Zephyr, fell down the precipice and was dashed to pieces.

Psyche meanwhile wandered day and night, without food or repose, in search of her husband. Casting her eyes on a lofty mountain having on its brow a magnificent temple, she sighed and said to herself, "Perhaps my love, my lord, inhabits there," and directed her steps thither.

She had no sooner entered than she saw heaps of corn, some in loose ears and some in sheaves, with mingled ears of barley. Scattered about, lay sickles and rakes, and all the instruments of harvest, without order, as if thrown carelessly out of the weary reapers' hands in the sultry hours of the day.

This unseemly confusion the pious Psyche put an end to, by separating and sorting everything to its proper place and kind, believing that she ought to neglect none of the gods, but endeavour by her piety to engage them all in her behalf. The holy Ceres, whose temple it was, finding her so religiously employed, thus spoke to her: "O Psyche, truly worthy of our pity, though I cannot shield you from the frowns of Venus, yet I can teach you how best to allay her displeasure. Go, then, and voluntarily surrender yourself to your lady and sovereign, and try by modesty and submission to win her forgiveness, and perhaps her favour will restore you the husband you have lost."

Psyche obeyed the commands of Ceres and took her way to the temple of Venus, endeavouring to fortify her mind and ruminating on what she should say and how best propitiate the angry goddess, feeling that the issue was doubtful and perhaps fatal.

Venus received her with angry countenance. "Most undutiful and faithless of servants," said she, "do you at last remember that you really have a mistress? Or have you rather come to see your sick husband, yet laid up of the wound given him by his loving wife? You are so ill-favoured and disagreeable that the only way you can merit your lover must be by dint of industry and diligence. I will make trial of your housewifery." Then she ordered Psyche to be led to the storehouse of her temple, where was laid up a great quantity of wheat, barley, millet, vetches, beans, and lentils prepared for food for her pigeons, and said, "Take and separate all these grains, putting all of the same kind in a parcel by themselves, and see that you get it done before evening." Then Venus departed and left her to her task.

But Psyche, in a perfect consternation at the enormous work, sat stupid and silent, without moving a finger to the inextricable heap.

While she sat despairing, Cupid stirred up the little ant, a native of the fields, to take compassion on her. The leader of the ant-hill, followed by whole hosts of his six-legged subjects, approached the heap, and with the utmost diligence taking grain by grain, they separated the pile, sorting each kind to its parcel; and when it was all done, they vanished out of sight in a moment.

Venus at the approach of twilight returned from the banquet of the gods, breathing odours and crowned with roses. Seeing the task done, she exclaimed, "This is no work of yours, wicked one, but his, whom to your own and his misfortune you have enticed." So saying, she threw her a piece of black bread for her supper and went away.

Next morning Venus ordered Psyche to be called and said to her, "Behold yonder grove which stretches along the margin of the water. There you will find sheep feeding without a shepherd, with golden-shining fleeces on their backs. Go, fetch me a sample of that precious wool gathered from every one of their fleeces."

Psyche obediently went to the riverside, prepared to do her best to execute the command. But the river god inspired the reeds with harmonious murmurs, which seemed to say, "O maiden, severely tried, tempt not the dangerous flood, nor venture among the formidable rams on the other side, for as long as they are under the influence of the rising sun, they burn with a cruel rage to destroy mortals with their sharp horns or rude teeth. But when the noontide sun has driven the cattle to the shade, and the serene spirit of the flood has lulled them to rest, you may then cross in safety, and you will find the woolly gold sticking to the bushes and the trunks of the trees."

Thus the compassionate river god gave Psyche instructions how to accomplish her task, and by observing his directions she soon returned to Venus with her arms full of the golden fleece; but she received not the approbation of her implacable mistress, who said, "I know very well it is by none of your own doings that you have succeeded in this task, and I am not satisfied yet that you have any capacity to make yourself useful. But I have another task for you. Here, take this box and go your way to the infernal shades, and give this box to Proserpine and say, 'My mistress Venus desires you to send her a little of your beauty, for in tending her sick son she has lost some of her own.' Be not too long on your errand, for I must paint myself with it to appear at the circle of the gods and goddesses this evening."

Psyche was now satisfied that her destruction was at hand, being obliged to go with her own feet directly down to Erebus. Wherefore, to make no delay of what was not to be avoided, she goes to the top of a high tower to precipitate herself headlong, thus to descend the shortest way to the shades below. But a voice from the tower said to her, "Why, poor unlucky girl, dost thou design to put an end to thy days in so dreadful a manner? And what cowardice makes thee sink under this last danger who hast been so miraculously supported in all thy former?" Then the voice told her how by a certain cave she might reach the realms of Pluto, and how to avoid all the dangers of the road, to pass by Cerberus, the three-headed dog, and prevail on Charon, the ferryman, to take her across the black river and bring her back again. But the voice added, "When Proserpine has given you the box filled with her beauty, of all things this is chiefly to be observed by you, that you never once open or look into the box nor allow your curiosity to pry into the treasure of the beauty of the goddesses."

Psyche, encouraged by this advice, obeyed it in all things, and taking heed to her ways travelled safely to the kingdom of Pluto. She was admitted to the palace of Proserpine, and without accepting the delicate seat or delicious banquet that was offered her, but contented with coarse bread for her food, she delivered her message from Venus. Presently the box was returned to her, shut and filled with the precious commodity. Then she returned the way she came, and glad was she to come out once more into the light of day.

But having got so far successfully through her dangerous task, a longing desire seized her to examine the contents of the box. "What," said she, "shall I, the carrier of this divine beauty, not take the least bit to put on my cheeks to appear to more advantage in the eyes of my beloved husband!" So she carefully opened the box, but found nothing there of any beauty at all, but an infernal and truly Stygian sleep, which being thus set free from its prison, took possession of her, and she fell down in the midst of the road, a sleepy corpse without sense or motion.

But Cupid, being now recovered from his wound, and not able longer to bear the absence of his beloved Psyche, slipping through the smallest crack of the window of his chamber which happened to be left open, flew to the spot where Psyche lay, and gathering up the sleep from her body closed it again in the box, and waked Psyche with a light touch of one of his arrows. "Again," said he, "hast thou almost perished by the same curiosity. But now perform exactly the task imposed on you by my mother, and I will take care of the rest."

Then Cupid, as swift as lightning penetrating the heights of heaven, presented himself before Jupiter with his supplication. Jupiter lent a favouring ear, and pleaded the cause of the lovers so earnestly with Venus that he won her consent. On this he sent Mercury to bring Psyche up to the heavenly assembly, and when she arrived, handing her a cup of ambrosia, he said, "Drink this, Psyche, and be immortal; nor shall Cupid ever break away from the knot in which he is tied, but these nuptials shall be perpetual."

Thus Psyche became at last united to Cupid, and in due time they had a daughter born to them whose name was Pleasure.

The fable of Cupid and Psyche is usually considered allegorical. The Greek name for a *butterfly* is Psyche, and the same word means the *soul*. There is no illustration of the immortality of the soul so striking and beautiful as the butterfly, bursting on brilliant wings from the tomb in which it has lain, after a dull, grovelling, caterpillar existence, to flutter in the blaze of day and feed on the most fragrant and delicate productions of the spring. Psyche, then, is the human soul, which is purified by sufferings and misfortunes, and is thus prepared for the enjoyment of true and pure happiness.

In works of art Psyche is represented as a maiden with the wings of a butterfly, along with Cupid, in the different situations described in the allegory.

Milton alludes to the story of Cupid and Psyche in the conclusion of his "Comus":

Celestial Cupid, her famed son, advanced,
Holds his dear Psyche sweet entranced,
After her wandering labours long,
Till free consent the gods among
Make her his eternal bride;
And from her fair unspotted side
Two blissful twins are to be born,
Youth and Joy; so Jove hath sworn.

The allegory of the story of Cupid and Psyche is well presented
in the beautiful lines of T. K. Harvey:

They wove bright fables in the days of old,
    When reason borrowed fancy's painted wings;
When truth's clear river flowed o'er sands of gold,
    And told in song its high and mystic things!
And such the sweet and solemn tale of her
    The pilgrim heart, to whom a dream was given,
That led her through the world,—Love's worshipper,—
    To seek on earth for him whose home was heaven!

In the full city,—by the haunted fount,—
    Through the dim grotto's tracery of spars,—
'Mid the pine temples, on the moonlit mount,
    Where silence sits to listen to the stars;
In the deep glade where dwells the brooding dove,
    The painted valley, and the scented air,
She heard far echoes of the voice of Love,
    And found his footsteps' traces everywhere.

But nevermore they met! since doubts and fears,
    Those phantom shapes that haunt and blight the earth,
Had come 'twixt her, a child of sin and tears,
    And that bright spirit of immortal birth;
Until her pining soul and weeping eyes
Had learned to seek him only in the skies;
Till wings unto the weary heart were given,
And she became Love's angel bride in heaven!

The story of Cupid and Psyche first appears in the works of
Apuleius, a writer of the second century of our era. It is therefore of

much more recent date than most of the legends of the Age of Fable. It is this that Keats alludes to in his "Ode to Psyche":

> O latest born and loveliest vision far
>   Of all Olympus' faded hierarchy!
> Fairer than Phœbe's sapphire-regioned star
>   Or Vesper, amorous glow-worm of the sky;
> Fairer than these, though temple thou hast none,
>   Nor altar heaped with flowers;
> Nor virgin choir to make delicious moan
>   Upon the midnight hours;
> No voice, no lute, no pipe, no incense sweet,
>   From chain-swung censer teeming;
> No shrine, no grove, no oracle, no heat
>   Of pale-mouthed prophet dreaming.

In Moore's "Summer Fête" a fancy ball is described, in which one of the characters personated is Psyche—

> . . . not in dark disguise tonight
> Hath our young heroine veiled her light;—
> For see, she walks the earth, Love's own.
>   His wedded bride, by holiest vow
> Pledged in Olympus, and made known
>   To mortals by the type which now
>   Hangs glittering on her snowy brow,
> That butterfly, mysterious trinket,
> Which means the soul, (though few would think it,)
> And sparkling thus on brow so white
> Tells us we've Psyche here tonight.

❦ ❧

WILLIAM JAMES

from *The Principles of Psychology*

Love.   Of all propensities, the sexual impulses bear on their face the most obvious signs of being instinctive, in the sense of blind, automatic, and untaught. The teleology they contain is often at variance with the wishes of the individuals concerned; and the actions are performed for no assignable reason but because Nature urges just that way. Here, if ever, then, we ought to find those characters of fatality, infallibility, and uniformity, which, we are told, make of actions done from instinct a class so utterly apart. But is this so? The facts are just the reverse: the sexual instinct is particularly liable to be checked and modified by slight differences in the individual stimulus, by the inward condition of the agent himself, by habits once acquired, and by the antagonism of contrary impulses operating on the mind. One of these is the ordinary shyness recently described; another is what might be called the *anti-sexual instinct,* the instinct of personal isolation, the actual repulsiveness to us of the idea of intimate contact with most of the persons we meet, especially those of our own sex. Thus it comes about that this strongest passion of all, so far from being the most "irresistible," may, on the contrary, be the hardest one to give rein to, and that individuals in whom the inhibiting influences are potent may pass through life and never find an occasion to have it gratified. There could be no better proof of the truth of that proposition with which we began our study of the instinctive life in man, that irregularity of behavior may come as well from the possession of too many instincts as from the lack of any at all.

from *The Varieties of Religious Experience*

I subjoin an additional document which has come into my possession, and which represents in a vivid way what is probably a very frequent sort of conversion, if the opposite of "falling in love," falling out of love, may be so termed. Falling in love also conforms frequently to this type, a latent process of unconscious preparation often preceding a sudden awakening to the fact that the mischief is irretrievably done. The free and easy tone in this narrative gives it a sincerity that speaks for itself.

> For almost two years of this time I went through a very bad experience, which almost drove me mad. I had fallen violently in love with a girl who, young as she was, had a spirit of coquetry like a cat. As I look back on her now, I hate her, and wonder how I could ever have fallen so low as to be worked upon to such an extent by her attractions. Nevertheless, I fell into a regular fever, could think of nothing else; whenever I was alone, I pictured her attractions, and

spent most of the time when I should have been working, in recalling our previous interviews, and imagining future conversations. She was very pretty, good humored, and jolly to the last degree, and intensely pleased with my admiration. Would give me no decided answer yes or no, and the queer thing about it was that whilst pursuing her for her hand, I secretly knew all along that she was unfit to be a wife for me, and that she would say yes. Although for a year we took our meals at the same boarding-house, so that I saw her continually and familiarly, our closer relations had to be largely on the sly, and this fact, together with my jealousy of another one of her male admirers, and my own conscience despising me for my uncontrollable weakness, made me so nervous and sleepless that I really thought I should become insane. I understand well those young men murdering their sweethearts, which appear so often in the papers. Nevertheless I did love her passionately, and in some ways she did deserve it.

The queer thing was the sudden and unexpected way in which it all stopped. I was going to my work after breakfast one morning thinking as usual of her and my misery, when, just as if some outside power laid hold of me, I found myself turning round and almost running to my room, where I immediately got out all the relics of her which I possessed, including some hair, all her notes and letters, and ambrotypes on glass. The former I made a fire of, the latter I actually crushed beneath my heel, in a sort of fierce joy of revenge and punishment. I now loathed and despised her altogether, and as for myself I felt as if a load of disease had suddenly been removed from me. That was the end. I never spoke to her or wrote to her again in all the subsequent years, and I have never had a single moment of loving thought towards one who for so many months entirely filled my heart. In fact, I have always rather hated her memory, though now I can see that I had gone unnecessarily far in that direction. At any rate, from that happy morning onward I regained possession of my own proper soul, and have never since fallen into any similar trap.

This seems to be an unusually clear example of two different levels of personality, inconsistent in their dictates, yet so well balanced against each other as for a long time to fill the lie with discord and dissatisfaction. At last, not gradually, but in a sudden crisis, the unstable equilibrium is resolved, and this happens so unexpectedly that it as as if, to use the writer's words, "some outside power laid hold."

꿍 ꩜

HENRY ADAMS

from *Mont Saint-Michel*

After worshipping at the shrines of Saint Michael on his Mount and of the Virgin at Chartres, one may wander far and wide over France, and seldom feel lost; all later Gothic art comes naturally, and no new thought disturbs the perfected form. Yet tourists of English blood and American training are seldom or never quite at home there. Commonly they feel it only as a stage-decoration. The twelfth and thirteenth centuries, studied in the pure light of political economy, are insane. The scientific mind is atrophied, and suffers under inherited cerebral weakness, when it comes in contact with the eternal woman—Astarte, Isis, Demeter, Aphrodite, and the last and greatest deity of all, the Virgin. Very rarely one lingers, with a mild sympathy, such as suits the patient student of human error, willing to be interested in what he cannot understand. Still more rarely, owing to some revival of archaic instincts, he rediscovers the woman. This is perhaps the mark of the artist alone, and his solitary privilege. The rest of us cannot feel; we can only study. The proper study of mankind is woman and, by common agreement since the time of Adam, it is the most complex and arduous. The study of Our Lady, as shown by the art of Chartres, leads directly back to Eve, and lays bare the whole subject of sex.

If it were worth while to argue a paradox, one might maintain that Nature regards the female as the essential, the male as the superfluity of her world. Perhaps the best starting-point for study of the Virgin would be a practical acquaintance with bees, and especially with queen bees. Precisely where the French man may come in, on the genealogical tree of parthenogenesis, one hesitates to say; but certain it is that the French woman, from very early times, has shown qualities peculiar to herself, and that the French woman of the Middle Ages was a masculine character. Almost any book which deals with the social side of the twelfth century has something to say on this subject, like the following page from M. Garreau's volume published in 1899, on the "Social State of France during the Crusades":—

> A trait peculiar to this epoch is the close resemblance between the manners of men and women. The rule that such and such feelings or acts are permitted to one sex and forbidden to the other was not fairly settled. Men had the right to dissolve in tears, and women that of talking without prudery. . . . If we look at their intellectual level, the women appear distinctly superior. They are more serious; more subtle. With them we do not seem dealing with the rude state of civilization that their husbands belong to. . . . As a rule, the women seem to have the habit of weighing their acts; of not yielding to momentary impressions. While the sense of Christianity is more developed in them than in their husbands, on the other hand they show more perfidy and art in crime. . . . One might doubtless prove by a series of examples that the maternal influence when it predominated in the education of a son gave him a marked superiority over his contemporaries. Richard Cœur-de-Lion the crowned poet, artist, the king whose noble manners and refined mind in spite of his cruelty exercised so strong an impression on his age, was formed by that brilliant Eleanor of Guienne who, in her struggle with her husband, retained her sons as much as possible within her sphere of influence in order to make party chiefs of them. Our great Saint Louis, as all know, was brought up exclusively by Blanche of Castile; and Joinville, the charming writer so worthy of Saint Louis's friendship, and apparently so superior to his surroundings, was also the pupil of a widowed and regent mother.

The superiority of the woman was not a fancy, but a fact. Man's business was to fight or hunt or feast or make love. The man was also the travelling partner in commerce, commonly absent from home for months together, while the woman carried on the business. The woman ruled the household and the workshop; cared for the economy; supplied the intelligence, and dictated the taste. Her ascendancy was secured by her alliance with the Church, into which she sent her most intelligent children; and a priest or clerk, for the most part, counted socially as a woman.

Both physically and mentally the woman was robust, as the men often complained, and she did not greatly resent being treated as a man. Sometimes the husband beat her, dragged her about by the hair, locked her up in the house; but he was quite conscious that she always got even with him in the end. As a matter of fact, probably she got more than even. On this point, history, legend, poetry, romance, and especially the popular fabliaux—invented to amuse the gross tastes of the coarser class—are all agreed, and one could give scores of volumes illustrating it. The greatest men illustrate it best, as one might show almost at hazard. The greatest men of the eleventh, twelfth, and thirteenth centuries were William the Norman; his great grandson Henry II Plantagenet; Saint Louis of France; and, if a fourth be needed, Richard Cœur-de-Lion. Notoriously all these men had as much difficulty as Louis XIV himself with the women of their family. Tradition exaggerates everything it touches, but shows, at the same time, what is passing in the minds of the society which *tradites*. In Normandy, the people of Caen have kept a tradition, told elsewhere in other forms, that one day, Duke William,—the Conqueror,—exasperated by having his bastardy constantly thrown in his face by the Duchess Matilda, dragged her by the hair, tied to his horse's tail, as far as the suburb of Vaucelles; and this legend accounts for the splendour of the Abbaye-aux-Dames, because William, the common people believed, afterwards regretted the impropriety, and atoned for it by giving her money to build the abbey. The story betrays the man's weakness. The Abbaye-aux-Dames stands in the same relation to the Abbaye-aux-Hommes that Matilda took towards William. Inferiority there was none; on the contrary, the woman was socially the superior, and William was probably more afraid of her than she of him, if Mr. Freeman is right in insisting that he married her in spite of her having a husband living, and certainly two children. If William was the strongest man in the eleventh century, his great-grandson, Henry II of England, was the strongest man of the twelfth; but the history of the time resounds with the noise of his battles with Queen Eleanor whom he, at last, held in prison for fourteen years. Prisoner as she was, she broke him down in the end. One is tempted to suspect that, had her husband and children been guided by her, and by her policy as peacemaker for the good of Guienne, most of the disasters of England and France might have been postponed for the time; but we can never know the truth, for monks and historians abhor emancipated women,—with good reason, since such women are apt to abhor them,—and the quarrel can never be pacified. Historians have commonly shown fear of women without admitting it, but the man of the Middle Ages knew at least why he feared the woman, and told it openly, not to say brutally. Long after Eleanor and Blanche were dead, Chaucer brought the Wife of Bath on his Shakespearean stage, to explain the woman, and as usual he touched masculine frailty with caustic, while seeming to laugh at woman and man alike—

> "My liege lady! generally," quoth he,
> "Women desiren to have soverainetee."

The point was that the Wife of Bath, like Queen Blanche and Queen Eleanor, not only wanted sovereignty, but won and held it. . . .

The twelfth century had the child's love of sweets and spices and preserved fruits, and drinks sweetened or spiced, whether they were taken for supper or for poetry; the true knight's palate was fresh and his appetite excellent either for sweets or verses or love; the world was young then; Robin Hoods lived in every forest, and Richard Cœur-de-Lion was not yet twenty years old. The pleasant adventures of Robin Hood were real, as you can read in the stories of a dozen outlaws, and men troubled themselves about pain and death much as healthy bears did, in the mountains. Life had miseries enough, but few shadows deeper than those of the imaginative lover, or the terrors of ghosts at night. Men's imaginations ran riot, but did not keep them awake; at least, neither the preserved fruits nor the mulberry wine nor the clear syrup nor the gingerbread nor the Holy Graal kept Perceval awake, but he slept the sound and healthy sleep of youth, and when he woke the next morning, he felt only a mild surprise to find that his host and household had disappeared, leaving him to ride away without farewell, breakfast, or Graal.

Christian wrote about Perceval in 1174 in the same spirit in which the workmen in glass, thirty years later, told the story of Charlemagne. One artist worked for Mary of Champagne; the others for Mary of Chartres, commonly known as the Virgin; but all did their work in good faith, with the first, fresh, easy instinct of colour, light, and line. Neither of the two Maries was mystical, in a modern sense; none of the artists was oppressed by the burden of doubt; their scepticism was as childlike as faith. If one has to make an exception, perhaps the passion of love was more serious than that of religion, and gave to religion the deepest emotion, and the most complicated one, which society knew. Love was certainly a passion; and even more certainly it was, as seen in poets like Dante and Petrarch,—in romans like "Lancelot" and "Aucassin,"—in ideals like the Virgin,—complicated beyond modern conception. For this reason the loss of Christian's "Tristan" makes a terrible gap in art, for Christian's poem would have given the first and best idea of what led to courteous love. The "Tristan" was written before 1160, and belonged to the cycle of Queen Eleanor of England rather than to that of her daughter Mary of Troyes; but the subject was one neither of courtesy nor of France; it belonged to an age far behind the eleventh century, or even the tenth, or indeed any century within the range of French history; and it was as little fitted for Christian's way of treatment as for any avowed burlesque. The original Tristan—critics say—was not French, and neither Tristan nor Isolde had ever a drop of French blood in their veins. In their form as Christian received it, they were Celts or Scots; they came from Brittany, Wales, Ireland, the northern ocean, or farther still. Behind the Welsh Tristan, which passed probably through England to Normandy and thence to France and Champagne, critics detect a far more ancient figure living in a form of society that France could not remember ever to have known. King Marc was a tribal chief of the Stone Age whose subjects loved the forest and lived on the sea or in caves; King Marc's royal hall was a common shelter on the banks of a stream, where every one was at home, and king, queen, knights, attendants, and dwarf slept on the floor, on beds laid down where they pleased; Tristan's weapons were the bow and stone knife; he never saw a horse or a spear; his ideas of loyalty and Isolde's ideas of marriage were as vague as Marc's royal authority; and all were alike unconscious of law, chivalry, or church. The note they sang was more unlike the note of Christian, if possible, than that of Richard Wagner; it was the simplest expression of rude and primitive love, as one could perhaps find it among North American Indians, though hardly so defiant even there, and certainly in the Icelandic Sagas hardly so lawless; but it was a note of real passion, and touched the deepest chords of sympathy in the artificial society of the twelfth century, as it did in that of the nineteenth. The task of the French poet was to tone it down and give it the fashionable dress, the pointed shoes and long sleeves, of the time. "The Frenchman," says Gaston Paris, "is specially interested in making his story entertaining for the society it is meant for; he is 'social'; that is, of the world; he smiles at the adventures he tells, and delicately lets you see that he is not their dupe; he exerts himself to give to his style a constant elegance, a uniform polish, in which a few neatly turned, clever phrases sparkle here and there; above all, he wants to please, and thinks of his audience more than of his subject."

In the twelfth century he wanted chiefly to please women, as Orderic complained; Isolde came out of Brittany to meet Eleanor coming up from Guienne, and the Virgin from the east; and all united in giving law to society. In each case it was the woman, not the man, who gave the law;—it was Mary, not the Trinity; Eleanor, not Louis VII; Isolde, not Tristan. No doubt, the original Tristan had given the law like Roland or Achilles, but the twelfth-century Tristan was a comparatively poor creature. He was in his way a secondary figure in the romance, as Louis VII was to Eleanor and Abélard to Héloïse. Everyone knows how, about twenty years before Eleanor came to Paris, the poet-professor Abélard, the hero of the Latin Quarter, had sung to Héloïse those songs which—he tells us—resounded through Europe as widely as his scholastic fame, and probably to more effect for his renown. In popular notions Héloïse was Isolde, and would in a moment have done what Isolde did (Bartsch, 107–08):—

> When King Marc had banned us both,
> And from his court had chased us forth,
> Hand in hand each clasping fast
> Straight from out the hall we passed;
> To the forest turned our face;
>
> Found in it a perfect place,
> Where the rock that made a cave
> Hardly more than passage gave;
> Spacious within and fit for use,
> As though it had been planned for us.

At any time of her life, Héloïse would have defied society or church, and would—at least in the public's fancy—have taken Abélard by the hand and gone off to the forest much more readily than she went to the cloister; but Abélard would have made a poor figure as Tristan. Abélard and Christian of Troyes were as remote as we are from the legendary Tristan; but Isolde and Héloïse, Eleanor and Mary were the immortal and eternal woman. The legend of Isolde, both in the earlier and the later version, seems to have served as a sacred book to the women of the twelfth and thirteenth centuries, and Christian's Isolde surely helped Mary in giving law to the Court of Troyes and decisions in the Court of Love. . . .

For us the poetry is history, and the facts are false. French art starts not from facts, but from certain assumptions as conventional as a legendary window, and the commonest convention is the Woman. The fact, then as now, was Power, or its equivalent in exchange, but Frenchmen, while struggling for the Power, expressed it in terms of Art. They looked on life as a drama,—and on drama as a phase of life—in which the bystanders were bound to assume and accept the regular stage-plot. That the plot might be altogether untrue to real life affected in no way its interest. To them Thibaut and Blanche were bound to act Tristan and Isolde. Whatever they were when off the stage, they were lovers on it. Their loves were as real and as reasonable as the worship of the Virgin. Courteous love was avowedly a form of drama, but not the less a force of society. Illusion for illusion, courteous love, in Thibaut's hands, or in the hands of Dante and Petrarch, was as substantial as any other convention;—the balance of trade, the rights of man, or the Athanasian Creed. In that sense the illusions alone were real; if the Middle Ages had reflected only what was practical, nothing would have survived for us. . . .

> There is no comfort to be found for pain
> Save only where the heart has made its home.
> Therefore I can but murmur and complain
> Because no comfort to my pain has come
> From where I garnered all my happiness.
> From true love have I only earned distress
>   The truth to say.
> Grace, lady! give me comfort to possess
>   A hope, one day.
>
> Seldom the music of her voice I hear
> Or wonder at the beauty of her eyes.
> It grieves me that I may not follow there
> Where at her feet my heart attentive lies.
> Oh, gentle Beauty without consciousness,
> Let me once feel a moment's hopefulness,
>   If but one ray!
> Grace, lady! give me comfort to possess
>   A hope, one day.
>
> Certain there are who blame upon me throw
> Because I will not tell whose love I seek;

But truly, lady, none my thought shall know,
None that is born, save you to whom I speak
In cowardice and awe and doubtfulness,
That you may happily with fearlessness
    My heart essay.
Grace, lady! give me comfort to possess
    A hope, one day.

                    —Thibaut of Champagne

G. K. Chesterton

Romantic Love

This morning I read an article in a very serious magazine, in which the writer quoted the remark of Byron that a certain sort of romantic love is woman's whole existence. The writer then said that the first people who ever challenged this view were the revolutionary Suffragettes at the end of the nineteenth century. The truth is that the first people who ever maintained this view were the revolutionary Romantics at the beginning of the nineteenth century. The habit of giving to romantic love this extravagant and exclusive importance in human life was itself an entirely modern and revolutionary thing, and dates from the romantic movement commonly traced to Rousseau; but I think much more truly to be traced to the influence of the German sentimentalists. Most people who curse Rousseau have never read Rousseau; or have only read the *Confessions* and not the *Contrat Social.* The critics read the *Confessions,* if only to condemn them; because the critics themselves are modern romantics and sentimentalists; men who like Confessions and dislike Contracts. The critics hate or avoid the *Contrat Social* not because it is sloppy and sentimental (for it is not) but because it his hard and clear and lucid and logical. Rousseau had his emotional weaknesses as an individual, like other individuals; but he was not an eighteenth-century philosopher for nothing. What the moderns dislike about him is not the silliness of his confessions, but the solidity of his convictions; and the fact that, like the old theologians, he could hold general ideas in a hard and fast fashion. When it comes to defining his fundamentals, Rousseau is as definite as Calvin. They were both ruthless theorists from Geneva; though one preached the theory of pessimism and the other the theory of optimism. I am not maintaining that I agree with either; but Rousseau would be as useful as Calvin in teaching some of his critics how to criticise.

But Rousseau is a parenthesis. Wherever the real Romantic Movement came from, whether from the German forests or the Geneva lake, it was a recent and revolutionary business, as compared with history as a whole. But it is obvious that the ordinary modern critic is entirely ignorant of history as a whole. He knows that his mother read Tennyson and his grandmother read Byron. Beyond that he can imagine nothing whatever; he supposes that his great-great-grandmothers and their great-great-great-grandmothers had gone on reading Byron from the beginning of the world. He imagines that Byron, who was a disinherited and disreputable rebel to the last, has been an established and conventional authority from the first. He therefore supposes that all women, in all ages, would have accepted the prehistoric Byronic commandment that the Byronic sort of romantic passion was the sole concern of their lives. Yet it is certain that women have had a great many other concerns and have been attached to a great many other convictions. They have been priestesses, prophetesses, empresses, queens, abbesses, mothers, great housewives, great letter-writers, lunatics founding sects, blue-stockings keeping salons, and all sorts of things. If you had said to Deborah the mother in Israel, or Hypatia the Platonist of Alexandria, or Catherine of Siena, or Joan of Arc, or Isabella of Spain, or Maria Theresa of Austria, or even to Hannah More or Joanna Southcott, that Byronic love was "woman's whole existence," they would all have been very indignant and most of them flown into a towering passion. They would have asked in various ways whether there was no such thing as honour, no such thing as duty, no such thing as glory, no such thing as great studies or great enterprises, no such thing as normal functions and necessary labours; incidentally, we may add, no such thing as babies. They differed a great deal in their type of vocation and even in their theory of virtue; but they all had some theory of virtue that went a little further than that. Up to a particular moment in the eighteenth century, practically every thinking person would have accepted the colossal common sense expressed by a French poet of the seventeenth century: "L'amour est un plaisir; l'honneur est un devoir." [Love is a pleasure; honor is a duty]

Then came the extreme emphasis on romance among the Victorians; for the Victorians were not notable for their emphasis on virtue, but for their emphasis on romance. Queen Victoria lived so long, and the Victorian Age was such an unconscionably long time dying, that by the

time Mr Bernard Shaw and others began what they called a realistic revolt against romance, the sentimental German movement seemed to be
not only as old as Victoria, but as old as Boadicea. It is highly typical, for
instance, that Mr Bernard Shaw, in one of his earliest criticisms, complained of the convention according to which anybody was supposed to
have "penetrated into the Holy of Holies" so long as he was content to
say that "Love is Enough." But, as a matter of fact, the very phrase "Love
is Enough" did not come to him from any conventional or classical authority; not even from any conventional or conservative Victorian. It
came from a book by a Socialist and Revolutionist like himself; from a
book by William Morris.

Of course the anti-romantic movement led by Shaw, like the romantic movement led by Byron, has gone forward blindly and blundered in every sort of way. The modern world seems to have no notion
of preserving different things side by side, of allowing its proper and
proportionate place to each, of saving the whole varied heritage of cul-
ture. It has no notion except that of simplifying something by destroy-
ing nearly everything; whether it be Rousseau breaking up kingdoms in
the name of reason; or Byron breaking up families in the name of romance; or Shaw breaking up romances in the name of frankness and the
formula of Ibsen. I myself value very highly the great nineteenth-century
illumination of romantic love; just as I value the great eighteenth-
century ideal of right reason and human dignity, or the seventeenth-
century intensity, or the sixteenth-century expansion, or the divine logic
and dedicated valour of the Middle Ages. I do not see why any of these
cultural conquests should be lost or despised; or why it is necessary for
every fashion to wash away all that is best in every other. It may be possible that one good custom would corrupt the world; but I never could
see why the second good custom should deny that the first good custom was good. As it is, those who have no notion except that of breaking away from romance are being visibly punished by breaking away
from reason. Every new realistic novel serves to show that realism, when
entirely emptied of romance, becomes utterly unreal. For romance was
only the name given to a love of life which was something much larger
than a life of love, in the Byronic or sentimental sense. And anything
from which it has passed is instantly corrupt and crawling with the
worms of death.

HAVELOCK ELLIS

from *Studies in the Psychology of Sex*

THE ORIGINS OF THE KISS

Manifestations resembling the kiss, whether with the object of expressing affection or sexual emotion, are found among various animals much
lower than man. The caressing of the antennae practiced by snails and
various insects during sexual intercourse is of the nature of a kiss. Birds
use their bills for a kind of caress. Thus, referring to guillemots and their
practice of nibbling each other's feet, and the interest the mate always
takes in this proceeding, which probably relieves irritation caused by insects, Edmund Selous remarks: "When they nibble and preen each other
they may, I think, be rightly said to cosset and caress, the expression and
pose of the bird receiving the benefit being often beatific." Among mammals, such as the dog, we have what closely resembles a kiss, and the dog
who smells, licks, and gently bites his master or a bitch, combines most
of the sensory activities involved in the various forms of the human
kiss.

As practiced by man, the kiss involves mainly either the sense of
touch or that of smell. Occasionally it involves to some extent both sensory elements.

The tactile kiss is certainly very ancient and primitive. It is common among mammals generally. The human infant exhibits, in a very
marked degree, the impulse to carry everything to the mouth and to lick
or attempt to taste it, possibly, as Compayre suggests, from a memory of
the action of the lips protruded to seize the maternal nipple. The affectionate child, as Mantegazza remarks, not only applies inanimate objects to its lips or tongue, but of its own impulse licks the people it likes.
Stanley Hall, in the light of a large amount of information he obtained
on this point, found that "some children insist on licking the cheeks,
necks, and hands of those they wish to caress," or like having animals lick
them. This impulse in children may be associated with the maternal impulse in animals to lick the young. "The method of licking the young
practiced by the mother," remarks S. S. Buckman, "would cause licking
to be associated with happy feelings. And, further, there is the allaying
of parasitical irritation which is afforded by the rubbing and hence results in pleasure. It may even be suggested that the desire of the mother

to lick her young was prompted in the first place by a desire to bestow on her offspring a pleasure she felt herself." The licking impulse in the child may thus, it is possible, be regarded as the evanescent manifestation of a more fundamental animal impulse, a manifestation which is liable to appear in adult life under the stress of strong sexual emotion. Such an association is of interest if, as there is some reason to believe, the kiss of sexual love originated as a development of the more primitive kiss bestowed by the mother on her child, for it is sometimes found that the maternal kiss is practiced where the sexual kiss is unknown.

The impulse to bite is also a part of the tactile element which lies at the origin of kissing. As Stanley Hall notes, children are fond of biting, though by no means always as a method of affection. There is, however, in biting a distinctly sexual origin to invoke, for among many animals the teeth (and among birds the bill) are used by the male to grasp the female more firmly during intercourse. This point has been discussed in the previous volume of these *Studies* in reference to "Love and Pain," and it is unnecessary to enter into further details here. The heroine of Kleist's *Penthesilea* remarks: "Kissing (Küsse) rhymes with biting (Bisse), and one who loves with the whole heart may easily confound the two."

The kiss, as known in Europe, has developed on a sensory basis that is mainly tactile, although an olfactory element may sometimes co-exist. The kiss thus understood is not very widely spread and is not usually found among rude and uncultured peoples. We can trace it in Aryan and Semitic antiquity, but in no very pronounced form; Homer scarcely knew it, and the Greek poets seldom mention it. Today it may be said to be known all over Europe except in Lapland. Even in Europe it is probably a comparatively modern discovery; and in all the Celtic tongues, Rhys states, there is no word for "kiss," the word employed being always borrowed from the Latin *pax*. At a fairly early historic period, however, the Welsh Cymri, at all events, acquired a knowledge of the kiss, but it was regarded as a serious matter and very sparingly used, being by law only permitted on special occasions, as at a game called rope-playing or a carousal; otherwise a wife who kissed a man not her husband could be repudiated. Throughout eastern Asia it is unknown; thus, in Japanese literature kisses and embraces have no existence. "Kisses and embraces are simply unknown in Japan as tokens of affection," Lafcadio Hearn states, "if we except the solitary fact that Japanese mothers, like mothers all over the world, lip and hug their little ones betimes. After babyhood there is no more hugging or kisses; such actions, except in the case of infants, are held to be immodest. Never do girls kiss one another; never do parents kiss or embrace their children who have become able to walk." This holds true, and has always held true, of all classes; hand-clasping is also foreign to them. On meeting after a long absence, Hearn remarks, they smile, perhaps cry a little, they may even stroke each other, but that is all. Japanese affection "is chiefly shown in acts of exquisite courtesy and kindness." Among nearly all of the black races of Africa lovers never kiss nor do mothers usually kiss their babies. Among the American Indians the tactile kiss is, for the most part, unknown, though here and there, as among the Fuegians, lovers rub their cheeks together. Kissing is unknown to the Malays. In North Queensland, however, Roth states, kissing takes place between mothers (not fathers) and infants, also between husbands and wives; but whether it is an introduced custom Roth is unable to say; he adds that the Pitta-pitta language possesses a word for kissing.

It must be remarked, however, that in many parts of the world where the tactile kiss, as we understand it, is usually said to be unknown, it still exists as between a mother and her baby, and this seems to support the view advocated by Lombroso that the lovers' kiss is developed from the maternal kiss. Thus, the Angoni Zulus to the north of the Zambesi, Wiese states, kiss their small children on both cheeks and among the Fuegians, according to Hyades, mothers kiss their small children.

Even in Europe the kiss in early mediæval days was, it seems probable, not widely known as an expression of sexual love; it would appear to have been a refinement of love only practiced by the more cultivated classes. In the old ballad of Glasgerion the lady suspected that her secret visitor was only a churl, and not the knight he pretended to be, because when he came in his master's place to spend the night with her he kissed her neither coming nor going, but simply got her with child. It is only under a comparatively high stage of civilization that the kiss has been emphasized and developed in the art of love. Thus the Arabic author of the *Perfumed Garden,* a work revealing the existence of a high degree of social refinement, insists on the great importance of the kiss, especially if applied to the inner part of the mouth, and he quotes a proverb that "A moist kiss is better than a hasty coitus." Such kisses, as well as on the face generally, and all over the body, are frequently referred to by Hindu, Latin, and more modern erotic writers as among the most efficacious methods of arousing love.

A reason which may have stood in the way of the development of the kiss in a sexual direction has probably been the fact that in the near

East the kiss was largely monopolized for sacred uses, so that its erotic potentialities were not easily perceived. Among the early Arabians the gods were worshiped by a kiss. This was the usual way of greeting the house gods on entering or leaving. In Rome the kiss was a sign of reverence and respect far more than a method of sexual excitation. Among the early Christians it had an all but sacramental significance. It retains its ancient and serious meaning in many usages of the Western and still more the Eastern Churches; the relics of saints, the foot of the pope, the hands of bishops, are kissed, just as the ancient Greeks kissed the images of the gods. Among ourselves we still have a legally recognized example of the sacredness of the kiss in the form of taking an oath by kissing the Testament.

So far we have been concerned mainly with the tactile kiss, which is sometimes supposed to have arisen in remote times to the east of the Mediterranean—where the vassal kissed his suzerain and where the kiss of love was known, as we learn from the Songs of Songs, to the Hebrews—and has now conquered nearly the whole of Europe. But over a much larger part of the world and even in one corner of Europe (Lapland, as well as among the Russian Yakuts) a different kind of salutation rules, the olfactory kiss. This varies in form in different regions and sometimes simulates a tactile kiss, but, as it exists in a typical form in China, where it has been carefully studied by d'Enjoy, it may be said to be made up of three phases: (1) the nose is applied to the cheek of the beloved person; (2) there is a long nasal inspiration accompanied by lowering of the eyelids; (3) there is a slight smacking of the lips without the application of the mouth to the embraced cheek. The whole process, d'Enjoy considers, is founded on sexual desire and the desire for food, smell being the sense employed in both fields. In the form described by d'Enjoy, we have the Mongolian variety of the olfactory kiss. The Chinese regard the European kiss as odious, suggesting voracious cannibals, and yellow mothers in the French colonies still frighten children by threatening to give them the white man's kiss. Their own kiss the Chinese regard as exclusively voluptuous; it is only befitting as between lovers, and not only do fathers refrain from kissing their children except when very young, but even the mothers only give their children a rare and furtive kiss. Among some of the hill-tribes of south-east India the olfactory kiss is found, the nose being applied to the cheek during salutation with a strong inhalation; instead of saying "Kiss me," they here say "Smell me." The Tamils, I am told by a medical correspondent in Ceylon, do not kiss during coitus, but rub noses and also lick each other's mouth and tongue. The olfactory kiss is known in Africa; thus, on the Gambia in inland Africa when a man salutes a woman he takes her hand and places it to his nose, twice smelling the back of it. Among the Jekris of the Niger coast mothers rub their babies with their cheeks or mouths, but they do not kiss them, nor do lovers kiss, though they squeeze, cuddle, and embrace. Among the Swahilis a smell kiss exists, and very young boys are taught to raise their clothes before women visitors, who thereupon playfully smell the penis; the child who does this is said to "give tobacco." Kissing of any kind appears to be unknown to the Indians throughout a large part of America: Im Thirn states that it is unknown to the Indians of Guiana, and at the other end of South America Hyades and Deniker state that it is unknown to the Fuegians. In North America the olfactory kiss is known to the Eskimo, and has been noted among some Indian tribes, as the Blackfeet. It is also known in Polynesia. At Samoa kissing was smelling. In New Zealand, also, the *hongi*, or nose-pressing, was the kiss of welcome, of mourning, and of sympathy. In the Malay archipelago, it is said, the same word is used for "greeting" and "smelling." Among the Dyaks of the Malay archipelago, however, Vaughan Stevens states that any form of kissing is unknown. In Borneo, Breitenstein tells us, kissing is a kind of smelling, the word for smelling being used, but he never himself saw a man kiss a woman; it is always done in private.

The olfactory kiss is thus seen to have a much wider extension over the world than the European (or Mediterranean) tactile kiss. In its most complete development, however, it is mainly found among the people of Mongolian race, or those yellow peoples more or less related to them.

❧ ☙

Sigmund Freud

from *Delusion and Dream*

Freud's interpretation of the romantic novel Gradiva, about a young archeologist, Norbert Hanold, and his sweetheart, Zoe

. . . our author has connected the treatment of the delusion and the breaking forth of the desire for love most closely with one another, and prepared the outcome in a love-affair as necessary. He knows the nature of the delusion even better than his critics; he knows that a component of amorous desire has combined with a component of resistance in the formation of the delusion, and he has the girl who undertakes the cure discover in Hanold's delusion the component referring to her. Only this insight can make her decide to devote herself to treating him, only the certainty of knowing herself loved by him can move her to confess to him her love. The treatment consists in restoring to him, from without, the repressed memories which he cannot release from within; it would be ineffective if the therapeutist did not consider the emotions; and the interpretation of the delusion would not finally be: "See; all that means only that you love me."

The procedure which our author has his Zoë follow for the cure of the delusion of the friend of her youth, shows a considerable resemblance, no, complete agreement, essentially, with a therapeutic method which Dr. J. Breuer and the present writer introduced into medicine in 1895, and to the perfection of which the latter has since devoted himself. This method of treatment, first called the "cathartic" by Breuer, which the present writer has preferred to designate as "analytic" consists in rather forcibly bringing into the consciousness of the patients who suffer from disturbances analogous to Hanold's delusion, the unconscious, through the repression of which they have become ill, just as Gradiva does with the repressed memories of their childhood relations. To be sure, accomplishment of this task is easier for Gradiva than for the physician; she is, in this connection, in a position which might be called ideal from many view-points. The physician who does not fathom his patient in advance, and does not possess within himself, as conscious memory, what is working in the patient as unconscious, must call to his aid a complicated technique in order to overcome this disadvantage. He must learn to gather with absolute certainty, from the patient's conscious ideas and statements, the repressed material in him, to guess the unconscious, when it betrays itself behind the patient's conscious expressions and acts. The latter then does something similar to what Norbert Hanold did at the end of the story, when he re-translates the name, Gradiva, into *Bertgang*. The disturbance disappears then by being traced back to its origin; analysis brings cure at the same time.

The similarity between the procedure of Gradiva and the analytic method of psychotherapy is, however, not limited to these two points, making the repressed conscious, and the concurrence of explanation and cure. It extends itself to what proves the essential of the whole change, the awakening of the emotions. Every disturbance analogous to

Hanold's delusion, which in science we usually designate as a psychoneurosis, has, as a preliminary, the repression of part of the emotional life, to speak boldly, of the sex-impulse, and at every attempt to introduce the unconscious and repressed cause of illness into consciousness, the emotional component necessarily awakens to renewed struggle with the forces repressing it, to adjust itself for final result, often under violent manifestations of reaction. In reawakening, in consciousness, of repressed love, the process of recuperation is accomplished when we sum up all the various components of sex-impulse as "love" and this reawakening is irremissible, for the symptoms on account of which the treatment was undertaken are nothing but the precipitations of former struggles of repression and recurrence and can be solved and washed away only by a new high-tide of these very passions. Every psychoanalytic treatment is an attempt to free repressed love, which has formed a miserable compromise-outlet in a symptom. Yes, the conformity with the therapeutic process pictured by the author in "Gradiva" reaches its height when we add that even in analytical psychotherapy, the reawakened passion, whether love or hate, chooses the person of the physician as its object every time.

Then, of course, appear the differences which make the case of Gradiva an ideal one such as the technique of physicians cannot attain. Gradiva can respond to the love which is pushing through from the unconscious into the conscious; the physician cannot; Gradiva was herself the object of the former repressed love; her person offers at once a desirable object to the freed erotic activity. The physician has been a stranger, and after the cure must try to become a stranger again; often he does not know how to advise the cured patient to apply in life her regained capacity for love. To suggest what resources and makeshifts the physician then employs to approach with more or less success the model of a love-cure which our author has drawn for us, would carry us too far away from our present task.

Now, however, the last question which we have already evaded answering several times. Our views about repression, the formation of delusion and related disturbances, the formation and interpretation of dreams, the role of erotic life, and the manner of cure for such disturbances are, of course, not by any means the common property of science, to say nothing of being the possession of educated people. If the insight which makes our author able to create his "Fancy" in such a way that we can analyze it like a real history of disease has for its foundation the above-mentioned knowledge, we should like to find out the source of it.

One of the circle who, as was explained at the beginning, was interested in the dreams of "Gradiva" and their possible interpretation, put the direct question to Wilhelm Jensen, whether any such similar theories of science had been known to him. Our author answered, as was to be expected, in the negative, and rather testily. His imagination had put into his mind the "Gradiva" in whom he had his joy; anyone whom she did not please, might leave her alone. He did not suspect how much she had pleased the readers.

It is easily possible that our author's rejection does not stop at that. Perhaps he denies knowledge of the rules which we have shown that he follows, and disavows all the intentions which we recognized in his production; I do not consider this improbable; then, however, only two possibilities remain. Either we have presented a true caricature of interpretation, by transferring to a harmless work of art tendencies of which its creator had no idea, and have thereby shown again how easy it is to find what one seeks and what one is engrossed with, a possibility of which most strange examples are recorded in the history of literature. Every reader may now decide for himself whether he cares to accept such an explanation; we, of course, hold fast to the other, still remaining view. We think that our author needed to know nothing of such rules and intentions, so that he may disavow them in good faith, and that we have surely found nothing in his romance which was not contained in it. We are probably drawing from the same source, working over the same material, each of us with a different method, and agreement in results seems to vouch for the fact that both have worked correctly. Our procedure consists of the conscious observation of abnormal psychic processes in others, in order to be able to discover and express their laws. Our author proceeds in another way; he directs his attention to the unconscious in his own psyche, listens to its possibilities of development and grants them artistic expression, instead of suppressing them with conscious critique. Thus he learns from himself what we learn from others, what laws the activity of this unconscious must follow, but he does not need to express these laws, need not even recognize them clearly; they are, as a result of his intelligent patience, contained incarnate in his creatures. We unfold these laws by analysis of his fiction as we discover them from cases of real illness, but the conclusion seems irrefutable, that either both (our author, as well as the physician) have misunderstood the unconscious in the same way or we have both understood it correctly. This conclusion is very valuable for us; for its sake, it was worth while for us to investigate the representation of the formation and cure of delusion, as well as the dreams, in Jensen's "Gradiva" by the methods of therapeutic psychoanalysis.

We have reached the end. An observant reader might remind us that, at the beginning, we had remarked that dreams are wishes represented as fulfilled and that we still owe the proof of it. Well, we reply, our arguments might well show how unjustifiable it would be to wish to cover the explanations which we have to give of the dream with the formula that the dream is a wish-fulfilment; but the assertion stands, and is also easy to demonstrate for the dreams in "Gradiva." The latent dream-thoughts—we know now what is meant by that—may be of numerous kinds; in "Gradiva" they are day-remnants, thoughts which are left over unheard, and not disposed of by the psychic activity of waking life. In order that a dream may originate from them the cooperation of a—generally unconscious—wish is required; this establishes the motive power for the dream-formation; the day-remnants give the material for it. In Norbert Hanold's first dream two wishes concur in producing the dream, one capable of consciousness, the other, of course, belonging to the unconscious, and active because of repression. This was the wish, comprehensible to every archaeologist, to have been an eye-witness of that catastrophe of 79. What sacrifice would be too great, for an antiquarian, to realize this wish otherwise than through dreams! The other wish and dream-maker is of an erotic nature: to be present when the beloved lies down to sleep, to express it crudely. It is the rejection of this which makes the dream an anxiety-dream. Less striking are, perhaps, the impelling wishes of the second dream, but if we recall its interpretation, we shall not hesitate to pronounce it also erotic. The wish to be captured by the beloved, to yield and surrender to her, as it may be construed behind the lizard-catching, has really a passive masochistic character. On the next day the dreamer strikes the beloved, as if under the sway of the antagonistic, erotic force; but we must stop or we may forget that Hanold and Gradiva are only creatures of our author.

❧ ❧

H. L. Mencken

The Wedding: A Stage Direction

The scene is a church in an American city of about half a million population, and the time is about eleven o'clock of a fine morning in early spring. The neighbourhood is

well-to-do, but not quite fashionable. That is to say, most of the families of the vici-
nage keep two servants (alas, more or less intermittently!), and eat dinner at half-past
six, and about one in four boasts a coloured butler (who attends to the fires, washes
windows and helps with the sweeping), and a last year's automobile. The heads of these
families are merchandise brokers; jobbers in notions, hardware and drugs; manufacturers of candy, hats, badges, office furniture, blank books, picture frames, wire goods
and patent medicines; managers of steamboat lines; district agents of insurance companies; owners of commercial printing offices, and other such business men of substance—and the prosperous lawyers and popular family doctors who keep them out
of trouble. In one block lives a Congressman and two college professors, one of whom
has written an unimportant textbook and got himself into Who's Who in America. In the block above lives a man who once ran for Mayor of the city, and came near
being elected.

The wives of these householders wear good clothes and have a liking for a reasonable gayety,
but few of them can pretend to what is vaguely called social standing, and, to do them
justice, not many of them waste any time lamenting it. They have, taking one with
another, about three children apiece, and are good mothers. A few of them belong to
women's clubs or flirt with the suffragettes, but the majority can get all of the intellectual stimulation they crave in the Ladies' Home Journal and the Saturday
Evening Post, with Vogue added for its fashions. Most of them, deep down in their
hearts, suspect their husbands of secret frivolity, and about ten per cent of them have
the proofs, but it is rare for them to make rows about it, and the divorce rate among
them is thus very low. Themselves indifferent cooks, they are unable to teach their servants the art, and so the food they set before their husbands and children is often such
as would make a Frenchman cut his throat. But they are diligent housewives otherwise; they see to it that the windows are washed, that no one tracks mud into the hall,
and that the servants do not waste coal, sugar, soap and gas, and that the family buttons are always sewn on. In religion these estimable wives are pious in habit but somewhat nebulous in faith. That is to say, they regard any person who specifically refuses
to go to church as a heathen, but they themselves are by no means regular in attendance, and not one in ten of them could tell you whether transubstantiation is a Roman
Catholic or a Dunkard doctrine ["Dunkards" were members of a Baptist sect which
believed in total immersion]. About two percent of them have dallied more or less gingerly with Christian Science, their average period of belief being one year.

The church we are in is like the neighbourhood and its people; well-to-do but not fashionable. It is Protestant in faith and probably Episcopalian. The pews are of thick, yellow-
brown oak, severe in pattern and hideous in colour. In each there is a long, removable
cushion of a dark, purplish, dirty hue, with here and there some of its hair stuffing
showing. The stained-glass windows, which were all bought ready-made and depict
scenes from the New Testament, commemorate the virtues of departed worthies of the
neighbourhood, whose names appear, in illegible black letters, in the lower panels. . . .

The organist is a tall, thin man of melancholy and uraemic aspect, wearing a black slouch hat with a wide brim and a yellow overcoat that barely reaches to his knees. A pupil, in his youth, of a man who had once studied (irregularly and briefly) with Charles-Marie Widor, he acquired thereby the artistic temperament, and with it a vast fondness for malt liquor. His mood this morning is acidulous and depressed, for he spent yesterday evening in a Pilsner ausschank with two former members of the Boston Symphony Orchestra, and it was 3 A.M. before they finally agreed that Johann Sebastian Bach, all things considered, was a greater man than Beethoven, and so parted amicably. Sourness is the precise sensation that wells within him. He feels vinegary; his blood runs cold; he wishes he could immerse himself in bicarbonate of soda. But the call of his art is more potent than the protest of his poisoned and quaking liver, and so he manfully climbs the spiral staircase to his organ-loft.

Once there, he takes off his hat and overcoat, stoops down to blow the dust off the organ keys, throws the electrical switch which sets the bellows going, and then proceeds to take off his shoes. This done, he takes his seat, reaches for the pedals with his stockinged feet, tries an experimental 32-foot CCC, and then wanders gently into a Bach toccata. It is his limbering-up piece: he always plays it as a prelude to a wedding job. It thus goes very smoothly and even brilliantly, but when he comes to the end of it and tackles the ensuing fugue he is quickly in difficulties, and after four or five stumbling repetitions of the subject he hurriedly improvises a crude coda and has done. Peering down into the church to see if his flounderings have had an audience, he sees two old maids enter, the one very tall and thin and the other somewhat brisk and bunchy.

They constitute the vanguard of the nuptial throng, and as they proceed; hesitatingly up the centre aisle, eager for good seats but afraid to go too far, the organist wipes his palms upon his trouser legs, squares his shoulders, and plunges into the program that he has played at all weddings for fifteen years past. It begins with Mendelssohn's Spring Song, pianissimo. Then comes Rubenstein's Melody in F, with a touch of forte towards the close, and then Nevin's "Oh, That We Two Were Maying," and then the Chopin waltz in A flat 69, No. 1, and then the Spring Song again, and then a free fantasia upon "The Rosary" and then a Moszkowski mazurka, and then the Dvořák Humoresque (with its heart-rending cry in the middle), and then some vague and turbulent thing (apparently the disjecta membra *of another fugue), and then Tschaikowsky's "Autumn," and then Elgar's "Salut d'Amour," and then the Spring Song a third time, and then something or other from one of the Peer Gynt suites, and then an hurrah or two from the Hallelujah chorus, and then Chopin again, and Nevin, and Elgar, and—*

But meanwhile there is a growing activity below. First comes a closed automobile bearing the six ushers and soon after it another automobile bearing the bridegroom and his best man. The bridegroom and the best man disembark before the side entrance of the church and make their way into the vestry-room, where they remove their hats and coats, and proceed to struggle with their cravats and collars before a mirror which hangs on the wall. The room is very dingy. A baize-covered table is in the centre of it, and around the table stand six or eight chairs of assorted designs. One wall is completely covered by a bookcase, through the glass doors of which one may discern piles of cheap Bibles, hymn-books and back numbers of the parish magazine. In one corner is a small washstand. The best man takes a flat flask of whiskey from his pocket, looks around him for a glass, finds it on the washstand, rinses it at the tap, fills it with a policeman's drink, and hands it to the bridegroom. The latter downs it at a gulp. Then the best man pours out one for himself. . . .

It is now a quarter to twelve, and of a sudden the vestibule fills with wedding guests. Nine-tenths of them, perhaps even nineteen-twentieths, are women, and most of them are beyond thirty-five. Scattered among them, hanging on to their skirts, are about a dozen little girls—one of them a youngster of eight or thereabouts, with spindle shanks and shining morning face, entranced by her first wedding. Here and there lurks a man. Usually he wears a hurried, unwilling, protesting look. He has been dragged from his office on a busy morning, forced to rush home and get into his cutaway coat, and then marched to the church by his wife. One of these men, much hustled, has forgotten to have his shoes shined. He is intensely conscious of them, and tries to hide them behind his wife's skirt as they walk up the aisle. Accidentally he steps upon it, and gets a look over the shoulder which lifts his diaphragm an inch and turns his liver to water. This man will be court-martialed when he reaches home, and he knows it. He wishes that some foreign power would invade the United States and burn down all the churches in the country, and that the bride, the bridegroom, and all the other persons interested in the present wedding were dead and in hell. . . .

To the damp funeral smell of the flowers of the altar, there has been added the cacodorous scents of forty or fifty different brands of talcum and rice paper. It begins to grow warm in the church, and a number of women open their vanity bags and duck down for stealthy dabs at their noses. Others, more reverent, suffer the agony of augmenting shines. One, a trickster, has concealed powder in her pocket handkerchief, and applies it dexterously while pretending to blow her nose.

The bridegroom in the vestry-room, entering on the second year (or is it the third?) of his long and ghastly wait, grows increasingly nervous, and when he hears the organist pass from the Spring Song into some more sonorous and stately thing he mistakes it for the wedding march from "Lohengrin," and is hot for marching upon the altar at once. The best man, an old hand, restrains him gently, and administers another sedative from the bottle. The bridegroom's thoughts turn to gloomy things. He remembers sadly that he will never be able to laugh at benedicts [newly married men] again; that his days of low, rabelaisian wit and carefree scoffing are over; that he is now the very thing he mocked so gaily but yesteryear. Like a drowning man, he passes his whole life in review—not, however, that part which is past, but that which is to come. Odd fancies throng upon him. He wonders what his honeymoon will cost him, what there will be to drink at the wedding breakfast, what a certain girl in Chicago will say when she hears of his marriage. . . .

The organist plunges into "Lohengrin" and the wedding procession gets under way:

The bride and her father march first. Their step is so slow (about one beat to two measures) that the father has some difficulty in maintaining his equilibrium, but the bride herself moves steadily and erectly, almost seeming to float. Her face is thickly encrusted with talcum in its various forms, so that she is almost a dead white. She keeps her eyelids lowered modestly, but is still acutely aware of every glance fastened upon her—not in the mass, but every glance individually. For example, she sees clearly, even through her eyelids, the still, cold smile of a girl in Pew 8 R—a girl who once made an unwomanly attempt upon the bridegroom's affections, and was routed and put to flight by superior strategy. And her ears are open, too: she hears every "How sweet!" and "Oh, lovely!" and "Ain't she pale!" from the latitude of the last pew to the very glacis of the altar of God. . . .

The bride arrives beside the bridegroom at the altar rail and they stand together, silently looking down at their feet.

Then the music, having died down to a faint murmur and a hush having fallen upon the assemblage, they look up.

Before them, framed by foliage, stands the reverend gentleman of God who will presently link them in indissoluble chains—the estimable rector of the parish. He has got there just in time; it was, indeed, a close shave. But no trace of haste or of anything else of a disturbing character is now visible upon his smooth, glistening, somewhat feverish face. That face is wholly occupied by his official smile, a thing of oil and honey all compact, a balmy, unctuous illumination—the secret of his success in life. Slowly his cheeks puff out, gleaming like soap-bubbles. Slowly he lifts his prayer-book from the prie-dieu and holds it droopingly. Slowly his soft caressing eyes engage it. There is an almost imperceptible stiffening of his frame. His mouth opens with a faint click. He begins to read.

The Ceremony of Marriage has begun.

❧ ☙

DENIS DE ROUGEMONT

from *Love in the Western World*

THE WARLIKE LANGUAGE OF LOVE

Already in Antiquity poets used warlike metaphors in order to describe the effects of natural love. The god of love is an *archer* who shoots *fatal arrows.* Woman *surrenders* to man, and he *conquers* her because he is the better warrior. The Trojan War was fought for the possession of a woman. And one of the oldest novels we possess—Heliodorus's *Theagenes and Chariclea,* written in the third century—already refers to the *"battles of love"* and to the "delightful *defeat"* suffered by the man who *"falls under the unerring shafts"* of Eros. Plutarch makes it clear that the sexual morals of the Lacedaemonians were determined by their military requirements. The eugenics of Lycurgus, and his detailed laws concerning the relations of husband and wife, had no other aim than to ensure the aggressive vigour of the soldiery.

All this confirms the natural—that is to say, the physiological— connection between the sexual and fighting instincts. But it would be idle to seek any kinship between the *tactics* of the Ancients and their notion of love. The two fields remained under quite distinct rules, and offered no ground for comparison. But this has not been true in Western Europe since the twelfth and thirteenth centuries. The language of love was then enriched with phrases and expressions which had unmistakably been borrowed from the art of giving battle and from contemporary military tactics. It is no longer a question of the more or less dim awareness of a common origin, but truly of a close similarity of detail. A lover *besieged* his lady. He delivered *amorous assaults* on her virtue. He *pressed her closely.* He *pursued* her. He sought to *overcome* the final *defences* of her modesty, and *to take them by surprise.* In the end the lady *surrendered to his mercy.* And thereupon, by a curious inversion typical enough of courtesy, he became the lady's *prisoner* as well as her *conqueror.* He became a *vassal* of this *suzerain,* in accordance with the laws of feudal warfare, as if it had been he who suffered defeat. It only remained for him to give proofs of his *valour.* So much for polite language. But slang, both military and civil, was rich in words and phrases which were rendered even more significant by their coarseness. And when firearms came into use, they gave rise to countless jokes of *double entendre.* Writers, indeed, delighted to take advantage of the resemblance, for it provided them with an inexhaustible rhetorical topic.

"O, all too fortunate captain [Brantôme writes], who at the front and in the towns hath fought and killed so many men who were the foes of God! And O, more and more fortunate still, you who hath fought and overcome in many other assaults and bouts such a lovely Lady under the banners of your bed!"

It is not surprising that, once such metaphors had become *commonplace,* mystical writers should have employed them and transposed them—in the way I have described earlier—to the key of divine love. Francisco de Ossuna—who was steeped in courtly rhetoric and was one of Saint Teresa's favourite authors—writes in his *Ley de Amor:*

"Do not believe that the battle of love is like other fights in which the clamour and fury of an appalling war prevail on either side; for love fights only by means of caresses and threatens only with tender words. Its arrows and blows are gifts and blessings. Its encounter is a most effective promise. Sighs make up its artillery. Its taking possession is an embrace. Its slaughter consists of giving one's life for the beloved."

It was shown earlier that courtly rhetoric began by expressing the *struggle* between Day and Night. The part played by *Death* is of capital importance: it marked the defeat of the world and the victory of the life of light. Love and death were connected by *askesis,* as instinct connects desire and war. But neither the religious origin nor the physiological kinship of the fighting and procreative instincts was enough to determine the *exact* use of warlike phrases in European erotic literature. What does account for everything is that there existed in the Middle Ages a rule actually applicable to the arts of both love and war—the rule called chivalry.

Translated by Montgomery Belgion

❧ ☙

FRANK GONZALEZ-CRUSSI

from *The Remedies of Love*

Could it be called a disease? Yes, since the patient obviously suffers. No, since it could not be called "contrary to nature," as required in early definitions. Yes, since the sufferer is clearly in pain. No, since the intervention of the physician is not really necessary. Yes, since the condition is potentially fatal. No, since it can cure of its own accord or by the satisfaction of a normal desire, as stated by the commonplace, "love is its own physician." This debate lasted for centuries and, like so many others, never really did receive a satisfactory resolution. Exhausted debaters simply ceased asking the question, and the question eventually lost relevance when all the terms of its formulation had changed. But as to the severity of the external manifestations of the disorder, no one doubted the rather frightening proportions. For in its most violent form, the love passion hits the victim with considerable impact. Reason is beclouded, the senses perturbed, and the imagination distorted. The lovelorn individual thinks of nothing if it does not touch his (or her) idol; and his monomania is amply reflected in the reiterative nature of his discourse. Mark the objective signs, as intense as the symptoms: pallor, lack of appetite, loss of weight, lassitude, sunken or reddened eyes with circular shadows about them, fear of accustomed routines, and tendency to seek solitary seclusion, there to brood and sigh. Pity this victim of love: All is lost for him, for he is fallen, prostrated, utterly without resources, divided between hope and fear, one minute buoyant, the next despairing; his heart has become a troubled sensor of the tempestuous commotions, and it beats now languorous, now quickened at the sight or at the mere mention of the object of his passion.

The worst feature of this disorder is that it is without remedy. At most, one can hope to extirpate it in the bud, before its roots grow deep and it becomes ineradicable. This was the conclusion at which the sages arrived. "Utterly hotheaded and reckless; as a man who would do a somersault into a ring of knives; as one who would jump into fire." So did Socrates speak of Critobolus when he heard that his disciple had kissed a youth of great beauty. The wise should keep their distance from the fair; for lovers were called "archers," seeing that their glances, like arrows, can hurt from afar. From Ovid on down, the admonition of the prudent is to avoid all sight and frequentation of the potential source of passion. And the stern Christian moralists enjoined us to vividly represent in our minds the perilous risk that erotic passion poses to our conscience, to our honor, to our estate, and more generally to our peace of mind. All to no avail. In sensitive dispositions, the slightest exposure suffices to kindle the conflagration. One glance, and the dart sinks into the target; and wherever the lover goes, the spear goes with him, as the arrow stays with the wounded deer, the feathered butt protruding from its flank, while point and shaft sink with each motion.

◦✦◦

ALBERT CAMUS

Losing a Loved One

Losing a loved one, uncertainty about what we are, these are deprivations that give rise to our worst suffering. We may be idealists, but we need what is tangible. It is by the presence of persons and things that we believe we recognize certainty. And though we may not like it, at least we live with this necessity. But the astonishing or unfortunate thing is that these deprivations bring us the cure at the same time that they give rise to pain. Once we have accepted the fact of loss, we understand that the loved one obstructed a whole corner of the possible, pure now as a sky washed by rain. Freedom emerges from weariness. To be happy is to stop. We are not here in order to stop. Free, we seek anew, enriched by pain. And the perpetual impulse forward always falls back again to gather new strength. The fall is brutal, but we set out again.

When some interest in our life crumbles beneath our feet, we transfer the interest we had accorded it to another possibility, and from this another, and again, without cease. An incessant need to believe, a perpetual projection ahead—such is the necessary comedy, and we shall enact it for a long time. Certain persons even play this pitiable game at the decisive moment. They review their whole life in order to persuade themselves of its nobility. A faint hope animates them: Who knows? the reward . . . or else. . . .

But why speak of comedy and games? Nothing of what is lived is a comedy. Our most cynical lies, our basest hypocrisies are worth the respect or the pity due to each living thing. After all, our life may indeed be our work. But if it is necessary to believe that living is nothing but creating, there is a peculiar refinement of cruelty in this gesture that gives rise to what crushes us. It is not easy to believe that without providence to do the bookkeeping of his pain, self-punishing man furnishes his own despair. And however fanatical he may be, the idealist necessarily forgets his philosophy when his son has died.

But such a man may believe he lost everything with the death of his wife. He realizes that once this misfortune has occurred a new life begins. And even if it should be a life of sorrow or self-denial, the pathos of such an existence still has its attractions. And rightly so; since at any moment it is given to us to be done with it: we are allowed not to live. It can be said of certain people that in any circumstance, happy or not, it is always better for them to die. But from the moment they live, they must accept the ridiculous as well as the sublime. And yet, let us not be mistaken! One can always uncover the ridiculous in the sublime; there are few examples the other way round.

This is why the sorrows we make so much of are, in reality, the least harmful. They are scratches compared to the unfathomable torment for which we believe we live. True pain is not so much to be frustrated over some good thing, but always to aspire in vain for the single good thing that tempts us. Doubtless we would not know how to describe it precisely. But the pain that the feeling of its absence gives rise to is the only thing that does not change. It is this pain that reveals its depths to experienced eyes, and about which we say we know nothing in reply to anxious questions. We wish with all our strength for some good thing we know not. And believing ourselves worthy of it makes us misjudge the only ends that we would be able to attain. What's to be done about it? One wave collapses and moans, is covered over by another lamentation, which is drowned beneath the desolation of a third.

And how can I not recall here the Dominican father who told me with great simplicity and in the plainest tone: "When we are in Paradise . . ." There are, then, men who live with such certainty while others seek for it at great cost? I also remember the youth and the gaiety of that father. His serenity had hurt me. In other circumstances it would have estranged me from God. It disturbed me then profoundly. Because doubtless one cannot become estranged from God when it is not he who wishes to keep us apart.

Yes, there are deprivations, there are the deprivations that give rise to our worst sorrows. But what does it truly matter what we lack when what we have is not used up. So many things are susceptible of being loved that surely no discouragement can be final. To know how to suffer, to know how to love, and, when everything collapses, to take everything up once more, simply, the richer from suffering, almost happy from the the awareness of our misery.

Translated by Ellen Conroy Kennedy

MURIEL SPARK

Love

There are many types of love. In ancient Greece from whence all ideas flow, there were seven main words for love. Maternal love is like, but not the same as, love of country or love between friends. And love of fellow men and women which the old Bibles called charity is also something akin to these, but different.

What I'm writing about here is exclusively the love we mean when we are "in love"; and it includes a certain amount of passion and desire, a certain amount of madness while it lasts. Its main feature is that you cannot argue about it. The most unlikely people may fall in love with each other; their friends, amazed, look for the reason. This is useless; there is no reason. The lovers themselves may try to explain it: "her beautiful eyes", "his lovely manners, his brains," and so on. But these claims never fit the case comprehensively. For love is inexplicable. It is something like poetry. Certainly, you can analyze it and expound its various senses and intentions, but there is always something left over, mysteriously hovering between music and meaning.

It is said that love is blind. I don't agree. I think that, on the contrary, love sharpens the perceptions. The lovers see especially clearly, but often irrationally; they like what they perceive even if, in anyone else, they wouldn't. They see the reality and something extra. Proust, one of the greatest writers on the subject of love, shows, in his love-story of Swann and Odette, how Swann, civilized, well-bred and artistic, saw perfectly clearly that Odette was vulgar, promiscuous and not at all a suitable partner for him in the Parisian world of his time. Right at the end of a section of the book Swann even resigned himself to the loss of Odette: "After all, she was not my style"; nevertheless, at the beginning of the next chapter Swann is already married to Odette, because he adored her, and couldn't resist her, even while unhappily knowing and loving the worst about her.

Falling in love is by nature an unforseen and chance affair, but it is limited by the factor of opportunity. The number of people in the world any one person can meet is comparatively few, and this is usually further limited by occasions of meeting. In *The Tempest*, Miranda exclaims when she first sees Ferdinand:

> I might call him
> A thing divine, for nothing natural
> I ever saw so noble.

But if she had never seen Ferdinand—if there had been no storm, no shipwreck, to bring him into her life? Undoubtedly this nubile maiden would eventually have become infatuated with Caliban. Even though she has said of him,

> 'Tis a villain, sir,
> I do not love to look on.

Miranda would inevitably have become enamoured of the monster, knowing him, by comparison with her father (who was taboo), to be hideous; because Caliban was the only available male within her range of opportunity. Prospero, of course, was aware of this danger.

Today there is an English aristocratic family, of which the four daughters have all married dukes and earls; and, goes the apochryphal story, when the mother is asked how she managed to marry her daughters "so well", she replies, "They never got to meet anyone else but dukes and earls." If the story isn't true, it's to the point.

Love is not blind and it is also not deaf. It is possible to fall in love with a voice, a timbre, a certain way of talking, a charming accent. Many inexplicable love affairs, especially those of the long past where we only have photographs or paintings to go by, would probably be better understood if we could hear the lovers speak. Many a warped-looking and ill-favoured Caliban has been endowed with a winning, mellow and irresistable voice. Many a shapely and gorgeous Ferdinand caws like an adenoidal crow. And the same with women—one often sees how a husky, sexy voice takes a raddled face further in love than does a little-girl twang issuing from a smooth-cheeked nymph.

The first time I was aware of two people in love was when an English master and an art mistress at my school got engaged. They observed the utmost discretion in front of the girls, but we registered their every move and glance when they happened to meet in the corridors. We exchanged endless information on this subject. These two teachers were not at all lover-like. Both were already middle-aged (and alas must now be dead, or else aged 99). He was tall and gawky with a long horselike face, and eyes, too, not unhorselike. She was dumpy, with the same shape over and under her waist, which was more or less tied-in round the middle. They were both pleasant characters. I liked him better, because he was fond of English literature; she, on the other hand, was inclined to stick her forefinger onto my painting and say, "What does it mean? It doesn't mean anything." Which of course was true, and I didn't take it amiss. The only puzzling thing about this love-affair was what he, or anybody, could see in her. What she could see in him was also difficult to place, but still, he had something you could call "personality." She, none. We pondered on this at the same time as we noted how he followed her with his eyes—they were dark, and vertically long—and how she, apparently oblivious of his enamoured long-eyed look, would stump off upon her stodgy way, on her little peg-like legs, with never a smile nor a light in her eyes. One thing we learned: love is incomprehensible. He saw the same person as we saw, but he saw something extra. It never occurred to us to think that perhaps she was an excellent cook, which might very likely have been the magic element in the love-affair. It might also have been the case that neither of them had really had time to meet anybody else.

Observing people in love has a certain charm and sometimes, entertainment value. But to my mind watching them actually making love is something different. I find it most unappealing to walk through a London park on a mild spring day and find the grass littered with couples making love. It turns me up, it turns me off. I don't understand how voyeurism turns people on.

With animals, strangely enough I feel the opposite. I live most of the time in the Italian countryside, and nothing is more attractive and moving than to look out of the window on a sunny morning, as I did recently; and see a couple of young hares making love. He hopped towards her, she hopped away. He hopped and she hopped through the long grass, till at last he hopped on. Then, too, not long ago, driving with a friend down a country road we had to stop while a horse mated with a mare. There were a number of cars but we all lined up respectfully and with deep interest for it was known that the owner of the horses, who was standing by, depended for his living on events like this, and was delighted that the horse had at last arrived at his decision, even in the middle of the road. The horse mounted the mare slowly, laid his nose dreamily along her flank, entered her precisely, and performed without bungle. The horse-coper radiated joy and success. The horse and mare moved off casually into a field and the caravan of cars went its way.

The aspects of love that one could discuss are endless. But certainly, as the old songs say, love is the sweetest thing, and it makes the world go round.

MEMOIRS
AND
LETTERS

Tomb inscription, Ancient Egypt

I breathe the sweet breath which comes forth from Thy mouth. I behold Thy beauty every day. It is my desire that I may hear Thy sweet voice, even on the north wind, that my limbs may be rejuvenated with life through love of Thee. Give me Thy hands, holding Thy spirit, that I may receive it and may live by it. Call Thou upon my name unto eternity, and it shall never fail.

SAPPHO TO ANACTORIA

Some say that the fairest thing upon the dark earth is a host of foot-soldiers, and others again a fleet of ships, but for me it is my beloved. And it is easy to make anyone understand this.

When Helen saw the most beautiful of mortals, she chose for best that one, the destroyer of all the house of Troy, and thought not much of children or dear parent but was led astray by love to bestow her heart far off, for woman is ever easy to lead astray when she thinks of no account what is near and dear.

Even so, Anactoria, you do not remember, it seems, when she is with you, one the gentle sound of whose footfall I would rather hear and the brightness of whose shining face I would rather see than all the chariots and mail-clad footmen of Lydia.

I know that in this world man cannot have the best, yet to pray for a part of what was once shared is better than to forget it.

❧❧

ANONYMOUS

The Alexandrian Erotic Fragment

From both of us was the choice: we were united. Cypris is the surety of our love. Grief holds me fast when I remember how he traitorously kissed me, meaning to desert me all the while, the contriver of inconstancy. Love, the stablisher of friendship, overcame me; I do not deny that I have him ever within my soul.

Ye dear stars, and thou, lady night, partner of my love, bring me even now to him to whom Cypris leads me as slave and the great love that has taken hold upon me: to light me on my way I have the great fire that burns in my soul: this is my hurt, this is my grief. He, the deceiver of hearts, he that was aforetime so proud and claimed that Cypris had nought to do with our love, hath brought upon me . . . this wrong that is done me.

I shall surely go mad, for jealousy possesses me, and I am all afire in my deserted state. Throw me the garlands—this at least I must have— for me to lie and hug them close, since I am all alone. My lover and lord, drive me not forth, take me in, the maid locked out. I have good will to serve thee zealously, all mad to see thee. Thy case hath great pain; thou must be jealous, keep thine own counsel, endure. If thou fix thy heart on one alone, thou must lose thy senses; a love of one, and one alone, makes mad.

Know that I have a heart unconquerable when hate takes hold upon me. Mad am I when I think that here I lie alone, while thou dost fly off to harlotry. But come, let us cease from this fury: yes, we must quickly be reconciled; why else have we common friends, but to judge who is in the wrong?

❧❧

PROPERTIUS

from *The Elegies*

TO TULLUS

Cynthia's eyes first took me, poor unfortunate, captive, previously affected by no passion; then did Love cast down my resolute, disdainful eyes, and set foot on my neck, till in time he taught me, desperate power! to despise chaste maidens, and to live recklessly. Even now, my present mad pursuit flags not after a whole year, though I am forced to have the gods opposed to me. Milanion, Tullus, by shrinking from no toils, broke down the stubborn cruelty of the daughter of Iasus: for once he roamed of yore crazed with love, amid the caves of Parthenius, and tracked the steps of shaggy wild beasts; stricken too by the club of Hylæus, he groaned, in pain, among Arcadian rocks. Therefore was he able to tame the swift-footed damsel. Such is the force of prayers and good deeds in love. In me slow-witted Love devises no plans, and forgets to travel, as before, in the beaten paths. Come ye, that are skilled in bringing the moon down from the sky, and whose dread work it is to solemnize sacred rites with magic fire, come and turn the heart of my mistress, and make her more pale than myself. Then I may believe you able to draw down the stars, and turn the course of rivers by Cytæan spells. And you, my friends, who attempt too late to cry me back who am already fallen, find some help for my wounded heart. I will bear the knife and torturing cautery unflinchingly: let me but have liberty to speak what my anger wills. Carry me to the end of the world, or over the seas, whither no woman can know my track. Remain ye, to whom the god lends a willing ear, and may ye meet with kindred feelings, and your love fear no danger. Me my Venus torments with bitter nights, and Love at no time grants me a respite. Avoid, I warn you, this woe; let each hold to his own beloved one, and let no one abandon his wonted love. But, if any one shall be slow to heed my warnings, alas! with how great grief will he remember my words!

To Cynthia

Like to the Gnossian maid as she lay, exhausted, on the solitary shore, whilst the ship of Theseus sped away; like to Andromeda, the daughter of Cepheus, as she slept in her first sleep, released, at length, from the hard rocks; or like as when a Bacchante, wearied with constant dancing, falls down on the banks of the grassy Apidanus: like to these did Cynthia, with her head resting at ease on her hands, seem to me to breathe softly in her slumber, while I, drunk with much wine, walked with tottering gait, and the boys shook the torches at the midnight hour. I tried to lay myself gently on the couch by her side, having not yet lost all my senses; and although doubly fired, and urged on one side by Love, on the other by Bacchus, each a powerful god, to place my arm under her gently as she lay, and to put my hand to her lips and steal a kiss; yet I dared not disturb the rest of my mistress, fearing her stinging reproaches that

I had before experienced, but I remained as I was, with my eyes fixed on her in ardent gaze, as Argus at the first sight of the horns of Io, the daughter of Inachus. At one time I loosened the chaplets from my forehead, and placed them on your temples, Cynthia; at another I amused myself by confining your truant tresses, or placing apples, stealthily, in the hollows of your hands; and I gave all my gifts to thankless sleep, gifts that often slipped from your slant bosom. And whenever at times your form moved and you heaved a sigh, my credulous soul was confounded by the idle presage, lest any unwonted vision was affrighting you; lest someone was forcing you against your will to be his. At length, piercing through the casement opposite her couch, the Moon, the officious Moon, with light that should have lingered, opened, by its gentle beams, her closed eyelids. Then resting on her elbow on the downy couch, "So, at last," she said, "another's contemptuous treatment has driven you from her closed doors, back to my bed. Where have you been spending the long hours of a night promised to me, and now come wearied to me, when the stars are gone? May you, wretch, endure the agony of such nights as you are constantly bidding me have, to my sorrow. At one time I tried to drive away sleep by my purple embroidery, and when tired of that, then with playing on my Orphean lyre. At one time, in my solitude, I kept quietly groaning over the long time spent by you in another's embrace: until, at last, slumber fanned me with his soft wings, and bade me yield; that was the last remedy for my tears."

TO PONTICUS

While you, Ponticus, sing of Cadmean Thebes and the fatal contest between the brothers, (and may I thrive as you are likely to rival Homer, chief in Epic song, if the Fates are gentle to your strains,) I, as is my wont, am pursuing my career of love, and trying to devise something for a stern mistress. I am forced to obey not so much my natural bent as my woe, and to complain of my hard fate in life. In this task my allotted span is consumed; this is my glory; it is from this that I hope my poetic fame will arise. Let me be celebrated as having been the sole favourite of an accomplished girl, and as having often endured her unjust reproaches. Let a despised lover, henceforth, read me constantly, and may the knowledge of my woes benefit him. If the boy Cupid shall have pierced you also with his unerring bow,—a disaster that I would fain wish the gods I obey may not have decreed,—you will weep, in sorrow, at your camp, your seven bands of heroes lying neglected in lasting mildew. In vain, too, will you be desirous of composing a tender strain; for Love, if he comes late, will dictate no verses to you. Then will you often praise me as no mean poet; then shall I be preferred to the other wits of Rome. Nor will the young men be able to refrain from saying over my tomb, "O great poet, interpreter of our pangs, thou art buried here." Beware then how you proudly despise my poetry. Love often comes late, and comes with a vengeance.

To Cynthia, on the Storminess of the Sea

Deservedly, since I have had the heart to leave my mistress, am I now addressing the solitary halcyons. Cassiope no longer, as is her wont, is going to look on my vessel, and all my vows fall unheeded on the thankless shore. Even when away from me, Cynthia, the winds favour thee. See how fierce and threatening is the chiding of the gale. Will not Fortune come and appease the storm? Is this small shore to cover my dead body? Do thou, however, change for the better thy angry complaints, let the darkness and the raging sea be vengeance enough for thee. Canst thou picture to thyself my disaster without shedding a tear? Canst thou endure to gather no bones of mine into thy bosom? May he perish who was the first to introduce ships and sails, and to make a voyage over the unwilling sea. Was it not better to conquer the temper of a fickle mistress,—though hard, yet was she the paragon of maids,—than to be looking, as now, on a shore surrounded by unknown forests, and to be wishing and gazing for the Tyndaridæ. Had any destiny buried my misery at Rome, and a stone, last tribute of affection, were standing over a lover's corpse, she would have sacrificed her hair, cherished as it is, to my grave, and would have fondly planted tender roses near my tomb; she would have exclaimed my name over the turn containing my dust, and would have prayed the earth to press lightly on me. But, O ye maidens, denizens of the ocean, children of the fair Doris, come in a protecting band, and speed us on our voyage. If ever Love has come down to your waters, spare me, a lover like yourselves, and make the shore kind.

To Cynthia

Cynthia, I fear not now the melancholy Manes, nor do I care for the fatal debt of death; but lest, perchance, my deathbed be without thy love,— this fear is more grievous than death itself. The winged boy has not stuck to my eyes so lightly as to allow my ashes to be oblivious of love. Down below, in the dismal region of the dead, the hero, the grandson of Phylacus, could not forget his beloved wife, but, desirous of folding his dear one within his phantom arms, he came, shade as he was, to his ancient Thessalian abode. There, whatever I may be, I shall always be called your image: extraordinary attachments survive even beyond the fatal shore. There let fair heroines come, given, by victory over Dardans, to Argive heroes, yet none of them shall prove dearer to me than your beauty, O Cynthia; and may the Earth kindly allow this. Although a destiny of long old age delays you, yet your bones will be always dear to my tears; and may you, on earth, feel the same, when my body has been burnt: then death, wherever it happen, will never be bitter to me. How I fear, lest, despising my tomb, merciless Love tear you away, alas, from my ashes, and force you, against your will, to dry your falling tears; even a true heart yields at last to importunity. Therefore, while we may, let us gladden each other with love: love is never long enough, last how long it may.

Translated by Gantillon

꧁ ꧂

PLINY TO CALPURNIA AND PAULINUS

TO CALPURNIA
It is incredible how I miss you; such is the tenderness of my affection for you, and so unaccustomed are we to a separation! I lie awake the greatest part of the night in conjuring up your image, and by day (to use a very common, but very true expression) my feet carry me of their own accord to your apartment, at those hours I used to visit you; but not finding you there, I return with as much sorrow and disappointment as an excluded lover. The only intermission my torment knows, is when I am engaged at the bar, and in the causes of my friends. Judge how wretched must *his* life be, who finds no repose but in toil, no consolation but in dealing with distress and anxieties. Farewell.

TO PAULINUS
Whether I have reason for my rage is not quite so clear; however, wondrous angry I am. But love, you know, will sometimes be irrational; as it is often ungovernable, and ever jealous. The occasion of this my formidable wrath is great, and I think, just: however, taking it for granted that there is as much truth as weight in it, I am most vehemently enraged at your long silence. Would you soften my resentment? Let your letters for

the future be very frequent, and very long; I shall excuse you upon no other terms; and as absence from Rome, or press of business, is a plea I can by no means admit; so that of ill health, the Gods, I hope, will not suffer you to allege. As for myself, I am enjoying at my villa the alternate pleasures of study and indolence; those happy privileges of retired leisure! Farewell.

TO CALPURNIA

You tell me, my absence is greatly uneasy to you, and that your only consolation is in conversing with my works, instead of their author, to which you frequently even give my own place by your side. How agreeable is it to me to know that you thus wish for my company, and support yourself under the want of it by these tender amusements! In return, I read over your letters again and again, and am continually taking them up as if I had just received them; but alas! they only serve to make me more strongly regret your absence: for how amiable must her conversation be, whose letters have so many charms?

❦ ❦

MARCUS AURELIUS TO FRONTO

Hail, my sweetest of masters.

We are well. I slept somewhat late owing to my slight cold, which seems now to have subsided. So from five A.M. till 9, I spent the time partly in reading some of Cato's *Agriculture*, partly in writing not quite such wretched stuff, by heavens, as yesterday. Then, after paying my respects to my father, I relieved my throat, I will not say by gargling—though the word *gargarisso* is, I believe, found in Novius and elsewhere—but by swallowing honey water as far as the gullet and ejecting it again. After easing my throat I went off to my father and attended him at a sacrifice. Then we went to luncheon. What do you think I ate? A wee bit of bread, though I saw others devouring beans, onions, and herrings full of roe. We then worked hard at grape-gathering, and had a good sweat, and were merry and, as the poet says, "still left some clusters hanging high as gleanings of the vintage." After six o'clock we came home.

I did but little work and that to no purpose. Then I had a long chat with my little mother as she sat on the bed. My talk was this: "What do you think my Fronto is now doing?" Then she: "And what do you think my Gratia is doing?" Then I: "And what do you think our little sparrow, the wee Gratia, is doing?" Whilst we were chattering in this way and disputing which of us two loved the one or other of you two the better, the gong sounded, an intimation that my father had gone to his bath. So we had supper after we had bathed in the oil-press room; I do not mean bathed in the oil-press room, but when we had bathed, had supper there, and we enjoyed hearing the yokels chaffing one another. After coming back, before I turn over and snore, I get my task done and give my dearest of masters an account of the day's doings, and if I could miss him more, I would not grudge wasting away a little more. Farewell, my Fronto, wherever you are, most honey-sweet, my love, my delight. How is it between you and me? I love you and you are away.

ᘐᕯ ᕲᘑ

ST. AUGUSTINE

from *The Confessions*

And what was it that I delighted in, but to love and to be beloved? But love kept not that moderation of one's mind loving another mind, as the lightsome bounder of true friendship; but out of that puddly concupiscence of my flesh, certain mists and bubblings of youth fumed up, which beclouded and so overcast my heart that I could not discern the beauty of a chaste affection from a fog of impure lustfulness. Both did confusedly boil in me, and ravished away my unstayed youth over the downfalls of unchaste desires, and drenched me over head and ears in the very whirlpool of most heinous impurities. . . .

　　There is comeliness now in all beautiful bodies, both in gold and silver, and all things; and in the touch of flesh, sympathy pleases much. Each other sense hath his proper object answerably tempered. Wordly honour hath also its grace, in commanding and overcoming by its own power; whence springs also the thirst of revenge. But yet, might a man obtain all these, he were not to depart from thee, O Lord, nor to decline from Thy Law. The life also which here we live hath its proper enticement, and that by reason of a certain proportion of comeliness of its own, and a correspondency with all these inferior beauties. That friendship also which is amongst societies, we see endeared with a sweet tie, even by reason of the union of many hearts. . . . For these low things have their delights, but nothing like my Lord God, who hath made these all. . . .

An impure love inflames the mind and summons the soul destined to perish to lust after earthly things, and to follow what is perishable, and precipitates it into the lowest places, and sinks it in the abyss; so holy love raiseth us, and inflames us to what is eternal, and excites the soul to those things which do not pass away and die, and from the depths of hell raiseth it to heaven. Yet all love hath a power of its own, nor can love in the soul of the lover be idle; it must needs draw it on. But dost thou wish to know of what sort love is? See whither it leadeth. We do not therefore warn you to love nothing; but that you love not the world, that you may freely love Him who made the world. For the soul when bound by the love of the earth, hath as it were birdlime on its wings; it cannot fly. But when purged from the sordid affections of the world, extending as it were its pair of wings, and freeing them from every impediment, flyeth upon them, that is to say, upon the two commandments of love unto God and our neighbour. Whither will it fly, but by rising in its flight to God? For it riseth by loving. Before it can do this, it groaneth on earth, if it hath already in it the desire for flight; and saith, "who will give me wings like a dove, and I will fly and be at rest.". . . From the midst of offences, then, from the medley of evil men, from the chaff mingled with the grain, it longeth to fly, where it may not suffer the society of any wicked one, but may live in the holy company of angels, the citizens of the eternal Jerusalem.

Translated by William Watts

✿ ✿

HELOISE TO ABELARD

Heloise, the lover and eventually the wife of philosopher Peter Abelard (1079–1142), made no pretence of why she entered a convent: to please Peter. The crime she refers to is their love affair, which resulted in a son born out of wedlock and the castration of Peter by Heloise's angry uncle. Heloise continued in her devotion to Peter even after decades as a nun, but she had a temper and a quick wit, as this letter shows.

TO *ABELARD* HER WELL BELOVED IN CHRIST JESUS, FROM *HELOISE* HIS WELL BELOVED IN THE SAME CHRIST JESUS.
I Read the Letter I received from you with abundance of Impatience: In spite of all my Misfortunes, I hoped to find nothing in it besides Argu-

ments of Comfort. But how ingenious are Lovers in tormenting themselves! Judge of the exquisite Sensibility and Force of my Love, by that which causes the Grief of my Soul. I was disturb'd at the Superscription of your Letter; Why did you place the Name of *Heloise* before that of *Abelard?* What means this cruel and unjust Distinction? 'Twas your Name only, the Name of a Father, and of a Husband, which my eager Eyes sought after. I did not look for my own, which I had much rather, if possible, forget, as being the cause of your Misfortune. The Rules of Decorum, and the Character of Master and Director which you have over me, opposed that Ceremonious manner of addressing me; and love commanded you to banish it: Alas! you know all this but too well.

Did you write thus to me before cruel Fortune had ruined my happiness? I see your heart has deserted me, and you have made greater Advances in the way of Devotion than I could wish. Alas! I am too weak to follow you; condescend at least to stay for me, and animate me with your Advice. Will you have the Cruelty to abandon me? The fear of this stabs my Heart. But the fearful Presages you make at the latter end of your Letter, those terrible Images you draw of your Death, quite distract me. Cruel *Abelard!* you ought to have stop'd my Tears, and you make them flow. You ought to have quieted the disorder of my Heart, and you throw me into Despair.

You desire that after your Death I should take care of your Ashes, and pay them the last Duties. Alas! in what Temper did you conceive these mournful Ideas? And how could you describe them to me? Did not the Apprehension of causing my present Death make the Pen drop from your Hand? You did not reflect, I suppose, upon all those Torments to which you were going to deliver me. Heaven, as severe as it has been against me, is not in so great a degree so, as to permit me to live one moment after you. Life, without my *Abelard,* is an unsupportable Punishment, and Death a most exquisite Happiness, if by that means I can be united with him. If Heaven hears the Prayers I continually make for you, your Days will be prolonged, and you will bury me.

Is it not your Part to prepare me by your powerful Exhortations against that great Crisis, which shakes the most resolute and confirmed Minds? Is it not your part to receive my last Sighs, take care of my Funerals, and give an Account of my Manners and Faith? Who but you can recommend us worthily to God, and by the Fervour and Merit of your Prayers, conduct those Souls to him which you have joined to his Worship by solemn Contracts? We expect these pious Offices from your Paternal Charity. After this you will be free from those Disquietudes which now disturb you, and you will quit Life with more Ease whenever it shall please God to call you away. You may follow us content with what you have done, and in a full assurance of our Happiness. But 'till then write not to me any such terrible things. Are we not already sufficiently miserable? Must we aggravate our Sorrows? Our Life here is but a languishing Death; will you hasten it? Our present Disgraces employ our Thoughts continually, and shall we seek for new Arguments of Grief in Futurities? How void of Reason are Men, said *Seneca*, to make distant Evils present by Reflection, and to take pains before Death to lose all the Comforts of Life?

When you have finished your Course here below, you say it is your Desire that your Body be carried to the House of the *Paraclete*; to the intent that being always exposed to my Eyes, you may be for ever present to my Mind; and that your dead Body may strengthen our Piety, and animate our Prayers. Can you think that the Traces you have drawn in my Heart can ever be worn out; or that any length of time can obliterate the Memory we have here of your Benefits? And what time shall I find for those Prayers you speak of? alas, I shall then be filled with other Cares. Can so heavy a Misfortune leave me a Moment's Quiet? Can my feeble Reason resist such powerful Assaults? When I am distracted and raving, (if I dare say it) even against Heaven it self, I shall not soften it by my prayers, but rather provoke it by my Cries and Reproaches! But how should I pray? Or how bear up against my Grief? I should be more urgent to follow you, than to pay you the sad Ceremonies of Burial. It is for you, for *Abelard*, that I have resolved to live; if you are ravished from me, what use can I make of my miserable Days? Alas! What Lamentations should I make if Heaven, by a cruel Pity, should preserve me 'till that moment? When I but think of this last Separation, I feel all the Pangs of Death; what shall I be then, if I should see this dreadful Hour? Forbear therefore to infuse into my Mind such mournful Thoughts, if not for Love, at least for Pity.

You desire me to give my self up to my Duty, and to be wholly God's, to whom I am consecrated. How can I do that, when you frighten me with Apprehensions that continually possess my Mind Day and Night? When an Evil threatens us, and it is impossible to ward it off, why do we give up our selves to the unprofitable fear of it, which is yet even more tormenting than the Evil it self?

What have I to hope for after the loss of you? What can detain me upon Earth, when Death shall have taken away from me all that was dear upon it? I have renounced without difficulty all the Charms of Life, preserving only my Love, and the secret pleasure of thinking incessantly of you, and hearing that you live. And yet, alas! you do not live for me, and I dare not even flatter my self with the hopes that I shall ever enjoy a sight of you more! This is the greatest of my Afflictions. Merciless Fortune! Hast thou not persecuted me enough? Thou dost not give me any Respite; thou hast exhausted all thy Vengeance upon me, and reserved thy self nothing whereby thou may'st appear terrible to others. Thou hast wearied thy self in tormenting me, and others have nothing now to fear from thy Anger. But to what purpose dost thou still arm thy self against me? The Wounds I have already received leave no room for new ones; why cannot I urge thee to kill me? Or dost thou fear, amidst the numerous Torments thou heapest on me, dost thou fear that such a Stroke would deliver me from all? Therefore thou preservest me from Death, in order to make me die every moment.

Dear *Abelard,* pity my Despair! Was ever any thing so miserable! The higher you raised me above other Women who envied me your Love, the more sensible am I now of the loss of your Heart. I was exalted to the top of Happiness, only that I might have a more terrible Fall. Nothing cou'd formerly be compared to my Pleasures, and nothing now can equal my Misery. My Glory once raised the Envy of my Rivals; my present Wretchedness moves the Compassion of all that see me. My fortune has been always in extremes, she has heaped on me her most delightful Favours, that she might load me with the greatest of her Afflictions. Ingenious in tormenting me, she has made the Memory of the Joys I have lost, an inexhaustible Spring of my Tears. Love, which possest was her greatest Gift, being taken away, occasions all my Sorrow. In short, her Malice has entirely succeeded, and I find my present Afflictions proportionably bitter as the Transports which charmed me were sweet.

But what aggravates my Sufferings yet more, is, that we began to be miserable at a time when we seemed the least to deserve it. While we gave our selves up to the Enjoyment of a Criminal Love, nothing opposed our vicious Pleasures. But scarce had we retrench'd what was unlawful in our Passion, and taken Refuge in Marriage against that Remorse which might have pursu'd us, but the whole Wrath of Heaven fell on us in all its Weight. But how barbarous was your Punishment? The very Remembrance makes me shake with Horror. Could an outrageous Husband make a Villain suffer more that had dishonoured his Bed? Ah! what right had a cruel Uncle over us? We were joined to each other even before the Altar, which should have protected you from the Rage of your Enemies. Must a Wife draw on you that Punishment which ought not to fall on any but an Adulterous Lover? Besides, we were separated; you were busy in your Exercises, and instructed a learned Auditory in Mysteries which the greatest Geniuses before you were not able to penetrate; and I, in obedience to you, retired to a Cloister. I there spent whole Days in thinking of you, and sometimes meditating on holy Lessons, to which I endeavoured to apply my self. In this very Juncture you became the Victim of the most unhappy Love. You alone expiated the Crime common to us both. You only were punished, tho' both of us were guilty. You, who were least so, was the Object of the whole Vengeance of a barbarous Man. But why should I rave at your Assassins? I, wretched I, have ruined you, I have been the Original of all your Misfortunes! Good Heav'n! Why was I born to be the occasion of so Tragical an Accident? How dangerous is it for a great Man to suffer himself to be moved by our Sex! He ought from his Infancy to be inured to Insensibility of Heart, against all our Charms. *Hearken, my Son,* (said formerly the wisest of Men) *attend and keep my Instructions; if a beautiful Woman by her Looks endeavour to intice thee, permit not thy self to be overcome by a corrupt Inclination; reject the Poison she offers, and follow not the Paths which she directs. Her House is the Gate of Destruction and Death.* I have long examined things, and have found that Death it self is a less dangerous Evil than Beauty. 'Tis the Shipwreck of Liberty, a fatal Snare, from which it is impossible ever to get free. 'Twas Woman which threw down the first Man from that glorious condition in which Heaven had placed him. She who was created in order to partake of his Happiness, was the sole Cause of his Ruin. How bright had been thy Glory, *Sampson,* if thy Heart had been as firm against the Charms of *Dalilah,* as against the Weapons of the *Philistines.* A Woman disarmed and betrayed thee, who hadst been a glorious Conqueror of Armies. Thou sawst thy self delivered into the Hands of thy Enemies; thou wast deprived of thy Eyes, those Inlets of Love into thy Soul. Distracted and despairing didst thou die, without any Consolation but that of involving thy Enemies in thy Destruction. *Solomon,* that he might please Women, forsook the Care of pleasing God. That King, whose Wisdom Princes came from all Parts to admire, he whom God had chosen to build him a Temple, abandon'd the Worship of those very Altars he had defended, and proceeded to such a pitch of Folly as even to burn Incense to Idols. *Job* had no Enemy more cruel than his Wife; what Temptations did he not bear? The evil Spirit who had declared himself his Persecutor, employed a Woman as an Instrument to shake his Constancy. And the same evil Spirit made *Heloise* an Instrument to ruin *Abelard!* All the poor Comfort I have is, that I am not the voluntary

Cause of your Misfortunes. I have not betray'd you; but my Constancy and Love have been destructive to you. If I have committed a Crime in having lov'd you with Constancy, I shall never be able to repent of that Crime. Indeed I gave my self up too much to the Captivity of those soft Errors into which my rising Passion seduced me. I have endeavour'd to please you, even at the Expence of my Virtue, and therefore deserve those Pains I feel. My guilty Transports cou'd not but have a Tragical End. As soon as I was persuaded of your Love, alas, I scarce delay'd a moment resigning my self to all your Protestations. To be beloved by *Abelard*, was, in my Esteem, too much Glory, and I too impatiently desired it, not to believe it immediately. I endeavoured at nothing but convincing you of my utmost Passion. I made no use of those Defences of Disdain and strict Honour; those Enemies of Pleasure which tyrannize over our Sex, made in me but a weak and unprofitable Resistance. I Sacrificed all to my Love, and I forc'd my Duty to yield to the Ambition of making happy the most gallant and learned Person of the Age. If any Consideration had been able to stop me, it would have been without doubt the Interest of my Love. I fear'd least having nothing further for you to desire, your Passion might become languid, and you might seek for new Pleasures in some new Conquest. But it was easy for you to cure me of a Suspicion so opposite to my own Inclination. I ought to have foreseen other more certain Evils; and to have consider'd that the Idea of lost Enjoyments wou'd be the trouble of my whole Life.

How happy should I be, could I wash out with my Tears the Memory of those Pleasures, which yet I think of with Delight? At least I will exert some generous Endeavour, and by smothering in my Heart those Desires to which the frailty of my Nature may give Birth, I will exercise the same Torments upon my self, as the Rage of your Enemies has made you suffer. I will endeavour by that means to satisfy you at least, if I cannot appease an angry God. For to show you what a deplorable Condition I am in, and how far my Repentance is from being available, I dare even accuse Heaven every moment of Cruelty, for delivering you into those Snares which were prepared for you. My Repinings kindle the Divine Wrath, when I shou'd endeavour to draw down Mercy.

In order to expiate a Crime, 'tis not sufficient that we bear the Punishment; whatever we suffer is accounted as nothing, if the Passions still continue, and the Heart is inflam'd with the same Desires. 'Tis an easy matter to confess a Weakness, and to inflict some Punishment upon our selves; but 'tis the last Violence to our Nature to extinguish the Memory of Pleasures, which by a sweet Habit have gain'd absolute Possession of our Minds. How many Persons do we observe who make an outward Confession of their Faults, yet far from being afflicted for them, take a new Pleasure in the relating them. Bitterness of Heart ought to accompany the Confession of the Mouth, yet that very rarely happens. I, who have experienced so many Pleasures in loving you, feel, in spite of my self, that I cannot repent of them, nor forbear enjoying them over again as much as is possible, by recollecting them in my Memory. Whatever Endeavours I use, on whatever side I turn me, the sweet Idea still pursues me, and every Object brings to my Mind what I ought to forget. During the still Night, when my Heart ought to be quiet in the midst of Sleep, which suspends the greatest Disturbances, I cannot avoid those Illusions my Heart entertains. I think I am still with my dear *Abelard*. I see him, I speak to him, and hear him answer. Charmed with each other, we quit our Philosophic Studies to entertain our selves with our Passion. Sometimes too I seem to be a Witness of the bloody Enterprise of your Enemies; I oppose their Fury, I fill our Apartment with fearful Cries, and in the moment I awake in Tears. Even into Holy Places before the Altar I carry with me the Memory of our guilty Loves. They are my whole business; and far from lamenting for having been seduced, I sigh for having lost them.

I remember (for nothing is forgot by Lovers) the Time and Place in which you first declared your Love to me, and swore you would love me 'till Death. Your Words, your Oaths, are all graven in my Heart. The Disorder of my Discourse discovers to every one the Trouble of my Mind. My Sighs betray me; and your Name is continually in my Mouth. When I am in this condition, why dost not thou, O Lord! pity my Weakness, and strengthen me by thy Grace? You are happy, *Abelard*, this Grace has prevented you; and your Misfortune has been the Occasion of your finding Rest. The Punishment of your Body, has cured the deadly Wounds of your Soul. The Tempest has driven you into the Haven. God, who seemed to lay his Hand heavily upon you, sought only to help you: He is a Father Chastizing, and not an Enemy Revenging; a wise Physician, putting you to some Pain in order to preserve your Life. I am a thousand times more to be lamented than you; I have a thousand Passions to combat with. I must resist those Fires which Love kindles in a young Heart. Our Sex is nothing but Weakness, and I have the greater difficulty to defend my self, because the enemy that attacks me pleases me; I doat on the Danger which threatens me, how then can I avoid falling?

In the midst of these struggles, I endeavour at least to conceal my

Weakness from those you have entrusted to my Care. All who are about me admire my Virtue, but could their Eyes penetrate into my Heart, what would they not discover? My Passions there are in a Rebellion; I preside over others, but cannot rule my self. I have but a false Covering, and this seeming Virtue is a real Vice. Men judge me praise-worthy, but I am guilty before God, from whose All-seeing Eye nothing is hid, and who views thro' all their foldings the Secrets of all Hearts. I cannot escape his Discovery. And yet it is a great deal to me to maintain even this appearance of Virtue. This troublesome Hypocrisy is in some sort commendable. I give no Scandal to the World, which is so easy to catch bad Impressions. I do not shake the virtue of these feeble Ones who are under my Conduct. With my Heart full of the Love of Man, I exhort them at least to love only God. Charmed with the Pomp of worldly Pleasures, I endeavour to show them that they are all Deceit and Vanity. I have just Strength enough to conceal from them my Inclinations, and I look upon that as a powerful effect of Grace. If it is not sufficient to make me embrace Virtue, 'tis enough to keep me from committing Ill.

And yet it is in vain to endeavour to separate these two things. They must be guilty who merit nothing; and they depart from Virtue who delay to approach it. Besides, we ought to have no other Motive than the Love of God; alas! what can I then hope for? I own, to my confusion, I fear more the offending a Man, than the provoking God, and study less to please him than you. Yes, 'twas your Command only, and not a sincere Vocation, as is imagined, that shut me up in these Cloisters. I sought to give you Ease, and not to sanctify my self. How unhappy am I? I tear my self from all that pleases me; I bury my self here alive, I exercise my self in the most rigid Fastings, and such Severities as cruel Laws impose on us; I feed my self with Tears and Sorrows; and notwithstanding this, I deserve nothing for all the Hardships which I suffer. My false Piety has long deceived you as well as others; you have thought me easy, yet I was more disturbed than ever. You persuaded yourself I was wholly taken up with my Duty, yet I had no business but Love. Under this mistake you desire my Prayers; alas! I must expect yours. Do not presume upon my Virtue and my Care. I am wavering, and you must fix me by your Advice. I am yet feeble, you must sustain and guide me by your Counsel.

What Occasion had you to praise me? Praise is often hurtful to those on whom it is bestowed. A secret Vanity springs up in the Heart, blinds us, and conceals from us Wounds that are ill cured. A Seducer flatters us, and at the same time aims at our Destruction. A sincere Friend disguises nothing from us, and far from passing a light Hand over the

Wound, makes us feel it the more intensly, by applying Remedies. Why do you not deal after this manner with me? Will you be esteemed a base dangerous Flatterer; or if you chance to see any thing commendable in me, have you no fear that Vanity, which is so natural to all Women, should quite efface it? But let us not judge of Virtue by outward Appearances, for then the Reprobate as well as the Elect may lay claim to it. An artful Impostor may by his Address gain more Admiration, than the true Zeal of a Saint.

The Heart of Man is a Labyrinth whose Windings are very difficult to be discover'd. The Praises you give me are the more dangerous, in regard that I love the Person who gives them. The more I desire to please you, the readier am I to believe all the Merit you attribute to me. Ah think rather how to support my Weaknesses by wholesome Remonstrances! Be rather fearful than confident of my Salvation; say our Virtue is founded upon Weakness, and that those only will be crowned, who have fought with the greatest Difficulties. But I seek not for that Crown which is the Reward of Victory, I am content to avoid only the Danger. It is easier to keep off, than to win a Battle. There are several Degrees in Glory, and I am not ambitious of the highest; those I leave to Souls of great Courage, who have been often Victorious. I seek not to Conquer, out of fear least I should be overcome: Happy enough, if I can escape Shipwreck, and at last gain the Port. Heaven commands me to renounce that fatal Passion which unites me to you; but oh! my Heart will never be able to consent to it. Adieu.

ABELARD TO BERNARD AND HELOISE

TO BERNARD
You perform all the difficult religious duties, you fast; you watch; you suffer; but you will not endure the easy ones—you do not love.

TO HELOISE
Thus, dear and venerable sister in God, he to whom you are united, after your tie in the flesh, by the better and stronger bond of the divine love; he, with whom, and under whom, you have served the Lord, the Lord now takes, in your place, like another you, and warms in His bosom; and, for the day of His coming, when shall sound the voice of

the archangel and the trumpet of God descending from Heaven, He keeps him to restore him to you. . . .

❧ ☙

DANTE ALIGHIERI

from *The New Life*

Nine times now since my birth, the heaven of light had turned almost to the same point in its own gyration, when the glorious Lady of my mind, who was called Beatrice by many who knew not what to call her, first appeared before my eyes. She had already been in this life so long that in its course the starry heaven had moved toward the region of the East one of the twelve parts of a degree; so that at about the beginning of her ninth year she appeared to me, and I near the end of my ninth year saw her. She appeared to me clothed in a most noble color, a modest and becoming crimson, and she was girt and adorned in such wise as befitted her very youthful age. At that instant, I say truly that the spirit of life, which dwells in the most secret chamber of the heart, began to tremble with such violence that it appeared fearfully in the least pulses, and, trembling, said these words: *Ecce deus fortior me, qui veniens dominabitur mihi* [Behold a god stronger than I, who coming shall rule over me].

At that instant the spirit of the soul, which dwells in the high chamber to which all the spirits of the senses carry their perceptions, began to marvel greatly, and, speaking especially to the spirit of the sight, said these words: *Apparuit jam beatitudo vestra* [Now has appeared your bliss].

At that instant the natural spirit, which dwells in that part where our nourishment is supplied, began to weep, and, weeping, said these words: *Heu miser! quia frequenter impeditus ero deinceps* [Woe is me, wretched! because often from this time forth shall I be hindered].

I say that from that time forward Love lorded it over my soul, which had been so speedily wedded to him: and he began to exercise over me such control and such lordship, through the power which my imagination gave to him, that it behoved me passing along a street, turned her eyes toward that place where I stood very timidly; and by her ineffable courtesy, which is today rewarded in the eternal world, saluted me with such virtue that it seemed to me then that I saw all the bounds of bliss. The hour when her most sweet salutation reached me was precisely the ninth of that day; and since it was the first time that her words came to my ears, I took in such sweetness, that, as it were intoxicated, I turned away from the folk; and, betaking myself to the solitude of my own chamber, I sat myself down to think of this most courteous lady.

And thinking of her, a sweet slumber overcame me, in which a marvellous vision appeared to me; for methought I saw in my chamber a cloud of the color of fire, within which I discerned a shape of a Lord of aspect fearful to whoso might look upon him; and he seemed to me so joyful within himself that a marvellous thing it was; and in his words he said many things which I understood not, save a few, among which I understood these: *Ego Dominus tuus* [I am thy Lord]. In his arms meseemed to see a person sleeping, naked, save that she seemed to me to be wrapped lightly in a crimson cloth; whom I, regarding very intently, recognized as the lady of the salutation, who had the day before deigned to salute me. And in one of his hands it seemed to me that he held a thing which was all on fire; and it seemed to me that he said to me these words: *Vide cor tuum* [Behold thy heart]. And when he had remained awhile, it seemed to me that he awoke her that slept; and he so far prevailed upon her with his craft as to make her eat that thing which was burning in his hand; and she ate it timidly. After this, it was but a short while before his joy turned into most bitter lament; and as he wept he gathered up this lady in his arms, and with her it seemed to me that he went away toward heaven. Whereat I felt such great anguish, that my weak slumber could not endure it, but was broken, and I awoke. And straightaway I began to reflect, and found that the hour in which this vision had appeared to me had been the fourth of the night; so that, it plainly appears, it was the first hour of the nine last hours of the night.

And thinking on what had appeared to me, I resolved to make it known to many who were famous poets at that time; and since I had already seen in myself the art of discoursing in rhyme, I resolved to make a sonnet in which I would salute all the liegemen of Love, and, praying them to give an interpretation of my vision, would write to them that which I had seen in my slumber. And I began then this sonnet:—

> To every captive soul and gentle heart
>   Unto whose sight may come the present word,
>   That they thereof to me their thoughts impart,
>   Be greeting in Love's name, who is their Lord.
> Now of those hours wellnigh one third had gone
>   What time doth every star appear most bright,

When on a sudden Love before me shone,
   Remembrance of whose nature gives me fright.
Joyful to me seemed Love, and he was keeping
   My heart within his hands, while on his arm
   He held my lady, covered o'er, and sleeping.
Then waking her, he with this flaming heart
   Did humbly feed her fearful of some harm.
   Thereon I saw him thence in tears depart.

This sonnet is divided into two parts. In the first part I offer greeting, and ask for a reply; in the second I signify to what the reply is to be made. The second part begins here: "Now of."

To this sonnet reply was made by many, and of diverse opinions. Among those who replied to it was he whom I call first of my friends, and he then wrote a sonnet which begins, "All worth, in my opinion, thou hast seen." And this was, as it were, the beginning of the friendship between him and me, when he knew that I was he who had sent it to him.

The true meaning of this dream was not then seen by any one, but now it is plain to the simplest.

After this vision my natural spirit began to be hindered in its operation, for my soul was wholly given over to the thought of this most gentle lady; whereby in brief time I fell into so frail and feeble a condition, that my appearance was grievous to many of my friends; and many full of envy eagerly sought to know from me that which above all I wished to conceal from others. And I, perceiving their evil questioning, through the will of Love, who commanded me according to the counsel of the reason, replied to them, that it was Love who had brought me to this pass. I spoke of Love, because I bore on my face so many of his signs that this could not be concealed. And when they asked me: "For whom has Love thus wasted thee?" I, smiling, looked at them and said nothing.

Translated by Charles Eliot Norton

✌🏵 🏵✌

MARGERY BREWS TO JOHN PASTON

TO MY RIGHT WELL-BELOVED COUSIN, JOHN PASTON, ESQUIRE, BE THIS LETTER DELIVERED, ETC.
Right worshipful and well-beloved Valentine, in my most humble wise I recommend me unto you, etc. And heartily I thank you for the letter

which that ye sent me by John Bickerton, whereby I understand and know that ye be purposed to come to Topcroft in short time, and without any errand or matter but only to have a conclusion of the matter betwixt my father and you. I would be most glad of any creature alive, so that the matter might grow to effect. And thereas ye say, an' ye come and find the matter no more towards you than ye did aforetime, ye would no more put my father and my lady my mother to no cost nor business for that cause a good while after; which causeth mine heart to be full heavy. And if that ye come, and the matter take to none effect, then should I be much more sorry and full of heaviness.

And as for myself, I have done and understood in the matter that I can or may, as God knoweth; and I let you plainly understand that my father will no more money part withal in that behalf, but £100 and 50 marks, which is right far from the accomplishment of your desire.

Wherefore, if that ye could be content with that good and my poor person, I would be the merriest maiden on ground. And if ye think not yourself so satisfied, or that ye might have much more good (as I have understood by you afore)—good, true, and loving Valentine, that ye take no such labour upon you as to come more for that matter, but let it pass, and never more to be spoken of, as I may be your true lover and beadswoman during my life.

No more unto you at this time, but Almighty Jesus preserve you both body and soul, etc.

By your Valentine,
Margery Brews

❧ ❧

PIETRO BEMBO TO LUCREZIA BORGIA

Today I would have come to pay tribute to your Ladyship, as was my obligation or my desire—I know not which the more, for both were vast and infinite—had it not been that the other night I woke with such pain in my neck that now I can only move it if I turn my entire body, and that with difficulty, and consequently it gives me no little annoyance. I believe it was a bad strain, and certainly it was very bad of it to choose to assail me at this time. But these past hours it has begun to perceive its error and appears to be relenting and preparing to be gone; and no sooner is this accomplished than I shall straightway come to your Ladyship, which will, I deem, be within two days. And should it defer its departure longer I shall come in any case, as I have no desire to follow this neckache with heartache, which is wont to be much more serious—although I fear I am already affected, seeing that I have delayed more than I should wish my coming to kiss your hand. Accordingly I shall come quickly whatever happens, if only to cure myself of this second malady. Here the heat is unusually intense and for my part I have never felt it stronger—I seem to be all aflame and turned to fire. I do not know whether you feel it to the same degree. In no wise, I must suppose, for where you are there is more shade than I have here, nor can I forget that by their nature women feel the heat less than men are wont to do. Craving your favour I kiss your Ladyship's hand, and beg my dear Madonna Lisabetta to say one prayer for me to her saintly mistress.

Ostellato 29 June 1503

I rejoice that each day to increase my fire you cunningly devise some fresh incitement, such as that which encircled your glowing brow today. If you do such things because, feeling some little warmth yourself, you wish to see another burn, I shall not deny that for each spark of yours untold Etnas are raging in my breast. And if you do so because it is natural for you to relish another's suffering, who in all justice could blame me if he but knew the reasons for my ardour? Truly I can do no sin if I put my faith in such a gospel and in so many miracles. Let Love wreak just revenge for me, if upon your brow you are not the same as in your heart.

Ferrara 14 July 1503

I am leaving, oh my dearest life, and yet I do not leave and never shall. If likewise you who stay were not to stay, I dare not speak for you, but truly "Ah, of all who love none more blest than I!" And what sweeter miracle could be wrought than this: to live in another and die in oneself? And oh, how truthfully I can swear I live in you! All this night, whether in dreams or lying awake, all this long night I was with you, and so far as this mortal condition can vouchsafe I hope it will be the same every night of my life. Do not, I entreat your Ladyship, disdain to attend most kindly and sweetly to that part of me which remains with you, and sometimes speak of it with my dear and saintly Lisabetta, in whose prayers I ask to be remembered. They say each has a good angel who prays for him, and I pray to that angel who can pray for me that he will pray f.f. for that which he knows will profit me. All I know is that faith as pure and as constant as mine deserves the favour of your goodness. And were I an angel, as he is, I should be consumed with great pity for any man who loved as much as I. My heart kisses your Ladyship's hand which so soon I shall come to kiss with these lips that are forever forming your name—or rather with this very soul which even now is telling me that at that instant it will want to leap to my lips, and so take sweet revenge for its sweet wound.

Ferrara 18 July 1503

Not because I am able to tell you what tender bitterness enfolds me at this parting do I write to you, light of my life, but only to entreat you to cherish yourself most dearly, and, lest my life perish, also your health, which would seem to be a little affected. That line which you had in part written upon my heart is now wholly engraved deep within, and it will admit nothing but the thought of you, so well have you deserved it. Alas, now I must depart. I kiss that tender hand which has slain me.

Ferrara 18 July 1503

Translated by Hugh Shankland

LUCREZIA BORGIA TO PIETRO BEMBO

I think were I to die
And with my wealth of pain
  Cease longing,
Such great love to deny
Could make the world remain
  Unloving.
When I consider this,
Death's long delay is all
  I must desire,
Since reason tells me bliss
Is felt by one in thrall
  To such a fire.

—LUCREZIA BORGIA

MY DEAREST MISSER PIETRO,

I know that the very expectation of something awaited is the greater part of satisfaction because the hope of possessing it inflames desire. The rarer it is, the more beautiful it seems, the commoner, the less so. I decided to put off writing to you until this moment, so for that, by awaiting some exquisite reward to your most exquisite letters, you have become the source of your own satisfaction; you are both creditor and payer.

Nevertheless I have in two of my letters, confessed to Monsignor Thesauriero of my debt to you and this may have constituted no small part of what I can pay. As far as the rest is concerned, I do not believe that I can be held bound. In your letters you express with such ease all that you feel for me, but, I, just because I feel so well disposed towards you, am unable to do so. It is this feeling of powerlessness which absolves me from the debt. However as it would be wrong for me to be both prosecutor and judge of my own cause, I submit to the weighty judgement of the aforesaid Monsignor Thesauriero, commending myself to his Lordship and you.

Ferrara the seventh day of August.
Your own Duchess of Ferrara

Translated by Hugh Shankland

❧ ❧

KING HENRY VIII TO ANNE BOLEYN

In debating with myself the contents of your letters I have been put to a great agony; not knowing how to understand them, whether to my disadvantage as shown in some places, or to my advantage as in others. I beseech you now with all my heart definitely to let me know your whole mind as to the love between us; for necessity compels me to plague you for a reply, having been for more than a year now struck by the dart of love, and being uncertain either of failure or of finding a place in your heart and affection, which point has certainly kept me for some time from naming you my mistress, since if you only love me with an ordinary love the name is not appropriate to you, seeing that it stands for an uncommon position very remote from the ordinary; but if it pleases you to do the duty of a true, loyal mistress and friend, and to give yourself body and heart to me, who have been, and will be, your very loyal servant (if your rigour does not forbid me), I promise you that not only the name will be due to you, but also to take you as my sole mistress, casting off all others than yourself out of mind and affection, and to serve you only; begging you to make me a complete reply to this my rude letter as to how far and in what I can trust; and if it does not please you to reply in writing, to let me know of some place where I can have it by word of mouth, the which place I will seek out with all my heart. No more for fear of wearying you. Written by the hand of him who would willingly remain your

HR

JOHN DONNE

In Kindness to an Absent Friend

SIR,

Your long silence, could never bring me to any doubt of having lost my Title to your friendship. It shall not be in your power, to be able, so to prescribe, even in your self, against me, but that still I will be making my continual claim to your love. For Friendship hath so much of Soveraignty, yea and of Religion too, that no prescription can be admitted against it. And as for losing you by any forfeit, or demerit on my part, I have been very carefull, and shall be watchfull still, to bless my self from such a curse, as that. And indeed, such care is all the merit, which can be hoped for, at the hands of a person, so useless as my self. And from this care now proceeds my haste, to thank you for your last Letter; and to begg a preservation of that love, which though, at first, it fell not directly, and immediately upon myself, but by way of reflection or Briccole, through your other Friends (to use the Metaphor of a Game, wherein I congratulate that excellency, to which my Lord *Clifford* tells me, you have arrived) yet now I dare conceive, that your love belongs to me, even as a kind of due; since I see, you now discern that I am so much in earnest in loving you.

❧ ☙

MAXIMILIEN DE BETHUNE, DUC DE SULLY

from *Memoirs*

Sully unwisely offers love advice to the Queen of King Henry IV of France

The reader may perceive that in my memoirs of the late years, I have faithfully observed the promise I had formerly made, to entertain him no more with the weaknesses of Henry. I carefully concealed from my secretaries, and all persons whatever, all that passed between Henry and me upon this subject, in those many long and secret conversations we had together: except the Duchess of Beaufort and the Marchioness of Verneuil, the name of no other woman has been mentioned in these "Memoirs," with the title of mistress to the King. I choose rather to suppress all the trouble I have suffered in this article, than make it known at the expense of my master's glory: probably I have carried this scruple too far. The public has heard so often the names of Madame de Moret; Mademoiselle des Essarts; old Madame d'Angoulême; the Countess of Sault; Mesdames de Ragny and de Chanlivault, two of my relations; the Commandeur de Sillery; Rambouillet; Marillac; Duret the physician . . . and many of the most considerable persons at court, all differently interested in these adventures of gallantry, either as principals or as parties concerned; that I might relate a great deal without saying anything new, which would be indeed but a cold repetition of little debates and love quarrels, such as those which I have already slightly mentioned. The following circumstance I have excepted from this rule, as it is of a nature that seems to require I should justify my part in it to the public.

On one of those occasions when Henry was most deeply affected with the uneasy temper of the Queen, it was reported that he had quitted her with some emotion, and set out for Chantilly without seeing her. This indeed was true; he took the arsenal in his way, and there opened his whole heart to me upon the cause of this dispute. The King pursued his journey, and I went in the afternoon to the Louvre, attended only by one of my secretaries, who did not follow me to the Queen's little closet, where she was then shut up. Leonora Conchini was at the door of this closet, her head bending down toward her neck, like a person who was sleeping, or at least in a profound reverie. I drew her out of it, and she told me that the Queen would not suffer her to enter her closet, the door of which, however, opened to me the moment I was named.

I found the Queen busy in composing a letter to the King, which she allowed me to read: it breathed an air of spleen and bitterness, which must inevitably have very bad effects. I made her so sensible of the consequences it was likely to produce, that she consented to suppress it, though with great difficulty; and upon condition that I should assist her in composing another, wherein nothing should be omitted of all that, as she said, she might with justice represent to the King her husband. There was a necessity for complying with this request, to avoid something worse. Many little debates arose between us, concerning the choice of expressions and the force of each term. I had occasion for all the presence of mind I was capable of exerting, to find out the means of satisfying this princess, without displeasing the King, or of being guilty of any disrespect in addressing him.

This letter, which was very long, I shall not repeat here. The Queen complained in it of the continual gallantries of the King her husband; but declared that she was excited to this only by the earnest desire she had to possess his heart entirely. If therefore she appeared to insist too absolutely upon his sacrificing his mistress to her, her quiet, her conscience, and her honor, the interest of the King, his health and his life, the good of the State, and the security of her children's succession to the throne, which the Marchioness de Verneuil took pleasure in rendering doubtful, were so many motives which reduced her, she said, to the disagreeable necessity of making such a demand. To awaken his tenderness, and excite his compassion, she added that she, together with the children she had by him, would throw themselves at his feet. She reminded him of his promises, and took God to witness, that if she could prevail upon him to keep them, she would, on her side, renounce all other vengeance against the Marchioness de Verneuil.

All my caution was scarce sufficient to avoid the extremes the Queen would have run into; and it is apparent, however, that I failed either in address or invention: for the King, when he received this letter, was mortally offended with it, and so much the more as he instantly perceived that it was not in the Queen's manner. I had a billet from him immediately, conceived in these terms: "My friend, I have received the most impertinent letter from my wife that ever was wrote. I am not so angry with her, as with the person that has dictated it; for I see plainly that it is not her style. Endeavor to discover the author of it: I never shall have any regard for him, whoever he be; nor will I see him as long as I live."

However secure I thought myself, I could not help being uneasy at this billet.

The King, on his arrival from Chantilly, three or four days afterward, came to the arsenal. I was sufficiently perplexed by the questions he asked me concerning this affair; for it was expressly for that purpose that he came.

"Well," said he, "have you yet discovered the person who composed my wife's letter?"

"Not yet certainly," replied I, making use of some little address, "but I hope to give you this satisfaction in two days; and probably sooner, if you will tell me what there is in it that displeases you."

"Oh," replied he, "the letter is mighty well written; full of reasons, obedience, and submission; but wounds me smiling, and while it flatters piques me. I have no particular exception to make to it; but, in general, I am offended with it, and shall be the more so if it comes to be public."

"But, sire," replied I, "if it be such as you say, it may have been written with a good intention, and to prevent something still worse."

"No! no!" interrupted Henry, "it is maliciously designed, and with a view to insult me. If my wife had taken advice from you, or from any of my faithful servants in it, I should not have been so much offended."

"What, sire," resumed I hastily, "if it was one of your faithful servants who had dictated it, would you not bear him some ill-will?"

"Not the least," returned the King; "for I should be very certain, that he had done it with a good intention."

"It is true, sire," said I. "Therefore you must be no longer angry; for it was I that dictated it, through an apprehension that something worse might happen: and when you know my reasons, you will confess that I was under a necessity of doing it. But to remove all your doubts, I will show you the original, written in my own hand, at the side of the Queen's." Saying this, I took the paper out of my pocket, and presented it to him.

The King, as he read it, made me observe some words, in the place of which the Queen, when she copied the letter, had substituted others far less obliging. "Well," said he, "since you are the author, let us say no more of it: my heart is at rest.

ANN HAMILTON AND BARBARA VILLIERS TO LORD CHESTERFIELD

MY LORD,
My friend and I are now abed together a-contriving how to have your company this afternoon. If you deserve this favour, you will come and seek us at Ludgate Hill about three a clock at Butler's shop, where we will expect you, but lest we should give you too much satisfaction at once, we will say no more; expect the rest when you see.

Your &c

MARGARET, DUCHESS OF NEWCASTLE

from *The Life of Newcastle*

"OF HIS NATURAL HUMOR AND DISPOSITION"

My Lord may justly be compared to Titus, the deliciae of mankind, by reason of his sweet, gentle, and obliging nature; for though his wisdom and experience found it impossible to please all men because of their different humors and dispositions, yet his nature is such that he will be sorry when he seeth that men are displeased with him out of their own ill natures without any cause, for he loves all that are his friends and hates none that are his enemies. He is a loyal subject, a kind husband, a loving father, a generous master, and a constant friend.

He is true and just both in his words and actions and has no mean or petty designs, but they are all just and honest.

He is full of charity and compassion to persons that are in misery and full of clemency and mercy; insomuch that when he was general of a great army he would never sit in council himself upon cause of life and death, but granted pardon to many delinquents that were condemned by his council of war; so that some were forced to petition him not to do it by reason it was an ill precedent for others. To which my Lord merrily answered that if they did hang all they would leave him none to fight.

His noble bounty is so manifest to all the world that should I light a candle to the sun if I should strive to illustrate it.

In short I know him not addicted to any manner of vice, except that he hath been a great lover and admirer of the female sex, which whether it be so great a crime as to condemn him for it, I'll leave to the judgment of young gallants and beautiful ladies.

SAMUEL PEPYS

from *The Diary*

THE DEB WILLET AFFAIR

September 30, 1667. So by coach home, and there found our pretty girl Willet come, brought by Mr. Batelier, and she is very pretty, and so grave as I never saw a little thing in my life. Indeed, I think her a little too good for my family, and so well carriaged as I hardly ever saw. . . .

October 5. Took my wife and Willet to the Duke of York's play-house. . . .

December 7. All the morning at the office, and at noon home to dinner with my clerks, and while we were at dinner comes Willet's aunt to see her and my wife; she is a very fine widow and pretty handsome but extraordinary well carriaged and speaks very handsomely and with extraordinary understanding, so as I spent the whole afternoon in her company with my wife, she understanding all the things of note touching plays and fashions and Court and everything and speaks rarely, which pleases me mightily, and seems to love her niece very well, and was so glad (which was pretty odd) that since she came hither her breasts begin to swell. . . .

December 22 (Lord's day). Up and my wife, poor wretch, still in pain, and then to dress myself and down to my chamber to settle some papers, and thither come to me Willet with an errand from her mistress, and this time I first did give her a little kiss, she being a very pretty humored girl, and so one that I do love mightily. . . .

March 31. I called Deb to take pen, ink and paper and write down what things came into my head for my wife to do in order to her going into the country, and the girl, writing not so well as she would do, cried, and her mistress construed it to be sullenness, and so away angry with her too, but going to bed she undressed me, and there I did give her good advice and *baiser la, elle* weeping still. . . .

June 19. I home, and there we to bed again, and slept pretty well, and about nine rose, and then my wife fell into her blubbering again, and at length had a request to make of me, which was, that she might go into France, and live there, out of trouble; and then all come out, that I loved pleasure and denied her any. . . .

October 25 (Lord's day). So home and to dinner, and after dinner all the afternoon got my wife and boy to read to me, and at night W. Batelier comes and sups with us; and, after supper, to have my head combed by Deb, which occasioned the greatest sorrow to me that ever I knew in this world, for my wife, coming up suddenly, did find me embracing the girl. . . . I was at a wonderful loss upon it, and the girl also, and I endeavored to put it off, but my wife was struck mute and grew angry, and so her voice came to her. . . . I did give no provocation, but did promise all fair usage to her and love, and forswore any hurt that I did with her, till at last she seemed to be at ease again, and so toward morning a little sleep, and so I with some little repose and rest. . . .

November 12. I to my wife and to sit with her a little and then called her and Willet to my chamber and there did, with tears in my eyes, which I could not help, discharge her and advise her to be gone as soon as she could, and never to see me, or let me see her more while she was in the house, which she took with tears too, but I believe understands me to be her friend, and I am apt to believe by what my wife hath of late told me is a cunning girl, if not a slut. Thence, parting kindly with my wife, I away by coach to my cozen Roger.

November 13. Thence I home, and there to talk, with great pleasure all the evening, with my wife, who tells me that Deb has been abroad today, and is come home and says she has got a place to go to, so as she will be gone tomorrow morning. This troubled me. But she will be gone and I not know whither. Before we went to bed my wife told me she would not have me to see her or give her her wages, and so I did give my wife ten pounds for her year, and half a quarter's wages, which she went into her chamber and paid her, and so to bed, and there, blessed be God! we did sleep well and with peace, which I had not done in now almost twenty nights together.

November 16. Up, and by water to White Hall. This being done I away to Holborne, about Whetstone's Park, where I never was in my life before, where I understand by my wife's discourse that Deb is gone, which do trouble me mightily that the poor girl should be in a desperate condition forced to go thereabouts, and there not hearing of any such man as Allbon, with whom my wife said she now was.

November 18. Lay long in bed talking with my wife, she being un-willing to have me go abroad, saying and declaring herself jealous of my going out for fear of my going to Deb, which I do deny, for which God forgive me, for I was no sooner out about noon but I did go by coach directly to Somerset House, and there inquired among the porters there for Dr. Allbon, and the first I spoke with told me he knew him, and that he was newly gone to Lincoln's Inn Fields, but whither he could not tell me. At last he comes back and tells me she is well, and that I may see her if I will, but no more. So I could not be commanded by my reason, but I must go this very night, and so by coach, it being now dark, I to her, close by my tailor's, and she did come into the coach to me, and *je* did *baiser* her. . . . I did nevertheless give her the best council I could, to have a care of her honour, and to fear God, and suffer no man *para avoir* to do *con* her as *je* have done, which she promised. *Je* did give her 20s. and di-rections *para laisser* sealed in paper at any time the name of the place of her being at Herringman's, my bookseller in the 'Change, by which I might go *par* her, and so bid her good night with much content to my mind, and resolution to look after her no more till I heard from her. And so home, and there told my wife a fair tale, God knows, how I spent the day. . . .

November 19. Up, and at the office all the morning, with my heart full of joy to think of what a safe condition all my matters now stand between my wife and Deb and me, and at noon running upstairs to see the upholsters. . . . I find my wife sitting sad in the dining room; which inquiring into the reason of, she begun to call me all false, rotten-hearted rogues in the world, letting me understand that I was with Deb yesterday, which, thinking it impossible for her ever to understand, I did a while deny, but at last did, for the ease of my mind and hers, and for-ever to discharge my heart of this wicked business, I did confess all, and above stairs in our bed chamber there I did endure the sorrow of her threats and vows and curses all the afternoon, and, what was worse, she swore by all that was good that she would slit the nose of this girl and be gone herself this very night from me. . . . W. Hewer . . . obtained what I could not, that she would be pacified. . . . there was, beyond my hopes as well as desert, a durable peace; and so to supper, and pretty kind words, and to bed, and did this night begin to pray to God upon my knees alone in my chamber, which God knows I cannot yet do heartily. . . .

March 12, 1669. . . . And so home, where, thinking to meet my wife with content, after my pains all this day, I find her in her closet, alone, in the dark, in a hot fit of railing against me, upon some news she has this day heard of Deb's living very fine, and with black spots, and speaking ill words of her mistress. . . . God knows, I know nothing of her, not what she do, nor what becomes of her, though God knows that my devil that is within me do wish that I could. But in her [his wife's] fit she did tell me upon putting off her handsome maid and hiring another that was full of the small pox, which did mightily vex me. . . .

April 13. I away home, and there sent for W. Hewer, and he and I by water to White Hall. . . . as God would have it, I spied Deb, which made my heart and head to work . . . and I run after her and her two women and a man. . . . she endeavored to avoid me, but I did speak to her and she to me, and did get her *pour dire me ou* she *demeurs* now, and did charge her *para* say nothing of me that I had *vu elle*, which she did promise, and so with my heart full of surprise and disorder I away. And so back to White Hall. . . . we home by water, to my wife, who is home from Deptford. But, God forgive me I hardly know how to put on confidence enough to speak as innocent, having had this passage today with Deb, though only, god knows, by accident. But my pain is lest God Almighty shall suffer met to find out this girl, whom indeed I love, and with a bad *amour*, but I will pray to God to give me grace to forbear it.

April 15. Up and to the office . . . by the Conduit, I did see Deb on foot going up the hill. I saw her, and she me, but she made no stop, but seemed unwilling to speak to me; so I away on, but then . . . overtook her at the end of Hosier lane in Smithfield, and without standing in the street desired her to follow me, and I led her into a little blind alehouse within the walls, and there she and I alone fell to talk and *baiser la* and *toker su mammailles.*

April 26. Creed, coming just now to see me, my wife, and he, and I out, and I set him down at Temple Bar, and myself and wife went down the Temple upon seeming business, only to put him off, and just at the Temple gate I spied Deb with another gentlewoman, and Deb winked on me and smiled, but undiscovered, and I was glad to see her.

❧ ❧

JOHN WILMOT, EARL OF ROCHESTER TO
MRS. BARRY

MADAM:
I know not well who has the worst on't, thou who love but a little, or I who dote to an extravagance. Sure, to be half kind is as bad as to be half

witted, and madness, both in love and reason, bears a better character than a moderate state of either. Would I could bring you to my opinion in this point. I would then confidently pretend you had too just exceptions either against me or my passion, the flesh, and the devil. I mean all the fools of my own sex and that fat, with the other lean, one of yours, whose prudent advice is daily concerning you: how dangerous it is to be kind to the man upon earth who loves you best. I, who still persuade myself by all the arguments I can bring, that I am happy, find this none of the least, that you are too unlike these people every way to agree with them in any particular. This is writ between sleeping and walking, and I will not answer for its being sense . . . remove my fears and make me as happy as I am faithful.

DEAR MADAM,
You are stark mad and therefore the fitter for me to love; and that is the reason, I think, I can never leave to be

Your Humble Servant,

MADAM,
There is now no minute of my life that does not afford me some new argument how much I love you. The little joy I take in everything wherein you are not concerned, the pleasing perplexity of endless thought which I fall into wherever you are brought to my remembrance, and lastly, the continual disquiet I am in during your absence, convince me sufficiently that I do you justice in loving you so as woman was never loved before.

MADAM,
Anger, spleen, revenge and shame are not yet so powerful with me as to make me disown this great truth, that I love you above all things in the world, But I thank God I can distinguish, I can see every woman in you and from yourself am convinced I have never been in the wrong in my opinion of women. 'Tis impossible for me to curse you, but give me leave to pity myself, which is more than ever you will do for me. . . .

WILLIAM CONGREVE TO ARABELLA HUNT

DEAR MADAM,

Not believe that I love you? You cannot pretend to be so incredulous. If you do not believe my tongue, consult my eyes, consult your own. You will find by yours that they have charms; by mine that I have a heart which feels them. Recall to mind what happened last night. That at least was a lover's kiss. Its eagerness, its fierceness, its warmth, expressed the God its parent. But oh! its sweetness, and its melting softness expressed him more. With trembling in my limbs, and fevers in my soul I ravish'd it. Convulsions, pantings, murmurings show'd the mighty disorder within me: the mighty disorder increased by it. For those dear lips shot through my heart, and thro' my bleeding vitals, delicious poison, and an avoidless but yet a charming ruin.

What cannot a day produce? The night before I thought myself a happy man, in want of nothing, and in fairest expectation of fortune; approved of by men of wit, and applauded by others. Pleased, nay charmed with my friends, my then dearest friends, sensible of every delicate pleasure, and in their turns possessing all.

But Love, almighty Love, seems in a moment to have removed me to a prodigious distance from every object but you alone. In the midst of crowds I remain in solitude. Nothing but you can lay hold of my mind, and that can lay hold of nothing but you. I appear transported to some foreign desert with you (oh, that I were really thus transported!), where, abundantly supplied with everything, in thee, I might live out an age of uninterrupted ecstasy.

The scene of the world's great stage seems suddenly and sadly chang'd. Unlovely objects are all around me, excepting thee; the charms of all the world appear to be translated to thee. Thus in this sad but oh, too pleasing state! my soul can fix upon nothing but thee; thee it contemplates, admires, adores, nay depends on, trusts on you alone.

If you and hope forsake it, despair and endless misery attend it.

DEAR MADAM,

May I presume to beg pardon for the fault I committed. So foolish a fault that it was below not only a man of sense but a man; and of which nothing could ever have made me guilty but the fury of a passion with which none but your lovely self could inspire me. May I presume to beg pardon for a fault which I can never forgive myself? To purchase that pardon what would I not endure? You shall see me prostrate before you, and use me like a slave while I kiss the dear feet that trample upon me. But if my crime be too great for forgiveness, as indeed it is very great, deny me not one dear parting look, let me see you once before I must never see you more.

Christ! I want patience to support that accursed thought, I have nothing in the world that is dear to me but you. You have made everything else indifferent; and can I resolve never to see you more? In spite of myself I must always see you. Your form is fixed by fate in my mind and is never to be remov'd. I see those lovely piercing eyes continually, I see each moment those ravishing lips which I have gazed on still with desire, and still have touch'd with transport, and at which I have so often flown with all the fury of the most violent love.

Jesus! from whence and whither am I fallen? From the hopes of blissful ecstasies to black despair! From the expectation of immortal transports, which none but your dear self can give me, and which none but he who loves like me could ever so much as think of, to a complication of cruel passions and the most dreadful condition of human life.

My fault indeed has been very great, and cries aloud for the severest vengeance. See it inflicted on me: see me despair and die for that fault. But let me not die unpardon'd, madam; I die for you, but die in the most cruel and dreadful manner. The wretch that lies broken on the wheel alive feels not a quarter of what I endure. Yet boundless love has been all my crime; unjust, ungrateful, barbarous return for it!

Suffer me to take my eternal leave of you; when I have done that how easy will it be to bid all the rest of the world adieu.

❧ ❧

GEORGE FARQUHAR TO ANNE OLDFIELD

Sunday, after Sermon

I came, I saw, and was conquered; never had man more to say, yet can I say nothing; where others go to save their souls, there have I lost mine; but I hope that Divinity which has the justest title to its service has received it; but I will endeavour to suspend these raptures for a moment, and talk calmly.——

Nothing on earth, madam, can charm, beyond your wit but your beauty: after this not to love you would proclaim me a fool; and to say I did when I thought otherwise would pronounce me a knave; if anybody called me either I should resent it; and if you but think me either I shall break my heart.

You have already, madam, seen enough of me to create a liking or an aversion; your sense is above your sex, then let your proceeding be so likewise, and tell me plainly what I have to hope for. Were I to consult my merits my humility would chide any shadow of hope; but after a sight of such a face whose whole composition is a smile of good nature, why should I be so unjust as to suspect you of cruelty. Let me either live in London and be happy or retire again to my desert to check my vanity that drew me thence; but let me beg you to receive my sentence from your own mouth, that I may hear you speak and see you look at the same time; then let me be unfortunate if I can.

If you are not the lady in mourning that sat upon my right hand at church, you may go to the devil, for I'm sure you're a witch.

Friday night, eleven o'clock

If you find no more rest from your thoughts in bed than I do, I could wish you, madam, to be always there, for there I am most in love. I went to the play this evening and the music roused my soul to such a pitch of passion that I was almost mad with melancholy. I flew thence to Spring Garden where with envious eyes I saw every man pick up his mate, whilst I alone walked like solitary Adam before the creation of Eve, but the place was no paradise to me, nothing I found entertaining but the nightingale which methought in sweet notes like your own pronounced the name of my dear Penelope—as the fool thinketh the bell clinketh. From hence I retired to the tavern where methought the shining glass represented your fair person, and the sparkling wine within it looked like your lovely wit and spirit. I met my dear mistress in everything, and I propose presently to see her in a lively dream, since the last thing I do is to kiss her dear letter, clasp her charming ideal in my arms, and so fall asleep—

My morning songs, my evening prayers,
My daily musings, nightly cares.

Adieu!

MADAM,

If I haven't begun thrice to write and as often thrown away my pen, may I never take it up again; my head and my heart have been at cuffs about you two long hours,—says my head, you're a coxcomb for troubling your noddle with a lady whose beauty is as much above your pretensions as your merit is below her love.

Then answers my heart,—Good Mr Head, you're a blockhead. I know Mr F———r's merit better than you; as for your part, I know you to be as whimsical as the devil, and changing with every new notion that offers, but for my share I am fixt, and can stick to my opinion of a lady's merit forever, and if the fair she can secure an interest in me, Monsieur Head, you may go whistle.

Come, come, (answered my head) you, Mr Heart, are always leading the gentleman into some inconvenience or other; was it not you that first enticed him to talk to this lady? Your damn'd confounded warmth made him like this lady, and your busy impertinence has made him write to her; your leaping and skipping disturbs his sleep by night and his good humour by day; in short, sir, I will hear no more on't; I am head, and will be obeyed.

You lie, sir, replied my heart (being very angry), I am head in matters of love, and if you don't give your consent, you shall be forced, for I am sure that in this case all the members will be on my side. What say you, gentlemen Hands!

Oh (say the hands), we would not forego the tickling pleasure of touching a delicious white soft skin for the world.

Well, what say you, Mr Tongue?

Zounds, says the linguist, there is more ecstasy in speaking three soft words of Mr Heart's suggesting than whole orations of Signior Head's, so I am for the lady, and here's my honest neighbour, Lips, will stick to't.

By the sweet power of kisses, that we will, (replied the lips) and presently some other worthy members, standing up for the Heart, they laid violent hands (*nemine contradicente*) on poor Head, and knocked out his brains. So now, madam, behold me, as perfect a lover as any in Christendom, my heart firmly dictating every word I say. The little rebel throws itself into your power, and if you don't support it in the cause it has taken up for your sake, think what will be the condition of the headless and heartless

Farquhar

ALEXANDER POPE TO TERESA BLOUNT

7 August 1716

MADAM,

I have so much Esteem for you, and so much of the other thing, that were I a handsome fellow I should do you a vast deal of good: but as it is, all I am good for is to write a civil letter, or to make a fine Speech. The truth is, that considering how often & how openly I have declared Love to you, I am astonished (and a little affronted) that you have not forbid my correspondence, & directly said, *See my face no more.* It is not enough, Madam, for your reputation that you keep your hands pure, from the Stain of Such Ink as might be shed to gratify a male Correspondent; Alas! while your heart consents to encourage him in this lewd liberty of writing, you are not (indeed you are not) what you would so fain have me think you, a Prude! I am vain enough to conclude (like most young fellows) that a fine Lady's Silence is Consent, and so I write on.

But in order to be as Innocent as possible in this Epistle, I'll tell you news. You have asked me News a thousand times at the first word you spoke to me, which some would interpret as if you expected nothing better from my lips: And truly 'tis not a sign Two Lovers are together, when they can be so impertinent as to enquire what the World does? All I mean by this is, that either you or I cannot be in love with the other; I leave you to guess which of the two is that stupid & insensible Creature, so blind to the others Excellencies and Charms. . . .

ESTHER VANHOMRIGH (VANESSA) TO JONATHAN SWIFT

London, 1 September 1712

Had I a correspondent in China, I might have had an answer by this time. I never could think till now that London was so far off in your thoughts and that twenty miles were by your computation equal to some thousands. I thought it a piece of charity to undeceive you in this point and to let you know, if you'll give yourself the trouble to write, I may probably receive your letter in a day. 'Twas that made me venture to take pen in hand the third time. Sure you'll not let it be to no purpose. You must needs be extremely happy where you are, to forget your absent friends; and I believe you have formed a new system and think there is no more of this world, passing your sensible horizon. If this be your notion I must excuse you; if not, you can plead no other excuse; and if it be so, I must reckon myself of another world; but I shall have much ado to be persuaded till you send me some convincing arguments of it. Don't dally in a thing of this consequence, but demonstrate that 'tis possible to keep up a correspondence between friends, though in different worlds, and assure one another, as I do you, that

    I am

> *Your most obedient & humble servant*
> *E. Vanhomrigh*

                             Dublin, 1714

Well, now I plainly see how great a regard you have for me. You bid me be easy, and you'd see me as often as you could. You had better said, as often as you could get the better of your inclinations so much, or as often as you remembered there was such a one in the world. If you continue to treat me as you do you will not be made uneasy by me long. 'Tis impossible to describe what I have suffered since I saw you last; I am sure I could have bore the rack much better than those killing, killing words of yours. Sometimes I have resolved to die without seeing you more; but those resolves, to your misfortune, did not last long. For there is something in human nature that prompts one so to find relief in this world, I must give way to it, and beg you'd see me and speak kindly to me; for I am sure you'd not condemn anyone to suffer what I have done, could you but know it. The reason I write to you is because I cannot tell i[t] you, should I see you; for when I begin to complain, then you are angry, and there is something in your look so awful, that it strikes me dumb. Oh! That you may but have so much regard for me left, that this complaint may touch your soul with pity. I say as little as ever I can: did you but know what I thought, I am sure it would move you. Forgive me, and believe I cannot help telling you this, and live.

✦✦✦

Jonathan Swift

Found in Esther Vanhomrigh's desk, after her death, in Swift's handwriting.

To Love

In all I wish, how happy should I be,
Thou grand deluder, were it not for thee!
So weak art thou, that fools thy power despise
And yet so strong, thou triumph'st o'er the wise.
Thy traps are laid with such peculiar art,
They catch the cautious, let the rash depart.
Most nets are filled by want of thought and care;
But too much thinking brings us to thy snare,
Where, held by thee, in slavery we stay,
And throw the pleasing part of life away.
But, what does most my indignation move,
Discretion! thou wert ne'er a friend to love:
Thy chief delight is to defeat those arts
By which he kindles mutual flames in hearts;
While the blind, loitering god is at his play,
Thou steal'st his golden-pointed darts away;
Those darts which never fail; and in their stead
Convey'st malignant arrows tipt with lead.
The heedless god, suspecting no deceits,
Shoots on, and thinks he has done wondrous feats;
But the poor nymph, who feels her vitals burn,
And from her shepherd can find no return,
Laments, and rages at the power divine,
When, curst Discretion, all the fault was thine.
Cupid and Hymen thou hast set at odds,
And bred such feuds between those kindred gods
That Venus cannot reconcile her sons;
When one appears, away the other runs.
The former scales, wherein he used to poise
Love against love, and equal joys with joys,
Are now filled up with avarice and pride,
Where titles, power and riches still subside.

Then, gentle Venus, to thy father run,
And tell him how thy children are undone;
Prepare his bolts to give one fatal blow,
And strike Discretion to the shades below.

❦ ❦

FRANÇOISE ATHENAIS, MARQUISE DE
MONTESPAN

from *Memoirs*

The Marquise is replaced in King Louis XIV's affections by Madame de Maintenon.

Today, when time and reflection, and, perhaps, that fund of contempt which is so useful, have finally revealed to me the insurmountable necessities of life, I can look with a certain amount of composure at the injury which the King did me. I had at first resolved to conclude, with the chapter which you have just read, my narrative or the more or less important things which have passed or been unfolded before my eyes. For long I did not feel myself strong enough to approach a narrative which might open up all my old wounds and make my blood boil again; but I finished by considering that our monarch's reign will be necessarily the subject of a multitude of commentaries, journals, and memoirs. All these confidential writings will speak of me to the generations to be; some will paint me as one paints an object whom one loves; others, as the object one detests. The latter, to render me more odious, will probably revile my character, and, perhaps, represent me as a cowardly and despairing mistress, who has descended even to supplications!! It is my part, therefore, to retrace with a firm and vigorous hand this important epoch of my life, where my destiny, at once kind and cruel, reduced me to treat the greatest of all kings both as my equal and as an inconstant friend, as a treacherous enemy, and as my inferior or subject. He had, at first, the intention of putting me to death—of that I am persuaded—but soon his natural gentleness got the better of his pride. He grasped the wounds in my heart from the deplorable commotion of my face. If his former friend was guilty in her speech, he was far more guilty by his actions. Like an equitable judge he pardoned neither of us; he did not forgive himself and he dared not condemn me.

Since this sad time of desertion and sorrow, into which the new state of things had brought me, MM. de Mortemart, de Nevers, and de Vivonne had been glad to avoid me. They found my humor altered, and I admit that a woman who sulks, scolds, or complains is not very attractive company.

One day the poor Maréchal de Vivonne came to see me; he opened my shutters to call my attention to the beauty of the sky, and, my health seeming to him a trifle poor, he suggested to me to embark at once in his carriage and to go and dine at Clagny. I had no will left that day, so I accompanied my brother.

Being come to Clagny, the marshal, having shut himself up with me in his closet, said to me the words which follow:

"You know, my sister, how all along you have been dear to me; the grief which is wearing you out does me almost as much harm as you. Today I wish to hurt you for your own good, and get you away from this locality in spite of yourself. Kings are not to be opposed as we oppose our equals; our King, whom you know by heart, has never suffered contradiction. He has had you asked, two or three times already, to leave his palace and to go and live on your estates. Why do you delay to satisfy him, and to withdraw from so many eyes which watch you with pity?"

"The King, I am very sure, would like to see me away," I replied to the marshal, "but he has never formally expressed himself, and it is untrue that any such wish has been intimated or insinuated to me."

"What! you did not receive two letters last year, which invited you to make up your mind and retire!"

"I received two anonymous letters; nothing is more true. Could those two letters have been sent to me by the King himself?"

"The Marquis de Chamarante wrote them to you, but beneath the eyes, and at the dictation, of his Majesty."

"Ah, God! What is it you tell me? What! the Marquis de Chamarante, whom I thought one of my friends, has lent himself to such an embassy!"

"The marquis is a good man, a man of honor; and his essential duty is to please his sovereign, his master. Moreover, at the time when the letters were sent you, time remained to you for deliberation. Today, all time for delay has expired; you must go away of your own free will, or receive the affront of a command, and a *lettre de cachet* in form."

"A *lettre de cachet* for me! for the mother of the Duc du Maine and the Comte de Toulouse! We shall see that, my brother! We shall see!"

"There is nothing to see or do but to summon here all your people, and leave tomorrow, either for my château of Roissy, or for your palace at Petit-Bourg; things are pressing, and the day after tomorrow I will explain all without any secrecy."

"Explain it to me at once, my brother, and I promise to satisfy you."

"Do you give me your word?"

"I give it you, my good and dear friend, with pleasure. Inform me of what is in progress."

"Madame de Maintenon, whom, having loved once greatly, you no longer love, had the kindness to have me summoned to her this morning."

"The kindness!"

"Do not interrupt me—yes, the kindness. From the moment that she is in favor, all that comes from her requires consideration. She had me taken into her small *salon*, and there she charged me to tell you that she has always loved you, that she always will; that your rupture with her has displeased the King; that for a long time, and on a thousand occasions, she has excused you to his Majesty, but that things are now hopeless; that your retreat is required at all costs, and that it will be joined with an annual pension of 600,000 livres."

"And you advise me—?" I said to my brother.

"I advise you, I implore you, I conjure you, to accept these propositions which save everything."

My course was clear to me on the instant. Wishing to be relieved of the importunities of the marshal (a courtier, if ever there was one), I embraced him with tears in my eyes. I assured him that, for the honor of the family and out of complacence, I accepted his propositions. I begged him to take me back to Versailles, where I had to gather together my money, jewels, and papers.

The Duc de Vivonne, well as he knew me, did not suspect my trickery; he applied a score of kisses to my "pretty little white hands," and his postilions, giving free play to their reins, speedily brought us back to the château.

All beaming with joy and satisfaction, he went to convey his reply to Madame de Maintenon, who was probably expecting him. Twenty minutes hardly elapsed. The King himself entered my apartment.

He came toward me with a friendly air, and, hardly remarking my agitation, which I was suppressing, he dared to address the following words to me: "The shortest follies are the best, dear marquise; you see things at last as they should be seen. Your determination, which the

Maréchal de Vivonne has just informed me of, gives me inexpressible pleasure; you are going to take the step of a clever woman, and everybody will applaud you for it. It will be eighteen years tomorrow since we took a fancy for each other. We were then in that period of life when one sees only that which flatters, and the satisfaction of the heart surpasses everything. Our attachment, if it had been right and legitimate, might have begun with the same ardor, but it could not have endured so long; that is the property of all contested affections.

"From our union amiable children have been born, for whom I have done, and will do, all that a father with good intentions can do. The act which acknowledged them in full Parliament has not named you as their mother, because your bonds prevented it, but these respectful children know that they owe you their existence, and not one of them shall forget it while I live.

"You have charmed by your wit and the liveliness of your character the busiest years of my life and reign. That pleasant memory will never leave me, and separated though we be, as good sense and propriety of every kind demands, we shall still belong to each other in thought. Athénaïs will always be to me the mother of my dear children. I have been mindful up to this day to increase at different moments the amount of your fortune: I believe it to be considerable, and wish, nevertheless, to add to it even more. If the pension that Vivonne had just suggested to you appear insufficient, two lines from your pen will notify me that I must increase it.

"Your children being proclaimed princes of France, the court will be their customary residence, but you will see them frequently, and can count on my commands. Here they are coming—not to say good-bye to you, but, as of old, to embrace you on the eve of a journey.

"If you are prudent, you will write first to the Marquis de Montespan, not to annul and revoke the judicial and legal separation which exists, but to inform him of your return to reasonable ideas, and of your resolve to be reconciled with the public."

With these words the King ceased speaking. I looked at him with a fixed gaze; a long sigh escaped from my heaving breast, and I had with him, as nearly as I can remember, the following conversation:

"I admire the *sang-froid* with which a prince who believes himself, and is believed by the whole universe, to be magnanimous, gives the word of dismissal to the tender friend of his youth—to that friend who, by a misfortune which is too well known, knew how to leave all and love him alone.

"From the day when the friendship which had united us cooled and was dissipated, you have resumed with regard to me that distance which your rank authorizes you, and on my side, I have submitted to see in you only my King. This revolution has taken effect without any shock, or noise, or scandal. It has continued for two years already; why should it not continue in the same manner until the moment when my last two children no longer require my eyes, and presence, and care? What sudden cause, what urgent motive, can determine you to exclude me? Does not, then, the humiliation which I have suffered for two years any longer satisfy your aversion?"

"What!" cried the prince, in consternation, "is your resolution no longer the same? Do you go back upon what you promised to your brother?"

"I do not change my resolution," I resumed at once; "the places which you inhabit have neither charm nor attraction for my heart, which has always detested treachery and falseness. I consent to withdraw myself from your person, but on condition that the odious intriguer who has supplanted me shall follow the unhappy benefactress who once opened to her the doors of this palace. I took her from a state of misery, and she plunges daggers into my breast."

"The kings of Europe," said the prince, white with agitation and anger, "have not yet laid down the law to me in my palace; you shall not make me submit to yours, madame. The person whom, for far too long, you have been offending and humiliating before my eyes, has ancestors who yield in nothing to your forefathers, and if you have introduced her to this palace, you have introduced here goodness, sweetness, talent, and virtue itself. This enemy, whom you defame in every quarter, and who every day excuses and justifies you, will abide near this throne, which her fathers have defended and which her good counsel now defends. In sending you today from a court where your presence is without motive and pretext, I wished to keep from your knowledge, and in kindness withdraw from your eyes an event likely to irritate you, since everything irritates you. Stay, madame, stay, since great catastrophes appeal to and amuse you; after tomorrow you will be more than ever a supernumerary in this château."

At these words I realized that it was a question of the public triumph of my rival. All my firmness vanished; my heart was, as it were, distorted with the most rapid palpitations. I felt an icy coldness run through my veins, and I fell unconscious upon my carpet.

My woman came to bring me help, and when my senses returned,

I heard the King saying to my intendant: "All this wearies me beyond endurance; she must go this very day."

"Yes, I will go," I cried, seizing a dessert knife which was on my bureau. I rushed forward with a mechanical movement upon my little Comte de Toulouse, whom I snatched from the hands of his father, and I was on the verge of sacrificing this child.

I shudder every time I think of that terrible and desperate scene. But reason had left me; sorrow filled my soul; I was no longer myself. My reader must be penetrated by my misfortune and have compassion on me.

Madame de Maintenon, informed probably of this storm, arrived and suddenly showed herself. To rush forward, snatch away the dagger and my child was but one movement for her. Her tears coursed in abundance; and the King, leaning on the marble of my chimney-piece, shed tears and seemed to feel a sort of suffocation.

My women had removed my children. My intendant alone had remained in the deep embrasure of a shutter; the poor man had affliction and terror painted on his face. Madame de Maintenon had slightly wounded herself in seizing my knife. I saw her tearing her handkerchief, putting on lavender-water in order to moisten the bandage. As she left me she took my hand with an air of kindness, and her tears began again.

The King, seeing her go out, retired without addressing me a word. I might call as much as I would; he did not return.

❧ ☙

ÉMILIE DU CHÂTELET TO DUC
DE RICHELIEU

It is the privilege of friendship to see one's friend in every condition of his soul. I love you sad, gay, lively, oppressed; I wish that my friendship might increase your pleasures, diminish your troubles and share them. There is no need on that account to have real misfortunes or great pleasures. No events are necessary, and I am as much interested in your moods and flirtations as other people are in the good fortune or bad fortune of the people they call their friends. . . .

I do not know whether it is flattering to you to say that you are as agreeable far off as near by; but I know very well that it is thought to be a great merit by a lonely person, who, in renouncing the world, does not wish to renounce friendship, and who would be very sorry if a necessary absence made a breach between her and you.

I discover in your mind all the charms and in your society all the delights which the whole world has agreed to find there; but I am sure that no one has felt more than I have the value of your friendship. Your heart has prepossessed mine. I believed there was none other but myself who knew friendship in a measure so keen, and I was provoked by the proofs I wished to give you of it, sometimes on account of my scruples, at other times from fear, always in defiance of myself.

I could not believe that anyone so amiable, so much sought after, would care to disentangle the sentiments of my heart from all my faults. I believed that I had known you too late to obtain a place in your heart; I believed, also, I confess it, that you were incapable of continuing to love anyone who was not necessary to your pleasures and could not be useful to you—you, unique and incomparable man, understand how to combine everything; delicious friendship, intoxication of love, all is felt by you and spreads the sweetest charm over your fine destiny.

I confess to you that if, after having made me give myself up to your friendship, you should cease—I do NOT say to love me—but to tell me of it; if you should allow such a breach to appear in your friendship, if the remarks or witticisms of people who find me pleasing today and who will perhaps be displeased with me tomorrow, make the least impression on you, I should be inconsolable. I should be most unfortunate if you do not keep your friendship for me, and if you do not continue to give me proofs of it. You would make me repent of the candor with which I speak, and my heart does not wish to know repentance.

Until I write again, dear friend, goodbye. There is no perfect happiness for me in the world until I can unite the pleasure of enjoying our friendship with that of loving him to whom I have devoted my life.

❧ ❦

THE EARL OF CHESTERFIELD

from *On the Fine Art of Becoming a Man of the World and a Gentleman*

Letters to his son

London, January 25, O. S. 1750.

My Dear Friend: It is so long since I have heard from you, that I suppose Rome engrosses every moment of your time; and if it engrosses it in the manner I could wish, I willingly give up my share of it. I would rather *prodesse quam conspici.* Put out your time, but to good interest; and I do not desire to borrow much of it. Your studies, the respectable remains of antiquity, and your evening amusements cannot, and indeed ought not, to leave you much time to write. You will, probably, never see Rome again; and therefore you ought to see it well now; by seeing it well, I do not mean only the buildings, statues, and paintings, though they undoubtedly deserve your attention: but I mean seeing into the constitution and government of it. But these things certainly occur to your own common sense.

How go your pleasures at Rome? Are you in fashion there? that is, do you live with the people who are?—the only way of being so yourself, in time. Are you domestic enough in any considerable house to be called *le petit Stanhope?* Has any woman of fashion and good breeding taken the trouble of abusing and laughing at you amicably to your face? Have you found a good *décrotteuse?* For those are the steps by which you must rise to politeness. I do not presume to ask if you have any attachment, because I believe you will not make me your *confident;* but this I will say, eventually, that if you have one, *il faut bien payer d'attentions et de petits soin,* if you would have your sacrifice propitiously received. Women are not so much taken by beauty as men are, but prefer those men who show them the most attention.

> Would you engage the lovely fair?
>   With gentlest manners treat her;
> With tender looks and graceful air,
>   In softest accents greet her.
>
> Verse were but vain, the Muses fall,
>   Without the Graces' aid;
> The God of Verse could not prevail
>   To stop the flying maid.
>
> Attention by attentions gain,
>   And merit care by cares;
> So shall the nymph reward your pain;
>   And Venus crown your prayers.

A man's address and manner weigh much more with them than his beauty; and, without them, the *Abbati* and *Monsignori* will get the better of you. This address and manner should be exceedingly respectful, but at the same time easy and unembarrassed. Your chit-chat or *entregent* with them neither can, nor ought to be very solid; but you should take care to turn and dress up your trifles prettily, and make them every now and then convey indirectly some little piece of flattery. A fan, a riband, or a headdress are great materials for gallant dissertations, to one who has got *le ton léger et aimable de la bonne compagnie.* At all events, a man had better talk too much to women, than too little; they take silence for dullness, unless where they think that the passion they have inspired occasions it; and in that case they adopt the notion, that

> Silence in love betrays more woe
>   Than words, though ne'er so witty;
> The beggar that is dumb, we know,
>   Deserves a double pity.

À propos of this subject: what progress do you make in that language, in which Charles the Fifth said that he would choose to speak to his mistress? Have you got all the tender diminutives, in *etta, ina,* and *ettina,* which, I presume, he alluded to? You already possess, and, I hope, take care not to forget, that language which he reserved for his horse. You are absolutely master, too, of that language in which he said he would converse with men; French. But, in every language, pray attend carefully to the choice of your words, and to the turn of your expression. Indeed, it is a point of very great consequence. To be heard with success, you must be heard with pleasure: words are the dress of thoughts; which should no more be presented in rags, tatters, and dirt, than your person should. By the way, do you mind your person and your dress sufficiently? Do you take great care of your teeth? Pray have them put in order by the best operator at Rome. Are you be-laced, be-powdered, and be-feathered, as other young fellows are, and should be? At your age, *il faut du brillant, et même un peu de fracas, mais point de médiocre; il faut un air vif, aisé et noble. Avec les hommes, un maintien respectueux et en même tems respectable; avec les femmes, un caquet léger, enjoué, et badin, mais toujours fort poli.*

To give you an opportunity of exerting your talents, I send you, here inclosed, a letter of recommendation from Monsieur Villettes to Madame de Simonetti at Milan, a woman of the first fashion and consideration there, and I shall in my next send you another from the same person to Madame Clerici, at the same place. As these two ladies' houses are the resort of all the people of fashion at Milan, those two recommendations will introduce you to them all. Let me know, in due time, if you have received these two letters, that I may have them renewed, in case of accidents.

Adieu, my dear friend! Study hard; divert yourself heartily; distinguish carefully between the pleasures of a man of fashion, and the vices of a scoundrel; pursue the former, and abhor the latter, like a man of sense.

JACQUES CASANOVA

from *The Memoirs*

From my landing in Chiozza up to my arrival in Naples, Fortune had seemed bent upon frowning on me; in Naples it began to show itself less adverse, and on my return to that city it entirely smiled upon me. Naples has always been a fortunate place for me, as the reader of my *Memoirs* will discover. My readers must not forget that in Portici I was on the point of disgracing myself, and there is no remedy against the degradation of the mind, for nothing can restore it to its former standard. It is a case of disheartening atony for which there is no possible cure.

I was not ungrateful to the good Bishop of Martorano, for, if he had unwittingly injured me by summoning me to his diocese, I felt that to his letter for M. Gennaro I was indebted for all the good fortune which had just befallen me. I wrote to him from Rome.

I was wholly engaged in drying my tears as we were driving through the beautiful Street of Toledo, and it was only after we had left Naples that I could find time to examine the countenance of my travelling companions. Next to me I saw a man of from forty to fifty, with a pleasing face and a lively air, but opposite to me two charming faces delighted my eyes. They belonged to two ladies, young and pretty, very well dressed, with a look of candour and modesty. This discovery was most agreeable, but I felt sad and wanted calm and silence. We reached Avessa without one word being exchanged, and, as the *vetturino* stopped there only to water his mules, we did not get out of the coach. From Avessa to Capua my companions conversed almost without interruption, and, wonderful to relate, I did not open my lips once. I was amused by the Neapolitan jargon of the gentleman and by the pretty accent of the ladies, who were evidently Romans. It was a most wonderful feat for me to remain five hours before two charming women without addressing one word to them, without paying them one compliment.

At Capua, where we were to spend the night, we put up at an inn and were shown into a room with two beds—a very usual thing in Italy. The Neapolitan, addressing himself to me, said, "Am I to have the honour of sleeping with the reverend gentleman?"

I answered in a very serious tone that it was for him to choose or to arrange it otherwise if he liked. The answer made the two ladies smile, particularly the one whom I preferred, and it seemed to me a good omen.

We were five at supper, for it is usual for the *vetturino* to supply his travellers with their meals unless some private agreement is made otherwise and to sit down at table with them. In the desultory talk which went on during the supper I found in my travelling companions decorum, propriety, wit and the manners of persons accustomed to good society. I became curious to know who they were, and, going down with the driver after supper, I asked him.

"The gentleman," he told me, "is an advocate, and one of the ladies is his wife, but I do not know which of the two."

I went back to our room and was polite enough to go to bed first, in order to make it easier for the ladies to undress with freedom; I likewise got up the first in the morning, left the room and returned only when I was called for breakfast. The coffee was delicious. I praised it highly, and the lady, the one who was my favourite, promised that I should have the same every morning during our journey. The barber came in after breakfast; the advocate was shaved, and the barber offered me his services, which I declined, but the rogue declared that it was slovenly to let one's beard grow.

When we had resumed our seats in the coach, the advocate made some remark upon the impudence of barbers in general.

"But we ought to decide first," said the lady, "whether or no it is slovenly to go bearded."

"Of course it is," said the advocate. "A beard is nothing but a dirty excrescence."

"You may think so," I answered, "but everybody does not share your opinion. Do we consider a dirty excrescence the hair of which we take so much care and which is of the same nature as the beard? Far from it; we admire the length and the beauty of the hair."

"Then," remarked the lady, "the barber is a fool."

"But after all," I asked, "have I any beard?"

"I thought you had," she answered.

"In that case I will begin to shave as soon as I reach Rome, for this is the first time that I have been reproached for having a beard."

"My dear wife," exclaimed the advocate, "you should have held your tongue; perhaps the reverend abbé is going to Rome with the intention of becoming a Capuchin friar."

The pleasantry made me laugh, but, unwilling that he should have the last word, I answered that he had guessed rightly, that such had been my intention, but that I had entirely altered my mind since I had seen his wife.

"Oh! you are wrong," said the joyous Neapolitan, "for my wife is very fond of Capuchins, and, if you wish to please her, you had better follow your original vocation."

Our conversation continued in the same tone of pleasantry, and the day passed off in an agreeable manner; in the evening we had a very poor supper at Garillan, but we made up for it by cheerfulness and witty conversation. My dawning inclination for the advocate's wife borrowed strength from the affectionate manner she displayed towards me.

The next day she asked me, after we had resumed our journey, whether I intended to make a long stay in Rome before returning to Venice. I answered that, having no acquaintance in Rome, I was afraid my life there would be very dull.

"Strangers are liked in Rome," she said. "I feel certain that you will be pleased with your residence in that city."

"May I hope, madame, that you will allow me to pay you my respects?"

"We shall be honoured by your calling upon us," said the advocate.

My eyes were fixed upon his charming wife. She blushed, but I did not appear to notice it. I kept up the conversation, and the day passed as pleasantly as the previous one. We stopped at Terracina, where they gave us a room with three beds—two single beds and a large one between the two others. It was natural that the two sisters should take the large bed; they did so and undressed while the advocate and I went on talking at the table, with our backs turned to them.

As soon as they had gone to rest, the advocate took the bed on which he found his nightcap, and I the other, which was only about one foot distant from the large bed. I remarked that the lady by whom I was captivated was on the side nearest my couch, and, without much vanity, I could suppose that it was not owing only to chance.

I put the light out and lay down, revolving in my mind a project which I could not abandon and yet durst not execute. In vain did I court sleep. A very faint light enabled me to perceive the bed in which the pretty woman was lying, and my eyes would, in spite of myself, remain open. It would be difficult to guess what I might have done at last (I had already fought a hard battle with myself for more than an hour), when I saw her rise, get out of her bed and go and lay herself down near her husband, who most likely did not wake up and continued to sleep in peace, for I heard nothing.

Vexed, disgusted, I tried to compose myself to sleep and did not wake until daybreak. Seeing the beautiful wandering star in her own bed, I got up, dressed in haste and went out, leaving all my companions fast asleep. I did not return to the inn until the time fixed for our departure, and I found the advocate and the two ladies already in the coach, waiting for me.

The lady complained in a very obliging manner of my not having cared for her coffee; I pleaded as an excuse a desire for an early walk and took care not to honour her even with a look; I feigned to be suffering from the toothache and remained in my corner, dull and silent. At Piperno she managed to whisper to me that my toothache was all sham; I was pleased with the reproach because it heralded an explanation which I craved for, in spite of my vexation.

During the afternoon I continued my policy of the morning. I was morose and silent until we reached Sermonetta, where we were to pass the night. We arrived early, and, the weather being fine, the lady said that she could enjoy a walk, and asked me politely to offer her my arm. I did so, for it would have been rude to refuse; besides, I had had enough of my sulking fit. An explanation could alone bring matters back to their original standing, but I did not know how to force it upon the lady. Her husband followed us at some distance with the sister.

When we were far enough in advance, I ventured to ask her why she had supposed my toothache to have been feigned.

"I am very candid," she said. "It is because the difference in your manner was so marked and because you were so careful to avoid looking at me through the whole day. A toothache would not have prevented you from being polite, and therefore I thought it had been feigned for some purpose. But I am certain that not one of us can possibly have given you any grounds for such a rapid change in your manner."

"Yet something must have caused the change, and you, madame, are only half sincere."

"You are mistaken, sir, I am entirely sincere; and, if I have given you any motive for anger, I am, and must remain, ignorant of it. Be good enough to tell me what I have done."

"Nothing, for I have no right to complain."

"Yes, you have; you have a right, the same that I have myself, the right which good society grants to every one of its members. Speak and show yourself as sincere as I am."

"You are certainly bound not to know, or to pretend not to know, the real cause, but you must acknowledge that my duty is to remain silent."

"Very well; now it is all over; but, if your duty bids you to conceal the cause of your bad humour, it also bids you not to show it. Delicacy sometimes enforces upon a polite gentleman the necessity of concealing certain feelings which might implicate either himself or others; it is a restraint for the mind, I confess, but it has some advantage when its effect is to render more amiable the man who forces himself to accept that restraint."

Her close argument made me blush for shame, and, carrying her beautiful hand to my lips, I confessed myself in the wrong.

"You would see me at your feet," I exclaimed, "in token of my repentance, were I not afraid of injuring you—"

"Do not let us allude to the matter any more," she answered.

And, pleased with my repentance, she gave me a look so expressive of forgiveness that, without being afraid of augmenting my guilt, I took my lips off her hand and raised them to her half-open, smiling mouth.

Intoxicated with rapture, I passed so rapidly from a state of sadness to one of overwhelming cheerfulness that during our supper the advocate enjoyed a thousand jokes upon my toothache, so quickly cured by the simple remedy of a walk.

On the following day we dined at Velletri and slept in Marino, where, although the town was full of troops, we had two small rooms and a good supper.

I could not have been on better terms with my charming Roman; for, although I had received but a rapid proof of her regard, it had been such a true one—such a tender one! In the coach our eyes could not say much; but I was sitting opposite to her, and our feet spoke a very eloquent language.

The advocate had told me that he was going to Rome on some ecclesiastical business and that he intended to reside in the house of his mother-in-law, whom his wife had not seen since her marriage two years before, and her sister hoped to remain in Rome, where she expected to marry a clerk at the Spirito Santo Bank. He gave me their address, with a pressing invitation to call upon them, and I promised to devote all my spare time to them.

We were enjoying our dessert when my beautiful lady-love, admiring my snuff-box, told her husband that she wished she had one like it.

"I will buy you one, dear."

"Then buy mine," I said. "I will let you have it for twenty ounces, and you can give me a note-of-hand payable to bearer in payment. I owe that amount to an Englishman and will give it him to redeem my debt."

"Your snuff-box, my dear abbé, is worth twenty ounces, but I cannot buy it unless you agree to receive payment in cash; I should be delighted to see it in my wife's possession, and she would keep it as a remembrance of you."

His wife, thinking that I would not accept his offer, said that she had no objection to give me the note-of-hand.

"But," exclaimed the advocate, "can you not guess that the Englishman exists only in our friend's imagination? He would never enter an appearance, and we would have the snuff-box for nothing. Do not trust the abbé, my dear, he is a great cheat."

"I had no idea," answered his wife, looking at me, "that the world contained rogues of this species."

I affected a melancholy air and said that I only wished myself rich enough to be often guilty of such cheating.

When a man is in love, very little is enough to throw him into despair and as little to enhance his joy to the utmost. There was but one bed in the room where supper had been served and another in a small closet leading out of the room, but without a door. The ladies chose the closet, and the advocate retired to rest before me. I bade the ladies good night as soon as they had gone to bed; I looked at my dear mistress and, after undressing, went to bed, intending not to sleep through the night. But the reader may imagine my rage when I found, as I got into the bed, that it creaked loud enough to wake the dead. I waited, however, quite motionless, until my companion should be fast asleep, and, as soon as his snoring told me that he was entirely under the influence of Morpheus, I tried to slip out of the bed; but the infernal creaking which took place whenever I moved woke my companion, who felt about with his hand and, finding me near him, went to sleep again. Half an hour after I tried a second time, but with the same result. I had to give it up in despair.

Love is the most cunning of gods; in the midst of obstacles he seems to be in his own element, but, as his very existence depends upon the enjoyment of those who ardently worship him, the shrewd, all-seeing, little blind god contrives to bring success out of the most desperate case.

I had given up all hope for the night and had nearly gone to sleep when suddenly we heard a dreadful noise. Guns are fired in the street, people, screaming and howling, are running up and down the stairs; at last there is a loud knocking at our door. The advocate, frightened out of his slumbers, asks me what it can all mean; I pretend to be very indifferent and beg to be allowed to sleep. But the ladies are trembling with fear and loudly calling for a light. I remain very quiet, the advocate jumps out of bed and runs out of the room to obtain a candle; I rise at once, I followed him to shut the door, but I slam it rather too hard, the double spring of the lock gives way, and the door cannot be reopened without the key.

I approach the ladies in order to calm their anxiety, telling them that the advocate would soon return with a light, and that we should then know the cause of the tumult, but I do not waste my time, and I meet with very little opposition. However, leaning rather too heavily, I break through the bottom of the bedstead, and we suddenly find ourselves all together in a heap on the floor. The advocate comes back and knocks at the door; the sister gets up; I obey the prayers of my charming friend and, feeling my way, reach the door and tell the advocate that I cannot open it and that he must get the key. The two sisters are behind me. I extend my hand, but am abruptly repulsed and judge that I have addressed myself to the wrong quarter; I go to the other side, and there I am better received. But the husband returns, the noise of the key in the lock announces that the door is going to be opened, and we return to our respective beds.

The advocate hurries to the bed of the two frightened ladies, thinking of relieving their anxiety, but, when he sees them buried in their broken-down bedstead, he bursts into a loud laugh. He tells me to come and have a look at them, but I am very modest and decline the invitation. He then tells me that the alarm has been caused by a German detachment attacking suddenly the Spanish troops in the city and that the Spaniards are running away. In a quarter of an hour the noise has ceased, and quiet is entirely re-established. The advocate complimented me upon my coolness, got into bed again and was soon asleep. As for me, I was careful not to close my eyes, and, as soon as I saw daylight, I got up in order to change my shirt.

I returned for breakfast, and, while we were drinking the delicious coffee which Donna Lucrezia had made, as I thought, better than ever,

I remarked that her sister frowned on me. But how little I care for her anger when I saw the cheerful, happy countenance and the approving looks of my adored Lucrezia! I felt a delightful sensation run through the whole of my body.

We reached Rome very early. We had taken breakfast at the Tour, and, the advocate being in a very gay mood, I assumed the same tone, loading him with compliments, and, predicting that a son would be born to him. I compelled his wife to promise it should be so. I did not forget the sister of my charming Lucrezia, and, to make her change her hostile attitude toward me, I addressed to her so many pretty compliments and behaved in such a friendly manner that she was compelled to forgive the fall of the bed. As I took leave of them, I promised to give them a call on the following day.

I was in Rome with a good wardrobe, pretty well supplied with money and jewellery, not wanting in experience and with excellent letters of introduction. I was free, my own master and just reaching the age in which a man can have faith in his own fortune, provided he is not deficient in courage and is blessed with a face likely to attract the sympathy of those he mixes with. I was not handsome, but I had something better than beauty—a striking expression which almost compelled a kind interest in my favour, and I felt myself ready for anything. I knew that Rome is the one city in which a man can begin from the lowest rung and reach the very top of the social ladder. This knowledge increased my courage, and I must confess that a most inveterate feeling of self-esteem, which on account of my inexperience I could not distrust, enhanced wonderfully my confidence in myself.

The man who intends to make his fortune in this ancient capital of the world must be a chameleon susceptible of reflecting all the colours of the atmosphere that surrounds him, a Proteus apt to assume every form, every shape. He must be supple, flexible, insinuating, close, inscrutable, often base, sometimes sincere, sometimes perfidious, always concealing a part of his knowledge, indulging in but one tone of voice, patient, a perfect master of his own countenance, as cold as ice when any other man would be all fire; and, if unfortunately he is not religious at heart—a very common occurrence for a soul possessing the above requisites—he must have religion in his mind, that is to say, on his face, on his lips, in his manners; he must suffer quietly, if he be an honest man, the necessity of knowing himself an arrant hypocrite. The man whose soul would loathe such a life should leave Rome and seek his fortune elsewhere. I do not know whether I am praising or excusing myself, but of all those qualities I possessed but one—namely, flexibility; for the rest, I was only an interesting, heedless young fellow, a pretty good-blooded horse, but not broken—or, rather, badly broken, and that is much worse.

❧ ❧

LAURENCE STERNE

Laurence Sterne to Catherine de Fourmantel

London, 176[0]

MY DEAR KITTY,

I have arrived here safe & sound, except for the Hole in my Heart, which you have made like a dear enchanting Slut as you are. I shall take Lodgings this morning in Picadilly or the Haymarket, & before I seal this letter, will let you know where to direct a Letter to me, which Letter I shall wait for by the return of the Post with great impatience; so write, my dear Love, without fail. I have the greatest honours paid me & most civilities shewn me, that were ever known from the Great; and am engaged all ready to ten Noble Men & Men of fashion to dine. Mr Garrick pays me all & more honour than I could look for. I dined with him today, & he has promised Numbers of great People to carry me to dine with 'em. He has given me an Order for the Liberty of his Boxes, and of every part of his House for the whole Season; & indeed leaves nothing undone that can do me either Service or Credit; he has undertaken the management of the Booksellers, & will procure me a great price—but more of this in my next.

       And now my dear, dear Girl! let me assure you of the truest friendship for you, that ever man bore towards a woman. Where ever I am, my heart is warm towards you, & ever shall be till it is cold for ever. I thank you for the kind proof you gave me of your Love, and of your desire to make my heart easy, in ordering yourself to be denied to you know who;—whilst I am so miserable to be separated from my dear, dear Kitty, it would have stabb'd my soul to have thought such a fellow could have the Liberty of coming near you. I therefore take this proof of your Love & good principles most kindly, & have as much faith & dependence upon you in it, as if I was at your Elbow;—would to God I was at it this moment! but I am sitting solitary & alone in my bed Chamber (ten o'-clock at night, after the Play), & would give a Guinea for a squeeze of your hand. I send my Soul perpetually out to see what you are ado-ing;—wish I could send my Body with it. Adieu, dear & kind Girl! and believe me ever your kind friend & most affte Admirer. I go to the Or-atorio this night.

Adieu! Adieu!

P.S. My service to your Mama.

Laurence Sterne to Lady P(ercy)

Mount Coffee-House, Tuesday, 3 o'clock [1765?]

There is a strange mechanical effect produced in writing a billet-doux within a stonecast of the lady who engrosses the heart and soul of an in-amorato—for this cause (but mostly because I am to dine in this neigh-bourhood) have I, Tristram Shandy, come forth from my lodgings to a coffee-house the nearest I could find to my dear Lady——'s house, and have called for a sheet of gilt paper, to try the truth of this article of my creed. Now for it—

O my dear lady—what a dishclout of a soul hast thou made of me? I think, by the bye, this is a little too familiar an introduction, for so unfamiliar a situation as I stand in with you—where heaven knows, I am kept at a distance—and despair of getting one inch nearer you, with all the steps and windings I can think of to recommend myself to you. Would not any man in his senses run diametrically from you—and as far as his legs would carry him, rather than thus causelessly, foolishly, and foolhardily expose himself afresh—and afresh, where his heart and rea-son tells him he shall be sure to come off loser, if not totally undone? Why would you tell me you would be glad to see me? Does it give you pleasure to make me more unhappy—or does it add to your triumph, that your eyes and lips have turned a man into a fool, whom the rest of the town is courting as a wit? I am a fool—the weakest, the most duc-tile, the most tender fool that every woman tried the weakness of—and the most unsettled in my purposes and resolutions of recovering my right mind. It is but an hour ago, that I kneeled down and swore I never would come near you—and after saying my Lord's Prayer for the sake of the close, *of not being led into temptation*—out I sallied like any Christian hero, ready to take the field against the world, the flesh, and the devil; not doubting but I should finally trample them all down under my feet. And now I am got so near you—within this vile stone's cast of your house— I feel myself drawn into a vortex, that has turned my brain upside down-wards; and though I had purchased a box ticket to carry me to Miss———'s benefit, yet I know very well, that was a single line directed to me to let me know Lady———would be alone at seven, and suffer me to spend the evening with her, she would infallibly see everything veri-fied I have told her. I dine at Mr C———r's in Wigmore-street, in this neighbourhood, where I shall stay till seven, in hopes you purpose to put me to this proof. If I hear nothing by that time, I shall conclude you are better disposed of—and shall take a sorry hack, and sorrily jog on to the play. Curse on the word. I know nothing but sorrow—except this one thing, that I love you (perhaps foolishly, but)

most sincerely,
L. Sterne

Laurence Sterne to Mrs H.

Coxwould, 12 October 1767

Ever since my dear H. wrote me word she was mine, more than ever woman was, I have been racking my memory to inform me where it was that you and I had that affair together. People think that I have had many, some in body, some in mind, but as I told you before, you have had me more than any woman—therefore you must have had me, [Hannah], both in mind, and in body. Now I cannot recollect where it was, nor ex-actly when—it could not be the lady in Bond-street, or Grosvenor-street, or———Square, or Pall Mall. We shall make it out, H., when we meet. I impatiently long for it—'tis no matter. I cannot now stand writing to you today. I will make it up next post—for dinner is upon table, and if I make Lord F———stay, he will not frank this. How do you do? Which parts of *Tristram* do you like best? God bless you.

Yours,
L. Sterne

NINON DE L'ENCLOS TO THE MARQUIS DE SÉVIGNÉ

Shall I tell you what renders love dangerous? It is the sublime idea which one often appears to have about it. But in exact truth, Love, taken as a passion, is only a blind instinct which one must know how to value correctly; an *appetite* which determines you for one object rather than for another, without being able to give any reason for one's preference; considered as a link of friendship, when reason presides over it, it is not a passion, it is no longer love, it is an affectionate esteem, in truth, but peaceful, incapable of leading you out of bounds; when, however, you walk in the traces of our ancient heroes of romance, you go in for the grand sentiments, you will see that this pretended heroism only makes of love a deplorable and often disastrous folly. It is a true fanaticism; but if you strip it of all those virtues of hearsay, it will soon minister to your happiness and to your pleasures. Believe me, that if it were reason or enthusiasm which governed affairs of the heart, love would become either insipid or a delirium. The only way to avoid these two extremes is to follow the path I indicate to you. You have need of being amused and you will only find what you require for that amongst the women I speak of. Your heart needs occupation; they are made to captivate it. . . .

Honesty in love, marquis! How can you think of that! Ah, you are a good man gone wrong. I shall take great care not to show your letter; you would be dishonoured. You could not, you say, take on yourself to employ the manoeuvre which I have counselled you. Your frankness, your grandiose sentiments would have made your fortune in the old days. Then one used to treat love as a matter of honour; but today, when the corruption of the century has changed everything, Love is no more than a play of whim and vanity. . . . How many occasions do you not find where a lover gains as much by dissimulating the excess of his passion, as he would in others, by displaying greater passion than he feels?

EDWARD GIBBON

from *Memoirs of My Life*

I hesitate from the apprehension of ridicule, when I approach the delicate subject of my early love. By this word I do not mean the polite attention, the gallantry without hope or design, which has originated from the spirit of chivalry, and is interwoven with the texture of French manners. I do not confine myself to the grosser appetite which our pride may affect to disdain, because it has been implanted by Nature in the whole animal creation: *Amor omnibus idem.* The discovery of a sixth sense, the first consciousness of manhood, is a very interesting moment of our lives: but it less properly belongs to the memoirs of an individual, than to the natural history of the species. I understand by this passion the union of desire, friendship and tenderness, which is inflamed by a single female, which prefers her to the rest of her sex, and which seeks her possession as the supreme or the sole happiness of our being. I need not blush at recollecting the object of my choice, and though my love was disappointed of success, I am rather proud that I was once capable of feeling such a pure and exalted sentiment. The personal attractions of Mademoiselle Suzanne Curchod were embellished by the virtues and talents of the mind. Her fortune was humble but her family was respectable: her mother, a native of France, had preferred her religion to her country; the profession of her father did not extinguish the moderation and philosophy of his temper, and he lived content with a small salary and laborious duty in the obscure lot of minister of Crassy, in the mountains that separate the Pays de Vaud from the County of Burgundy. In the solitude of a sequestered village he bestowed a liberal and even learned education on his only daughter; she surpassed his hopes by her proficiency in the sciences and languages; and in her short visits to some relations at Lausanne, the wit and beauty and erudition of Mademoiselle Curchod were the theme of universal applause. The report of such a prodigy awakened my curiosity; I saw and loved. I found her learned without pedantry, lively in conversation, pure in sentiment, and elegant in manners; and the first sudden emotion was fortified by the habits and knowledge of a more familiar acquaintance. She permitted me to make her two or three visits at her father's house: I passed some happy days in the mountains of Burgundy; and her parents honourably encouraged a connection which might raise their daughter above want and dependence. In a calm retirement the gay vanity of youth no longer fluttered in her bosom: she listened to the voice of truth and passion; and I might presume to hope that I had made some impression on a virtuous heart.

At Crassy and Lausanne I indulged my dream of felicity; but on my return to England I soon discovered that my father would not hear of this strange alliance, and that without his consent I was myself destitute and helpless. After a painful struggle I yielded to my fate: the remedies of absence and time were at length effectual; and my love subsided in friendship and esteem. The minister of Crassy soon afterwards died; his stipend died with him. His daughter retired to Geneva where, by teaching young ladies, she earned a hard subsistence for herself and her mother; but in her lowest distress she maintained a spotless reputation and a dignified behaviour. The Duchess of Grafton (now Lady Ossory) has often told me that she had nearly engaged Mademoiselle Curchod as a governess, and her declining a life of servitude was most probably blamed by the wisdom of her short-sighted friends. A rich banker of Paris, a citizen of Geneva, had the good fortune and good sense to discover and possess this inestimable treasure; and in the capital of taste and luxury, she resisted the temptations of wealth as she had sustained the hardships of indigence. The genius of her husband has exalted him to the most conspicuous station in Europe; in every change of prosperity and disgrace he has reclined on the bosom of a faithful friend; and Mademoiselle Curchod is now the wife of M. Necker, the Minister and perhaps the legislator of the French Monarchy.

❧❧

BENJAMIN FRANKLIN

from *The Autobiography*

Mrs. Godfrey projected a match for me with a relation's daughter, took opportunities of bringing us often together, till a serious courtship on my part ensued, the girl being in herself very deserving. The old folks encouraged me by continued invitations to supper and by leaving us together, till at length it was time to explain. Mrs. Godfrey managed our little treaty. I let her know that I expected as much money with their daughter as would pay off my remaining debt for the printing house, which I believe was not then above a hundred pounds. She brought me word they had no such sum to spare. I said they might mortgage their house in the Loan Office. The answer to this after some days was that they did not approve the match; that on inquiry of Bradford they had been informed the printing business was not a profitable one, the types would soon be worn out and more wanted; that S. Keimer and D. Harry had failed one after the other, and I should probably soon follow them; and therefore I was forbidden the house, and the daughter shut up. Whether this was a real change of sentiment or only artifice, on a supposition of our being too far engaged in affection to retract and therefore that we should steal a marriage, which would leave them at liberty to give or withhold what they pleased, I know not. But I suspected the motive, resented it, and went no more. Mrs. Godfrey brought me afterwards some more favorable accounts of their disposition and would have drawn me on again, but I declared absolutely my resolution to have nothing more to do with that family. This was resented by the Godfreys, we differed, and they removed, leaving me the whole house, and I resolved to take no more inmates. But this affair having turned my thoughts to marriage, I looked round me and made overtures of acquaintance in other places, but soon found that the business of a printer being generally thought a poor one, I was not to expect money with a wife, unless with such a one as I should not otherwise think agreeable. In the meantime that hard-to-be-governed passion of youth had hurried me frequently into intrigues with low women that fell in my way, which were attended with some expense and great inconvenience, besides a continual risk to my health by a distemper, which of all things I dreaded, though by great good luck I escaped it.

A friendly correspondence as neighbors and old acquaintances had continued between me and Miss Read's family, who all had a regard for me from the time of my first lodging in their house. I was often invited there and consulted in their affairs, wherein I sometimes was of service. I pitied poor Miss Read's unfortunate situation, who was generally dejected, seldom cheerful, and avoided company. I considered my giddiness and inconstancy when in London as in a great degree the cause of her unhappiness, though the mother was good enough to think the fault more her own than mine, as she had prevented our marrying before I went thither and persuaded the match in my absence. Our mutual affection was revived, but there were now great objections to our union. That match was indeed looked upon as invalid, a preceding husband being said to be living in England; but this could not easily be proved because of the distance. And though there was a report of his death, it was not certain. Then, though it should be true, he had left many debts which his successor might be called upon to pay. We ventured, however, over all these difficulties, and I took her to wife, Sept. I, 1730. None of the inconveniences happened that we had apprehended; she proved a good and faithful helpmate, assisted me much by attending the shop; we throve together and ever mutually endeavored to make each other happy. Thus I corrected that great erratum as well as I could.

Benjamin Franklin to Madame Helvetius

Mortified at the barbarous resolution pronounced by you so positively yesterday evening, that you would remain single the rest of your life, as a compliment due to the memory of your husband, I retired to my chamber. Throwing myself upon my bed, I dreamt that I was dead, and was transported to the Elysian Fields.

I was asked whether I wished to see any persons in particular; to which I replied, that I wished to see the philosophers. "There are two who live here at hand in this garden; they are good neighbors, and very friendly towards one another." "Who are they?" "Socrates and Helvetius." "I esteem them both highly; but let me see Helvetius first, because I understand a little of French, but not a word of Greek." I was conducted to him; he recieved me with much courtesy, having known me, he said, by character, some time past. He asked me a thousand questions relative to the war, the present state of religion, of liberty, of the government in France. "You do not inquire, then," said I, "after your dear friend, Madame Helvetius; yet she loves you exceedingly; I was in her company not more than an hour ago." "Ah," said he, "you make me recur to my past happiness, which ought to be forgotten in order to be happy here. For many years I could think of nothing but her, though at length I am consoled. I have taken another wife, the most like her that I could find; she is not indeed altogether so handsome, but she has a great fund of wit and good sense; and her whole study is to please me. She is at this moment gone to fetch the best nectar and ambrosia to regale me; stay here awhile and you will see her." "I perceive," said I, "that your former friend is more faithful to you than you are to her; she has had several good offers, but refused them all. I will confess to you that I loved her extremely; but she was cruel to me, and rejected me peremptorily for your sake." "I pity you sincerely," said he, "for she is an excellent woman, handsome and amiable. But do not the Abbé de la Roche and the Abbé Morelett visit her?" "Certainly they do; not one of your friends has dropped her acquaintance." "If you had gained the Abbé Morelett with a bribe of good coffee and cream, perhaps you would have succeeded; for he is as deep a reasoner as Duns Scotus or St. Thomas; he arranges and methodizes his arguments in such a manner that they are almost irresistible. Or, if by a fine edition of some old classic, you had gained the Abbé de la Roche to speak *against* you, that would have been still better; as I always observed, that when he recommended anything to her, she had a great inclination to do directly the contrary." As he finished these words the new Madame Helvetius entered with the nectar, and I recognized her immediately as my former American friend, Mrs. Franklin! I reclaimed her, but she answered me coldly: "I was a good wife to you for forty-nine years and four months, nearly half a century; let that content you. I have formed a new connection here, which will last to eternity."

Indignant at this refusal of my Eurydice, I immediately resolved to quit those ungrateful shades, and return to this good world again, to behold the sun and you! Here I am: let us *avenge ourselves!*

❦ ❧

WOLFGANG AMADEUS MOZART TO HIS WIFE

8th April, 1789, Budweis.

DEAREST LITTLE WIFE!

While the Prince is engaged in bargaining for horses, I joyfully seize the occasion to write you a few lines, little wife of my heart! How goes it with you? Do you think of me as often as I do of you? Every moment I look at your portrait and weep, half for joy, half for sorrow! Look after your precious health, which means so much to me, my dear, and farewell!—Do not be anxious on my account, for I am suffering no hardships or inconveniences on this journey, save that of *thy* absence, which, since it can't be cured must be endured. I write with eyes full of tears. *Adjeu.* I will write you a longer and more legible letter from Prague when I shall not be in such haste. *Adjeu.* I kiss you a million times most tenderly, and am ever thine, true till death,

stu—stu—Mozart.

Kiss Karl for me, and all kind remembrances to Herr and Frau von Puchberg. More very soon.

> Dresden, 13th April,I 1789
> 7 o'clock in the morning.

DEAREST, BEST LITTLE WIFE!

We expected to reach Dresden after dinner on Saturday, but did not arrive till six o'clock on Sunday evening, as the roads are so bad. Yesterday I went to the Neumanns', where Madame Duschek is staying, to deliver her husband's letter. They live on the third story overlooking the road so that they can see from their room who is coming. When I reached the door Herr Neumann was there before me, and asked me with whom he had the honour to be speaking. "I will tell you at once who I am," I replied, "only pray be so good as to have Madame Duschek summoned so that my joke may not be spoiled." But at the same moment Madame Duschek stood before me, for she had recognised me from the window, and had said at once: "There comes someone who looks like Mozart!" They were all delighted. The company was large and consisted entirely of ugly women, but they make up for lack of beauty here by virtue. Today the Prince and I go out to breakfast, then to see Neumann, then to the chapel. Tomorrow or the day after we shall leave here for Leipzig. After receiving this letter you must write to Berlin, *poste restante.* I hope you got my letter from Prague safely. The Neumanns and Duscheks send their kind regards to you and also to Herr and Frau Lang.

Dearest little wife, if only I had a letter from you! If I were to tell you all the things I do with your dear portrait you would often laugh, I think! For instance, when I take it out of its case, I say, "Good morrow, Stanzerl! Good day, little rogue!—pussy-wussy! saucy one!—good-for-nothing!—dainty morsel!" And when I put it back I slip it in little by little saying all the time, *"Nu—nu—nu—nu!"* with just the peculiar emphasis this very meaningful word demands, and then, just at the last, quickly, "Good night, little pet—sleep sound!" Well, I suppose that what I have written is folly (to the world, at least) but to us, loving each other as devotedly as we do, it is *not* folly. Today is the sixth since I left you, and, by God, it seems a year! I expect you will often find it hard to read my letters, as I write in haste, and therefore rather badly. *Adieu,* my dear, my only love.

❧❧

JAMES BOSWELL

from *Life of Samuel Johnson*

BOSWELL. "Pray, Sir, do you not suppose that there are fifty women in the world, with any one of whom a man may be as happy, as with any one woman in particular?" JOHNSON. "Ay, Sir, fifty thousand." BOSWELL. "Then, Sir, you are not of opinion with some who imagine that certain men and certain women are made for each other; and that they cannot be happy if they miss their counterparts?" JOHNSON. "To be sure not, Sir. I believe marriages would in general be as happy, and often more so, if they were all made by the Lord Chancellor, upon a due consideration of characters and circumstances, without the parties having any choice in the matter."

❧❧

LORD NELSON TO LADY HAMILTON

I am so agitated that I can write nothing. I knew it would be so, and you can't help it. Why did you not tell Sir William? Your character will be gone. Good God! he will be next you, and telling you soft things. If he does, tell it out at table, and turn him out of the house. Do not sit long. If you sing a song, I know you cannot help it, do not let him set next you, but at dinner he will hob glasses with you. I cannot write to Sir William, but he ought to go to the Prince and not suffer your character to be ruined by him. O, God, that I was dead! But I do not, my dearest Emma, blame you, nor do I fear your inconstancy. I tremble, and God knows how I write. Can nothing be thought of? I am gone almost mad, but you cannot help it. It will be in all the newspapers with hints. Recollect what the villain said to Mr Nisbet, *how you hit his fancy.* I am mad, almost dead, but ever forever yours to the last moment, your, only your, &c.

I could not write another line if I was to be made King. If I was in town nothing should make me dine with you that damned day, but, my dear Emma, I do not blame you, only remember your poor miserable friend, that you must be singing and appear gay. I shall that day have no one to dinner; it shall be a fast day to me. He will put his foot near you.

I pity you from my soul, as I feel confident you wish him in hell. Have plenty of people and do not say a word you can help to him. He wishes, I dare say, to have you alone. Don't let him touch, nor yet sit next you; if he comes, get up. God strike him blind if he looks at you—this is high treason, and you may get me hanged by revealing it. Oh, God! that I were. I have read your letter, your resolution never to go where the fellow is, but you must have him at home. Oh, God! but you cannot, I suppose, help it, and you cannot turn him out of your own house. He will stay and sup and sit up till 4 in the morning, and the fewer that stay the better. Oh, God! why do I live? But I do not blame you; it is my misfortune. I feel nobody uses me ill. I am only fit to be second, or third, or 4, or to black shoes. I want no better part than I have. I see your determination to be on your guard, and am as fixed as fate. If you'll believe me, don't scold me; I am more dead than alive, to the last breath yours. If you cannot get rid of this I hope you will tell Sir William never to bring the fellow again.

I send a note for Mrs T.

❦ ❧

SIR WILLIAM HAMILTON TO LADY HAMILTON

I have passed the last 40 years of my life in the hurry & bustle that must necessarily be attendant on a public character. I am arrived at the age when some repose is really necessary, & I promised myself a quiet home, & altho' I was sensible, & said so when I married, that I should be superannuated when my wife would be in her full beauty and vigour of youth. That time is arrived, and we must make the best of it for the comfort of both parties. Unfortunately our tastes as to the manner of living are very different. I by no means wish to live in solitary retreat, but to have seldom less than 12 or 14 at table, & those varying continually, is coming back to what was become so irksome to me in Italy during the latter years of my residence in that country. I have no connections out of my own family. I have no complaint to make, but I feel that the whole attention of my wife is given to Lord Nelson and his interest at Merton. I well know the purity of Lord Nelson's friendship for Emma and me, and I know how very uncomfortable it would make his Lordship, our best friend, if a separation should take place, & am therefore determined to do all in my power to prevent such an extremity, which would be *essentially detrimental* to all parties, but would be more sensibly felt by our dear friend than by us. Provided that our expences in housekeeping do not increase beyond measure (of which I must own I see some danger), I am willing to go on upon our present footing; but as I cannot expect to live many years, every moment to me is precious, & I hope I may be allow'd sometimes to be my own master, & pass my time according to my own inclination, either by going my fishing parties on the Thames or by going to London to attend the museum, Royal Society, the Tuesday club, & auctions of pictures. I mean to have a light chariot or post chaise by the month, that I may make use of it in London and run backwards and forwards to Merton or to Shepperton, &c. This is my plan, & we might go on very well, but I am fully determined not to have more of the very silly altercations that happen between us but too often and embitter the present moments exceedingly. If really one cannot live comfortably together, a wise and well concerted separation is preferable; but I think, considering the probability of my not troubling any party long in this world, the best for us all would be to bear those ills we have rather than fly to those we know not of. I have fairly stated what I have on my mind. There is not time for nonsense or trifling. I know and admire your talents & many excellent qualities, but I am not blind to your defects, & confess having many myself; therefore let us bear and forbear for God's sake.

❦ ❦

NAPOLEON BONAPARTE TO JOSEPHINE BONAPARTE

Nice, 10 Germinal, year IV [1796]

TO CITIZEN BONAPARTE
CARE OF CITIZEN BEAUHARNAIS
6, RUE CHANTEREINE, PARIS.

I have not spent a day without loving you; I have not spent a night without embracing you; I have not so much as drunk one cup of tea without cursing the pride and ambition which force me to remain apart from the moving spirit of my life. In the midst of my duties, whether I am at the head of my army or inspecting the camps, my beloved Josephine stands alone in my heart, occupies my mind, fills my thoughts. If I am moving away from you with the speed of the Rhône torrent, it is only that I may see you again more quickly. If I rise to work in the middle of the night, it is because this may hasten by a matter of days the arrival of my sweet love. Yet in your letter of the 23rd and 26th Ventôse, you call me *vous. Vous* yourself! Ah! wretch, how could you have written this letter? How cold it is! And then there are those four days between the 23rd and the 26th; what were you doing that you failed to write to your husband? . . . Ah, my love, that *vous,* those four days make me long for my former indifference. Woe to the person responsible! May he, as punishment and penalty, experience what my convictions and the evidence (which is in your friend's favour) would make me experience! Hell has no torments great enough! Nor do the Furies have serpents enough! *Vous! Vous!* Ah! how will things stand in two weeks? . . . My spirit is heavy; my heart is fettered and I am terrified by my fantasies. . . . You love me less; but you will get over the loss. One day you will love me no longer; at least tell me; then I shall know how I have come to deserve this misfortune. . . . Farewell, my wife: the torment, joy, hope and moving spirit of my life; whom I love, whom I fear, who fills me with tender feelings which draw me close to Nature, and with violent impulses as tumultuous as thunder. I ask of you neither eternal love, nor fidelity, but simply . . . *truth,* unlimited honesty. The day when you say "I love you less," will mark the end of my love and the last day of my life. If my heart were base enough to love without being loved in return I would tear it to pieces. Josephine! Josephine! Remember what I have sometimes said to you: Nature has endowed me with a virile and decisive character. It has built yours out of lace and gossamer. Have you ceased to love me? Forgive me, love of my life, my soul is racked by conflicting forces.

My heart, obsessed by you, is full of fears which prostrate me with misery . . . I am distressed not to be calling you by name. I shall wait for you to write it.

Farewell! Ah! if you love me less you can never have loved me. In that case I shall truly be pitiable.

Bonaparte

P.S.—The war this year has changed beyond recognition. I have had meat, bread and fodder distributed; my armed cavalry will soon be on the march. My soldiers are showing inexpressible confidence in me; you alone are a source of chagrin to me; you alone are the joy and torment of my life. I send a kiss to your children, whom you do not mention. By

God! If you did, your letters would be half as long again. Then visitors at ten o'clock in the morning would not have the pleasure of seeing you. Woman!!!

JOHN KEATS TO FANNY BRAWNE

[Wednesday, 13 October 1819]

MY DEAREST GIRL,
This moment I have set myself to copy some verses out fair. I cannot proceed with any degree of content. I must write you a line or two and see if that will assist in dismissing you from my Mind for ever so short a time. Upon my Soul I can think of nothing else. The time is passed when I had power to advise and warn you against the unpromising morning of my Life. My love has made me selfish. I cannot exist without you. I am forgetful of every thing but seeing you again—my Life seems to stop there—I see no further. You have absorb'd me. I have a sensation at the present moment as though I was dissolving—I should be exquisitely miserable without the hope of soon seeing you. I should be afraid to separate myself far from you. My sweet Fanny, will your heart never change? My love, will it? I have no limit now to my love—You[r] note came in just here—I cannot be happier away from you. 'Tis richer than an Argosy of Pearls. Do not threat me even in jest. I have been astonished that Men could die Martyrs for religion—I have shudder'd at it. I shudder no more—I could be martyr'd for my Religion—Love is my religion— I could die for that. I could die for you. My Creed is Love and you are its only tenet. You have ravish'd me away by a Power I cannot resist; and yet I could resist till I saw you; and even since I have seen you I have endeavoured often "to reason against the reasons of my Love." I can do that no more—the pain would be too great. My love is selfish. I cannot breathe without you.

Yours forever
John Keats

SWEETEST FANNY,
You fear, sometimes, I do not love you so much as you wish? My dear Girl I love you ever and ever and without reserve. The more I have known

you the more have I lov'd. In every way—even my jealousies have been agonies of Love, in the hottest fit I ever had I would have died for you. I have vex'd you too much. But for Love! Can I help it? You are always new. The last of your kisses was ever the sweetest; the last smile the brightest; the last movement the gracefullest. When you pass'd my window home yesterday, I was fill'd with as much admiration as if I had then seen you for the first time. You uttered a half complaint once that I only lov'd your Beauty. Have I nothing else then to love in you but that? Do not I see a heart naturally furnish'd with wings imprison itself with me? No ill prospect has been able to turn your thoughts a moment from me. This perhaps should be as much a subject of sorrow as joy—but I will not talk of that. Even if you did not love me I could not help an entire devotion to you: how much more deeply then must I feel for you knowing you love me. My Mind has been the most discontented and restless one that ever was put into a body too small for it. I never felt my Mind repose upon anything with complete and undistracted enjoyment—upon no person but you. When you are in the room my thoughts never fly out of window: you always concentrate my whole senses. The anxiety shown about our Loves in your last note is an immense pleasure to me: however you must not suffer such speculations to molest you any more: nor will I any more believe you can have the least pique against me. Brown is gone out—but here is Mrs. Wylie—when she is gone I shall be awake for you.—Remembrances to your Mother.

Your affectionate
J. Keats

᭝᭝ ᭝᭝

STENDHAL (HENRI BEYLE) TO MADAME
DEMBOWSKI

Varese, the 7th of June 1819

MADAME,
You throw me into despair. You repeatedly accuse me of failing in delicacy—as if, on your lips, this accusation were nothing. Who would have thought, when I parted from you at Milan, that the first letter you wrote to me would begin with "monsieur," or that you would accuse me of failing in delicacy?

Ah, madame, it is easy for a man who has no passion to conduct himself always with moderation and prudence. I, too, when I can hearken to my own counsel, I believe that I am not lacking in discretion. But I am dominated by a fatal passion that leaves me no longer master of my actions. I had sworn to myself to take coach, or at least not to see you, and not to write to you until you returned: a force more powerful than all my resolutions dragged me to the places where you were. I perceive all too well that henceforth this passion is to be the great concern of my life. All interests, all considerations have paled before it. This fatal need I have of seeing you carries me away, dominates me, transports me. There are moments, in the long, solitary evenings, when, if it were necessary to commit a murder that I might see you, I would become a murderer.

In all my life I have had only three passions: ambition, from 1800–1811; love of a woman who deceived me, from 1811 to 1818; and, during the past year, this passion that dominates me and ceaselessly grows. At all seasons and amidst all distractions, anything unrelated to my passion has meant nothing to me: whether happy or unhappy, it has occupied every moment. And do you suppose that the sacrifice I have made to your conventions, of not seeing you this evening, is a little thing? Assuredly, I do not wish to make a merit of it. I present it to you only as an expiation of the wrongs of which I may have been guilty two days [a]go. This expiation means nothing to you, madame: but for me, who have spent so many frightful evenings deprived of you and without seeing you, it is a sacrifice more difficult to endure than the most horrible tortures; it is a sacrifice which, in the extreme pain of the victim, is worthy of the sublime woman to whom it is offered.

In the midst of the confusion of my whole being, into which I am thrown by the imperious necessity of seeing you, there is nevertheless one quality which I have preserved, and which I pray that destiny will continue to preserve for me, unless it seeks to plunge me, in my own esteem, into the underworld of abjection—the quality of perfect truthfulness. You tell me, madame, that I so greatly "compromised" matters on Saturday morning, that in the evening it was necessary for you to act as you did. It is the word "compromised" that wounds me to the bottom of my soul; and, if I had the good fortune to be able to pluck out the fatal affection that pierces my heart, it would be this word "compromised" that gave me the strength to do so.

But no, madame, your soul has too much nobility not to have understood mine. You were offended, and you used the first word that came to the end of your pen. I shall accept as judge, between your accusation and myself, a person whose evidence you will not reject. If Madame Dembowski, if the noble and sublime Métilde, *believes* that my conduct of Saturday morning was the least in the world *calculated* to force her, out of a just care for her reputation in this country, to take some further step, then I confess that this infamous conduct was mine, that there is a being in the world who can say that I fail in delicacy. I shall go further: I have never had any talent for seduction except in respect of women whom I did not love at all. As soon as I am in love I become timid—as you can judge from the manner in which I am always out of countenance in your presence.

If I had not started prattling on Saturday evening, everybody, even including the good padre Rettore, would have perceived that I was in love. But even if I had had a talent for seduction, I would not have employed it upon you. If success depended only upon the making of vows, I would still wish to win you for myself, and not for another being whom I had set up in my place. I would blush, I would have no more happiness, I think, even though you loved me, if I could suspect that you loved a being who was not myself. If you had faults, I could say that I did not see them. I would say, and say in truth, that I adored them: and, indeed, I can say I adore that extreme susceptibility which causes me to spend such horrible nights. It is thus that I would wish to be loved, it is thus that true love is created: it rejects in horror the idea of seduction, as a means unworthy of it, and, together with seduction, it rejects every calculation, every stratagem—including the least thought of "compromising" the beloved object in order to force her to certain further steps to its own advantage.

Had I the talent to seduce you—and I do not believe that such a talent exists—I would not use it. Sooner or later you would perceive that you had been deceived; and to lose you after having possessed you would be still more frightful, I think, than if heaven had condemned me to die without ever having been loved by you.

When a being is dominated by an extreme passion, all that he says or does in a particular situation proves nothing concerning him: what bears witness for him is the entirety of his life. Thus, madame, were I to vow all day long at your feet that I loved you, or that I hated you, this should have no influence upon the degree of credence that you decided to grant me. It is the entirety of my life that should speak. Now, although I am very little known, and still less interesting to the people who know me, yet you might enquire—for lack of another topic of conversation—whether I am known to lack either pride or constancy.

I have now been in Milan for five years. Let us assume that all that is said about my previous life is false. Five years—from the age of thirty-one to the age of thirty-six—are a fairly important interval in a man's life, especially when during these five years he has been tested by difficult circumstances. If ever you deign, madame—for lack of a better occupation—to think about my character, then deign to compare these five years of my life with five years taken from the life of any other individual. You will find lives much more brilliantly talented, lives much more fortunate; but that you will find a life more full of honour and constancy than mine, this I do not believe. How many mistresses had I in Milan, in five years? How many times have I weakened on a point of honour? Well, I would have disgracefully failed in honour if, in my relations with a being who cannot make me draw my sword, I had in the least sought to "compromise" her.

Love me if you will, divine Métilde, but in God's name do not despise me. Such torment is beyond my strength to endure. In your manner of thinking, which is very just, if you despised me it would be impossible for you ever to love me.

With a soul as lofty as yours, what surer way could there be of earning your displeasure than that which you accuse me of having taken? I so much fear to displease you that the moment when I first saw you, on the evening of the 3rd—the moment which should have been the sweetest of my life—was, on the contrary, one of my most wretched, by reason of the fear I had of displeasing you.

❦ ❦

JANE CLAIRMONT TO LORD BYRON

You bid me write short to you and I have much to say. You also bade me believe that it was a fancy which made me cherish an attachment for you. It cannot be a fancy since you have been for the last year the object upon which every solitary moment led me to muse.

I do not expect you to love me, I am not worthy of your love. I feel you are superior, yet much to my surprise, more to my happiness, you betrayed passions I had believed no longer alive in your bosom. Shall I also have to ruefully experience the want of happiness? Shall I reject it when it is offered? I may appear to you imprudent, vicious; my opinions detestable, my theory depraved; but one thing, at least, time shall show you: that I love gently and with affection, that I am incapable of anything approaching to the feeling of revenge or malice; I do assure you, your future will shall be mine, and everything you shall do or say, I shall not question.

Have you then any objection to the following plan? On Thursday Evening we may go out of town together by some stage or mail about the distance of ten or twelve miles. There we shall be free and unknown; we can return early the following morning. I have arranged everything here so that the slightest suspicion may not be excited. Pray do so with your people.

Will you admit me for two moments to settle with you where? Indeed I will not stay an instant after you tell me to go. Only so much may be said and done in a short time by an interview which writing cannot effect. Do what you will, or go where you will, refuse to see me and behave unkindly, I shall never forget you. I shall ever remember the gentleness of your manners and the wild originality of your countenance. Having been once seen, you are not to be forgotten. Perhaps this is the last time I shall ever address you. Once more, then, let me assure you that I am not ungrateful. In all things have you acted most honourably, and I am only provoked that the awkwardness of my manner and something like timidity has hitherto prevented my expressing it to you personally.

Clara Clairmont

Will you admit me now as I wait in Hamilton Place for your answer?

❦ ❦

LORD BYRON TO THE COUNTESS GUICCIOLI

Venice, December 3rd, 1819

You are, and ever will be, my first thought, but at this moment, I am in a state most dreadful, not knowing which way to decide:—on the one hand, fearing that I should compromise you forever, by my return to Ravenna, and the consequences of such a step, and, on the other, dreading that I shall lose both you and myself, and all that I have ever known or tasted of happiness, by never seeing you more, I pray of you, I implore you to be comforted, and to believe that I cannot cease to love you but with my life. . . .

I go to save you, and leave a country insupportable to me without you. Your letters to F. and myself do wrong to my motives—but you will yet see your injustice. It is not enough that I must leave you—from motives of which ere long you will be convinced—it is not enough that I must fly from Italy, with a heart deeply wounded, after having passed all my days in solitude since your departure, sick both in body and mind—but I must also have to endure your reproaches without answering them and without deserving them. Farewell!—In that one word is comprised the death of my happiness.

Venice, December 9th, 1819

F. will already have told you, *with her accustomed sublimity*, that Love has gained the victory. I could not summon up resolution enough to leave the country where you are, without at least once more seeing you. On *yourself,* perhaps, it will depend, whether I ever again shall leave you. Of the rest we shall speak when we meet. You ought, by this time, to know which is most conducive to your welfare, my presence or my absence. For myself, I am a citizen of the world—all countries are alike to me. You have ever been, since our first acquaintance, *the sole object of my thoughts.* My opinion was, that the best course I could adopt, both for your peace and that of all your family, would have been to depart and go far, *far* away from you;—since to have been near and not approach you would have been, for me, impossible. You have, however, decided that I am to return to Ravenna. I shall accordingly return—and shall *do*—and *be* all that you wish. I cannot say more.

❧ ❧

THOMAS MEDWIN

from *Conversations of Lord Byron*

"I have often wished," said I to Lord Byron one day, "to know how you passed your time after your return from Greece in 1812."

"There is little to be said about it," replied he. "Perhaps it would have been better had I never returned! I had become so much attached to the Morea, its climate, and the life I led there, that nothing but my mother's death and my affairs would have brought me home. However, after an absence of three years, behold! I was again in London. My Second Canto of 'Childe Harold' was then just published; and the impersonation of myself, which, in spite of all I could say, the world would discover in that poem, made everyone curious to know me, and to discover the identity. I received everywhere a marked attention, was courted in all societies, made much of by Lady Jersey, had the *entré* at Devonshire-house, was in favour with Brummell, (and that was alone enough to make a man of fashion at that time;) in fact, I was a lion—a ballroom bard—a *hot-pressed* darling! 'The Corsair' put my reputation *au comble*, and had a wonderful success, as you may suppose, by one edition being sold in a day.

"Polidori, who was rather vain, once asked me what there was he could not do as well as I? I think I named four things:—that I could swim four miles—write a book, of which four thousand copies should be sold in a day—drink four bottles of wine—and I forget what the other was, [dupe four women—ed] but it was not worth mentioning. However, as I told you before, my 'Corsair' was sufficient to captivate all the ladies.

"About this period I became what the French call *un homme à bonnes fortunes*, and was engaged in a *liaison*,—and, I might add, a serious one.

"The lady had scarcely any personal attractions to recommend her. Her figure, though genteel, was too thin to be good, and wanted that roundness which elegance and grace would vainly supply. She was, however, young, and of the first connections. *Au reste*, she possessed an infinite vivacity, and an imagination heated by novel-reading, which made her fancy herself a heroine of romance, and led her into all sorts of eccentricities. She was married, but it was a match of *convenance*, and no couple could be more fashionably indifferent to, or independent of one another, than she and her husband. It was at this time that we happened to be thrown much together. She had never been in love—at least where the affections are concerned,—and was made without a heart, as many of the sex are; but her head more than supplied the deficiency.

"I was soon congratulated by my friends on the conquest I had made, and did my utmost to show that I was not insensible to the partiality I could not help perceiving. I made every effort to be in love, expressed as much ardour as I could muster, and kept feeding the flame with a constant supply of *billets-doux* and amatory verses. In short, I was in decent time duly and regularly installed into what the Italians call *service*, and soon became, in every sense of the word, a *patito*.

"It required no Oedipus to see where all this would end. I am easily governed by women, and she gained an ascendancy over me that I could not easily shake off. I submitted to this thraldom long, for I hate *scenes,* and am of an indolent disposition; but I was forced to snap the knot rather rudely at last. Like all lovers, we had several quarrels before we came to a final rupture. One was made up in a very odd way, and without any verbal explanation. She will remember it."

* * *

Calling on Lord Byron one evening after the opera, we happened to talk of *Cavalieri Serventi,* and Italian women; and he contended that much was to be said in excuse for them, and in defence of the system.

"We will put out of the question," said he, "a *Cavalier Serventeism;* that is only another term for prostitution, where the women get all the money they can, and have (as is the case in all such contracts) no love to give in exchange.—I speak of another, and of a different service."

"Do you know how a girl is brought up here?" continued he. "Almost from infancy she is deprived of the endearments of home, and shut up in a convent till she has attained a marriageable or marketable age. The father now looks out for a suitable son-in-law. As a certain portion of his fortune is fixed by law for the dower of his children, his object is to find some needy man of equal rank, or a very rich one, the older the better, who will consent to take his daughter off his hands, under the market price. This, if she happen to be handsome, is not difficult of accomplishment. Objections are seldom made on the part of the young lady to the age, and personal or other defects of the intended, who perhaps visits her once in the parlour as a matter of form or curiosity. She is too happy to get her liberty on any terms, and he her money or her person. There is no love on either side. What happiness is to be expected, or constancy, from such a *liaison?* Is it not natural, that in her intercourse with a world, of which she knows and has seen nothing, and unrestrained mistress of her own time and actions, she should find somebody to like better, and who likes her better, than her husband? The Count Guiccioli, for instance, who is the richest man in Romagna, was sixty when he married Teresa; she sixteen. From the first they had separate apartments, and she always used to call him *Sir.* What could be expected from such a preposterous connection? For some time she was an Angiolina, and he a Marino Faliero, a good old man; but young women, and your Italian ones too, are not satisfied with your good old men. Love is not the same dull, cold, calculating feeling here as in the North. It is the business, the serious occupation of their lives; it is a want, a necessity. Somebody properly defines a woman, 'a creature that loves.' They die of love; particularly the Romans: they begin to love earlier, and feel the passion later than the Northern people. When I was at Venice, two dowagers of sixty made love to me.—But to return to the Guiccioli. The old Count did not object to her availing herself of the privileges of her country; an *Italian* would have reconciled him to the thing: indeed for some time he winked at our intimacy, but at length made an exception against me, as a foreigner, a heretic, an Englishman, and, what was worse than all, a liberal.

"A circumstance took place in Greece that impressed itself lastingly on my memory. I had once thought of founding a tale on it; but the subject is too harrowing for any nerves,—too terrible for any pen! An order was issued at Yanina by its sanguinary Rajah, that any Turkish woman convicted of incontinence with a Christian should be stoned to death! Love is slow at calculating dangers, and defies tyrants and their edicts; and many were the victims to the savage barbarity of this of Ali's. Among others a girl of sixteen, of a beauty such as that country only produces, fell under the vigilant eye of the police. She was suspected, and not without reason, of carrying on a secret intrigue with a Neapolitan of some rank, whose long stay in the city could be attributed to no other cause than this attachment. Her crime (if crime it be to love as they loved) was too fully proved; they were torn from each other's arms, never to meet again: and yet both might have escaped,—she by abjuring her religion, or he by adopting hers. They resolutely refused to become apostates from their faith. Ali Pacha was never known to pardon. She was stoned by those dæmons, although in the fourth month of her pregnancy! He was sent to a town where the plague was raging, and died happy in not having long outlived the object of his affections!

❧ ☙

GEORGE SAND TO ALFRED DE MUSSET

15–17 April, 1834.

. . . Never, never believe, Alfred, that I could be happy if I thought I had lost your heart. Whether I have been mistress or mother to you, what does that matter? Whether I have inspired you by love or by friendship, whether I have been happy or unhappy with you—nothing of this affects the present state of my mind. I know that I love you, that is all. . . . To watch over you, to keep you from all harm, from all friction; to surround you with distractions and pleasures, that is the need which awakens regret in me since I lost you. Why has a task so sweet, a task which I should have undertaken so joyfully, become little by little so bitter, and then suddenly impossible? What fate has intervened to turn my remedies into poisons? How is it that I, who would have given all my vitality to give you a night's repose and peace, have become a torment, a scourge, a spectre to you? When these atrocious memories besiege me (and at what hour do they leave me in peace?), I go nearly mad, I soak my pillow with tears; I hear in the silence of the night your voice calling me. Who will call me now? Who will need me to keep watch? How am I to use up the strength which I had accumulated for you and which now turns against me? Oh, my child, my child! How much I need your tenderness and your forgiveness! Never ask me for mine, and never say you have wronged me: how did I know? I remember nothing except that we have been very unhappy and have parted; but I know, I feel, that all our lives we shall love one another from our heart, from our intelligence, and that we shall by a holy affection try to cure ourselves mutually of the ills that we have each suffered for the other.

Alas, no! we were not to blame; we obeyed our destiny, for our natures, more impulsive than others', prevented us living the life of ordinary lovers; but we were born to know and to love each other, be sure of that. Had it not been for your youth and the weakness which your tears produced in me one morning, we should have remained brother and sister. . . .

You were right, our embraces were an incest, but we knew it not; we threw ourselves innocently and sincerely into each other's arms. Well now, have those embraces left us a single remembrance which is not chaste and holy? On a day of fever and delirium you reproached me with never having made you feel the pleasures of love. I shed tears at that, but now I am well content that there should have been something true in that speech. I am well content that those pleasures have been more austere, more veiled than any you will find elsewhere. At least you, in the arms of other women, will not be reminded of me. But when you are alone, when you feel the need to pray and to shed tears, you will think of your George, of your true comrade, of your sick-nurse, of your friend, of something better than that. For the sentiment which unites us is combined of so many things, that it can compare to none other. The world will never understand it at all; so much the better. We love each other and we can snap our fingers at it.

Good-bye, good-bye, my dearest little one. Write me very often, I beg of you. Oh that I knew you arrived safe and sound in Paris! Remember that you have promised to take care of yourself. Good-bye, my Alfred, love your George. Send me, I beg, twelve pairs of glacé gloves, six yellow and six of colour. Send me, above all, the verses you have made. All, I have not a single one!

❧ ☙

BLACK ELK

High Horse's Courting

You know, in the old days, it was not so very easy to get a girl when you wanted to be married. Sometimes it was hard work for a young man and he had to stand a great deal. Say I am a young man and I have seen a young girl who looks so beautiful to me that I feel all sick when I think about her. I can not just go and tell her about it and then get married if she is willing. I have to be a very sneaky fellow to talk to her at all, and after I have managed to talk to her, that is only the beginning.

Probably for a long time I have been feeling sick about a certain girl because I love her so much, but she will not even look at me, and her parents keep a good watch over her. But I keep feeling worse and worse all the time; so maybe I sneak up to her tepee in the dark and wait until she comes out. Maybe I just wait there all night and don't get any sleep at all and she does not come out. Then I feel sicker than ever about her.

Maybe I hide in the brush by a spring where she sometimes goes to get water, and when she comes by, if nobody is looking, then I jump out and hold her and just make her listen to me. If she likes me too, I can tell that from the way she acts, for she is very bashful and maybe will not say a word or even look at me the first time. So I let her go, and then maybe I sneak around until I can see her father alone, and I tell him how many horses I can give him for his beautiful girl, and by now I am feeling so sick that maybe I would give him all the horses in the world if I had them.

Well, this young man I am telling about was called High Horse, and there was a girl in the village who looked so beautiful to him that he was just sick all over from thinking about her so much and he was getting sicker all the time. The girl was very shy, and her parents thought a great deal of her because they were not young any more and this was the only child they had. So they watched her all day long, and they fixed it so that she would be safe at night too when they were asleep. They thought so much of her that they had made a rawhide bed for her to sleep in, and after they knew that High Horse was sneaking around after her, they took rawhide thongs and tied the girl in bed at night so that nobody could steal her when they were asleep, for they were not sure but that their girl might really want to be stolen.

Well, after High Horse had been sneaking around a good while and hiding and waiting for the girl and getting sicker all the time, he finally caught her alone and made her talk to him. Then he found out that she liked him maybe a little. Of course this did not make him feel well. It made him sicker than ever, but now he felt as brave as a bison bull, and so he went right to her father and said he loved the girl so much that he would give two good horses for her—one of them young and the other one not so very old.

But the old man just waved his hand, meaning for High Horse to go away and quit talking foolishness like that.

High Horse was feeling sicker than ever about it; but there was another young fellow who said he would loan High Horse two ponies and when he got some more horses, why, he could just give them back for the ones he had borrowed.

Then High Horse went back to the old man and said he would give four horses for the girl—two of them young and the other two not hardly old at all. But the old man just waved his hand and would not say anything.

So High Horse sneaked around until he could talk to the girl again, and he asked her to run away with him. He told her he thought he would just fall over and die if she did not. But she said she would not do that; she wanted to be bought like a fine woman. You see she thought a great deal of herself too.

That made High Horse feel so very sick that he could not eat a bite, and he went around with his head hanging down as though he might just fall down and die any time.

Red Deer was another young fellow, and he and High Horse were great comrades, always doing things together. Red Deer saw how High Horse was acting, and he said: "Cousin, what is the matter? Are you sick in the belly? You look as though you were going to die."

Then High Horse told Red Deer how it was, and said he thought he could not stay alive much longer if he could not marry the girl pretty quick.

Red Deer thought awhile about it, and then he said: "Cousin, I have a plan, and if you are man enough to do as I tell you, then everything will be all right. She will not run away with you; her old man will not take four horses; and four horses are all you can get. You must steal her and run away with her. Then afterwhile you can come back and the old man cannot do anything because she will be your woman. Probably she wants you to steal her anyway."

So they planned what High Horse had to do, and he said he loved the girl so much that he was man enough to do anything Red Deer or anybody else could think up.

So this is what they did.

That night late they sneaked up to the girl's tepee and waited until it sounded inside as though the old man and the old woman and the girl were sound asleep. Then High Horse crawled under the tepee with a knife. He had to cut the rawhide thongs first, and then Red Deer, who was pulling up the stakes around that side of the tepee, was going to help drag the girl outside and gag her. After that, High Horse could put her across his pony in front of him and hurry out of there and be happy all the rest of his life.

When High Horse had crawled inside, he felt so nervous that he could hear his heart drumming, and it seemed so loud he felt sure it would 'waken the old folks. But it did not, and afterwhile he began cutting the thongs. Every time he cut one it made a pop and nearly scared him to death. But he was getting along all right and all the thongs were cut down as far as the girl's thighs, when he became so nervous that his knife slipped and stuck the girl. She gave a big, loud yell. Then the old folks jumped up and yelled too. By this time High Horse was outside, and he and Red Deer were running away like antelope. The old man and some other people chased the young men but they got away in the dark and nobody knew who it was.

Well, if you ever wanted a beautiful girl you will know how sick High Horse was now. It was very bad the way he felt, and it looked as though he would starve even if he did not drop over dead sometime.

Red Deer kept thinking about this, and after a few days he went to High Horse and said: "Cousin, take courage! I have another plan, and I am sure, if you are man enough, we can steal her this time." And High

Horse said: "I am man enough to do anything anybody can think up, if I can only get that girl."

So this is what they did.

They went away from the village alone, and Red Deer made High Horse strip naked. Then he painted High Horse solid white all over, and after that he painted black stripes all over the white and put black rings around High Horse's eyes. High Horse looked terrible. He looked so terrible that when Red Deer was through painting and took a good look at what he had done, he said it scared even him a little.

"Now," Red Deer said, "if you get caught again, everybody will be so scared they will think you are a bad spirit and will be afraid to chase you."

So when the night was getting old and everybody was sound asleep, they sneaked back to the girl's tepee. High Horse crawled in with his knife, as before, and Red Deer waited outside, ready to drag the girl out and gag her when High Horse had all the thongs cut.

High Horse crept up by the girl's bed and began cutting at the thongs. But he kept thinking, "If they see me they will shoot me because I look so terrible." The girl was restless and kept squirming around in bed, and when a thong was cut, it popped. So High Horse worked very slowly and carefully.

But he must have made some noise, for suddenly the old woman awoke and said to her old man: "Old Man, wake up! There is somebody in this tepee!" But the old man was sleepy and didn't want to be bothered. He said: "Of course there is somebody in this tepee. Go to sleep and don't bother me." Then he snored some more.

But High Horse was so scared by now that he lay very still and as flat to the ground as he could. Now, you see, he had not been sleeping very well for a long time because he was so sick about the girl. And while he was lying there waiting for the old woman to snore, he just forgot everything, even how beautiful the girl was. Red Deer who was lying outside ready to do his part, wondered and wondered what had happened in there, but he did not dare call out to High Horse.

Afterwhile the day began to break and Red Deer had to leave with the two ponies he had staked there for his comrade and girl, or somebody would see him.

So he left.

Now when it was getting light in the tepee, the girl awoke and the first thing she saw was a terrible animal, all white with black stripes on it, lying asleep beside her bed. So she screamed, and then the old woman screamed and the old man yelled. High Horse jumped up, scared almost to death, and he nearly knocked the tepee down getting out of there.

People were coming running from all over the village with guns and bows and axes, and everybody was yelling.

By now High Horse was running so fast that he hardly touched the ground at all, and he looked so terrible that the people fled from him and let him run. Some braves wanted to shoot at him, but the others said he might be some sacred being and it would bring bad trouble to kill him.

High Horse made for the river that was near, and in among the brush he found a hollow tree and dived into it. Afterwhile some braves came there and he could hear them saying that it was some bad spirit that had come out of the water and gone back in again.

That morning the people were ordered to break camp and move away from there. So they did, while High Horse was hiding in his hollow tree.

Now Red Deer had been watching all this from his own tepee and trying to look as though he were as much surprised and scared as all the others. So when the camp moved, he sneaked back to where he had seen his comrade disappear. When he was down there in the brush, he called, and High Horse answered, because he knew his friend's voice. They washed off the paint from High Horse and sat down on the river bank to talk about their troubles.

High Horse said he never would go back to the village as long as he lived and he did not care what happened to him now. He said he was going to go on the war-path all by himself. Red Deer said: "No, cousin, you are not going on the war-path alone, because I am going with you."

So Red Deer got everything ready, and at night they started out on the war-path all alone. After several days they came to a Crow camp just about sundown, and when it was dark they sneaked up to where the Crow horses were grazing, killed the horse guard, who was not thinking about enemies because he thought all the Lakotas were far away, and drove off about a hundred horses.

They got a big start because all the Crow horses stampeded and it was probably morning before the Crow warriors could catch any horses to ride. Red Deer and High Horse flew with their herd three days and nights before they reached the village of their people. Then they drove the whole herd right into the village and up in front of the girl's tepee. The old man was there, and High Horse called out to him and asked if he thought maybe that would be enough horses for his girl. The old man did not wave him away that time. It was not the horses that he wanted. What he wanted was a son who was a real man and good for something. So High Horse got his girl after all, and I think he deserved her.

As told to John G. Neihardt

❧ ❧

NATHANIEL HAWTHORNE TO SOPHIA HAWTHORNE

Boston, 17 April 1839

MY DEAREST,

I feel pretty secure against intruders, for the bad weather will defend me from foreign invasion; and as to Cousin Haley, he and I had a bitter political dispute last evening, at the close of which he went to bed in high dudgeon, and probably will not speak to me these three days. Thus you perceive that strife and wrangling, as well as east-winds and rain, are the methods of a kind Providence to promote my comfort,—which would not have been so well secured in any other way. Six or seven hours of cheerful solitude! But I will not be alone. I invite your spirit to be with me,—at any hour and as many hours as you please,—but especially at the twilight hour, before I light my lamp. I bid you at that particular time, because I can see visions more vividly in the dusky glow of firelight than either by daylight or lamplight. Come, and let me renew my spell against headache and other direful effects of the east-wind. How I wish I could give you a portion of my insensibility! and yet I should be almost afraid of some radical transformation, were I to produce a change in that respect. If you cannot grow plump and rosy and tough and vigorous without being changed into another nature, then I do think, for this short life, you had better remain just what you are. Yes; but you will be the same to me, because we have met in Eternity, and there our intimacy was formed. So get well as soon as you possibly can, and I shall never doubt that you are the same Sophie who have so often leaned upon my arm and needed its superfluous strength. I never, till now, had a friend who could give me repose; all have disturbed me, and, whether for pleasure or pain, it was still disturbance. But peace overflows from your heart into mine. Then I feel that there is a Now, and that Now must be always calm and happy, and that sorrow and evil are but phantoms that seem to flit across it. . . .

When this week's first letter came, I held it a long time in my hand, marvelling at the superscription. How did you contrive to write it? Several times since I have pored over it, to discover how much of yourself mingled with my share of it; and certainly there is grace flung over the facsimile, which never was seen in my harsh, uncouth autograph, and yet none of the strength is lost. You are wonderful.

What a beautiful day! and I had a double enjoyment of it—for your sake and my own. I have been to walk, this afternoon, to Bunker's Hill and the Navy Yard, and am tired, because I had not your arm to support me.

God keep you from east-winds and every other evil.

> *Your own friend,*
> *N.H.*

Boston, July 24th, 1839—8 o'clock P.M.

MINE OWN,

I am tired this evening, as usual, with my long day's toil; and my head wants its pillow—and my soul yearns for the friend whom God has given it—whose soul He has married to my soul. Oh, my dearest, how that thought thrills me! We *are* married! I felt it long ago; and sometimes, when I was seeking for some fondest word, it has been on my lips to call you—"Wife"! I hardly know what restrained me from speaking it—unless a dread (for *that* would have been an infinite pang to me) of feeling you shrink back from my bosom, and thereby discovering that there was yet a deep place in your soul which did not know me.

Mine own Dove, need I fear it now? Are we not married? God knows we are. Often, while holding you in my arms, I have silently given myself to you, and received you for my portion of human love and happiness, and have prayed Him to consecrate and bless the union. And any one of our innocent embraces—even when our lips did but touch for a moment, and then were withdrawn—dearest, was it not the symbol of a bond between our Souls, infinitely stronger than any external rite could twine around us?

Yes—we are married; and as God Himself has joined us, we may trust never to be separated, neither in Heaven nor on Earth. We will wait patiently and quietly, and He will lead us onward hand in hand (as He has done all along) like little children, and will guide us to our perfect happiness—and will teach us when our union is to be revealed to the world. My beloved, why should we be silent to one another—why should our lips be silent—any longer on this subject? The world might, as yet, misjudge us; and therefore we will not speak to the world; but when I hold you in my arms, why should we not commune together about all our hopes of earthly and external, as well as our faith of inward and eternal union?

Farewell for tonight, my dearest—my soul's bride! Oh, my heart is thirsty for your kisses; they are the dew which should restore its freshness every night, when the hot sunshiny day has parched it. Kiss me in your dreams; and perhaps my heart will feel it.

❦

SOPHIA HAWTHORNE TO NATHANIEL HAWTHORNE

31 December 1839

BEST BELOVED,

I send you some allumettes wherewith to kindle the taper. There are very few but my second finger could no longer perform extra duty. These will serve till the wounded one be healed, however. How beautiful is it to provide even this slightest convenience for you, dearest! I cannot tell you how much I love you, in this back-handed style. My love is not in this attitude,—it rather bends forward to meet you.

What a year has this been to us! My definition of Beauty is, that it is love, and therefore includes both truth and good. But those only who love as we do can feel the significance and force of this.

My ideas will not flow in these crooked strokes. God be with you. I am very well, and have walked far in Danvers this cold morning. I am full of the glory of the day. God bless you this night of the old year. It has proved the year of our nativity. Has not the old earth passed away from us?—are not all things new?

Your Sophie

QUEEN VICTORIA

Journal entries

15 October 1839

At about 1/2 past 12 I sent for Albert; he came to the Closet where I was alone, and after a few minutes I said to him, that I thought he must be aware why I wished [him] to come here, and that it would make me too happy if he would consent to what I wished (to marry me); we embraced each other over and over again, and he was so kind, so affectionate; Oh! to feel I was, and am, loved by such an Angel as Albert was too great delight to describe! he is perfection; perfection in every way—in beauty—in everything! I told him I was quite unworthy of him and kissed his dear hand—he said he would be very happy and was so kind and seemed so happy, that I really felt it was the happiest brightest moment in my life, which made up for all I had suffered and endured. Oh! how I adore and love him, I cannot say!! how I will strive to make him feel as little as possible the great sacrifice he has made; I told him it was a great sacrifice,—which he wouldn't allow . . . I feel the happiest of human beings.

11 February 1840

When day dawned (for we did not sleep much) and I beheld that beautiful angelic face by my side, it was more than I can express! He does look so beautiful in his shirt only, with his beautiful throat seen. We got up at 1/4 past 8. When I had laced I went to dearest Albert's room, and we breakfasted together. He had a black velvet jacket on, without any neck-cloth on, and looked more beautiful than it is possible for me to say. . . . At 12 I walked out with my precious Angel, all alone—so delightful, on the Terrace and new Walk, arm in arm! Eos our only companion. We talked a great deal together. We came home at one, and had luncheon soon after. Poor dear Albert felt sick and uncomfortable, and lay down in my room. . . . He looked so dear, lying there and dozing.

12 February 1840

Already the 2nd day since our marriage; his love and gentleness is beyond everything, and to kiss that dear soft cheek, to press my lips to his, is heavenly bliss. I feel a purer more unearthly feel than I ever did. Oh! was ever woman so blessed as I am.

13 February 1840

My dearest Albert put on my stockings for me. I went in and saw him shave; a great delight for me.

Queen Victoria to King Leopold

11 February 1840

I write to you from here [Windsor] the happiest, happiest Being that ever existed. Really, I do not think it possible for anyone in the world to be happier, or as happy as I am. He is an Angel, and his kindness and affection for me is really touching. To look in those dear eyes, and that dear sunny face, is enough to make me adore him. What I can do to make him happy will be my greatest delight. Independent of my great personal happiness, the reception we both met with yesterday was the most gratifying and enthusiastic I ever experienced; there was no end of the crowds in London, and all along the road. I was a good deal tired last night.

Osborne, 20 December 1861

My *own* dearest, kindest *Father,*—For as such have I *ever* loved you! The poor fatherless baby of eight months is now the utterly broken-hearted and crushed widow of forty-two! My *life* as a *happy* one is *ended!* the world is gone for *me!* If I *must live* on (and I will do nothing to make me worse than I am), it is henceforth for our poor fatherless children—for my unhappy country, which has lost *all* in losing him—and in *only* doing what I know and *feel* he would wish, for he *is* near me—his spirit will guide and inspire me! But oh! to be cut off in the prime of life—to see our pure, happy, quiet, domestic life, which *alone* enabled me to bear my *much* disliked position, CUT OFF at forty-two—when I *had* hoped with such instinctive certainty that God never *would* part us, and would let us grow old together (though *he* always talked of the shortness of life)—is *too awful,* too cruel! And yet it *must* be for *his* good, his happiness! His purity was too great, his aspiration *too high* for this poor, *miserable* world! His great soul is *now only* enjoying *that* for which it *was* worthy! And I will *not* envy him—only pray that *mine* may be perfected by it and fit to be with him eternally, for which blessed moment I earnestly long. Dearest, dearest Uncle, *how* kind of you to come! It will be an unspeakable *comfort*, and you *can do* much to tell people to do what they ought to do. As for my *own good, personal* servants—poor Phipps in particular—nothing can be more devoted, heartbroken as they are, and anxious only to live as *he* wished!

Good Alice has been and is wonderful.

The 26th will suit me perfectly. Ever your devoted, wretched Child,

Victoria R.

꿔ꩢ ꩢꩯ

ROBERT BROWNING TO ELIZABETH BARRETT

Friday, 10 January 1845

I love your verses with all my heart, dear Miss Barrett,—and this is no offhand complimentary letter that I shall write,—whatever else, no prompt matter-of-course recognition of your genius and there a graceful and natural end of the thing: since the day last week when I first read your poems, I quite laugh to remember how I have been turning and turning again in my mind what I should be able to tell you of their effect upon me—for in the first flush of delight I thought I would this once get out of my habit of purely passive enjoyment, when I do really enjoy, and thoroughly justify my admiration—perhaps even, as a loyal fellowcraftsman should, try and find fault and do you some little good to be proud of hereafter!—but nothing comes of it all—so into me has it gone, and part of me has it become, this great living poetry of yours, not a flower of which but took root and grew—oh, how different that is from lying to be dried and pressed flat and prized highly and put in a book with a proper account at top and bottom, and shut up and put away . . . and the book called a 'Flora', besides! After all I need not give up the thought of doing that, too, in time; because even now, talking with whoever is worthy, I can give a reason for my faith in one and another excellence, the fresh strange music, the affluent language, the exquisite pathos and true new brave thought—but in this addressing myself to you, your own self, and for the first time, my feeling rises altogether. I do, as I say, love these books with all my heart—and I love you too: do you know I was once not very far from seeing—really seeing you? Mr Kenyon said to me one morning would you like to see Miss Barrett?—then he went to announce me,—then he returned . . . you were too unwell—and now it is years ago—and I feel as at some untoward passage in my travels—as if I had been close, so close, to some world's-wonder in chapel or crypt, only a screen to push and I might have entered, but there was some slight . . . so it now seems . . . slight and just-sufficient bar to admission, and the half-opened door shut, and I went home my thousands of miles, and the sight was never to be!

Well, these Poems were to be—and this true thankful joy and pride with which I feel myself

Yours ever faithfully,
Robert Browning

I p.m. Saturday [postmark, 12 September 1846]

You will only expect a few words—what will those be? When the heart is full it may run over, but the real fulness stays within.

You asked me yesterday "if I should repent?" Yes—my own Ba,— I could wish all the past were to do over again, that in it I might somewhat more,—never so little more, conform in the outward homage to the inward feeling. What I have professed . . . (for I have performed nothing) seems to fall short of what my first love required even—and when I think of *this* moment's love . . . I could repent, as I say.

Words can never tell you, however,—form them, transform them anyway,—how perfectly dear you are to me—perfectly dear to my heart and soul.

I look back, and in every one point, every word and gesture, *every* letter, every silence—you have been entirely perfect to me—I would not change one word, one look.

My hope and aim are to preserve this love, not to fall from it—for which I trust to God who procured it for me, and doubtlessly can preserve it.

Enough now, my dearest, dearest, own Ba! You have given me the highest, completest proof of love that ever one human being gave another. I am all gratitude—and all pride (under the proper feeling which ascribes pride to the right source) all pride that my life has been so crowned by you.

God bless you prays your very own R.

I will write tomorrow of course. Take every care of *my life* which is in that dearest little hand; try and be composed, my beloved.

Remember to thank Wilson for me.

ELIZABETH BARRETT TO ROBERT BROWNING

> January 15, 1846
> Thursday night

Ever dearest—how you can write touching things to me—& how my whole being vibrates, as a string, to these!—How have I deserved from God and you all that I thank you for? Too unworthy I am of all! Only, it was not, dearest beloved, what you feared, that was "horrible," . . . it was you *supposed*, rather!—It was a mistake of yours. And now we will not talk of it anymore.

> Friday morning

. . . For the rest, I will think as you desire: but I have thought a great deal, & there are certainties which I know; & I hope we *both* are aware that nothing can be more hopeless than our position in some relations & aspects, though you do not guess perhaps that the very approach to the subject is shut up by dangers, & that from the moment of a suspicion entering *one mind*, we should be able to meet never again in this room, nor to have intercourse by letter through the ordinary channel. I mean, that letters of yours, addressed to me here, would infallibly be stopped & destroyed—if not opened. Therefore it is advisable to hurry on nothing— on these grounds it is advisable.

What should I do if I did not see you nor hear from you, without being able to feel that it was for your happiness? What should I do for a month even? And then, I might be thrown out of the window or its equivalent—I look back shuddering to the dreadful scenes in which poor Henrietta was involved who never offended as I have offended . . . years ago which seem as present as today. She had forbidden the subject to be referred to until that consent was obtained—& at a word she gave up all—at a word. In fact she had no true attachment, as I observed to Arabel at the time: a child never submitted more meekly to a revoked holiday. Yet how she was made to suffer—Oh, the dreadful scene!—only because she had seemed to feel a little. I told you, I think, that there was an obliquity . . . an eccentricity—or something beyond . . . on one class of subjects. I hear how her knees were made to ring upon the floor, now!—she was carried out of the room in strong hysterics, & I, who rose up to follow her, though I was quite well at that time & suffered only by sympathy, fell flat down upon my face in a fainting-fit. Arabel thought I was dead.

I have tried to forget it all—but now I must remember—& throughout our intercourse *I have remembered.* It is necessary to remember so much as to avoid such evils as are evitable, & for this reason I would conceal nothing from you. Do *you* remember, besides, that there can be no faltering on my "part," & that, if I should remain well, which is not proved yet, I will do for you what you please & as you please to have it done. But there is time for considering!

Only . . . as you speak of "counsel," I will take courage to tell you that my SISTERS KNOW—. Arabel is in most of my confidences, & being often in the room with me, taxed me with the truth long ago—she saw that I was affected from some cause—& I told her. We are as safe with both of them as possible—& they thoroughly understand that if *there should be any change it would not be* YOUR *fault* . . . I made them understand that thoroughly. From themselves I have received nothing but the most smiling words of kindness & satisfaction—(I thought I might tell you so much,—) they have too much tenderness for me to fail in it now. My brothers, it is quite necessary not to draw into a dangerous responsibility: I have felt that from the beginning, & shall continue to feel it—though I hear, & can observe that they are full of suspicions & conjectures, which are never unkindly expressed. I told you once that we held hands the faster in this house for the weight over our heads. But the absolute *knowledge* would be dangerous for my brothers: with my sisters it is different, & I could not continue to conceal from *them* what they had under their eyes—and then, Henrietta is in a like position—It was not wrong of me to let them know it?—no?—

Yet of what consequence is all this to the other side of the question? What, if *you* should give pain & disappointment where you owe such pure gratitude—But we need not talk of these things now. Only you have more to consider than *I,* I imagine, while the future comes on. . . .

My life was ended when I knew you, & if I survive myself it is for your sake:—*that* resumes all my feelings & intentions in respect to you. No "counsel" could make the difference of a grain of dust in the balance. It *is so,* & not otherwise. If you changed towards me, it would be better for you I believe—& I should be only where I was before. If you do *not* change, I look to you for my first affections & my first duty—& nothing but your bidding me, could make me look away.

Sunday [postmark, 14 September 1846]

My Own Beloved, if ever you should have reason to complain of me in things voluntary and possible, all other women would have a right to tread me underfoot, I should be so vile and utterly unworthy. There is my answer to what you wrote yesterday of wishing to be better to me . . . you! What could be better than lifting me from the ground and carrying me into life and the sunshine? I was yours rather by right than by gift (yet by gift also, my beloved!); for what you have saved and renewed is surely yours. All that I am, I owe you—if I enjoy anything now and henceforth, it is through you. You know this well. Even as *I*, from the beginning, knew that I had no power against you . . . or that, if I *had* it was for your sake.

Dearest, in the emotion and confusion of yesterday morning, there was yet room in me for one thought which was not a feeling—for I thought that, of the many, many women who have stood where I stood, and to the same end, not one of them all perhaps, not one perhaps, since that building was a church, has had reasons strong as mine, for an absolute trust and devotion towards the man she married,—not one! And then I both thought and felt, that it was only just, for them . . . those women who were less happy . . . to have that affectionate sympathy and support and presence of their nearest relations, parent or sister . . . which failed to *me*, . . . needing it less through being happier!

❦ ❧

SARAH MARGARET FULLER, MARCHIONESS D'OSSOLI

Fuller, a nineteenth-century feminist and reformer, was one of the first American women to earn her living as a writer and journalist. In 1847 she met and married the Italian revolutionary, Angelo Ossoli. In the midst of their very passionate marriage, she continued to write reports of the devastating war and revolution in Rome.

from letters and memoirs

Earth, our mother, always finds strange, unexpected ways to draw us back to her bosom,—to make us seek a new a nutriment which has never failed to cause us frequent sickness.

This brings me to the main object of my present letter,—a piece of intelligence about myself, which I had hoped I might be able to communicate in such a way as to give you *pleasure.* That I cannot,—after suffering much in silence with that hope,—is like the rest of my earthly destiny.

The first moment, it may cause you a pang to know that your eldest child might long ago have been addressed by another name than yours, and has a little son a year old.

But, beloved mother, do not feel this long. I do assure you, that it was only great love for you that kept me silent. I have abstained a hundred times, when your sympathy, your counsel, would have been most precious, from a wish not to harass you with anxiety. Even now I would abstain, but it has become necessary, on account of the child, for us to live publicly and permanently together; and we have no hope, in the present state of Italian affairs, that we can do it at any better advantage, for several years, than now.

My husband is a Roman, of a noble but now impoverished house. His mother died when he was an infant; his father is dead since we met, leaving some property, but encumbered with debts, and in the present state of Rome hardly available, except by living there. He has three older brothers, all provided for in the Papal service,—one as Secretary of the Privy Chamber, the other two as members of the Guard Noble. A similar career would have been opened to him, but he embraced liberal principles, and, with the fall of the Republic, has lost all, as well as the favor of his family, who all sided with the Pope. Meanwhile, having been an officer in the Republican service, it was best for him to leave Rome. He has taken what little money he had, and we plan to live in Florence for the winter. If he or I can get the means, we shall come together to the United States, in the summer;—earlier we could not, on account of the child.

He is not in any respect such a person as people in general would expect to find with me. He had no instructor except an old priest, who entirely neglected his education; and of all that is contained in books he is absolutely ignorant, and he has no enthusiasm of character. On the other hand, he has excellent practical sense; has been a judicious observer of all that passed before his eyes; has a nice sense of duty, which, in its unfailing, minute activity, may put most enthusiasts to shame; a very sweet temper, and great native refinement. His love for me has been unswerving and most tender. I have never suffered a pain that he could not relieve. His devotion, when I am ill, is to be compared only with yours. His delicacy in trifles, his sweet domestic graces, remind me of E——. In him I have found a home, and one that interferes with no tie. Amid many ills and cares, we have had much joy together, in the sympathy with natural beauty,—with our child,—with all that is innocent and sweet.

I do not know whether he will always love me so well, for I am the elder, and the difference will become, in a few years, more perceptible than now. But life is so uncertain, and it is so necessary to take good things with their limitations, that I have not thought it worthwhile to calculate too curiously.

However my other friends may feel, I am sure that *you* will love him very much, and that he will love you no less. Could we all live together, on a moderate income, you would find peace with us. Heaven grant, that, on returning, I may gain means to effect this object. He, of course, can do nothing, while we are in the United States, but perhaps I can; and now that my health is better, I shall be able to exert myself, if sure that my child is watched by those who love him, and who are good and pure.

What shall I say of my child? All might seem hyperbole, even to my dearest mother. In him I find satisfaction, for the first time, to the deep wants of my heart. Yet, thinking of those other sweet ones fled, I must look upon him as a treasure only lent. He is a fair child, with blue eyes and light hair; very affectionate, graceful, and sportive. He was baptized, in the Roman Catholic Church, by the name of Angelo Eugene Philip, for his father, grandfather, and my brother. He inherits the title of marquis.

Write the name of my child in your Bible, ANGELO OSSOLI, *born September 5, 1848.* God grant he may live to see you, and may prove worthy of your love!

About Ossoli I do not like to say much, as he is an exceedingly delicate person. He is not precisely reserved, but it is not natural to him to talk about the objects of strong affection. I am sure he would not try to describe me to his sister, but would rather she would take her own impression of me; and, as much as possible, I wish to do the same by him. I presume that, too many of my friends, he will benothing, and they will not understand that I should have life in common with him. But I do not think he will care;—he has not the slightest tinge of self-love. He has, throughout our intercourse, been used to my having many such ties. He has no wish to be anything to persons with whom he does not feel spontaneously bound, and when I am occupied, is happy in himself. But some of my friends and my family, who will see him in the details of practical life, cannot fail to prize the purity and simple strength of his character; and, should he continue to love me as he has done, his companionship will be an inestimable blessing to me. I say *if,* because all human affections are frail, and I have experienced too great revulsions in my own, not to know it. Yet I feel great confidence in the permanence of his love. It has been unblemished so far, under many trials; especially as I have been more desponding and unreasonable, in many ways, than I ever was before, and more so, I hope, than I ever shall be again. But at all such times, he never had a thought except to sustain and cheer me. He is capable of the sacred love,—the love passing that of woman. He showed it to his father, to Rome, to me. Now he loves his child in the same way. I think he will be an excellent father, though he could not speculate about it, nor, indeed, about anything.

Our meeting was singular,—fateful, I may say. Very soon he offered me his hand through life, but I never dreamed I should take it. I loved him, and felt very unhappy to leave him; but the connection seemed so every way unfit, I did not hesitate a moment. He, however, thought I should return to him, as I did. I acted upon a strong impulse, and could not analyze at all what passed in my mind. I neither rejoice nor grieve;—for bad or for good, I acted out my character. Had I never connected myself with any one, my path was clear; now it is all hid; but, in that case, my development must have been partial. As to marriage, I think the intercourse of heart and mind may be fully enjoyed without entering into this partnership of daily life. Still, I do not find it burdensome. The friction that I have seen mar so much the domestic happiness of others does not occur with us, or, at least, has not occurred. Then, there is the pleasure of always being at hand to help one another.

Still, the great novelty, the immense gain, to me, is my relation with my child. I thought the mother's heart lived in me before, but it did not;—I knew nothing about it. Yet, before his birth, I dreaded it. I thought I should not survive; but if I did, and my child did, was I not cruel to bring another into this terrible world? I could not, at that time, get any other view. When he was born, that deep melancholy changed at once into rapture; but it did not last long. Then came the prudential motherhood. I grew a coward, a caretaker, not only for the morrow, but, impiously faithless, for twenty or thirty years ahead. It seemed very wicked to have brought the little tender thing into the midst of cares and perplexities we had not feared in the least for ourselves. I imagined everything;—he was to be in danger of every enormity the Croats were then committing upon the infants of Lombardy;—the house would be burned over his head; but, if he escaped, how were we to get money to buy his bibs and primers? Then his father was to be killed in the fighting, and I to die of my cough, &c. &c.

During the siege of Rome, I could not see my little boy. What I endured at that time, in various ways, not many would survive. In the burning sun, I went, every day, to wait, in the crowd, for letters about him. Often they did not come. I saw blood that had streamed on the wall where Ossoli was. I have a piece of a bomb that burst close to him. I sought solace in tending the suffering men; but when I beheld the beautiful fair young men bleeding to death, or mutilated for life, I felt the woe of all the mothers who had nursed each to that full flower, to see them thus cut down. I felt the *consolation*, too,—for those youths died worthily. I was a Mater Dolorosa, and I remembered that she who helped Angelino into the world came from the sign of the Mater Dolorosa. I thought, even if he lives, if he comes into the world at this great troubled time, terrible with perplexed duties, it may be to die thus at twenty years, one of a glorious hecatomb, indeed, but still a sacrifice! It seemed then I was willing he should die.

✳   ✳   ✳

My love for Ossoli is most pure and tender, nor has any one, except my mother or little children, loved me so genuinely as he does. To some, I have been obliged to make myself known; others have loved me with a mixture of fancy and enthusiasm, excited by my talent at embellishing life. But Ossoli loves me from simple affinity;—he loves to be with me, and to serve and soothe me. Life will probably be a severe struggle, but I hope I shall be able to live thorugh all that is before us, and not neglect my child or his father. He has suffered enough since we met;—it has ploughed furrows in his life. He has done all he could, and cannot blame himself. Our outward destiny looks dark, but we must brave it as we can. I trust we shall always feel mutual tenderness, and Ossoli has a simple, childlike piety, that will make it easier for him.

❧ ❧

HARRIET BEECHER STOWE TO CALVIN STOWE

January 1, 1847

MY DEAREST HUSBAND

. . . I was at that date of marriage a very different being from what I am now and stood in relation to my Heavenly Father in a very different attitude. My whole desire was to live in love, absorbing passionate devotion to one person. Our separation was my first trial—but then came a note of comfort in the hope of being a mother. No creature ever so longed to see the face of a little one or had such a heart full of love to bestow. Here came in trial again sickness, pain, perplexity, constant discouragement—wearing wasting days and nights—a cross, deceitful, unprincipled nurse—husband gone . . . When you came back you came only to increasing perplexities.

Ah, how little comfort I had in being a mother—how was all that I proposed met and crossed and my way ever hedged up! . . . In short, God would teach me that I should make no family be my chief good and portion and bitter as the lesson has been I thank Him for it from my very soul. One might naturally infer that from the union of two both morbidly sensitive and acute, yet in many respects exact opposites—one hasty and impulsive—the other sensitive and brooding—one the very personification of exactness and routine and the other to whom everything of the kind was an irksome effort—from all this what should one infer but some painful friction.

But all this would not after all have done so very much had not Providence as if intent to try us throws upon the heaviest external pressure . . . but still where you have failed your faults have been to me those of one beloved—of the man who after all would be the choice of my heart still were I to choose—for were I now free I should again love just as I did and again feel that I could give up all to and for you—and if I do not love never can love again with the blind and unwise love with which I married I love quite as truly tho far more wisely. . . .

In reflecting upon our future union—our marriage—the past obstacles to our happiness—it seems to me that they are of two or three kinds. Ist those from physical causes both in you and in me—such on your part as hypocondriac morbid instability for which the only remedy is physical care and attention to the laws of health—and on my part an excess of sensitiveness and of confusion and want of control of mind and memory. This always increases on my part in proportion as I blamed and found fault with and I hope will decrease with returning health. I hope that we shall both be impressed with a most solemn sense of the importance of a wise and constant attention to the laws of health.

Then in the second place the want of any definite plan of mutual watchfulness, with regard to each other's improvement, of a definite time and place for doing it with a firm determination to improve and be improved by each other—to confess our faults one to another and pray one for another that we may be healed. . . .

Yours with much love
H.

JOHN RUSKIN

John Ruskin to Effie Gray

Folkestone, 30 November 1847

MY BELOVED EFFIE,
I never thought to have felt time pass slowly any more—but—foolish that I am, I cannot help congratulating myself on this being the last day of November—Foolish, I say—for what pleasure soever may be in store for us, we ought not to wish to lose the treasure of time—nor to squander away the heap of gold even though its height should keep us from seeing each other for a little while. But your letter of last night shook all the philosopher out of me. That little undress bit! Ah—my sweet Lady—What naughty thoughts had I. Dare I say?—I was think-ing—thinking, naughty—happy thought, that you would soon have— someone's arms to keep you from being cold! Pray don't be angry with me. How *culd* I help it?—how can I? I'm thinking so just now, even. Oh—my dearest—I am not so "scornful" neither, of all that I hope for—Alas—I know not what I would not give for one glance of your fair eyes—your fair—saucy eyes. You cruel, cruel girl—now that was *just* like you—to poor William at the Ball. I can see you at this moment—*hear* you. "If you wanted to dance with *me*, William! *If!*" You saucy—wicked—witching—malicious—merciless—mischief loving— torturing—martyrizing—unspeakably to be feared and fled—moun-tain nymph that you are—"If!" When you knew that he would have given a year of his life for a touch of your hand. Ah's me—what a world this is, when its best creatures and kindest will do such things. What a sad world. Poor fellow,—How the lights of the ballroom would darken and its floor sink beneath him—Earthquake and eclipse at once, and to be "if'd" at by you, too; Now—I'll take up his injured cause— I'll punish you for that—Effie—sometime—see if I don't—*If* I don't. It deserves—oh—I don't know what it doesn't deserve—nor what I can do.

P.S. Ah—my mysterious girl—I forgot one little bit of the letter— but I can't forget *all*, though "a great many things."

My heart is yours—my thoughts—myself—all but my memory, but that's mine. Now it is cool—as you say—to give me all that pain—

and then tell me—"Never mind, I won't do it again." Heaven forbid! How could you—puss? You are not thinking of saying that you have "been thinking about it—" or "writing to a friend"—and that you won't have me now! Are you?

John Ruskin to Lady Mount-Temple

4 October 1872

MY DEAREST ISOLA,

The good that you may be sure you have done me remember, is in my having known, actually, for one whole day, the *perfect* joy of love. For I think, to be *quite* perfect, it must still have *some* doubt and pain—the pride of war and patience added to the intense actual pleasure. I don't think any *quite* accepted & beloved lover could have the Kingly and Servantly joy together, as I had it in that ferry boat of yours, when she went into it herself, and stood at the stern, and let me stop it in mid-stream and look her full in the face for a long minute, before she said "Now go on"—The beautiful place—the entire peace—nothing but birds & squirrels near—the trust, which I had then in all things being—finally well—yet the noble fear mixed with the enchantment—her remaining still above me, not mine, and yet mine.

And this after ten years of various pain—and thirst. And this with such a creature to love—For you know. Isola, people may think her pretty or not pretty—as their taste may be, but she is a *rare* creature, and that kind of beauty happening to be *exactly* the kind I like,—and my whole life being a worship of beauty,—fancy how it intensifies the whole.

Of course, every lover, good for anything, thinks his mistress perfection—but what a difference between this instinctive, foolish—groundless preference, and my deliberate admiration of R, as I admire a thin figure in a Perugino fresco, saying "it is the loveliest figure I know after my thirty years study of art"—Well—suppose the Perugino—better than Pygmalions statue,—holier—longer sought, *had* left the canvas—come into the garden—walked down to the riverside with me—looked happy—been happy, (—for she *was*—and said she was)—in being with me.

Was'nt it a day, to have got for me?—all your getting.

And clear gain—I am no worse now than I was,—a day or two

more of torment and disappointment are as nothing in the continued darkness of my life. But that day is worth being born and living seventy years of pain for.

And I can still read my Chaucer, and write before-breakfast letters—Mad, or dead, she is still mine, now.

ॐॐ

KWEI-LI TO HER HUSBAND

19th Century China

MY DEAR ONE,
The house on the mountain-top has lost its soul. It is nothing but a palace with empty windows. I go upon the terrace and look over the valley where the sun sinks a golden red ball, casting long purple shadows on the plain. Then I remember that thou art not coming from the city to me, and I say to myself that there can be no dawn that I care to see, and no sunset to gladden my eyes, unless I share it with thee.

But do not think I am unhappy. I do everything the same as if thou wert here, and in everything I say, "Would this please my master?" Meh-ki wished to put thy long chair away, as she said it was too big; but I did not permit it. It must rest where I can look at it and imagine I see thee lying in it, smoking thy water pipe; and the small table is always near by, where thou canst reach out thy hand for thy papers and the drink thou lovest. Meh-ki also brought out the dwarf pine-tree and put it on the terrace, but I remembered thou saidst it looked like an old man who had been beaten in his childhood, and I gave it to her for one of the inner courtyards. She thinks it very beautiful, and so I did once; but I have learned to see with thine eyes, and I know now that a tree made straight and beautiful and tall by the Gods is more to be regarded than one that has been bent and twisted by man.

Such a long letter I am writing thee. I am so glad that thou madest me promise to write thee every seventh day, and to tell thee all that passes within my household and my heart. Thine Honourable Mother says it is not seemly to send communication from mine hand to thine. She says it was a thing unheard of in her girlhood, and that we younger generations have passed the limits of all modesty and womanliness. She wishes me to have the writer or thy brother send thee the news of thine household; but that I will not permit. It must come from me, thy wife. Each one of these strokes will come to thee bearing my message. Thou wilt not tear the covering roughly as thou didst those great official letters; nor wilt thou crush the papers quickly in thy hand, because it is the written word of Kwei-li, who sends with each stroke of her brush a part of her heart.

MY DEAR ONE,

My first letter to thee was full of sadness and longing because thou wert newly gone from me. Now a week has passed, the sadness is still in my heart, but it is buried deep for only me to know. I have my duties which must be done, my daily tasks that only I can do since thine Honourable Mother has handed me the keys of the rice-bin. I realise the great honour she does me, and that at last she trusts me and believes me no child as she did when I first entered her household.

Can I ever forget that day when first I came to my husband's people? I had the one great consolation of a bride, my parents had not sent me away empty-handed. The procession was almost a *li* in length and I watched with a swelling heart the many tens of coolies carrying my household goods. There were the silken coverlets for the beds, and they were folded to show their richness and carried on red lacquered tables of great value. There were the household utensils of many kinds, the vegetable dishes, the baskets, the camphor-wood baskets containing my clothing, tens upon tens of them; and I said within my heart as they passed me by, "Enter my new home before me. Help me to find a loving welcome." Then at the end of the chanting procession I came in my red chair of marriage, so closely covered I could barely breathe. My trembling feet could scarce support me as they helped me from the chair, and my hand shook with fear as I was being led into my new household. She stood bravely before you, that little girl dressed in red and gold, her hair twined with pearls and jade, her arms heavy with bracelets and with rings on each tiny finger, but with all her bravery she was frightened—frightened. She was away from her parents for the first time, away from all who loved her, and she knew if she did not meet with approval in her new home her rice-bowl would be full of bitterness for many moons to come.

After the obeisance to the ancestral tablet and we had fallen upon our knees before thine Honourable Parent, I then saw for the first time the face of my husband. Dost thou remember when first thou raised my veil and looked long into my eyes? I was thinking, "Will he find me beautiful?" and in fear I could look but for a moment, then my eyes fell and I would not raise them to thine again. But in that moment I saw that thou wert tall and beautiful, that thine eyes were truly almond, that thy skin was clear and thy teeth like pearls. I was secretly glad within my heart, because I have known of brides who, when they saw their husbands for the first time, wished to scream in terror, as they were old or ugly. I thought to myself that I could be happy with this tall, strong young man if I found favour in his sight, and I said a little prayer to Kwan-yin. Because she has answered that prayer, each day I place a candle at her feet to show my gratitude.

I think thine Honourable Mother has passed me the keys of the household to take my mind from my loss. She says a heart that is busy cannot mourn, and my days are full of duties. I arise in the morning early, and after seeing that my hair is tidy, I take a cup of tea to the Aged One and make my obeisance; then I place the rice and water in their dishes before the God of the Kitchen, and light a tiny stick of incense for his altar, so that our day may begin auspiciously. After the morning meal I consult with the cook and steward. The vegetables must be regarded carefully and the fish inspected, and I must ask the price that has been paid, because often a hireling is hurried and forgets that a bargain is not made with a breath.

I carry the great keys and feel much pride when I open the door of the storeroom. Why, I do not know, unless it is because of the realisation that I am the head of this large household. If the servants or their children are ill, they come to me instead of to thine Honourable Mother, as in former times. I settle all difficulties, unless they be too rare or heavy for one of my mind and experience.

Then I go with the gardener to the terrace and help him arrange the flowers for the day. I love the stone-flagged terrace, with its low marble balustrade, resting close against the mountain to which it seems to cling.

I always stop a moment and look over the valley, because it was from here I watched thee when thou went to the city in the morning, and here I waited thy return. Because of my love for it and the rope of remembrance with which it binds me, I keep it beautiful with rugs and flowers.

It speaks to me of happiness and brings back memories of summer days spent idling in a quiet so still that we could hear the rustle of the bamboo grasses on the hillside down below; or, still more dear, the evenings passed close by thy side, watching the lingering moon's soft touch which brightened into jade each door and archway as it passed.

I long for thee, I love thee, I am thine.

Thy Wife

MY DEAR ONE,

It will soon be the Feast of the Springtime. Even now the roads are covered with the women coming to the temple carrying their baskets of spirit money and candles to lay before the Buddha.

Spring will soon be truly here; the buds are everywhere. Everything laughs from the sheer joy of laughter. The sun looks down upon the water in the canal and it breaks into a thousand little ripples from pure gladness. I too am happy, and I want to give of my happiness. I have put a great *kang* of tea down by the rest-house on the tow-path, so that they who thirst may drink. Each morning I send Chang-tai, the gate-keeper, down to the man who lives in the little reed hut he has builded by the grave of his father. For three years he will live there, to show to the world his sorrow. I think it very worthy and filial of him, so I send him rice each morning. I have also done another thing to express the joy that is deep within my heart. The old abbot, out of thankfulness that the tall poles were not erected before the monastery gateway, has turned the fields back of the temple into a freeing-place for animals. There one may acquire merit by buying a sheep, a horse, a dog, a bird, or a snake that is to be killed, and turning it loose where it may live and die a natural death, as the Gods intended from the beginning. I have given him a sum of money, large in his eyes but small when compared to my happiness, to aid him in this worthy work. I go over in the morning and look at the poor horses and the dogs, and wonder whose soul is regarding me from out of their tired eyes.

Let me hear that thou art coming, man of mine, and I will gather dewdrops from the cherry-trees and bathe me in their perfume to give me beauty that will hold thee close to me.

I am
Thy Wife

MY DEAR ONE,

Thou askest me if I still care for thee, if the remembrance of thy face has grown less dear with the passing of the days. Dear one, thou knowest we Chinese women are not supposed to know of love, much less to speak of it. We read of it, we know it is the song of all the world, but it comes not to us unless by chance. We go to you as strangers, we have no choice, and if the Gods withhold their greatest gift, the gift of love, then life is grey and wan as the twilight of a hopeless day. Few women have the joy I feel when I look into my loved one's face and know that I am his and he is mine, and that our lives are twined together for all the days to come.

Do I love thee? I cannot tell. I think of thee by day and I dream of thee by night. I never want to hurt thee nor cause thee a moment's sorrow. I would fill my hands with happiness to lay down at thy feet. Thou art my life, my love, my all, and I am thine to hold through all the years.

Translated by Elizabeth Cooper

❧ ❧

CHARLOTTE BRONTË TO CONSTANTINE HEGER

November 18th, 1845

MONSIEUR,

The six months of silence have run their course. It is now the 18th of November; my last letter was dated (I think) the 18th of May. I may therefore write to you without failing in my promise.

The summer and autumn seemed very long to me; truth to tell, it has needed painful efforts on my part to bear hitherto the self-denial which I have imposed on myself. You, Monsieur, you cannot conceive what it means; but suppose for a moment that one of your children was separated from you, 160 leagues away, and that you had to remain six months without writing to him, without receiving news of him, without hearing him spoken of, without knowing aught of his health, then you would understand easily all the harshness of such an obligation.

I tell you frankly that I have tried meanwhile to forget you, for the remembrance of a person whom one thinks never to see again, and whom, nevertheless, one greatly esteems, frets too much the mind; and when one has suffered that kind of anxiety for a year or two, one is ready to do anything to find peace once more. I have done everything; I have sought occupations; I have denied myself absolutely the pleasure of speaking about you—even to Emily; but I have been able to conquer neither my regrets or my impatience. That, indeed, is humiliating—to be unable to control one's own thoughts, to be the slave of a regret, of a memory, the slave of a fixed and dominant idea which lords it over the mind. Why cannot I have just as much friendship for you, as you for me—neither more nor less? Then should I be so tranquil, so free—I could keep silence then for ten years without an effort.

My father is well but his sight is almost gone. He can neither read nor write. Yet the doctors advise waiting a few months more before attempting an operation. The winter will be a long night for him. He rarely complains; I admire his patience. If Providence wills the same calamity for me, may He at last vouchsafe me as much patience with which to bear it! It seems to me, Monsieur, that there is nothing more galling in great physical misfortunes than to be compelled to make all those about us share in our sufferings. The ills of the soul one can hide, but those which attack the body and destroy the faculties cannot be concealed. My father allows me now to read to him and write for him; he shows me, too, more confidence than he has ever shown before, and that is a great consolation.

Monsieur, I have a favour to ask of you: when you reply to this letter, speak to me a little of yourself, not of me; for I know that if you speak of me it will be to scold me, and this time I would see your kindly side. Speak to me therefore of your children. Never was your brow severe when Louise and Claire and Prosper were by your side. Tell me also something of the School, of the pupils, of the Governesses. Are Mesdemoiselles Blanche, Sophie, and Justine still at Brussels? Tell me where you travelled during the holidays—did you go to the Rhine? Did you not visit Cologne or Coblentz? Tell me, in short, my master, what you will, but tell me something. To write to an ex-assistant governess (No! I refuse to remember my employment as assistant governess—I repudiate it)— anyhow, to write to an old pupil cannot be a very interesting occupation for you, I know; but for me it is life.

Your last letter was stay and prop to me—nourishment for half a year. Now I need another and you will give it me; not because you bear me friendship—you cannot have much—but because you are compassionate of soul and you would condemn no one to prolonged suffering to save yourself a few moments' trouble. To forbid me to write to you, to refuse to answer me, would be to tear from me my only joy on earth, to deprive me of my last privilege—a privilege I never shall consent willingly to surrender. Believe me, my master, in writing to me it is a good deed that you will do. So long as I believe you are pleased with me, so long as I have hope of receiving news from you, I can be at rest and not too sad. But when a prolonged and gloomy silence seems to threaten me with the estrangement of my master—when day by day I await a letter, and when day by day disappointment comes to fling me back into over-whelming sorrow, and the sweet delight of seeing your handwriting and reading your counsel escapes me as a vision that is vain, then fever claims me—I lose appetite and sleep—I pine away.

May I write to you again next May: I would rather wait a year, but it is impossible—it is too long.

I must say one word to you in English. I wish I could write to you more cheerful letters, for when I read this over I find it to be somewhat gloomy—but forgive me, my dear master—do not be irritated at my sad-ness—according to the words of the Bible, "Out of the fulness of the heart, the mouth speaketh," and truly I find it difficult to be cheerful so long as I think I shall never see you more. You will perceive by the de-fects in this letter than [sic] I am forgetting the French language—yet I read all the French books I can get, and learn daily a portion by heart—but I have never heard French spoken but once since I left Brussels—and then it sounded like music in my ears—every word was most precious to me because it reminded me of you—I love French for your sake with all my heart and soul.

Farewell, my dear Master—may God protect you with special care and crown you with peculiar blessings.

C.B.

⁕

❧ ❧

GEORGE ELIOT

George Eliot (Mary Ann Evans) to Herbert Spencer

July 1852

I know this letter will make you very angry with me, but wait a little, and don't say anything to me while you are angry. I promise not to sin any more in the same way.

My ill health is caused by the hopeless wretchedness which weighs upon me. I do not say this to pain you, but because it is the simple truth which you must know in order to understand why I am obliged to seek relief.

I want to know if you can assure me that you will not forsake me, that you will always be with me as much as you can and share your thoughts and feelings with me. If you become attached to someone else, then I must die, but until then I could gather courage to work and make life valuable, if only I had you near me. I do not ask you to sacrifice any-thing—I would be very good and cheerful and never annoy you. But I find it impossible to contemplate life under any other conditions. If I had your assurance, I could trust that and live upon it. I have struggled—in-deed I have—to renounce everything and be entirely unselfish, but I find myself utterly unequal to it. Those who have known me best have always said, that if ever I loved anyone thoroughly my whole life must turn upon that feeling, and I find they said truly. You curse the destiny which has made the feeling concentrate itself on you—but if you will only have patience with me you shall not curse it long. You will find that I can be satisfied with very little, if I am delivered from the dread of losing it.

I suppose no woman ever before wrote such a letter as this—but I am not ashamed of it, for I am conscious that in the light of reason and true refinement I am worthy of your respect and tenderness, whatever gross men or vulgar-minded women might think of me.

George Eliot (Mary Ann Evans) to John Cross

The Heights, Witley, Nr. Godalming.
October 16, 1897, Thursday.

Best loved and loving one—the sun it shines so cold, so cold, when there are no eyes to look love on me. I cannot bear to sadden one mo-ment when we are together, but *wenn Du bist nicht da* [when you are not there] I have often a bad time. It *is* a solemn time, dearest. And why should I complain if it is a painful time? What I call my pain is almost a joy seen in the wide array of the world's cruel suffering. Thou seest I am grumbling today—got a chill yesterday and have a headache. All which, as a wise doctor would say, is not of the least consequence, my dear Madam.

Through everything else, dear tender one, there is the blessing of trusting in thy goodness. Thou dost not know anything of verbs in Hiphil and Hophal or the history of metaphysics or the position of Kepler in science, but thou knowest best things of another sort, such as belong to the manly heart—secrets of lovingness and rectitude. O I am flattering. Consider what thou wast a little time ago in pantaloons and black hair.

Triumph over me. After all, I have *not* the second copy of the deed. What I took for it was only Foster's original draft and my copy of it. The article by Sully in the *New Quarterly* is very well done.

I shall think of thee this afternoon getting health at Lawn Tennis, and I shall reckon on having a letter by tomorrow's post.

Why should I compliment myself at the end of my letter and say that I am faithful, loving, more anxious for thy life than mine? I will run no risks of being "inexact"—so I will only say *"varium et mutabile semper"* [ever fickle and changeable] but at this particular moment thy tender

Beatrice.

❦ ❦

CHARLES BAUDELAIRE TO APOLLONIE
SABATIER

Monday, May 9, 1853

Really, Madame, I ask your pardon a thousand times for this stupid, anonymous doggerel which smacks horribly of childishness; but what can I do about it? I am as egoistic as a child or as an invalid. I think of persons I love when I suffer. Usually I think of you in verse and when the verse are finished, I cannot resist the desire to have them read by the person who inspired them.—At the same time, I hide myself like someone who is terribly afraid of appearing ridiculous.—Isn't there something essentially comic in love?—especially for those who are not involved.

But I swear to you that this is really the last time I shall expose myself to ridicule; and if my ardent friendship for you lasts as long as it had lasted before I said a word to you about it, we shall both be old.

However absurd all this may seem to you, remember there is a heart which it would be cruelty to mock and in which your image is always alive.

Once, only once, beloved and gentle lady,
    Upon my arms you leaned your arm of snow,
And on my spirit's background, dim and shady,
    That memory flashes now.

The hour was late, and like a medal gleaming
    The full moon showed her face,
And the night's splendour over Paris streaming
    Filled every silent place.

Along the houses, in the doorways hiding,
    Cats passed with stealthy tread
And listening ear, or followed, slowly gliding,
    Like ghosts of dear ones dead.

Sudden, amid our frank and free relation,
    Born of that limpid light,
From you, rich instrument, whose sole vibration
    Was radiancy and light—

From you, joyous as bugle-call resounding
    Across the woods at morn,
With sharp and faltering accent strangely sounding,
    Escape one note forlorn.

Like some misshapen infant, dark, neglected,
    Its kindred blush to own,
And long have hidden, by no eye detected,
    In some dim cave unknown.

Your clashing note cried clear, poor, prisoned spirit,
    That nothing in the world is sure or fast,
And that man's selfishness, though decked as merit,
    Betrays itself at last.

That hard the lot to be the queen of beauty,
    And all is fruitless, like the treadmill toil
Of some paid dancer, fainting at her duty,
    Still with her vacant smile.

That if one build on hearts, ill shall befall it,
    That all things crack, and love and beauty flee,
Until oblivion flings them in his wallet,
    Spoil of eternity.

Oft have I called to mind that night enchanted,
  The silence and the languor over all,
And that wild confidence, thus harshly chanted,
  At the heart's confessional.

✥ ✥

WALT WHITMAN TO ANNE GILCHRIST

Washington, November 3, 1871

DEAR FRIEND,
I have been waiting quite a long while for time & the right mood to answer your letter in a spirit as serious as its own, & in the same unmiti-
gated trust & affection. But more daily work than ever has fallen upon
me to do the current season, & though I am well & contented, my best
moods seem to shun me. I wished to give to it a day, a sort of Sabbath
or holy day apart to itself, under serene & propitious influences—confident that I could then write you a letter which would do you good, &
me too. But I must at least show, without further delay, that I am not insensible to your love. I too send you my love. And do you feel no disappointment because I now write but briefly. My book is my best letter, my
response, my truest explanation of all. In it I have put my body & spirit.
You understand this better & fuller & clearer than any one else. And I
too fully & clearly understand the loving & womanly letter it has evoked.
Enough that there surely exists between us so beautiful & delicate a relation, accepted by both of us with joy.

Walt Whitman

✥ ✥

EMILY DICKINSON TO "MASTER"

Summer, 1861

MASTER,
If you saw a bullet hit a Bird—and he told you he was'nt shot—you
might weep at his courtesy, but you would certainly doubt his word. One
drop more from the gash that stains your Daisy's bosom. . . . God made

me, Master. I didn't be myself. *I* don't know how it was done. He built
the heart in me. Bye and bye it outgrew me—and like the little mother
with the big child—I got tired holding him. I heard of a thing called
"Redemption"—which rested men and women. You remember I asked
you for it—you gave me something else. I forgot the Redemption . . . (I
did'nt tell you for a long time—but I knew you had altered me) and was
tired. . . . I am older—tonight, Master—but the love is the same—so are
the moon and the crescent. If it had been God's will that I might breathe
where you breathed and find the place—myself—at night—if I never
forget that I am not with you—and that sorrow and frost are nearer than
I—if I wish with a might I cannot repress—that mine were the Queen's
place—the love of the Plantagenet is my only apology— . . .

These things are holy, Sir, I touch them hallowed, but persons
who pray—dare remark "Father!" You say I do not tell you all. Daisy
"confessed—and denied not."

Vesuvius dont talk—Etna—dont— . . . One of them—said a
syllable—a thousand years ago, and Pompeii heard it, and hid forever.
She could'nt look the world in the face, afterward—I suppose—Bashful Pompeii! "Tell you of the want"—you know what a leech is, dont
you—and you have felt the horizon hav'nt you—and did the sea—never
come so close as to make you dance?

I dont know what you can do for it—thank you—Master—but if
I had the Beard on my cheek—like you—and you—had Daisy's petals—
and you cared so for me—what would become of you? Could you forget me in fight, or flight—or the foreign land? . . . I used to think when
I died—I could see you—so I died as fast as I could—but the "corporation" are going too—so Heaven wont be sequestered at all.

Say I may wait for you—

Say I need go with no stranger to the to me—untried country. I
waited a long time—Master—but I can wait more—wait till my hazel
hair is dappled and you carry the cane—then I can look at my watch—
and if the Day is too far declined—we can take the chances for Heaven.

What would you do with me if I came "in white"? Have you the
little chest—to put the alive—in?

I want to see you more—Sir—than all I wish for in this world—
and the wish—altered a little—will be my only one—for the skies.

Could you come to New England this summer? Would you come
to Amherst—Would you like to come—Master?

Would it do harm—yet we both fear God? Would Daisy disappoint you—no—she would'nt—Sir—it were comfort forever—just to

look in your face, while you looked in mine—then I could play in the woods—till Dark—till you take me where sundown cannot find us— and the true keep coming—till the town is full. (Will you tell me if you will?)

I did'nt think to tell you, you did'nt come to me "in white"—nor ever told me why—

No Rose, yet felt myself a'bloom,
No Bird—yet rode in Ether.

❧❧

SULLIVAN BALLOU TO SARAH BALLOU

July 14, 1861
Camp Clark, Washington, D.C.

MY VERY DEAR SARAH,

The indications are very strong that we shall move in a few days, perhaps tomorrow. And lest I should not be able to write you again, I feel impelled to write a few lines that may fall under your eyes when I am no more.

I have no misgivings about or lack of confidence in the cause in which I am engaged and my courage does not halt or falter. I know how American Civilization now leans on the triumph of the Government and how great a debt we owe to those who went before us through the blood and suffering of the Revolution. And I am willing, perfectly willing, to lay down all my joys in this life to help maintain this government and to pay that debt.

Sarah, my love for you is deathless. It seems to bind me with mighty cables that nothing but Omnipotence can break. And yet my love of Country comes over me like a strong wind and bears me irresistibly, with all these chains, to the battlefield.

The memories of all the blissful moments I have enjoyed with you come creeping over me, and I feel most deeply grateful to God and you that I have enjoyed them so long. And hard it is for me to give them up and burn to ashes the hopes of future years when, God willing, we might still have lived and loved together and seen our boys grown up to honorable manhood around us. I have, I know, but few and small claims upon Divine Providence, but something whispers to me—perhaps it is the wafted prayer of my little Edgar, that I shall return to my loved ones unharmed.

If I do not return, my dear Sarah, never forget how much I loved you, nor that when my last breath escapes me on the battlefield, it will whisper your name. Forgive my many faults and the many pains I have caused you. How thoughtless, how foolish I have sometimes been! How gladly would I wash out with my tears every little spot upon our happiness.

But, O Sarah! If the dead can come back to this earth and flit unseen around those they loved, I shall always be near you; in the gladdest days and in the darkest nights . . . *always* always, and if there be a soft breeze upon your cheek, it shall be my breath, as the cool air fans your throbbing temple, it shall be my spirit passing by. Sarah, do not mourn me dead; Think I am gone and wait for thee, for we shall meet again. . . .

❦ ❦

GEORGE SAND TO GUSTAVE FLAUBERT

About Charles Marchal

14 September, 1871, Nohant

And what, you want me to stop loving? You want me to say that I have been mistaken all my life, that humanity is contemptible, hateful, that it has always been and always will be so? And you chide my anguish as a weakness, and puerile regret for a lost illusion? You assert that the people has always been ferocious, the priest always hypocritical, the bourgeois always cowardly, the soldier always brigand, the peasant always stupid? You say that you have known all that ever since your youth and you rejoice that you never have doubted it, because maturity has not brought you any disappointment; have you not been young then? Ah! We are entirely different, for I have never ceased to be young, if being young is always loving.

What, then, do you want me to do, so as to isolate myself from my kind, from my compatriots, from my race, from the great family in whose bosom my own family is only one ear of corn in the terrestrial field? And if only this ear could ripen in a sure place, if only one could, as you say, live for certain privileged persons and withdraw from all the others!

But it is impossible, and your steady reason puts up with the most unrealizable of Utopias. In what Eden, in what fantastic Eldorado will you hide your family, your little group of friends, your intimate happiness, so that the lacerations of the social state and the disasters of the country shall not reach them? If you want to be happy through certain people—those certain people, the favorites of your heart, must be happy in themselves. Can they be? Can you assure them the least security?

Will you find me a refuge in my old age which is drawing near to death? And what difference now does death or life make to me for myself? Let us suppose that we die absolutely, or that love does not follow into the other life, are we not up to our last breath tormented by the desire, by the imperious need of assuring those whom we leave behind all the happiness possible? Can we go peacefully to sleep when we feel the shaken earth ready to swallow up all those for whom we have lived? A continuous happy life with one's family in spite of all, is without doubt relatively a great good, the only consolation that one could and that one would enjoy. But even supposing external evil does not penetrate into our house, which is impossible, you know very well, I could not approve of acquiescing in indifference to what causes public unhappiness.

All that was foreseen. . . . Yes, certainly, I had foreseen it as well as anyone! I saw the storm rising. I was aware, like all those who do not live without thinking, of the evident approach of the cataclysm. When one sees the patient writhing in agony is there any consolation in understanding his illness thoroughly? When lightning strikes, are we calm because we have heard the thunder rumble a long time before?

No, no, people do not isolate themselves, the ties of blood are not broken, people do not curse or scorn their kind. Humanity is not a vain word. Our life is composed of love, and not to love is to cease to live.

❧ ❧

LEWIS CARROLL TO GERTRUDE

Christ Church, Oxford, 28 October 1876

MY DEAREST GERTRUDE:
You will be sorry, and surprised, and puzzled, to hear what a queer illness I have had ever since you went. I sent for the doctor, and said, "Give

me some medicine. for I'm tired." He said, "Nonsense and stuff! You don't want medicine: go to bed!" I said, "No; it isn't the sort of tiredness that wants bed. I'm tired in the *face*." He looked a little grave, and said, "Oh, it's your *nose* that's tired: a person often talks too much when he thinks he nose a great deal." I said, "No, it isn't the nose. Perhaps it's the *hair*." Then he looked rather grave, and said, "*Now* I understand: you've been playing too many hairs on the pianoforte." "No, indeed I haven't!" I said, "and it isn't exactly the *hair:* it's more about the nose and chin." Then he looked a good deal graver, and said, "Have you been walking much on your chin lately?" I said, "No." "Well!" he said, "it puzzles me very much. Do you think that it's in the lips?" "Of course!" I said. "That's exactly what it is!"

Then he looked very grave indeed, and said, "I think you must have been giving too many kisses." "Well," I said, "I did give one kiss to a baby child, a little friend of mine." "Think again," he said; "are you sure it was only one?" I thought again, and said, "Perhaps it was eleven times." Then the doctor said, "You must not give her any more till your lips are quite rested again." "But what am I to do?" I said, "because you see, I owe her a hundred and eighty-two more." Then he looked so grave that the tears ran down his cheeks, and he said, "You may send them to her in a box." Then I remembered a little box that I once bought at Dover, and thought I would some day give it to *some* little girl or other. So I have packed them all in it very carefully. Tell me if they come safe or if any are lost on the way.

❧ ❧

SARAH ORNE JEWETT TO ANNIE FIELDS

Sunday night, November, 1884

I am getting sleepy, for I must confess that it is past bedtime. I went to church this morning, but this afternoon I have been far afield, way over the hill and beyond, to an unusual distance. Alas, when I went to see my beloved big pitch-pine tree that I loved best of all the wild tress that lived in Berwick, I found only the broad stump of it beside the spring, and the top boughs of it scattered far and wide. It was a real affliction, and I thought you would be sorry, too, for such a mournful friend as sat down and counted the rings to see how many years old her tree was, and saw the broad rings when good wet summers had helped it grow and narrow

ones when there had been a drought, and read as much of its long bi-
ography as she could. But the day was very lovely. . . . I found such a good
little yellow apple on one of the pasture trees, and I laughed to think how
you would be looking at the next bite. It was *very* small but I nibbled it
like a squirrel. . . . I was in some underbrush, going along the slope, and
saw a crow come toward me flying low, and when I stood still he did not
see me and came so close that I could hear his wings creak their feathers. . . . I wished for you so much, it was a day you would have loved.

SAMUEL BUTLER

from *The Notebooks*

LOVING AND HATING

I have often said that there is no true love short of eating and consequent
assimilation; the embryonic processes are but a long course of eating and
assimilation—the sperm and germ cells, or the two elements that go to
form the new animal, whatever they should be called, eat one another up,
and then the mother assimilates them, more or less, through mutual
inter-feeding and inter-breeding between her and them. But the curious
point is that the more profound our love is the less we are conscious of
it as love. True, a nurse tells her child that she would like to eat it, but
this is only an expression that shows an instinctive recognition of the fact
that eating is a mode of, or rather the acme of, love—no nurse loves her
child half well enough to want really to eat it; put to such proof as this
the love of which she is so profoundly, as she imagines, sentient proves
to be but skin deep. So with our horses and dogs: we think we dote upon
them, but we do not really love them.

What, on the other hand, can awaken less consciousness of warm
affection than an oyster? Who would press an oyster to his heart, or pat
it and want to kiss it? Yet nothing short of its complete absorption into
our own being can in the least satisfy us. No merely superficial temporary contact of exterior form to exterior form will serve us. The embrace
must be consummate, not achieved by a mocking environment of draped
and muffled arms that leaves no lasting trace on organisation or consciousness, but by an enfolding within the bare and warm bosom of an
open mouth—a grinding out of all differences of opinion by the sweet
persuasion of the jaws, and the eloquence of a tongue that now convinces

all the more powerfully because it is inarticulate and deals but with the one universal language of agglutination. Then we become made one with what we love—not heart to heart, but protoplasm to protoplasm, and this is far more to the purpose.

The proof of love, then, like that of any other pleasant pudding, is in the eating, and tested by this proof we see that consciousness of love, like all other consciousness, vanishes on becoming intense. While we are yet fully aware of it, we do not love as well as we think we do. When we really mean business and are hungry with affection, we do not know that we are in love, but simply go into the love-shop—for so any eating-house should be more fitly called—ask the price, pay our money down, and love till we can either love or pay no longer.

And so with hate. When we really hate a thing it makes us sick, and we use this expression to symbolise the utmost hatred of which our nature is capable; but when we know we hate, our hatred is in reality mild and inoffensive. I, for example, think I hate all those people whose photographs I see in the shop windows, but I am so conscious of this that I am convinced, in reality, nothing would please me better than to be in the shop windows too. So when I see the universities conferring degrees on anyone, or the learned societies moulting the yearly medals as peacocks moult their tails, I am so conscious of disapproval as to feel sure I should like a degree or a medal too if they would only give me one, and hence I conclude that my disapproval is grounded in nothing more serious than a superficial, transient jealousy.

Union and Separation

In the closest union there is still some separate existence of component parts; in the most complete separation there is still a reminiscence of union. When they are most separate, the atoms seem to bear in mind that they may one day have to come together again; when most united, they still remember that they may come to fall out some day and do not give each other their full, unreserved confidence.

The difficulty is how to get unity and separateness at one and the same time. The two main ideas underlying all action are desire for closer unity and desire for more separateness. Nature is the puzzled sense of a vast number of things which feel they are in an illogical position and should be more either of one thing or the other than they are. So they will first be this and then that, and act and re-act and keep the balance as near equal as they can, yet they know all the time that it isn't right and, as they incline one way or the other, they will love or hate.

When we love, we draw what we love closer to us; when we hate a thing, we fling it away from us. All disruption and dissolution is a mode of hating; and all that we call affinity is a mode of loving.

✿❧

OSCAR WILDE TO LORD ALFRED DOUGLAS

Savoy Hotel, London, March 1893

DEAREST OF ALL BOYS,
Your letter was delightful, red and yellow wine to me; but I am sad and out of sorts. Bosie, you must not make scenes with me. They kill me, they wreck the loveliness of life. I cannot see you, so Greek and gracious, distorted with passion. I cannot listen to your curved lips saying hideous things to me. I would sooner be blackmailed by every renter in London than have you bitter, unjust, hating. I must see you soon. You are the divine thing I want, the thing of grace and beauty; but I don't know how to do it. Shall I come to Salisbury? My bill here is £49 for a week. I have also got a new sitting-room over the Thames. Why are you not here, my dear, my wonderful boy? I fear I must leave; no money, no credit, and a heart of lead.

Your own Oscar

Courtfield Gardens, 20 May 1895

MY CHILD,
Today it was asked to have the verdicts rendered separately. Taylor is probably being judged at this moment, so that I have been able to come back here. My sweet rose, my delicate flower, my lily of lilies, it is perhaps in prison that I am going to test the power of love. I am going to see if I cannot make the bitter warders sweet by the intensity of the love I bear you. I have had moments when I thought it would be wiser to separate. Ah! moments of weakness and madness! Now I see that that would have mutilated my life, ruined my art, broken the musical chords which make a perfect soul. Even covered with mud I shall praise you, from the deepest abysses I shall cry to you. In my solitude you will be with me. I am determined not to revolt but to accept every outrage through devotion to love, to let my body be dishonoured so long as my soul may al-

ways keep the image of you. From your silken hair to your delicate feet you are perfection to me. Pleasure hides love from us, but pain reveals it in its essence. O dearest of created things, if someone wounded by silence and solitude comes to you, dishonoured, a laughing-stock, Oh! you can close his wounds by touching them and restore his soul which unhappiness had for a moment smothered. Nothing will be difficult for you then, and remember, it is that hope which makes me live, and that hope alone. What wisdom is to the philosopher, what God is to his saint, you are to me. To keep you in my soul, such is the goal of this pain which men call life. O my love, you whom I cherish above all things, white narcissus in an unmown field, think of the burden which falls to you, a burden which love alone can make light. But be not saddened by that, rather be happy to have filled with an immortal love the soul of a man who now weeps in hell, and yet carries heaven in his heart. I love you, I love you, my heart is a rose which your love has brought to bloom, my life is a desert fanned by the delicious breeze of your breath, and whose cool spring are your eyes; the imprint of your little feet makes valleys of shade for me, the odour of your hair is like myrrh, and wherever you go you exhale the perfumes of the cassia tree.

Love me always, love me always. You have been the supreme, the perfect love of my life; there can be no other.

I decided that it was nobler and more beautiful to stay. We could not have been together. I did not want to be called a coward or a deserter. A false name, a disguise, a hunted life, all that is not for me, to whom you have been revealed on that high hill where beautiful things are transfigured.

O sweetest of all boys, most loved of all loves, my soul clings to your soul, my life is your life, and in all the world of pain and pleasure you are my ideal of admiration and joy.

Oscar

H.M. Prison, Reading

Dear Bosie, After long and fruitless waiting I have determined to write to you myself, as much for your sake as for mine, as I would not like to think that I had passed through two long years of imprisonment without ever having received a single line from you, or any news or message even, except such as gave me pain.

Our ill-fated and most lamentable friendship has ended in ruin and public infamy for me, yet the memory of our ancient affection is often with me, and the thought that loathing, bitterness and contempt should forever take that place in my heart once held by love is very sad to me: and you yourself will, I think, feel in your heart that to write to me as I lie in the loneliness of prison-life is better than to publish my letters without my permission or to dedicate poems to me unasked, though the world will know nothing of whatever words of grief or passion, of remorse or indifference you may choose to send as your answer or your appeal.

I have no doubt that in this letter in which I have to write of your life and of mine, of the past and of the future, of sweet things changed to bitterness and of bitter things that may be turned into joy, there will be much that will wound your vanity to the quick. If it prove so, read the letter over and over again till it kills your vanity. If you find in it something of which you feel that you are unjustly accused, remember that one should be thankful that there is any fault of which one can be unjustly accused. If there be in it one single passage that brings tears to your eyes, weep as we weep in prison where the day no less than the night is set apart for tears. It is the only thing that can save you. If you go complaining to your mother, as you did with reference to the scorn of you I displayed in my letter to Robbie, so that she may flatter and soothe you back into self-complacency or conceit, you will be completely lost. If you find one false excuse for yourself, you will soon find a hundred, and be just what you were before. Do you still say, as you said to Robbie in your answer, that I *"attribute unworthy motives"* to you? Ah! you had no motives in life. You had appetites merely. A motive is an intellectual aim. That you were *"very young"* when our friendship began? Your defect was not that you knew so little about life, but that you knew so much. The morning dawn of boyhood with its delicate bloom, its clear pure light, its joy of innocence and expectation you had left far behind. With very swift and running feet you had passed from Romance to Realism. . . .

❧❧

JACK LONDON TO CHARMIAN KITTREDGE

Oakland
Thursday, Sept. 24, 1903

Nay, nay, dear Love, not in my eyes is this love of ours a small and impotent thing. It is the greatest and most powerful thing in the world. The relativity of things makes it so. That I should be glad to live for you or to die for you is proof in itself that it means more to me than life or death, is greater, far greater, than life or death.

That you should be the one woman to me of all women; that my hunger for you should be greater than any hunger for food I have ever felt; that my desire for you should bite harder than any other desire I have ever felt for fame and fortune and such things;—all, all goes to show how big is this our love.

As I tell you repeatedly, you cannot possibly know what you mean to me. The days I do not see you are merely so many obstacles to be got over somehow before I see you. Each night as I go to bed I sigh with relief because I am one day nearer you. So it has been this week, and it is only Monday that I was with you. Today I am jubilant, my work goes well. And I am saying to myself all the time, "Tonight I shall see her! Tonight I shall see her!"

My thoughts are upon you always, lingering over you always, caressing you always in a myriad ways. I wonder if you feel those caresses sometimes!

Our love small! Dear, it might be small did the love of God enter into my heart, and the belief in an eternity of living and an eternity of the unguessed joys of Paradise. But remember my philosophy of life & death, and see clearly how much my love for you & your love for me must mean to me.

Ah Love, it looms large. It fills my whole horizon. Wherever I look I feel you, see you, touch you, and know my need for you. And there is no love of God to lessen my love for you. I love you, you only & wholly. And there are no joys of a future life to make of less value the joy I know and shall know through you. I clutch for you like a miser for his gold, because you are everything and the only thing. Remember, I must die, and go into the ground, and cease to feel and joy & know; and remember, each moment I am robbed of you, each night & all nights I am turned away from you, turned out by you, give me pangs the exquisiteness of which must be measured by the knowledge that they are moments and nights lost, lost, lost forever. For my little space of life is only so long. Tomorrow or next day I cease forever; and the moment I am robbed of you and the night I must be away from you will never, never come again. There is no compensation. It is all dead and utter loss.

So I live from day to day like an unwilling prodigal. I am wasting my substance and I cannot help it—nor am I wasting it even in riotous living. My fortune of life is only so large. How large I know not, but no matter how large, the sum of the hours & moments which compose it is determined. Each lost moment, is a moment squandered. My fortune is diminished that much without return. And so, day by day, helplessly, I watch the bright-minted moments flowing out and see the day of my bankruptcy approaching which is the day when I shall have no more moments perforce must die.

But it is even harder. For I know I am twenty-seven, at the high-tide of my life and vigor; and I know that these wasted moments now are the brightest-minted of all my moments.

I have not wandered through all this in order to plead for something I have not & might have, but to show how large to me, in the scheme of life, bulks this love of ours.

❦ ❦

RAINER MARIE RILKE

from *Letters to a Young Poet*

Rome, May 14th, 1904

MY DEAR MR. KAPPUS,
Much time has gone by since I received your last letter. Do not hold that against me; first it was work, then interruptions and finally a poor state of health that again and again kept me from the answer, which (so I wanted it) was to come to you out of quiet and good days. Now I feel somewhat better again (the opening of spring with its mean, fitful changes was very trying here too) and come to greet you, dear Mr. Kappus, and to tell you (which I do with all my heart) one thing and another in reply to your letter, as well as I know how.

You see—I have copied your sonnet, because I found that it is lovely and simple and born in the form in which it moves with such quiet decorum. It is the best of those of your poems that you have let me read. And now I give you this copy because I know that it is important and full of new experience to come upon a work of one's own again written in a strange hand. Read the lines as though they were someone else's, and you will feel deep within you how much they are your own.

It was a pleasure to me to read this sonnet and your letter often; I thank you for both.

And you should not let yourself be confused in your solitude by the fact that there is something in you that wants to break out of it. This very wish will help you, if you use it quietly, and deliberately and like a tool, to spread out your solitude over wide country. People have (with the help of conventions) oriented all their solutions toward the easy and toward the easiest side of the easy; but it is clear that we must hold to what is difficult; everything alive holds to it, everything in Nature grows and defends itself in its own way and is characteristically and spontaneously itself, seeks at all costs to be so and against all opposition. We know little, but that we must hold to what is difficult is a certainty that will not forsake us; it is good to be solitary, for solitude is difficult; that something is difficult must be a reason the more for us to do it.

To love is good, too: love being difficult. For one human being to love another: that is perhaps the most difficult of all our tasks, the ultimate, the last test and proof, the work for which all other work is but preparation. For this reason young people, who are beginners in everything, cannot yet know love: they have to learn it. With their whole being, with all their forces, gathered close about their lonely, timid, upward-beating heart, they must learn to love. But learning-time is always a long, secluded time, and so loving, for a long while ahead and far on into life, is—solitude, intensified and deepened loneness for him who loves. Love is at first not anything that means merging, giving over, and uniting with another (for what would a union be of something unclarified and unfinished, still subordinate—?), it is a high inducement to the individual to ripen, to become something in himself, to become world, to become world for himself for another's sake, it is a great exacting claim upon him, something that chooses him out and calls him to vast things. Only in this sense, as the task of working at themselves ("to hearken and to hammer day and night"), might young people use the love that is given them. Merging and surrendering and every kind of communion is not for them (who must save and gather for a long, long time still), is the ultimate, is perhaps that for which human lives as yet scarcely suffice.

But young people err so often and so grievously in this: that they (in whose nature it lies to have no patience) fling themselves at each other, when love takes possession of them, scatter themselves, just as they are, in all their untidiness, disorder, confusion.... And then what? What is life to do to this heap of half-battered existence which they call their communion and which they would gladly call their happiness, if it were possible, and their future? Thus each loses himself for the sake of the other and loses the other and many others that wanted still to come. And loses the expanses and the possibilities, exchanges the approach and flight of gentle, divining things for an unfruitful perplexity out of which nothing can come any more, nothing save a little disgust, disillusionment and poverty, and rescue in one of the many conventions that have been put up in great number like public refuges along this most dangerous road. No realm of human experience is so well provided with conventions as this: life-preservers of most varied invention, boats and swimming-bladders are here; the social conception has managed to supply shelters of every sort, for, as it was disposed to take love-life as a pleasure, it had also to give it an easy form, cheap, safe and sure, as public pleasures are.

It is true that many young people who love wrongly, that is, simply with abandon and unsolitarily (the average will of course always go on doing so), feel the oppressiveness of a failure and want to make the situation in which they have landed viable and fruitful in their own personal way—; for their nature tells them that, less even than all else that is important, can questions of love be solved publicly and according to this or that agreement; that they are questions, intimate questions from one human being to another, which in any case demand a new, special, *only* personal answer—: but how should they, who have already flung themselves together and no longer mark off and distinguish themselves from each other, who therefore no longer possess anything of their own selves, be able to find a way out of themselves, out of the depth of their already shattered solitude?

They act out of common helplessness, and then, if, with the best intentions, they try to avoid the convention that occurs to them (say, marriage), they land in the tentacles of some less loud, but equally deadly conventional solution; for then everything far around them is—convention; where people act out of a prematurely fused, turbid communion, *every* move is convention: every relation to which such entanglement leads has its convention, be it ever so unusual (that is, in the ordinary sense immoral); why, even separation would here be a conventional step, an impersonal chance decision without strength and without fruit.

Whoever looks seriously at it finds that neither for death, which is difficult, nor for difficult love has any explanation, any solution, any hint or way yet been discerned; and for these two problems that we carry wrapped up and hand on without opening, it will not be possible to discover any general rule resting in agreement. But in the same measure in which we begin as individuals to put life to the test, we shall, being individuals, meet these great things at closer range. The demands which the difficult work of love makes upon our development are more than life-size, and as beginners we are not up to them. But if we nevertheless hold out and take this love upon us as burden and apprenticeship, instead of losing ourselves in all the light and frivolous play, behind which people have hidden from the most earnest earnestness of their existence— then a little progress and an alleviation will perhaps be perceptible to those who come long after us; that would be much.

We are only just now beginning to look upon the relation of one individual person to a second individual objectively and without prejudice, and our attempts to live such associations have no model before them. And yet in the changes brought about by time there is already a good deal that would help our timorous novitiate.

The girl and the woman, in their new, their own unfolding, will but in passing be imitators of masculine ways, good and bad, and repeaters of masculine professions. After the uncertainty of such transitions it will become apparent that women were only going through the profusion and the vicissitude of those (often ridiculous) disguises in order to cleanse their own most characteristic nature of the distorting influences of the other sex. Women, in whom life lingers and dwells more immediately, more fruitfully and more confidently, must surely have become fundamentally riper people, more human people, then easygoing man, who is not pulled down below the surface of life by the weight of any fruit of his body, and who, presumptuous and hasty, undervalues what he thinks he loves. This humanity of woman, borne its full time in suffering and humiliation, will come to light when she will have stripped off the conventions of mere femininity in the mutations of her outward status, and those men who do not yet feel it approaching today will be surprised and struck by it. Some day (and for this, particularly in the northern countries, reliable signs are already speaking and shining), some day there will be girls and women whose name will no longer signify merely an opposite of the masculine, but something in itself, something that makes one think, not of any complement and limit, but only of life and existence: the feminine human being.

This advance will (at first much against the will of the outstripped men) change the love-experience, which is now full of error, will alter it from the ground up, reshape it into a relation that is meant to be of one human being to another, no longer of man to woman. And this more human love (that will fulfill itself, infinitely considerate and gentle, and kind and clear in binding and releasing) will resemble that which we are preparing with struggle and toil, the love that consists in this, that two solitudes protect and border and salute each other.

And this further: do not believe that that great love once enjoined upon you, the boy, was lost; can you say whether great and good desires did not ripen in you at the time, and resolutions by which you are still living today? I believe that that love remains so strong and powerful in your memory because it was your first deep being-alone and the first inward work you did on your life.—All good wishes for you, dear Mr. Kappus!

Yours:
Rainer Maria Rilke

COLETTE

from *Earthly Paradise*

PART TWO 1893–1910

I often went to see her in her dressing room. If we did not go on to a tavern with M. Willy to eat her favorite supper, which was my favorite too—a big wedge of cheese with the knob of a round loaf and a glass of red wine—we would say goodbye at the stage door of the *"Bouffes."* Already she was no longer the carefree, happy Claudine; her mood had darkened.

"Goodbye, Colette. Good night."

"Sleep well, Polaire."

"Oh, I don't sleep much, you know. I lie and wait."

"Who for?"

"Nobody! I wait and wait for tomorrow's performance."

She was telling the truth. Every real passion has its ascetic side, and her passion for her art made Polaire neglectful of love. Her neglect was deeply mortifying to the handsome young man, the rich young "blood," who loved "Popo" in his simple, frank, sometimes rather brutal fashion.

She went so far as to banish Pierre L—— from "her" theatre, even forbidding him, except on rare occasions, to come there at midnight and fetch her away.

"What would people say," she cried indignantly, "if gentlemen called for me here? They'd say I wasn't serious, they'd say I was only thinking of having fun!"

So she often went home alone, springing lightly into her victoria, when the weather was fine, her tiny toy terrier clasped to her breast. Her carriage was drawn by two piebald horses, like something out of a fairy story or a traveling circus, and away she drove, a strange young woman who had no need of true beauty to put all other women in the shade, an inspired actress to whom training and study were equally unnecessary. The hem of her pale-colored dress swept like a curling wave about her ankles, hiding or curving up over her high white boots—boots such as a hunting nymph might have worn, or a lion tamer at a fair—and the passers-by turned to stare at "Claudine."

One night M. Willy was awakened by the violent ringing of the telephone. He lifted the receiver and heard a confused noise of sobs and muffled cries: "Vili! Oh Vili! . . . Come quick! I'm dying."

A short outburst of curses, and M. Willy leapt from his bed, flung a topcoat over his Russian-embroidered nightgown and hurried off, calling a few brief orders to me over his shoulder:

"Dress. Get there as soon as you can. I don't know what's up at Polaire's, but it looks as if tonight's takings were bitched."

He found, we found, Polaire on the floor of her bedroom, half under the bed. Sitting on the bed, and most admirably lit by a pink-frilled table lamp, was a young man in pajamas, Pierre L——. His eyes glowered, and with arms folded on his chest, he was breathing quickly through his nostrils like a boxer at the end of a round.

Down for the count, Polaire lay prostrate, if indeed the word "prostrate" can be applied to the stricken serpent, the frantic panther, to every live creature that can writhe and toss and buckle madly, tear the ground with its claws, sob, roar. The young man looked down at her in silence, motionless, making no attempt to help or soothe.

"Good God!" gasped M. Willy. "Whatever is the matter with her?"

Pierre L——'s handsome mouth remained grimly closed, but an answer issued, panting and incoherent, from underneath the bed:

"Vili! He hit me! . . . The brute! The brute! . . . Here . . . and here . . . and here! . . . Vili! I want to die! . . . Oh! Oh! Oh! Oh! I'm *so* unhappy! . . . Get a policeman! Get a policeman! I'll have him sent to prison! I'll have him put in irons!"

M. Willy wiped his forehead and inquired anxiously (first things first):

"Is she badly hurt?"

Pierre L—— shrugged his shoulders.

"Hurt? Don't be funny! A couple of wallops . . ."

The prostrate victim sprang to her feet. Crowned with curl papers large as the largest Roman snails, puffed with tears, swollen with sighs and cries, she still glowed, in her long nightdress, like some fiery Eastern sorceress; nothing that was excessive or frenzied could ever make her ugly.

"A couple of wallops?" she repeated. "And what about this? . . . And this?"

She pointed to her arms, her neck, her shoulder, her thighs that were made to grip the bare flanks of a horse.

"The police!" she whispered childishly. "Call the police."

Tears of exhaustion and defeat overcame her, and she sank to the ground again. M. Willy, much relieved, sat down on the bed beside Pierre L——.

"My dear old fellow! This sort of thing isn't decent. You must forgive me if I tell you, as a friend, that a decent-hearted man, a man of feeling . . ."

The dear fellow laid a large, white, well-kept hand upon his unfeeling heart:

"In the first place I don't care a damn," he declared, "whether I'm decent or not. As for tonight—she said something I couldn't stand. No!" he suddenly shouted. "No! I can't and I won't stand it!"

He got up, scrabbling with his fingers in his thick, ash-gold hair.

"Can't you tell me what happened?" suggested M. Willy in a conciliatory tone. "You know you can trust me."

"She said—" began Pierre L—— at the top of his voice. "She said—that I wasn't gentle!"

Below him, on the carpet, Polaire stirred feebly, shook her cluster of monster snails, moaned.

"That—I—was—not—gentle!" Pierre L—— barked out. "When I heard that, I saw red. . . . Not gentle! I! I!"

He struck his fine chest with his fists.

"I—! Everybody knows it! I'm the midlest of men! *I*, not gentle! . . ."

Groans came from the carpet, broken and despairing. . . .

"No, you're not. You're not gentle. . . . You don't understand anything. . . . You don't know what gentleness and understanding are. . . . What a woman really wants from love isn't what you think it is. . . . It's . . ."

"Do you hear her?" Pierre L—— thundered. "She's at it again! My God!"

He threw off his pajama jacket, bent over the floor. M. Willy was about to intervene when two amber arms rose and closed about the smooth neck of the mildest of men.

"Pierre . . . I'm so unhappy. . . . Nobody loves me. . . . Pierre . . ."

"My little duck . . . My lovey girl. . . . Popo, darling. . . . Who said nobody loved you?"

He picked her up, held her slung across his breast like a dark gazelle, carried her, humming softly, back and forth about the great Louis XV bed. M. Willy turned to me:

"I feel that our presence is no longer essential. But they did give me a turn! They're killing, don't you think?"

He wiped his forehead and laughed, but I could not do the same. Standing there, unwanted, almost in silence, I had had ample time to watch a strange, unknown sight—love in its youth and its violence, an outraged lover, naked to the waist, the silky woman's skin above the perfect muscles, the rippling play of light upon the proud, careless body, his easy assurance as he stepped over and then picked up the fallen body of Polaire.

I saw the back of his trim, well-shaped neck and the ash-gold hair falling like rain over Polaire's hidden face. Her arms about him, he rocked his victim gently, and she had forgotten we were there.

"Hey! Young Pierrot! Can you promise not to try our star's nerves too hard? Not to give her advice so—er—convincingly?"

The young head lifted and we saw the flushed, ferocious face, the mouth still moist from the interrupted kiss.

"Only when it's absolutely necessary, old man. I promise. . . ."

I joined M. Willy, who, by the way of being funny, was tripping to the door on tiptoe, and we went out.

M. Willy, his mind now entirely at rest, seemed greatly amused by our night's adventure. I was not so entertained.

"Are you cold? You don't want to go home on foot, do you?"

No, I was not cold. Yes, I was cold. All the same, I would have liked to go home on foot. Or not to go home at all. Walking beside him, I looked back in my mind at the room we had just left. I can see something of it still—highlights of pale blue against a dim background, lamps that shone pink in their little embroidered shades, the tumbled, white expanse of a lovers' bed. I have kept the memory of a prolonged, uneasy sadness that I ought, perhaps, to call jealousy.

Colette to Marguerite Moreno

Paris, June 21, 1925

Ah! La la, and la la again! And never la enough! Your friend is very proper, believe it. She is in a fine, agreeable mess, and up to her chin, her eyes, and farther than that! Oh! the satanism of tranquil creatures—and I'm speaking of the kid Maurice. Do you want to know what he is? He's a skunk, and a this and a that, and at the same time a chic chap with a satiny hide. That's the mess I'm in. . . .

Paris, late Saturday Evening, July 11, 1925

. . . Whom shall I thank? You, the lord of Chance, and who or what else? The Chiwawa has finally beheld us together; and all she could see was two tranquil comrades who looked like friends. Oh, the luxury of also being friends! It's hardly believable. And when she phones me asking, "What is Maurice doing? Where is he?" I can truthfully answer, "I have no idea. We never call each other during the day." And it's true, absolutely true. We wait for evening to bring us together. . . . He leaves for London tomorrow and we have just said our goodbyes without fuss. He plans to return Wednesday or Thursday—a small but certain test. . . .

Beauvallon, August 5, 1925

. . . the sparrow owls are hooting under the full moon and I sleep on the terrace. . . . The sea and the sand have become my native elements. So is love. Am I not an abominable creature? (I need you to assure me otherwise.) Because it's three o'clock in the afternoon, my charming companion is sleeping, but I don't need a siesta, I sleep so well at night. One always feels a little guilty writing next to someone who is asleep, even when it is only to acknowledge that he is charming and that one loves him. Tell me, wasn't it last winter that you warned me that during a voyage I would meet a man "who would change my life"?

Kensington Hotel, La Croix (Var) January 3, 1928

. . . Moonlight, a wood fire, my own good lamp. What can I complain about? Only the absence of those I love. . . . For the new year, my Marguerite, I wish you—whatever suits you best. The same torments—less sharp, less attached to the state of health and of your "bad boy" Pierre; the same joys indissolubly mixed with the same torments—all to continue as they have been. Isn't that better than any change? I also wish you wealth and tranquility—and at the same time your work. Yes, of course, I'm being contradictory. But I am not illogical. And I love you tenderly. Oh, how happy I'd be to have you here for a few days!

Colette to Pierre Moreno

Paris, April 13, 1949

I've been very ill, and I've never thought so much about Marguerite. During my bad days and coughing fits, I cling to her memory and image. What bitterness and sweetness are combined in a fidelity as involuntary as ours! I have missed Helene Picard and her richly provincial genius, but in all the losses I've known, nothing can compare with the shock I feel every time I remember Marguerite. . . .

Monte Carlo, March 8, 1952

. . . Yesterday I was talking at length about Marguerite. Happily, the remembrance of what I have loved best remains intact. . . .

✥ ✥

AGNES VON KUROWSKY TO ERNEST
HEMINGWAY

March 7, 1919

ERNIE, DEAR BOY,
I am writing this late at night after a long think by myself, & I am afraid it is going to hurt you, but, I'm sure it won't harm you permanently.

For quite awhile before you left, I was trying to convince myself it was a real love-affair, because, we always seemed to disagree, & then arguments always wore me out so that I finally gave in to keep you from doing something desperate.

Now, after a couple of months away from you, I know that I am still very fond of you, but, it is more as a mother than as a sweetheart. It's alright to say I'm a Kid, but, I'm not, & I'm getting less & less so every day.

So, Kid (still Kid to me, & always will be) can you forgive me some day for unwittingly deceiving you? You know I'm not really bad, & don't mean to do wrong, & now I realize it was my fault in the beginning that you cared for me, & regret it from the bottom of my heart. But, I am now & always will be too old, & that's the truth, & I can't get away from the fact that you're just a boy—a kid.

I somehow feel that some day I'll have reason to be proud of you, but, dear boy, I can't wait for that day, & it is wrong to hurry a career.

I tried hard to make you understand a bit of what I was thinking on that trip from Padua to Milan, but, you acted like a spoiled child, & I couldn't keep on hurting you. Now, I only have the courage because I'm far away.

Then—& believe me when I say this is sudden for me, too—I expect to be married soon. And I hope & pray that after you have thought things out, you'll be able to forgive me & start a wonderful career & show what a man you really are.

> *Ever admiringly & fondly*
> *Your friend,*
> *Aggie*

❧ ☙

ALINE BERNSTEIN TO THOMAS WOLFE

> Berlin
> Hotel Esplanade
> August 11, 1928

MY DEAR:
We arrived yesterday, could not get rooms at Adlon Hotel, a nasty place anyway, and came here which is lovely.—Your letter came here, I was so afraid you would come to the Adlon and miss me that I bribed every official and flunkey in the place, so when I came in at lunchtime I found a boy waiting with your letter.

I had been hoping so desperately that you would come although I knew it would be very difficult for both of us, and very disquieting. I am in a constant agony of longing for you, and it seems so strange to me, if you love me so, that you would not take this journey to see me, even if you do not care to see Berlin (a very peculiar reason, isn't it?) I do not seem to be able to put into words the love and longing I have for you. I feel now that I will never be satisfied with this loving friendship you talk so much about. The phrase stings me to helpless anger.

I am your true love until I die, how dare you write me to make "other arrangements for my happiness." That is what you wrote. Have you no sense! Ever since you parted from me, you write that you love me, and never once have you said you would come back to me. Except in "loving friendship." Well, once for all, that means nothing and you know it.

As you see, I feel bitter, angry and horribly discouraged. This whole summer has been a prolonged agony, except for the times I have been able to lose myself in pictures, and what will be the consequence of it all. God knows I only hope that you will benefit by it. I am also discouraged that you drift so endlessly. How about your work? Wasn't that the idea behind our separation this summer? Tom dear forgive me, but I am so hurt that you didn't come to meet me here, when you could.

For heaven's sake do something, you are now in the most precious time of your life, and it seems to me you are doing the same thing you did four years ago, aimlessly wandering. Possibly I am wrong and that sort of thing is necessary to you. I think I know, but must be mistaken.

—We came from Prague here by aeroplane yesterday. It was a strange and terrible experience, and I hoped several times the God damn plane would smash and go down. This is not fancy talk as you call it, but the truth. The wind was blowing a gale, and we had what is called a very rough passage. It was terrible, nothing that a ship does in the most violent storm could compare to the plunges and leaps of the plane. The earth was wonderful to look at from above, so perfectly designed. I felt deathly sick but could not vomit, and for the last hour of the ride had a steady sharp pain in my heart and was a beautiful indigo blue color when we landed. . . . The strangest thing was that I had no sensation of fear at all. And if it weren't for the awful sickness it must be a marvellous way to travel. I had some tea when we got settled in the hotel, and stayed nearly an hour in a very hot bath, finally got warm, and went to bed. But the bed swayed, and my head nearly cracked all night. No more flying for me for some time.—I wish to God I could sink into some state of insensibility.

I don't know what to do if I go on being wracked this way by my feeling. I wish I could be so noble that I would be happy just because you have your freedom, or whatever you choose to call it, and are doing what you please. I'm not that noble, in spite of the Carlsbad cure. As I feel I don't think it is in me to do any more beautiful shows, in spite of your advice. I also do not think it is in me to make another home for my family, and root up my old one. Isn't it funny to have reached my age and be all at sea! And here I go giving advice to you about settling to work. More people than I, have lived through it. Without you I am finished with it.

You must dread getting a letter from me now, they are all so painful, but I guess not so painful as to see me. Do you think you ever will again?—When I think that you are being untrue to me with women, I have murder in my heart.—I am true to you and me and love forever. I went to the museum here for an hour this morning, it is very fine. Some magnificent paintings. My head hurt so from the flight I couldn't stay very long. Fortunately I can get off by myself, occasionally. Phil comes along, when I look at pictures. I am sending you a lovely Egyptian head. Berlin is much lovelier than I had thought, I took a little one horse hack and drove around. I will get up very early tomorrow, as the galleries all close at one o'clock Saturday and 3 other days. The pictures seem to be grand. Will know better tomorrow.

I hope you will let me know where to write you, will go on sending mail to Munich till further notice. You will find a great collection from me there. If I feel no happier soon what shall I do? Just go on. Well, my darling an ache only aches the person who has it, I found that out by now. Time is a dream—

I love you
Aline

❧ ❧

KATHERINE ANNE PORTER TO MATTHEW
JOSEPHSON

Jan 7 1931

When I first knew you, you were just emerging from the Zola period. . . . Later, remember, you were the man of action warring single-handed against great cities. Later when you feared I might stubbornly keep on being in love with you when the occasion that called for me had passed, you wrote that "our emotional feats" were of no consequence compared to the realistic businesses of life such as running a household, begetting young and writing books. We were to be machines, I remember distinctly, functioning with hair's breadth precision. I wasn't deceived then, dear Matthew, and still I'm not when you decide that we must all be romantic rather than decorous. One might be both if one's nature was such? I think it means merely that you have found someone or something new to play with, and this point of view may be for the moment useful to you? You are like a good golfer who chooses just the right club to hit the ball in a certain way?

*　*　*

You do wrong to be so angry with a friend who loves you as I do, and you mustn't burst into abuse, elegies and eternal farewells regularly as you do whenever I forget myself and take the liberty of writing to you as frankly and freely as I do to other persons. Why cannot you grant to your friends the freedom you give yourself of criticism and comment. And as for MY rhetoric? I am being continually humbled and confounded by the complicated brilliance of your style. It wasn't acid and brimstone—not at all these. I was in an excellent but I see now foolhardy humor. And it wasn't pretty of you—I can't say graceful, for that word is gradually being destroyed for me—to answer by a general flight under cover of such words as psychosis, vengeance, vomiting, spewing—oh, come now, Matthew. You'll have to do better than this. I did not mean to insult you; I was perfectly aware I was writing a provocative letter, but it was not a bitter one. But this has happened before. You have written frightfully wounding things to me, or have said them. And then I answered with edged words, and you were grieved and astonished and wounded, and wounded that I was wounded—and yes, really, to flee is one answer for such persistent wronging of the human heart.

Let me answer your thousandth farewell with the thousand and first. But I do not mean it and you need not. Am I among all your friends to be the only one not permitted to quarrel even a little with you, and make it up again. . . .

Out of this well-renovated bosom of tenderness I send you my affection. In the hope that Mr. Rousseau will make a fine book. Better than *The Portrait*, and *The Portrait* was better than Zola . . . and remember what we thought of Zola.

Above all, no more good-byes.

HENRY MILLER TO ANAÏS NIN

Hotel Central, Paris
March 10, 1932, 1:30 A.M.

ANAÏS:

I was stunned when I got your note this morning. Nothing I can ever say will match these words. To you the victory—you have silenced me—I mean so far as expressing these things in writing goes. You don't know how I marvel at your ability to absorb quickly and then turn about, rain down the spears, nail it, penetrate it, envelop it with your intellect. The experience dumbed me. I felt a singular exaltation, a surge of vitality, then of lassitude, of blankness, of wonder, of incredulity . . . everything, everything. Coming home I kept remarking about the Spring wind—everything had grown soft and balmy, the air licked my face, I couldn't gulp down enough of it. And until I got your note I was in a panic. . . . I was afraid you would disavow everything. But as I read—I read very slowly because each word was a revelation to me—I thought back to your smiling face, to your sort of innocent gaiety, something I had always sought for in you but never quite realized. There were times you began this way—at Louveciennes—and then the mind crashed through and I would see the grave, round eyes and the set purse of your lips, which used almost to frighten me, or, at any rate, always intimidated me.

You make me tremendously happy to hold me undivided—to let me be the artist, as it were, and yet not forgo the man, the animal, the hungry, insatiable lover. No woman has ever granted me all the privileges I need—and you, why you sing out so blithely, so boldly, with a laugh even—yes, you invite me to go ahead, be myself, venture anything. I adore you for that. That is where you are truly regal, a woman extraordinary. What a woman you are! I laugh to myself now when I think of you. I have no fear of your femaleness. And that you burned—I want that—I would not have it otherwise. You see, in spite of all my intimations, I was not quite prepared for the tempest you invoked. That moment in the room when, standing and swaying, you clung to me with your very womb, it seemed, that blinded me. And then do you know what happened later—you will forgive me, I hope—the blood on your face kept reminding me of the garden scene in *L'Age d'Or* and I was growing frantic and hysterical. Then I remember vividly your dress, the color and the texture of it, the voluptuous airy spaciousness of it—precisely what I would have begged you to wear had I been able to anticipate the moment. I was aware, too, of all that you hint at but tremendously relieved that you treated these things (I am about to say brazenly)—but no, it was nonchalantly.

And today, in the most precious good health, I had very langurous, pleasurable sensations of aches in my arms—from holding you so tightly. It dawned on me very very slowly. I wish I could retain it.

Anaïs, I am sending you this note to the other address. In my crude way I have a certain feeling of delicacy which prevents me from sending such things to Louveciennes. You will understand, I hope. I am enclosing more of Fred's manuscript, and some more of mine, too. Note how you were anticipating what I wrote today—I refer to your words about "caricature . . . hate etc." I will call around noon tomorrow, and if I don't succeed in getting you I *may* phone you again in the evening. I am timid about that sort of thing, or is it false delicacy? I don't know. When I phone I shall be able to say if it is possible to meet tomorrow—you see I am not yet straightened out with the police about my working card—the red tape is endless.

Henry

ANAÏS NIN

from *The Diary of Anaïs Nin, Vol. Two, 1934–1939*

Someday I'll be locked up for love insanity. "She loved too much." This could be on my tombstone. What I feel intensely and always respond to is the aloneness of the others, their needs. Which love makes the great closeness, the fraternal, the friendship, the passion, the intellectual harmony, the tender one, devotion, the lover, the brother, the husband, the father, the son, the friend. So many kinds of fusions! What is it that annihilates the loneliness? The understanding of Rank, devotion, ardor, creative harmony?

Break and shatter loneliness forever!

I am never close enough; I want some impossible communion.

I must accept intermittences. Loneliness in between.

Dreams, dreams. I arrive in a dilapidated taxi because I knew nobody else would take such a taxi. The floor of the taxi was so worn the street showed through the cracks. I could have counted the cobblestones. I wondered whether in the end I would fall through and be left sitting in the middle of the street like a newborn baby fallen out of a crib, or an egg from a hen. And there would be the street, suddenly, without time to have prepared myself for adventure. I was a believer in preparation. I liked to sit in a taxi and watch myself in the little mirror in front. I would talk to myself: I would say I need greatly to have heavy objects put on myself, on my head and feet, something like lead chains and boots. That way I would not leave the earth so easily. It is amazing with what facility I outdistance things, with what ease I float away, and soar away, and am carried thousands of miles from the spot where I stand, in such a way that I assure you I don't hear what is being said to me, I do not see the person who is there, and I am not aware of myself anymore. I feel so light, so light at times, vaporous, like steam on a window which can be erased with a careless finger. Put a lot of heavy things on me so that I will stay on earth. Put warm blankets on me because heat attracts me and makes me want to stay where I am. Turn on a strong warm voice. A strong voice which comes from the stomach also makes me want to stay on earth. As a matter of fact, there are many things which might detain me, hold me down, like the smell of coffee in the morning and a mauve glass bottle with a neck like a man with a goiter, and the moment in the taxi when I am going somewhere and I have time to imagine what this somewhere will be like, time to invent it, time to prepare myself for it. I was going to say this to him, with a strange face in which the features do not seem to belong together, a face where the eyes seem to spark away from each other and the radiance of the cheeks depart in many directions, like a broken halo, and the smile falls apart. I made this face in the mirror, just like the face, I thought, you see sometimes on people when they are about to go insane. It is all unrelated. The eyes are not connected to the meaning of the phrase which is spoken, and neither does the expression conform to the contents of the phrase. There is a kind of panic through it all, they are all wavering as if in a panic, and each is saying a different thing. The eyes do not reflect the mood of the moment, but that blanketlike past hovering behind the present eternally, like the traces of an ancient disease, and the voice has in it still the terror of many years ago and not the courage of today. It is all confused, while the woman is saying with today's mood: I will say to him I happened to come here because when the bottom of the taxi fell out I found myself in front of your house. I would like life to be always as casual as that. There would never be any engagements. I dropped in her like a package left at the *con-*

signe. Will you give me a receipt please, give me a receipt. I have no confidence, you see, I like to hear from people what they think of me, how I look to them, even what I have said to them. You would have to write on the receipt at this hour there came a woman who looked exotic and talked with a foreign accent. I don't mean that she was born elsewhere, in another country, but that she has the intonation of never having been born at all to our language, to the language of other women. I received from her very grave words said in a bantering tone, a bantering uttered with a sadness I cannot understand. It was all very foreign because she made one feel so. She herself must have enjoyed feeling not at home. She liked to have the illusion of the uncommon, the never-lived-before. I really think she believed it. Now this receipt will prove to me that at five o'clock I was in your house and we did exchange words which you pretended not to have heard before, this receipt would be a great comfort to me. I will fold it and wear it against my breast. It is like a certainty. I would like also when you love me you should note it all down. I feel that from the very beginning life played a terrible conjurer's trick on me. I lost faith in it. It seems to me that every moment now it is playing tricks on me. So that when I hear love I am not sure it is love, and when I hear gaiety I am not sure it is gaiety, and when I have eaten and loved and I am all warm from wine, I am not sure it is either love or food or wine, but a strange trick being played on me, an illusion, slippery and baffling and malicious, and a magician hangs behind me watching the ecstasy I feel at the things which happen so that I know deep down it is all fluid and escaping and may vanish at any moment. Don't forget to write me a letter and tell me I was here, and I saw you, and loved you, and ate with you. It is all so evanescent and I love it so much, I love it as you love the change in the days. I would prefer to move away where I could not sense the movements of life passing, somewhere in space and distance where I might divine that ultimately it is I who will abandon life and separate myself from it, not life leaving me, and it will be like the old taxi that was falling apart and dropped its contents like an egg, and maybe this egg is a book, and not me, and I am safe behind paper and ink and words and stories and only counting cobblestones, not having arrived anywhere yet because of the painstaking preparations involved, for you see in the mirror I am practicing a certain expression and when I arrive it is generally not needed. For the person is another from the one I invented, and I have to adapt my soul anew.

❧ ❧

VLADIMIR NABOKOV
First Love

I

In the early years of this century, a travel agency on Nevski Avenue displayed a three-foot-long model of an oak-brown international sleeping
car. In delicate verisimilitude it completely outranked the painted tin of
my clockwork trains. Unfortunately it was not for sale. One could make
out the blue upholstery inside, the embossed leather lining of the compartment walls, their polished panels, inset mirrors, tulip-shaped reading lamps, and other maddening details. Spacious windows alternated
with narrower ones, single or geminate, and some of these were of
frosted glass. In a few of the compartments, the beds had been made.

The then great and glamorous Nord Express (it was never the
same after World War One when its elegant brown became a nouveau-
riche blue), consisting solely of such international cars and running but
twice a week, connected St. Petersburg with Paris. I would have said: directly with Paris, had passengers not been obliged to change from one
train to a superficially similar one at the Russo-German frontier (-
Verzhbolovo-Eydtkuhnen), where the ample and lazy Russian sixty-and-
a-half-inch gauge was replaced by the fifty-six-and-a-half-inch standard
of Europe and coal succeeded birch logs.

In the far end of my mind I can unravel, I think, at least five such
journeys to Paris, with the Riviera or Biarritz as their ultimate destination. In 1909, the year I now single out, our party consisted of eleven
people and one dachshund. Wearing gloves and a traveling cap, my father
sat reading a book in the compartment he shared with our tutor. My
brother and I were separated from them by a washroom. My mother and
her maid, Natasha, occupied a compartment adjacent to ours. Next
came my two small sisters, their English governess, Miss Lavington, and
a Russian nurse. The odd one of our party, my father's valet, Osip
(whom, a decade later, the pedantic Bolsheviks were to shoot, because he
appropriated our bicycles instead of turning them over to the nation),
had a stranger for companion.

Historically and artistically, the year had started with a political
cartoon in *Punch:* goddess England bending over goddess Italy, on whose

head one of Messina's bricks has landed—probably, the worst picture *any* earthquake has ever inspired. In April of that year, Peary had reached the North Pole. In May, Shalyapin had sung in Paris. In June, bothered by rumors of new and better Zeppelins, the United States War Department had told reporters of plans for an aerial Navy. In July, Blériot had flown from Calais to Dover (with a little additional loop when he lost his bearings). It was late August now. The firs and marshes of Northwestern Russia sped by, and on the following day gave way to German pinewoods and heather.

At a collapsible table, my mother and I played a card game called *durachki*. Although it was still broad daylight, our cards, a glass, and on a different plane the locks of a suitcase were reflected in the window. Through forest and field, and in sudden ravines, and among scuttling cottages, those discarnate gamblers kept steadily playing on for steadily sparkling stakes. It was a long, very long game: on this gray winter morning, in the looking glass of my bright hotel room, I see shining the same, the very same, locks of that now seventy-year-old valise, a highish, heavyish *nécessaire de voyage* of pigskin, with "H.N." elaborately interwoven in thick silver under a similar coronet, which had been bought in 1897 for my mother's wedding trip to Florence. In 1917 it transported from St. Petersburg to the Crimea and then to London a handful of jewels. Around 1930, it lost to a pawnbroker its expensive receptacles of crystal and silver leaving empty the cunningly contrived leathern holders on the inside of the lid. But that loss has been amply recouped during the thirty years it then traveled with me—from Prague to Paris, from St. Nazaire to New York and through the mirrors of more than two hundred motel rooms and rented houses, in forty-six states. The fact that of our Russian heritage the hardiest survivor proved to be a traveling bag is both logical and emblematic.

"Ne budet-li, ti ved' ustal [Haven't you had enough, aren't you tired]?" my mother would ask, and then would be lost in thought as she slowly shuffled the cards. The door of the compartment was open and I could see the corridor window, where the wires—six thin black wires—were doing their best to slant up, to ascend skywards, despite the lightning blows dealt them by one telegraph pole after another; but just as all six, in a triumphant swoop of pathetic elation, were about to reach the top of the window, a particularly vicious blow would bring them down, as low as they had ever been, and they would have to start all over again.

When, on such journeys as these, the train changed its pace to a dignified amble and all but grazed housefronts and shop signs, as we passed through some big German town, I used to feel a twofold excitement, which terminal stations could not provide. I saw a city, with its toy-like trams, linden trees, and brick walls enter the compartment, hobnob with the mirrors, and fill to the brim the windows on the corridor side. This informal contact between train and city was one part of the thrill. The other was putting myself in the place of some passer-by who, I imagined, was moved as I would be moved myself to see the long, romantic, auburn cars, with their intervestibular connecting curtains as black as bat wings and their metal lettering copper-bright in the low sun, unhurriedly negotiate an iron bridge across an everyday thoroughfare and then turn, with all windows suddenly ablaze, around a last block of houses.

There were drawbacks to those optical amalgamations. The wide-windowed dining car, a vista of chaste bottles of mineral water, miter-folded napkins, and dummy chocolate bars (whose wrappers—Cailler, Kohler, and so forth—enclosed nothing but wood), would be perceived at first as a cool haven beyond a consecution of reeling blue corridors; but as the meal progressed toward its fatal last course, and more and more dreadfully one equilibrist with a full tray would back against our table to let another equilibrist pass with another full tray, I would keep catching the car in the act of being recklessly sheathed, lurching waiters and all, in the landscape, while the landscape itself went through a complex system of motion, the day-time moon stubbornly keeping abreast of one's plate, the distant meadows opening fanwise, the near trees sweeping up on invisible swings toward the track, a parallel rail line all at once committing suicide by anastomosis, a bank of nictitating grass rising, rising, rising, until the little witness of mixed velocities was made to disgorge his portion of *omelette aux confitures de fraises.*

It was at night, however, that the *Compagnie Internationale des Wagons-Lits et des Grands Express Européens* lived up to the magic of its name. From my bed under my brother's bunk (Was he asleep? Was he there at all?), in the semidarkness of our compartment, I watched things, and parts of things, and shadows, and sections of shadows cautiously moving about and getting nowhere. The woodwork gently creaked and crackled. Near the door that led to the toilet, a dim garment on a peg and, higher up, the tassel of the blue, bivalved night light swung rhythmically. It was hard to correlate those halting approaches, that hooded stealth, with the headlong rush of the outside night, which I knew *was* rushing by, spark-streaked, illegible.

I would put myself to sleep by the simple act of identifying myself with the engine driver. A sense of drowsy well-being invaded my veins as soon as I had everything nicely arranged—the carefree passengers in their rooms enjoying the ride I was giving them, smoking, exchanging knowing smiles, nodding, dozing; the waiters and cooks and train guards (whom I had to place somewhere) carousing in the diner; and myself, goggled and begrimed, peering out of the engine cab at the tapering track, at the ruby or emerald point in the black distance. And then, in my sleep, I would see something totally different—a glass marble rolling under a grand piano or a toy engine lying on its side with its wheels still working gamely.

A change in the speed of the train sometimes interrupted the current of my sleep. Slow lights were stalking by; each, in passing, investigated the same chink, and then a luminous compass measured the shadows. Presently, the train stopped with a long-drawn Westinghousian sigh. Something (my brother's spectacles, as it proved next day) fell from above. It was marvelously exciting to move to the foot of one's bed, with part of the bedclothes following, in order to undo cautiously the catch of the window shade, which could be made to slide only halfway up, impeded as it was by the edge of the upper berth.

Like moons around Jupiter, pale moths revolved about a lone lamp. A dismembered newspaper stirred on a bench. Somewhere on the train one could hear muffled voices, somebody's comfortable cough. There was nothing particularly interesting in the portion of station platform before me, and still I could not tear myself away from it until it departed of its own accord.

Next morning, wet fields with misshapen willows along the radius of a ditch or a row of poplars afar, traversed by a horizontal band of milky-white mist, told one that the train was spinning through Belgium. It reached Paris at 4 P.M., and even if the stay was only an overnight one, I had always time to purchase something—say, a little brass *Tour Eiffel*, rather roughly coated with silver paint—before we boarded, at noon on the following day, the Sud-Express, which, on its way to Madrid, dropped us around 10 P.M. at the La Négresse station of Biarritz, a few miles from the Spanish frontier.

2

Biarritz still retained its quiddity in those days. Dusty blackberry bushes and weedy *terrains à vendre* bordered the road that led to our villa. The Carlton was still being built. Some thirty-six years had to elapse before

Brigadier General Samuel McCroskey would occupy the royal suite of the Hôtel du Palais, which stands on the site of a former palace, where, in the sixties, that incredibly agile medium, Daniel Home, is said to have been caught stroking with his bare foot (in imitation of a ghost hand) the kind, trustful face of Empress Eugénie. On the promenade near the Casino, an elderly flower girl, with carbon eyebrows and a painted smile, nimbly slipped the plump torus of a carnation into the buttonhole of an intercepted stroller whose left jowl accentuated its royal fold as he glanced down sideways at the coy insertion of the flower.

The rich-hued Oak Eggars questing amid the brush were quite unlike ours (which did not breed on oak, anyway), and here the Speckled Woods haunted not woods, but hedges and had tawny, not pale-yellowish, spots. Cleopatra, a tropical-looking, lemon-and-orange Brimstone, languorously flopping about in gardens, had been a sensation in 1907 and was still a pleasure to net.

Along the back line of the *plage*, various seaside chairs and stools supported the parents of straw-hatted children who were playing in front on the sand. I could be seen on my knees trying to set a found comb aflame by means of a magnifying glass. Men sported white trousers that to the eye of today would look as if they had comically shrunk in the washing; ladies wore, that particular season, light coats with silk-faced lapels, hats with big crowns and wide brims, dense embroidered white veils, frill-fronted blouses, frills at their wrists, frills on their parasols. The breeze salted one's lips. At a tremendous pace a stray Clouded Yellow came dashing across the palpitating *plage*.

Additional movement and sound were provided by venders hawking *cacahuètes*, sugared violets, pistachio ice cream of a heavenly green, cachou pellets, and huge convex pieces of dry, gritty, waferlike stuff that came from a red barrel. With a distinctness that no later superpositions have dimmed, I see that waffleman stomp along through deep mealy sand, with the heavy cask on his bent back. When called, he would sling it off his shoulder by a twist of its strap, bang it down on the sand in a Tower of Pisa position, wipe his face with his sleeve, and proceed to manipulate a kind of arrow-and-dial arrangement with numbers on the lid of the cask. The arrow rasped and whirred around. Luck was supposed to fix the size of a sou's worth of wafer. The bigger the piece, the more I was sorry for him.

The process of bathing took place on another part of the beach. Professional bathers, burly Basques in black bathing suits, were there to help ladies and children enjoy the terrors of the surf. Such a *baigneur* would place the *client* with his back to the incoming wave and hold him by the hand as the rising, rotating mass of foamy, green water violently descended from behind, knocking one off one's feet with one mighty wallop. After a dozen of these tumbles, the *baigneur*, glistening like a seal, would lead his panting, shivering, moistly snuffling charge landward, to the flat foreshore, where an unforgettable old woman with gray hairs on her chin promptly chose a bathing robe from several hanging on a clothesline. In the security of a little cabin, one would be helped by yet another attendant to peel off one's soggy, sand-heavy bathing suit. It would plop onto the boards, and, still shivering, one would step out of it and trample on its bluish, diffuse stripes. The cabin smelled of pine. The attendant, a hunchback with beaming wrinkles, brought a basin of steaming-hot water, in which one immersed one's feet. From him I learned, and have preserved ever since in a glass cell of my memory, that "butterfly" in the Basque language is *misericoletea*—or at least it sounded so (among the seven words I have found in dictionaries the closest approach is *micheletea*).

3

On the browner and wetter part of the *plage*, that part which at low tide yielded the best mud for castles, I found myself digging, one day, side by side with a little French girl called Colette.

She would be ten in November, I had been ten in April. Attention was drawn to a jagged bit of violet mussel shell upon which she had stepped with the bare sole of her narrow long-toed foot. No, I was not English. Her greenish eyes seemed flecked with the overflow of the freckles that covered her sharp-featured face. She wore what might now be termed a playsuit, consisting of a blue jersey with rolled-up sleeves and blue knitted shorts. I had taken her at first for a boy and then had been puzzled by the bracelet on her thin wrist and the corkscrew brown curls dangling from under her sailor cap.

She spoke in birdlike bursts of rapid twitter, mixing governess English and Parisian French. Two years before, on the same *plage*, I had been much attached to Zina, the lovely, sun-tanned, bad-tempered little daughter of a Serbian naturopath—she had, I remember (absurdly, for she and I were only eight at the time), a *grain de beauté* on her apricot skin just below the heart, and there was a horrible collection of chamber pots, full and half-full, and one with surface bubbles, on the floor of the hall in her family's boardinghouse lodgings which I visited early one morning to be given by her, as she was being dressed, a dead humming-bird moth found by the cat. But when I met Colette, I knew at once that this was the real thing. Colette seemed to me so much stranger than all my other chance playmates at Biarritz! I somehow acquired the feeling that she was less happy than I, less loved. A bruise on her delicate, downy forearm gave rise to awful conjectures. "He pinches as bad as my mummy," she said, speaking of a crab. I evolved various schemes to save her from her parents, who were *"des bourgeois de Paris"* as I heard somebody tell my mother with a slight shrug. I interpreted the disdain in my own fashion, as I knew that those people had come all the way from Paris in their blue-and-yellow limousine (a fashionable adventure in those days) but had drably sent Colette with her dog and governess by an ordinary coach-train. The dog was a female fox terrier with bells on her collar and a most waggly behind. From sheer exuberance, she would lap up salt water out of Colette's toy pail. I remembered the sail, the sunset, and the lighthouse pictured on that pail, but I cannot recall the dog's name, and this bothers me.

During the two months of our stay at Biarritz, my passion for Colette all but surpassed my passion for Cleopatra. Since my parents were not keen to meet hers, I saw her only on the beach; but I thought of her constantly. If I noticed she had been crying, I felt a surge of helpless anguish that brought tears to my own eyes. I could not destroy the mosquitoes that had left their bites on her frail neck, but I could, and did, have a successful fistfight with a red-haired boy who had been rude to her. She used to give me warm handfuls of hard candy. One day, as we were bending together over a starfish, and Colette's ringlets were tickling my ear, she suddenly turned toward me and kissed me on the cheek. So great was my emotion that all I could think of saying was, "You little monkey."

I had a gold coin that I assumed would pay for our elopement. Where did I want to take her? Spain? America? The mountains above Pau? *"Là-bas, là-bas, dans la montagne,"* as I had heard Carmen sing at the opera. One strange night, I lay awake, listening to the recurrent thud of the ocean and planning our flight. The ocean seemed to rise and grope in the darkness and then heavily fall on its face.

Of our actual getaway, I have little to report. My memory retains a glimpse of her obediently putting on rope-soled canvas shoes, on the lee side of a flapping tent, while I stuffed a folding butterfly net into a brown-paper bag. The next glimpse is of our evading pursuit by entering a pitch-dark *cinéma* near the Casino (which, of course, was absolutely out of bounds). There we sat, holding hands across the dog, which now and then gently jingled in Colette's lap, and were shown a jerky, drizzly, but highly exciting bullfight at St. Sebástian. My final glimpse is of myself being led along the promenade by Linderovski. His long legs move with a kind of ominous briskness and I can see the muscles of his grimly set jaw working under the tight skin. My bespectacled brother, aged nine, whom he happens to hold with his other hand, keeps trotting out forward to peer at me with awed curiosity, like a little owl.

Among the trivial souvenirs acquired at Biarritz before leaving, my favorite was not the small bull of black stone and not the sonorous sea shell but something which now seems almost symbolic—a meerschaum penholder with a tiny peephole of crystal in its ornamental part. One held it quite close to one's eye, screwing up the other, and when one had got rid of the shimmer of one's own lashes, a miraculous photographic view of the bay and of the line of cliffs ending in a lighthouse could be seen inside.

And now a delightful thing happens. The process of recreating that penholder and the microcosm in its eyelet stimulates my memory to a last effort. I try again to recall the name of Colette's dog—and, triumphantly, along those remote beaches, over the glossy evening sands of the past, where each footprint slowly fills up with sunset water, here it comes, here it comes, echoing and vibrating: Floss, Floss, Floss!

Colette was back in Paris by the time we stopped there for a day before continuing our homeward journey; and there, in a fawn park under a cold blue sky, I saw her (by arrangement between our mentors, I believe) for the last time. She carried a hoop and a short stick to drive it with, and everything about her was extremely proper and stylish in an autumnal, Parisian, *tenue-de-ville-pour-fillettes* way. She took from her governess and slipped into my brother's hand a farewell present, a box of sugar-coated almonds, meant, I knew, solely for me; and instantly she was off, tap-tapping her glinting hoop through light and shade, around and around a fountain choked with dead leaves, near which I stood. The leaves mingle in my memory with the leather of her shoes and gloves, and there was, I remember, some detail in her attire (perhaps a ribbon on her Scottish cap, or the pattern of her stockings) that reminded me then of the rainbow spiral in a glass marble. I still seem to be holding that wisp of iridescence, not knowing exactly where to fit it, while she runs with her hoop ever faster around me and finally dissolves among the slender shadows cast on the graveled path by the interlaced arches of its low looped fence.

❦ ❧

BRENDA PETERSEN

Sex as Compassion—A New Eros in a Time of AIDS

When I was nineteen and in my freshman year at the University of California, Davis, I took part in a 1968 experimental program called "Self and Society." Inspired by the '60s novel *The Harrad Experiment*, our program included sexual relations studies and introduced the college's first co-ed dorm, with males and females sharing everything from bathrooms to bedrooms. Oddly enough, familiarity between the sexes bred neither contempt nor couples; instead, most of us found ourselves living side by side like siblings. Out of the two hundred young men and women in my dorm, there were only five or six couples; the rest found romance outside our sociology program.

My boyfriend, Daniel, and I were one of those few couples who met sharing the same bathroom mirror, he shaving and I putting on makeup. Daniel was from Hawaii, part-Polynesian, with lustrous black curls I imagined twirling around my fingers long before I ever touched him. He was dark-skinned, his face wide open and his body muscular, compact. Dreamy and imaginative, he could play more deeply than anyone I had ever met. In a dorm where every exit stairwell was filled with drug deals, antiwar folksingers, or intense encounters of the psychological kind, Daniel and I would escape to his room and read novels together. We'd act out the dialogue and love scenes. Sometimes we'd even switch gender roles, taking turns playing virile hero and shy virgin. We were, in fact, both virgins. I was on the health clinic's waiting list for birth control pills and was very afraid of pregnancy in this time of illegal abortions. Daniel did not trust condoms, having himself been born as a result of that more risky method. We both wanted the protection of the pill. This meant that for four months we would have to figure out how to make love without intercourse.

One day Daniel showed me an old Chinese Taoist pillow book he had found in Hawaii. It was an instructional manual usually given to newlyweds for practicing sexual arts. Illustrated with elegant watercolors and indecipherable Chinese characters, the book did have one English inscription in delicate penmanship: "Practice with careful tenderness. Breathe together."

We lay propped up over the exquisite picture book: Here were couples gazing tenderly into each other's dark eyes, their delicate limbs entwined in elegant postures of worship, abandon, and surrender as they stroked thighs, toes, bellies, gently sloped backs, or graceful buttocks. Their sensual play was artful, their bedrooms adorned with silken beds and painted scrolls—a brilliant, mineral blue-green seascape, a benevolent Taoist master's portrait serenely watching over the lovers. Our favorite picture was a couple in a garden, languid willow falling over their pallet as the woman lay back, contented and trusting, against the man's chest. Embracing her from behind, his hands held her breasts as if they were the most precious porcelain vases held up to golden daylight. At her feet a pink lotus burst open with their pleasure.

Another favorite was a bathing picture that Daniel and I decided to recreate every weekend. During the week I spent hours in health food stores buying lavender soap, loofa sponges, and an East Indian bubble elixir called Treasures of the Sea, whose beads turned the bath a hot blue like the turquoise waters of Daniel's island homeland. He brought volcanic pumice stone for my feet, his mother's homemade tropical shampoo for my hair, and coconut massage oil for my sunburned skin. Because he was deeply interested in geology, he made a life-size topographical map of my body, naming his favorite places—my back, hands, and neck—after mountains and valleys he'd studied on maps of the ancient world. I wrote him primitive poetry, reciting it in our bath as we faced each other, encircled by candles. In our glowing water cave, we were two initiates, learning the luxurious language of touch and time.

Some weekends studying our pillow book, we'd play my Miriam Makeba album, with its African drumming, or listen to recordings of Tibetan chants. We didn't understand the words, just the rhythm. It flowed through our bodies—drum with our heartbeats, chants with our breath. The music moved our hands as we slowly caressed each other. One night I washed Daniel's feet with my hair; another night he washed my hair and stroked it one hundred times, each stroke a prayer murmured for me. Another night, as we embraced, we imagined we were snakes in a slow-motion dance under the earth; in our play we were all the animals we loved, making love. And in our animal selves we glimpsed that this intimacy was a prayer for the whole Earth.

Sometimes we'd sit naked, back to back, like the pillow book illustrated, and simply breathe together. I could feel his heartbeat through my backbone, and I trembled to hear his pulse in my body. Then, turning face to face, we let waves of energy wash over us, and our bellies rose and fell together like molten lava. Each time Daniel felt himself on the edge of orgasm, we'd both keep still, our bodies against one another. Daniel discovered, quite by accident, that he could stop the urge to ejaculate by pressing on a sensitive point between his scrotum and anus for several seconds. This pressure would only increase his pleasure, allowing him to build wave after arousing wave. Instinctively, I would place my hand on top of his head, the other on his buttocks. It was like holding the whole of him between my hands. After a moment, we'd both grow calm and tenderly draw away from the fire in our genitals.

"Breathe, breathe," we'd say, and inhale in sync. The energy moved to our heads and feet all at once like an ecstatic undertow, a sensual, slow flow that awakened arms, tingled in legs, and sang along our spines. "Bottom of the ocean" we called this joy, as our bodies tumbled together, sinking deep, settling at last on the seabed where the pulse of something greater like the sea rocked us. Our skin smelled salty, and our naked bodies gleamed like phosphorescent fishes. We gave off our own light, our own spinning gravity. Sometimes I'd fall asleep, my body stretched on top of Daniel; sometimes I'd wake to find him resting atop me like a comforter made of soft skin. Even when we were apart during the day, we'd carry one another's bodies against our own like a fragrance, sweet and spicy.

It is a great irony of my youth that Daniel and I parted before I obtained the birth control pills to allow us *actual* intercourse. But in all our erotic explorations, we hardly missed "going all the way," since we had found so many other pleasurable ways. Only years later, after much spiritual exploration, did I recognize those months with Daniel as an intuitive blend of tantra, Taoist, and kundalini partner yoga. Daniel and I were very sad to part when he left school to study with a local guru. Mourning him, I finally got the pill, my own little compact wheel-of-life, and I lost my virginity then with a young man who was kind but less inspired than Daniel. But I consider Daniel my first lover; even without intercourse or procreation, we made something alive and holy between us. We made love.

☙ ❧

JAMES MCCONKEY

Idyll

Toward the middle of my career as a college teacher, I had an unexpected classroom insight. Unlike my undergraduates, I had been born long before Auschwitz and Buchenwald, before the invention of the nuclear bomb, television, birth control pills, or even of Scotch tape and Band-aids; before the epidemic of mind-altering drugs, or the shocking collapse of our cities into burgeoning suburbs for the well-to-do and ghettoes for the poor. My advanced years made me, in a crucial way, younger—surely more innocent—than my students, burdened as they were almost from birth with historical knowledge that came to me in increments long after my formative years.

Like nearly all other revelations, this one—that the older we are, the younger we are—was far less original than for years I thought it to be; shortly before my retirement, I learned, in an essay by Stephen Jay Gould that relies upon Robert K. Merton's book *On the Shoulders of Giants*, that my insight is known as the Baconian Paradox, in honor of the popular formulation of it made by Francis Bacon in 1605—even though its origin can be traced as far back as an apocryphal book of the Vulgate Bible. In my case, the insight came to me as the consequence of a student's offhand remark about sex that led me to remember a respite from military duties that I shared with my fiancée at Mammoth Cave National Park one Christmas during World War II.

Not until our fiftieth wedding anniversary—one celebrated far from home—was I able to see our holiday as something more than a self-enclosed idyll, one not only too intimate to mention but isolated by its very poignancy from our later domestic experiences. Idylls, of course, *are* intimate, and *do* demand isolation. Idylls require that their participants separate themselves from historical necessity—from a world they can hold momentarily in obeyance. The world we were keeping in check then was a world at war, with all of its bloody chaos. War commands unthinking obedience from its soldiers on military duty, but relaxes societal proscriptions, particularly those concerned with sexual conduct. Like much else that was part of Jean's and my cultural heritage—including a belief in human brotherhood that made war itself abhorrent—the moral requirement of chastity before marriage had already been subject to rapid revision. So I suppose we were naive even for the times in managing to resist a consummation of our desires—wilfully innocent, perhaps, since neither of us believed that a government should have the power to legislate rules about intimate behavior, mandating an official document in advance of a permanent relationship.

Shortly before my induction into the Army in May 1943, Jean and I were engaged; we were students at the same downtown school, Cleveland College, both of us on the editorial staff of the undergraduate newspaper. For basic infantry training, I was sent to an Army camp in Georgia, as a member of a special battalion. Everybody in that battalion had just graduated from college; indeed, we had all enrolled a couple of years earlier in the Army Specialized Training Program for the same reason: to delay our military service long enough for us to get our degrees. I resented the regimentation, the training to make me an efficient killer; in body as well as mind, I felt a revulsion toward the exercises designed to teach me how to thrust a bayonet into an enemy's guts. For the first time in my life, I was unable to accomplish satisfactorily what was expected of me. Most of the others managed to succeed, and yet in every other way we seemed peers—all of us from similar cultural backgrounds, all of us members of a generation told almost from birth about the horrors of war, and whose history texts in public school, written by Charles and Mary Beard, informed their young readers that economics and not idealism had motivated our past American wars, including the Revolution itself. Now, as college graduates in a specialized program, we attended any number of classroom lectures, but none of them was designed to tell us that *this* war had a moral necessity lacking from the earlier ones. References of German atrocities to Jews were missing, though like all other soldiers the trainees in my battalion were shown graphic slides of what could happen to our penises if we engaged in casual sex without using the condoms available without cost in every day room.

From all those incredibly long days and weeks of basic training, I have but one sharp memory, all of its details made vivid by the happiness I felt. On an extended nighttime march, I broke step to plant one foot firmly on a ribbon of steel at a railroad crossing near a darkened Georgia hamlet, thinking that to do so connected me through a variety of switches and tracks to the passenger depot in East Cleveland, Ohio, a block or two from the house where my beloved lay sleeping.

Upon the completion of basic training, the majority of soldiers in my battalion were sent back to college, to learn foreign languages and advanced skills in mathematics; a handful of us, dropped from the program as inept soldiers, were assigned as infantry privates to a division preparing for combat at a base in southern Kentucky, near the Tennessee border. Long before Christmas, I reserved a room for Jean at the base's guest house for the holiday period, since the brevity of my pass would prevent me from returning to Cleveland. Travel was chiefly by train in those days, and the majority of the rolling stock of the railroads had been requisitioned for military use; train service for civilians was erratic and largely limited to antique passenger cars with straw seats and tulip-shaped overhead lamp brackets. Jean's 425-mile journey from Cleveland took eighteen hours, including a stopover in Cincinnati; the train from Cincinnati to Clarksville, Tennessee, was so crowded that she and many others sat on their suitcases, which wouldn't have been so difficult, she told me, if she and the others in the aisles hadn't had to rise and push aside their suitcases so often, to let the vendors of apples and soft drinks pass. She arrived the night preceding Christmas Eve, tired and smudged with soot but happy that we would be together.

Only the kind intercession of a USO volunteer kept Jean from returning to Cleveland the next evening. Her reservation at the guest house was abruptly cancelled late in the afternoon of her first full day on the base, apparently to accommodate a last-moment request by officers for their wives or friends; the few hotels and rooming houses in the nearby towns had long since been booked to capacity. I packed my weekend bag on the unlikely chance that something would turn up; harried as she was, the woman at the USO housing desk in Clarksville took a particular interest in our predicament, intensified as it was by our wish for separate rooms, and was able to secure reservations for us at the hotel within Mammoth Cave National Park, only ninety miles away. Darkness had long since fallen, and we had to rush to the station to catch the northbound train—the same one that Jean would have taken by herself, if we'd not found a place to stay. Shortly before midnight on Christmas Eve, the train stopped, just for us—for an infantry private and his fiancée!—at a little trackside sign marked "Cave City."

The helpfulness of nearly everybody we met, from the USO volunteer onward, contributed to the specialness of our brief holiday. The conductor held up the train in the apparent emptiness of the Kentucky countryside long enough to point out a path through the weeds that would take us across a road to a light that marked a telephone booth, where we could call a taxi. I called the after-hours number of the taxi company; the driver's wife, who answered the phone, said the family had just begun to open their Christmas presents, so we'd need to be patient. Less than ten minutes later, though, the taxi arrived: the driver thought the weather (we hadn't even noticed that a cold drizzle had started to fall) too miserable to leave us waiting long. The hotel was a two-story frame building maybe ten minutes away; a large evergreen near the entrance glowed with colored lights. The driver carried Jean's bag into the lobby. He refused a tip, wishing us and the clerk at the registration desk—a boy of about fifteen—a merry Christmas. In an alcove off the lobby, a log fire was burning in a stone hearth; the alcove was just large enough for a couple of upholstered chairs and a small table with a checkerboard. A pair of white-framed and many-paned glass doors separated the lobby from the much larger dining room—empty of guests at this hour of course, but with another Christmas tree that lit up a series of linen-covered tables, each decorated with its own miniature tree.

Breakfast would be waiting for us in that dining room, the clerk said; he'd have to wake us quite early, in order for us to take the day-long Christmas trip led by a park ranger through the cave. For servicemen, the guided tour was free. Since Mammoth Cave itself was the only reason for the hotel's existence, he took it for granted that we would go: as I remember, he gave us our tickets after we'd signed the registration book. He led us down a long corridor to our first-floor rooms. It turned out that they were connected, as was the case throughout the hotel, by a bathroom serving both rooms. The clerk said he could lock the deadbolt of one of the bathroom doors if we wished him to, though it meant that one of us would have to use the lavatory at the far end of the hall. How strange it now seems that both of us were embarrassed, and that the adolescent clerk himself—no doubt a high school student brought in as a holiday substitute—was blushing!

Jean and I decided the deadbolt lock wasn't necessary. On that first night, we slept in our separate rooms, but with both bathroom doors open. I woke on occasion to hear laughter and music from a party down the hall, or the sound of the rain at the window, and imagined I could hear Jean stirring in her sleep.

At breakfast, the guests included those partying the night before, two WAC officers and their male civilian companions. It was still raining—as it did for most of our stay—but it didn't matter, since we and the other guests spent the daylight hours of Christmas Day underground, with a box lunch provided for us on picnic tables in a vast cavern. We had crossed three counties, the ranger said as we came to the surface by a country road where a bus was waiting to transport us back to the hotel. My recollection of our exploration of underground spectacles is far less distinct than are my memories of sitting across the table from Jean that night in the hotel restaurant, with its white linen, courteous attendants bearing platters of holiday food, and its Christmas tree, whose colored lights were reflected in her eyes; afterwards, of sitting opposite her again, this time in the lobby alcove's upholstered chairs, where we played checkers before the log fire; and finally of lying next to her on her bed or mine (she in her nightgown and I in my khaki Army shorts) where we talked long into the night about whatever came into our minds. We argued about which one of us was better at checkers; we reminisced about our first meeting (a janitorial assistant at the college, I had been assigned an early-morning task of dusting the tops of the lockers in the women's lavatory area: embarrassed that a young woman had entered who might or might not see me crouched above her on the lockers, I called out, "Don't mind me: I'm just working my way through college"); and we imagined what we might do after the war ended. We could, for example, move to some town with lovely old houses set far back from the tree-lined streets, a town in which we would raise a family while editing together the weekly newspaper.

Jean said she needed to warn me about one thing, after we'd married and moved to that little town—since childhood, she'd twisted about a lot in bed. "Like this," she said, rolling over and over so rapidly that even I became dizzy, from laughing as well as from watching her whirl. "But that's because you've been sleeping alone," I said, pulling her close. She pretended to roll again, but lay quietly, her head resting on my shoulder. (The two couples down the hall had resumed their riotous partying and whatever else it led up to; only momentarily was our own resolute chastity in serious doubt.) I woke in the morning, smelling the sweetness of Jean's hair on the pillow we shared.

We had arranged with the taxi driver to pick us up at nightfall the day after Christmas for the longer ride to Bowling Green, where Jean would board the train taking her home and I the one returning me to Clarksville. We dawdled over meals, and walked along the gravel paths of the hotel grounds, despite the rain; and we let the warmth of the log fire dry the dampness from our clothes while we played more aimless games of checkers. We didn't speak much; just to hold hands while looking into the other's eyes brought us close to the tears of imminent loss. But when the taxi driver asked us if we had enjoyed our stay, we smiled and said words like Yes, very much—words which, however true, couldn't begin to indicate how we truly felt. In Bowling Green, the train station was packed with travelers heading either north or south. Jean's train was the first to arrive. Swept aboard in the jostling army of passengers eager for a seat, she made her way down an aisle already crowded with standees; sometimes from the platform I could see only the tip of the jaunty feather of her hat. My sense of loss turned into anguish at the thought that she probably wouldn't find a seat; I prayed that she would. I remember nothing about my own train ride back to Clarksville.

About four months later—on May 6, 1944—we were married,

during the furlough granted all members of my division preceding our departure for Europe.

To celebrate our fiftieth anniversary, Jean and I spent a couple of weeks in New Zealand. We went there for a number of reasons. We wanted to go somewhere by ourselves, partly to prevent the fuss our three sons and extended family members would make if we had stayed at home; since childhood, Jean had dreamed of visiting those far-away islands; and New Zealand, according to the guidebooks, was a reasonably prosperous and peaceful democracy that had not despoiled the landscapes—glacier-topped mountains, rainswept fjords, green valleys filled with sheep, rugged coasts with pristine beaches—that made it one of the most beautiful places in the world.

Though graffiti were beginning to appear on city walls, we felt as if we had been transported back in time to the idealized America of our childhood, if not earlier than that. (In one town we watched a group of adolescents dismount from their bicycles long enough to pick up some litter in the street, tossing it into a nearby basket.) The kindness bestowed upon us was like that given us long ago by a USO volunteer, a train conductor, and a taxi driver; but then it had much to do with the Christmas season, and with what had to be obvious to anybody who saw us—we were young and in love, and I was in uniform. Now, of course, almost everybody was much younger than we, and maybe we reminded others of their grandparents; as for the people our own age that we met, their generosity might have come from the fact that I had been an American soldier in a distant war. "We're still grateful to you Yanks, for saving us from the Japs," a silver-haired pharmacist told me; for, by the time of Pearl Harbor, the majority of New Zealand's own troops were fighting for Britain in Europe. "Yip, we know we're a kindly people," a mechanic who had come to rescue us from a car breakdown told Jean with disarming frankness. "That's because there's still so few of us in a free and beautiful land." The low population density of that land—less than three-and-a-half million people in a pair of islands a bit larger than the Great Britain from which the ancestors of almost everybody not a Maori had come—has something to do with its remoteness from the West; the consideration its people give to strangers may also be a consequence of their knowledge that loneliness is bonded to their good luck.

Loneliness has far more than an alliterative connection with love as well as luck. Loneliness—that response to a separation either real or portended—is what we feel most strongly, during the first and painful stirrings of adolescent love; it is what we would assuage in marriage. But the luckier and longer the marriage, the greater the awareness of the inevitable separation. On the morning of our last day in New Zealand, I was having thoughts—if feelings can be called thoughts—of this kind. We had checked out of our hotel in Queenstown, a resort on the South Island nestled between the mountains and a lake. While waiting for the local flight that would take us to the international airport at Christchurch, we took a stroll in Queenstown Gardens, where the late roses were still in full bloom; at home, our buds would just be opening. That last day was also the anniversary day of our wedding. Just before the ceremony, the minister, who disapproved of wartime marriages, said he supposed his advice that we postpone ours had come too late to do any good. During the ritual itself, his words and our responses echoed in the vast emptiness of a vaulted auditorium: only members of our immediate families were in attendance. We were still standing on the altar, for I had just finished kissing the bride, when a girl of six or seven—much as all Italians do in their cathedrals, this American child was taking a shortcut home through the church—looked at the sudden paleness on my face and asked me if I wanted a glass of water. But the expectations and anxieties of a previously chaste couple on their wedding day, as well as the gratified release that follows, are so extraordinary that they provide few if any of the later associations so necessary to the reverberations of memory; it was Christmas at Mammoth Cave that I was now remembering, as if that idyll had been merely a prelude, a forshadowing of what was yet to come. The association was a quick and simple one: having crossed through the gardens, we were standing on the lake shore, uncertain of where to go next. We sat on a rock. I grasped Jean's hand, we looked into each other's eyes, and for a moment we were sitting before the hearth in the alcove of a friendly old hotel, pretending to be engrossed in checkers while waiting for the taxi we didn't want to come. Is it sentimental to acknowledge that one's own marriage, whatever its problems, has been the idyll, all along? I don't think so, given the anguish that idylls bring. Jean, while not privy to the particular associations that had taken her with me so far back in time, still knew the reason for my sudden grief.

Mammoth Cave Hotel, I've heard, was long ago replaced by a brick motel with all the modern conveniences: it has vanished from Earth, along with our innocence. About that innocence, I'm of two minds, knowing that innocence is relative to its time, and often is the result of moral blindness; while also believing that the trust of young lovers in each other's integrity—despite (or because of) the vagaries, the hypocrisies, and the growing problems of the world beyond them—is essential to whatever happiness they conceivably will find. "I am older, hence I am younger" is a paradox that allows us some defiance against a relentless forward chronology; still, the children who are our elders have a vulnerable innocence of their own that time itself will undo. Aphorisms cling to us like barnacles, as we age.

On our way home, Jean and I, having crossed the International Date Line before reaching our stopover in Tahati, were able to celebrate our fiftieth anniversary for a second consecutive day. This may not have been a logical paradox, but it was an unexpected delight to toast each other with champagne from a hotel balcony that evening, while watching the volcanic mass of a neighboring island turn into a scattering of mysterious lights across the darkening tropical sea.

JAN MORRIS

God, Love and Abysinnian Cats

I have been a pagan all my life, and more exactly a pantheist, believing that the divine is not merely manifest in nature, but is actually nature itself. What else, after all, is the Christians' Holy Ghost? This unsophisticated conviction was supernaturally confirmed to me one day after I had been listening, as I washed my hair in my Sunday morning bath, to a radio sermon. "God is love," the preacher had declared, and I had countered him aloud through the shampoo. It should be the other way round, I told him. It's not that God is love, but that love is God.

Later that morning, as I walked down a lane on my daily exercise, I found myself debating that proposition too. How could I reconcile it with my own naturist beliefs? Nature certainly wasn't simply love—it was teeth, claw, decay, competition, blood, sex and hunger. But suddenly, truly as in revelation, I had an answer from nature itself. Suddenly every tree leaned kindly toward me, every bush seemed to be smiling, and from the grass and the flowers beside the road, from the sheep over the stone wall and the mountains beyond, I felt a glow of reassurance. Yes, they all seemed to me saying, love is the emotional figure of God, but the whole grand panoply of the natural order, fierce and placid, carnivorous or herbivore, crumbling into senility or awakening into new life, is the physical embodiment of love. Trust us! Keep walking!

I do trust them, and I believe that any cruelty and indignity practised upon the natural world, whether it be chemical farming or animal vivisection, is a direct affront to love and thus to the divine. And since this concept is necessarily woolly, like all religious conviction, I concentrate my thoughts about it upon the animals.

Long ago I came to realize that every single living creature, from a saint to a slug, from a rose to the most ragged weed, was of equal value in the eye of nature. We are all comrades, not waiting for some resurrected unity in the hereafter, but united now, and we should treat one another if not necessarily with affection, at least with respect. "Why should I hurt thee?" said Sterne's Uncle Toby, releasing a fly through the window. "This world is surely wide enough to hold both thee and me," and I agree with him. Flies are safe with me—mosquitoes too, if they don't press their luck.

Nature is scarcely love in the Christian, turn-the-other-cheek sense. The tiger suffers not the little children, as she springs for the jugular of a baby antelope, and the whale gobbles up several million of its algaic fellow creatures, I am told, in every mouthful of sustenance. It is the heedless and unnecessary violation of natural laws that is evil: a man may eat a lamb with dignity, as a fox eats a mouse—may even give to the act some sacramental virtue if he thinks of it, between munches, as a symbolic affirmation of fellowship.

All this has made of me an animal liberationist of almost atavistic passion. A mild-mannered American Episcopalian bishop, talking on Hong Kong radio one day about "the sanctity of human life," found himself when he left the studio fallen upon by me with vituperative fury, so blind did the phrase declare him to be to the sanctity of life as a whole. In New York once I tried exclaiming loudly, when I saw a woman in the street wearing a mink or a Persian lamb, "Oh, the poor animals," until I found that nobody took the slightest notice, assuming me to be merely another crazed bag lady.

But if my obsession with animals has caused me anguish and bitterness, it has brought me infinite joy too, and this has been expressed above all in the companionship of Abyssinian cats.

It might have been goats, wittiest and most potent of the beasts, who have affected the course of empires in their time, and who are destined one day to take over the world in partnership with left-handed humans. It might have been donkeys: we had a couple for years, living wild on our brackeny hillside in South Wales, and I greatly respected their calm and kind intelligence. However I don't want the destiny of my own garden goat-governed too, and it is hard to establish intimacy with feral asses, so instead I have thrown in my lot with the cats. I remember as if it were yesterday the moment I set eyes on my own first Abyssinian, bought for me as a present and sent to me in Wales by rail, all by himself in a basket. I met the train at Bangor station, and opening the lid of the basket, saw looking up at me with extreme confidence and cheerfulness what appeared to be a very small wild creature, ticked and gold-brown like a hare, with little tufts on the end of his ears. He gave me the impression that he had arranged the journey himself, having decided to emigrate out of a forest somewhere, and from that day to this I have regarded my Abyssinian cats as generous visitors from outer nature, kindly spending their lives with me.

Only the cat can give us this sensation. Dogs are disciplined, horses are enslaved, cows and pigs are exploited. Only cats join us as opportunistic partners. They do things for us, we do things for them, and when both sides feel like it we share the pleasure of each others' company. I find this arrangement exciting enough with any cat, even with the most homely of farmyard toms, descended from generations of cats next door; but with Abyssinians I find it thrilling, for they seem to bring into the house with them a suggestion of nature at its most defiantly untamable.

Not that the Abyssinian cat himself is in the least untamed. He is the most affectionate and easygoing of animals. But his form is so lithe, elegant and exotic, his manners are so sensually graceful, and the look in his eye is sometimes so infinitely unfathomable, sometimes so mocking, that I can easily imagine him at nighttime, or when I am away from home, leading another life that is altogether his own. The cats of the ancient Egyptians, whom they mummified as sacred, were very like Abyssinians, and there are certain forest cats of Africa who appear to be close relatives.

The origin of the breed is in fact uncertain. I belong to a school— of course I do—which claims that the first examples came to Britain in the kitbags of soldiers returning from Lord Napier's punitive expedition to Ethiopia in 1868. There are some however, who maintain they originated in other parts of Africa, or in Asia, and even a few numbskulls who say they are descended merely from very refined and skillfully bred English tabbies. I made a special journey once to see the famous sacred cats of Aksum, in northern Ethiopia, in the hope that I would find them to be obvious relatives of our Abyssinians. In those days they were officially maintained by the Cathedral of St. Mary of Zion, on the grounds that their ancestors had been brought to Aksum by the Virgin Mary herself, and each cat was supported by a particular patch of revenue-bearing land. There were six sacred cats when I was there, and I easily persuaded myself that their manner of mixed irony and bravado was very like that of the little creature in the basket at Bangor station; if I could not honestly claim they looked much like him, being a good deal plumper and more complacent, well, who would look lithe, thin and Pharaonic after a thousand years of episcopal bounty?

Whatever their roots, I like to think that my Abyssinians have given me an intimate link with the command post of nature, a chain of communication with headquarters. They have lived with me now through four cat generations, and though they have come to me with preposterous breeders' names, I have renamed them one and all after figures of Ethiopian myth or history: Theodore, Menelik, Solomon, Prester John—names of a wild grandeur, I like to think, by which I pay my own tribute to their other, private lives.

I am aware nevertheless that my cats are compromised. I do not entirely trust them—they may be spies, like dolphins, reporting to some unknown authority. When I want to experience the impartial immensity of nature I escape their surveillance and go down to the river in the evening. It is called the Dwyfor, and rising in the mountains seven or eight miles above my house, debouches into Cardigan Bay a couple of miles below. It is not very wide or deep, but it is very fast, and on a summer evening especially, for all the ravages of silage farming and air pollution, it is still full of life. I never see glow-worms nowadays, and toads seem rarer than they were, but there are still plenty of bats and dragonflies, and sometimes a heron rises ghostlike in the evening and flaps off into the dusk.

There as darkness falls I sit on a rock to watch the water, and feel I am looking into the heart of all things. I know that when the night draws on the heroic sea trout, making their way upstream to spawn in the mountain pools, will be swimming by me in urgent instinct, battling their way against rapid and waterfall, swift and bold and muscular: and thinking of them with admiration, though I cannot see them, I realize that nature's first message, the message of that Sunday morning revelation, is that love is strenuous and risky, comes in all kinds, and moves mysteriously.

PERMISSIONS

Ackerman, Diane. "Beija-Flor," "Zoë," "Ode to the Alien" from *Jaguar of Sweet Laughter.* Random House, 1991. Excerpt from *A Natural History of Love,* Random House, 1994. Reprinted by permission of the publisher.

Adams, Alice. "Complicities." Copyright © 1996 by Alice Adams. Reprinted by permission of International Creative Management, Inc. Originally published in the *Michigan Quarterly Review.*

Addonizio, Kim. "Survivors," copyright © Kim Addonizio. Reprinted with the permission of the author. This story originally appeared in the *Gettysburg Review* and *Micro Fiction* (W. W. Norton, 1996).

Appleman, Marjorie. "Love," and "Another Beginning" from *Against Time.* Birnham Wood Press, 1994. Copyright © 1994 Marjorie Appleman. Used by permission of the author.

Appleman, Philip. "Crystal Anniversary" and "A Priest Forever" from *New and Selected Poems, 1956–1996.* University of Arkansas Press, 1996. Copyright © 1996 by Philip Appleman. Reprinted with the permission of the author.

Ashbery, John. "A Blessing in Disguise" from *Rivers and Mountains.* Holt, Rinehart & Winston, 1966. Copyright © 1962, 1963, 1964, 1966 by John Ashbery. Reprinted by permission of Georges Borchardt, Inc., for the author. "Just Walking Around" from *A Wave.* Viking, 1984.

cert" from *Loving a Woman in Two Worlds* by Robert Bly. Copyright © 1985 by Robert Bly. Used by permission of Doubleday, a division of Bantam Doubleday Dell Publishing Group, Inc.

Borgia, Lucretia, and Pietro Bembo. Letters from *Messer Pietro Mio— Letters between Lucrezia Borgia and Pietro Bembo.* Copyright © 1985, 1987 by Hugh Shankland and Libanus Press, Marlborough.

Browning, Robert, and Elizabeth Barrett. Letters from *The Letters of Robert Browning and Elizabeth Barrett,* edited by Elvan Kintner. Cambridge, Mass.: Harvard University. Copyright © 1969 by the President and Fellows of Harvard College.

Camus, Albert. "Losing a Loved One" from *Youthful Writings* by Albert Camus, trans. Ellen Conroy Kennedy (Hamish Hamilton, 1977). Copyright © Editions Gallimard, 1974. Translation copyright © 1976 by Alfred A. Knopf, Inc. Reprinted by permission of the publishers.

Capellanus, Andreas. Excerpt from *The Art of Courtly Love* by Andreas Capellanus, copyright © 1960 by the Columbia University Press. Reprinted with the permission of the publisher.

Caputi, Anthony. Excerpt from the novel-in-progress *To Know the Wind is Mortal,* copyright © 1996 by Anthony Caputi. Reprinted with the permission of the author.

Cedering, Siv. "Ukiyo-E" from *Letters from the Floating World.* University of Pittsburgh Press, 1984. Copyright © 1984 by Sic Cedering. "Crossing the Sound" by Siv Cedering, copyright © 1997 by Siv Cedering. "Country Music" by Siv Cedering, *The Georgie Review,* Winter, 1992. Copyright © 1992 by Siv Cedering.

Chesterton, G. K. "Romantic Love" from *A G. K. Chesterton Selected Anthology.* Reprinted with the permission of A. P. Watt Ltd. on behalf of The Royal Literary Fund.

Christopher, Nicholas. "Sleep" from a book-in-progress. Copyright © Nicholas Christopher, 1996. Reprinted with permission of Nicholas Christoper. "Rice Wine" from a book-in-progress. Copyright Nicholas Christopher, 1996. Reprinted by permission of Nicholas Christopher.

Ciardi, John. "Men Marry What They Need" from *Poems of Love and Marriage.* University of Arkansas Press. Copyright © 1989. Reprinted by permission of the publisher.

Colette. Excerpt from *Earthly Paradise* by Colette, edited by Robert Phelps. Translation copyright © 1956, renewed 1994 by Farrar, Straus & Giroux, Inc. Reprinted by permission of Farrar, Straus & Giroux, Inc. and Reed International Books Limited. Letters from *Letters from Co-*

Song" from *Firekeeper: New and Selected Poems* by Pattiann Rogers. Copyright © 1994 by Pattiann Rogers. Reprinted with permission from Milkweed Editions.

Sand, George. Letter to Gustave Flaubert, from *The George Sand—Gustave Flaubert Letters,* translated by Aimee L. McKenzie. Translation copyright © 1921 by Boni & Liveright, Inc., renewed 1949 by Aimee L. McKenzie. Reprinted by permission of Liveright Publishing Corporation.

Schulz, Bruno. "Spring" from *Sanatorium Under the Sign of the Hour Glass.* Reprinted by permission of Walker and Company.

Scott, Joanna. Excerpt from *The Manikin,* by Joanna Scott. Copyright © 1996 by Joanna Scott. Reprinted by permission of Henry Holt & Co., Inc.

Sexton, Anne. "The Ballad of the Lonely Masturbator" from *Love Poems.* Copyright © 1967, 1968, 1969 by Anne Sexton. Reprinted by permission of Houghton Mifflin Company. All rights reserved.

Simpson, Louis. "The Birch" from *At the End of the Open Road.* Copyright © 1963 by Wesleyan University Press. Reprinted by permission of University Press of New England. "Dvonya" from *Adventures of the Letter I* by Louis Simpson. Copyright © 1971 by Louis Simpson. Used by permission of the author.

Snyder, Gary. "Cross-Legg'd" from *Mountains and Rivers Without End.* Counterpoint, 1996. Reprinted with permission.

Spark, Muriel. "Love." Copyright © 1984 by Muriel Spark. Reprinted by permission of Georges Borchardt, Inc. and David Higham Associates.

Spender, Stephen. "Daybreak" from *The Collected Poems: 1929–1953.* Reprinted by permission of Random House.

Steiner, Stan. "Must We Live Weeping?: A Father's Advice to His Daughter" from *Aztlan: An Anthology of Mexican American Literature,* edited by Luis Valdez and Stan Steiner. Copyright © 1972 by Vintage Books. Used by permission of Vera Steiner, literary executor.

Stern, Gerald. "Both of Them Were Sixty-five" and "June First," which originally appeared in the *The Red Coal* (Houghton Mifflin) and were republished in *Leaving Another Kingdom, Selected Poems.* Harper. Used with the permission of the author.

Stowe, Harriet Beecher. Letter reprinted from *The Limits of Sisterhood: The Beecher Sisters on Women's Rights and Women's Sphere,* by Jeanne Boydston, Mary Kelley, and Anne Margolis. Copyright © 1988 by the University of North Carolina Press. Used by permission of the publisher.

Strand, Mark. "Our Masterpiece is the Private Life." Copyright ©

INDEX

A

Abelard, Peter, 641
A bright moon illumines the high building, 278
A charming girl, full of dejected love, 280
Ackerman, Diane, 448
Adams, Alice, 187
Adams, Henry, 592
Addison, Joseph, 538
Addonizio, Kim, 193
Advising a Young Man as to the Selection of a Mistress, 537
Aeneid, The, 287
Aethiopica, The, 19
After the clash of elevator gates, 379
After we had loved each other intently, 453
Age of Fable, 580
A Harmony, 350
Air and Fire, 405
Alas, my love, you do me wrong, 305
Alexandrian Erotic Fragment, The, 626
Ali, Agha Shahid, 483
All for Love: Baby Doe and Silver Dollar, 252
All in the merry month of May, 311

All right. I may have lied to you and about you, and made a few pronounce-
ments a bit too sweeping, perhaps, and possibly forgotten to tag the bases
here or there, 367
All's over, then: does truth sound bitter, 349
All the long night we talked of your long hair, 297
All thoughts, all passions, all delights, 337
Almanac Branch, The, 238
A man and a woman sit near each other, and they do not long, 453
A man and woman lie on a white bed, 478
A mighty pain to love it is, 321
A month or twain to live on honeycomb, 334
Amorist, An, 530
Anacreon, 321
Anatomy of Melancholy, The, 531
And here's a portrait of my granddaughter Una, 371
Andreas Capellanus, 508
And what is love? It is a doll dress'd up, 329
And wilt thou have me fashion into speech, 348
Anna Karenina, 105
Annabel Lee, 342
Another Beginning, 391
Antigone, 281
Antony and Cleopatra, 301
Appleman, Marjorie, 390
Appleman, Philip, 386
Apuleius of Madaura, 12
Aristotle, 495
Arnold, Matthew, 335
Arouet, François-Marie, *see* **Voltaire**
Art of Courtly Love, The, 508
As a man and woman make, 477
As bamboo chill drifts into the bedroom, 279
Ashbery, John, 481
A surprise siren wakes, 391
A sweet disorder in the dress, 319
At dawn she lay with her profile at that angle, 365
Athenais, François, Marquise de Montespan, 666
At the Cookout, 418
At the Mouth of a Creek, 437
At the Wedding March, 351
Aubade (Goldstein), 421
Aucassins and Nicolette, 23
Auden, W. H., 368
Augustine, Saint, 632
Austen, Jane, 75
Autobiography, The (Franklin), 688
Awake at four, 454
Awakening at dawn thirty-, 396

B

Bachelor's Banquet, The, 525
Bachelor's Complaint of the Behavior of Married People, A, 550
Bacon, Francis, 526
Balaban, John, 440
Balaban, Lonnie, 439
Ballad of the Lonely Masturbator, The, 376
Ballou, Sullivan, 742
Barbara Allen, 311
Barker, George, 372
Barrett, Elizabeth, *see* Browning, Elizabeth Barrett
Barter, 377
Baudelaire, Charles, 738
Beast, I've known you, 449
Beast of the Haitian Hills, The, 178
Beauty alone will not account for her, 296
Because, like the sun, 436
Because I Never Learned the Names of Flowers, 461
Beckett, Samuel, 360
Before Parting, 334
Before Us, 427
Behn, Aphra, 45
Beija-Flor, 448
Bell, Marvin, 467
Bembo, Pietro, 645
Be My Mistress Short or Tall, 319
Bernstein, Aline, 762
Berry, Wendell, 402
Berryman, John, 364
Bethune, Maximilien de, Duc de Sully, 650
Beyle, Marie-Henri, *see* Stendhal
Bialosky, Jill, 474
Bible, The, 277, 498
Birch, 441
Birch tree, you remind me, 441
Birthday Poem, A, 396
Black Elk, 708
Blake, William, 333
Blessing, A, 362
Blessing in Disguise, A, 482
Bly, Robert, 453
Boethius, 505
Bonaparte, Napoleon, *see* Napoleon I, Emperor of France
Book of Laughter and Forgetting, The, 225
Book of the Courtier, The, 523
Book of the Thousand Nights and a Night, The, 132
Borgia, Lucrezia, 647

Boswell, James, 693
Both of Them Were Sixty-five, 469
Bracelet, Thimble and Hoof, 467
Bradstreet, Anne, 329
Brews, Margery, 644
Broken Heart, The, 557
Brontë, Charlotte, 76, 734
Brontë, Emily, 86
Browning, Elizabeth Barrett, 348, 720
Browning, Robert, 349, 718
Bulfinch, Thomas, 580
Burney, Fanny, 62
Burns, Robert, 340
Burton, Richard, 132
Burton, Robert, 531
Busy old fool, unruly Sun, 307
Butler, Samuel, 746
But soft, what light through yonder window breaks!, 303
Byron, Lord (George Gordon), 334, 702
By the side of the lake where last summer, 444

C

Caline, 148
Camus, Albert, 617
Capellanus, Andreas, *see* Andreas Capellanus
Caputi, Anthony, 193
Carew, Thomas, 321
Carlyle, Thomas, 94
Carroll, Lewis, 744
Cartwright, William, 316
Casanova, Jacques, 675
"Cascade is my favorite word," she said, 421
Cascando, 360
Castiglione, Count Baldesar, 523
Cather, Willa, 150
Catullus, 294
Cedering, Siv, 405
Cervantes Saavedra, Miguel de, 37
Charm to Quell a Rival, 275
Châtelet, Émilie du, 671
Chekhov, Anton, 115
Chesterfield, Earl of, 672
Chesterton, G. K., 599
Chopin, Kate, 148
Christopher, Nicholas, 445

Ciardi, John, 372
Clairmont, Jane, 701
Clare, John, 320
Clemens, Samuel, *see* Twain, Mark
Clerestory, 436
Cloister, The, 457
Coleridge, Samuel Taylor, 337, 548
Colette, 756
Colman, George, 541
Come live with me and be my love, 324
Coming into the high room again after years, 426
Coming of Light, The, 382
Complicities, 187
Confessions, The, 632
Congreve, William, 659
Coningsby, 97
Consolation of Philosophy, The, 505
Conversations of Lord Byron, 703
Conversations on Marriage, 533
Cooking for C., 457
Corinthians 13, 498
Cottager to Her Infant, The, 340
Count Rumford: His Book, 197
Country Music, 405
Country of Marriage, The, 402
Country of the Pointed Firs, The, 143
Cowley, Abraham, 321
Crime of Sylvestre Bonnard, The, 129
Crossing, The, 276
Crossing Over, 411
Crossing the Sound by Ferry One Night During the Gulf War, 408
Cross-Legg'd, 475
Cross-Legg'd under the low tent roof, 475
Crystal Anniversary, 390
Cummings, E. E., 358

D

Daisy Miller: A Study, 147
Dangerous Adventure, A, 385
Dante Alighieri, 642
d'Arblay, Madame, *see* Burney, Fanny
David Copperfield, 98
Daybreak, 365
Dedication to My Wife, A, 369
Deep in a glassy ball, the future looks

Definition of Love, The, 315
Defoe, Daniel, 52
Dekker, Thomas, 525
Delbanco, Nicholas, 197
Delight in Disorder, 319
Delusion and Dream, 606
Desire, 337
Diary, The (Pepys), 654
Diary of Adam and Eve, The, 104
Diary of Anaïs Nin, Volume Two, 1934–1939, The, 767
Dickens, Charles, 98
Dickinson, Emily, 344, 740
Disraeli, Benjamin, 97
Doctrow, E. L., 199
does not show his, 473
Doing, a Filthy Pleasure Is, and Short, 290
Donne, John, 306, 532, 649
Don Quijote de la Mancha, 37
Dove, Rita, 473
Dover Beach, 335
Dreamland, 478
Dream Songs, The, 364
Drifting Duckweed, 279
Drifting duckweed floats on the clear water, 279
Drinking Song, A, 361
Drink to Me Only with Thine Eyes, 304
Dry Time, 432
Dvonya, 441

E

Earthly Paradise, 756
Earth Tremors Felt in Missouri, 426
Ecstasy, The, 309
Edge, The, 484
Einsteinian Love, 412
Elegies, The (Propertius), 626
Elegy 5 (Ovid), 293
Eliot, George, 101, 736
Eliot, T. S., 369
Elizabeth I, Queen of England, 298
Ellis, Havelock, 602
Emerson, Ralph Waldo, 351, 563
Empedocles, xxxv
Enabling love, roof of this drafty hutch, 409
Envoi (Pastan), 437

Eros in Long Beach, 421
Ethica Nicomachea, 495
Evans, Mary Ann, *see* **Eliot, George**
Evelina, or A Young Lady's Entrance into the World, 62
Even this late it happens, 382

F

Farquhar, George, 660
Father's Advice to His Daughter, from the Aztec Codices, A, 491
Fearing, Kenneth, 367
Fear Not, Dear Love, 322
February 14th, 396
Filling her compact & delicious body, 364
first: I'm driving home when BOOMER cuts me off, 464
First Love (Clare), 320
First Love (Nabokov), 770
First Love (Turgenev), 112
Fisherman's Wife, 444
Flaubert, Gustave, 90
Flea, The, 306
Fling this useless book away, 326
Floodplain, 437
Flow gently, sweet Afton! among thy green braes, 341
For C., 379
For her candor, salt, 457
For My Wife, 280
France, Anatole, 129
France, Marie de, 24
Frankenstein, or The Modern Prometheus, 69
Franklin, Benjamin, 537, 688
Freud, Sigmund, 606
From a long bottle with a curved neck, 445
From my wife and household and fields, 405
From out of the earth I dig this plant, an herb of most effectual power, 275
From Pent-up, Aching Rivers, 353
Fuller, Sarah Margaret, Marchioness D'Ossoli, 722

G

Gather ye rosebuds while ye may, 318
Gay, John, 312
Ghazal (Ali), 483
Ghosts of the House, The, 409
Gibbon, Edward, 687

Gift, The, 460
Gift of another day!, 460
Gift of the Magi, The, 171
Gilgamesh, 5
Gill, John, 476
Give All to Love, 351
Give me more love, or more disdain, 321
Glück, Louise, 477
Go and catch a falling star, 308
God, Love and Abysinnian Cats, 788
God with honour hang your head, 351
Gold, 472
Goldbarth, Albert, 462
Goldstein, Laurence, 421
Gonzalez-Crussi, Frank, 616
Graham, Jorie, 423
Granddaughter, 371
Greensleeves, 305

H

Had we but world enough, and time, 314
Hafiz, 296
Hall, Donald, 471
Hamilton, Ann, 653
Hamilton, Sir William, 694
Happiness, 478
Hardy, Thomas, 141, 357
Harteis, Richard, 412
Hawthorne, Nathaniel, 86, 713
Hawthorne, Sophia, 715
Hazlitt, William, 562
Heart Exchange, 323
Heat of Snow, 442
Hecht, Anthony, 396
He cleansed his weapons, he polished his arms, 5
Helen, thy beauty is to me, 342
Heliodorus, 19
Heloise, 633
Henry, O., 171
Henry VIII, King of England, 648
Heptameron, The, 33
Herbert, George, 326
Herrick, Robert, 317
Herrin, Lamar, 205
Her slender body moves among the herd, 438

Her window looks upon the lane, 374
High Horse's Counting, 708
High on this whitest place, 443
His Reply, 440
His Shirt, 473
History of Clarissa Harlowe, The, 58
History of the Lover's Leap, 538
Hoffman, Roald, 468
Hogan, Linda, 419
Hollander, John, 442
Homer, 282
Hongo, Garrett Kaoru, 401
Hopkins, Gerard Manley, 351
Housman, A. E., 375
Howard, Richard, 429
How do I love thee? Let me count the ways, 348
Hower, Edward, 210
How It Grows, 468
Ho Xuan Huong, 347
Hugh of Saint Victor, 506
Hummingbird: A Seduction, The, 466
Hundred Secret Senses, The, 249
Hunt, Leigh, 357

I

I abhor the slimy kiss, 318
I am alone tonight, 392
I am the rose of Sharon, and the lily of the valleys, 277
I can feel she has got out of bed, 416
I cannot live with You—, 344
I cry your mercy—pity—love!—aye, love!, 330
I dreamed this mortal part of mine, 317
I dream of you walking at night along the streams, 402
Idyll (McConkey), 780
If all the world and love were young, 325
If a loving belief, an artless heart, 295
If ever two were one then surely we, 329
If in my mind I marry you every year, 425
If I were a female hummingbird perched still, 466
If I Were Tickled by the Rub of Love, 370
Ignatow, David, 476
I grieve and dare not show my discontent, 298
I Knew a Woman, 373
i like my body when it is with your, 358
I'll give myself an hour, I said, and then it was over, 467

I married my shy mistress, the one who made two eggs, bacon and toast, 468
Imperfect Enjoyment, The, 327
Importance of Being Ernest, The, 164
I'm so ripe I could drop, 476
"I'm thirty-six," 412
In all I wish, how happy should I be, 665
I ne'er was struck before that hour, 320
In her room at the prow of the house, 380
In Kindness to an Absent Friend, 649
In love are we made visible, 378
In Love Made Visible, 378
Inscription in the tomb of Queen Ahmose, wife of Tuthmosis I, 5
In summer's heat and mid-time of the day, 293
In the Dark, 395
In the Gold Room, 350
In the last light of a summer day facing the Canadian shore, 395
In the town of Odessa, 441
In this blue room, behind salt-streaked shutters, my wife sleeps, 447
In this brief space I try, 437
In this strange spring—, 437
Ironweed, 220
Irving, Washington, 557
Is there something down by the water keeping itself from us, 381
It always comes, and when it comes they know, 393
It fleeth away, my heart, quickly, 275
I think were I to die, 647
It is all right. All they do, 363
it is moonlight and white where, 461
It Is the Season, 486
I took my TV and bass fiddle to the pawnshop, 417
It's all right, together with me tonight, 465
It's not really enough, 478
It's such a little thing to weep—, 346
It was many and many a year ago, 342

J

Jacobsen, Josephine, 484
James, Henry, 147
James, William, 589
Jane Eyre, 76
Janowitz, Phyllis, 444
Jeffers, Robinson, 371
Jellema, Rod, 461
Jenny Kissed Me, 357
Jewett, Sarah Orne, 143, 745

Johannes Secundus, 517
Jong, Erica, 454
Jonson, Ben, 304
Journal (Victoria), 716
June First, 470
Justice, Donald, 393
Just off the highway to Rochester, Minnesota, 362
Just Walking Around, 481

K

Kamal ud-Din, 281
Kama Sutra, The, 503
Keats, John, 329, 697
Kennedy, William, 220
Killed, the sand, 432
King's Son, The, 3
Kinnell, Galway, 415
Kiss, The, 115
Kisses, The, 517
Kisses Loathsome, 318
Kizer, Carolyn, 460
Kumin, Maxine, 383
Kundera, Milan, 225
Kurowsky, Agnes von, 761
Kwei-li, 730

L

Lamb, Charles, 550
Last Thing I Say, The, 467
Late Love Songs, 436
Late Loving, 425
Late Spring, 426
Launcelot with Bicycle, 374
Lay of the Two Lovers, The, 24
Lay your sleeping head, my love, 368
Leaving the book of love poems beside you, 408
l'Enclos, Ninon de, 686
Let me not to the marriage of true minds, 300
Let's say that I was called away, 440
Letter (Ballou, Sullivan): To Sarah Ballou, 742
Letter (Baudelaire): To Apollonie Sabatier, 738
Letter (Bernstein): To Thomas Wolfe, 762
Letter (Borgia): To Pietro Bembo, 647

Letter (Brews): To John Paston, 644
Letter (Brontë, Charlotte): To Constantine Heger, 734
Letter (Carroll): To Gertrude, 744
Letter (Châtelet): To Duc de Richelieu, 671
Letter (Clairmont): To Lord Byron, 701
Letter (Dickinson): To "Master," 740
Letter (Franklin): To Madame Helvetius, 690
Letter (Hamilton, Sir William): To Lady Emma Hamilton, 694
Letter (Hamilton and Villiers): To Lord Chesterfield, 653
Letter (Hawthorne, Sophia): To Nathaniel Hawthorne, 715
Letter (Heloise): To Peter Abelard, 633
Letter (Henry VIII): To Anne Boleyn, 648
Letter (Jewett): To Annie Fields, 745
Letter (Kurowsky): To Ernest Hemingway, 761
Letter (l'Enclos): To the Marquis de Sévigné, 686
Letter (London): To Charmian Kittredge, 750
Letter (Marcus Aurelius): To Fronto, 631
Letter (Miller): To Anaïs Nin, 766
Letter (Napoleon I): To Josephine Bonaparte, 695
Letter (Nelson): To Lady Emma Hamilton, 693
Letter (Pope): To Teresa Blount, 663
Letter (Porter): To Matthew Josephson, 764
Letter (Sappho): To Anactoria, 625
Letter (Stendhal): To Madame Dembowski, 698
Letter (Stowe, Harriet Beecher): To Calvin Stowe, 726
Letter (Whitman): To Anne Gilchrist, 740
Letters (Abelard): To Bernard, 641; To Heloise, 641
Letters (Barrett [Browning], Elizabeth): To Robert Browning, 720, 722
Letters (Bembo): To Lucrezia Borgia, 645, 646, 647
Letters (Browning, Robert): To Elizabeth Barrett, 718, 719
Letters (Byron): To the Countess Guiccioli, 702, 703
Letters (Colette): To Marguerite Moreno, 760; To Pierre Moreno, 761
Letters (Congreve): To Arabella Hunt, 659
Letters (Eliot, George): To Herbert Spencer, 736; To John Cross, 737
Letters (Farquhar): To Anne Oldfield, 660, 661, 662
Letters (Hawthorne, Nathaniel): To Sophia Hawthorne, 713, 714
Letters (Keats): To Fanny Brawne, 697
Letters (Kwei-li): To her husband, 730, 731, 733
Letters (Mozart, Wolfgang Amadeus): To Constanze Weber Mozart, 691, 692
Letters (Pliny): To Calpurnia, 630, 631; To Paulinus, 630
Letters (Ruskin): To Effie Gray, 728; To Lady Mount-Temple, 729
Letters (Sand): To Alfred de Musset, 706; Gustave Flaubert, 743
Letters (Sterne): To Catherine de Fourmantel, 683; To Lady Percy, 684;
    To Mrs H., 685
Letters (Vanhomrigh): To Jonathan Swift, 663, 664
Letters (Victoria): To King Leopold, 717
Letters (Wilde): To Lord Alfred Douglas, 748, 749

Letters (Wilmot): To Mrs. Barry, 657, 658
Letters and Memoirs (Fuller), 722
Letters to a Young Poet, 752
Let Us Live and Love, 294
Levine, Philip, 395
Liber Amoris, 562
Lies Boys Tell, The, 205
Life has loveliness to sell, 377
Life of Newcastle, The, 653
Life of Samuel Johnson, 693
Life with Swan, 255
Lifted Veil, The, 101
Light, The, 460
Like a small cloud, like a little hovering ghost, 396
L'Invitation au Voyage, 429
Listen, they are applauding, 458
Listening to the Köln Concert, 453
Liu Hsiao-wei, 280
Lives of the Noble Grecians and Romans, The, 500
London, Jack, 750
Longus, 8
Losing a Loved One, 617
Lost Mistress, The, 349
Love (Appleman), 390
Love (Coleridge), 337
Love (Emerson), 563
Love (Herbert), 326
Love (Spark), 619
Love, never foiled in fight!, 281
Love, we are a small pond, 383
Love: Three Pages from a Sportsman's Book, 136
Love and Janus Zyvka, 243
Love and Strife, xxxv
Love and the Creatures, 289
Love bade me welcome, yet my soul drew back, 326
Love in the Western World, 614
Love Is a Powerful Attraction, 555
Love is not all: it is not meat nor drink, 366
Love Letters Between a Noble-Man and His Sister, 45
Love refines, 321
Lover Showeth Wherefore He Is Abandoned of the Beloved He Sometime Enjoyed, Even in Sleep, The, 431
love's function is to fabricate unknownness, 359
Loves of Daphnis and Chloe, The, 8
Love Song (Rogers), 465
Love's Philosophy, 333
Love 20¢ the First Quarter Mile, 367

Lucretius, 286
Lurie, Alison, 227

M

Mackin, Jeanne, 230
Madame Bovary, 90
Make no mistake, you cannot take, 476
Malory, Sir Thomas, 28
Manikin, The, 246
Marcelin, Pierre, 178
March Haiku, 437
Marcus Aurelius, 631
Margaret, Duchess of Newcastle, 653
Margaret, Queen of Navarre, 33
Mark but this flea, and mark in this, 306
Marked Playing Cards, 417
Marlowe, Christopher, 324
Marvell, Andrew, 314
Matthews, William, 457
Maupassant, Guy de, 136
McConkey, James, 780
McGinley, Phyllis, 374
McHugh, Heather, 432
Mediocrity in Love Rejected, 321
Medwin, Thomas, 703
Meeting at Night, 349
Memoirs (Athenais), 666
Memoirs (Bethune), 650
Memoirs, The (Casanova), 675
Memoirs of My Life (Gibbon), 687
Mencken, H. L., 610
Men Marry What They Need, 372
Men You've Loved, The, 476
Merchant of Venice, The, 302
Meredith, William, 409
Merwin, W. S., 426
Metamorphoses or Golden Ass, The, 12
Millay, Edna St. Vincent, 366
Miller, Henry, 766
Milton, John, 321
mind is its own beautiful prisoner, the, 359
Miriamu and the King, 210
Modern Love, 329
Moll Flanders, 52
Montaigne, Michel de, 511

Mont Saint-Michel, 592
Morgan, Robert, 235
Morris, Jan, 788
Morrow, Bradford, 238
Morte D'Arthur, Le, 28
Most near, most dear, most loved and most far, 372
Mozart, Wolfgang Amadeus, 691
My Felisberto, 384
My felisberto is handsomer than your mergotroid, 384
My God, my lotus, my love, 276
My life closed twice before its close—, 344
My Love, 278
My love is of a birth as rare, 315
My mistress' eyes are nothing like the sun, 298
My silks and fine array, 333
My sweetest Lesbia, let us live and love, 294
Myth of Cupid, The, 526
My true love hath my heart, and I have his, 323

N

Nabokov, Vladimir, 770
Naked she lay, clasped in my longing arms, 327
Napoleon I, Emperor of France, 695
Nelson, Lord (Horatio), 693
Neutral Tones, 357
New Life, The, 642
Nightingale and the Rose, The, 166
Nin, Anaïs, 767
No Platonic Love, 316
Notebooks, The (Butler), 746
Note to Marina Marquez of El Paso, Who Sublet My Apartment for the Summer, 462
Nothing, 420
Nothing sings in our bodies, 420
Now sleeps the crimson petal, now the white, 338
Nude Descending a Staircase, 480
Nymph's Reply to the Shepherd, The, 325

O

Oates, Joyce Carol, 458
Ode 147 (Hafiz), 296
Ode 173 (Hafiz), 297
Ode to the Alien, 449
Odyssey, The, 282

Of course, the familiar rustling of programs, 399
Of like importance is the posture too, 286
Of Love (Bacon), 528
Of Love (Stendhal), 561
Of the Nature of Love, 506
Oh! ye bright Stars! that on the Ebon fields, 295
Old Man's Love, An, 98
O Love, Thy Hair!, 281
O love, thy hair! thy locks of night and musk!, 281
On an Anniversary, 394
Once, only once, beloved and gentle lady, 738
"One little kiss, sweet maid!" I cry—, 518
One way I need you, the way I come to need, 434
On Falling in Love, 573
On Grief for Lost Friends, 499
On Monsieur's Departure, 298
Ono no Yoshiki, 278
On Sharing a Husband, 347
On Superstitions in Love, 541
On the Fine Art of Becoming a Man of the World and a Gentleman, 672
On the soft neck, or blooming cheek exprest, 519
ordinarily I wouldn't be introducing Aaron Copland to Ida Stern, 469
Origins of Corn, The, 419
Our Masterpiece Is the Private Life, 381
Overbury, Sir Thomas, 530
Ovid, 291

P

Pale gold of the walls, gold, 472
Paradise Lost, 321
Passion and Order, 548
Passionate Shepherd to His Love, The, 324
Pastan, Linda, 435
Pepys, Samuel, 654
Perfect Woman, 339
Peripeteia, 399
Petersen, Brenda, 778
Petrarch, 295
Petronius, 290
Phaedrus, 492
Philosophical Dictionary, A, 545
Pinsky, Robert, 434
Plato, 492
Pliny, 630
Plutarch, 500
Poe, Edgar Allan, 342

Poem (Meredith), 410
Poet's Wife Sends Him a Poem, The, 439
Poleskie, Stephen F., 243
Pope, Alexander, 663
Porter, Katherine Anne, 764
Porter, William Sydney, *see* Henry, O.
Posture, The, 286
Press Close Bare-Bosom'd Night, 353
Pride and Prejudice, 75
Priest Forever, A, 386
Principle, The, 476
Principles of Psychology, The, 589
Propertius, 626
Proverbs 30, 498
Public Love, 458
P'u Sung-ling, 41

R

Ralegh, Sir Walter, 325
Rapture, 416
Relearning the Language of April, 383
Remedies of Love, The, 616
Report of Health, 392
Restless Night (Tu Fu), 279
Restless Night, A (Hongo), 401
Resurrection (Tolstoy), 110
Resurrection, A (Cather), 150
Reunion with Jake at Still Pond Creek, 445
Rice Wine, 445
Richardson, Samuel, 58
Rilke, Rainer Marie, 752
Robinson, Clement, 305
Roethke, Theodore, 373
Rogers, Pattiann, 465
Romantic Love, 599
Romeo and Juliet, 303
Rougemont, Denis de, 614
Ruskin, John, 728

S

Sanatorium Under the Sign of the Hourglass, 177
Sand, George, 706, 743
Sappho, 295, 625
Sartor Resartus: The Life and Opinions of Herr Teufelsdröckh, 94

Scarlet Letter, The, 86
Schulz, Bruno, 177
Scott, Joanna, 246
Screw the fate that makes you share a man, 347
Secundus, Johannes, *see* Johannes Secundus
Seneca, 499
Sentient, 454
Seriema Song, 462
Sex as Compassion—A New Eros in a Time of AIDS, 778
Sexton, Anne, 376
Shakespeare, William, 298
Shall I compare thee to a summer's day?, 299
She kissed him, pissing, 390
Shelley, Mary Wollstonecraft, 69
Shelley, Percy Bysshe, 333, 555
She Walks in Beauty, 331
She was a phantom of delight, 339
Sidney, Sir Philip, 323
Simic, Charles, 417
Simpson, Louis, 441
6/16/94, 476
Sleep, 447
Snow piles up these lonely nights, 439
Snyder, Gary, 475
Some blossoms are so white and luscious, when they, 470
Something Borrowed, Something Blue, 227
somewhere i have never travelled,gladly beyond, 358
Song ("Go and catch a falling star"—Donne), 308
Song ("My silks and fine array"—Blake), 333
Song of Solomon, The, 277
Sonnet XXVII (Sappho), 295
Sonnet CCXXIV (Petrarch), 295
Sonnets from the Portuguese, XIII, 348
Sophocles, 281
Sorrow, in Seven, 278
Sounds of the Resurrected Dead Man's Footsteps #9, 467
Soup, Toast and Elbow, 468
So we'll go no more a-roving, 332
Spark, Muriel, 619
Spender, Stephen, 365
Stand Fast, O My Heart, 275
Star Trek III, 414
Steele, Sir Richard, 533
Stendhal, 561, 698
Stern, Gerald, 469
Sterne, Laurence, 683
Stevenson, Robert Louis, 573
Stowe, Harriet Beecher, 726

Strand, Mark, 381
Studies in Secrecy, 423
Studies in the Psychology of Sex, 602
Summer, 175
Summer Night, 338
Sundays, 265
Sun Rising, The, 307
Survivors, 193
Sweet Afton, 341
Swenson, May, 378
Swift, Jonathan, 665
Swinburne, Algernon Charles, 334

T

Talking with my beloved in New York, 415
Tan, Amy, 249
Tate, James, 384
Teasdale, Sara, 377
Telephoning in Mexican Sunlight, 415
Tell me no more of minds embracing minds, 316
Tennyson, Alfred, Lord, 338
Tess of the D'Urbervilles, 142
Thackeray, William Makepeace, 85
That Our Desires Are Increased by Difficulty, 511
That's what love is like. The whole river, 411
That Women Ought to Paint, 532
The barge she sat in, like a burnish'd throne, 301
The Belovéd will leave you behind from the start, 483
The chinese windchimes, 485
The days are cold, the nights are long, 340
The edge? The edge is, 484
The end of the affair is always death, 376
The fantasy spaceman, 414
The first time?, 386
The flamingo delouses its belly with the easy speed, 462
The fountains mingle with the river, 333
The grey sea and the long black land, 349
The last light of a July evening drained, 457
The men you've loved are one man, 476
the mind is its own beautiful prisoner, 359
The moon shines bright. In such a night as this, 302
The night surrounds me in a dark grey fog, 401
The quake last night was nothing personal, 426
There is much unsaid, though the edges of the said, 433
There were nights the snow began as powder, 412
The Rose did caper on her cheek—, 346

The sea is calm tonight, 335
The secret we don't know we're trying to find, the thing *un-*, 423
The swans on the river, a great, 410
The tongue of the waves tolled in the earth's bell, 435
The wives of my friends, 418
The woman I love is typing in a nearby room, 385
They Flee from Me, 322
They flee from me, that sometime did me seek, 322
Third Body, A, 453
Thirty years and more go by, 394
This creek, as old as rain, flows past our fire, 437
This is the female corn, 419
Thoby-Marcelin, Philippe, 178
Thomas, Dylan, 370
Thornton, Bonnel, 541
Thus every creature, and of every kind, 289
Time of Year, the Time of Day, The, 434
to a thirteen-year-old sleeping, 467
To a Young Lady, with Some Lampreys, 312
To every captive soul and gentle heart, 643
To Helen, 342
To His Coy Mistress, 314
To His Mistress, 291
To Know the Wind Is Mortal, 193
To Love (Swift), 665
To My Dear and Loving Husband, 329
Tolstoy, Leo, 105
Tomb Inscription, Ancient Egypt, 625
To My Mother, 372
Tonight (the moonless kind), 431
To the Muse, 363
To the Virgins, to Make Much of Time, 318
To wake embedded in warm weight of limbs, 460
To whom I owe the leaping delight, 369
Trollope, Anthony, 98
Truest Pleasure, The, 235
Ts'ao Chih, 278
Tu Fu, 279
Turgenev, Ivan, 112
Twain, Mark, 104
Two Parts of the Day Are, The, 464

U

Ukiyo-E, 407
Ultimate immigrant, 451

Under the Greenwood Tree, 141
Untitled (McHugh), 433
Updike, John, 392
Upon Julia's Clothes, 319

V

Van Duyn, Mona, 425
Vanhomrigh, Esther (Vanessa), 663
Vanity Fair, 85
Varieties of Religious Experience, The, 590
Vatsyayana, 503
Vernon, John, 252
Victoria, Queen of England, 716
Villiers, Barbara, 653
Vine, The, 317
Virgil, 287
Voltaire, 545

W

Wagoner, David, 437
Wandering with you the shore, 429
Want Bone, The, 435
We Are, 383
We are becoming martyrs to our spirits, 445
Web and the Rock, The, 184
Wedding: A Stage Direction, The, 610
Weeds and Peonies, 471
We Learned, 455
We learned the decorum of fire, 455
We'll Go No More A-Roving, 332
We miss each other by just an eyelash, 462
We're made to, 480
West, Paul, 255
We stood by a pond that winter day, 357
We Two Boys Together Clinging, 356
Wharton, Edith, 175
What explanation is given for the phosphorus light, 407
What lips my lips have kissed, and where, and why, 366
What name do I have for you?, 481
Whenas in silks my Julia goes, 319
When I Heard at the Close of the Day, 355
When in disgrace with fortune and men's eyes, 300
When I Was One-and-Twenty, 375

When my love swears that she is made of truth, 299
When she, laughing, plastered a snowball on me, 442
when we learn, 486
When We Two Parted, 331
When You Are Old, 362
When you are old and gray and full of sleep, 362
When you kiss me, moths flutter in my mouth, 448
Where, like a pillow on a bed, 309
Where I see the marooned Pike, 421
Where the creek bed turns, 468
Where this man walks his fences, 383
Where true Love burns Desire is Love's pure flame, 337
White Above Green, 443
White Lilies, The, 477
White petals, not snow, 437
Whitman, Walt, 353, 740
Why does the woman lay her head so far, 474
why not merely the despaired of, 360
Wier, Dara, 478
Wilbur, Richard, 379
Wilde, Oscar, 164, 350, 748
Wildflowers, 435
Wild Nights—Wild Nights!, 346
Willi, 199
Wilmot, John, Second Earl of Rochester, 326, 657
Wind in the Sunporch, The, 485
Wine comes in at the mouth, 361
Winter Lesson, 412
Wise and Foolish Virgins, The, 230
With lovers 'twas of old the fashion, 312
Without, 474
Wolfe, Thomas, 184
Wolitzer, Hilma, 265
Woman Photographing Holsteins, A, 438
Women in Love, 393
Wordsworth, William, 339
Wright, James, 362
Writer, The, 380
Written in a Lady's Prayer Book, 326
Wuthering Heights, 86
Wyatt, Thomas, 322

Y

Yeats, William Butler, 361
Ye Flowery Banks, 340

Yes, they are alive and can have those colors, 482
You ask why thus I sport in wanton strains, 518
You gave me dandelions, 435
You must be imagining walls, 459
Young Lady of the Tung-T'ing Lake, The, 41
Your husband will be with us at the treat, 291
Your peonies burst out, white as snow squalls, 471
You say you like whales, and I surface, spout, 405
You were there all the time and I saw only, 427
You / Your, 459

Z

Zoë, 451